Microsoft® Exchange Server 2007 Administrator's Companion

Walter Glenn
Scott Lowe
Joshua Maher

PUBLISHED BY
Microsoft Press
A Division of Microsoft Corporation
One Microsoft Way
Redmond, Washington 98052-6399

Library of Congress Control Number: 2007926319

Printed and bound in the United States of America.

1 2 3 4 5 6 7 8 9   QWT   2 1 0 9 8 7

Distributed in Canada by H.B. Fenn and Company Ltd.

A CIP catalogue record for this book is available from the British Library.

Microsoft Press books are available through booksellers and distributors worldwide. For further information about international editions, contact your local Microsoft Corporation office or contact Microsoft Press International directly at fax (425) 936-7329. Visit our Web site at www.microsoft.com/mspress. Send comments to mspinput@microsoft.com.

Acquisitions Editor: Martin DelRe
Developmental Editor: Karen Szall
Project Editor: Melissa von Tschudi-Sutton
Editorial Production: Abshier House
Technical Reviewer: Randall Galloway; Technical Review services provided by Content Master, a member of CM Group, Ltd.

Body Part No. X13-72721

For my father, Bill English.

– Walter

For Amy. Thank you for your help and dedication in this and in everything.

– Scott

To my family for their unending support, John, Robin, Quentin, and Gabriel.

– Josh

Contents at a Glance

Table of Contents

Part II
Planning Your Deployment

Part III
Installation and Deployment

Part IV
Management

Part V
Maintenance

Part VI
Security

Part VII
Clients

Part VIII
Appendices

Introduction

Welcome to the *Microsoft Exchange Server 2007 Administrator's Companion*! Whether you are an experienced Exchange administrator or just learning this product, you are going to be impressed with its new features, increased flexibility, and expanded information management capabilities. The development team at Microsoft has done an outstanding job of continuing the Exchange tradition of offering superior messaging services—Exchange Server 2007 really is the best ever!

Microsoft Exchange Server 2007 is designed to meet the messaging and collaboration needs of businesses of all sizes. The *Microsoft Exchange Server 2007 Administrator's Companion* is designed to not only bring you up to speed in setting up the various features of Exchange Server 2007, but also to show you how these features work and why you might want to use them. We also offer advice from first-hand experience in the real world of Exchange organizations.

It's impossible to cover every element of Exchange Server 2007 in detail in one book. However, this Administrator's Companion is a great place to start as you consider implementing Exchange Server 2007 in your organization. This book can be used in several different ways. You can read it as a

- Guide to planning and deployment
- Ready reference for day-to-day questions
- Source of information needed to make decisions about the network
- Thorough introduction to the particulars of Exchange Server 2007

We assume that the reader has a fundamental understanding of networking concepts and of Microsoft Windows Server 2003. We have attempted to provide background at appropriate points as well as references to additional resources.

What's in This Book

The *Microsoft Exchange Server 2007 Administrator's Companion* is divided into multiple parts, each roughly corresponding to a stage in the implementation of an Exchange organization or covering a particular functionality.

Part I: Introduction

We begin by outlining the new features of Exchange Server 2007. Then we dive in for a closer look at the program's storage and routing architecture. Chapter 1, "Overview of Microsoft Exchange Server 2007," is designed to get you up to speed quickly on what Exchange Server is and some of the features it offers. This first chapter also serves as a roadmap for the rest of the book. Chapter 2, "Active Directory for Exchange Administrators," explains the tight integration between Exchange Server 2007, Active Directory, and Windows Domain Name System (DNS). Chapter 3, "Exchange Server 2007 Architecture," details the storage and transport architecture of Exchange Server 2007.

Part II: Planning Your Deployment

Every successful implementation of a messaging system requires good planning, and Exchange Server 2007 is no exception. Two chapters are devoted to planning issues. Chapter 4, "Assessing Needs," looks at methods for taking stock of a current network and assessing the needs of users on that network prior to an Exchange Server 2007 deployment. Chapter 5, "Planning for Development," examines ways to create an actual deployment plan, based on the needs-assessment methods outlined in Chapter 4.

Part III: Installation and Deployment

After learning about the architecture of Exchange Server 2007 and how to plan for its deployment, you're ready to get your hands dirty. In this part, we outline how to install Exchange Server 2007 and how to implement its various features in the way that best suits your organization. Chapter 6, "Installing Exchange Server 2007," details the various methods of installing Exchange Server 2007. This chapter also shows how to make sure a server is ready for Exchange Server 2007 installation. Chapter 7, "Coexisting with Previous Versions of Exchange Server," shows you how to install Exchange Server 2007 into an organization that uses previous versions of Exchange Server. Chapter 8, "Transitioning to Exchange Server 2007," details how to transition an organization running a previous version of Exchange Server to using only Exchange Server 2007. Chapter 9, "High Availability in Exchange Server 2007," looks at the installation and configuration of local continuous replication, cluster continuous replication, and single copy clusters.

Part IV: Management

After learning about Exchange Server 2007 deployment, we turn our attention to issues of management. Chapter 10, "Managing Exchange Server 2007," introduces you to Microsoft Management Console (MMC)—the management interface included with Windows Server 2003. This chapter also provides a tour of the two primary interfaces for managing Exchange Server 2007: Exchange Management Console and Exchange Management Shell.

The next group of chapters—Chapter 11, "Creating and Managing Recipients," through Chapter 14, "Unified Messaging"—covers a whole host of other topics: creation and management of recipients (users, contacts, groups, and public folders), storage groups, and configuration of the new Unified Messaging feature.

Part V: Maintenance

Every system—even Exchange Server 2007—needs maintenance. We address the most important maintenance tasks in this section. Chapter 15, "Troubleshooting Exchange Server 2007," looks at how to perform basic troubleshooting for a server. Chapter 16, "Disaster Recovery," covers the critical topic of backup and restoration of your databases. Chapter 17, "Tuning Exchange Server 2007 Performance," examines how to tune your Exchange servers for maximum performance.

Part VI: Security

Security is a primary concern of any network administrator, and Exchange Server 2007 in collaboration with Windows Server 2003 offers enhanced options for protecting your organization. Although this is another topic that could easily fill a book of its own, in this part, we offer as comprehensive a look at security as this space permits. Chapter 18, "Security Policies and Exchange Server 2007," looks at planning Exchange security policies. Chapter 19, "Exchange Server Security Basics," covers the basics of Exchange Server security. Chapter 20, "Antivirus and Anti-Spam," looks at new features in Exchange Server 2007 that help you to combat malicious software. Chapter 21, "Securing Exchange Server 2007 Messages," looks at methods for securing messaging in an Exchange organization.

Part VII: Clients

The best implementation of Exchange Server 2007 won't do your organization much good if there aren't any clients to connect to it and use it. In this section, we provide an overview of the clients for Exchange Server 2007. The topics presented here could easily be expanded into their own book, so we cover the more important topics and reference other materials where appropriate. Chapter 22, "Overview of Exchange Clients," gives a general introduction to the various types of clients that can be used to connect to an Exchange server. Chapter 23, "Deploying Microsoft Office Outlook 2007," focuses on Microsoft Office Outlook 2007 and examines the issues surrounding its deployment. Chapter 24, "Supporting Outlook Web Access," covers the use of Outlook Web Access.

Chapter 25, "Supporting Other Clients," details the configuration of basic Internet protocols: POP3 and IMAP4. We go over the basic commands of each and discuss how to use the logging features for troubleshooting purposes.

How to Use This Book

Within the chapters, we've tried to make the material accessible and readable. You'll find descriptive passages, theoretical explanations, and step-by-step examples. We've also included a generous number of graphics that make it easy to follow the written instructions. The following reader's aids are common to all books in the Administrator's Companion series.

Real World

Everyone can benefit from the experiences of others. "Real World" sidebars contain elaboration on a theme or background based on the experiences of others who used this product during the beta testing period.

Note   Notes include tips, alternative ways to perform a task, or some information that needs to be highlighted.

More Info   Often there are excellent sources for additional information on key topics. We use these boxes to point you to a recommended resource.

Important   Boxes marked Important shouldn't be skipped. (That's why they're called Important.) Here you'll find security notes, cautions, and warnings to keep you and your network out of trouble.

Best Practices   Best Practices provide advice for best practices that this book's authors have gained from our own technical experience.

Security Alert   Nothing is more important than security when it comes to a computer network. Security elements should be carefully noted and acted on.

System Requirements

The following are the minimum system requirements to run the companion CD provided with this book:

- Microsoft Windows XP, with the latest service pack installed and the latest updates installed from Microsoft Update Service

- CD-ROM drive

- Internet connection

- Display monitor capable of 1024 x 768 resolution

- Microsoft Mouse or compatible pointing device

- Adobe Reader for viewing the eBook (Adobe Reader is available as a download at *http://www.adobe.com*)

About the Companion CD

The companion CD contains the fully searchable electronic version of this book. We've also included pointers to white papers, tools, webcasts, virtual labs, and other information we found useful while we were writing this book.

Support

Every effort has been made to ensure the accuracy of this book and companion CD content. Microsoft Press provides corrections to this book through the Web at the following location:

http://www.microsoft.com/learning/support

To connect directly to the Microsoft Knowledge Base and type a query regarding a question or issue that you may have, go to the following address:

http://www.microsoft.com/learning/support/search.asp

If you have comments, questions, or ideas regarding the book or companion CD content, or if you have questions that are not answered by querying the Knowledge Base, please send them to Microsoft Press using either of the following methods:

E-Mail:

mspinput@microsoft.com

Postal Mail:

Microsoft Press
Attn: Microsoft Exchange Server 2007 Administrator's Companion Editor
One Microsoft Way
Redmond, WA, 98052-6399

Please note that product support is not offered through the preceding mail addresses. For support information, please visit the Microsoft Product Support Web site at the following address:

http://support.microsoft.com

Part I
Introduction

Chapter 1
Overview of Microsoft Exchange Server 2007

Microsoft Exchange Server has been a leading collaborative product since its introduction in April 1996. Exchange Server is one of the best-selling server applications in Microsoft's history. With each new release, Microsoft adds functionality to enhance Exchange Server's capabilities. The latest version, Microsoft Exchange Server 2007, builds on the superior performance and features that Exchange users have come to expect.

This chapter provides an overview of the capabilities and structure of Exchange Server, discussing basic concepts of Exchange Server—in particular, how components are organized and how they interact to provide a comprehensive messaging system. It also offers a look at some of the powerful new features of Exchange Server 2007. Exchange Server is a complex program, but with a little dissection, you will see how its complexity can benefit any enterprise.

What Is Exchange Server?

So, what is Exchange Server? Ask three different administrators, and you're liable to get three different answers. Is it a messaging system? Is it a groupware product? Is it a development platform? The answer to all three questions is yes.

As a messaging system, Exchange Server 2007 represents the state of the art in reliability, scalability, and performance. Over the past couple of decades, electronic messaging has become one of the dominant methods of business communication, and Exchange Server is one of the most popular messaging systems in the world.

The term *groupware* was coined in the 1980s to describe products that could be used to create collaborative applications in which people share access to a collection of centralized documents and resources. These days, it is just called *collaborative software*. Exchange Server 2007 lets you store and share virtually any type of document within the Exchange system. Exchange Server can also automatically send copies of documents to different physical information stores, making the use of shared documents across an organization much more efficient.

Microsoft Office Outlook 2007 is the newest version of Microsoft's premier messaging and collaboration client for use with Exchange Server 2007. It allows users to send and receive messages that include many different types of data, to share scheduling and contact information, to participate in public folder discussions, and even to access both network and local file systems. You'll learn more about Outlook 2007 in Chapter 23, "Deploying Outlook 2007."

Exchange Server is also increasingly being used as a development platform—that is, as a basis for creating applications and systems to address the specific needs of organizations. For example, you can use it to create forms that extend the capabilities of a simple message. You can even attach application logic to those forms and then configure Exchange Server to route the forms to specific users or destinations, where they can undergo further modification. Additional tools allow you to access and manipulate the information stored in Exchange Server or to take advantage of Exchange Server's delivery services.

As you can see, Exchange Server is a multifaceted and complex product. By the time you complete this book, you will fully understand how to use Exchange Server to implement and administer all these features, and you will be equipped to exploit Exchange Server to its fullest.

Editions of Exchange Server 2007

Microsoft provides two distinct editions of Exchange Server 2007. Each is basically identical in function but includes a slightly different set of features. The two editions are Exchange Server 2007 Standard Edition and Exchange Server 2007 Enterprise Edition.

Exchange Server 2007 Standard Edition

The standard edition is designed to meet the basic messaging needs of small- to medium-sized companies. The standard edition may also be useful in branch offices of larger installations or for particular server roles. Exchange Server 2007 Standard Edition has the following limitations:

- It offers support for only five storage groups per server; each storage group can contain only five databases.

■ Local Continuous Replication is supported, but neither Single Copy Clusters nor Cluster Continuous Replication is supported.

Exchange Server 2007 Enterprise Edition

The enterprise edition is designed to meet enterprise-level messaging and collaboration needs. Exchange Server 2007 Enterprise Edition includes all the features in Exchange Server 2007 Standard Edition plus the following:

■ It offers support for up to 50 storage groups per server. Each storage group can contain up to 50 databases.

■ Single Copy Clusters and Cluster Continuous Replications are supported.

More Info   You can learn more about Exchange Server editions and client access licenses at *http://www.microsoft.com/exchange/evaluation/editions.mspx*.

Note   This book refers to Exchange Server in different ways, and each has a different meaning. Typically, the software product is referred to as "Exchange Server" (note the uppercase *s* in "server"). If you see this term, you can take it to mean Microsoft Exchange Server 2007 Enterprise Edition. When necessary, "Exchange Server 2007" is also used to draw attention to the fact that a feature that is new or has changed in the most recent version of the product is being discussed. Each of these terms means essentially the same thing. Any references to previous versions of Exchange Server call out the specific version, such as "Exchange 2000 Server" or "Exchange Server 2003." Finally, the term "Exchange server" (note the lowercase *s* in "server") refers to an actual server computer, as in "There are two Exchange servers configured with the Mailbox server role."

Understanding Basic Concepts

Chapter 3, "Exchange Server 2007 Architecture," gives you an in-depth look at the architecture of Exchange Server 2007. Before learning the specifics of Exchange Server, however, you need to understand some of the concepts that form its foundation. This section describes the basics of messaging systems, how an Exchange Server environment is organized, and how Exchange Server stores information.

Messaging Systems

When most people think of electronic messages, they first think of e-mail, but an electronic messaging system can do more than just deliver e-mail. The term *electronic messaging* describes a more generalized process that can be used to deliver many different types of information to many different locations. A messaging system has several specific characteristics. First, it involves the participation of at least two parties: the sender and one or more recipients. Second, when a sender dispatches a message, the sender can count on the message being delivered. If the messaging system cannot deliver a message to a recipient immediately, it keeps trying. If, after repeated tries, the messaging system fails to deliver the message, the least it should do is inform the sender of this failure.

Although a standard messaging system can guarantee the reliable delivery of messages, it cannot guarantee exactly how long it will take to deliver a particular message. This uncertainty is due to the asynchronous nature of a messaging system. In an *asynchronous system*, two related events are not dependent on each other; in a messaging system, for example, the sending of a message and the receipt of the message are not tied together in any fixed span of time.

There are two basic types of messaging systems: shared-filed systems and client/server systems. Although client/server systems have almost entirely replaced shared-file systems in modern messaging products, administrators need to have a good understanding of both.

Shared-File Systems

Many older messaging products, such as Microsoft Mail, are shared-file systems. A *shared-file* e-mail system, as shown in Figure 1-1, works fairly simply. A messaging server contains a shared folder (a mailbox) for each user of the system. When a user sends a message, that user's e-mail client places a copy of the message into the shared folders of any designated recipients. Clients are generally configured to check their shared folders at set intervals. If the recipient client finds a new message in the folder, it alerts the user. Shared-file systems are generally referred to as *passive* systems, in that it is up to the messaging software running on the client to carry out the operations of the e-mail transaction. The messaging server itself plays no active role (other than housing the e-mail system's shared folders) in passing the message from sender to recipient.

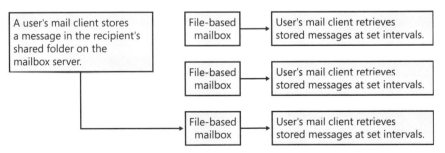

Figure 1-1   A shared-file e-mail system

Client/Server Systems

An Exchange-based system is a form of *client/server* system (see Figure 1-2). This type of system is referred to as an *active* system because the server takes a much more active role than it does in a shared-file system. In an Exchange-based messaging system, client software delivers outbound messages to a service on an Exchange server. That service places the messages in the recipient's mailbox or in a queue destined for another Exchange server or for a foreign messaging system. Exchange Server itself is then responsible for alerting users that new messages await them. In addition, Exchange Server takes on many other responsibilities. For example, each Exchange server (depending on its role) may do the following:

- Manage the messaging database

- Manage the connections to other Exchange servers and messaging systems

- Index the messaging database for better performance

- Receive new messages and transfer them to their destinations

To provide these services, Exchange Server is typically installed on more powerful server machines than those used for shared-file messaging systems, which means that a client/server system such as Exchange Server is inherently more scalable than a shared-file system. The server-based agents that implement Exchange Server can also provide a higher level of security, reliability, and scalability than a simple shared-file messaging system can. All these features allow Exchange Server to support many more users than simple file-based systems.

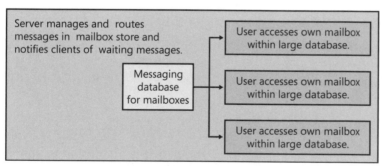

Figure 1-2   The Exchange client/server system

As the name implies, a client/server system has two distinct components: a client and a server. The client and the server use a specific interface to cooperate. The fact that Exchange Server distributes functions between the client and the server means that more processing power is available systemwide for messaging in general. In comparison, a shared-file system depends on the client to constantly check and pull mail, a process that can result in poorer performance as well as increased network traffic on a workstation client. (Exchange Server is the server component of an Exchange system, but the server does not exist in a vacuum. You also learn about the clients that participate in an Exchange system.)

Multiple clients can access a server at the same time. As a result, a server must be designed to handle many types of requests from many sources simultaneously. The need to service many clients is one of the primary factors that led to the architecture used to implement Exchange Server, in which several separate processes in the server cooperate to handle client requests. (These server processes and the way they interact are described later in this chapter.) Each Exchange Server process handles one type of task. This structure means that Exchange Server can execute different functions simultaneously rather than sequentially, as a monolithic, single-process messaging architecture would do.

The Organization of an Exchange Environment

In versions of Exchange Server prior to Exchange 2000 Server, each group of Exchange servers was known as a *site*, and each site defined the group's boundaries for both administration and routing. Exchange 2000 Server and Exchange Server 2003 did away with sites and instead separated the boundaries by allowing Exchange servers to be grouped into administrative groups and routing groups. Exchange Server 2007 now does away with routing and administrative groups specific to Exchange and instead relies fully upon the routing and administrative architecture of Windows Active Directory. This section outlines the basic organizational features of Exchange Server 2007.

Servers

Server is the term used in the Microsoft Exchange topology to refer to an individual computer that has the Microsoft Exchange Server messaging application installed and running on it. The name of the server is the same as the name of the Windows computer that hosts the Exchange Server application.

There are no hard-and-fast rules as to how many servers you should have within a particular site or organization or how powerful those servers should be. The size and number of servers is largely determined by the number of clients in the organization and the location of those clients, as well as by other roles that the Exchange server plays. In addition, put some thought into which servers to place users on. When individual users on the same server communicate through Exchange Server, they do not add to network bandwidth because the message does not need to move across the network between separate physical machines. Grouping users according to how they interact with one another improves the Exchange server's performance and even the performance of the entire messaging system.

Server Roles

Exchange Server 2007 introduces role-based deployment that provides more flexibility in how multiple servers within an organization are used. In Exchange Server, a *server role* works similarly to how roles work within Windows Server 2003. A server role allows you to split the functions of Exchange Server and place those functions on different physical servers.

In Exchange 2003, you could designate a server as a front-end server that accepted requests from outside the company network or as a mailbox server that provided typical Exchange functions. Exchange Server 2007 takes this concept further by introducing five server roles:

- **Mailbox**   The Mailbox server role hosts mailbox databases containing user mailboxes. The Mailbox server role is required to host mailboxes or public folders.

- **Client Access**   The Client Access role accepts connections from a number of different clients, including Outlook Web Access, mobile clients using ActiveSync, and e-mail clients that use Post Office Protocol v3 (POP3) or Internet Message Access Protocol v4 (IMAP4). The Client Access role also supports services like the AutoDiscover service and Web services.

- **Edge Transport**   The Edge Transport role is designed to be deployed in an organization's perimeter network as a stand-alone server with no other roles installed. The Edge Transport role handles all Internet mail flow for an organization, helping to reduce the attack surface of the Exchange organization. The server that has the Edge Transport role installed does not have access to Active Directory. Instead, configuration and recipient information is stored on the Edge Transport server using the Active Directory Application Mode (ADAM) service. This information is synchronized with information in Active Directory.

- **Hub Transport**   The Hub Transport role handles message routing and mail flow within an organization. This role also applies transport rules, applies journaling policies, and delivers messages to recipients' inboxes. If an organization does not have an Edge Transport server, the Hub Transport role can also relay Internet messages.

- **Unified Messaging**   The Unified Messaging role interfaces with a telephony network to provide voice messaging and fax services. This allows voice messages, faxes, and e-mail messages to arrive in a single Inbox.

You can configure a single Exchange server with multiple roles (as will be the case on a network with one Exchange server). The exception to this is that the Edge Transport role requires a separate server. You can also configure each role individually on separate computers, creating a highly scalable messaging solution. For example, you might create an organization with a single Mailbox server, a separate Hub Transport server in each site, a

Client Access server to handle OWA connections, and an Edge Transport server to handle Internet-facing communications.

Recipients

Although the recipient is the lowest level of the Exchange hierarchy, it is a critical component of the Exchange organization. As the name implies, a *recipient* is an entity that can receive an Exchange message. Most recipients are associated with a single, discrete mailbox, although this mailbox can be represented by several addresses, depending on the addressing types implemented within Exchange.

Installing Exchange Server 2007 adds Exchange-related functionality to the user objects in Active Directory and to the interface in the Active Directory Users and Computers snap-in. This tie to Active Directory means that, in addition to mailboxes, Exchange Server 2007 supports other types of recipients, including groups and contacts.

Mailboxes

A *mailbox* is an area of an Exchange server's mailbox store database in which a particular user's private messages are stored. An Active Directory user object that has been given a mailbox is referred to as *mailbox-enabled*. Only user objects can be mailbox-enabled.

Note   You can make other objects participate in Exchange Server 2007 routing simply by giving them an e-mail address. Such objects are referred to as *mail-enabled* and are not associated with an actual mailbox.

Distribution Groups

A *distribution group* is a collection of users, mail contacts, and even other distribution groups that is able to receive messages. When a distribution group receives a message, Exchange Server sends a copy of the message to each of the recipients within the group. The term *group* also refers to an Active Directory security object that is a collection of users and other groups. An Exchange group is always based upon an Active Directory group. A group is the functional equivalent of a distribution list in previous versions of Exchange Server.

Mail Contacts

A *mail contact* is an Active Directory object that is not an actual user and thus, cannot log on to the network. Contacts can receive e-mail from Exchange users, just as standard Exchange recipients can, after their addresses are defined in the Exchange system's Global Address List. Through the use of mail contacts, you can integrate external recipients, such as Internet e-mail addresses, into the address list of your Exchange system.

Note   Mail contacts are the functional equivalent of custom recipients in some previous versions of Exchange Server.

Address Lists

An *address list* is simply a list of recipients. The Global Address List is the list of all Exchange Server recipients in the entire Exchange organization. Exchange Server uses address lists to hold and organize the names of the recipients associated with the system.

An Exchange system can have hundreds of thousands of recipients, making it difficult for a user to locate an individual recipient's name. In addition, e-mail addresses can be somewhat cryptic. Various legacy messaging systems have restrictions on the length of the user's mailbox name, and some administrators assign puzzling mailbox names. All in all, it can be difficult to guess a user's email address. The primary purpose of an address list, from a user's point of view, is to provide a way to locate an e-mail address for a recipient. When the administrator of an Exchange environment creates a recipient, the person's name—not a cryptic e-mail address—appears in the Global Address List, making it easier for Exchange users to locate and send e-mail to recipients.

In addition to the Global Address List maintained by Exchange Server, individual users can create their own personal address lists, called *address books*. Personal address books, which are stored by Outlook locally on a user's computer and can contain a portion of the Global Address List as well as other custom addresses added by the user, make it easier to access the addresses the user needs most frequently.

Connectors

You should understand one more piece of the Exchange Server topology before moving on: connectors. A *connector* is a piece of software that acts as a gateway between an Exchange Server 2007 environment and an environment using a previous version of Exchange Server or another messaging system. A connector enables the Exchange system to interact directly with the other system, as though its users are part of your Exchange environment. Connectors can integrate foreign address lists into the Global Address List, enable message exchange, provide access to shared messaging folders, and make other functions available. Some connectors simply enable a consistent mail-forwarding and receipt operation. In addition to providing a link between Exchange Server and other messaging systems, a connector can be extremely useful if you are in the process of migrating to Exchange Server. You learn more about connectors and coexistence in Chapter 7, "Coexisting with Previous Versions of Exchange Server."

Exchange Server Storage

Exchange Server uses *message databases* to hold the messages that make up its information environment. Within these databases, Exchange Server organizes the messages and other material in folders. A folder has the same relationship to its messages that a directory in a file system has to its files. Because Exchange Server manages the storage of its own data, there is not a strict one-to-one relationship between a folder in an Exchange

Server database and a directory in the operating system. Exchange Server uses two types of databases: a mailbox database and a public folder database.

When you install an Exchange server, you have to specify locations for the public folder database and the mailbox database.

Mailbox Database

The *mailbox database* manages the data within the mailboxes it contains, tracking deleted messages and mailbox sizes and assisting in message transfers. A *private folder* is a secured folder component within a mailbox for an Exchange Server recipient. Each private folder holds information that is available only to a single Exchange user and to others to whom that user has granted access permissions.

Exchange maintains private folders and the mailboxes that contain them within the mailbox database of the associated Exchange server. Although the folders are "secured" in the sense that an Exchange user must have an account and a password to access each mailbox, Exchange Server does manage the contents of mailboxes. For example, the mailbox database is included in standard Exchange Server backup and recovery operations.

Exchange users are not limited to using Outlook to access their mailboxes. They can also access private stores through various Internet mail protocols and even through a standard Web browser, if the Exchange environment is configured to allow those types of access.

> **Note**   Many companies using Exchange also make use of *personal stores*, which are databases of messages controlled by a messaging client rather than by Exchange Server. Typically, personal stores reside on a user's local machine or on a shared network volume. After materials are placed in a personal folder, they are the exclusive responsibility of the user. Other users cannot access the materials in a personal folder. If users create or modify any of the documents in the personal folder and want others to access these documents, they have to explicitly place these documents in a private or public folder in order to put them back under the care of an Exchange server.

Public Folder Database

The *public folder database* is a database that stores public folders, indexes their contents, and assists in the replication of the folders with other Exchange servers. As the name implies, a public folder is accessible to more than one user. Administrators can define the specific security restrictions on a public folder to limit the types of users who have access to it. Public folders are mostly used to keep information that is accessed by large numbers of people. If, for example, your organization has marketing materials or human resources policies that you want to make available to everyone as soon as they are created, you can put them in a public folder.

The reason for the separation between the public folder database and the mailbox database lies in the way Exchange Server treats the information in the public folder database. Because everyone in what could be a widely dispersed organization can access public folders, Exchange Server allows you to set up automatic replication of the contents of public folders. Exchange Server handles the replication of documents in a public folder with no intervention on the part of an administrator after the replication is defined. Users who request a document in a public folder retrieve it from the closest copy of the public folder rather than from a single location. In this way, public folders help expand the scalability of Exchange Server by reducing the bandwidth requirements for the access of common documents.

Real World   Public Folders are De-emphasized in Exchange Server 2007

Since the early versions of Exchange Server, public folders have provided an ideal way to store documents and messages that need to be accessed by a large number of people. However, with the advent of Microsoft SharePoint Server, public folders have lost some of their relevance. SharePoint does a much better job at not only storing documents centrally, but making them accessible in a way that's easy to locate and work on them. SharePoint also provides advanced features like document tracking, security, and versioning.

In response to this, public folders have been de-emphasized in Exchange Server 2007. For example:

- You can no longer manage public folders using the Exchange Management graphical interface. You must use the Exchange Management Shell.

- Public folders are no longer accessible using the Network News Transfer Protocol (NNTP) or IMAP.

To use either of these features, you must keep a computer running Exchange 2000 or Exchange 2003 in your organization.

What's New in Exchange Server 2007

Exchange Server 2007 provides a number of new features and enhancements to existing features in the areas of reliability, management, and security. This section takes a look at the important enhancements to Exchange Server 2007.

Active Directory Site Routing

Previous versions of Exchange required an extra layer of routing configuration in the form of routing groups to determine how servers communicated with one another and how clients communicated with servers. Exchange Server 2007 does away with routing groups, instead building on the site topology of Active Directory itself. Exchange Server 2007 uses Active Directory sites to determine how servers communicate.

Split Permissions Model

Exchange Server 2007 also no longer uses administrative groups, which in previous versions of Exchange were used to define the administrative topology of an Exchange organization. Instead, Exchange Server 2007 uses a split permissions model based on Universal Security Groups (USG), which allows you to more easily split the Exchange administrative permissions from other Windows administrative permissions. Combined with more specific administrator roles, the split permissions model offers more flexibility in assigning permissions throughout the Exchange organization.

Exchange Server 2007 Setup Wizard

The new Exchange Server 2007 Setup Wizard now performs readiness checks on a server to ensure that the server is prepared for a successful Exchange Server 2007 installation. If the server is not properly prepared, the Setup Wizard offers guidance and best practices for configuring the server. The Setup Wizard also allows you to customize the server roles that are installed on a server. You learn more about installing the Setup Wizard in Chapter 6, "Installing Exchange Server 2007."

Exchange Management

Exchange Server 2007 offers two rich management interfaces:

■ **Exchange Management Console**   Based on the Microsoft Management Console (MMC) 3.0, the Exchange Management Console provides a powerful new interface for managing Exchange Server 2007. The Exchange Management Console is fully redesigned and is actually based on the Exchange Management Shell.

■ **Exchange Management Shell**   Built on Microsoft Windows PowerShell technology, the Exchange Management Shell provides a command-line interface that offers full functionality for managing an Exchange organization. The Exchange Management Shell can not only perform every task available in the Exchange Management Console, but also some tasks that are not available in the console.

You learn more about the Exchange Management Console and the Exchange Management Shell in Chapter 10, "Managing Exchange Server 2007."

Exchange Server Roles

Server roles provide more flexibility and scalability within an organization by allowing you to split the functions of Exchange Server and place those functions on different physical servers. You can learn more about server roles in the section "Defining the Role of Your Server" earlier in this chapter and in Chapter 6.

Unified Messaging

Unified Messaging allows Exchange Server 2007 to connect to a telephony system (such as a PBX) to combine e-mail messages, voice messaging, and fax into a single infrastructure. When the Unified Messaging server role is deployed and connected to a telephony system, users can receive voice messages, faxes, and e-mail messages to a single inbox that they can access from a variety of devices. Unified Messaging also allows users to access messages in their mailboxes via telephone using Outlook Voice Access. You learn more about Unified Messaging in Chapter 14, "Unified Messaging."

Messaging Policy and Compliance

Legal requirements and internal company policy have made it more important than ever that messaging systems filter, store, and create rules for messages within an organization. Exchange Server 2007 adds a number of features that help administrators ensure compliance:

- **Transport rules** Transport rules govern how messages are transmitted and stored. They can also be used to add disclaimers or other text to messages, as well as enforce message journaling. Exchange Server 2007 supports two kinds of transport rules:

   - ❑ *Edge transport rules* control messages sent to or received from the Internet.

   - ❑ *Hub transport rules* control messages sent between users in the Exchange organization.

- **Records management** Exchange Server 2007 also allows you to create managed folders, which are inboxes to which item retention policies are applied.

You learn more about messaging policies and compliance in Chapter 21, "Messaging Security."

Anti-Spam and Antivirus

Exchange Server 2007 adds new or improved features for connection and content filtering, spam quarantine, recipient filtering, support for Sender ID and Sender reputation, and aggregation of Outlook Junk E-Mail filter lists. You learn more about the anti-spam and antivirus features of Exchange Server 2007 in Chapter 20, "Antivirus and Anti-Spam."

64-Bit Architecture

The 64-bit architecture used by Exchange Server 2007 provides for an increase in performance and stability over previous versions of Exchange Server. The 64-bit architecture also allows for an increase in the number of storage groups and databases allowable on an Exchange server. Exchange Server 2007 supports up to 50 storage groups on a server with up to 50 databases per storage group (a dramatic increase from the four storage groups and five database limit in Exchange Server 2003).

The 64-bit architecture requires that Exchange Server be installed on a server with 64-bit hardware that is running a 64-bit version of Windows Server 2003. Because previous versions of Exchange were 32-bit only, this requirement means that you cannot perform an in-place upgrade from any previous version to Exchange Server 2007. Instead, upgrading an organization from previous versions means installing new servers running Exchange Server 2007 and then transitioning the organization from existing servers. This is covered in Chapter 8, "Transitioning to Exchange Server 2007," and Chapter 7.

> **Note**   A 32-bit version of Exchange Server 2007 is available for testing purposes but is not supported for production use. Only the 64-bit version of Exchange Server 2007 is supported in production.

Outlook Web Access

Outlook Web Access (OWA) has been significantly enhanced in Exchange Server 2007. OWA comes in two versions: Outlook Web Access Premium and Outlook Web Access Light. Outlook Web Access Premium takes advantage of features in Microsoft Internet Explorer to provide features such as secure messaging, rules, spell-checking, and reminders. Outlook Web Access Light can be used with any Web browser but does not support all the features of the Outlook Web Access Premium. You learn more about Outlook Web Access in Chapter 24, "Supporting Outlook Web Access."

> **More Info**   For a more detailed look at the new features in Exchange Server 2007 (all of which are also covered throughout this book) and at discontinued features, check out the What's New section of the Microsoft Exchange Server 2007 TechNet center at *http://technet.microsoft.com/en-us/library/aa996018.aspx*.

Summary

This chapter introduced you to Exchange Server 2007, giving you the background you need to delve into the Exchange Server architecture in detail. It described basic concepts, including how an Exchange environment is organized, how different types of information are stored, and how services work behind the scenes to accomplish the many tasks that Exchange Server performs. In addition, the chapter gave an overview of the new features in Exchange Server 2007. The next two chapters take a deeper look into the Exchange Server/Active Directory integration and into Exchange Server 2007 architecture.

Chapter 2
Active Directory for Exchange Administrators

In the Chapter 1, "Overview of Microsoft Exchange Server 2007," you learned about some of the basic components of an Exchange organization. This chapter builds on that knowledge by describing how Exchange Server 2007 integrates with Microsoft Windows Server 2003 and how it uses the services in Windows Server 2003 to its advantage. It begins with a brief overview of the Windows Server 2003 Active Directory service and finishes by describing how Exchange Server 2007 uses Active Directory and discussing some of the more important Internet information protocols.

Brief Overview of Active Directory

A full explanation of Active Directory is outside the scope of this book, but a brief overview is warranted. Because Exchange Server 2007 is heavily dependent on the underlying network operating system, it is important to have a basic understanding of Windows Server 2003 Active Directory.

> **More Info**   For a more thorough discussion of Active Directory and the other concepts discussed in this chapter, see *Microsoft Windows Server 2003 Administrator's Companion*, Second Edition, by Charlie Russel, Sharon Crawford, and Jason Gerend (Microsoft Press, 2006).

Directory Structure in Active Directory

Before beginning the discussion on what Active Directory is, you should first understand what a directory is. As an analogy, think of a generic file system. Perhaps in this file system, you have a C drive, and on that drive, you have a root folder named Memos. Under C:\Memos, you have a folder for each of the 12 months of the year, so you would find a folder in the structure named July. Under C:\Memos\July, you have a folder named Departments; the full pathname to Departments is C:\Memos\July\Departments. This is a hierarchy of folders in a file system.

A directory is no different from a folder list, except that the hierarchy consists not of folders but of objects. An *object* is an entity that is described by a distinct, named set of attributes. Instead of using Windows Explorer to search through this hierarchy of objects, you'll be using a protocol designed to search a directory, called the *Lightweight Directory Access Protocol* (LDAP).

Note   The original protocol for accessing a directory was called Directory Access Protocol (DAP), but it had a high overhead and tended to be slow. *Lightweight Directory Access Protocol* (LDAP) is an improved version that is faster and requires less overhead.

With Active Directory, Microsoft has made significant improvements to the directory concept, such as dynamic DNS. The "Active" in Active Directory describes the flexibility and extensibility that have been built into Microsoft's directory service.

Logical Structure of Active Directory

The components that form the logical structure of Active Directory include domains, organizational units, trees, and forests.

Domains

A *domain* is the core unit in Active Directory and is made up of a collection of computers that share a common directory database. The computers that share this common directory database are called domain controllers. A *domain controller* is a Windows Server 2003 server that has Active Directory installed. It can authenticate users for its own domain. Each domain controller holds a complete replica of the domain naming partition for the domain to which it belongs and a complete replica of the configuration and schema naming partitions for the forest. Dcpromo.exe is the utility used to promote a Windows Server 2003 server to a domain controller. Partitions are discussed later in this chapter.

All Active Directory domain names are identified by a DNS name as well as by a NetBIOS name. The following is an example of the two types of names:

- DNS-style domain name: contoso.com

- NetBIOS name: CONTOSO

Generally, the NetBIOS name is the same as the first naming component in the DNS name. However, a NetBIOS name can be only 15 characters in length, whereas each name in the DNS naming convention can have up to 64 characters. During installation, both names can be configured to meet your needs. In the initial release of Windows Server 2003, Active Directory names could be changed. Although there are tools available that allow you to change a domain name, it is a complex undertaking. It is better to be careful when initially creating your naming scheme.

> **More Info**   To read more about and download the Windows Server 2003 Active Directory Domain Rename Tools, visit *http://www.microsoft.com/technet/downloads /winsrvr/domainrename.mspx.*

The domain is also a security boundary in Active Directory. Administrators in a domain have the permissions and rights to perform administrative functions in that domain. However, because each domain has its own security, administrators must be given explicit permissions to perform administrative tasks in other domains. Members of the Enterprise Admins group have rights to perform administrative tasks in all domains across the forest. Hence, you can have domain administrators and a higher level of administration from the Enterprise administrators.

A Windows Server 2003 Active Directory domain can be in either mixed mode or native mode. The default installation is mixed mode. In mixed mode, a Windows Server 2003 domain controller acts like a Microsoft Windows NT 4 domain controller. Active Directory domains in mixed mode have the same limitations on the security accounts database as Windows NT 4 domain controllers. For example, in mixed mode, the size of the directory is limited to 40,000 objects, the same restriction imposed by Windows NT 4. These limitations allow Windows NT 4 backup domain controllers to exist on the network and connect to and synchronize with the Windows Server 2003 domain controllers.

> **Note**   Exchange Server 2007 requires that an Active Directory be in native mode prior to installation. You'll learn more about that in Chapter 6, "Installing Exchange Server 2007."

The PDC Emulator is one of the five Flexible Single Master Operation (FSMO) roles that make Windows Server 2003 look like a Windows NT 4 PDC. Only one Windows Server

2003 domain controller can act as the PDC Emulator. By default, the PDC Emulator role, like all other FSMO roles, is installed on one domain controller in each domain – by default, on the first domain controller of each domain. (FSMO roles are discussed in a moment.) To run Windows Server 2003 in native mode, you must not have any reason or desire to connect to a Windows NT 4 backup domain controller. In other words, when you decide to run Windows Server 2003 in native mode, you won't be able to use a Windows NT backup domain controller again on your network, and no applications running on your network will be able to use Windows NT to operate. The switch to native mode is a one-time, one-way switch and is irreversible. Native mode allows your Windows Server 2003 domain controllers to have millions of objects per domain. In addition, native mode allows the nesting of groups, something that is advantageous if you anticipate large distribution groups in Exchange Server 2007.

A Windows Server 2003 network running in native mode can accommodate Windows NT 4 stand-alone and member servers. Windows NT 4 workstations must be upgraded to Windows 2000 Professional, Windows XP Professional, or Windows Vista to participate in Active Directory, or you must install the Directory Service Client. Windows Server 2003 implements Active Directory in a multimaster model because objects in Active Directory can be modified on any domain controller, which accounts for the emphasis on directory replication between domain controllers. However, some roles are either too sensitive to security issues or too impractical to perform in a multimaster model because of potential conflicts that could arise from the replication traffic. An understanding of these roles is important: if a domain controller that is performing a particular role becomes unavailable, the function it performs is not available in Active Directory. These roles are schema master, domain naming master, relative identifier master, PDC emulator, and infrastructure master.

Schema Master

The *schema* is the set of object classes (such as users and groups) and their attributes (such as full name and phone number) that form Active Directory. The schema master controls all aspects of updates and modifications to the schema. To update the schema, you must have access to the schema master. There can be only one schema master in the forest at any given time.

Domain Naming Master

The domain naming master controls the addition and removal of domains in the forest. This is the only domain controller from which you can create or delete a domain. There can be only one domain naming master in the forest at any given time.

Relative Identifier Master

The relative identifier (RID) master allocates sequences of RIDs to each of the domain controllers in its domain. Whereas the schema master and domain naming master perform forestwide functions, one RID master is assigned per domain. Because each domain controller can create objects in Active Directory, the RID master allocates to each domain controller a pool of 500 RIDs from which to draw when creating the object. When a domain controller has used more than 400 RIDs, the RID master gives it another batch of 500 RIDs.

Whenever a new user, group, or computer object is created, the object inherits the security identifier (SID) of the domain.The RID is appended to the end of the of the domain SID to make up a unique SID for the object. In addition, when an object is moved from one domain to another, its SID changes, because it receives a new SID (made up of both the domain SID and the RID) in the destination domain. By allowing only the RID master to move objects between domains, Windows Server 2003 ensures SID uniqueness, even across domains. Objects maintain a SID history for security access to resources.

PDC Emulator

Each domain in the forest must have one domain controller that acts as the PDC emulator. If Active Directory is running in mixed mode with Windows NT 4 domain controllers on the same network, the PDC emulator is responsible for synchronizing password changes and security account updates between the Windows NT 4 servers and the Windows Server 2003 servers. Moreover, the PDC emulator appears to downlevel clients, such as Windows 95, Windows 98, and Windows NT 4, as the PDC of the domain. It functions as the domain master browser, is responsible for replication services to the BDCs, and performs directory writes to the Windows NT 4 domain security database.

In native mode, the PDC emulator receives the urgent updates to the Active Directory security accounts database, such as password changes and account lockout modifications. These urgent changes to user accounts are immediately replicated to the PDC emulator, no matter where they are changed in the domain. If a logon authentication fails at a domain controller, the credentials are first passed to the PDC emulator for authentication before the logon request is rejected.

Infrastructure Master

The infrastructure master is responsible for tracking group-to-user references whenever the user and the group are not members of the same domain. The object that resides in the remote domain is referenced by its GUID and SID. If an object is moved from one domain to another, it receives a new SID, and the infrastructure master replicates these changes to other infrastructure masters in other domains.

Organizational Units

An *organizational unit* (OU) is a container object that is used to organize other objects within a domain. An OU can contain user accounts, printers, groups, computers, and other OUs.

More Info   The design of Active Directory is based on the X.500 standard, which can be procured from *www.itu.org*. The standard is rather short—around 29 pages—but reading it will give you a great background for understanding Active Directory and, for that matter, Novell Directory Services.

OUs are strictly for administrative purposes and convenience. They are transparent to the user and have no bearing on the user's ability to access network resources. OUs can be used to create departmental or geographical boundaries. They can also be used to delegate administrative authority to users for particular tasks. For example, you can create an OU for all of your printers and then assign full control over the printers to your printer administrator.

OUs can also be used to limit administrative control. For example, you can give your help desk support personnel the permission to change the password on all user objects in an OU without giving them permissions to modify any other attributes of the user object, such as group membership or names.

Because an Active Directory domain can hold millions of objects, upgrading to Windows Server 2003 allows companies to convert from a multiple-domain model to a single-domain model and then use organizational units to delegate administrative control over resources.

Trees and Forests

The first Windows Server 2003 domain that you create is the root domain, which contains the configuration and schema for the forest. You add domains to the root domain to form the tree. As Figure 2-1 illustrates, a *tree* is a hierarchical grouping of Windows Server 2003 domains that share a contiguous namespace. A *contiguous namespace* is one that uses the same root name when naming additional domains in the tree.

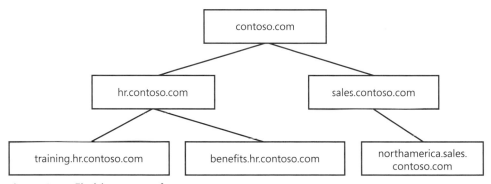

Figure 2-1   Fictitious tree of contoso.com

A collection of trees that does not share a contiguous namespace can be placed in the same forest. They then share a common configuration, schema, and Global Catalog (GC). By default, the name of the root domain becomes the name of the forest, even though other trees will not share the same name as the root domain.

Even though they don't share the same name, transitive trust relationships are automatically established between the root domain servers in each tree, as long as they are members of the same forest. Figure 2-2 shows two trees—contoso.com and litwareinc.com—in the same forest.

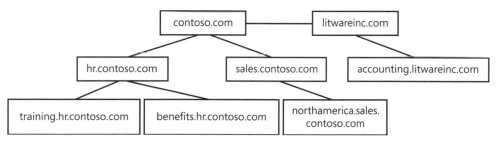

Figure 2-2   Forest consisting of contoso.com and litwareinc.com

The schema and configuration partitions for Active Directory are replicated to all domain controllers in each domain. Whereas a domain represents a boundary for security and the logical grouping of objects, a forest represents the boundary for Active Directory and the Exchange Server 2007 organization.

In addition, other domain names cannot be represented above the first domain name. For example, if your root domain name is sales.contoso.com, you can never install a domain named contoso.com in the same forest. You can join other domain names to the forest, such as litwareinc.com, as long as they are in a different namespace.

Groups

In Windows Server 2003, groups are used to reduce administrative effort and to enable the management of many user accounts simultaneously. Windows Server 2003 uses groups to reduce the number of objects that require direct administration.

There are basically two kinds of groups in Windows Server 2003. Each has its own advantages and restrictions that you must take into account when using them. Exchange Server 2007 uses both kinds of groups from Windows Server 2003:

- **Security groups**   Security groups host security principles within Active Directory. They are used to group users or computers for the purpose of reducing the points of administration and providing permissions to network resources.

■ **Distribution groups**   Distribution groups are meant to perform distribution functions. You cannot use them to assign permissions to network resources.

Global Groups

Global groups, in mixed mode, can contain users only from the domain in which they are hosted. In native mode, they can contain users and global groups from the local domain in which they were created. However, they can be used to assign permissions to resources in any domain. Global groups can contain users, computers, and global groups from the local domain. They can be members of any other type of group.

Typically, you'll use global groups for administering user membership that has permissions to a network resource. The group itself is replicated as part of the Global Catalog, but its membership is not. This restriction means that adding user accounts to or removing user accounts from a global group does not trigger a new replication of the Global Catalog. Global groups can be converted to universal groups (discussed shortly) as long as the global groups do not contain other global groups and the domain is in native mode.

Domain Local Groups

Domain local groups in native mode can contain other domain local groups, users, global groups, and universal groups from any domain in the forest, but they can be granted permissions only in the domain in which they reside. In mixed mode, they can contain only user and global group accounts.

You grant permissions to domain local groups only for objects in the local domain. The existence of the domain local group is replicated to the Global Catalog server, but its membership is not replicated. Domain local groups are flexible in that you can use any other security principle inside the domain local group (when running in native mode) to reduce administrative effort. You can convert a domain local group to a universal group in native mode as long as it does not contain other domain local groups.

Universal Groups

Universal groups can contain users, global groups, and other universal groups from any Windows Server 2003 domain in the forest. The domain must be operating in native mode to create security groups with universal scope. You can grant permissions to resources anywhere in the forest to a universal group.

Universal group membership must be determined at the time of logon. Because the scope of the universal group is universal, this group is propagated through the Global Catalog. Hence, not only is the group itself propagated in the Global Catalog, but its membership is propagated as well. A universal group with a large membership generates additional replication overhead if the membership changes. Universal groups as security groups are available only in native mode. Table 2-1 summarizes group membership rules.

Table 2-1   Comparison of Various Types of Groups

Group scope	In mixed mode can contain	In native mode can contain	Can be a member of	Can be granted permissions for
Domain local	User accounts and global groups from any domain	User accounts, global groups, and universal groups from any domain in the forest, and domain local groups from the same domain	Domain local groups in the same domain	The domain in which the domain local group exists
Global	User accounts	User accounts and global groups from the same domain	Universal and domain local groups in any domain and global groups in the same domain	All domains in the forest
Universal	Not applicable	User accounts, global groups, and other universal groups from any domain in the forest	Domain local and universal groups in any domain	All domains in the forest

Other Active Directory Components

Active Directory is a complex system that includes far more than the basic logical structure just described. This section highlights several other components that play a critical role within Active Directory.

Naming Partitions

You can think of Active Directory as being divided into three distinct directories, or partitions: the domain partition, the configuration partition, and the schema partition. Each partition is a self-contained section of Active Directory that can have its own properties, such as replication configuration and permissions structure. A Windows Server 2003 domain controller always holds three naming partitions in its database file (Ntds.dit). These are the default LDAP paths for these partitions:

- Configuration: cn=configuration,dc=sales,dc=contoso,dc=com
- Schema: cn=schema,cn=configuration,dc=sales,dc=contoso,dc=com
- Domain: dc=sales,dc=contoso,dc=com

In a multidomain structure, domain controllers belong to different domains. These servers share a common configuration and schema naming partition but have a unique domain naming partition. Exchange Server 2007 stores most of its information in the configuration naming partition, which is replicated throughout the forest.

Sites

A *site* within Active Directory is a collection of Internet protocol (IP) subnets that enjoy permanent, high-bandwidth connectivity. Active Directory assumes that all computers in the same site have permanent, high-speed connectivity with one another. Sites tend to map to the physical structure of your network: slow WAN links will be considered outside your sites, and high-speed links will form your sites.

Site and domain topologies are not dependent upon each other; a single domain can span multiple sites, or multiple domains can be located in a single site. Because the bandwidth between sites is assumed to be slow or unreliable, it stands to reason that some type of connector is needed to connect the sites. That connector is called a *site link*.

Site links are built manually by the administrator and form the physical topology of the network. To create replication paths between domain controllers across the site links (as well as between domain controllers within the same site), Windows Server 2003 employs the knowledge consistency checker (KCC), which runs automatically but can be configured manually, if necessary. The KCC creates *connection objects* on each domain controller in the configuration naming partition; these connection objects form the overall replication topology over which Active Directory information can be replicated. The KCC is a service that runs on each domain controller to create the connection objects for that domain controller.

Location Service Providers

In Windows Server 2003, DNS provides the role of server service locator, helping the client find the services it needs on the network. Dynamic DNS is supplied with Windows Server 2003 and is a standard part of the Active Directory installation. With dynamic DNS, clients query DNS service (SRV) records to locate services on the network and can also update the DNS records if their own location changes.

Global Catalog Servers

In a multidomain environment, it is reasonable to assume that some users will need access to objects outside of their own domains. For example, a user in domain A might need access to a color printer located in domain B. Because domain controllers maintain only a replica of objects in their own domain, a special service is needed in the forest to gain access to objects located in remote domains. The Global Catalog server performs this function. This server holds a replica of all objects in the forest, with a limited set of attributes for those objects. The schema defines which attributes are listed for each object in the Global Catalog. The Global Catalog is not a separate file; it is instead held inside the NTDS.DIT file. The GC will be roughly 40 percent of the size of your active directory, or the size of the NTDS.DIT file on a non-GC domain controller.

Note   By default, there is only one Global Catalog server in the entire forest, and that is the first domain controller installed in the first domain of the first tree. All other Global Catalog servers need to be configured manually. You can do this by opening the Active Directory Sites And Services snap-in, navigating to the NTDS settings on the server on which you want to install this service, right-clicking NTDS Settings, choosing Properties, and selecting the Global Catalog Server check box.

In addition to users needing access to services outside their domain, some applications need access to a forestwide listing of objects. Exchange Server 2007 is one of those applications. For example, a user might want to browse the Global Address List, which is generated by the Global Catalog server. The Global Catalog server gathers each mail-enabled object into a list and returns this list to the user inside the address book interface.

Even in a single-domain environment, Exchange clients are referred to the Global Catalog server for address book lookups. In this scenario, the default is to refer all those lookups to the root domain controller. You should plan for an increase in network traffic between Global Catalogs and Exchange Server 2007 servers. This increase may be sizeable if you are taking full advantage of all the new features and roles in Exchange Server 2007.

It is helpful to note that a Global Catalog server passes back different attributes depending on the TCP port used for the query. For example, a query to port 389 (the default LDAP port) allows a client to search for objects only within the home domain, with the full set of attributes for the object being returned. In contrast, a query over port 3268 allows a client to search for domain objects from all domains in the forest, including the home domain of the Global Catalog server. However, a query over this port returns only a subset of the attributes available, even if the object is in the home domain of the Global Catalog server.

Client Authentication

When a client attempts to log on to the domain, it queries DNS SRV records to locate a domain controller. DNS attempts to match the client's IP address to an Active Directory site and then returns a list of domain controllers that can authenticate the client. The client chooses a domain controller at random from the list and then pings it before sending the logon request. In native mode, the authenticating domain controller passes the client's credentials to the local Global Catalog server so that the Global Catalog can enumerate universal security group access.

Active Directory Names

Both users and applications are affected by the naming conventions that a directory uses. To locate a network resource, you need to know its name or one of its properties. Active Directory supports many naming schemes for the different formats that can access Active Directory.

Distinguished Name

Each object in the directory has a *distinguished name* (DN) that identifies where the object resides in the overall object hierarchy. For example:

cn=dhall,cn=users,dc=contoso,dc=com

This example indicates that the user object dhall is in the Users container that is located in the contoso.com domain. If the dhall object is moved to another container, its DN changes to reflect its new position in the hierarchy. Distinguished names are guaranteed to be unique in the forest. You cannot have two objects with the same distinguished name.

Relative Distinguished Name

The *relative distinguished name* of an object is the part of the distinguished name that is an attribute of the object. In the former example, the relative distinguished name of the dhall object is dhall. The relative distinguished name of the parent organizational unit is Users. Active Directory does not allow two objects with the same relative distinguished name under the same parent container.

User Principal Name

The *user principal name* that is generated for each object is in the form username@DNS-domainname. Users can log on with their user principal name, and an administrator can define suffixes for user principal names if desired. User principal names are required to be unique, but Active Directory does not enforce this requirement. It's best, however, to formulate a naming convention that avoids duplicate user principal names.

Globally Unique Identifier

Some applications require that an object be referred to by an identifier that remains constant. This is achieved by adding an attribute called the *globally unique identifier* (GUID), a 128-bit number that is guaranteed to be unique. A GUID is assigned to an object when it is created, and it never changes, even if the object is moved between containers in the same domain.

Exchange Server 2007 and Active Directory

Exchange Server 2007 is tightly integrated with the Windows Server 2003 Active Directory service. Integration with Windows Server 2003 provides several benefits, including the following:

- **Centralized object management**   Administration is unified for Exchange Server 2007 and Windows Server 2003. Directory objects can be managed from one location, with one management tool, and by one team.

- **Simplified security management**   Exchange Server 2007 uses the security features of Windows Server 2003, such as the discretionary access control list (DACL). Changes to security principles (such as user or group accounts) apply to data stored in both Exchange Server 2007 and Windows Server 2003 file shares.

- **Simplified creation of distribution lists**   Exchange Server 2007 automatically uses Windows Server 2003 security groups as distribution lists, eliminating the need to create a security group for each department and a corresponding distribution group for the same department. Distribution groups can be created in those instances when e-mail distribution is the only desired function of the group.

- **Easier access to directory information**   LDAP is the native access protocol for directory information.

Exchange Server 2007 and Active Directory Site Topology

In Exchange 2000 Server and Exchange Server 2003, Exchange requires the configuration of routing groups to govern how messages and other Exchange-related traffic are routed throughout an organization. Exchange Server 2007 no longer uses routing groups, instead relying on the routing technology built into Active Directory site topology.

All computers within a single Active Directory site are considered well connected, with a high-speed, reliable network connection. By default, when you first deploy Active Directory on a network, it creates a single site named (by default) *Default-First-Site-Name*. All server and client computers in the forest are made members of this first site. When you define more than one site, you must define the network subnets that are present on the network and associate each of those subnets with Active Directory sites.

In Active Directory, *IP site links* define the relationship between sites. An IP site link connects two or more Active Directory sites. Each IP site link is associated with a cost that helps dictate how Active Directory should consider using that link in relation to the costs of other available site links. You (or the Active Directory administrator) assign the cost to a link based on relative network speed and available bandwidth compared to other available connections.

Exchange Server 2007 uses the cost assignment for an IP site link to determine the lowest cost route for traffic to follow when multiple paths exist to a destination. The cost of the route is determined by aggregating the cost of all site links in the path. For example, assume that a computer in Site A must communicate with a computer in Site C. Site A is connected by an IP site link with a cost of 10 to Site B. Site B is connected by an IP site link to Site C with a cost of 5. The cost of the full route from Site A to Site C would be 15.

Active Directory clients assume site membership by matching their assigned IP address to a subnet associated with a particular site.

Because Exchange Server 2007 is now a site-aware application, it can determine its own Active Directory site membership and the Active Directory site membership of other servers. All Exchange Server 2007 server roles use site membership to determine which domain controllers and Global Catalog servers to use for processing Active Directory queries. In addition, Exchange Server 2007 also tries first to retrieve information about recipients from directory servers that are in the same site as the Exchange Server 2007 server.

The Exchange Server 2007 server roles use Active Directory site membership information as follows:

- The Mailbox server role uses Active Directory site membership information to determine which Hub Transport servers are located in the same Active Directory site as the Mailbox servers. The Mailbox server submits messages for routing and transport to a Hub Transport server that has the same Active Directory site membership as the Mailbox server. The Hub Transport server performs recipient resolution and queries Active Directory to match an e-mail address to a recipient account. The Hub Transport server delivers the message to the Mailbox server within its same Active Directory site, or it relays the message to another Hub Transport server for delivery to a Mailbox server that is outside the Active Directory site. If there are no Hub Transport servers in the same Active Directory site as a Mailbox server, mail can't flow to that Mailbox server.

- Active Directory site membership and IP site link information is used to prioritize the list of servers that are used for public folder referrals. Users are directed first to the default public folder database for their mailbox database. If a replica of the public folder being accessed does not exist in the default public folder database, the Mailbox store where the default public folder database resides provides a prioritized referral list of Mailbox servers that hold a replica to the client. Public folder databases that are in the same Active Directory site as the default public folder database are listed first, and additional referral locations are prioritized based on Active Directory site proximity.

■ The Unified Messaging (UM) server role uses Active Directory site membership information to determine which Hub Transport servers are located in the same Active Directory site as the Unified Messaging server. The Unified Messaging server submits messages for routing and transport to a Hub Transport server that has the same Active Directory site membership as the Unified Messaging server. The Hub Transport server delivers the message to a Mailbox server within its same Active Directory site, or it relays the message to another Hub Transport server for delivery to a Mailbox server that is outside the Active Directory Site.

■ When the Client Access server role receives a user connection request, it queries Active Directory to determine which Mailbox server is hosting the user's mailbox. The Client Access server then retrieves the Active Directory site membership of that Mailbox server. If the Client Access server that received the initial user connection is not located in the same site as the user's Mailbox server, the connection is redirected to a Client Access server in the same site as the Mailbox server.

■ Exchange Server 2007 Hub Transport servers retrieve information from Active Directory to determine how mail should be routed inside the organization. If the recipient's mailbox is located on a Mailbox server in the same Active Directory site as the Hub Transport server, the message is delivered directly to that mailbox. If the recipient's mailbox is located on a Mailbox server in a different Active Directory site, the message is relayed to a Hub Transport server in that site and then delivered to the Mailbox server.

Management Shell

You can use the `Set-AdSiteLink` cmdlet in the Exchange Management Shell to configure an Exchange-specific cost to an Active Directory IP site link. The Exchange-specific cost is a separate attribute that is used instead of the Active Directory-assigned cost to determine the Exchange routing path. This configuration is useful when the Active Directory IP site link costs do not result in an optimal Exchange message routing topology.

Storing Exchange Server 2007 Data in Active Directory

It was mentioned earlier that Active Directory is divided into three naming partitions: configuration, schema, and domain. This section discusses how Exchange Server 2007 uses each of these partitions and which kind of data is stored in them.

Domain Naming Partition

In the domain naming partition, all domain objects for Exchange Server 2007 are stored and replicated to every domain controller in the domain. Recipient objects, including users, contacts, and groups, are stored in this partition. Exchange Server 2007 exploits Active Directory by adding attributes to user, group, and contact objects for messaging purposes.

Designing a Group Implementation Strategy

Exchange Server 2007 uses distribution groups to send the same message to a large number of recipients. Any user accounts that are placed inside the distribution group will receive the message. In Windows Server 2003 native mode, groups can be nested inside of other groups, effectively creating a multitiered distribution list. The two types of groups you will use most often for large distribution of a message are global and universal.

The largest downside to universal groups is that membership is fully replicated to each Global Catalog server, which means that replication traffic occurs whenever a Universal Group's membership changes. Therefore, it is best to populate a universal group with other global groups so that when membership changes in the global group, the universal group is not changed and traffic is not replicated.

Global groups can also be mail-enabled for message distribution. If you choose not to use universal groups, you can mail-enable global groups. Membership for a global group is not promoted to the Global Catalog server, which presents some issues to consider when working in a multidomain environment.

When a message is sent to a global group in a remote domain, the expansion server must connect to a domain controller in the group's home domain and retrieve the membership list. In addition, the expansion server must have IP connectivity to a domain controller in the group's home domain. If bandwidth between the two domains is slow or unreliable, retrieving membership from a remote domain might take time and slow down message delivery, which affects overall performance. It is best if Exchange Server 2007 is in the remote domain. Then you can set the expansion server to be the remote Exchange Server 2007 server instead of retrieving the membership remotely and expanding the group membership locally.

When deciding which group type to select, consider the following implications:

- **Are you using a single-domain or multiple-domain environment?**   If you have a single domain, you don't need to use universal groups, because all of the domain objects are local. When you have multiple domains, use universal groups if the membership is fairly static (that is, global groups as opposed to individual users), and remember that users might not have access to all object attributes from other domains in universal groups.

- **Is direct IP connectivity possible between all domains?**   If you have IP connectivity, use global groups when membership changes frequently or you have Exchange servers in each domain that can act as expansion servers. Otherwise, use universal groups, because membership is static, and the local expansion server can expand the list.

- **Will membership change frequently?**   If membership changes often, use global groups. If membership changes infrequently, use universal groups.

Microsoft Outlook users will not be able to view the user memberships of a group that has been created in a remote domain. They can view membership only in global groups and domain local groups that have been created in their home domain.

An Expansion server, which has been mentioned several times, requires some explanation. When a message is sent to a mail-enabled group, the message needs to be expanded and individually addressed to each member of the group. By default, the local server performs the expansion and uses LDAP to contact the Global Catalog server to deliver the message to each member of the group. If the message is intended for a local group in the domain, the local Global Catalog server is contacted. If the local server is not available for expansion, another server in the site is used.

You can select a specific server in an organization to be an expansion server. The advantage of doing this is that you can offload the sometimes resource-intensive process of expanding large distribution groups to a dedicated server, removing the load from the mailbox server. The disadvantage of specifying an expansion server is that if that expansion server is not available, messages to the distribution group are not delivered, as Exchange does not try another server. For this reason, if you choose to designate an expansion server, take steps to ensure high availability for that server.

Configuration Naming Partition

The configuration partition of Active Directory stores information regarding how your Exchange Server 2007 system is organized. Because this information is replicated to all domain controllers in the forest, the Exchange Server 2007 configuration is also replicated throughout the forest. The configuration information includes the Exchange Server 2007 topology, connectors, protocols, and service settings.

Schema Naming Partition

The schema partition contains all object types and their attributes that can be created in Active Directory. This information is replicated to all domain controllers in the forest. During the first installation of Exchange Server 2007 in the forest, the Active Directory schema is extended to include new object classes and attributes that are specific to Exchange Server 2007. These new classes start with "msExch" or "ms-Exch" and are derived from the LDAP Data Interchange Format (LDIF) information in the Exchange Server 2007 installation files.

Given that these extensions represent more than 1000 changes to the schema and that these changes are replicated to all the domain controllers in your forest, you should prepare the forest for Exchange Server 2007 at the beginning of a period of time when you anticipate that network activity will be relatively light—for example, on a Friday night. This schedule gives the domain controllers time to replicate all the schema changes into their own databases.

Note   You can install Exchange Server 2007 using the */prepare AD* switch, which writes the new Exchange object classes and attributes to the schema but does not install Exchange itself. Plan on this activity taking anywhere from 30 to 90 minutes, depending on the speed and capacity of your hardware. Also, generally, the earlier in an Active Directory deployment that you extend schema, the better, because as domain controllers are added to the forest, they inherit the extended schema, thus reducing replication traffic when */prepare AD* is run. For more information on installing Exchange Server 2007, consult Chapter 6.

Exchange Server 2007 and Forest Boundaries

Because Exchange Server 2007 stores much of its information in the configuration naming partition, an Exchange Server 2007 organization cannot be extended past the boundaries of the forest. This is one area in which your Active Directory structure directly influences your Exchange topology. Having multiple forests in a company incurs the following limitations:

- You have separate Exchange organizations to administer.

- You have separate Global Address Lists, with no automatic directory replication between them.

- All e-mail system features are not available between forests.

Cross-Forest authentication is available, however. See Chapter 21, "Messaging Security," for a discussion about this topic.

Although using a single forest is the recommended way to set up an Exchange Server 2007 organization, if you want to synchronize directory information among multiple forests, you can use one of two scenarios:

- **Resource forest**   In this scenario, one forest is dedicated to running Exchange Server 2007 and hosting mailboxes. User accounts associated with those mailboxes are contained in separate forests. The disadvantage of using this scenario is higher cost associated with configuring the additional forest, domain controllers, and

Exchange servers. You must also ensure that when objects are created in one forest, corresponding placeholder objects are created in the other forests.

■ **Cross-forest**   Exchange Server 2007 runs in multiple forests, and e-mail functionality is configured between forests. The primary disadvantage of this scenario is reduced e-mail functionality between forests.

Configuration Partition and Directory Data

The two Active Directory services that an Exchange server uses most often are the Global Catalog server for address book lookups and the configuration naming partition for routing information. It is possible that two different domain controllers will be referenced, depending on the type of request being made by the Exchange server.

When an Exchange server starts up, it establishes a number of LDAP connections to domain controllers and Global Catalog servers. If it needs routing information to route a message, it can contact any domain controller to obtain this information, because each domain controller in the forest has a full copy of the configuration naming partition. If the Exchange server needs to obtain the Global Address List, it contacts the closest Global Catalog server. Best practice is to place a Global Catalog server near the Exchange server and make sure that they are in the same site and domain.

DNS Configuration

On the Internet (or on any TCP/IP network, for that matter), every device is represented by an IP address—using a four-part dotted-decimal notation, such as 192.168.0.1. A device with a TCP/IP address is called a *host* and is assigned a host name, which is a character-based name that is easier for humans to recognize and remember than its numeric IP address. The format of the host name is *hostname.domain.com*. When a host name identifies a resource on a TCP/IP network, computers must translate that host name into an IP address because computers communicate using only IP addresses. This translation is called *name resolution*.

Two basic methods exist for resolving host names to IP addresses on a TCP/IP network. The first involves using a Hosts file. The Hosts file is a single, flat file that simply lists hosts on a network and each host's IP address. To use the SMTP with a Hosts file, enter into that file the domain name and IP address of the hosts to which the IMS might need to transfer messages. As you might imagine, this process can be time consuming.

The second method of resolving names is more efficient. It involves the Domain Name System (DNS), a hierarchical, distributed database of host names and IP addresses. In order to run Exchange Server 2007, you must have already installed Windows Server

2003 Active Directory and DNS services on your network. Although host files are still available in Windows Server 2003, given the dynamic nature of the new implementation of DNS, there are few times when you'll want to use them.

You are likely to want outside SMTP hosts to be able to transfer messages to your SMTP service. To enable this capability, create two records in the DNS database so that those outside hosts can resolve your server's IP address. The first record you must create is an address record, or a record for your Exchange server. This can be registered dynamically with DNS in Windows Server 2003. The second record is a mail exchanger record, or MX record, which is a standard DNS record type used to designate one or more hosts that process mail for an organization or site. This record must be entered manually in your DNS tables.

More Info   This chapter provides a simple discussion of configuring TCP/IP and DNS, but these topics actually encompass a monstrous amount of material. If you need more information about using TCP/IP and DNS in the Windows Server 2003 environment, see *Microsoft Windows Server 2003 Administrator's Companion*, Second Edition, by Charlie Russel, Sharon Crawford, and Jason Gerend (Microsoft Press, 2006).

Summary

This chapter described the ways in which Exchange Server 2007 is integrated with Windows Server 2003. It gave an overview of how Active Directory is structured and described how Exchange Server 2007 works with Active Directory. It also discussed the Internet information protocols installed with Windows Server 2003 as well as services available in Exchange Server 2007, such as Outlook Web Access. In the Chapter 3, "Exchange Server 2007 Architecture," you learn more about the Exchange Server 2007 architecture.

Chapter 3
Exchange Server 2007 Architecture

This chapter describes the architecture of Microsoft Exchange Server 2007. This chapter covers each of the Exchange Server 2007 roles, the database file structure, the Extensible Storage Engine (ESE), and the way Exchange Server 2007 handles public folders. Additionally, you learn about indexing and how clients access Exchange Server 2007 stores, as well as the various server roles available in Exchange Server 2007. You also get an overview of the storage needs of Exchange Server 2007. Finally, you take a look at how Exchange Server 2007 differs from older versions of Exchange when it comes to analyzing the message routing topology.

The Role of Exchange Server 2007 Roles

With the release of Exchange Server 2007, Microsoft introduces significant flexibility and further secures the product through the overhaul of a role-based architecture. Although the Exchange Server product has supported roles for quite some time, Exchange Server

2007 takes the paradigm to a new level, providing, among other things, the following benefits:

- Enhanced security by reducing the attack surface of the Exchange Server to only those services absolutely necessary to perform the functions of a particular role

- Improved ability of administrators to make better use of hardware by targeting roles while not having to worry about a drain on system resources by services not necessary for a particular function through installation flexibility

- Streamlined and simplified administration by providing Exchange Server administrators with a role-based concept that maps more to a more natural way to handle tasks

Exchange Server 2007 includes five distinct roles, each supporting a specific set of features. All five roles are discussed in the following sections.

Mailbox Server Role

The Mailbox server role is the foundational server role in Exchange Server 2007. The mailbox server is responsible for hosting mailbox and public folder databases. The Mailbox server role also provides scheduling services for Outlook users. The Mailbox server role also handles communication with Outlook clients, except when such clients connect using RPC-over-HTTP, now known as Outlook Anywhere. This role can be installed in three ways:

- **Mailbox Role Only (no clustering)**   When installed without a clustering option, the Mailbox role can coexist with any of the other server roles, with the exception of the Edge Transport role, which must always be installed by itself.

- **Active Clustered Mailbox Role**   If you opt for one of the clustered mailbox options, you cannot install any other roles on the server. The first mailbox server you create in a new cluster must be an active node because it initially houses the mailbox database.

- **Passive Clustered Mailbox Role**   Subsequent Exchange Server 2007 installations on other servers support installation of the Passive Clustered Mailbox role, which is a standby backup of your cluster's active node.

The clustered mailbox roles support both cluster continuous replication (CCR) and single copy clusters (SCC). CCR is a high-availability feature that has no single point of failure and that can be deployed in a geographically redundant fashion. SCC is akin to Exchange's traditional clustering options in that the clustered Exchange servers share a single copy of the database, which is housed on some kind of shared storage mechanism, such as a storage area network (SAN) array. For more information about clustering in Exchange Server 2007, see Chapter 9, "High Availability in Exchange Server 2007."

Client Access Server Role

If the Mailbox server role provides the foundation for your new Exchange Server 2007 infrastructure, the Client Access server role provides your users with a doorway into that new structure. As such, at least one server running this access-enabling role is required. The Client Access server role is responsible for almost all client-facing activity in your Exchange Server 2007 organization, including the following:

■ **Outlook Anywhere**   Formerly called RPC-over-HTTP, the newly named Outlook Anywhere service provides the services that the feature's new name implies—namely, by enabling this Client Access server role-based feature, users can connect Outlook clients from anywhere, including outside your organization's firewall. Of course, in order to use this feature, you need an appropriately configured firewall. Outlook Anywhere is discussed further in Chapter 23, "Deploying Microsoft Office Outlook 2007."

> **Note**   The Client Access server role does not directly serve Outlook clients, but does serve these clients when they connect to Exchange Server via Outlook Anywhere. MAPI-based connections to Exchange Server are a function of the Mailbox server role.

■ **Outlook Web Access**   Outlook Web Access (OWA) in Exchange Server 2007 has undergone a tremendous transformation for users of all browsers and operating system platforms. The Premium OWA client, supported by Internet Explorer 6 and above, boasts such enhancements as direct access to file shares and more. The Light OWA client, which provides OWA capability to non-Internet Explorer browsers and to older versions of Internet Explorer, has been completely overhauled. OWA 2007 alone is worth the price of admission to the world of Exchange Server 2007. Outlook Web Access is discussed in detail in Chapter 24, "Supporting Outlook Web Access."

■ **POP3 Access**   The venerable Post Office Protocol version 3 (POP3) protocol is still found in this latest version of Exchange Server. POP3 is a function of the Client Access server role. POP3 is a message retrieval mechanism that is discussed in detail in Chapter 25, "Supporting Other Clients."

■ **IMAP4 access**   Internet Message Access Protocol version 4 (IMAP4) is a popular way for users to connect to Exchange Server using clients other than Outlook. IMAP4, supported via the Client Access server role, provides users with the flexibility of reading mail from almost anywhere while leaving messages on the server. Learn all about IMAP by reading to Chapter 25.

■ **Exchange ActiveSync**   The use of mobile devices for message retrieval has exploded since the introduction of Exchange Server 2003. Although ActiveSync, the mechanism by which mobile devices can automatically synchronize e-mail between the device and an Exchange Server computer, was supported in Exchange Server 2003 and later enhanced through a service pack, Exchange Server 2007 provides full support for this synchronization technology from the beginning. Mobile users must connect to a server running the Client Access server role in order to synchronize their mobile devices.

- **The AutoDiscover Service** Exchange Server 2007, along with Outlook 2007, provides an easier way for users and administrators to connect to Exchange-based mailboxes—the AutoDiscover service. Using the AutoDiscover service, you can simply provide Outlook 2007 with e-mail address and password for a mailbox, and Outlook 2007 automatically accesses a Client Access Server to obtain the rest of the details necessary to complete the configuration of the Outlook 2007 client.

- **The Availability Service** In Exchange Server 2003, user availability, or free/busy, information was stored in a public folder, a mechanism that resulted in a lag of up to 15 minutes for updates to be made to recipient free/busy data. Further, this free/busy information was subject to replication rules that could break...and did so from time to time. Anyone who has been managing any semicomplex Exchange organization for any significant amount of time has probably run into dreaded free/busy public folder replication or corruption problems. The Exchange Server 2007 Availability service aims to fix all of these problems and is integrated into the Client Access server role. Under Exchange Server 2007 and Outlook 2007, availability information is no longer stored in a public folder. Instead, when an Outlook 2007 or Outlook Web Access 2007 user needs to retrieve calendar information, individual mailboxes are polled in real time. The advantages: no more replication, no more lag, and a significantly simplified architecture. Of course, this feature depends on both Exchange Server 2007 and Outlook 2007. Older versions of Outlook still expect to find a public folder for free/busy information, so the Availability service continues to serve this role as well.

- **Unified Messaging features** The Client Access server is also the front end into some of the unified features of Exchange Server 2007, such as Play on phone. Play on phone is a way to tell Exchange Server that you want to play a voice mail message on your phone. When you enable this feature, you can request that Exchange Server call your phone to play a voice message to you.

Hub Transport Server Role

Another required role, the Hub Transport server is responsible for all message delivery in your Exchange Server organization. The Hub Transport server role also has the following responsibilities:

- **Message Submission**   Message submission is the process of placing messages into submission queues on a Hub Transport server. The message submission service is also responsible for gathering mail from users' Outbox folders as they are sent as well as for submitting messages received through an SMTP receive connector.

- **Mail Flow**   Every message sent in your organization passes through a Hub Transport server, thus underscoring the necessity for this role's existence in every Exchange Server 2007 organization. Even messages that are sent between mailboxes in the same mailbox database are sent through a Hub Transport server in order that transport rules, such as the addition of an e-mail disclaimer, can be applied to each message.

- **Message Delivery**   The Hub Transport server role handles all local and remote delivery of messages. For remote delivery, the Hub Transport server is responsible for sending the message to the remote Active Directory site. For e-mail destined for Internet sites, the Hub Transport server either sends the message to an Edge server or is configured to directly send mail to remote SMTP hosts.

- **Transport Rules**   The Hub Transport server handles the application of rules to messages traversing your Exchange organization. Such rules can include the addition of disclaimers to e-mail, rights management, and more. In fact, *all* messages sent in the organization are sent through the Hub Transport role, providing you a high degree of predictability regarding the application of transport rules.

- **Antivirus and Anti-spam**   In the absence of an Edge Transport server, which is better suited to handle message protection, a Hub Transport server can provide antivirus and anti-spam services to the organization.

Unified Messaging Server Role

Perhaps the most noticeable addition to Exchange Server 2007 is the inclusion of all-new Unified Messaging capabilities. Unified messaging allows all of a user's e-mail, voice mail messages, and fax communications to be stored in a single mailbox. The services provided by this role also allow the various types of messages to be accessible from a number of points, including from Outlook, Outlook Web Access, from a compatible mobile device, and the telephone. The Unified Messaging role in Exchange Server 2007 has the following features:

- **Outlook Voice Access**   An addition to the Outlook line, Outlook Voice Access provides voice-based access into a user's Unified Messaging-enabled mailbox. Contents of the mailbox can then be managed either via voice commands or touch-tone input.

- **Auto Attendant**   Most companies today put callers into an automated menu system so that the customer's call can be routed most efficiently to the right person or department. The Unified Messaging role in Exchange Server 2007 provides this same technology.

- **Traditional Voice Mail Operations**   When most people think of voice mail, what comes to mind is calling someone and getting the voice mail system when that person fails to pick up the phone or is on another call. In these instances, the voice mail system plays the person's personal message and then records a voice mail message that is then played back when the person is available. Unified Messaging provides all of these traditional voice mail functions.

- **Faxing**   Using Unified Messaging, users can receive faxes in their inbox.

You learn all about the Unified Messaging capabilities in Exchange Server 2007 in Chapter 14, "Unified Messaging."

Edge Transport Server Role

Also new to Exchange Server is the Edge Transport server role, whose primary responsibility is to protect your messaging environment from viruses and spam and to ensure regulatory compliance. The Edge Transport role provides a wide variety of functionality to help your organization protect electronic assets. Among the features included with the Edge Transport role are:

- **Address Rewriting**   Address rewriting allows you to modify sender and recipient addresses on messages to and from your organization. As an example, suppose one organization has merged with another. You can use address rewriting to present a unified face to the world by rewriting the addresses of the merged organization to match the address of the acquiring company.

- **Sender ID**   Sender ID uses the IP address of the sending server and the Purported Responsible Address of the sender to help determine whether or not the incoming message has a spoofed sender. This is useful in cutting down on phishing expeditions.

- **Filtering**   The Edge Transport server provides attachment filtering, connection filtering, content filtering, recipient filtering, and sender filtering. Attachment filtering filters messages based on the name of the file, the file extension, or content type. Connection filtering looks up the IP address of the sending server and runs it against block lists and allow lists to determine whether the message should be allowed. Content filtering uses the Intelligent Message Filter-based Microsoft SmartScreen technology to assess the contents of a message. This service recognizes key indicators of both legitimate messages and spam messages to accurately assess the probability that an inbound e-mail message is legitimate. Recipient and sender filtering can block a message based on addresses in the To or From lines.

■ **Transport rules**   You can use transport rules to reduce the number of viruses that enter your organization and to reduce the effect of denial-of-service attacks and to prevent infected internal computers from spreading.

The Edge Transport server role is described in detail in Chapter 20, "Antivirus and Anti-spam."

Storage Design Goals in Exchange Server 2007

The storage architecture of Exchange Server 2007 has three goals. The first goal is to allow a single server to host more users than is pragmatically possible in 32-bit versions of Microsoft Exchange Server, thus driving down the overall cost of storage. Storage alone can consume up to 80 percent of an Exchange project's budget. Depending on how you have your server storage configured, the 64-bit architecture of Exchange Server 2007 allows you to use up to 75 percent fewer disks to achieve performance levels comparable to older versions of Exchange. Thus, you can make the choice between supporting the same number of users on one-quarter of the disks of your old servers; you can choose to add 300 percent more users to a single server; or you can support a number of users with much larger mailboxes. Any way you look at it, however, Exchange Server 2007 provides much better per-server scalability than was possible under a 32-bit architecture.

A second goal related to storage architecture on Exchange Server 2007 is to enhance the overall reliability of the infrastructure. This goal is accomplished in a number of ways. First, Microsoft singificantly enhanced the stores/storage groups architecture in Exchange Server 2007. By increasing the number of storage groups, more users can exist on a single server. Because the databases are smaller, creating more databases on each server allows each server to host more users. For example, it is easier to manage six databases with 1,000 users per database than it is to manage one database of 6,000 users. Not only can backup and restore times be scheduled individually and run faster, but if one database becomes corrupted, only 1,000 users are affected instead of 6,000 users. In addition, Exchange Server 2007 can group multiple databases into a single storage group and host multiple storage groups on a single server. In total, Exchange Server 2007 can support up to 50 databases per server. This is a dramatic increase over older versions of Exchange Server, which support a maximum of 20 databases on a single server. Table 3-1 shows you how the number of stores and storage groups has changed with each iteration of Exchange Server.

Note   Although the 32-bit version of Exchange Server 2007 is not supported in a production environment, it is widely used for testing. During testing, be aware that the 32-bit version supports a maximum of five storage groups and five databases per server.

A third goal for Exchange Server 2007 was enhancing the infrastructure's recoverability in the event of a disaster. Through the use of various forms of clustering, a technology that has been signficiantly improved in Exchange Server 2007, those that upgrade realize shorter downtimes and greater productivity for users because data can more easily and more quickly be recovered from a clustered copy.

Table 3-1   Exchange Server Storage Comparison

	2000 Std.	2000 Ent.	2003 Std.	2003 Ent.	2007 Std.	2007 Ent.
Storage Groups	1	4	1	4	5	50
Stores per group	2 (1 mailbox, 1 public)	5	2 (1 mailbox, 1 public)	5	5	50
Stores per server	2	20	2	20	5	50
Database size limit	16 GB	16 TB	75 GB	16 TB	16 TB	16 TB
Recovery Group	No	No	Yes	Yes	Yes	Yes

You got an introduction to some of the clustering options in Exchange Server 2007 in the discussion of the Mailbox server role earlier in this chapter. Here are some additional notes regarding the clustering capabilities of Exchange Server 2007.

- **Local Continuous Replication**   Local continuous replication (LCR) is a feature that uses asynchronous log shipping to maintain a locally housed copy of your databases. With LCR, you can manually cut over to the clustered database.

- **Continuous Cluster Replication (CCR)**   Continuous cluster replication (CCR) is similar to LCR, except that the database copy is housed on a separate server either in the same data center or in a remote data center.

- **Single Copy Clusters**   A single copy cluster (SCC) is very similar to legacy Exchange clustering techniques in that a single copy of a database is housed on shared storage that is used by multiple Exchange servers.

Stores and Storage Groups

When talking about Exchange Server storage, it's important that you understand what is meant by the terms store and storage group. In Exchange, a store is the entity in which user mailboxes are located. A *store* also has its own associated database file in which mailbox contents are saved. *Storage groups*, first introduced in Exchange 2000 Server as a means to achieve more reasonable scalability, are collections of individual stores. The version and edition of Exchange server in use at your organization dictates the level to which you can utilize stores and storage groups. Table 3-1, which you saw earlier, outlines the storage capabilities of various versions of Exchange Server.

In Table 3-1, take special notice of the *Stores per server* values in the two editions of Exchange Server 2007. Under Exchange Server 2003, the value for the maximum stores allowed on a single server was a simple mathematical operation that multiplied the maximum number of storage groups and the maximum stores per storage group. Partially due to the 64-bit nature of Exchange Server 2007, these two values have been drastically increased in both editions of Exchange Server 2007. However, the maximum stores per server is no longer a function of stores and storage groups per server. Instead, the standard edition of Exchange Server 2007 supports a maximum of five stores on a server while the enterprise edition supports up to 50 stores on a single server. There are no artificial database size restrictions on the Standard Edition of Exchange Server 2007.

Note   The terms *store, information store,* and *database* are more or less interchangeable.

Storage in Exchange Server 2007 can be configured in a number of ways, but there are a few things that can't change, such as the need for stores and storage groups. A storage group in an Exchange Server 2007 system resides in a Mailbox server role server and consists of a set of up to 50 databases (stores) for the Enterprise Edition and five for the Standard Edition. Housed in each separate store is a single database file and other information, including data definitions, indices, and other information associated with user mailboxes or public folders.

As was the case in older versions of Exchange, log files belong to the storage group and not to each individual store. All the databases in a storage group use the same transaction log files. Each database in Exchange Server 2007 consists of a single file, the database, sometimes referred to as the .edb file after the name of the actual file's extension. This file is managed by the Information Store service. Take special note that the streaming file (.stm file) that used to be associated with each information store has been eliminated. All content is now stored in the database, resulting in a smaller overall I/O footprint for Exchange, which was one of the design considerations of Exchange Server 2007 and is part of the reason that Exchange Server 2007 can support many more users per server. In addition, the Exchange Installable File System (ExIFS) is now completely gone from the product.

These days, it is not uncommon to find Exchange databases that are massive—approaching 100 GB or more. The time necessary to back up these databases can exceed several hours. The problem with this is not the time it takes to back up the database, but the time it takes to restore such a large database. During the restoration, of course, your users' productivity with regard to e-mail approaches zero. Under Exchange Server 2007, these delays can also impact a user's use of voice mail. In essence, the entire communication flow in your organization can come to a grinding halt if you don't take appropriate time to plan your storage architecture. In Exchange Server database planning, the old cliché is a good one: *Always plan for failure so that you can succeed*. You'll find that prudent use of storage groups will help you succeed during disaster recovery.

As you read earlier, in implementing storage groups and allowing multiple databases per Exchange Server 2007 server, Microsoft has made some tremendous changes to the Extensible Storage Engine (ESE) database architecture since Exchange Server 2003, changes that are even more dramatic when you go back as far as Exchange Server 5.5 (see Table 3-1). These changes significantly enhance recoverability and maximize productivity when an Exchange database becomes corrupted. In addition, storage groups offer several key benefits that are listed here and discussed in the sections that follow:

- Each server can host more users than before.
- Each database can be backed up and restored individually.
- Each server can host multiple businesses.
- A separate store can be used for special mailboxes that may require different limits than users in other stores.

Increased User Support

Probably the largest benefit of storage groups is that they allow you to spread users across databases and storage groups on the same Exchange Server 2007 server. This scenario provides three distinct advantages:

- **You can support more users on a single server than was possible in earlier versions of Exchange.**   This is particularly true when you look at the way Exchange Server 2007 is architected. The 64-bit capability of the product makes significantly more memory available, thus increasing the number of potential users per server.
- **You have less downtime when a database becomes corrupted.**   By breaking up your users into separately managed groups, you keep the overall database size lower for each individual group, thereby reducing the amount of time it takes to restore after a failure.
- **You can host more users on an Exchange server because you can keep your databases to a manageable size.**   As you create more storage groups, they become separately managed entities and are backed up and restored separately. If a database becomes corrupt, you will affect fewer users.

As mentioned earlier, each server can house up to 50 storage groups, and within a storage group, you can have up to 50 databases. However, each server can have a maximum of 50 databases in total, no matter how many storage groups you create. Bear in mind that this is just for Exchange Server 2007 Enterprise Edition. The standard edition has lower limits, which were detailed in Table 3-1.

There are some good reasons to refrain from creating the maximum number of databases possible in a single storage group. First, a log file problem could then bring down all of the databases in that storage group, resulting in an ugly situation for your help desk, not to mention the impact on business operations. Further, when you run the Information Store Integrity Checker (Isinteg.exe) on a database, you must dismount that individual database's information store. In addition, Isinteg.exe needs a second database for temporary use while the tool works its magic. When you plan for your Exchange Server 2007 storage needs, make sure that you leave a database slot available in the event that you need to run Isinteg.exe. Having your users spread out across multiple databases means that only a subset of your users is affected if one of your databases goes offline for some reason. The other users can continue to work because their databases are up and running. A database that is offline is considered to be *dismounted*. Its icon appears with a down arrow in the Exchange Management Console, as shown in Figure 3-1. Also, the database's status is explicitly listed as Dismounted.

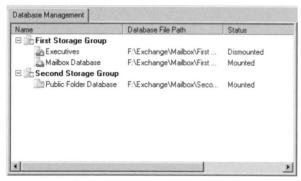

Figure 3-1   Online databases and an offline database (Executives) in a single storage group

Individual Backup and Restore

Because each individual database can be mounted or dismounted, you can back up and restore databases individually while other databases in the same storage group are mounted and running. Consider a scenario in which you have created four mailbox stores in the same storage group, one for each of four departments. If one of those stores becomes corrupted, the other three can remain mounted while you restore the fourth store from backup and then mount it again. You are not required to dismount all the stores in a storage group in order to restore one of them. And if one store becomes corrupted and cannot be mounted, it does not stop other stores in the same storage group from being mounted and available to users.

Database File Structure

Exchange Server 2007 databases (also called mailbox stores) consist of a single file that has an .edb extension. The database file holds everything related to a user's mailbox, including e-mail messages, voice mail messages, faxes, Message Application Programming Interface (MAPI) content, attachments, and more. Exchange Server 2007 no longer relies on the streaming (.stm) file to hold non-MAPI content. Exchange Server databases are stored in an Extensible Storage Engine (ESE) database format. (ESE is discussed later in this chapter.)

The .edb database holds messages from MAPI clients such as Microsoft Outlook. MAPI clients access these messages without a conversion process running on the server. The rich text file is the same as the Exchange 5.5 information store. It is an .edb file that uses transaction logging just as it did in Exchange 5.5.

On-Demand Content Conversion

When a MAPI client attempts to read a message from the database, no conversion is necessary when the message format was originally rich text or plain text, because the message is in the client's native format. However, if another type of client, such as an HTTP client, attempts to read a rich text or plain text message from the database, Exchange converts the message to the requested format. This process, in which messages are converted for dissimilar clients, is known as *on-demand conversion*.

Client Access servers and Hub Transport servers handle the brunt of the content conversion tasks. However, for legacy Outlook Web Access clients, content conversion is handled by a Mailbox server. In situations in which a client requests data that needs to use a Client Access server for conversion, such data is accessed and converted by the Mailbox server and then sent to the Client Access server.

Single-Instance Message Store

Exchange Server 2007 databases continue to support the Single-Instance Message Store (SIS) feature, meaning that a message sent to multiple recipients is stored only once as long as all the recipients are located in the same database. SIS is not maintained when a mailbox is moved to a different database, even if it still resides in the same storage group. Moreover, SIS does not span multiple databases in a single storage group.

Here is an example of how SIS works. Laura Owen, the Exchange administrator at a company named Contoso, has deployed two storage groups consisting of four databases each. Each group contains two mailbox stores and two public folder stores. John Peoples, a user in Laura's network, sends a 1-MB message to a distribution group of 40 recipients, all of them residing in the first storage group, with 30 of them in mailbox store 1 and the other 10 in mailbox store 2.

Without SIS, the message would be copied 42 times (40 copies for 40 users plus 1 copy for the transaction log plus 1 copy in the Sent Items folder of the sender), requiring a whopping 42 MB of total disk space to store the message. However, as Figure 3-2 shows, with SIS only three copies of the message are held: one in the database of mailbox store 1, one in the database of mailbox store 2, and one temporarily in the transaction log. Hence, sending this message to these 40 recipients requires only 3 MB of total disk space, saving 38 MB.

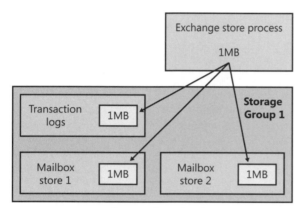

Figure 3-2   How the Single-Instance Message Store feature works

Data Recovery and Transaction Logs

Three of the top 10 questions that Microsoft's technical support receives are related to the Extensible Storage Engine (ESE) and data recovery. This section discusses the role of transaction logs and describes how they are used in the recovery of your databases in the event of a catastrophe. It also covers why databases fail and looks at some of the common error messages that accompany a database failure. See Chapter 16 for a step-by-step description of how to restore a database.

The Extensible Storage Engine

The Extensible Storage Engine is a transaction logging system that ensures data integrity and consistency in the event of a system crash or media failure. The design of the ESE was guided by four criteria. The first was a question: "What happens if there's a crash?" Every development was guided by the notion that it should improve recoverability in the event of a disaster. The second criterion was to reduce the number of I/O operations that ESE performs, and every effort was made to do so. Three I/O operations are better (faster) than four, and four are better than five. Even if it means expanding an I/O operation to include additional calculations, eliminating one I/O operation greatly improves performance. The third criterion was for the database engine to be as self-tuning as possible. Finally, ESE is designed to provide an uptime as close to 24 hours a day, 7 days a week as possible. Achieving the online maintenance level will enhance the success of this last goal.

The main function of ESE is to manage transactions. ESE applies four tests to the databases to ensure their integrity. They are sometimes referred to as ACID tests:

- **Atomic**   Either all the operations performed in a transaction must be completed, or none will be completed.

- **Consistent**   A transaction must start with a database in a consistent state and leave the database in a consistent state when finished.

- **Isolated**   Changes are not visible until all operations within the transaction are completed. When all operations are completed and the database is in a consistent state, the transaction is said to have been *committed*.

- **Durable**   Committed transactions are preserved even if the system experiences significant stress such as a system crash.

Note   Durability can be seen when the system crashes during the performance of the operations. If some of the operations were completed before a system crash (for example, if the e-mail was deleted from the Inbox and copied to the Private folder but the item count on each folder was not updated), when the Store.exe process starts on reboot, it will detect that the database is in an inconsistent state and will roll back the operations. This precaution means that the e-mail message cannot be lost while it is being moved, nor will there be two copies of the message upon reboot. ESE ensures that, when restarted, the database is in the same state it was in immediately before the operations began.

Real World   What Happens When a Change Is Made to a Page in the Database?

Let's say that you move an important e-mail message from your Inbox to a private folder named Private. The following operations occur to complete this transaction:

- Inserting the e-mail message into the Private folder
- Deleting the e-mail message from the Inbox folder

- Updating the information about each folder to correctly display the number of items in each folder

- Committing the transaction in the temporary transaction log file

Because these operations are performed in a single transaction, Exchange either performs all of them or none of them. This is the Atomic test. The commit operation cannot be carried out until all the operations have been performed successfully. Once the transaction is committed, the Isolated test is passed. And because the database is left in a consistent state, the Consistent test is passed. Finally, after the transaction is committed to the database, the changes are preserved even if there is a crash. This meets the Durable test.

How Data Is Stored

In an ESE database file, data is organized in 8-KB sections called *pages*. Information is read from an ESE database file and loaded into memory in the form of a page. Each page contains data definitions, data, indexes, checksums, flags, timestamps, and other B-tree information. The pages are numbered sequentially within the database file to maximize performance. Pages contain either the actual data or pointers to other pages that contain the data. These pointers form a B-tree structure, and rarely is the tree more than three or four levels deep. Hence, the B-tree structure is wide but shallow.

More Info   If you want to learn more about the B-tree database structures, you can find plenty of information on the Internet. Start by going to *http://www.bluerwhite.org/btree*. As always, a Google search on "B-tree" yields other sites with more information than you'll be able to read in a single sitting.

A *transaction* is a series of modifications to a page in a database. Each modification is called an *operation*. When a complete series of operations has been performed on an object in a database, a transaction is said to have occurred.

To actually commit a transaction, the operations must be written to the transaction log buffer before being written to the transaction logs on disk. ESE uses "write-ahead" logging, which means that before ESE makes a change to the database, it notes what it's going to do in the log file. Data is written to a cached version of the log in the log buffer area; the page in memory is modified; and a link is created between these two entries. Before the modifications of the page can be written to disk, the change recorded in the log buffer must first be written to the log file on disk.

When a page is first read from disk and stored in memory, it is considered *clean*. Once an operation has modified the page, the page is marked as *dirty*. Dirty pages are available for further modifications if necessary, and multiple modifications can be made to a dirty page before it is written back to disk. The number of modifications to a page has no bearing on when the page will be written back to disk. This action is determined by other measures, which are discussed later in this chapter.

While the operations are being performed, they are being recorded in the version store. The version store keeps a list of all of the changes that have been made to a page but have not yet been committed. If your server loses power before the series of operations can be committed, the version store is referenced when ESE starts again to roll back, or undo, the unfinished operations. The version store is a virtual store—you won't find a Version Store database on the hard drive. The version store is held in RAM and really constitutes versioned pages of a single page that was read from the disk to memory. Figure 3-3 illustrates this process.

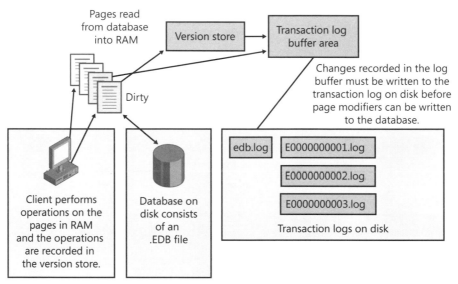

Figure 3-3   How ESE handles transactions

Note   One operation can hang or be so large that the version store takes up hundreds of megabytes. This situation can occur if your operation is indexing a large table or writing a very large file to the database. Because the version store keeps track of all changes that occurred to the database since the oldest transaction began, you might get the following error: "-1069 error (JET_errVersionStoreOutOfMemory)." If this happens, consider moving your databases and stores to another disk with more free disk space and consider increasing the RAM on your system.

Often, the cached version of the changes to the pages is not written to disk immediately. This does not present a problem, because the information is recorded in the log files.

Should the modifications in memory be lost, when ESE starts, the log files are replayed (a process discussed in more detail in the section "How Log Files Are Replayed during Recovery" later in this chapter), and the transactions are recorded to the disk. Moreover, not writing cached information to the database right away can improve performance. Consider the situation in which a page is loaded from memory and then modified. If it needs to be modified again soon thereafter, it does not need to be reread from the disk because it is already in memory. Thus, the modifications to the database can be batched to increase performance.

Database Files

Eventually, all transactions are written to one of these files. Before a page is written to disk, however, a checksum is calculated for that page, and the checksum is then written to the page along with the data. When the page is read from disk, the checksum is recalculated, and the page number is verified to be sure that it matches the requested page number. If the checksum fails or if there is a mismatch on the page number, a **-1018** error is generated. This error means that what was written to disk is not what was read by ESE from the disk into memory.

Note   Beginning with Service Pack 2 (SP2) in Exchange Server 5.5 and continuing in Exchange Server 2007, ESE attempts to read the data 16 times before generating a -1018 error, reducing the chance that a transient event might cause a problem. Hence, if you receive a -1018 error, you know that ESE attempted to read the data repeatedly before warning you.

ESE and Memory Management

Before it can load a page into memory, ESE reserves an area in memory for its own use. *Dynamic buffer allocation* (DBA) is the process of increasing the size of the database buffer cache before the memory is needed. More than a few Exchange administrators have complained that Exchange eats up all the memory on their servers. This situation is by design, although the design doesn't necessarily call for using all the memory, nor is the memory allocated to Exchange unavailable for other system processes. If other processes need more memory, Exchange releases the memory to that process so that it can run efficiently. This happens on the fly, and the methods used by ESE are not configurable.

In Exchange 4 and 5.0, the size of the cache was set by the Performance Optimizer. In Exchange 5.5, the process was changed to be dynamic: ESE observes the system and adjusts the size of the database cache as necessary. To observe how much of your RAM is being reserved by the Store process, use the Cache Size performance counter.

At this point, it might be helpful to take a look at the overall design goals of the DBA process. Understanding these will answer any questions you might have about memory management in Exchange Server 2007. The two design goals of DBA are

- **Maximize System Performance**   The Store process uses the amount of overall paging and I/O activity, among other factors, to determine how much RAM to allocate for the database buffer. Overall system performance really is the focus of this goal. It does no good to have Exchange running quickly if the operating system is constantly paging.

- **Maximize Memory Utilization**   Unused system memory is wasted dollars. ESE allocates to itself as much memory as it can without negatively impacting other applications. If a new application starts that needs additional memory, ESE releases memory so that the other application can run efficiently.

As you can see, you don't need to be alarmed if you go into Task Manager and see that, for example, out of the 1 GB of RAM on your system, only 200 MB are left, and the Store.exe process is using 800 MB of RAM. You're not running out of memory, and the Store.exe process does not have a memory leak. All it means is that the DBA feature of ESE has allocated additional RAM to increase your system performance. Figures 3-4 and 3-5 illustrate what this looks like in Task Manager. In Figure 3-4, you can see both the Store.exe and Mad.exe processes using more memory than most of the other processes. This figure was shot on a server that was not busy and still the Store.exe process was at the top of the memory usage list. Figure 3-5 shows that only 84,028 KB is available in physical memory. Look under the Physical Memory (K) box for the Available value.

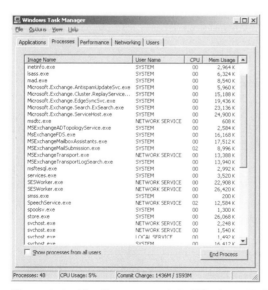

Figure 3-4   The Processes tab in Windows Task Manager, showing the memory allocated to Store.exe and Mad.exe

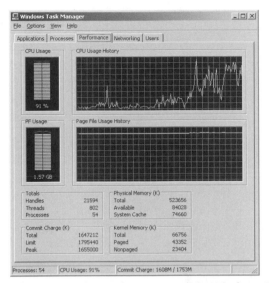

Figure 3-5   The Performance tab in Windows Task Manager, showing memory usage and availability

Transaction Log Files

In theory, the transaction log file could be one ever-expanding file. But it would grow so big that it would consume large amounts of disk space, thus becoming unmanageable. Hence, the log is broken down into *generations*–that is, into multiple files, each 1 MB in size and each representing a generation.

In Exchange Server 2007, the size of each log file is actually *reduced*. In older versions of Exchange, when each log file hit 5 MB in size, a new sequential log file was created. Under Exchange Server 2007, this limit is 1 MB. To address the potential problem of running out of log file names, which used to happen at just over a million log files, the log file name length is increased. Formerly, a log file had the name "E+sg+#####.log," but without the plus signs. The "sg" in the name is a storage group identifier, while the number signs represent a hexademical number that was up to five characters in length. Under Exchange Server 2007, this naming convention is now "E+nn+########.log." After doing some ESE math, this works out to 2,147,483,628 possible log files for each individual storage group. By ESE math, it's important to note that you can't have a log file named with all "f" characters. The maximum log file name is "7fffffec." This is an internal ESE limitation.

The Exx00000001.logfile is the highest generation. When it becomes full, it is renamed with the next hexadecimal number in sequence. As this happens, a temporary log file, Edbtemp.log, is created to hold transactions until a new log can be created.

Each log file consists of two sections: the header and the data. The header contains hard-coded paths to the databases that it references. In Exchange Server 2007, multiple databases can use the same log file, because the log files service the entire storage group. From an administrative perspective, this arrangement simplifies recovery. No matter which database in a storage group you're restoring, you reference the same log files for that group. The header also contains a signature matched to the database signature. This keeps the log file from being matched to a wrong but identically named database.

You can dump the header information of a log file with the command ESEUTIL /ML (see Figure 3-6). The dump displays the generation number, the hard-coded database paths, and the signatures. The data portion of the log file contains the transactional information, such as BeginTransaction, Commit, or Rollback information. The majority of it contains low-level, physical modifications to the database. In other words, it contains the records that say, "This information was inserted on this page at this location."

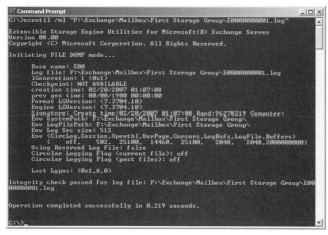

Figure 3-6   A header dump produced using ESEUTI /ML

When a database is modified, several steps occur. First, the page is read into the database cache, and then the timestamp on the page is updated. This timestamp is incremented on a per-database basis. Next, the log record is created, stating what is about to be done to the database. This occurs in the log cache buffer. Then the page is modified and a connection is created between these two entries so that the page cannot be written to disk without the log file entry being written to disk first. This step guarantees that a modification to the database is first written to the log file on disk before the database on disk is updated.

Hence, there is legitimate concern over the write-back caching that can be enabled on a log file disk controller. Essentially, *write-back caching* means that the hardware reports back to ESE a successful disk write even though the information is held in the disk buffer of the controller to be written to disk at a later time. Write-back caching, while improving performance, can also ruin the ESE process of writing changes to the log file before they are written to the database. If a controller or disk malfunction of some sort occurs, you could experience a situation in which the page has been written to disk but not recorded in the log file—which will lead to a corrupted database.

How Log Files Are Replayed during Recovery

After you restore your database, the logs are replayed when you start the Store.exe process. Replaying logs and then rolling back operations constitute the "starting" of the Store process; this is often referred to as the recovery process. Replaying the transaction logs is the first part of the recovery process, and it consumes most of the time necessary to start the Store.exe process.

Replaying the transaction log files means that for each log record, the page is read out of the database that the record references, and the timestamp on the page read from the database is compared to the timestamp of the log entry that references that page. If, for example, the log entry has a timestamp of 12 and the page read from the database has a timestamp of 11, ESE knows that the modification in the log file has not been written to disk, and so it writes the log entry to the database. However, if the timestamp on the page on disk is equal to or greater than the timestamp on the log entry, ESE does not write that particular log entry to disk and continues with the next log entry in the log file.

In the second and last phase of the recovery process, any uncommitted operations are rolled back: if a piece of e-mail was transferred, it is untransferred. If a message was deleted, it is restored. This is called *physical redo, logical undo*. Recovery runs every time the Store.exe process starts. If you stop and then start the Store process five times, the recovery process runs five times.

Even though the recovery process is run on the log files and not on the databases, if you move your databases, recovery won't work because the hard-coded path to the database in the header of the log file no longer points to the database. At the end of recovery, the process appears to have been successful, but when you attempt to use that database, you get an error with an event ID of 9519 from MSExchangeIS in the application log, indicating an error in starting your database (see Figure 3-7).

If you move the database back to the location where the log file expects to find it and then start the Store process, you should find that recovery brings your database to a consistent and usable state.

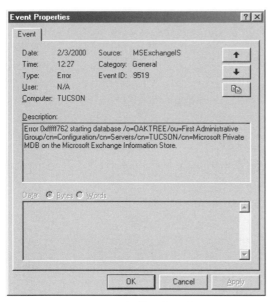

Figure 3-7   Message indicating that an error occurred when starting the database

Checkpoint File

The *checkpoint file* is an optimization of the recovery process. It records which entries in the log files have already been written to disk. If all the entries in the log files have been written to disk, the log files don't need to be replayed during recovery. The checkpoint file can speed up recovery time by telling ESE which log file entries need to be replayed and which do not.

Faster recovery of a database is sometimes why circular logging is enabled. *Circular logging* deletes log files older than the current checkpoint location. The problem with circular logging is that you lose the ability to roll forward from a backup tape. If some of your log files since the last full backup have been deleted by circular logging, you are able to recover only to the last full backup. However, if you have all your old log files, restoring the last full backup of your database from tape allows for a full restore up to the point of your disaster, because all the log files can be replayed into the restored database. Remember that in order for a full restore to work, the database must be in the same physical condition as it was when the log files were written. A physically corrupt database cannot service a restore process.

Important   Never, never, never delete your log files! Here's why: Assume that log file 9 contains a command to insert a new page at a particular place in the database. Log file 10 contains a command to delete this page. Now suppose that an administrator deletes log file 9, perhaps thinking that the file's timestamp is too old and deletes the checkpoint file. The administrator then needs to reboot the system for unrelated reasons. When the Store.exe process is started, ESE automatically enters recovery mode. Finding no checkpoint file, ESE has no choice but to replay all the log files. When log file 10 is replayed, the delete command is carried out on that page, and its contents are destroyed. ESE won't know that there was an earlier command to insert a new page in that location in the database because log file 9 was deleted. Your database will be corrupted. Whatever you do, *do not delete your log files*. Furthermore, be aware that *write-back caching can have the effect of deleting log files*. The best practice is to disable write-back caching and never delete your log files or checkpoint file.

How Log Entries Are Written to the Database

As mentioned earlier, modified pages in memory and committed transactions in the log buffer area are not written immediately to disk. Committed transactions in the transaction log file are copied to the database when one of the following occurs:

- The checkpoint falls too far behind in a previous log file. If the number of committed transactions in the log files reaches a certain threshold, ESE flushes these changes to disk.

- The number of free pages in memory becomes too low, possibly affecting system performance. In this case, committed transactions in memory are flushed to disk to free up pages in memory for system use.

- Another service is requesting additional memory, and ESE needs to free up some of the memory it is currently using. ESE flushes pages from memory to the database and then updates the checkpoint file.

- The database service is shutting down. In this case, all updated pages in memory are copied to the database file.

Bear in mind that pages are not copied from memory in any particular order and might not all be copied at the same time. The random order in which the pages are copied back to disk means that if there is a system crash while pages are being written to disk, the database file might have only portions of a committed transaction updated in the actual file. In this event, when the Store.exe process starts, the transaction is replayed from the transaction log files, and the database is updated completely.

Installable File System

In Exchange 2000 Server, the ExIFS was mounted by default and was a recommended method of managing users' data. As you might recall, the Installable File System allowed users to place any kind of document in the old native content file (the streaming file) and then access it from almost any client, regardless of whether that client was a browser, a MAPI client, or Microsoft Internet Explorer.

However, Microsoft has backed off from using the IFS for data and file management. In Exchange Server 2003, the IFS was not mounted by default, and ExIFS has been completely removed from Exchange Server 2007.

The Web Folder Client

WebDAV (Web Development Authoring and Versioning) is an extension of the HTTP protocol and represents a standards-based layer that is built on top of HTTP 1.1. Specifically, it supports a more complex command structure, adding commands such as COPY or MOVE that manipulate individual objects on a Web server. In addition, this new protocol allows read/write access to the information store over HTTP using the browser as your client. It supports relational database structures, semistructured databases (such as Exchange databases), and standard file systems. Furthermore, WebDAV clients can be synchronized to server-side stores over the Internet through replication, allowing efficient online access and offline usage of data. This feature enables you to, for example, publish an hourly update of current inventory to a nationwide sales force. Each salesperson would be able to view this information over the Internet, enter orders and comments, and have current information at a client site as long as Internet access is available.

WebDAV can accommodate all types of content, which means users can use WebDAV to work collaboratively on a word processing document, a spreadsheet, or an image file. Potentially, anything you can put in a file can be authored using WebDAV. WebDAV makes the Web, from the point of view of the client, a writable medium. Microsoft Internet Explorer 5 and later and Microsoft Office 2000 (and later) are compatible with WebDAV. Here are some features of WebDAV:

- **Overwrite Protection (file locking)**   Users can write, edit, and save shared documents without overwriting another person's work, regardless of which software program or Internet service they are using. This is a key collaborative support feature.

- **Namespace Management**   Users can conveniently manage Internet files and directories, including moving and copying files. This process is similar to file management in Explorer.

- **Property (metadata) Access**   Users can index and search metadata information about a document, such as the author's name, copyright, publication date, or keywords, to find and retrieve relevant documents. (For more information about this, see the "Indexing" section later in this chapter.)

Web folders are designed to let clients access a Web server in the same way they access a file server. Exchange Server 2007 allows a client to access public folders just as it would access them on a file server and to manage the data in the Web folder as if it were a file server. The Web Folder client ships with Microsoft Windows 2000 Professional, Microsoft Windows XP, and Microsoft Windows Vista.

To create a Web Folder to a resource in the Exchange store, use the Add Network Place Wizard in My Network Places and enter one of the following:

- The server share location using a Universal Naming Convention (UNC), such as \\servername\sharename

- A Uniform Resource Locator, such as *http://www.microsoft.com*

- An FTP site using this syntax: *ftp://ftp.microsoft.com*

Once created, the Web Folder client can be used to access information by an application, Windows Explorer, or other client-side utilities.

In Exchange Server 2007, WebDAV support is de-emphasized. This fancy word has a very simple meaning: start finding another solution because this one probably won't make it to the next version of Exchange Server. Fortunately, Microsoft has decided to leave the technology intact for Exchange Server 2007 but is beginning to push users toward a SharePoint-centric solution to replace both WebDAV and public folders. If you get a chance to take a look at the Windows SharePoint Services service from Microsoft, you'll find that file management is itself moving away from a file server–based architecture to a database architecture. This shift is part of an overall strategy to move away from what is traditionally thought of as LAN-based technologies to Web services–based technologies. This shift is well underway and is represented in nearly every new platform that Microsoft is introducing.

Public Folders

What if you've been using Exchange 2000 Server or Exchange Server 2003, and you've dumped a truckload of documents into public folders? Well, in Exchange Server 2007, you can continue to leave those documents in public folders. However, note that at some point in the future, Microsoft will release a version of Exchange server absent these features. The Web Storage System as you know it will give way to the next big database engine, which will be SQL-based. You might want to consider planning for this impending change now.

In Exchange Server 2007, public folders are still present, although their use will be somewhat hindered until Microsoft releases Service Pack 1 (SP1) for Exchange Server 2007. Until SP1 is released, the following conditions are true:

- Administration of public folders can be accomplished only from the command line-based Exchange Management Shell.

- Public folders are not accessible in OWA 2007.

Public folders in Exchange Server 2007 have these traits, which are also true for public folders in Exchange Server 2003:

- Public folder trees are far more scalable and flexible than they were in the past. You can now create public folder trees by geography, department, or function. The next section, "Multiple Public Folder Trees," discusses this feature in more detail.

- Public folders are integrated with Active Directory, which means that e-mail entries enable you to send messages to a public folder instead of posting them directly to the public folder.

- Public folders use the users and groups in the Active Directory directory service for security.

- Referrals are enabled by default. Public folder referrals enable clients to gain access to any folder in the organization because referrals between routing groups are now enabled by default.

Multiple Public Folder Trees

In Exchange Server 2007, you can create multiple public folder trees for a variety of purposes. For example, suppose that you have a project team composed of three internal LAN clients, two users in your company at remote locations, and three consultants outside your organization. You can create a public folder tree for these users that is separate from the default public folder tree.

Each public folder tree stores its data in a single public folder store on a per-server basis. You can replicate specific folders in the tree to every server in your company that has a public folder store associated with that public folder tree. The default public folder tree is available via MAPI and IMAP4.

Indexing

One area that has seen significant improvement in Exchange Server 2007 is indexing and searching. In fact, these functions have been rewritten from the ground up. Exchange Server 2007 now uses the same search/indexing engine as SQL Server 2005.

In previous versions of Exchange Server, the information store was periodically scanned and an index was simultaneously updated. However, this crawl method was slow, rarely current, and used up significant server resources. In fact, the indexing service in Exchange Server 2003 is initially disabled as a way to help boost system performance.

Under Exchange Server 2007, the following changes have been made:

- Indexing is automatically enabled on all new mailbox stores.

- The search component now uses MS Search 3.0—the same as SQL Server 2005. The result is much faster and much more efficient indexing.

- Partial-word matches are supported. So, if you search for "admin" the search service could return "admin," "administrator," or "administration."

- The index is always current. As soon as a message is written to the database, it is indexed, thus making the message contents immediately searchable. Further, because the message is so recent, it's also still in cache, meaning that the indexing process results in a minimal I/O hit.

- A crawl-type indexing process is still used, but only when you mount a new database, move a database, or move mailboxes between databases. However, this indexing method automatically throttles back in response to needs of other, more critical components.

- Attachments are also indexed, as long as they are of a supported type.

- Public folders are not indexed.

- Localization is now supported.

- The index is word-based, not character-based.

The new search in Exchange Server 2007 is most valuable for those users that run Outlook in online mode, as opposed to cached mode. In cached mode, in Outlook 2007, Microsoft has added Windows Desktop Search capability, which provides a local index against which searching can take place. Older versions of Outlook must rely on either third-party desktop search clients or on a linear scan of the entire mailbox. This can be very slow.

Server-based search also works with mobile clients. The mobile client does not need to perform the index search. Instead, results from the server-based indexing process are sent down to a mobile client for review.

The search/indexing function in Exchange Server 2007 supports dozens of different file types., including, as you would expect, Microsoft Office documents, and much more. You can search for files with any of the following extensions:

*.ascx	*.dot	*.inf	*.rc
*.asm	*.h	*.ini	*.reg
*.asp	*.hhc	*.inx	*.rtf
*.aspx	*.hpp	*.js	*.stm
*.bat	*.htm	*.log	*.txt
*.c	*.html	*.m3u	*.url
*.cmd	*.htw	*.mht	*.vbs
*.cpp	*.htx	*.odc	*.wtx
*.cxx	*.hxx	*.pl	*.xlc
*.def	*.ibq	*.pot	*.xls
*.dic	*.idl	*.ppt	*.xlt
*.doc	*.inc		

Index Catalogs

Index catalog files are created during the indexing process. They are located by default in each individual storage group directory and start with the name CatalogData. The full name of the directory is CatalogData-<db-guid>-<instance-guid>. The db-guid is the GUID for the database while the instance-guid is the instance of the database, which helps an index to distinguish between nodes in a clustered mailbox environment. Figure 3-8 gives you a look at the index folders that are housed in each storage group folder. Note that there are two folders in this shot. A separate index is created for each individual database.

Figure 3-8 An index folder is created for each database in the storage group

Index Size

In Exchange Server 2007, make every attempt to plan your storage space in order to take into account the size of the index files. Plan on your indexes to take up space equivalent to about 5 percent of the size of your database. Therefore, plan for 10 percent...just in case!

Exchange Server Storage Design

Now that you have a picture outlining how Exchange Server 2007 stores and storage groups work, it's a good time to discuss some best practices to consider when you design the physical storage infrastructure that supports your Exchange Server 2007 environment.

Supported Storage Technologies

First, before you get into designing your storage architecture, you should understand what storage technologies are supported by Exchange Server 2007. The supported storage technologies are

■ Direct-attached Serial ATA (SATA) or Serial Attached SCSI (SAS) disks.

■ iSCSI. This is the only network-based storage supported by Exchange Server 2007. Exchange Server 2007 no longer supports Network Attached Storage (NAS).

■ Fibre Channel.

Real World   RAID levels

Depending on how you look at things, there are a wide variety of RAID levels available for use in your Exchange storage environment. Table 3-2 gives you a look at five common RAID levels and how they compare against one another.

Table 3-2   RAID Levels

	Speed	Capacity utilization	Rebuild performance	Disk failure performance	I/O performance
RAID 10	Excellent	Poor	Excellent	Excellent	Excellent
RAID 5	Good	Best	Poor	Poor	Poor
RAID 6	Poor	Good	Poor	Poor	Poor
RAID 1	Excellent	Poor	Excellent	Excellent	Excellent

Exchange Server 2007 has significant storage requirements, and there are a number of best practices associated with various aspects of the Exchange infrastructure.

Choosing a RAID Level

In small Exchange Server environments, you'll probably simply place everything Exchange on a single disk array and use a single RAID level for that storage. However, for an optimal Exchange Server experience, you will customize the RAID level for each particular aspect of your Exchange infrastructure. The best place to start is with an overview of what Microsoft considers best practices related to your Exchange storage:

- **Transaction Logs**   Microsoft recommends that transaction logs be placed on a battery-backed RAID 1 or RAID 10 array. Transaction log performance is critical for Exchange Server. Of all of the reasonable RAID levels, RAID 1 and RAID 10 both provide the best write latency. Further, both RAID levels work very well with large capacity disks.

- **Databases**   When it comes to the actual Exchange Server databases, RAID 5 might be enough, but, even though you lose half your storage capacity, RAID 10 is better. In Exchange Server 2003, RAID 5 was sufficient for the Exchange Server databases. Under Exchange Server 2007, Microsoft indicates that RAID 5 may not be sufficient, particularly in the event of a rebuild due to disk failure, during which performance is severely degraded. When possible, Microsoft recommends that you use RAID 10, but RAID 5 is sufficient.

- **Operating System**   The disks on which you install the operating system for Exchange Server 2007 should use RAID 1. This RAID level provides the best protection against failure while supporting very high performance levels.

Real World   Storage Requirements Calculator

Creating an overall Exchange Server 2007 storage architecture is hard work and can be very complex if you want to adhere to all of the recommendations provided by Microsoft. If you want a cheat sheet that helps you to completely design your Exchange Server 2007 storage architecture, including the recommended number of storage groups, the recommended LUN layout, IOPS calculations based on mailbox size and number of users, and a whole lot more information, look at the storage calculator tool developed by the Microsoft Exchange team. Besides helping you figure out how much disk space your Exchange infrastructure requires, the tool helps you to determine, on other tabs, how many stores your intended configuration requires. It even goes so far as to provide a recommended physical storage layout. Finally, the tool uses all of the information you provide and figures out how much RAM you need for your server.

Download the tool from *http://msexchangeteam.com/archive/2007/01/15 /432207.aspx*.

Planning for Disk Space

When planning disk space capacities for your Exchange Server 2007 infrastructure, there are several key factors to consider:

- The number of users to be housed on a given Exchange server

- The average workload of users to be housed on a given Exchange server

- The amount of time it takes to recover from a failure (recovery time objective)

- The average size of an e-mail and an attachment and the number of attachments that your users will need to send and receive

- The number and size of public folders

The next two sections describe how to calculate the disk space needs of your Exchange server.

Calculating Required Mailbox Disk Space

Messaging activity by your users can be difficult to forecast. Some users send and receive only a few e-mails each day while others are at the opposite end of the spectrum, sending and receiving dozens of e-mails each day, some with large attachments. Obviously, given the same hardware specifications, you can house more light-usage users in a single mailbox store than you can heavy-usage users. Although it might seem trivial to do so, it's best to develop some type of classification system for your environment and then perform calculations to determine the best number of users per store, per storage group, and finally, per server. If you can get a somewhat accurate picture of your current messaging usage, you'll be better able to predict hardware and storage group needs.

A good way to do this is to pick a random sample of your users—at least 15 percent—and then conduct an audit of their current e-mail usage. Be sure they are saving copies of their sent e-mails in the Sent Items folder so that you can get an idea as to how many e-mails they send each day and the size of their emails. You can also see how many e-mails had attachments and, by opening the e-mails, you can see the sizes of the attachments. Security concerns might keep you from getting the information you need from some users, and in those cases you can give them a short survey to fill out.

Note Microsoft has released a tool that can help you gather data about your organization's messaging activity in a much more organized fashion, and include all of your user mailboxes in the results so you can perform Exchange Server 2007 storage calculations with much more information on hand. The tool, the Profile Analyzer, is available for download from Microsoft's Web site at *http:// www.microsoft.com/downloads/details.aspx?FamilyId=8F575F60-BD80-44AA-858B-A1F721108FAD&displaylang=en.*

After you collect your data, you need to analyze it. This part simply involves performing some calculations based on the data that you capture. Consider this example: assume that you conducted your analysis on 300 users over a 60-day period, and you find that the average number of e-mails per day for each user is 20, with an average size of 10K, with 2 attachments per user per day, each averaging 200 KB. The numbers would look like this:

- 20 e-mails × 10 KB = 200 KB per day in e-mail.

- 2 attachments × 200 KB = 400 KB per day in attachments.

- Total average disk space usage per day.

- Total average disk space usage: 1.2 MB per day (600 KB for the store, 600 KB for the transaction logs).

- 1.2 MB × 300 users = 360 MB of disk space per day for all 300 users. Over a 60-day period, there will be 44 working days, so 15,840 MB, or 15.8 GB of disk space is required to house all of the data.

This final figure of 15.8 GB is somewhat misleading because the transaction logs will not be retained forever and users will likely delete some of the messages they receive. Eventually, Exchange will delete the old logs, freeing up disk space to be used again by the transaction logs. Therefore, assume that Exchange keeps only a week's worth of logs, or 5 × 600 KB = 3 MB. Thus, after two months of activity, you need only about 7.74 GB (44 days × 600 KB average usage × 300 users, plus 3 MB for the logs) of disk space to run Exchange Server 2007.

Note that this figure does not take into consideration any of the advanced opportunities offered by Exchange Server 2007. Use of such advanced features as replication and content indexing, the use of a dedicated restore disk, your deleted item retention period (default is 14 days in Exchange Server 2007), and other factors play a significant part in your storage design. Further, decisions regarding the type of storage, such as Fibre Channel, iSCSI storage, or directly attached disks, as well as your backup window, backup methodology, hardware backup speed, and more, go into planning your storage architecture. After all, if you can't reliably back up your stores in the time allotted for your backup window, you don't have a good plan.

In addition to all of these facts, you still need to consider how much storage space is necessary for public folders if you plan to continue using them in Exchange Server 2007.

Logical Unit Number (LUN) Layout

Be aware that Microsoft's documentation makes liberal use of the term "LUN." A logical unit number (LUN) is an address for an individual hard drive in your server. When used in relation to a Storage Area Network (SAN), the term LUN may not refer to actual physical disks, but rather to volumes that you create on the SAN. An LUN may also refer to a volume created as a part of a RAID set.

Microsoft recommends that each individual database, or information store, should be stored on the same physical LUN. However, this only holds true if you place a single database into each storage group. Although Microsoft recommends that you try to maintain this one store per storage group configuration in Exchange Server 2007, if you decide to place multiple stores in a storage group, you should make every attempt to place the all of the database files on the same LUN.

Further, you should consider a "two LUNs per storage group" design. One LUN houses your database and the second houses your log files. Under this design, and depending on your physical disk configuration, you run less risk of losing both your log files and database in the event of a storage problem.

Other Storage Notes

There are a number of other things you should keep in mind when it comes to designing your Exchange Server 2007 storage architecture. Some of Microsoft's recommendation and observations are

- Unless you are using one of the continuous replication features in Exchange Server 2007, keep your individual database sizes less than 100 GB. If you use continuous replication, keep databases smaller than 200 GB.

- Try to maintain a storage architecture that keeps one database in each storage group.

- When creating databases, try to maintain an overhead rate of 20 percent on top of all other requirements.

- When repairing a database, you need capacity that equals the size of the database plus 10 percent. In your design plans, try to maintain enough free space that allows you to repair your largest database.

- The Indexing process in Exchange Server 2007 results in much less I/O overhead than in previous versions of Exchange so it requires much less thought.

- The Database Dumpster's retention time has increased to 14 days from 7 days. The Database Dumpster stores deleted items that have been deleted from Delete Items folders.

- Requiring Outlook 2007 clients to use Cached Mode can reduce I/O operations by up to 70 percent when compared with similar operations under Outlook 2003 and Exchange Server 2003.

Testing Your Storage Architecture

After you make your storage decisions, test your plans to make sure that your storage architecture can stand up to the abuse that will be visited upon it by your users. The first step in this process is to understand what you're trying to achieve. When it comes to Exchange Server 2007, your measurements are often measured in I/O operations per second (IOPS). Make sure you understand your performance needs. Use the calculator tool developed by the Exchange team to help you in your efforts. Table 3-3 shows you some guidelines provided by Microsoft that can help you determine the average IOPS per user/mailbox in your organization.

Table 3-3 IOPS Guidelines

User type (usage profile)	Send/receive per day approximately Assumes average 50KB message size	Estimated IOPS per user
Light	5 sent/20 received	0.11
Average	10 sent/40 received	0.18
Heavy	20 sent/80 received	0.32
Very heavy	30 sent/120 received	0.48

Testing your storage infrastructure can be accomplished even when you have no users connected to your Exchange server. Microsoft provides three tools that will help you make sure your storage is up to the task. All of the tools are available for download from Microsoft's Web site.

- **Exchange Server Jetstress** Jetstress is a tool that simulates I/O characteristics in Exchange Server 2007 to verify the performance and stability of your storage infrastructure. Jetstress simulates Exchange database and log file loads produced by a specific number of users, which closely matches the number of users in your organization. When combined with Performance Monitor and ESEUTIL, you can verify that your storage meets or exceeds your requirements or the recommendations provided by the Exchange team's calculator.

- **Exchange Load Generator** Exchange Load Generator is a simulation tool that measures the impact of MAPI clients on an Exchange Server 2007 server. Load Generator simulates a real mail load so that you can determine whether your servers and storage can handle the anticipated user load.

- **Exchange Server Profile Analyzer** The Exchange Server Profile Analyzer collects estimated information from a mailbox store or across your Exchange Server organization. This data can then be used to analyze the performance and health of mailbox servers and the related storage.

Transport Architecture

In Exchange Server 2007, Microsoft has completely eliminated the redundant routing group architecture. You might be wondering what is meant by "redundant." In short, in most instances, your legacy routing group topology should fairly closely mimic your network structure or Active Directory topology. Under older versions of Exchange Server, you were forced to create an additional routing layer used only by Exchange Server. Microsoft, with Exchange Server 2007, has eliminated this additional layer by allowing you to use a structure that must already be in place and working in an organization—the Active Directory site topology. In order to support coexistence between a legacy routing group and an Exchange Server 2007 environment, you can use a routing group connector. Routing group connectors are discussed at length in Chapter 7, "Coexisting with Previous Versions of Exchange Server."

In this section, you learn about how Exchange Server 2007 handles message routing. It's important to note that the two primary roles that handle message routing in Exchange Server 2007 are the Hub Transport server and the Edge Transport server. However, the Hub Transport server handles the brunt of the work and is the focus of this discussion.

SMTP Connectors

Before you get too deep into a transport discussion, here are definitions for a couple of terms and concepts that are important in this section:

- **Send Connector** A Send connector represents a logical gateway through which outbound messages are sent from an Exchange Server 2007 Hub Transport server or Edge Transport server. With the exception of a Send connector created to send mail to the Internet, most Send connectors have complementary Receive connectors. Although no explicit SMTP Send connectors are created upon installation of Exchange Server 2007, implicit and invisible Send connectors are created based on the structure of your Active Directory site topology. SMTP Send connectors are used to route mail between Hub Transport servers in your Active Directory site. Send connectors created on servers with the Hub Transport role installed are stored in Active Directory and made available to all Hub Transport role servers in the organization.

- **Receive Connector** An SMTP Receive connector is an inbound connection point for SMTP traffic into a particular Hub Transport server or Edge Transport server. Receive connectors actively listen for connections that match the connector's parameters, which include the originating IP address and port. A Receive connector is valid only on the server on which the connector is created.

- **Foreign Connector**   The third type of SMTP connector in Exchange Server 2007 is the Foreign connector, which allows Exchange Server to send messages to a local mail system that does not use SMTP for its communication mechanism.

Creating SMTP Connectors

There are three ways in which SMTP connectors are created in Exchange Server 2007:

- **Manually/Explicitly**   As the Exchange Server administrator, you can intentionally create an SMTP connector. You see how to create an SMTP Send connector in Chapter 7.

- **Implicitly**   Implictly created SMTP connectors in Exchange Server 2007 are created based on the Active Directory site topology. These types of connectors do not show up in the Exchange Management Console or in the Exchange Management Shell.

- **Automatically**   During setup and during the process of subscribing an Edge Transport server to the environment, SMTP connectors are created that enable end-to-end mail flow. You see this in action in Chapter 20, "Antivirus and Anti-Spam."

In reality, you can go through your entire Exchange Server 2007 administration career and never touch the SMTP connector configuration in your Exchange environment. If you use an Edge Transport server and don't need to perform any cross-forest mail transfers, Exchange Server 2007 provides the complete end-to-end routing scenario for you.

Message Routing

In Exchange Server 2007, all message routing is handled using a direct-relay method. In other words, the Hub Transport server establishes a direct IP connection to another Hub Transport server (which, in turn, connects to a Mailbox server) in order to complete message delivery. In doing so, Hub Transport servers rely on the capability of the underlying IP networks' ability to reroute in the event of a network failure.

Note   Hub Transport servers in the same site communicate with one another using MAPI/RPC. Hub Transport servers that are not in the same site communicate with one another using SMTP/SSL.

Real World   What Happened to Link State Routing and Routing Groups?

In Exchange Server 2003, the only way that individual servers knew whether the links between routing groups were alive was by using link state tables, hence the term link state routing. In Exchange Server 2007, Hub Transport servers use deterministic routing and no longer rely on these link state tables. As a result, Exchange Server 2007 doesn't make any use of link state information. Deterministic routing means that the transmission route is determined before transmission occurs.

Exchange Server 2003 and Exchange 2000 Server relied heavily on routing groups as a critical component of the overall transport architecture. Routing groups are still supported in Exchange Server 2007—to a point. In order to provide interoperability with legacy Exchange environments, Exchange Server 2007 allows the creation of a single legacy routing group whose sole purpose is to create a connection between your legacy Exchange routing groups and your new Exchange Server 2007 environment. This legacy routing group is discussed at length in Chapter 7.

Whenever possible, Exchange Server 2007 routes messages using the physical IP network or, if such connectivity is not available, uses your already configured Active Directory sites to find a path by which to deliver messages. Hub Transport servers attempt to make connections directly to Hub Transport servers in the destination site, thus avoiding intermediate relay sites that add no value and just slow down the process. The use of the Active Directory site topology by Exchange Server 2007 makes it easier for administrators because there is no redundant routing topology to worry about and manage. In fact, Exchange Server 2007 automatically configures its routing topology and creates default connectors based on your existing Active Directory topology. Figure 3-9 gives you a look at a direct connection in action. In Figure 3-9, a message is being sent from a user in Site 1 to another user in Site 5. In this instance, the Hub Transport server in Site 1 establishes a direct SMTP connection with a Hub Transport server in Site 5 and the message is delivered to the recipient.

Although Exchange Server 2007 makes every attempt to avoid using intermediate Hub Transport servers in favor of connecting directly to the destination site, there are cases in which it is preferable for Exchange Server to use an intermediate site. For example, suppose that the link between Site 3 and Site 5 goes down, as shown in Figure 3-10. The Hub Transport server in Site 1 is aware that a path to Site 5 is not available at the moment. Because of its knowledge of the Active Directory site topology, however, Site 1's Hub Transport server knows that Site 3 is the next closest site to Site 5. In this instance, Site 1 relays the message to a Hub Transport server in Site 3. Once the IP link to Site 5 is back up, Site 3 handles the delivery of the message to Site 5. This process, queuing the message at the source of the problem, provides an efficient way to get messages as close as possible to their destinations.

If multiple IP links fail and the message cannot even leave the local site, it is queued locally until such time as the IP network becomes available again.

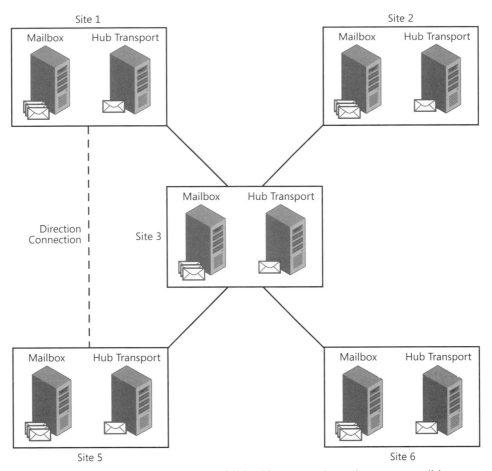

Figure 3-9 A direct connection is established between sites whenever possible.

One more scenario: suppose you have a message that is being sent to multiple recipients in multiple sites. In this case, a message is sent from a user in Site 1 to users in Site 5 and Site 6. In Figure 3-11, note that this scenario results in three separate direct connections being made. The first direct connection is from the Hub Transport server in Site 1 to a Hub Transport server in Site 3. What gives?

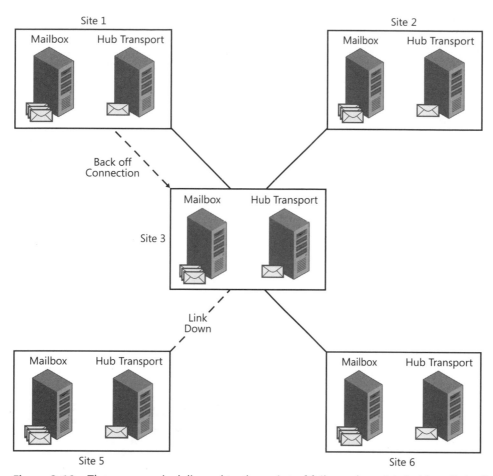

Figure 3-10 The message is delivered to the point of failure where it is held until the link is reestablished.

In this instance, the most efficient course, from a bandwidth perspective, is not to create direct connections from Site 1 to Site 5 and from Site 1 to Site 6. Instead, Exchange Server 2007 calculates the last point along the line in which there is a shared site. The originating Hub Transport server then establishes a direct connection with that site's Hub Transport server, which, in turn, relays the messages to each of the other two sites. This intermediary is known as the *bifurcation point*.

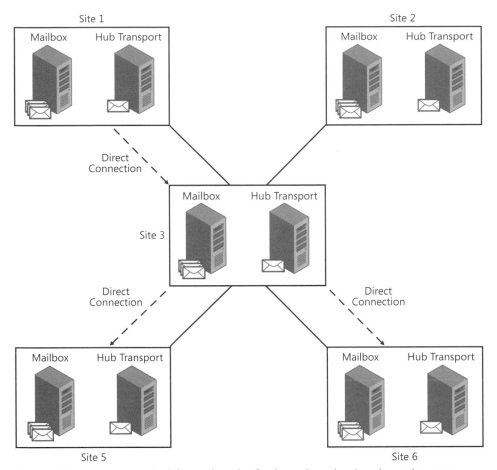

Figure 3-11   A message is delivered to the farthest shared point along the route.

Message Transport Scenarios

There are four common message routing scenarios to talk about and describe:

- A message is sent to a user in the same mailbox database or on a mailbox database on the same server.

- A message is sent to a user in a mailbox database housed on a different mailbox server. The receiving server is in the same Active Directory site as the sending server.

- A message is sent to a user in a mailbox database housed on a different mailbox server. The receiving server is in a different Active Directory site.

- A message is sent to the Internet.

All four of these scenarios are covered in the following sections.

Sending Mail between Users on the Same Server

Sending mail between users on the same server is the simplest of transport tasks in Exchange Server 2007, but still involves fairly significant message routing to take place. In this scenario, the Hub Transport server and the Mailbox server may share physical hardware, or the two roles may be physically separate. The end result, however, is the same. Figure 3-12 shows you a transport diagram in an environment in which both the Mailbox and Hub Transport server roles are on the same hardware.

In these instances, any messages sent between mailboxes on the same Mailbox server are sent to the Hub Transport in order for transport rules to be applied. Once that takes place, the message is sent back to the Mailbox server for delivery to the recipient's mailbox.

Figure 3-12 Sending mail between users on a single server

Sending Mail between Users in the Same Site

The second scenario is still limited to a single site but the sender and recipient mailboxes are housed on different Mailbox servers. This scenario is almost identical to the previous, except that there's an additional Mailbox server involved. Again, all messages sent, even between users in the same mailbox database, must traverse a Hub Transport server before they can be delivered to a recipient's mailbox. The communication transport used for message delivery is MAPI/RPC. Figure 3-13 gives you a look at this scenario.

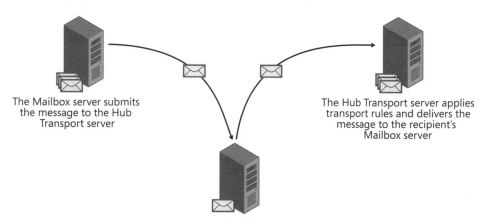

Figure 3-13 Sending mail between users on separate mailbox servers

Sending Mail between Users in Different Sites

The most complex transport scenario involves sending mail between users whose mailboxes are located on mailbox servers in different sites. In this scenario, a message is submitted to a Mailbox server. The Hub Transport server in that site picks up the message via MAPI/RPC and then initiates an SMTP/SSL connection to a Hub Transport server in the destination site. The receiving Hub Transport server then uses MAPI/RPC and delivers the message to the appropriate mailbox server. See Figure 3-14 for a look at this scenario.

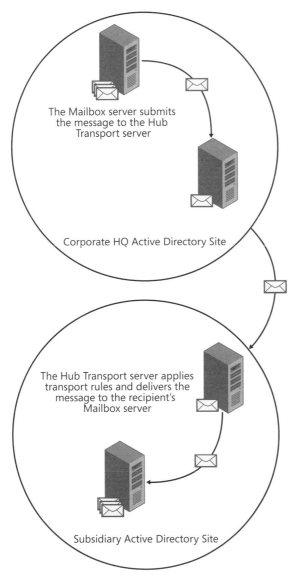

Figure 3-14   Sending mail between users on a separate Mailbox servers in different sites

This scenario can be significantly expanded and made much more complicated as you begin to introduce the need for cross-forest message delivery. You get a small taste of this complexity a little later in the section on transport protocols.

Sending Mail to the Internet

Sending mail to the Internet is supported by the addition of an SMTP Send connector on at least one Hub Transport server. This connector is provided with a global scope and all Internet-destined mail will flow through this connector. In Chapter 8, "Transitioning to Exchange Server 2007," you see how to accomplish the creation of this Internet-facing Send connector.

Transport Protocols

Depending on the communication entities involved, the following list outlines the communication method used:

- Communication between Mailbox servers and Hub Transport servers is accomplished via MAPI/RPC.

- Communication between Mailbox servers and Client Access servers is also accomplished via MAPI/RPC.

- Communication between Hub Transport servers in different sites is accomplished via SMTP.

- Communication between a Hub Transport server and a legacy Exchange server accessible via a routing group connector is accomplished via SMTP.

- Communication between Hub Transport servers in the same site is accomplished via SMTP/TLS.

- Communication between Hub Transport servers and Edge Transport servers is accomplished via SMTP/TLS.

- Clients, of course, use a wide variety of communication protocols, including HTTP, HTTPS, MAPI, POP3, IMAP, and RPC over HTTP/S.

Figure 3-15 gives you a relatively simplistic look at the protocols that are used in various communications in your Exchange environment. When you look at the diagram in Figure 3-15, keep the following points in mind:

- All e-mail is routed by a Hub Transport server, even e-mail destined for a mailbox on the same server as the sender.

- Although a Mailbox server will prefer to use a Hub Transport server that is installed on the same server, the Mailbox server will use any Hub Transport server that it can find in the local site.

- The Hub Transport server role automatically load balances in the local site, thus preventing a single server from holding up mail delivery.

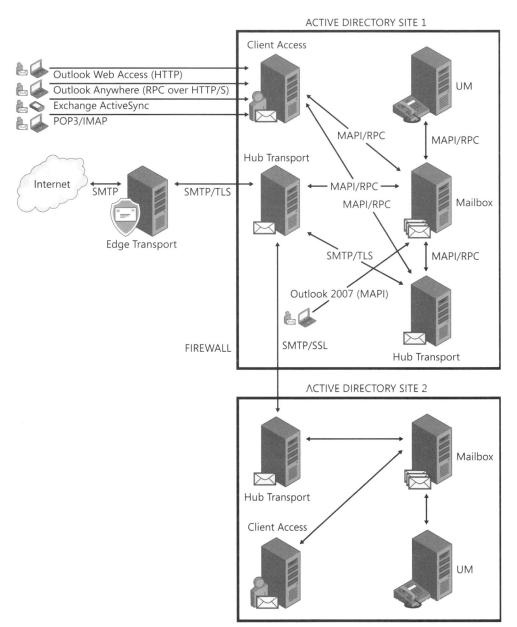

Figure 3-15   A simplistic look at the transport architecture in Exchange Server 2007

In short, the routing mechanism in Exchange Server 2007 provides an efficient, fault-tolerant, and easier-to-administer routing platform.

Summary

This chapter brought you up to speed on the storage and transport architecture used in Exchange Server 2007. You learned, for example, that the Store.exe process can manage many databases on a single server and that databases are divided into stores, each of which can hold up to 50 databases. You also learned that maxing out the number of stores in a storage group is not considered a best practice. Importantly, you also learned some design tips for your storage infrastructure. Finally, you were provided with a routing overview explaining how Exchange Server 2007 gets messages to different places in your organization.

Part II
Planning Your Deployment

Chapter 4
Assessing Needs

Proper planning is valuable in any project, but in a Microsoft Exchange Server 2007 deployment, planning is especially critical. Many Exchange Server components are difficult or impossible to change after installation. Poor planning can cause problems that range from inadequate performance to outright failure of components.

Discussion of planning is broken into two chapters. This chapter helps you gather the information you need to plan your implementation of Exchange Server 2007. It looks at the business requirements of the enterprise, examines how to assess the needs of future Exchange users, and describes how to evaluate the resources of the current environment for the new messaging system. Chapter 5, "Planning for Deployment," discusses how to plan specific elements of your Exchange organization based on those assessments. Exchange Server is a complex program, but with suitable preparation, implementation of the new Exchange organization becomes a much easier task.

If you are reading this book from start to finish, you might want to skim these two planning chapters and then read the rest of the book. After you have a firm understanding of how the various components in an Exchange organization work, come back and read these two chapters more carefully. In the real world, planning should always come before implementation, but it helps to understand the implementation before working on your plan.

More Info   This chapter and Chapter 5 provide an overview of planning an Exchange Server 2007 deployment that, coupled with the specific component knowledge you find throughout this book, should put you well on your way to designing an effective Exchange organization. If you are transitioning from a previous version of Exchange, you'll also be interested in Chapter 8, "Transitioning to Exchange Server 2007."

Defining User Needs

Your first step in designing any system should be to determine what that system needs to accomplish. In an Exchange system, this means asking several questions:

- Will the system provide basic messaging services, that is, a way for users to send e-mail to one another?

- Will the system provide access to Internet resources? Can users send and receive Internet e-mail?

- Do you plan to offer public folders as a means of group discussion?

- Do you plan to offer wireless access or synchronization for your users?

- Are there any custom applications for which you want to use Exchange Server 2007?

- Do you plan to link Exchange Server 2007 to your company's phone system so that users can receive voice messages and faxes in their inboxes?

Your goals at this stage include gathering business requirements and understanding the corporate culture and technical environment—including the network topology and desktop systems—in which you will use Exchange Server 2007. When designing an Exchange organization, you must also find out what services and functionality your users require. After you answer the questions presented in the following sections, you can effectively group users according to their needs. You can then use those groups to plan Exchange Server resources to accommodate user needs, as described in Chapter 5.

Messaging

Exchange Server 2007 is typically implemented as a messaging system. Ask the following questions to help describe the specific needs of your users:

- **To whom will most users be sending messages?**   Messaging on most networks follows a fairly typical pattern. Users tend to send messages primarily to other users in their organization. Users also need to send messages to outside recipients, such as people on the Internet. Developing a picture of these traffic patterns can help you plan user and server placement.

- **How much e-mail do users expect to generate and receive?**   Some users rarely use e-mail; others send and receive dozens of messages per day. Knowing the average volume of messages for your users allows you to plan the capacity of your servers, message delivery settings, and the bandwidth requirements of your network.

- **Will users exchange scheduling and contact information?**   Microsoft Office Outlook 2007 provides the ability to share scheduling and contact information dynamically between users. This generates extra messaging traffic and needs to be accounted for when designing your system.

■ **What kind of messages and attachments will you allow users to send?**   If your users transfer large files to one another using e-mail, you must make allowances for this volume. Some organizations put limits on the amount of information that can be transmitted in a single message or the disk space that mailboxes can consume. Others put limits only on specific mailboxes. Executives, for example, might be given more flexibility than other employees.

■ **Will user messages be stored primarily on an Exchange server or in local personal folders?**   If server-based storage is to be the primary repository of user messages, how much space do you intend to allot for your mailbox stores? Your organization might have business policies that require e-mail to be stored for long periods of time. For example, some government units must store e-mail forever. Such information can help you plan hardware capacity for both servers and clients.

■ **What kind of security will users need?**   Do your users need to encrypt or digitally sign messages and attachments? If so, you need to implement some sort of certificate server and Public Key Infrastructure (PKI) on your network, such as Microsoft Certificate Services. Exchange security is covered in Part VI, "Security."

Public Folders

In previous versions of Exchange Server, public folders formed a foundation for collaboration within an organization. Exchange Server 2007 deemphasizes public folders because an organization can gain much more collaborative functionality with a dedicated product like Microsoft SharePoint Server. Still, public folder support is available in Exchange Server 2007, and if you are transitioning from a previous version of Exchange Server, you may already have a public folder infrastructure you need to maintain.

In addition to planning storage capacity for the Exchange servers that will hold public folder replicas, you must plan public folder replication and user access to public folder servers. The following questions will assist you in assessing public folder usage in the new Exchange organization:

■ **Are there users of Outlook versions prior to Outlook 2007 in your organization?** Outlook 2003 and previous versions require at least one public folder database to exist so that they can connect to Exchange Server 2007, as well as share free/busy information. During Exchange Server 2007 installation, you are asked whether any client uses a previous version of Outlook. If you answer yes, a public folder database is created. If you answer no, no database is created. If no database exists in the organization, users of Outlook 2003 and previous versions will not be able to connect until you create one.

- **Which users will need access to which public folders?** Some workgroups will collaborate on certain documents and messages more than others. This information helps you decide where replicas of certain folders need to be placed and how often replication needs to occur.

- **Which users should be allowed to create public folders?** By default, top-level public folders in a public folder tree are created on the home server of the user who creates them. Subfolders are created on the same server as the top-level folder in which they are created. By restricting which users can create top-level folders, you can govern the placement of public folders on servers. Such restrictions also help you keep the structure of public folder trees manageable.

- **How much information do users expect to post within those public folders?** Both the type of information—documents, forms, executable files, or simple messages—and the size of a typical file help you determine the storage capacity required for public folder stores.

- **How long will the average message need to remain in a public folder?** This information helps you determine the storage space that your public folder stores consume and the load that users place on your servers when accessing the public folders.

- **How often will users access the public folders?** This information helps you further determine the load that your public folder servers must meet and to schedule public folder replication.

Connections to Other Systems

Will any of your users need to access the Internet or a pre-existing messaging system such as Lotus Notes? Having this information can help you plan the placement of users and foreign messaging connectors. If one group of users tends to use a connector heavily, you might want to place those users on the server on which the connector is installed, to reduce the number of hops that messages must take from your users to the foreign system. Any Exchange server can host a foreign messaging connector, and that messaging connector can be made available to all users in the organization. You might want to configure more than one connector to the foreign system to help balance the messaging load to that system.

You must decide between connector types when multiple connectors can support the same system. You will need to consider the types of foreign systems and the types of connectors they support, as well as the performance that those connectors are expected to provide.

Connectors also vary in the additional services they provide. A connector that enables the use of shared storage might be preferable to one that enables only e-mail between users.

If you use a connector only to migrate from one version of Exchange Server to another, it will be a temporary addition to the Exchange organization. In such cases, choose the connector that makes the transition easiest for the users. In many cases, you can migrate the users transparently, with little interruption to their daily business, just by selecting the right connector.

Remote Access

Often, you will want to allow users to access private and public folders from a remote location. In planning an Exchange organization, you need to take the requirements of these remote users into account. This information can help you plan the placement of users, as well as plan virtual private network (VPN) access or Internet-based access for your network. Various manufacturers offer solutions that can enable remote access to Exchange. This information is also valuable in security planning. Ask these questions to assess the remote access needs of the organization:

- Which users need to be able to access the Exchange organization remotely?

- Will users dial in to an RRAS server or access your network over the Internet? Dialing directly into an RRAS server usually provides better control and security. Accessing the network over the Internet is often much cheaper and more convenient, and new features increase the level of security on Internet-based access.

- Where will you locate your RRAS server?

- On average, how many users need simultaneous access to the network? This information helps you determine the number of RRAS servers you need and the number of modems and phone lines.

Custom Applications

Do your users have special needs that can be met only by custom-tailored applications? If so, can the users themselves design these applications, or will you need to hire special personnel? The time to think about custom applications is during the planning stage. The use of custom applications could change many of the answers to the questions in this section.

Training and Support Services

Your users will likely need special training in using the new system. Don't make the mistake of assuming that e-mail is simple to use. Outlook 2007 and other messaging clients are sophisticated programs. Users might need to be taught how to use public folders or how to sign and encrypt messages. Do you plan to have users install the mail clients themselves? If so, they need training, and you might need to set up a convenient way for them to do so, such as using the Office Customization Tool to create an automated installation point. The Office Customization Tool is covered in Chapter 23, "Deploying Microsoft Office Outlook 2007."

Remember that users are often called upon to learn new things, including new versions of operating systems and software. Take the time to make sure that your users understand the system you are putting in place and know who their contact is for questions or problems. You can use public folders or a SharePoint site to organize and store training materials so that they are available to all users.

Assessing Current Resources

After you determine the needs of your users, the next step in planning your organization is to assess your current resources. To make this assessment, put together three diagrams: one of your company's geographic profiles, another of your network topology, and a third of your Active Directory networking model.

Defining Your Geographic Profile

The easiest place to start your assessment is with a geographic profile of your company. Get out a pen and paper and start drawing maps. If your network is global, start with all the countries in which your company has offices. Work your way through states, cities, buildings, and even in-building locations.

Defining Your Software Environment

After you have a firm idea of how your company is laid out geographically, gather information on where users and resources are located within those geographical regions. This information helps you determine where the users are, where the computers are, whether the computers are ready for Exchange Server 2007 or your chosen messaging client, and how many licenses you need. Consider the following along the way:

- Where are existing servers located?
- What are the servers' names and roles?
- What versions of which software are installed on the servers?
- How many workstations are in each location?
- What operating systems and software are used on those workstations?
- How many users are in each location?
- What are the users' needs?

Defining Your Network Topology

After you create diagrams of your company's geographic profile, diagram your company's network. Unlike the geographic profile, a network topology tells you exactly how your network is put together physically. When reviewing the geographic topology of the network, mark out the wide area network (WAN) links between the various locations and their bandwidths. This step helps you assess the network boundaries, the connectors required between locations, and the replication schedules. Figure 4-1 shows an example of a network diagram for a companywide WAN.

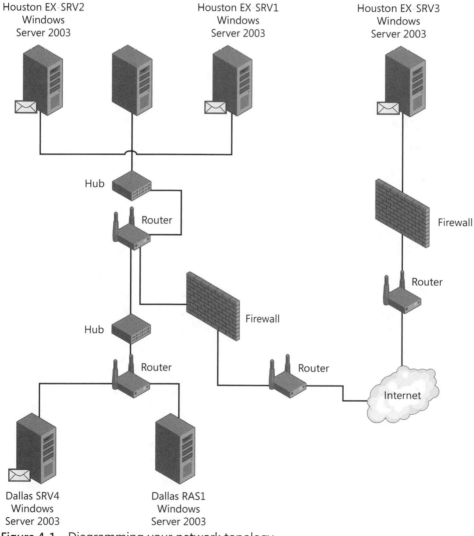

Figure 4-1   Diagramming your network topology

Real World   Systems Management Server

Ideally, you already have a detailed inventory of your existing network assets. A comprehensive inventory includes a list of all the hardware and software on all of the computers on your network. The inventory should also take into account how your network is constructed and maybe even some of the network's use statistics.

If you don't already have a network inventory, you can go to all the computers on your network with a notebook in hand, but a better method is to use an automatic inventory system such as that built into Windows Server 2003 or, for larger networks, Microsoft Systems Management Server (SMS) 2003. You can use Windows and SMS to gather hardware and software information automatically from computers on your network. You can also use SMS to push installations of software (such as messaging clients) to workstations throughout the network from a central location, to control and support client software remotely, and even to keep track of licensing information on your network. SMS really is must-have software for any up-and-coming Exchange administrator.

Note, however, that SMS is not a simple install-and-run application. It is a comprehensive, enterprise-capable network-management software package. SMS requires Microsoft SQL Server to provide the underlying database that captures and manages the network's data. To implement SMS and SQL Server, you should define and execute a project plan and systems design. Also, with the release of the next version of SMS, the product will be rolled into the Microsoft System Center family of products and its name will change to System Center Configuration Manager 2007.

For more details on the systems management capabilities built into Windows Server 2003, see your product documentation. For more information on using Systems Management Server, check out the *Microsoft Systems Management Server 2003 Administrator's Companion* by Steven D. Kaczmarek (Microsoft Press, 2004).

A clear definition of your network's topology allows you to plan server locations and server roles and also to understand replication issues. Whether your network is a single local area network (LAN) within one office building or a WAN connecting thousands of users around the world, design the Exchange organization to optimize its messaging functions over the network topology.

Areas that can be optimized include the following:

- Server and server role placement
- Global Catalog locations
- Message routing

The first step in defining a network topology is to determine the size of your network. The size of your network dictates how you make many planning decisions. On a large WAN, for example, especially one that is geographically dispersed, your Active Directory topology may consist of several sites connected by relatively slow links. If you set up a relatively small LAN, all computers may be part of a single site that enjoys high bandwidth connectivity throughout.

In a small company, all your computers are likely to be connected on one high-speed LAN. In larger companies, networks usually consist of many small LANs connected in various ways to form larger, interconnected LANs or WANs. In your network topology diagram, include all segments that make up your network. Figure 4-2 shows an example of a simple network diagram for a LAN.

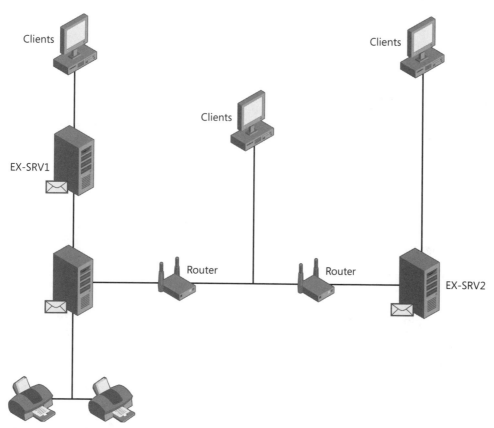

Figure 4-2 Diagramming a LAN

For each segment, ask yourself the following questions:

- How big is the segment? How many computers are there? How large a geographic area does the segment cover?

- How is the segment wired? Does it use shared or switched Ethernet, 10 Mbps or 100 Mbps, Fiber Distributed Data Interface (FDDI), or something else?

- What is the bandwidth of the segment? Determine the optimal bandwidth according to the type of network being used.

- How is the segment connected to other segments? Is the network segment connected to the rest of the network directly; is it connected through a router, switch, or bridge; or is it connected through a WAN link? Is the connection permanent or switched? What is the bandwidth of the connection?

- What protocols are used on the network?

- What are the traffic patterns on the network segment? At what times of day is network traffic within the segment heaviest? What application and operating system functions account for this traffic?

- What are the traffic patterns between this segment and other segments? At what times of day is network traffic heaviest between segments? What application and operating system functions account for this traffic?

Note   Although doing so can be somewhat tricky, determine the available bandwidth of each segment of your network. The available bandwidth is the amount of bandwidth not consumed by average network activity. For example, if the throughput of a WAN link is 1.544 Mbps and the bandwidth consumed on that link can peak at 1.544 Mbps but averages around 512 Kbps (equivalent to 0.5 Mbps), the available bandwidth will be 1.544 Mbps through 0.5 Mbps, or 1.044 Mbps. You subtract the average value, not the peak value, because all network links experience peaks that don't represent the usual network bandwidth consumption.

Defining Your Active Directory Model

The final step in assessing your current resources is to document the Active Directory model in use on the network. Again, constructing a diagram is helpful. Whereas the topology diagram illustrates the physical layout of your network (cables, routers, and so on), the diagram of the networking model illustrates the logical layout of your network. This logical layout includes the forests in your Active Directory structure, how many domains your network has, how those domains are configured to interact, and the functions of those domains and the servers in them. Figure 4-3 shows a basic example of an Active Directory model.

Exchange Server 2007 relies on Active Directory site topology for message routing and also on domains and domain controllers to perform essential security operations. For example, to access an Exchange mailbox, a user must log in to a domain using a valid user account. Because Exchange Server services are Windows services, they too need to be authenticated by a domain controller before they can perform their functions. Each server in an Exchange organization is configured with a special user account called the Site Services account, which is used to validate Exchange services. For a detailed look at the integration of Exchange Server 2007 and Active Directory, see Chapter 2, "Active Directory for Exchange Administrators."

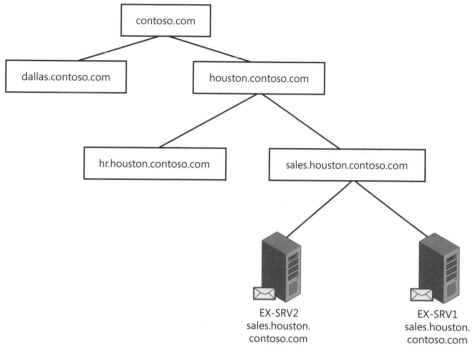

Figure 4-3 Diagramming a networking model

If your network contains only a single domain, the task of diagramming the networking model is easy. If your network consists of multiple domains, for each domain on your network, ask the following questions:

- What is the name of the domain?
- What is the function of the domain?
- Are any special trusts configured?
- How many user accounts are configured in this domain?
- What resources are configured in this domain?
- Who are the administrators of this domain?
- In what domain are the user accounts of the administrators configured?

Defining Administrative Needs

Your last step in the assessment stage of the planning process is to determine how administration will be handled. In versions of Exchange Server prior to Exchange 2000 Server, Exchange administration was mostly separate from other forms of network management. With the introduction of Exchange 2000 Server came extensive integration with Active Directory, and that continues in Exchange Server 2007; Windows and Exchange administrators must learn to get along.

In a small organization, one or two administrators are likely able to handle administration for both Active Directory and the Exchange organization. Planning the administration of larger networks requires a bit more thought. Here are a few factors to consider:

- **User management**   Since Exchange and Windows share Active Directory, it usually makes sense to let one person or group manage Active Directory users and their Exchange mailboxes (and usually other recipients, as well). Because the same interface is used to manage both, little extra training is required.

- **Routing**   You will likely need one person or group to be responsible for managing routing in your organization. Responsibilities of this group include defining and maintaining sites, site links, and link costs, as well as applying user and system policies, and managing permissions. You can think of this group as your core Exchange administrative unit.

- **Public folders**   If your organization has a large public folder infrastructure, designating a separate person or group to manage public folders and public folder replication is often useful. You might even want to designate a person to manage each distinct public folder tree. You can often leave basic administrative tasks on public folders up to expert users or to the people that manage the information stored in them.

Summary

Good planning can make or break your deployment of Exchange Server 2007. This chapter covered the first stage of planning an Exchange organization: assessing your current situation. It described how to assess the needs of your users and how to document your current resources by creating a geographic profile as well as profiles of the physical and logical layout of your current network. It also discussed considerations in planning how your Exchange system will be administered in an Active Directory environment. Now that you have collected the information you need, it's time to put that information to work. In Chapter 5, you learn how to plan the actual Exchange organization.

Chapter 5
Planning for Deployment

In Chapter 4, "Assessing Needs," you learned how to assess the needs of your users and how to take stock of your current network situation. In this chapter, you learn how to put that information to use.

The task of planning a Microsoft Exchange organization is divided into two distinct sub-tasks: designing the overall Exchange organization and placing individual Exchange servers in sites to optimize the messaging system. This approach provides you with a logical placement of resources developed with users' needs in mind.

Beginning at the organizational level, you establish organization-wide naming conventions, determine the number of routing groups you need and the boundaries of those groups, and plan how to link those groups. At the server level, you determine the functions each server performs and plan the server configuration to accommodate those functions.

Planning the Organization

The best place to start planning an Exchange organization is at the top—that is, you determine how your system will look. Planning at this level primarily involves establishing a convention for naming the various elements of the organization, planning for public folders, and planning for foreign gateways.

Establishing a Naming Convention

The requirement that names be unique is common to any system with a directory of users, resources, and servers. If you are migrating from Lotus Notes, duplication can occur when different organizations are migrated to an Exchange system. Review the systems for possible duplication and take appropriate precautions—such as changing a name or deleting old accounts—before migrating multiple systems to Exchange Server 2007.

Large Exchange systems can grow to include thousands of users worldwide and many routing groups and servers. Most names cannot be changed once an object has been created. Certain objects, such as user mailboxes, have different types of names as well. Before you install your first Exchange server, establish a convention for naming the primary types of objects in your Exchange organization: the organization, groups, servers, and recipients.

Establishing a naming convention for distribution groups, as well as for users and contacts that appear in Active Directory, is a great help to Exchange users. Furthermore, distributing administration among multiple administrators in different regions can help to apply a naming standard to connectors and other Exchange objects.

Important   Network and messaging systems should avoid using invalid characters in their names. Some systems do not understand invalid characters, and other systems misinterpret them as special codes (sometimes called escape sequences). This misinterpretation can cause these systems to try to interpret the remainder of a name as a command of some sort. The result, of course, is failure to communicate electronically and, perhaps, errors on the network or messaging systems. Although the list of invalid characters can vary, most systems consider some or all of the following, along with the space character (entered by pressing the spacebar on the keyboard), invalid characters:

\ / [ ] : | < > + = ~ ! @ ; , " ( ) {}' # $ % ^ & * - _

Avoid using invalid characters in any names, even if you find that Windows or Exchange Server allows you to do so.

Organization Names

The organization is the largest element of an Exchange system, and its name should typically reflect the largest organizational element of your company. Usually, an organization is named after the enterprise itself, although it is possible to create multiple organizations in an enterprise and for the organizations to communicate with one another. Organization names can contain up to 64 characters, but to facilitate administration, limiting their length is good practice. Keep in mind that users of external messaging systems might need to type the organization name manually, as part of the Exchange users' e-mail addresses.

Important   When you install the first production Exchange server, be sure that the organization name you specify is correct, even if this means waiting for management's approval. Changing the organization name later is possible but requires a good bit of reconfiguration. Also, be aware that the Simple Mail Transport Protocol (SMTP) address space uses the organization and routing group names to construct e-mail addresses for the Internet. The SMTP address space can be changed, but doing so can be a hassle and a cause of confusion for other Exchange administrators later.

Server Names

The server name for an Exchange server is the same as the NetBIOS name of the Windows server on which Exchange Server 2007 is installed. Therefore, establish naming conventions for servers before installing Windows. NetBIOS server names cannot be more than 15 characters long.

When installing an Exchange server in an enterprise network, one recommendation for naming the server is to use its location and/or the type of function that the server will provide. You can end the name with one or two digits to allow multiple Windows servers in the same location providing the same network function. For example, an Exchange server in a company's London office could be named LON-EX01.

Recipient Names

Recipient names work a bit differently from the names of the other objects. Exchange Server allows several types of recipients, including users, contacts, groups, and public folders. (Public folders are discussed later in this chapter.) Each of the other types of recipients actually has four key names, which are shown on the General tab of the object's property sheet (see Figure 5-1):

- **First Name**   The full first name of the user.
- **Initials**   The middle initial or initials of the user.

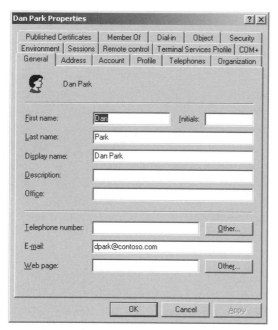

Figure 5-1   Elements of a recipient's name

- **Last Name**   The full last name of the user.

- **Display Name**   A name that is automatically constructed from the user's first name, middle initial or initials, and last name. The display name appears in address books and in the Exchange System snap-in, so it is the primary way Exchange users search for other users. Display names can be up to 256 characters long.

A naming convention should take into account the outside systems to which the Exchange organization might be connecting. Many legacy messaging and scheduling systems restrict the length of recipient names within their address lists. Although Exchange Server 2007 allows longer mailbox names, the legacy system might truncate or reject them, resulting in duplicates or missing recipients. In addition, messages could appear in the wrong mailboxes or might not be transmitted at all. A common length restriction in legacy systems is eight characters. You can avoid many problems if you keep mailbox names to eight characters or fewer.

Real World   Naming Conventions and Addressing

The names that you establish for objects in your Exchange organization determine the addresses that users of external messaging systems use to send messages to your recipients. Foreign systems do not always use the same addressing conventions as Exchange Server. Therefore, Exchange Server must have a way of determining where to send an inbound message from a foreign system. For each type of messaging system to which it is connected, Exchange Server maintains an address space consisting of information on how foreign addressing information should be used to deliver messages within the Exchange organization.

Suppose you set up Exchange Server so that your users can exchange e-mail with users on the Internet. In this situation, Exchange Server supports the SMTP address space by maintaining an SMTP address for each recipient object. A user on the Internet would then address messages to your users in the typical SMTP format—something like user@organization.com. (You learn how this works in Chapter 25, "Supporting Other Clients." For now, you need to understand that the way you name the objects in your organization has fairly far-reaching effects.)

Planning Public Folders

Public folders in Exchange Server can be put to several uses, including as discussion forums, as public collections of documents, and even as the basis for custom applications. Exchange Server allows you to configure multiple public folder trees, each of which can contain any number of public folders. Folders created in the root level of a public folder tree are referred to as top-level folders. When a user creates a top-level folder, it is placed on that user's home server. When a user creates a lower-level folder, it is placed on the same server as the folder in which it is created. The contents of a public folder can be stored on a single server, or the contents can be replicated to other servers in the routing group and organization. (Chapter 12, "Creating and Managing Public Folders," covers the creation, storage, and replication of public folders in detail.) A few aspects of public folders are pertinent to routing group planning:

- Decide how many different public folder trees you want to maintain. For example, each department could manage its own tree, or you could have one companywide tree.

- Decide whether to distribute public folders on multiple servers throughout your routing group or to maintain them all on a single server.

- Decide whether to dedicate certain servers to public folders by having them contain only public folder stores or to have servers that contain both public folders in public folder stores and private folders such as mailboxes in mailbox stores.

- Determine which users will use public folders for collaborative applications and whether those applications will require other services or special security.

- If users in remote routing groups need to access public folders in a local routing group, decide whether to replicate the contents to a server in the remote routing group to keep intergroup network traffic down.

- Consider which users should be allowed to create top-level folders in a public folder tree. Limiting the number of users who can create top-level folders allows you to control both the servers on which public folders are created and the basic organization of the public folder hierarchy.

- When naming public folders, you have a bit more license than with the names of other recipients. Public folder names can be up to 256 characters. However, when you name a folder, keep in mind that only a small portion of the name actually appears in your users' client software, and very long names could become a real hassle. Also, some users might occasionally need to type the name of a public folder, and smaller names will be greatly appreciated.

Planning Gateways

Any server can be configured with a connector to a foreign system. All other servers in the organization are then able to route messages over that gateway. When possible, create a foreign messaging connector on the server that maintains the actual physical connection to the foreign system. Also, if one group of users makes primary use of a foreign connection, consider placing those users on the server on which the connector is installed.

Planning Servers

After you plan the general structure of your organization, you can plan your servers. The number of servers you need depends on the number of users in a site and the services that you plan to provide to those users.

Depending on your needs and resources, you are likely to have decided whether to concentrate your services on just a few powerful servers or instead to distribute the services among a larger number of less powerful servers. What is important is that you make a plan. After you make that plan, you can begin to estimate the hardware requirements for your servers.

When estimating the performance of an Exchange server, consider four distinct categories of hardware: disk, processor, memory, and network. The sections that follow discuss each of these categories in turn.

Disk Considerations

You must take into account a number of considerations when planning storage. First and foremost, you should always invest in high performance disks and spindles. It is better to have smaller capacity disks that utilize each spindle's performance than to use fewer spindles with large capacity. Fast storage with a sufficient amount of spindles is one of the most important investments you can make in your messaging infrastructure.

Your server also needs adequate disk space for Windows Server 2003, Exchange Server 2007, directory information, transaction logs, and information stores. The speed at which Exchange Server can access your disks is another important consideration. Having sufficient disk capacity is critical because when a disk containing the transaction logs runs out of space, it causes all the databases in that storage group to go offline.

Following is a generally accepted formula for determining the size of a mailbox:

Mailbox Size = Mailbox Quota + White Space + (Weekly Incoming Mail * 2)

For example, if mailboxes are configured with a 2-GB storage quota and there is 50 MB of weekly incoming mail on average, the average mailbox size would follow the formula:

Mailbox Size = 2000 MB + 10 MB + (50 MB * 2) = 2110 MB (about 5% larger than the quota)

Real World   Calculating Disk Space

When you plan the amount of disk space your server needs, consider these factors:

- Windows Server 2003, Enterprise Edition takes up about 1.5 GB, depending on the options you install.

- At least 1.2 GB of available disk space is needed on the drive on which you install Exchange Server 2007. An additional 500 MB of available disk space is needed for each Unified Messaging (UM) language pack that you plan to install.

- In addition to these figures, factor in the number of user mailboxes and public folders on your server and the amount of space you plan to allow each type of store to consume.

- Transaction logs are relatively small (1 MB each), but you should use a separate drive for them.

Finally, take into account any additional services you need to run on the server, including Exchange extensions such as virus and filtering programs.

If you use multiple drives, you might also want to consider a hardware-based redundant array of independent disks (RAID), to offer some level of fault tolerance. Keep in mind when implementing any form of hardware-based RAID that the RAID configuration and management is handled by firmware created and supported by the hardware manufacturer Recommended types of RAID are:

- **RAID-5**   A RAID-5 set is also known as a striped set with distributed parity. All but one drive in a RAID-5 set must be present, meaning that if a single disk fails, data on that disk can be reconstructed from the parity information.

- **RAID-6**   RAID-6, also known as a striped set with dual distributed parity, works much like RAID-5, but uses two disks of the set for parity instead of just one disk. This significantly increases the reliability of the set.

- **RAID-10**   RAID-10 is a combination of two RAID types: RAID 1 (which is a striped set) and RAID 0 (which is a mirrored set). A striped set offers no fault tolerance, but does offer increased read and write times from disk. A mirrored set offers fault tolerance by creating full mirror copies of the primary disk. RAID-10 (which is essentially RAID 1+0) is a striped set of mirrored sets, which offers both increased speed and fault tolerance.

Another factor you must take into account is how disk Input/Output (I/O) is generated on an Exchange server. You can learn the details of storage architecture in Chapter 3,

"Exchange Server 2007 Architecture," but simply put, the two biggest factors in generating disk I/O are database reads/writes and recording of transaction logs. Additional factors in generating disk I/O include content indexing, SMTP mail transmission, memory paging, the number of mailboxes, and the number of items those mailboxes contain. Disk I/O is typically measured in Input/Output Per Second (IOPS). You can estimate IOPS before deployment by using the Exchange Load Generator, which simulate a user load on a test Exchange server, or on an existing server using the Performance tool. Both of these tools are discussed in Chapter 17, "Tuning Exchange Server 2007 Performance."

Although it might seem tempting to throw as much storage space at the Exchange server as you can, don't do it. Instead, think about the storage needs over time, speed of disks, and the capability of the backup system. If the storage space might exceed the capacity of the backup system, you might need additional servers instead. Many gigabytes of data can accrue on an Exchange server over time. You may need to retune your backup system to ensure that it can keep up with a growing organization. When defining the storage for a server, ensure that the backup system is adequate to fully back up the information stores, transaction logs, and operating system files. A large information store can take several tapes, and a very long time, to back up on a daily basis. A restore can take several hours. Multiple servers with smaller information stores provide an inherent tolerance to failure: the failure would affect fewer users for a shorter period of time because the restore process is shorter.

As the amount of data on an Exchange server grows, performance can diminish. Exchange Server manages a number of background tasks for the information stores. These tasks take longer to execute when there are more messages in the information store to manage; hence, performance degrades across the server as a whole. One way to keep the mailbox store from growing too large is to configure the server to limit the size of users' mailboxes. Another way is to configure multiple mailbox stores, which you learn how to do in Chapter 13, "Creating and Managing Storage Groups."

> **More Info**   You can learn more about planning disk storage by reading "Planning Disk Storage" in the TechNet Library at *http://technet.microsoft.com/en-us /library/bb124518.aspx*.

Processor Considerations

Since Exchange Server 2007 supports only production servers with the 64-bit version, you must choose a 64-bit processor that works with the x64-based version of Windows Server 2003. These include Intel processors that support Intel Extended Memory 64 Technology or AMD processors that support AMD64. You cannot use Intel Itanium processors with the x64-based version of Windows Server 2003. Regardless of which processor you choose, the server product must have the Designed for Windows logo to be supported.

Using multiple processors or multicore processors significantly increases a server's performance. Having a dual-core processor or adding a second full processor to a server, however, does not double its performance. The processors still share a motherboard, adapters, storage, and other components, and data can face a bottleneck in these components. However, Windows Server 2003 does support symmetric multiprocessing, and Exchange Server 2007 is a multithreaded application. Therefore, multiple pieces of the Exchange system can run simultaneously on different processors within the same system, significantly increasing response time.

In larger environments where you expect larger mail volume, you will want to choose the processing power of your Exchange servers accordingly. For a Hub Transport server, Client Access server, Unified Messaging server, Mailbox server, or a server performing multiple roles, a single core processor is adequate for a small organization. For a larger organization, you may want to move to two- or even four-core processors. In very large organizations where mail volume is heavy, eight processor cores might be the proper choice. Obviously, the choice of processing power largely depends on the following criteria:

- How many users the server will support and whether those users are light e-mail users (5 to 10 messages sent per day, 20 to 40 received) or heavy users (20 to 30 messages sent per day, 80 to 120 received)

- Whether the server performs multiple roles

- Whether the server performs additional duties (such as a Hub Transport server that also runs antivirus and anti-spam applications)

- Whether the server uses local continuous replication (the additional processor overhead being about 20 percent)

- Whether mailbox servers are accessed by Forefront Security for Exchange Server or other non-Microsoft security products

Whether Outlook clients are working online continuously or using Cached Exchange Mode, Table 5-1 shows the recommended processor configurations for Exchange Server roles.

Table 5-1 Suggested Processor Configurations Based on Exchange Server Roles

Server role	Minimum	Recommended	Maximum
Edge Transport	1 x processor core	2 x processor core	4 x processor core
Hub Transport	1 x processor core	4 x processor core	8 x processor core
Client Access	1 x processor core	4 x processor core	4 x processor core
Unified Messaging	1 x processor core	4 x processor core	4 x processor core
Mailbox	1 x processor core	4 x processor core	8 x processor core
Multiple roles	1 x processor core	4 x processor core	4 x processor core

Memory Considerations

Memory (RAM) is used to run active processes on a computer. When physical memory is not sufficient, the system supplements it by using a paging file on the computer's hard drive. Ideally, you should have enough physical memory on a server to avoid excessive use of the paging file. Right now, memory is the cheapest way to increase the performance of any computer. Having at least 2 GB of RAM on any Exchange server as the bare minimum is recommended; use 4 GB or more from the start if at all possible. Because Exchange Server 2007 runs on the x64-based version of Windows Server 2003, a server running Exchange Server 2007 can use 32 GB of memory or more in some situations.

Table 5-2 shows the recommended memory configurations for Exchange servers based on server roles.

Table 5-2   Suggested Memory Configurations Based on Exchange Server Roles

Server role	Minimum	Recommended	Maximum
Edge Transport	2 GB	1 GB per core (2 GB minimum)	16 GB
Hub Transport	2 GB	1 GB per core (2 GB minimum)	16 GB
Client Access	2 GB	1 GB per core (2 GB minimum)	8 GB
Unified Messaging	2 GB	1 GB per core (2 GB minimum)	4 GB
Mailbox	2 GB; also depends on number of storage groups	2 GB plus from 2 MB through 5 MB per mailbox (depending on activity level of users)	32 GB
Multiple roles	2 GB; also depends on number of storage groups	4 GB plus from 2 MB through 5 MB per mailbox (depending on activity level of users)	8 GB

More Info   For more detailed information, see "Planning Processor and Memory Configurations" in the TechNet Library at *http://technet.microsoft.com/en-us /library/aa998874.aspx.*

Network Considerations

The network interface cards on your servers should be fast enough to handle traffic coming from and going to clients and other servers. Fast servers can take advantage of multiple network interface cards, providing the ability to host connections to several other clients or servers at the same time. Furthermore, many server platforms allow you to merge network interface cards into a pool; then, should one of the cards in the pool fail, another card takes over.

Ways to Add Fault Tolerance

Some standard precautions can be taken to ensure that Exchange servers stay online, even when there are failures. An uninterruptible power supply (UPS) is a common way to ensure that the server does not go offline if the power in the building fails. A UPS can also prevent power surges from damaging the server components.

As already mentioned, a server can have multiple hard drives, multiple processors, and multiple network interface cards. These redundant components provide increased performance, load balancing, and failover options, depending on how they are configured. A server can also have dual power supplies, controller cards, and error-correcting RAM. Whenever a server has redundant internal components, it is better able to tolerate faults in those components. Server-class machines typically come with software that is able to monitor the servers' hardware components from a central management machine.

In addition to establishing redundancy for server components, you can establish redundancy for the server itself. Exchange servers can be configured to take advantage of a shared storage system using clustering. *Clustering* is a system in which multiple servers are configured in a cluster, so that if one server has a problem, the system fails over to the redundant server. You learn about clustering in Chapter 9, "Clustering."

Summary

In the previous chapter, you learned how to assess the needs of your organization. In this chapter, you learned how to put that to use in designing an Exchange organization. The design of an organization happens at two distinct levels: the organizational level and the server level. At the organization level, you learned how to establish a naming convention, plan public folders, and plan gateways. At the server level, you learned how to plan for the major hardware subsystems of a server: disk, processor, memory, and network.

Part II of this book, "Planning Your Deployment," has shown you how to collect and use information about your situation when planning your Exchange organization. Chapter 6, "Installing Exchange Server 2007," begins Part III, "Installation and Deployment," which looks at the deployment of Exchange Server 2007. In Chapter 6, you learn how to install Exchange Server.

Part III
Installation and Deployment

Chapter 6
Installing Exchange Server 2007

So far, you've learned a bit about what Microsoft has added to Exchange Server 2007 and about how Exchange Server is architected. In this chapter, and in the next few chapters, you put hands to keyboard and install Exchange Server. You do this in eight basic stages:

1. Prepare the Active Directory environment by adding the objects required for a functional Exchange infrastructure.

2. Decide which Exchange Server 2007 roles belong on which servers.

3. Decide whether you want to support your Exchange Server 2007 environment through the use of the product's new clustering options, such as clustered mailbox servers, local continuous replication or cluster continuous replication.

4. Make sure your servers are suitable for the installation. Exchange Server 2007 has a few software prerequisites that must be met.

5. When preparation is finished, run the Exchange Server 2007 Setup program, click a few buttons, and supply some information about your environment.

6. Verify that the new Exchange Server 2007 services are up and running.

7. Take care of some postinstallation chores, such as creating a postmaster mailbox.

8. Apply other software that might need to be integrated with Exchange Server, such as Exchange Server service packs, backup software, and virus-detection software.

Regardless of whether you install Exchange Server as the first server or as a subsequent server within the Exchange Server messaging system, you'll find that if you are prepared, Exchange Server 2007 is not difficult to install. If you are not prepared and choose the wrong options, however, you might end up having to reinstall the software or, worse, wreak a bit of havoc on your existing system. For anyone involved in installing Exchange Server 2007, this is a critical chapter.

Note   Exchange Server 2007 includes a number of server roles. The foundational server role is the Mailbox server role, however, and all other roles build from it. Where necessary, this chapter points out server role differences but focuses mostly on the Mailbox server role.

Preparing for the Installation

Although it's tempting (and easy enough) to insert the Exchange Server CD-ROM and go through the Setup routine, it's best to take care of a few chores first. Verify that your server is correctly configured, gather some information, decide which server roles will go where, and set up special accounts. If you create a good deployment plan, you probably have all the information you need.

Real World   Taking Exchange Server 2007 for a Test Drive

If you are considering transitioning your Exchange organization to Exchange Server 2007 from a previous version, try the new version on a nonproduction or virtual server first to get a feel for its new features. Although not supported for production use, Microsoft makes available a 32-bit version of Exchange Server 2007 suitable for just this purpose. You might also want to test-drive the software even if you are creating a new system rather than upgrading. Testing Exchange Server 2007 before deployment can help you plan the best ways to implement some of the features offered by the new version as those decisions come up during the "real" installation.

If you decide to take Exchange Server 2007 for a test drive, set up a test network or virtual lab that is physically (or virtually) separate from your actual network. If you do not have the physical resources for a separate network, consider using Microsoft Virtual PC or Microsoft Virtual Server to develop a virtual lab that mirrors your production server network.

Gathering Information

The following is a checklist of critical questions you should ask yourself before starting an Exchange Server installation. The answers to some of them might seem a bit obvious, but taking the time to study them before you begin will prevent problems during or after installation:

- Does the computer on which you plan to install Exchange Server 2007 meet the hardware requirements? (See the next section, "Verifying Hardware Requirements.")

- Is the computer on which you plan to install Exchange Server 2007 running a 64-bit version of Windows Server 2003 SP1 or Windows Server 2003 R2?

- Does your server have access to a domain controller and Global Catalog server running Windows Server 2003 SP1 or higher within the local Active Directory site? Is this DC/GC server running a 64-bit version of Windows? Although a 64-bit operating system is not required for domain controllers and Global Catalog servers in an Exchange Server 2007 environment, a 64-bit operating system improves overall directory service performance.

- Do you have access to a user account with the appropriate administrative rights? You must be a local server administrator on the server on which you will install Exchange Server 2007.

- Do you know which Exchange Server 2007 server roles you intend to install on which server? Bear in mind that Exchange Server 2007 uses server roles to determine what server will handle which duties. See "The Role of Roles" later in this chapter for details about Exchange Server 2007 roles.

- Do you have rights that allow you to modify the Active Directory schema? You must be a member of the Enterprise Admins and Schema Admins groups in order to run the Active Directory preparation portion of the installation. The Active Directory preparation command, **PrepareSchema** and **PrepareAD**, replace the Exchange 2003 **domainprep** and **forestprep** commands. If you do not have necessary rights, you can have an administrator who does have rights modify the schema before you begin installing your first Exchange Server 2007 into a domain. (See the section "Installing Exchange Server 2007 in a New Organization" later in this chapter.)

Note   If you have appropriate rights, the domain preparation steps are handled automatically during installation.

- Is Transmission Control Protocol/Internet Protocol (TCP/IP) correctly configured on your Windows server, and do you have access to DNS servers? (See the "TCP/IP" section later in this chapter.)

- What is the name of the organization you will create or join?

■ What connectors will you need to install support for your Exchange Server setup? If your Exchange Server 2007 server will coexist with Exchange 2000 Server or Exchange Server 2003 servers, a mail flow connector is required, although this is handled semiautomatically by the installer. See Chapter 7, "Coexisting with Previous Versions of Exchange Server," for more information about coexistence.

■ What is the disk configuration of the computer on which you are installing Exchange Server? Even though Exchange runs fine on a server with a single large hard drive, for best performance, you should separate responsibilities among multiple hard drives, including the operating system, the page file, the Exchange server software itself, the Exchange mailbox databases, and the log files associated with each storage group. For small organizations, you can safely combine all of these elements onto a single hard drive or RAID set.

■ Is Microsoft Internet Information Services (IIS) 6.0 or later running on the computer? This requirement is discussed further in this chapter because not every Exchange Server 2007 server role requires IIS components.

■ Do you have Simple Mail Transfer Protocol (SMTP) and Network News Transfer Protocol (NNTP) services installed on your server? If you do, remove them. In earlier versions of Exchange, SMTP was the default messaging transport mechanism in Exchange Server. In Exchange Server 2007, both SMTP and Messaging Application Programming Interface (MAPI) are used for message communication, depending on the server roles involved. For example, when messages are transferred between a Mailbox server and a Hub Transport server, the MAPI protocol is used. However, Exchange uses SMTP when messages are sent and received between Hub Transport servers.

Note The Exchange installer program provides you with a step-by-step list of prerequisites and performs a complete system check before any components are installed. So, if you miss something, don't fret. The installer notifies you and gives you the opportunity to fix the problem.

Verifying Hardware Requirements

Before installing Exchange Server 2007, make sure your server meets the minimum hardware requirements and is listed in the Hardware Compatibility List located at *www.windowsservercatalog.com*. Table 6-1 details the Microsoft minimum and recommended configurations for a computer running Exchange Server 2007. Keep in mind that these requirements indicate the configurations on which Exchange Server 2007 will run, not those on which it will run *well*. Many Exchange servers require multiple processors and more memory to execute the desired services.

Table 6-1   Minimum and Recommended Hardware Configurations

Hardware	Minimum	Recommended
Processor	64-bit processor (EM64T/AMD64) A fast 32-bit processor can be used for testing only.	2 or 4 multi-core 64-bit processors (EM64T/AMD64) for a total of 4 to 8 cores. Server role dependent.
Memory	2 GB	2 GB + 5 MB per mailbox. 4 GB for multiple server roles on a single server.
Disk space	1.2 GB on the drive where you install Exchange Server 2007; 200 MB on the system drive.	Space for e-mail and public folders; multiple physical disks configured as a stripe set or stripe set with parity.
Page file	Size equal to RAM + 10 MB.	Size equal to RAM + 10 MB.
Drive	DVD drive or network installation point.	DVD drive or network installation point.
Display	VGA or higher.	VGA or higher.

More Info   To allow you to verify that your hardware and software are compatible with a given Microsoft product, Microsoft publishes hardware and software compatibility lists. Because these lists are published for various Microsoft operating systems and applications and are updated often, Microsoft publishes them online in searchable form at *http://www.windowsservercatalog.com*.

Getting Service Packs

For five years after the release of a products, Microsoft provides associated service packs online for free and on DVD for a small charge. A *service pack* is an update to an operating system or application that encompasses the solutions for multiple problems. In contrast, hotfixes, or *updates*, are solutions to single, immediate problems with an operating system or application. Although service packs often include all hotfixes up to the point that the service pack is released, this is not always the case, and you should regularly check for hotfixes that solved specific problems you might be having. Service packs and hotfixes ensure you quick access to the latest improvements for your operating system or applications.

To get the latest service pack or set of hotfixes from Microsoft, downloading is the way to go. Be aware, however, that although hotfixes are usually small and quick to download, a service pack is typically many megabytes (sometimes hundreds of megabytes) in size and can take a very long time to download, even with a fast Internet connection. Most—but not all—service packs include the contents of past service packs within them. Check to make sure that the service pack you are downloading does include past service packs if you do not already have them installed on your system. This information can be found in the Microsoft Knowledge Base article associated with the service pack.

After you download a service pack, it is important that you test it on another system before implementing it in your production environment. Test it on the exact same type of hardware you have running in your environment.

Defining the Role of Your Server

Unless you work in a very small environment, a minimally configured Exchange Server computer is not sufficient for anything other than a test server. A production Exchange Server 2007 system must run on 64-bit hardware, and the more RAM the better. Even then, performance depends on what you're doing with the server. For optimal performance, run Exchange Server 2007 on a computer that is not also functioning as an Active Directory domain controller for your network. All domain controllers experience some capacity loss because of the overhead required to manage security for the domain. The amount of this overhead is determined by the size and activity of the domain. For best performance and to eliminate the chances for conflict between servers, you should run only the Exchange Server software on servers you designate for messaging.

That said, although an Exchange server performs better if it is running on a server that is dedicated to Exchange messaging, it is not uncommon in small networks to have one server serve as both a domain controller and an Exchange server because it saves the expense of an extra server. Saving on the cost of an extra server, however, might result in meager performance for both Microsoft Windows Server and Exchange Server 2007.

If your computer needs to play the dual role of both Exchange server and domain controller, you'll want more powerful hardware than that listed in Table 6-1. Also, running Exchange Server 2007 on the domain controller means that administrators of that server must be administrators on all domain controllers, thus introducing a potential security weakness.

The Exchange Server 2007 architecture was developed to participate in an Active Directory network. In fact, you can install Exchange Server 2007 only in an Active Directory domain; the Exchange server must also have access to a Global Catalog server. All domain controllers and Global Catalog servers that Exchange Server 2007 uses must be running Windows Server 2000 or Windows Server 2003 with at least a single domain controller running Windows Server 2003 SP1 or Windows Server 2003 R2. Moreover, the domain controller that houses the schema master Windows role must be running Windows Server 2003 SP1 or Windows Server 2003 R2. Also on the domain side, the domain functional level must be Windows 2000 Server native or higher. If you are still running

Exchange Server 5.5 in your environment, you must first transition that complete environment to Exchange 2000 Server or Exchange Server 2003 and eliminate any NT-based domain controllers before you can raise the domain functional level.

You must have Domain Name System (DNS) resolution running in your domain, as DNS is used as a service locator by Active Directory and Exchange Server 2007. The network can have one or more Active Directory forests, each with multiple domain trees in it, and each domain tree can consist of one or more child domains. Each Exchange Server 2007 server must be a member of an Active Directory domain or a be a domain controller in the domain. Although it might be necessary in a small environment to install Exchange Server 2007 on a domain controller, and even though this deployment scenario is supported, for security and performance reasons, it is not recommended. In any case, the Exchange server must be able to access a domain controller in order to function.

Specifying the role of a server involves more than simply configuring it as a domain controller or as a member server. It also includes indicating the services that the server provides to the network. One of these services is IIS. Hardware capacity is even more critical if your server is also running IIS or other network applications. IIS, which is required on Exchange Server 2007 servers with the Mailbox server role, uses considerable memory and processing power; the exact requirements depend on its configuration. For example, if IIS is configured to provide File Transfer Protocol (FTP) service as well as the typical web server role, it uses more CPU cycles and more hard drive space than if it did not provide those services. When determining your hardware requirements, list the services that the server will host and the hardware requirements of the various applications. Start with the application with the largest hardware requirements and then increment the RAM, processor speed, and storage capacity for each additional service by about half again its own recommendation. That provides a fair idea of your server's hardware needs. For more information on planning your server hardware, see Part II, "Planning Your Deployment."

Note   Unlike previous versions of Exchange, Exchange Server 2007 no longer requires the prior installation of the IIS SMTP and NNTP services. Exchange Server 2007 includes its own SMTP server and uses MAPI for internal communication. Further, IIS is not necessarily required on all of your Exchange servers. Only Exchange Server 2007 servers with the Mailbox Server or Client Access server roles require IIS.

Optimizing Hardware through Configuration

Increasing the speed of your processor and the amount of storage and memory on your computer are effective ways of making your Exchange server more powerful. You can also optimize your existing hardware to help boost the performance of an Exchange server if you configure the operating system in the following ways:

- If possible, use one physical disk and disk controller for your operating system and another for your pagefile. You can also increase the size of your pagefile to 50 MB or 100 MB beyond the size of your physical memory.

- Before installing Exchange Server 2007, designate separate physical disks or volumes to house your information stores and transaction log files. This separation allows your log files to be written more quickly to disk. The reason for this increase in speed is that logs are written to disk sequentially, while the Exchange database is written randomly. Having the logs and the database on the same physical disk affects storage performance because of the extra time required to continually reposition the head. Furthermore, when combined with an appropriate backup method, keeping the logs on a separate disk can assist you if the database disk crashes because the logs are used to recover the database.

- You can also use a mirror consisting of two disks (RAID 1) or a stripe set consisting of multiple physical disks (RAID 5, 10, or 50) to house the Exchange information stores and other main components, allowing the various components to be accessed most efficiently. These storage methods have the additional advantage of providing fault tolerance. Because messaging data is considered critical to most businesses, avoid striping without parity (RAID 0) because using it increases the chances of losing all data at once. Hardware RAID using striping with parity provides better performance than software RAID because the operating system does not have the burden of managing the disk activity.

More Info   The *Microsoft Windows Server 2003 Administrator's Companion*, Second Edition by Charlie Russel, Sharon Crawford, and Jason Gerend (Microsoft Press, 2006) has complete details about configuring RAID arrays on Windows servers. The Microsoft TechNet site, available at *http://technet.microsoft.com*, has a plethora of information concerning RAID arrays as well. Search for "Planning Disk Storage for Exchange Server 2007" on the TechNet site or browse to *http://technet.microsoft.com/en-us/library/bb124518.aspx*.

Verifying System Requirements

In addition to making sure that your computer's hardware can handle Exchange Server 2007, check certain other settings before proceeding with your setup.

Windows Server 2003

Exchange Server 2007 runs under only Windows Server 2003 x64 or Windows Server 2003 R2 x64. Make sure the NetBIOS name given to your Windows server is the name you want your Exchange server to have. It is simple enough to change the name of a member server before installing Exchange Server 2007, but it's more difficult to do so afterward. You can change the name beforehand by clicking Change on the Computer Name tab of the System Properties dialog box, which is accessed by clicking the System icon in Control Panel. This displays the Computer Name Changes dialog box, as shown in Figure 6-1.

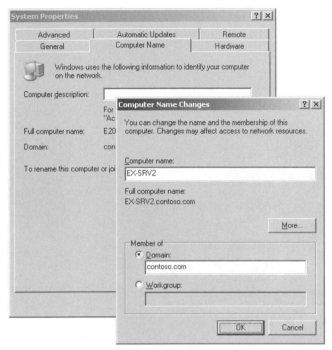

Figure 6-1   Changing the name of your Windows server

Active Directory Domains and Forests

When you install the first Exchange server in an organization, you also create a new Exchange organization and administrative group. If you are installing Exchange Server 2007 on a single-domain network or if your new Exchange infrastructure will not cross any domain boundaries, you should have no problems. However, if your new routing group will cross domain boundaries, you need to make sure appropriate security has been established before you start Setup.

Earlier in this chapter, you read that your domain must be in a functional mode of Windows 2000 native mode or higher. What's really important here is that neither your domain nor forest be running in mixed mode.

From one of your domain controllers, start the Active Directory Domains And Trusts tool. Raise your domain functional level before you raise the forest functional level. Right-click your domain and choose Raise Domain Functional Level to open the dialog box shown in Figure 6-2. Choose a functional level that is at least Windows 2000 native and click Raise. Windows warns you that the change is irreversible. Make sure to heed this warning! Make sure no domain controllers in your organization are still running Windows NT.

> **Important**   Make sure your domain is eligible for raising its functional level. If you have Windows 2000 domain controllers, for example, you cannot raise your domain to Windows Server 2003. Unless there is a problem, Windows lets you know that the raising was successful.

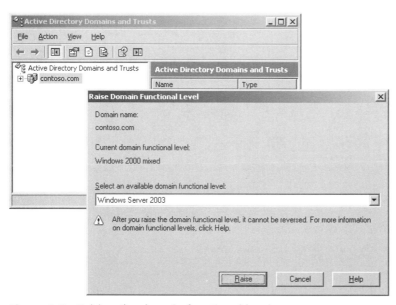

Figure 6-2   Raising the domain functional level

After your domains are raised, check your forest functional level. In Active Directory Domains And Trusts, right-click the Active Directory Domains And Trusts text. Choose Raise Forest Functional Level to open the dialog box shown in Figure 6-3. Again, Windows lets you know whether the change is successful. If you have a lot of domain controllers, give the forest and domain some time to propagate the changes.

> **Note**   Are you the impatient type? You don't have to wait for Active Directory to replicate before moving on to the next steps. Forcing replication is easy. From the command line of a domain controller, type **repladmin /syncall**.

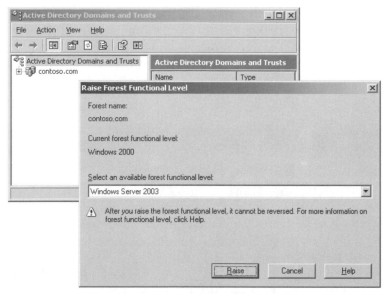

Figure 6-3   Raising the forest functional level

TCP/IP

Exchange Server 2007 includes support for many Internet protocols, including SMTP and HTTP. Exchange's supported protocols rely on the TCP/IP suite to operate. To configure TCP/IP on your Windows server, open the TCP/IP properties of the network connection you are using or use the Ipconfig utility, as shown in Figure 6-4. Note that each server's Ipconfig output reflects the actual IP configuration of that server—and varies widely from server to server.

Figure 6-4   Using the `Ipconfig /All` command to verify TCP/IP configuration

More Info   For more information on configuring Windows networking, consult your Windows product documentation. You might also want to check out the *Microsoft Windows Server 2003 Administrator's Companion*, Second Edition, by Charlie Russel, Sharon Crawford, and Jason Gerend (Microsoft Press, 2006).

Clustering

Previous versions of Microsoft Exchange Server relied on Windows to achieve the high availability afforded by clustering. The success of clustering using this method was mixed. Some organizations had great success, and others did not. Exchange Server 2007 includes all-new and more reliable clustering capabilities. For more information about clustering Exchange Server 2007 systems, see Chapter 9, "High Availability in Exchange Server 2007."

Real World   Curing Clustering Chaos

In earlier versions of Microsoft Exchange, clustering could be chaotic, complicated, and didn't always produce the desired results. Further, Exchange clustering could create significant administrative overhead when it came to updating servers with patches and service packs. As such, many organizations were wary of Exchange clusters and many reverted back to nonclustered servers in an attempt to simplify the messaging environment. Exchange Server 2007 greatly improves this important high availability solution, and you will hopefully be reading about huge Exchange clustering success stories! The moral here: look before you leap.

Internet Information Services

In Exchange Server 2007, IIS is not always required. It depends on which server role or roles you intend to assign to a server. In fact, only two server roles—Mailbox Server and Client Access—require IIS components. If your server doesn't use either one of these components, you can skip the IIS requirement.

This is a good place to reiterate that, unlike in previous versions of Exchange, you should not install the SMTP or NNTP components of IIS. Although these were critical components in Exchange 2000 Server and Exchange Server 2003, Exchange Server 2007 has its own SMTP component and does not use NNTP for communication.

If you install an Exchange Server 2007 server with the Mailbox Server or Client Access server roles, install the Windows Application server role (a Windows server role as opposed to an Exchange server role) before you install Exchange Server 2007. To install this Windows server role, from the Start menu, choose Manage Your Server and follow the instructions.

Creating the Exchange Administrator's Account

Exchange administration and Windows administration are handled separately. Just because an account has administrative privileges in Windows does not necessarily mean the account has full administrative privileges in Exchange. When you install Exchange Server 2007, one user account is given permission to administer Exchange: the account that you log on with when you start the installation. If you want to enable other Exchange administrators, you must do so manually, using Active Directory Users and Computers.

For this reason, make sure that when you start the Exchange Server installer that you are logged on from the account you want to use for initial Exchange administration. This account can be the preconfigured Administrator account, your own account, or a special one you create just for the task. It should be a member of the following Active Directory security groups: Domain Admins, Enterprise Admins, and Schema Admins. Later, you can assign administrative privileges to other accounts or groups.

Alternately, you can have an enterprise administrator run the domain preparation tools (discussed later in the chapter) and assign your account the Full Exchange Administrator permission. You still need to have local administrative permissions on the server, as well.

Note   The Exchange Server 2007 installer adds a number of groups to Active Directory that make it easier to administer Exchange. These groups are Exchange Organization Administrators, Exchange Recipient Administrators, Exchange Server Administrators and Exchange View-Only Administrators. Like any other Active Directory group, add users to these groups to provide users with enhanced Exchange administration rights.

Playing It Safe

It should go without saying, but here it is anyway. Back up your system before you perform any action as major as installing Exchange Server 2007. You can use the Backup utility provided with Windows (which you can find in the Accessories folder). Just start the Automated System Recovery Wizard from the Welcome page of Backup to back up everything on the system and create a floppy disk you can use to start the restore process. You will need one formatted 1.44 MB floppy disk in addition to the media used in performing a backup. Should something go wrong during the installation, you'll be glad you took the extra time to perform a backup. Chapter 16, "Disaster Recovery," discusses the procedure for backing up an Exchange server by using the Backup Utility for Windows. Although the procedure for backing up a Windows server is a bit different than the one described there, you can use that chapter as a tutorial for backing up your system prior to installing Exchange Server 2007 as well.

Performing the Installation

Finally! You actually get to run Exchange Server Setup. You can run Setup from either the Exchange Server 2007 DVD or a shared network installation point. If you are using the DVD, you have only to insert the disc and watch Setup start automatically. If you install over the network, find and run the Setup program yourself. There could be multiple versions of the installation files for different encryption levels and for different languages.

Be sure you find the right files for your situation. If you perform a typical installation of Exchange Server 2007, the setup program is found in the root folder of the DVD.

If you insert the Exchange Server 2007 DVD and the Autorun feature is enabled on your system, a splash screen appears from which you can install the Exchange prerequisites and access other Exchange features, such as documentation and updated tools on the Web. If Autorun is disabled, you must run Setup.exe manually from the DVD.

For now, close the splash screen window as you need to first prepare the Active Directory for Exchange Server 2007.

Preparing the Active Directory Environment

Note Unless you don't have the rights to update the Active Directory schema (see "What If You're Not Allowed to Update the Schema?" on the next page) or you have a complex Active Directory structure, you can skip this step because the Exchange installer will prepare Active Directory for you.

Preparing Active Directory for an Exchange Server 2007 implementation consists of a single command-line step, which requires that the account you're using be a member of the Enterprise Admins group. Further, make sure to run this command from a computer that is in the same domain and the same Active Directory site as the Schema Master.

To prepare Active Directory, follow these steps:

1. Open a command prompt.

2. Insert the Exchange Server 2007 DVD (optional).

3. Change to the drive from which you will be installing Exchange Server 2007. This can be from the Exchange Server 207 DVD or from a network sharepoint.

4. Execute this command:

```
setup /prepareAD
```

This command actually performs three tasks. First, if you have any Exchange 2000 or Exchange Server 2003 servers in your organization, the **prepareAD** command also prepares the Active Directory environment with legacy Exchange permissions so that the Exchange Server 2003 or Exchange 2000 Server Recipient Update Service functions correctly after you update the Active Directory schema for Exchange Server 2007. Second, this command updates the Active Directory schema with Exchange Server 2007 specific attributes. Finally, global Exchange objects in Active Directory are configured and Exchange Universal Security Groups are created.

Note that it may take some time for the changes produced by this command, as shown in Figure 6-5, to replicate throughout the Active Directory environment. For that reason, wait for at least a complete replication cycle before continuing.

Figure 6-5   Preparing Active Directory from the command line

Note   There are a total of five switches, including **/prepareAD**, available to prepare the Active Directory environment. The first switch **/preparelegacyexchangepermissions** (or **/pl**) is used to maintain the proper operation of the Exchange 2003 or Exchange 2000 Recipient Update Service after the Active Directory schema is extended with Exchange Server 2007 attributes. The second switch, **/prepareschema** (or **/ps**), updates the Active Directory schema with the objects used by Exchange Server 2007. Third, **/preparedomain** (or **/pd**), prepares the local domain for Exchange Server 2007. This switch can be modified with the name of another domain (**/pd:<domain FQDN>**) to update that domain instead. Finally, **/prepareall domains** (or **/pad**) prepares all of your domains for Exchange. But, you don't necessarily have to use any of these switches, except maybe **/prepareAD**. **/prepareAD** handles all of this for you. Even better, the Exchange installer will set up Active Directory for you with no intervention. In order to make these changes, you must be a member of Domain Administrations, Enterprise Administrators, or Schema Administrators.

Real World   What If You're Not Allowed to Update the Schema?

In some large companies, or those with tight administrative policies, only a select few administrators might have permission to mess around with the Active Directory Schema. How, then, are you to get your installation job done? Take heart—there is a way. You can run Exchange Setup from the command line, using a switch that causes Setup only to update the Active Directory Schema without actually installing any Exchange Server components. The command for doing this is **Setup /prepareAD**. This means that you can hand the Exchange DVD to an administrator who has permission to update the schema and let him or her update the schema for you. The administrator could also update the schema by using Exchange files on a shared network installation point. Once the schema is updated, you can install Exchange Server 2007 yourself, provided you have permission. There is a bonus to having someone else update the schema: you don't have to wait around for the update to finish.

Installing Exchange Server 2007 in a New Organization

This section assumes that you're creating a new organization. If you're joining an existing Exchange organization, see the section "Installing in an Existing Organization" later in this chapter for a description of the slight differences between the two procedures.

The meat of this section lies in the Install portion of the splash screen. Get started by either reinserting your Exchange Server 2007 DVD or executing Setup.exe. In either case, the first thing you see is the splash screen shown in Figure 6-6.

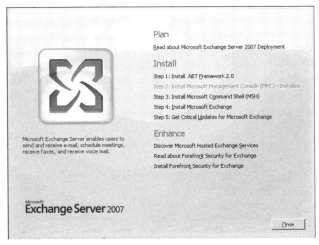

Figure 6-6 The opening splash screen

The real work happens in the tasks under the Install heading. Just as it appears, Exchange Server 2007 walks you step by step through the installation process. Items your configuration already satisfies are dimmed while unsatisfied requirements are black. To perform one of the steps, just click the step in the list. As you saw in Figure 6-6, before you install Exchange, you need:

- The .NET Framework 2.0 (x64 edition).

- The latest Microsoft Management Console. If you've kept up with server updates, the latest management console may already be installed on your server, as it is in Figure 6-6.

- The new Microsoft Command Shell.

If you are missing a prerequisite, click the text next to the step number. The Exchange installer takes you to the appropriate download location. Once the prerequisites are in place, you can move on to installing Exchange. Click Step 4: Install Microsoft Exchange. to start an interactive installation process that consists of seven steps:

- Introduction
- License Agreement

- Error Reporting

- Installation Type

- Readiness Checks

- Progress

- Completion

At least look at the Introduction and License Agreement steps, but they're not all that important when it comes to installation. Error Reporting asks you how much information you want to send to Microsoft should your Exchange server encounter an error. You can choose to send (or not to send) diagnostic information. The upside to sending error information to Microsoft is that you may get faster resolution to a problem. The downside is that an error report may inadvertently contain personal information. Verify that, by sending this fairly innocuous information, your organization's security and privacy policies permit this action.

The most important selection you make during the installation process has to do with the type of installation you want: Typical or Custom, as shown in Figure 6-7. A Typical Exchange Server 2007 installation installs the Hub Transport, Client Access, and Mailbox roles as well as the Exchange Management Tools. At the end of the process, you have a fully functional Exchange system capable of handling mail and client connections. Use the Custom option to better segregate server roles—which are discussed in "The Role of Roles" later in this chapter—among multiple servers, to install server roles not available in a typical installation or to install just the Exchange Management Tools to another system.

Figure 6-7   Choosing an installation type

The Role of Roles

Exchange Server 2007 borrows rom the Windows Server 2003 playbook with how the software handles component distribution, effectively doing away with the old concept of front-end and back-end servers. Exchange Server 2007 uses a new server roles concept, providing much more granularity for decisions as to what runs where. Even though this adds some complexity for Exchange organizations, Microsoft keeps things simple for less intricate Exchange organizations by providing a "typical" installation option that installs just the server roles you need for a completely functional Exchange environment. However, for larger or more complex Exchange environments, to improve overall efficiency and to simplify management, Microsoft provides the capability to install any of five distinct server roles on any given server. Each server role installs only what it needs to operate—and nothing more. By operating this way, your Exchange server's security is improved because there are no unnecessary components open to attack.

Table 6-2   Exchange Server 2007 Server Roles

Server role name	Description	Notes
Mailbox Server	This server role provides the foundation of your Exchange environment and hosts the mailbox and public folder databases. If you have installed Microsoft Cluster Services on your server, through the Exchange Server 2007 installer, you can install this server role in a clustered environment. In such a cluster scenario, the Mailbox server role cannot coexist with other roles.	This server role alone does not provide complete Exchange functionality, but you must have at least one server supporting this server role.
Client Access Server	The Client Access Server role is responsible for most client-based communication with the Mailbox Server-hosted databases. The Client Access Server role provides accessibility to the Exchange environment for clients using Outlook Web Access (OWA), Outlook Anywhere, POP3, and IMAP4.	This server role provides Outlook Web Access (OWA), ActiveSync, Outlook Anywhere (formerly called RPC over HTTP), AutoDiscover (the service responsible for automatically configuring Microsoft Office Outlook 2007 and supported mobile clients). Note that Outlook 2007 clients communicate directly with the Mailbox Server, but functionality such as Outlook Anywhere and the offline address book require the Client Access Server role. At least one server with this server role is required and this role cannot be installed on the same server as a clustered mailbox.

Table 6-2   Exchange Server 2007 Server Roles (Continued)

Server role name	Description	Notes
Edge Transport Server	The Edge Transport Server role is deployed into your company's perimeter network and handles all mail from the outside world. This server role handles message security, including attachment filtering, connection filtering, content filtering, sender and recipient filtering, spam and virus protection, and more. You can use rules provided by a server with the Edge Transport Server role to granularly prohibit messages from entering your Exchange system.	This server role cannot coexist with any other Exchange server role. The Hub Transport Server role can assume some of the functionality provided by the Edge Transport Server role. This server role is not required for a complete Exchange deployment.
Hub Transport Server	The Hub Transport Server role is required for all of Exchange Server 2007's internal mail flow. This server role's responsibilities include message delivery both to a local recipient's mailbox, to recipients in remote Active Directory sites, and, through the use of a special connector, to mailboxes residing on servers running an earlier version of Exchange.	The Hub Transport Server role can be configured to take the place of the Edge Transport Server's role in handling Internet mail communication, although you forgo most the protection offered by the Edge Transport Server. At least one server with the Hub Transport Server role is required in a fully functional Exchange Server 2007 system.
Unified Messaging Server	Introduced in Exchange Server 2007, the Unified Messaging Server role enables the storage of voice and fax messages in a user's Exchange mailbox, the contents of which then become accessible either via telephone or computer.	This server role is not required for a functional Exchange system.

From the Installation Type screen, you also can choose the location to which you want to install Exchange. Bear in mind that Exchange works best when it's separated from the operating system disks and has separate spindles for the database and log files. You can designate the drive on which you would like Exchange Server 2007 installed by selecting the Microsoft Exchange component and clicking the Drive drop-down menu to the right. You can also specify the installation path on that drive by clicking Browse. All components you select to be installed are installed on the drive you choose; you cannot install individual components to different drives.

The Custom Option

If you are wondering exactly what the differences are between a typical and a custom Exchange server installation, look no further. The two options are almost identical with a few minor exceptions. First, you have the option to install any Exchange Server 2007 server role you like onto your server. Second, a custom installation provides the ability to install the Mailbox server role in an active or passive cluster. Finally, the custom option makes it possible to install just the Exchange Server 2007 Management Tools. Figure 6-8 gives you a look at the custom installation options.

Figure 6-8   Exchange Server 2007 custom installation options and server role selection

Creating an Organization

After you select an installation type, you need to create the Exchange organization you've been planning. You can choose either to create a new Exchange organization or to join an existing Exchange 2000 or Exchange Server 2003 organization. If you join an Exchange 2000 or Exchange Server 2003 organization, you will want to check out Chapter 7, "Coexisting with Previous Versions of Exchange Server," and Chapter 8, "Transitioning to Exchange Server 2007." If you want to create a new Exchange organization, type the name of the new Exchange organization on the screen, as shown in Figure 6-9. Do not take this task lightly. Although you can change an organization name later, it's better to get it right first. If you haven't decided on the name, you haven't properly planned your organization. See Chapter 4, "Assessing Needs," and Chapter 5, "Planning for Deployment," for more information on planning and naming your organization. Click Next after you type the name.

Figure 6-9   Specifying a name for a new organization

Note   This section assumes that you're creating a new organization. If you're joining an existing Exchange organization, see the section "Installing in an Existing Organization" later in this chapter for a description of the slight differences between the two procedures.

Client Settings Option

The next step of the installer asks whether you have computers in your company that are running Microsoft Office Outlook 2003 or earlier. If you do have client computers that are running Outlook 2003 or earlier, and you select "Yes," Exchange Server 2007 creates a public folder database on the Mailbox server. If you've already upgraded to Outlook 2007 on your client systems, public folders are optional in Exchange Server 2007. Selecting "No" results in Exchange Server 2007 not creating a public folder database. You can add a public folder database later if you need to, though.

Note   In Exchange Server 2007, organizations with all clients running Outlook 2007 do not need public folders unless they are needed for organizational information sharing. In previous versions of Exchange and Outlook, public folders housed critical information, such as the free/busy data used to schedule meetings. Exchange Server 2007 replaces this functionality with the Availability Service, which gathers free/busy information directly from users' mailboxes.

Readiness Check

After you select your installation type, name your organization, and tell the installer about your client computers, the readiness check process begins. This process runs through the prerequisites and makes sure that they have been met. For example, if you failed to install IIS before you ran the installer and selected a server role that requires IIS, the readiness check tells you that you need to exit the installer and try again after you install IIS.

A series of green checkmarks means good news. It means that all of the readiness checks were successful, and you can continue with the installation. Click Install to continue. But, before you click Install, make sure you've made no mistakes in your choices. After installation begins, the Cancel button is unavailable!

Installation

Setup begins copying files. Depending on the components you selected for installation, this can take several minutes. After installation files are copied, the setup program installs the server roles you selected during installation.

During the process, Setup might notify you that it needs to extend the Active Directory schema. This happens if you are installing Exchange Server 2007 and did not run the prepareAD tool prior to installation. If you are logged on with a user account that has appropriate permissions to do this, Setup handles this step for you. Don't be alarmed if it seems as though it's taking some time to complete this process. The schema updating process can take quite a bit of time (sometimes hours), depending on your situation. (This might be a great chance to go get some lunch!) When Setup completes the task, the setup program indicates that the installation was successful, as shown in Figure 6-10.

Figure 6-10   The Exchange Server 2007 installation completed successfully.

Installing in an Existing Organization

Installing Exchange Server 2007 in an existing Exchange organization is nearly identical to installing it as the first server in an organization. You need to be aware of only a couple of small differences in the procedure as well as one important prerequisite: the existing Exchange organization must be running in native mode.

You start Setup the same way: from either the DVD or a network installation point. The first difference you notice is that the installer pops up a Mail Flow Settings option and asks you to select the Exchange 2000 Server or Exchange Server 2003 server to which the Exchange Server 2007 routing group connector will attach. Click Browse and identify the server to which you want to direct mail originating from an Exchange Server 2007 server that is destined for a mailbox in the Exchange 2000 or Exchange Server 2003 organization.

Second, you are not able to select an organization into which to install the new server. The Exchange Server 2007 server is installed into the existing Exchange 2000 or Exchange Server 2003 organization.

After you identify the server to use for mail flow, the rest of the process is no different from the one you used to install the first server in an organization.

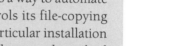

Real World   Automating Exchange Server 2007 Setup

If you plan to deploy a large number of Exchange servers in your enterprise or if you need to deploy servers remotely, you will be glad to know there is a way to automate the setup process. Setup places all the information that controls its file-copying process in a file named Setup.ini. The file is customized for a particular installation when you make choices in the various Installation Wizard pages described previously.

You can create your own Setup.ini files using tools and samples included in the Exchange Server 2007 Resource Kit. You can then create a batch script that runs the Setup program, using the information in your customized file. If you deploy Exchange Server 2007 on existing Windows servers in your enterprise, you can also use Microsoft Systems Management Server or a similar application to further automate the process.

More Info   To learn more about automating Exchange Server Setup, including all the parameters for customizing the Setup.ini files, consult the online product documentation.

Verifying Your Installation

You've installed Exchange Server, but don't pat yourself on the back just yet. You still need to perform some basic postinstallation tasks to make sure everything is running well. The first thing you should do is restart your server. After you do so, check the Windows application event logs for any problems. Each Exchange component that makes up your new server runs as Windows services. However, because of the role-based nature of Exchange Server 2007, you need to match server roles with service names and make sure the appropriate services are running. You can verify that these services are running by using the Services tool, available from the Administrative Tools folder on the Start menu. Figure 6-11 shows the Services console window. Table 6-3 outlines the services that should be running for each individual server role.

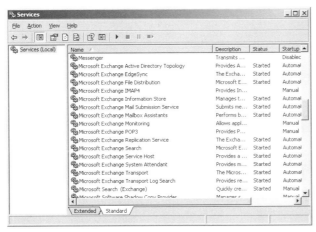

Figure 6-11   The Services console window

Table 6-3   **Exchange Server 2007 Service Summary**

Server role	Services
Mailbox	Microsoft Exchange Active Directory Topology
	Microsoft Exchange Management
	Microsoft Exchange Information Store
	Microsoft Exchange Mail Submission Service
	Microsoft Exchange Mailbox Assistants
	Microsoft Exchange Replication Service
	Microsoft Search (Exchange)
	Microsoft Exchange System Attendant

Table 6-3   Exchange Server 2007 Service Summary (Continued)

Server role	Services
Client Access	Microsoft Exchange Active Directory Topology
	Microsoft Exchange System Attendant
	Microsoft Exchange IMAP4
	Microsoft Exchange POP3
	IIS Admin
	HTTP SSL
	World Wide Web Publishing Services
Hub Transport	Microsoft Exchange Active Directory Topology
	Microsoft Exchange Administration Service
	Microsoft Exchange Management
	Microsoft Exchange Transport
Edge Transport	Microsoft Exchange Transport
	MSExchangeAdam
Unified Messaging	Microsoft Exchange Active Directory Topology
	Microsoft Exchange Unified Messaging
	Microsoft Exchange Speech Engine

Depending on the optional components you installed with Exchange Server 2007, you might also see several other Microsoft Exchange services running.

Management Shell

Checking the services list isn't the only trick you can use to see whether Exchange installed properly onto your server. For Exchange Server 2007, Microsoft has enabled a complete command-line interface using Microsoft Shell. In short, pretty much anything you can do from the Exchange Management Console you can do from the Exchange Management Shell. This is welcome news for those who like to script tasks. You will be seeing a lot of this command-line tool throughout this book, starting right now. From the Start menu, choose All Programs, Microsoft Exchange Server 2007, Exchange Management Shell. A window appears that looks a lot like a command window. At the prompt, type the following command and press Enter:

```
Get-ExchangeServer | Format-Table Name, ServerRole
```

This command returns a list of your Exchange servers along with the server roles that are installed on each, as you can see in Figure 6-12.

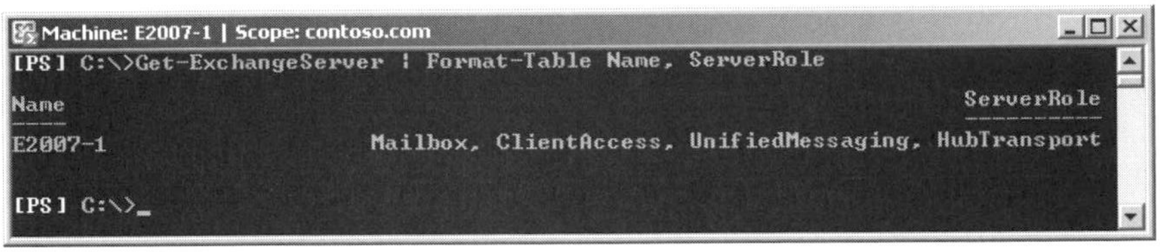

Figure 6-12   The Exchange Management Shell in action

Finalizing Exchange Server 2007 Deployment

Technically, your Exchange Server 2007 system is ready to go at this point. If you are so inclined, go ahead and dive into the Exchange Management Console, which should have opened automatically after installation. The console provides a number of recommended action steps, including:

- Creating a postmaster mailbox or assigning an existing user account postmaster duties

- Making sure that your Offline Address Book settings are configured properly

Management Shell

The steps you need to perform depend on the server roles you install to your server. To help further familiarize you with the Exchange Management Shell, you can use that tool to manage some of your postdeployment tasks. To check whether your Exchange server has a postmaster mailbox, from the Exchange Management Shell, execute the following command:

```
Get-TransportServer
```

The shell returns the name of your server along with, if configured, an account named postmaster@yourdomain.com under the heading of ExternalPostMasterAddress.

This doesn't mean that you're done, though. By default, there is no account associated with this postmaster e-mail address. As such, you need to either create a special postmaster account or designate an account that will serve as the postmaster for your domain. Your choice just depends on how diligent you are in monitoring items—such as nondelivery reports (NDRs)—generally sent to postmaster accounts.

To assign an existing account the role of postmaster for your domain with the secondary address of postmaster, follow these steps:

1. Open the Exchange Management Console (the GUI version).

2. Expand the Recipient Configuration option.

3. Choose Mailbox.

4. From the Results pane (the middle pane), right-click the user to which you want to add the postmaster account and, from the shortcut menu, choose Properties.

5. From the Properties page, click the E-mail Addresses tab.

6. Click Add.

7. In the SMTP Address box, type **postmaster@*contoso.com***, replacing *contoso.com* with your domain. When you finish, the new address appears in the SMTP section of the Address box, as shown in Figure 6-13.

8. Click OK.

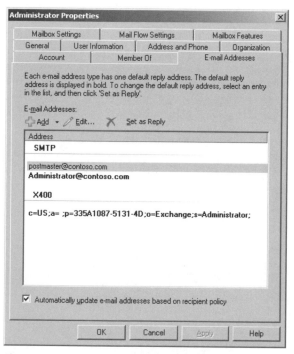

Figure 6-13   The new address appears in the list.

Or, if you prefer the postmaster to be a completely separate account, you can create a new user mailbox by following these steps:

1. Open the Exchange Management Console (the GUI version).

2. Select the Recipient Configuration option.

3. From the Actions pane at the right side of the window, choose New Mailbox to start the New Mailbox wizard.

4. On the Introduction page, choose User Mailbox, and click Next.

5. On the User Type page, click New user, and click Next.

6. On the Mailbox Information page, complete, at a minimum, the Name, User logon name (User Principal Name), User logon name (Pre-Windows 2000), and password fields. You should name this user **postmaster**. Click Next.

7. On the Mailbox Settings page, make sure the settings meet with your approval. This page gives you a place to specify the server on which the postmaster account should be created. From here, you can also decide which storage group and mailbox database will house the account. Click Next.

8. On the New Mailbox page, review the summary and, when ready, click New.

9. Finally, on the Completion page shown in Figure 6-14, look for information regarding the success or failure of the mailbox creation process. This page also displays the Exchange Management Shell command that was used to create the mailbox. This provides a great way to quickly learn how to script your own mailbox creation commands.

10. Click Finish.

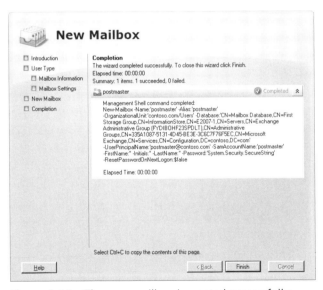

Figure 6-14 The new mailbox is created successfully.

Apart from making sure the postmaster account is configured, bear in mind that Exchange Server 2007 handles the offline address book differently depending on the version of Outlook your users use. Outlook 2003 and earlier clients continue to use public folders to handle offline address book synchronization while Outlook 2007 clients use a

Web-based distribution mechanism that does not rely on public folders. In the case of Outlook 2007 clients, Exchange points the client to a client access server that has an offline address book virtual directory.

If you select the option indicating that you have Outlook 2003 clients in your organization, the Exchange installer creates your public folder database for you. If, however, you do not do this and you have Outlook 2003 clients, you need to create a public folder database, or offline address book functionality, along with other things, is not available to your clients.

To check this, follow these steps:

1. Open the Exchange Management Console.

2. Expand the Server Configuration tree.

3. Select Mailbox.

4. If you do not see a Public Folder Database entry, continue with these steps. Otherwise, you are all set.

5. From the Actions pane, choose New Public Folder Database. This starts a wizard that walks you through the database creation process.

6. All you have to do is specify the name of the public folder database and the database file path.

Note   Don't worry if you accidentally try to create a second public folder database. The wizard will fail and tell you that multiple public folder databases are not allowed on the server.

If you have clients running Exchange Server 2007, you should be all set as long as you have one server with the Client Access Server role installed. The virtual directory housing the offline address book is created automatically when you install this server role. However, the Web-based offline address book distribution still needs to be enabled in order to work.

To enable the Web-based offline address book distribution, follow these steps:

1. Open the Exchange Management Console.

2. Expand the Organization Configuration branch.

3. Choose Mailbox.

4. Click the Offline Address Book tab.

5. Right-click the Default Offline Address Book entry and choose Properties. You should see a screen similar to the one shown in Figure 6-15.

6. Click the Distribution tab.

7. Under the Distribution Points header, select the check box next to Enable Web-based Distribution.

8. Click the Add button.

9. Select the Web site from which you want to distribute the offline address book and click OK.

10. From the Offline Address Properties page, click OK again.

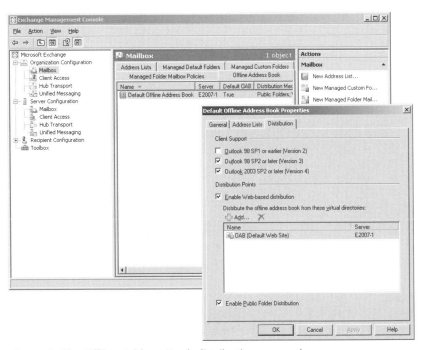

Figure 6-15   Offline Address Book distribution properties

Keeping Exchange Healthy

Microsoft releases service packs for Exchange Server, just as it does for Windows. To avoid possible problems later on, it is best to install the latest available Exchange Server service pack. See the section "Getting Service Packs" earlier in this chapter for more information. If you are concerned about the latest service pack introducing new problems, consider testing the service pack on a nonproduction (or virtual) server first. After you install the service pack, restart the system. When the server is back online, check the Services console window to ensure that the Exchange Server services are up and running.

Your new Exchange server is ready to be used. Now you can pat yourself on the back. And now that you've installed Exchange Server 2007, you're ready to apply the other software you need to integrate your Exchange environment, such as third-party backup software, virus-detection utilities, or content-filtering applications—unless you opt to use Exchange Server 2007's new features, of course.

Note   To verify that services are running on a remote Exchange server, you can use the Connect To Another Computer feature of the Computer Management snap-in.

One of the first things you might be tempted to do after successfully installing Exchange Server 2007 is poke around the system to see what was put where. This is fine, of course, and it's a great way to learn more about how Exchange is laid out.

Summary

This chapter described how to install Exchange Server 2007. It discussed how to prepare your Windows server for the installation, including how to verify that the hardware on the server meets requirements for installing Exchange Server 2007 in the desired config-uration. It then took you step by step through the installation process and described how to verify the installation after the setup routine is finished. Of course, the new server, single-server scenario focused on in this chapter is not necessarily the same scenario you face. In the next chapters, you learn how to make Exchange Server 2007 work with earlier versions of Exchange and how to migrate to a 100 percent Exchange Server 2007-based messaging system.

Chapter 7

Coexisting with Previous Versions of Exchange Server

In previous editions of this book, the chapter that immediately followed Installation was Upgrade/Migration and then Coexistence with Older Versions of Exchange Server. However, Microsoft Exchange Server 2007 does not support an upgrade path, as was possible with older versions of the product. Why?

Simply put, you can't directly upgrade an Exchange 2000 Server or Exchange Server 2003 server to Exchange Server 2007. Exchange 2000 Server and Exchange Server 2003 runs only under a 32-bit version of Windows whereas Exchange Server 2007 is a 64-bit-only affair and runs atop only 64-bit hardware and Windows. So, Exchange Server 2007 can't run on the 32-bit Windows that you run in your existing Exchange 2000 Server or Exchange Server 2003 computer.

If you currently run Exchange 2000 Server or Exchange Server 2003 and want to move to Exchange Server 2007, you must run a coexistence scenario before you can take the final plunge to a full Exchange Server 2007 environment. That is, Exchange Server 2007 must be installed on new hardware side by side with your existing Exchange Server 2000/Exchange Server 2003 organization. Once Exchange Server 2007 is in place, you can begin the actual transition process from Exchange 2000 Server or Exchange Server 2003 to Exchange Server 2007—the topic of Chapter 8, "Transitioning to Exchange Server 2007."

Chapter Background

This chapter focuses on coexisting with Exchange Server 2003. In this chapter, the word *coexistence* describes a configuration in which different versions of Exchange Server are installed in the same Exchange organization at the same time. Where points differ, however, it is pointed out what you should expect when coexisting with Exchange 2000 Server. Some of the information in this chapter overlaps with information from Chapter 6, "Installing Exchange Server 2007." This is by design and is intended to make this chapter as stand-alone as possible. This chapter does not cover any scenarios that involve upgrading from Exchange 5.5. Exchange Server 2007 does not support upgrades or migrations directly from Exchange 5.5, nor does Exchange Server 2007 support coexistence with Exchange 5.5. In order to move from Exchange 5.5 to Exchange Server 2007, first migrate to Exchange Server 2003, after which you can migrate to Exchange Server 2007.

This chapter assumes that mail to and from the Internet will continue to be handled by your Exchange Server 2003 servers and then passed on, through a legacy routing group connector, to mailboxes housed in your Exchange Server 2007 organization. In Chapter 8, you learn about moving all remaining services from Exchange Server 2003 to Exchange Server 2007 and removing Exchange Server 2003 from your organization.

Finally, in this and the next chapter, everything is based around the Hub Transport server. In other words, the Edge Transport server role server is not used in either of these chapters. The reason is simple: the Edge Transport server role server is brand-new to Exchange Server 2007. The Edge Transport server role server is introduced in Part 6, "Security." In that part, you learn how to best integrate the services provided by the Edge Transport sole server service into your newly transitioned Exchange Server 2007 organization.

Terminology

Notice the use of the words "transition" and "transitioning" in this chapter. There are other words that could be used, such as "migration," "upgrade," and so forth. However, Microsoft uses specific terminology for specific scenarios. As explained before, an upgrade is not possible with Exchange Server 2007. A migration, on the other hand, is the method used when moving from a non-Exchange messaging system to Exchange Server 2007. Microsoft reserves the word "transition" specifically for the scenario being discussed in this chapter— an upgrade from an earlier version of Exchange to Exchange Server 2007.

A part of your transition will also include a coexistence phase. During this phase, both of your legacy Exchange servers and your Exchange Server 2007 computers will run in a side-by-side configuration. Mail will be transferred between systems through a special connector, and mailboxes can be moved between organizations as a part of your overall transition.

Exchange Server 2007 Coexistence Deployment Considerations

As you can probably tell, Exchange Server 2007 is all new. With this newest release, Microsoft has jettisoned some of the product's legacy support in order to streamline and simplify an increasingly complex product. As such, there are a few things that you need to consider before you deploy Exchange Server 2007 into an existing legacy Exchange organization. Note that everything here applies to both Exchange 2000 Server and Exchange Server 2003. Where this information indicates Exchange Server 2003, the information also covers Exchange 2000 Server. Exchange Server 2007 also supports coexistence with and transition from Exchange 2000 Server and Exchange Server 2003 organizations.

Exchange Server 2003 Native Mode

First, Exchange Server 2007 can coexist with Exchange 2000 Server or Exchange Server 2003 only when the legacy Exchange organization is operating in native mode. A native mode Exchange Server 2000/Exchange Server 2003 organization can be created when the following conditions have been realized:

- You have read Chapter 6 and understand the Active Directory domain steps that must be taken in order to install Exchange Server 2007 into your environment.

- No Exchange Server version 5.5 exists in the Exchange Server 2000/Exchange Server 2003 organization.

- If you're upgrading from Exchange Server 5.5, you have decommissioned the Site Replication Service.

- All Active Directory connectors have been taken out of service.

- You understand that this is an irreversible decision. If you ever need to add an Exchange Server 5.5 server to your organization, you will be unable to do so.

- If you are running Exchange 2000 Server and intend to coexist with Exchange Server 2007, make sure all Exchange 2000 Server servers, including systems to which you have installed only the Exchange 2000 Server management tools, are running at least Exchange 2000 Server Post-Service Pack 3 (SP3) Update Rollup in order to avoid possible object corruption.

Note   You can install Exchange Server 2007 only into a native mode Exchange organization. If you create a new forest in which to install Exchange Server 2007, you cannot later add earlier versions of Exchange, as this scenario is not supported.

After these items are removed, convert your Exchange organization to native mode by following these steps:

1. From one of your Exchange 2000 Server or Exchange Server 2003 computers, start the Exchange System Manager.

2. Right-click the organization and, from the resulting shortcut menu, choose Properties.

3. From the Properties page (see Figure 7-1), click Change Mode.

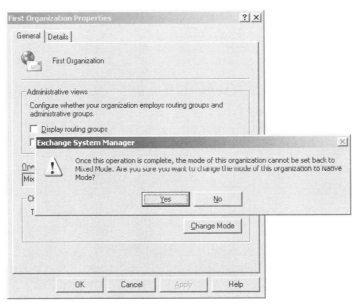

Figure 7-1   Change the Exchange organization to native mode.

4. A pop-up window appears to tell you that the change to native mode is an irreversible operation. Click Yes if you are ready to make this change.

5. When complete, the Operation mode portion of the Properties window is updated, indicating that your Exchange organization is running in native mode.

Automatic Coexistence Tasks

Before you continue with your Exchange Server 2007 deployment plans, you should have a firm understanding of the steps that the Exchange Server 2007 installer takes in order to support coexistence with your Exchange Server 2003 organization. Even though these steps are automated through the installer, you can also perform the steps manually if you like. This section explains the automated steps taken by the installer and, throughout the chapter some of the manual processes behind these actions are outlined in detail.

When you install Exchange Server 2007 in an existing Exchange Server 2003 organization, Setup performs the following coexistence-specific tasks:

- An Active Directory universal security group named ExchangeLegacyInterop is created. This group is necessary in order to allow Exchange Server 2003 and Exchange 2000 Server servers to send e-mail to the Exchange Server 2007 servers.

- The Exchange Server 2007 administrative group named Exchange Administrative Group (FYDIBOHF23SPDLT) is created.

  > **Important** It is important to note that you cannot move Exchange Server 2007 servers out of this administrative group, nor should you rename the administrative group. Exchange Server 2007 uses this administrative group for configuration data storage, and the product expects to find the database using this name.

- The Exchange Server 2007 routing group named Exchange Routing Group (DWBGZMFD01QNBJR) is created. Exchange Server 2007 uses this routing group for communication with your legacy Exchange servers.

  > **Important** As is the case with the newly created administrative group, you should not move Exchange Server 2007 servers out of this new routing group, nor should you rename this routing group.

- Because Exchange Server 2003 and Exchange Server 2007 use different routing topologies, a two-way routing group connector between Exchange Server 2007 and one of your Exchange Server 2003 bridgehead servers is created. This routing group connector is required in order to enable mail flow between Exchange Server 2007 and Exchange Server 2003.

Global Settings

Learn how the Exchange Server 2007 setup process handles the global settings that exist in your legacy Exchange organizations. These items include delegation permissions, recipient policies, message formats, SMTP connectors, and more. Global settings are transferred automatically to your new Exchange organization when you install Exchange Server 2007. So, if you create any of these items, you don't need to worry about re-creating them in the new Exchange Server 2007 organization.

Installing Exchange Server 2007 into an Existing Exchange Server 2003 Organization

Before you get started with the process of installing Exchange Server 2007 into your existing Exchange Server 2003 organization, read Chapter 6. Pay particular attention to the sections "Preparing for the Installation," "Active Directory Domains and Forests," "Preparing the Active Directory Environment," and "Installing in an Existing Organization." You will see some repetition of this information, for completeness.

> **Note**   In this section, a Typical installation of Exchange Server 2007 into an existing Exchange Server 2003 organization is performed. A Typical installation includes the Hub Transport server role, the Client Access server role, and the Mailbox server role, as well as the Exchange Management Tools.

The first difference you notice is that the installer pops up a Mail Flow Settings option and asks you to select the Exchange 2000 Server or Exchange Server 2003 server to which the Exchange Server 2007 routing group connector will attach (see Figure 7-2). In Exchange Server 2007–only organizations, routing groups have been eliminated in favor of using the Active Directory Site configuration for message routing. In these single-version organizations, all Exchange Server 2007 servers in the same Active Directory site can communicate with one another without the use of connectors through the use of Active Directory IP Site Links. Exchange Server 2007 only uses old-style routing group connectors when the new server communicates with Exchange Server 2003 or Exchange 2000 Server servers that exist in the same Exchange organization. During the Exchange Server 2007 installation, bidirectional routing group connectors are created between the Exchange Server 2007 routing group and a selected Exchange Server 2003 or Exchange 2000 Server routing group. The Exchange Server 2003 or Exchange 2000 Server server that you select during setup determines with which routing group the connection is made. Be aware that all of your Exchange Server 2007 computers are automatically added to this coexistence routing group.

> **Note**   You might ask why you can't just install your Exchange Server 2007 computer into one of your existing Exchange Server 2003 routing groups and just avoid all of this connector nonsense. The simple answer is that Exchange Server 2007 servers are placed automatically into the routing group named Exchange Routing Group (DWBGZMFD01QNBJR). Exchange Server 2007 servers cannot be placed in other routing groups and older Exchange servers cannot be placed into this Exchange Server 2007-only routing group. So... connectors are a must!

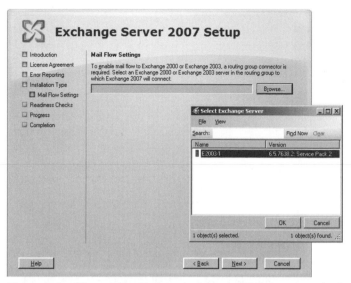

Figure 7-2   Choose the Exchange Server 2003 computer in the routing group to which Exchange Server 2007 will connect.

When you select the bridgehead server to which you want to install the Exchange Server 2007 routing group connector, try to choose a server somewhere near your hub routing group, assuming your routing groups are configured in a hub-and-spoke format. Bear in mind that all mail that is sent between Exchange Server 2003 servers and Exchange Server 2007 servers runs through these newly created connectors, so an appropriate selection is critical. Consider the following scenario: your organization has offices in New York, London, and Houston. All three offices have Exchange infrastructures with each one in a separate Exchange routing group. All three offices are connected with point-to-point connections, but the connections are pretty well utilized, with little room for additional traffic. The Houston office has two servers and is being upgraded to Exchange Server 2007; the first server selected for upgrade houses about half of the Houston users. The e-mail administrator in Houston accidentally chooses an Exchange server in New York as the bridgehead/mail flow server. Now, all mail between users on different servers in Houston is routed to New York and then back to Houston. Further, all mail to Exchange Server 2007 users in Houston must be routed through New York first. You can probably tell why appropriate selection of the mail flow server is so important. Of course, you can always create additional connectors as necessary. This task is covered later.

In the Exchange Server 2007 setup, click Browse and identify the server to which you want to direct mail originating from an Exchange Server 2007 server that is destined for a mailbox in the Exchange 2000 or Exchange Server 2003 organization.

> **Note** Intersite messaging in Exchange Server 2007 is handled by Exchange Server 2007 servers that have the Hub Transport role installed on them.

Second, you will notice that you are not able to select an organization into which to install the new server. The Exchange Server 2007 server will be installed into the existing Exchange 2000 Server or Exchange Server 2003 organization.

After you identify the server to use for mail flow, the rest of the process is no different from the one you used to install the first server in an organization. Go through the remainder of the setup process as described in Chapter 6.

Coexistence Administration Issues

There are some important points to make about using the Exchange System Manager and the Exchange Management Console or the Exchange Management Shell. Only the Exchange Management Console or the Exchange Management Shell can be used to manage Exchange Server 2007. Also, some Exchange Server 2003 objects can be edited from within these Exchange Server 2007 tools. On the flip side, the Exchange Server 2003 Exchange System Manager can view many Exchange Server 2007 objects, but cannot manage these objects. Further, although you can remove Exchange Server 2003 features with the Exchange Server 2007 Exchange Management Console/Shell, new Exchange Server 2003 objects can't be created with the new tools. Figure 7-3 gives you a look at the Exchange Server 2003 Exchange System Manager with Exchange Server 2007 objects visible. Note that there are two connectors—one in each administrative group. Figure 7-4 shows you these same routing group connectors from the other side of the link.

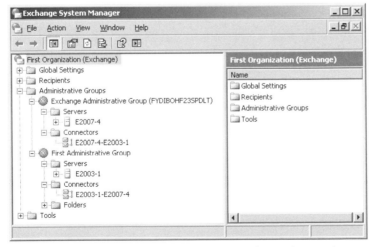

Figure 7-3 The Exchange System Manager shows the newly created Exchange Server 2007 objects.

Figure 7-4 The get-routinggroupconnector command in the Exchange Management Shell displays the installed routing group connectors.

Creating Additional Routing Group Connectors

Earlier in this chapter, you read that you can create additional routing group connectors as needed in order to create the most efficient mail flow possible between your Exchange Server 2003 and Exchange Server 2007 organizations. Routing group connectors must be created from an Exchange Server 2007 computer using the Exchange Management Shell. New routing group connectors cannot be created using the GUI-based Exchange Management Console.

Management Shell

A new routing group connector might be just what you need in order to improve message flow between your new and old messaging infrastructures. A new routing group connector can be created only from the Exchange Management Shell using the `new-routinggroupconnector` cmdlet.

The following command provides an example that creates a routing group connector between a new Exchange Server 2007 computer and the server named e2003-2, which resides in the Exchange Server 2003 organization in a second routing group.

```
new-routinggroupconnector -Name "Example RCG - RG 2"
-sourcetransportservers "e2007-4.contoso.com" -targettransportservers
"e2003-2.contoso.com" -cost 100 -bidirectional $true
-publicfoldersreferralsenabled $true
```

You notice that there are a number of other parameters associated with this command. First, note the `bidirectional $true` parameter. This indicates that new connectors should be created going in both directions. At the end of the command line, `publicfolderreferralsenabled $true` indicates that users can use this routing group connector to access public folders located on servers in the target routing group when those public folders are not available in the source routing group. The cost parameter assigns a cost to the connector to assist in determining the least cost path between organizations.

After you submit this command, the Exchange Management Shell returns the names of the newly created routing group connectors.

Real World   Preventing Routing Loops

Before you create additional routing group connectors, it's important to ensure that message routing loops do not take place and that earlier versions of Exchange use least-cost routing without trying to calculate alternate routes. Therefore, suppress minor link state updates on your Exchange Server 2003 servers. To do so:

1. Start the registry editor.

2. Browse to HKEY_LOCAL_MACHINE\System\CurrentControlSet\Services \RESvc\Parameters.

3. Right-click Parameters and, from the shortcut menu, choose New, and then choose DWORD value.

4. Name the new DWORD value SuppressStateChanges.

5. Double-click the newly created value.

6. In the Value Data field, type 1 and click OK.

7. When done, close the registry editor.

For the changes to take effect, restart the Simple Mail Transfer Protocol (SMTP) service, the Microsoft Exchange Routing Engine service, and the Microsoft Exchange MTA Stacks services.

Coexistence Issue: Version-Specific Administration

Once you are running your Exchange environment in this dual fashion, administration of that environment becomes a little more difficult. For the most part, you need to manage individual Exchange servers and Exchange objects using their native management tools. So, Exchange Server 2003 servers and others must be managed using the Exchange System Manager while Exchange Server 2007 routing group connectors and others must be managed using either the Exchange Management Console or the Exchange Management Shell. Here are some other important points to bear in mind when managing a mixed Exchange Server 2003/Exchange Server 2007 environment:

- You can view the properties for most supported Exchange Server 2007 objects from within the Exchange System Manager. However, when you open an Exchange Server 2007 object in the ESM, the ESM returns an informational error message (see Figure 7-5) indicating that the object can be managed only with Exchange System Manager 8.0 or higher. In these cases, "Exchange System Manager 8.0" refers to the Exchange Management Console and indicates that the object can be managed only from Exchange Server 2007.

Figure 7-5   A newer version of the Exchange System Manager is required to manage this object.

- Exchange 2000/2003 features that are not supported in Exchange Server 2007 can be managed only from the older management tools.

- Server properties can be managed only from native version management tools.

- Exchange Server 2003 tools cannot be used to move mailboxes to or from Exchange Server 2007 servers.

- Although it appears that some Exchange Server 2007 mailbox/recipient properties, such as storage limits/quotas, can be managed from within the Exchange System Manager, you should refrain from doing so. Active Directory Users and computers and the Exchange System Manager do not provide full management capability for Exchange Server 2007-based mailboxes.

■ Conversely, some Exchange Server 2003 mailbox properties can be managed from within any of the three management tools, as well. Figure 7-6 shows a list of mailboxes that exist within the Exchange messaging environment. Note that some of the mailboxes are listed as Legacy Mailbox (not on an Exchange Server 2007 server), while one mailbox—Robert Zare's—is listed as a User Mailbox (housed on an Exchange Server 2007 server). Also note that the server that houses the mailbox is also listed. These examples use the Exchange server version in the server name to make it easy to determine which Exchange version is housing a particular mailbox.

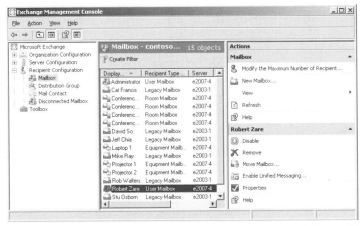

Figure 7-6   Organizational mailboxes can be managed from within Exchange Server 2007 management tools.

SMTP Connectors and Internet E-Mail

Both Exchange Server 2003 and Exchange Server 2007 support SMTP connectors, and either version can route messaging traffic to a connector housed on the other version. However, during this interversion communication, some version-specific settings are ignored and can possibly cause problems. Table 7-1 lists each SMTP connector feature for which there are version differences so that you can be prepared for these possible problems.

Table 7-1   SMTP Connector Features and Administration

SMTP connector feature	Version support	Comment
Connector scope	2003, 2007	Unless you have introduced further restrictions, in Exchange Server 2003, servers in a particular routing group are the only computers able to make use of that routing group's connectors. Because Exchange Server 2007 does away with routing groups in favor of Active Directory sites, this means that Exchange Server 2007 connectors are available to any Exchange Server 2007 server in the Active Directory site.

Table 7-1   SMTP Connector Features and Administration (Continued)

SMTP connector feature	Version support	Comment
Enabled/disabled property	2007	Exchange Server 2003 cannot tell when a particular Exchange Server 2007 connector is disabled and will continue routing, even if a connector is not enabled.
Maximum message size	2003, 2007	All messages passing through either connector are subject to message size limits set on either connector.
Message priority	2003	Exchange Server 2007 doesn't use message priority and bypasses these restrictions.
Message type	2003	Exchange Server 2007 doesn't assign message types. Exchange Server 2007 bypasses message type restrictions set through Exchange Server 2003 SMTP connectors.
Per user delivery restriction	2003	Exchange Server 2007 can route messages to Exchange Server 2003 connectors even if those Exchange Server 2003 connectors do not allow connections from the sending user.

Handling Internet E-Mail

One task that you need to perform is the configuration of an SMTP connector in order to handle Internet e-mail. However, before you learn about this topic, you need to understand how the introduction of Exchange Server 2007 into your environment can affect Internet mail flow.

Before you install Exchange Server 2007 into your organization, Internet mail flow is pretty simple, at least for small- and medium-sized organizations that have not created SMTP connectors in the organization. All Internet mail is directed through the SMTP virtual server, which uses its own DNS capabilities to look up the names of remote servers. Of course, should you install an SMTP connector into the legacy Exchange organization to handle Internet e-mail, the SMTP virtual server no longer handles this task, because it is now relegated to the new SMTP connector, and you should have no problems when you install Exchange Server 2007 into the organization. Either way, Internet e-mail flow is up and running.

Thanks to its role-based nature, Exchange Server 2007 throws a wrench into the works if you depend on Exchange Server 2003's SMTP virtual server to handle Internet e-mail. Upon installation, the Exchange Server 2007 Hub Transport server role resides inside the Exchange organization and is installed with just enough default SMTP functionality to communicate with other Exchange Server 2007 servers. Although the Hub Transport role (or the Edge Transport role) is responsible for handling Internet e-mail, this functionality is not enabled by default. In other words, a default Exchange Server 2007 installation cannot communicate with the outside world.

During the process of introducing Exchange Server 2007 into your legacy Exchange organization, remember that a routing group connector was created in order to facilitate communication between your legacy and new Exchange servers. With this introduction, your legacy Exchange environment now ignores the SMTP virtual server in favor of this new universal SMTP connector. All mail sent to the Internet now flows through this connector and to your Exchange Server 2007 organization, where it simply sits until you create an external SMTP connector in that organization. Of course, you can also create a new Internet-facing SMTP connector in the legacy Exchange organization. This chapter shows you how to create a new connector in the legacy Exchange organization in order to facilitate communication with the Internet. In Chapter 8, you learn how to create a functionally identical connector in the Exchange Server 2007 organization. Later, during the full transition process, this connector is removed in favor of a new one in the Exchange Server 2007 organization.

Adding an SMTP Connector to Your Legacy Exchange Organization

If you have already created an Internet-facing SMTP connector in your legacy Exchange organization, you can skip this step. If you have not created his SMTP connector and you install Exchange Server 2007 into the organization, Internet e-mail flow will stop once the required routing group connector is installed during installation of the Hub Transport role.

To avoid this, create an SMTP connector in the legacy Exchange organization. This connector stays in place until you perform a full transition to Exchange Server 2007 at which time you create a new connector in the Exchange Server 2007 organization. To install an Internet mail SMTP connector into your legacy Exchange organization, follow these steps:

1. From a legacy Exchange server, start the Exchange System Manager.

2. Expand First Organization (Exchange), then Administrative Groups, then First Administration Group, and then Connectors.

3. Right-click Connectors and, from the shortcut menu, choose New, and then choose SMTP Connector. Once you do so, you're presented with the connector's property sheet with the General tab displayed (see Figure 7-7), in which you name the connector and make some choices regarding DNS.

4. Provide a name for the new connector. Make it something useful, such as Internet.

Look through the following sections to complete the configuration of the new SMTP connector.

General Tab

The General tab for the new SMTP connector (see Figure 7-7) houses general options that pertain to the operation of the connector. As mentioned earlier, this is the tab on which you name the new connector.

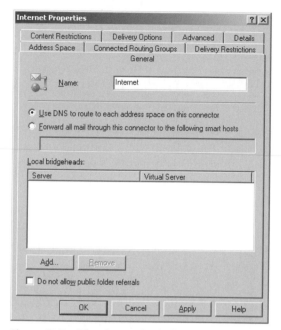

Figure 7-7   The General tab for the new SMTP connector

There are a few other important options on this tab as well:

- **Use DNS To Route To Each Address Space On This Connector**   Configures the connector to work with DNS to make direct connections to destination SMTP servers, based on MX records and preference values.

- **Forward All Mail Through This Connector To The Following Smart Hosts**   If you would rather forward e-mail upstream because multiple direct connections either take too long or are too costly, select the option. Into the field below this option, you can type either the fully qualified domain name (FQDN) of the smart host or its IP address. If you choose to type the IP address, place it inside brackets—for example, [192.168.2.200]. Also, the value you specify here overrides the value in the Smart Host setting in the Advanced Delivery dialog box, which you display by clicking Advanced on the Delivery tab of the SMTP virtual server's property sheet.

- **Local Bridgeheads**   Click the Add button below the Local Bridgeheads option and choose the server that has the SMTP virtual server through which this connector's mail will be sent.

- **Do Not Allow Public Folder Referrals**   On each connector, you can prevent public folder referrals. Public folder referrals provide clients with a way to access public folders in remote routing groups.

Address Space Tab

When you connect to a foreign system, such as the Internet, you must specify an address space that the connector will use. An *address space* is a set of address information associated with a connector or gateway that specifies the domains to which this connector sends messages. Typically, an address space is a subset of a complete address; usually, it is just the domain name.

Specify the address space on the Address Space tab of the connector's property sheet (see Figure 7-8). Because this SMTP connector is used for your organization's Internet e-mail, use "*" as the address space, which means that any string of characters is valid, and messages can be routed to any domain over this connector.

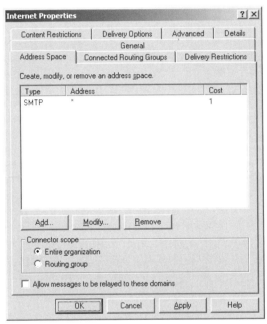

Figure 7-8   Address Space tab of the SMTP connector's property sheet

You can prevent messaging relay by not selecting the Allow Messages To Be Relayed To These Domains check box. This ensures that unsolicited e-mails cannot be routed through your SMTP server back out to the Internet. However, if this SMTP connector is used as a relay point between two foreign SMTP systems, select this check box and add to the address space area the destination name of the domain to which messages should be relayed.

Finally, if you want to limit the use of this SMTP connector to those servers that are members of the same routing group, select the Routing Group option in the Connector Scope area. The default is to allow all servers in the organization to use this connector. Because servers that are not in the same routing group are assumed to exist across either a slow connection or a nondedicated connection, it is a good idea to enable this setting to keep servers in remote routing groups from routing messages to the Internet or a foreign e-mail system over this connector.

Advanced Tab

Figure 7-9 shows the Advanced tab of the SMTP connector's property sheet, which has a number of important configuration options that you need to consider as you set up the connector.

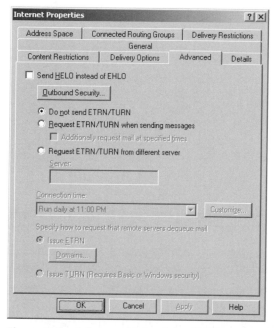

Figure 7-9   Advanced tab of the SMTP connector's property sheet

First, you can set the SMTP connector to Send HELO Instead Of EHLO. Traditionally, when an SMTP client connects to an SMTP server, the first command that is sent is the HELO command. This command starts the session and identifies the sender of the coming message. By default, Exchange Server 2003 sends the EHLO command, which is a start command that also indicates that the Exchange server is able to use the Extended SMTP (ESMTP) commands. Not all SMTP servers are capable of communicating using these extended commands. If you need to connect to an SMTP server that doesn't understand ESMTP commands, select this check box to have Exchange Server send the HELO start command instead.

Real World   Setting Up the SMTP Server as a Relay Server

Assume that your organization is known by two different names in the marketplace: contosopharma.com and contoso.com. Further assume that you want all messages to enter the organization through the SMTP connector on a server that is a member of the contosopharma.com domain. Here are the steps you would take to make sure that all messages for both domain names are routed correctly:

1. Enter an A record in DNS for this server's host name and IP address.

2. Enter two MX records in DNS, one for each domain, both pointing to this server's IP address.

3. Create the SMTP connector for the contosopharma.com domain.

4. Add contoso.com as a valid address space.

5. Select the Allow Messages To Be Relayed To These Domains check box.

6. Create an MX record and an A record in your internal DNS tables to point to the internal SMTP server that is serving the contoso.com domain.

Now messages addressed to either contoso.com or contosopharma.com will be routed to the same server.

Public Folders

First, the bad news: Beginning with Exchange Server 2007, Microsoft is working to de-emphasize the use of public folders in favor of a SharePoint-based solution. In fact, in the initial release of Exchange Server 2007's Outlook Web Access, public folders are not supported at all. That said, when used with the full Outlook client, public folders are alive and well. Further, if you've been using Exchange for any length of time, you probably have quite a bit of information in public folders that needs to be maintained even during the coexistence phase of your Exchange Server 2007 migration.

> **Note**   Exchange Server 2007 organizations with all clients running Microsoft Office Outlook 2007 do not need public folders unless they are needed for organizational information sharing. In previous versions of Exchange and Outlook, public folders housed critical information, such as the free/busy data used to schedule meetings. Exchange Server 2007 replaces this functionality with the Availability Service, which gathers free/busy information directly from users' mailboxes. This means that, unless your organization uses public folders for data sharing, and all of your clients are running Outlook 2007 or later, you don't even need a Public Folder database in Exchange Server 2007.

Public Folder Replication

If your organization has information stored in public folders that needs to be maintained throughout the transition process, take steps to ensure that the public folder database is replicated throughout both the legacy and the new Exchange organizations.

Note If you continue to use legacy Outlook clients—that is, Outlook 2007 or earlier, all the way back to Outlook 97—you need to maintain a public folder database in any organization in which these clients' mailboxes reside. Legacy Exchange clients use Public Folders to share free/busy information.

To replicate individual public folders, follow these steps:

1. From an Exchange Server 2003 server, start the Exchange System Manager.

2. Expand First Administrative Group, then Folders, and then Public Folders.

3. Right-click the public folder you want to replicate and choose Properties, as shown in Figure 7-10.

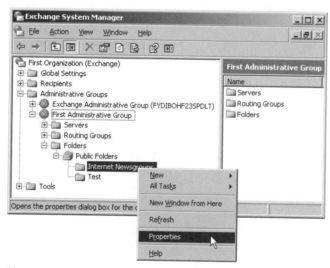

Figure 7-10 Open the Properties page for one of your public folders.

4. From the Properties page (see Figure 7-11) for the selected public folder, choose the Replication tab.

5. Click Add and, from the Select a Public Store window, select the server to which you want to replicate this folder's contents.

6. Click OK and return to the Exchange System Manager.

7. Now, from the Exchange Management Shell on the target Exchange Server 2007 server, issue the command `get-publicfolderstatistics`. The newly replicated public folder appears on the folder list (see Figure 7-11).

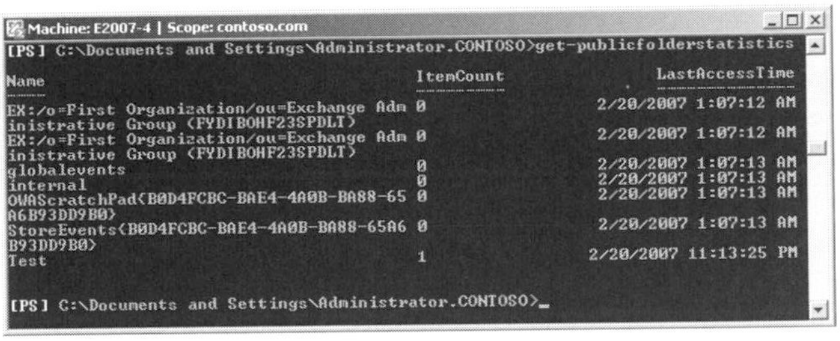

Figure 7-11   Take note of the *test* public folder that appears in this list.

Handling Public Folder Referrals

In a coexistence scenario, or if client computers in your organization are running older versions of the Outlook client, free/busy information for mailboxes on Exchange 2000/2003 servers is still published in public folders in order to be made accessible to all clients. As such, make sure you still have public folder stores on your Exchange servers in order to support the use of free/busy information in your organization.

By default, public folder referrals are enabled on the routing group connector between Exchange Server 2007 and earlier versions of Exchange Server. If you disable public folder referrals, end-users with mailboxes on Exchange Server 2003 or Exchange 2000 Server may not be referred to servers in the new Exchange Server 2007 organization over this routing group connector.

If you want to disable public folder referrals on the default routing group connector, you can do so in one of two ways. From Exchange Server 2003, follow these steps:

1. Start the Exchange System Manager.

2. Expand Administrative Groups, then Exchange Administrative Group (FYDIBOHF23SPDLT), then Routing Groups, then Exchange Routing Group (DWBGZMFD01QNBJR), and then Connectors.

3. Right-click a routing group connector.

4. From the shortcut menu, choose Disallow Public Folder Referrals (see Figure 7-12).

You can also disable public folder referrals from the other end of the connector by following these instructions:

1. Start the Exchange System Manager.

2. Expand Administrative Groups, then First Administrative Group, then Routing Groups, then Routing Group in which the mail flow server resides, and then Connectors.

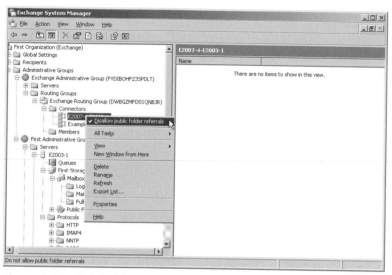

Figure 7-12   Public folder referrals can be enabled or disabled from the Exchange System Manager.

3.   Right-click a routing group connector.

4.   From the shortcut menu, choose Disallow Public Folder Referrals.

Management Shell

Changing the configuration of a routing group connector to support or disable support for public folder referrals is easily accomplished from the Exchange Management Shell. Although public folder referrals are enabled on the connector between your two Exchange organizations, there may come a time when you want to disable these referrals. Using the `set-routinggroupconnector` command, modify the `publicfolderreferralsenabled` parameter to accomplish your goal.

```
set-routinggroupconnector -identity "E2003-1-E2007-4"
-publicfolderreferralsenabled $true
```

Through the use of the `identity` parameter, this command specifies the name of the connector that will be modified. The `publicfolderreferralsenabled` parameter can be set to either `$true` or `$false`. `$true` enables public folder referrals over the connector while `$false` disables them.

Administering Public Folders

At the present time, there is no Exchange Server 2007 GUI-based method for managing public folders, although this GUI element is slated to be added to the product at some point. In a mixed Exchange Server 2003/Exchange Server 2007 environment, public folders should be administered from the Exchange Server 2003 Exchange System Manager, although it is also possible to manage public folders from the command-line–based Exchange Management Shell.

Management Shell

Although Microsoft has de-emphasized public folders in Exchange Server 2007, these folders still remain in use in the new product and are manageable from within the product. However, although at this point Microsoft has not provided an Exchange Server 2007 GUI-based means for managing public folders, the Exchange Management Shell does have the cmdlets necessary to manage these archives. Bear in mind that, in the Exchange Management Shell, there are a few prefixes for each type of command, with the most common being:

- **New**   Creates an Exchange object.

- **Set**   Manages the attributes of an existing Exchange object.

- **Get**   Polls objects of the specified type and returns their attributes.

Here is a list of each public folder management command along with its function and examples for using the commands:

- **New-PublicFolder, Remove-PublicFolder, Set-PublicFolder, Update-PublicFolder, Get-PublicFolder**   The New-, Set- and Get-PublicFolder commands create and manage public folder databases. Update-PublicFolder starts the public folder synchronization process.

  ```
  New-PublicFolder -Name NewPublicFolder -Server e2007-4
  Set-PublicFolder "\NewPublicFolder" -ReplicationSchedule Always
  Update-PublicFolder "\NewPublicFolder" -Server "e2007-4"
  ```

- **Enable-MailPublicFolder, Disable-MailPublicFolder, Set-MailPublicFolder, Get-MailPublicFolder**   The Enable- and Disable-MailPublicFolder cmdlets specify that a specific public folder should be enabled or disabled for direct e-mail delivery, respectively.

  ```
  Enable-MailPublicFolder "\NewPublicFolder"
  Disable-MailPublicFolder "\NewPublicFolder"
  Set-MailPublicFolder "\NewPublicFolder" -
  PublicFolderType GeneralPurpose
  ```

- **New-PublicFolderDatabase, Set-PublicFolderDatabase, Remove-PublicFolderDatabase, Get-PublicFolderDatabase** The `*-PublicFolderDatabase` commands manage the creation, management, and deletion of new public folder databases in your Exchange environment.

  ```
  Set-PublicFolderDatabase -Name "Sample Public Folder Database"
  -IssueWarningQuota 100MB
  ```

- **Add-PublicFolderAdministrativePermission, Remove-PublicFolderAdministrativePermission, Get-PublicFolderAdministrativePermission** The `PublicFolderAdministrativePermission` cmdlets manage administrative permissions present on your public folders and your public folder hierarchies.

  ```
  Add-PublicFolderAdministrativePermission -User cat.francis
  -Identity \NewPublicFolder -AccessRights ViewInformationStore
  ```

- **Add-PublicFolderClientPermission, Remove-PublicFolderClientPermission, Get-PublicFolderClientPermission** These commands provide the same functionality as `*-PublicFolderAdministrativePermission`, except on the client side of the equation.

  ```
  Add-PublicFolderClientPermission -Identity "\NewPublicFolder"
  -User david.so -AccessRights CreateItems
  ```

- **Suspend-PublicFolderReplication, Resume-PublicFolderReplication** These two commands start and stop public folder replication between servers.

- **Update-PublicFolderHierarchy** Starts synchronization of the content in the public folder hierarchy.

Recipient Update Service

Originally introduced in Exchange 2000 Server, the Recipient Update Service is an asynchronous service that completes the provisioning process each time you create a new Exchange user. The Recipient Update Service (RUS) in Exchange 2000 Server and Exchange Server 2003 is made up of two parts. The first part of RUS is an API that determines which properties are necessary for a particular object. The second part of RUS is a subservice that runs in the Exchange System Attendant. This subservice looks for the recipients that are in need of updating and applies the API-calculated properties to the object. It is this second part of RUS that is of interest in a coexistence scenario.

In Exchange Server 2007, the Exchange System Attendant–based asynchronous service that runs and looks for new mailboxes has been removed from the product. The reason: in Exchange Server 2007, new accounts are fully provisioned as soon as they are created, so there is no longer a need for this asynchronous service. The creation API that determines what properties are necessary for a particular object is built directly into the Exchange Server 2007 management cmdlets.

Besides completing the provisioning of new mailboxes in Exchange, RUS performed some other functions that have been modified in Exchange Server 2007, including the following tasks:

- Set permissions that hide distribution lists: Hidden distribution list membership has been made obsolete in Exchange Server 2007, so there is no need for this capability.

- Maintain Exchange Enterprise Server group membership: Exchange Enterprise Server group membership is not used in Exchange Server 2007.

- Set permissions on objects in the Exchange System Objects container in Active Directory to support delegation: Objects in the Exchange System Objects container are now set during the Exchange Server 2007 forestprep process and are not altered during delegation.

More Info For more information on exactly what is handled by RUS in Exchange 2000 Server and Exchange Server 2003, visit *http://support.microsoft.com/kb/253770*.

When running an organization with coexisting Exchange Server 2003 and Exchange Server 2007, you must continue using the Exchange Server 2003 Exchange System Manager to create and manage a Recipient Update Service policy for each domain that has Exchange mailboxes. This includes domains with only Exchange Server 2007 servers and users present, as long as Exchange 2000 Server or Exchange Server 2003 servers are installed.

One very important thing to keep in mind is that you can't make an Exchange Server 2007 server the source for a Recipient Update Service policy. Because Exchange Server 2007 does not include all of the RUS functionality that is found in older versions of Exchange Server, specifying an Exchange Server 2007 server effectively breaks an RUS. Figure 7-13 shows you the location of this item in Exchange Server 2003 Exchange System Manager so you know what not to change.

Complete Coexistence Notes

Running in a coexistence scenario can present challenges when it comes to trying to figure out which management tool to use for a particular job and what features work between software versions. Microsoft has made available a complete list of Exchange Server 2003 features along with management version compatibility notes. Table 7-2 lists Exchange Server 2003 features and, if present, those features' Exchange Server 2007 counterparts. Further, because Exchange Server 2003 is managed from both the Exchange System Manager and the Active Directory Users and Computers tool, Table 7-3 lists the ADUC-based features of Exchange Server 2003 along with Exchange Server 2007 equivalencies.

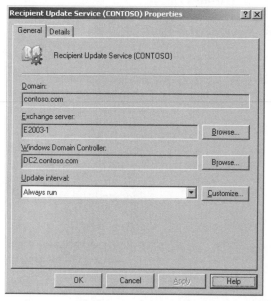

Figure 7-13   Don't target an Exchange Server 2007 computer with an RUS policy.

Table 7-2   Exchange Server 2003 ESM Features to Exchange Server 2007 Feature Summary

Exchange Server 2003 feature	Exchange Server 2007 equivalent feature name	Administer from Exchange Server 2007	Administer from Exchange Server 2003	Comments
Delegate Control	NA	No	Yes	Delegation control rights for Exchange Server 2003 must be administered in Exchange Server 2003.
Internet Mail Wizard	NA	No	Yes	In cases where an Exchange Server 2007 Edge Transport server is identified, this feature will not work.
Stop Public Folder Content Replication	NA	Yes	Yes	Exchange Server 2003 Service Pack 2 and later will use this setting.

Table 7-2   Exchange Server 2003 ESM Features to Exchange Server 2007
Feature Summary (Continued)

Exchange Server 2003 feature	Exchange Server 2007 equivalent feature name	Administer from Exchange Server 2007	Administer from Exchange Server 2003	Comments
Internet Message Format	Remote Domains	Yes	Yes	This feature is directly replaced by the Remote Domains feature in Exchange Server 2007. The feature can be managed from either version of Exchange. However, after they have been edited by Exchange Server 2007, the object is considered upgraded and cannot be edited by Exchange Server 2003.
Message Delivery Properties—Sender Filtering, Recipient Filtering	Sender Filtering and Recipient Filtering	No	Yes	The Exchange Server 2003 global message delivery settings are replaced by new entries in Exchange Server 2007. These settings are managed in the Exchange Management Console on an Edge Transport server or in the Exchange Management Shell on a Hub Transport server.
Message Delivery Properties—Connection Filtering	IP Allow List, IP Block List, IP Allow List Providers, IP Block List Providers	Yes	No	The Exchange Server 2003 global message delivery settings are replaced by new entries in Exchange Server 2007. These settings are managed in the Exchange Management Console on an Edge Transport server or in the Exchange Management Shell on a Hub Transport server.

Table 7-2   Exchange Server 2003 ESM Features to Exchange Server 2007 Feature Summary (Continued)

Exchange Server 2003 feature	Exchange Server 2007 equivalent feature name	Administer from Exchange Server 2007	Administer from Exchange Server 2003	Comments
Intelligent Mail Filter— Gateway Blocking Threshold	Edge Transport Server Content Filtering—Actions	No	Yes	Exchange Server 2003 stores the Intelligent Mail Filter threshold and action configuration in a different location than Exchange Server 2007. Therefore, each Exchange server's threshold actions must be maintained separately as two independent settings.
Intelligent Mail Filter Store Junk E-Mail Configuration settings	Set-OrganizationConfig *SCLJunkThreshold*	Yes	Yes	This property can be maintained from either Exchange Server 2007 or Exchange Server 2003.
Sender ID Filtering	NA	No	Yes	There is no interoperability of this feature. Exchange Server 2003 objects must be maintained in Exchange Server 2003 and Exchange Server 2007 objects must be maintained in Exchange Server 2007.
Mobile Services	NA	No	Yes	In Exchange Server 2007 Outlook Mobile Access, Always-up-to-date (AUTD) System Management Server (SMS), Exchange ActiveSync, and DirectPush have been moved into each of the respective sections in the Exchange Management Console for the Client Access servers. Exchange Server 2003 objects must be maintained by Exchange Server 2003 and Exchange Server 2007 objects must be maintained in Exchange Server 2007.

Table 7-2   Exchange Server 2003 ESM Features to Exchange Server 2007 Feature Summary (Continued)

Exchange Server 2003 feature	Exchange Server 2007 equivalent feature name	Administer from Exchange Server 2007	Administer from Exchange Server 2003	Comments
Details Templates and Address Templates	NA	No	Yes	Exchange server's details and addresses templates must be maintained separately as two independent settings.
Global Address List / Address Lists	NA	Yes	Yes	You can edit global address list (GAL) and address list objects from Exchange Server 2003 or Exchange Server 2007. However, you must upgrade Exchange Server 2003 objects before they can be edited by Exchange Server 2007. After you upgrade the object, it cannot be edited by Exchange Server 2003.
Offline Address Book	NA	Yes	Yes	You can edit the Exchange Server 2003 offline address book (OAB) from Exchange Server 2003 or Exchange Server 2007. However, to administer the OAB from Exchange Server 2007, it must be moved to the Exchange Server 2007 server by using the Exchange Server 2007 tools. When the object has been moved to Exchange Server 2007, the object is considered upgraded and cannot be edited by Exchange Server 2003 unless it is moved back to Exchange Server 2003 by using the Exchange Server 2007 tools.

Table 7-2   Exchange Server 2003 ESM Features to Exchange Server 2007 Feature Summary (Continued)

Exchange Server 2003 feature	Exchange Server 2007 equivalent feature name	Administer from Exchange Server 2007	Administer from Exchange Server 2003	Comments
Offline Address Book— Rebuild Action	Update-OfflineAddressBook	Yes	Yes	You can use Exchange Server 2003 or 2007 to update or rebuild the Exchange server 2003 offline address book. In addition, you can trigger the update or rebuild action of an Exchange Server 2007 offline address book from Exchange Server 2003.
Recipient Update Service	Udate-AddressList and Update-EmailAddressPolicy	No	Yes	The Recipient Update Service does not exist as a service for Exchange Server 2007; therefore, you cannot configure an Exchange Server 2007 server as a Recipient Update Service server. However, Exchange Server 2007 servers appear in the list of Recipient Update Service servers because the filter searches for all Exchange servers that are not front-end servers. Setting an Exchange Server 2007 server as a Recipient Update Service server will cause the Recipient Update Service to cease functioning.

Table 7-2   Exchange Server 2003 ESM Features to Exchange Server 2007
Feature Summary (Continued)

Exchange Server 2003 feature	Exchange Server 2007 equivalent feature name	Administer from Exchange Server 2007	Administer from Exchange Server 2003	Comments
Recipient Policies	E-mail Address Policy and Accepted Domains	See comment	See comment	In Exchange Server 2003, the recipient policy object defines both the proxy addresses that are stamped onto the recipient objects and the set of domains for which e-mail is accepted into the organization for an authoritative domain. In Exchange Server 2007, these two concepts are separated into E-mail address policies and accepted domains. They are completely separate settings in Exchange Server 2007; however, any accepted domains will be available to the e-mail address policy.
Recipient Policies	Accepted Domains	Yes	No	You can add recipient policies from Exchange Server 2003; however, accepted domains must be manually added as Exchange Server 2007 acceptable domains, or they will not be routable.
				If you add a new accepted domain in Exchange Server 2007, you must manually add any accepted domains from Exchange Server 2007 into Exchange Server 2003 recipient policies to be able to have Exchange Server 2003 servers route for them.

Table 7-2   Exchange Server 2003 ESM Features to Exchange Server 2007 Feature Summary (Continued)

Exchange Server 2003 feature	Exchange Server 2007 equivalent feature name	Administer from Exchange Server 2007	Administer from Exchange Server 2003	Comments
Recipient Policies	E-mail Address Policy	Yes	Yes	E-mail address policies can be edited from Exchange Server 2003 or Exchange Server 2007. However, to administer the e-mail address policy from Exchange Server 2007, you must first upgrade the object. When the e-mail address policy has been upgraded, it cannot be edited from Exchange Server 2003.
				If you add a new e-mail address policy in Exchange Server 2007, you must link it to an existing Exchange Server 2007 accepted domain. This ensures that all routing created in Exchange Server 2007 is properly reflected by Exchange Server 2003. Although Exchange Server 2007 ignores the fact that the e-mail address policy implies an accepted domain, Exchange Server 2003 does not.

Table 7-2   Exchange Server 2003 ESM Features to Exchange Server 2007
Feature Summary (Continued)

Exchange Server 2003 feature	Exchange Server 2007 equivalent feature name	Administer from Exchange Server 2007	Administer from Exchange Server 2003	Comments
Recipient Policy— "Apply this policy now" action	E-mail Address Policy—Update-E-mailAddressPolicy	Yes	Yes	The stamping behavior for Exchange Server 2003 Recipient Update Service is different than address provisioning in Exchange Server 2007. If the change is made in Exchange Server 2003, then the change will not take effect until the Recipient Update Service applies the changes to the objects.
				If the change is made in Exchange Server 2007, then Exchange Server 2007 will always stamp the updated proxy addresses after the policy is changed.
Mailbox Manager Policy	N/A	Yes	Yes	Although the Exchange Server 2007 mailboxes are stamped with the mailbox manager policy, processing against these Exchange Server 2007 mailboxes does not take place.

Table 7-2   Exchange Server 2003 ESM Features to Exchange Server 2007
Feature Summary (Continued)

Exchange Server 2003 feature	Exchange Server 2007 equivalent feature name	Administer from Exchange Server 2007	Administer from Exchange Server 2003	Comments
Queues	Queue Viewer	No	Yes	The Exchange System Manager queue viewer functionality uses Windows Management Instrument (WMI), which has been removed from Exchange Server 2007. Therefore, Exchange System Manager queue viewer will not work against an Exchange Server 2007 server. However, you will still be able to view Exchange Server 2007 servers in the Exchange Server 2003 Queue Viewer. If you attempt to access the connection, you will receive an error stating that Exchange "failed to retrieve the queues."
Storage Group	NA	No	Yes	You must use Exchange System Manager to maintain the Exchange Server 2003 storage group settings.
Mailbox Store	NA	No	Yes	You must use Exchange System Manager to maintain the Exchange Server 2003 mailbox store settings.
Public Folder Store	NA	No	Yes	You must use Exchange System Manager to maintain the Exchange Server 2003 public folder store settings

Table 7-2   Exchange Server 2003 ESM Features to Exchange Server 2007 Feature Summary (Continued)

Exchange Server 2003 feature	Exchange Server 2007 equivalent feature name	Administer from Exchange Server 2007	Administer from Exchange Server 2003	Comments
Protocols— X.400 Connectors and Mail Transfer Agent (MTA) Object	NA	No	Yes	X.400 connectors and the MTA object in Exchange System Manager are deprecated in Exchange Server 2007. However, because the configuration is ignored by Exchange Server 2007 servers, you can use Exchange System Manager to manage X.400 connectors and MTA objects that are located in Exchange Server 2003 routing groups.
SMTP Virtual Server	Receive Connector	No	Yes	SMTP virtual servers are deprecated in Exchange Server 2007. However, you can use Exchange System Manager to manage SMTP virtual servers that are configured on Exchange Server 2003 servers.
SMTP Virtual Server— Resolve anonymous e-mail	Receive Connector— externally secured with Exchange Servers permission group configured	No	Yes	You can create an Exchange Server 2007 object that has the same functionality as an Exchange Server 2003 SMTP virtual server that is configured to resolve anonymous e-mail. Create a new Receive connector, or modify an existing Receive connector, on an Exchange Server 2007 Hub Transport server. Configure the Receive connector to assign the Exchange Servers permission group and to use Externally Secured as the authentication mechanism.

Table 7-2   Exchange Server 2003 ESM Features to Exchange Server 2007 Feature Summary (Continued)

Exchange Server 2003 feature	Exchange Server 2007 equivalent feature name	Administer from Exchange Server 2007	Administer from Exchange Server 2003	Comments
Routing Group	NA	No	Yes	The Exchange routing group (DWBGZMFD01QNBJR) can't be modified. It can contain only Exchange Server 2007 servers. Placing Exchange Server 2003 and Exchange Server 2007 servers in the same routing group is not supported.
Routing Group Connectors	Routing group connectors	Yes	Yes	A routing group connector that is configured to use an Exchange Server 2007 server as a source or target server can't be managed by using Exchange System Manager. You must use the New-RoutingGroupConnector and Set-RoutingGroupConnector cmdlets in Exchange Management Shell if an Exchange Server 2007 server is specified in the routing group connector configuration.
SMTP Connectors	Send Connectors	No	Yes	Due to differences in schema configuration, you must manage these connectors by using the tools specific to the server version on which the connector is created. You cannot apply Exchange Server 2007 Send connector settings to Exchange Server 2003 SMTP connectors. Exchange Server 2007 also does not recognize Exchange Server 2003 SMTP connector settings that do not exist in Exchange Server 2007.

Table 7-3   Exchange Server 2003 ADUC Commands to Exchange Server 2007 Feature Summary

Exchange Server 2003 Active Directory Users and Computers feature	Exchange Server 2007 equivalent feature name	Can be administered from Exchange Server 2007	Can be administered from Exchange Server 2003
Outlook Mobile Access: Enable or Disable	Exchange ActiveSync	No	Yes
ActiveSync and Up-to-Date Notifications	Exchange ActiveSync	No	Yes
Protocols—Outlook Web Access, POP3, and IMAP4: Enable or Disable	NA	No	Yes
Mailbox Rights	Set-MailboxPermission	No	Yes
Delivery Restrictions	Set-MailboxPermission	No	Yes
Delivery Options	Set-MailboxPermission	No	Yes
Storage Limits	Set-MailboxPermission	Yes	Yes
Move Mailbox	Move-Mailbox	No	Yes
Establish E-Mail Address	Enable-Mailbox	No	Yes
Enable Mailbox	Enable-Mailbox	No	Yes
Delete Mailbox	Disable-Mailbox	No	Yes
Configure Exchange Features	Set-Mailbox or New-Mailbox	No	Yes
Remove Exchange Attributes	Disable-Mailbox	No	Yes
Establish E-Mail Address	Enable-MailContact	No	Yes
Delete E-Mail Addresses	Disable-MailContact	No	Yes
Remove Exchange Attributes	Disable-mailContact	No	Yes
Add E-Mail Addresses	NA	Yes	Yes
Delete E-Mail Addresses	NA	Yes	Yes
Add Query-Based Distribution Group to the Group	NA	Yes	Yes
Add Public Folder to the Group	NA	Yes	Yes

Summary

In this chapter, you learned about coexistence between Exchange Server 2003 and Exchange Server 2007. You learned about the requirements of Exchange Server 2007 that the product be installed only into a native-mode legacy Exchange organization as well as about some of the tasks that are automatically performed when you create a coexistence environment. Further, you learned about the importance of Exchange Server 2007 legacy routing group connectors and about how SMTP connectors are affected when running different versions of Exchange side by side. Probably most important, you learned from where specific Exchange features should be administered in order to avoid significant problems in your Exchange organization as well as how to enable and disable public folder referrals between Exchange versions.

In the next chapter, you learn what you need to do in order to eliminate this coexistence situation and return to a single-version Exchange organization.

Chapter 8
Transitioning to Exchange Server 2007

In Chapter 7, "Coexisting with Previous Versions of Exchange Server," you learned about your coexistence options between Microsoft Exchange Server 2003 and Exchange Server 2007. Coexistence is the first step in a full transition to Exchange Server 2007. Because Exchange Server 2007 does not support a direct in-place upgrade mechanism from older versions of Exchange, your transition project plan must include a coexistence phase. This book assumes that your coexistence phase does not include migrating mailboxes or changing any of your SMTP connectors to the outside world. In short, it is assumed that you simply brought up your first Exchange Server 2007 server, followed the details provided in the previous chapter, and then made your way to this chapter.

In this chapter, you follow a complete transition from Exchange Server 2003 to Exchange Server 2007, with illustrations explaining how to move users and public folders to Exchange Server 2007 as well as instructions to completely decommission your legacy Exchange environment. A thorough book on transitioning would be at least as long as this entire book, so this chapter covers the more common tools and provides a sufficient roadmap for your transition from Exchange Server 2003 to Exchange Server 2007.

Before you continue, note that all of the examples in this chapter make use of servers using the Hub Transport role server. As it is completely new to Exchange Server 2007, the Edge Transport role is not used in any of these examples. The introduction of the services provided by this new feature is covered in Part VI, "Security."

The Example Scenario

The examples in this chapter follow a fairly simply scenario: transition from two Exchange Server 2003 servers to a new Exchange Server 2007 server. In the previous chapter, you learned how to handle the coexistence period, which allows for a phased and more manageable transition to Exchange Server 2007. In this chapter, you learn how to do the following:

- Move mailboxes between versions of Exchange Server.

- Re-home your Internet-based mail feed from Exchange Server 2003 to Exchange Server 2007.

- Make sure that all functionality remains working during the coexistence phase of the transition.

- Decommission legacy Exchange servers.

Here are the relevant details regarding the servers used in the sample transition:

- The Active Directory domain controller is named DC2 and is running Microsoft Windows Server 2003 x64 Enterprise Edition.

- There are two Exchange Server 2003 servers, named E2003-1 and E2003-2. Both house mailboxes for users in the organization.

- There is an Exchange Server 2007 server installed in the organization as well, but it does not yet have any mailboxes.

The transition process can be broken down into a few major objectives. Here is what you will accomplish in this chapter, in order:

1. Install Exchange Server 2007 into the environment. This procedure is covered in Chapter 7.

2. Create public folder replicas in the Exchange Server 2007 environment. Again, the process is covered in Chapter 7.

3. Create an SMTP send connector in the Exchange Server 2007 organization in order to enable sending e-mail to the Internet.

4. Configure the default SMTP receive connector on your Exchange Server 2007 Hub Transport role server to allow incoming mail from the Internet.

5. Move all the mailboxes from the two Exchange Server 2003 servers to the new Exchange Server 2007 server.

6. Fully move all public folders to an Exchange Server 2007 server.

7. Remove connectors to legacy Exchange routing groups.

8. Configure the Recipient Update Service to run on an Exchange Server 2007 Mailbox server role server.

9. Remove the Exchange Server 2003 servers from the organization.

10. Remove legacy Exchange routing groups.

11. Keep a server around that runs the Exchange System Manager.

In this chapter, the examples assume that you have already prepared your environment (by upgrading your organization to Exchange native mode and so forth) and installed at least one Exchange Server 2007 server that coexists with an Exchange Server 2003 computer.

Transition Options

You can choose to perform your transition in a number of ways:

- Mimic, as closely as possible, your existing Exchange environment. Install the exact same number of Exchange Server 2007 servers as you have Exchange Server 2003 servers and perform a 1:1 migration of user mailboxes between servers.

- Use the transition as an opportunity to "clean up" your existing Exchange environment. Over time, large organizations in particular tend to become less organized.

- Begin the process of consolidating your Exchange environment onto fewer servers. The 64-bit architecture of Exchange Server 2007 provides for much larger amounts of RAM. Between this and other improvements to the product, Exchange Server 2007 can reliably support significantly more users per server than older versions of Exchange. These architectural improvements can save you money on hardware costs. The Exchange Server 2007 team has put together an outstanding storage requirements calculator that includes information that helps you to size your servers. Visit to download the calculator.

Transition Limitations

Some features from previous versions of Exchange have been eliminated from Exchange Server 2007, including:

- Novell GroupWise connector
- Network News Transfer Protocol (NNTP)

- Microsoft Mobile Information Server

- Instant Messaging service

- Exchange Chat Service

- Exchange 2000 Conferencing Server

- Key Management Service

- cc:Mail connector

- MS Mail connector

There are a number of ways you can plan around these eliminated services:

- **Acquire the new product that includes the service**   Since the release of Exchange 2000 Server and Exchange Server 2003, Microsoft has made a number of changes to its product line. For example, instant messaging is now included in Live Communications Server 2005. Research your specific feature needs and determine whether there is an applicable product change that can meet the need.

- **Eliminate the feature**   In some cases, you may need to eliminate a feature from your messaging organization. For example, if you are intent on transitioning to a full Exchange Server 2007 environment, and are also migrating from GroupWise, first complete the GroupWise to legacy Exchange conversion and then perform the transition to Exchange Server 2007.

- **Maintain a semi-coexistence environment**   If you absolutely require one of the eliminated features and cannot buy a new product that offers that feature, you may be required to continue to maintain an Exchange 2000 Server computer or Exchange Server 2003 server until such time that you can carry out one of the other options. You can still move all of your legacy Exchange user mailboxes to Exchange Server 2007, but cannot take the final steps that involve removing all of the legacy Exchange servers from the environment.

Microsoft's official documentation recommends that you deploy servers with the Client Access Role installed as your first foray into a transition to Exchange Server 2007. However, the information in this chapter assumes that you have deployed a full Exchange Server 2007 server into the legacy Exchange organization. This server will include the Client Access server role, the Hub Transport server role, and the Mailbox server role.

Move Internet Mail to Exchange Server 2007

In the previous chapter, you learned how to create an SMTP connector in your legacy Exchange organization in order to avoid breaking outbound Internet e-mail after the introduction of the Exchange Server 2007 routing group connector.

Unless you have already created an Internet-facing SMTP connector in your Exchange Server 2007 organization, outgoing Internet mail that originates from mailboxes in the new Exchange Server 2007 organization has no way to exit the organization. As a part of your transition process, and before you move mailboxes from the legacy Exchange organization, you must create an SMTP send connector in your new Exchange Server 2007 organization. Exchange Server 2007 uses SMTP send connectors to deliver messages to the next hop on their way to the final destination. By default, no send connectors are created when the Hub Transport role server is installed.

Note   Although no explicit SMTP send connectors are created upon installation of Exchange Server 2007, implicit and invisible send connectors are created based on the structure of your Active Directory site topology. SMTP send connectors are used to route mail between hub transport servers in your Active Directory site. Send connectors created on servers with the Hub Transport Role installed are stored in Active Directory and made available to all Hub Transport Role servers in the organization.

Your best option is to first create the new SMTP send connector in the Exchange Server 2007 organization and then, after moving all of your mailboxes to the new organization, eliminate the Internet-facing SMTP connector in your legacy Exchange organization. If you're not using an Edge Transport role server to handle e-mail communication with the Internet, you must also reconfigure the default SMTP receive connector on the Hub Transport role server to allow anonymous connections, which allows it to receive mail from any other SMTP server out on the Internet.

Note   In smaller Exchange organizations, you may be able to get away with deleting the legacy Internet-facing SMTP connector even before you complete moving all of your mailboxes to the new Exchange organization. After you delete an Internet-facing SMTP connector in your legacy Exchange organization, mail destined for the Internet routes through the Exchange Server 2007 routing group connector and then out through your new SMTP send connector. The reason: after you delete your legacy Internet-facing connector, the SMTP virtual server resumes these duties, but the new Exchange Server 2007 routing group connectors take precedence, so all Internet mail is sent through it to your new Exchange Server 2007 organization.

Allow Mail to Flow to the Internet

Until you create an SMTP send connector in your Exchange Server 2007 organization, all Internet-destined e-mail that originates in the Exchange Server 2007 organization is stuck until you create an SMTP send connector in the new Exchange organization. To create a new send connector that handles Internet mail, follow these steps:

1. From an Exchange Server 2007 server, start the Exchange Management Console.

2. Expand the Organization Configuration option.

3. Under Organization Configuration, choose Hub Transport.

4. From the Action pane, select New Send Connector. This starts a wizard that walks you through the creation process.

5. The Introduction page of the wizard asks for a name for the connector as well as for you to define the intended use of the new Send connector. Give the connector a descriptive name, such as To Internet and indicate that this connector is to be Internet-based, as shown in Figure 8-1. Click Next to continue to the next step.

Figure 8-1 The send connector needs a name and intended use.

6. The Address Space page provides a place for you to indicate the scope for the new send connector. On this page, shown in Figure 8-2, click Add and, in the Add Address Space window, type * and click OK. Click Next to continue.

7. On the Network Settings page (see Figure 8-3), select the Use Domain Name System (DNS) "MX" Records To Route Mail Automatically option. Or, if you want to replay all of your mail through an upstream smart host, select the Route Mail Through The Following Smart Hosts option and then click Add to add smart hosts. Hosts can be added by either name or IP address. Further, if your local DNS does not resolve hosts on the Internet, select the Use Domain Name System (DNS) To Route Mail Automatically option.

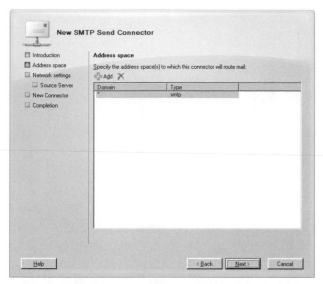

Figure 8-2   Provide a scope for the new send connector.

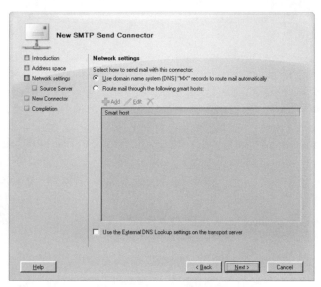

Figure 8-3   Decide how you want the new connector to handle DNS lookups.

8. The Source Server page (see Figure 8-4) of the wizard asks you to select the server with which this send connector is to be associated. Choose the server that should handle this task. The next couple of screens are informational only. When you are done, mail should be able to flow from your Exchange Server 2007 organization to the Internet.

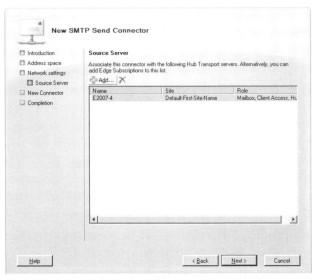

Figure 8-4 Associate the new connector with one of your Hub Transport servers.

Management Shell

In order for mail to be able to flow from Exchange Server 2007–based mailboxes to the Internet, you must install an SMTP send connector into the Exchange Server 2007 organization. Your legacy Exchange organization will continue to use the Internet-facing connector you created earlier. To create an SMTP send connector in your organization using the Exchange Management Shell, use the following command, replacing **E2007-4** with the name of one of your Exchange Server 2007 servers on which you have installed the Hub Transport server role. Also note that, if you need to use different DNS settings than those assigned to the Exchange server's network adapters, you will need to adjust the **UseExternalDNSServersEnabled** setting.

```
new-SendConnector -Name 'To Internet' -Usage 'Internet'
-AddressSpaces 'smtp:*;1' -DNSRoutingEnabled $true
-UseExternalDNSServersEnabled $false -SourceTransportServers 'E2007-4'
```

Allow Incoming Mail from the Internet

Upon initial installation, there is no SMTP receive connector in your Exchange Server 2007 organization configured to allow incoming mail from the Internet. Unless you make use of an Edge Transport role server, as a part of your transition, you need to add an appropriate connector or update an existing connector to allow outside connections to your Exchange Server 2007 organization. The easiest action to take is to allow the receive connector named Default *<server name>* to accept mail from the Internet.

Security Alert Keep in mind that allowing direct connections to your Exchange server is a security risk. Make sure you take appropriate precautions, including implementing a correctly configured firewall, antivirus software, and anti-spam filters.

To modify the default SMTP receive connector to allow anonymous connections, follow these steps:

1. From one of your Exchange Server 2007 servers, start the Exchange Management Console.

2. Expand Server Configuration and select Hub Transport.

3. In the Work pane, select the Exchange Server 2007 server that houses the receive connector you want to modify.

4. From the Action menu, under the name of the server you selected, select the Properties option.

5. In the Properties window, click the Permission Groups tab.

6. On the Permission Groups tab, shown in Figure 8-5, select the Anonymous Users check box, and then click OK.

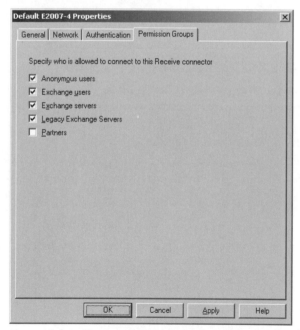

Figure 8-5 Allow anonymous users access to this receive connector.

Note Instead of modifying the default receive connector, you could also create a new SMTP receive connector that handles incoming Internet mail. However, you would also need to change the scope of the default receive connector in order to avoid overlapping the address space. Two connectors cannot service the same IP address range and port at the same time.

Management Shell

In order to receive mail from the Internet, you must configure an SMTP receive connector on the server on which you wish to receive Internet mail. The best way to proceed is to reconfigure the default SMTP receive connector that is automatically installed during the installation of Exchange Server 2007. Use the **set-receiveconnector** command to accomplish this goal.

```
Set-ReceiveConnector -Identity "Default E2007-4" -
PermissionGroups AnonymousUsers,ExchangeUsers,ExchangeServers,ExchangeLegacy
Servers
```

By default, the listed groups, except anonymous users, already have access to this connector. This command adds anonymous users to the list.

Moving Mailboxes to Exchange Server 2007

At some point in the coexistence phase of your transition project, you need to make the decision as to when you plan to transition mailboxes from your legacy Exchange environment to your Exchange Server 2007 environment. This is where your users begin to notice that something is happening with regard to their mail.

Note At this point, begin notifying users of the pending transition. After all, any problems that you face in your transition will directly affect the ability for your users to accomplish their goals.

Now, when it comes to the actual act of moving a mailbox into the Exchange Server 2007 organization, the task can be performed in just a few simple steps. To carry out this goal, do the following:

1. From an Exchange Server 2007 server, start the Exchange Management Console.

2. Expand the Recipient Configuration. A list of all of the mailboxes in your Exchange organization appears in the middle pane. Mailboxes that reside on your Exchange 2000 Server or Exchange Server 2003 servers are tagged with the phrase Legacy Mailbox in the Recipient Type Details column, as shown in Figure 8-6.

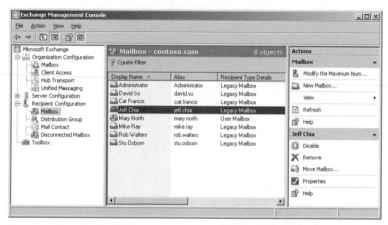

Figure 8-6   The Exchange Management Console lists both native and legacy Exchange mailboxes.

3. Select the mailbox for the legacy mailbox user that you want to transition. You can also select multiple mailboxes by holding down the Ctrl key while you select mailboxes.

4. From the Action menu, under the name of the user you selected, click Move Mailbox. This starts the Move Mailbox Wizard.

5. On the Introduction page of the wizard, as shown in Figure 8-7, you're asked to select the Server, Storage Group, and Mailbox Database to which you want to move the legacy user's mailbox. Use the drop-down arrows next to each option to make your selection. Click Next after you make your selections.

6. The Move Options page of the wizard, shown in Figure 8-8, asks how you want to handle corruption in a user's mailbox. Unfortunately, an Exchange database is susceptible to database corruption, and the time that it's most likely to appear is when you browse through every record in a mailbox, which is exactly what takes place when you move a mailbox. It is recommended that, for the first pass, you select the Skip The Mailbox option. If you have corruption problems with a lot of mailboxes, check the integrity of the database as a whole before you continue. If, however, you have corruption only now and then, select the Skip The Corrupted Messages option instead and specify how many messages can be corrupt before the

entire mailbox is skipped. Click Next after you decide how you want to handle possible corruption.

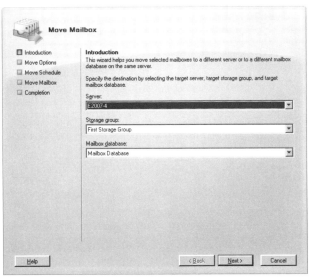

Figure 8-7 Choose the Server, Storage Group, and Mailbox Database that will house the user's mailbox.

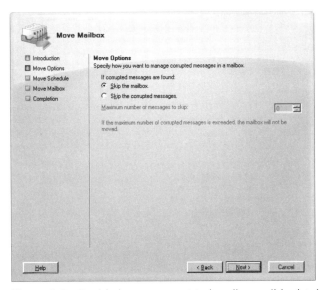

Figure 8-8 Decide how you want to handle possible database corruption.

7. In an effort to prevent the Move Mailbox function from affecting the overall performance of your Exchange infrastructure, the wizard provides the ability to schedule the time during which the move takes place. There are three options on this screen, as shown in Figure 8-9—two of which control the move schedule. The first option, Immediately, does exactly what it implies. As soon as you finish with the wizard, the process begins. The second option, At The Following Time, provides date and time drop-down selectors you can use to choose the time when the mailbox will be moved. Finally, the Cancel Tasks That Are Still Running After (Hours) check box provides a way for you to let the Move Mailbox task run overnight and stop before people start coming into the office. This option is especially useful if you select multiple mailboxes to move. Once you select your scheduling options, click Next.

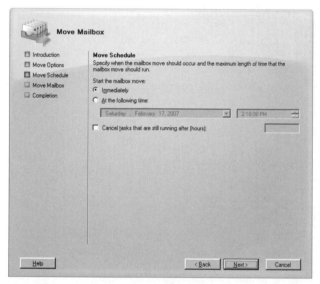

Figure 8-9   Schedule the mailbox to be moved either immediately or during off-peak hours.

8. Before the mailbox is actually moved, you are given an opportunity to review the options you have selected. Do so and, after you verify your selections, click Move, as shown in Figure 8-10.

9. Throughout the move process, you are kept informed about the status of the operation, as shown in Figure 8-11. At the end of the process, a completion status window appears indicating success or failure and a clock telling you how long the operation took. Click Finish when you're done.

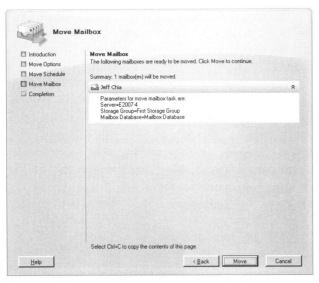

Figure 8-10   Review your selected Move Mailbox options.

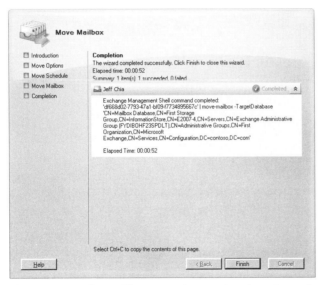

Figure 8-11   The mailbox move is completed as planned.

Moving Mailboxes from the Command Line

Moving mailboxes from legacy Exchange servers to Exchange Server 2007 can easily be accomplished from the command line using the **move-mailbox** command. As is the case with the GUI, you are able to schedule the mailbox move and decide how you want to handle bad items. The following command will stop moving the user mailbox into the Exchange Server 2007 organization after hitting five bad items. Also, note the confirm parameter. If you omit this parameter, you are prompted as to whether or not you want to move the mailbox. By passing $false to the confirm parameter, you bypass this confirmation prompt. Also note that the default name of Exchange Server 2007 coexistence administrative group is Exchange Administrative Group (FYDIBOHF23SPDLT). This name cannot be changed.

```
move-mailbox -identity contoso\garth.fort -BadItemLimit '5'
-TargetDatabase 'CN=Mailbox Database,CN=First Storage Group,
CN=InformationStore,CN=E20074,CN=Servers,CN=Exchange Administrative
Group (FYDIBOHF23SPDLT),CN=Administrative Groups,CN=First Organization,
CN=Microsoft Exchange,CN=Services,CN=Configuration,DC=contoso,
DC=com' -confirm:$false
```

At the end of the process, the command reports back to you with the complete status of the mailbox move. The pertinent output from the preceding command is shown here.

Identity : contoso.com/Users/Garth Fort

DistinguishedName: CN=Garth Fort,CN=Users,DC=contoso,DC=com

DisplayName: Garth Fort

Alias: garth.fort

LegacyExchangeDN : /o=First Organization/ou=First Administrative Group/cn=Recipients/cn=garth.fort

PrimarySmtpAddress : garth.fort@contoso.com

SourceServer : E2003-1.contoso.com

SourceDatabase : Mailbox Store (E2003-1)

SourceGlobalCatalog: DC2.contoso.com

SourceDomainController : DC2.contoso.com

TargetGlobalCatalog: DC2.contoso.com

TargetDomainController : DC2.contoso.com

TargetMailbox:

TargetServer : E2007-4.contoso.com

TargetDatabase : E2007-4\First Storage Group\Mailbox Database

MailboxSize: 116KB

IsResourceMailbox: False

MoveType : IntraOrg

MoveStage: Completed

StartTime: 2/12/2007 3:31:01 PM

EndTime: 2/12/2007 3:31:27 PM

StatusCode : 0

StatusMessage: This mailbox has been moved to the target database.

Real World   Recipient Policies and Mailbox Moves

Under Exchange 2000 Server and Exchange Server 2003, recipient policies were a tricky proposition. Depending on how you manage new recipient policies, it was possible that new recipient policies would never be applied to mailboxes created before the new recipient policy went into place. Or, if the new policy was manually applied to all mailboxes, it was possible that a recipient's primary e-mail address would change as an unintended consequence. Why did this situation exist?

Simply put, an administrator had a choice as to whether or not to actually apply a recipient policy. If a policy was not applied, it would be applicable only to mailboxes created after the new policy was created. If the policy was manually applied by the administrator, a person's Reply To address could be unintentionally changed.

Under Exchange Server 2007, this situation has changed in a big way. The administrator is no longer provided the choice as was the case in legacy Exchange systems. When an administrator creates a new recipient policy—called an E-mail Address Policy in Exchange Server 2007—policy membership is evaluated and reapplied if necessary. Where does this fit into your mailbox migration?

As you move mailboxes from your legacy Exchange servers to Exchange Server 2007, your organizational e-mail address policies are evaluated against the mailbox. If you have not manually applied particular recipient policies in your legacy Exchange organization, these policies are applied during the mailbox move. So, your users could find themselves with different primary e-mail addresses, or policies that you did not intend for a particular mailbox may be automatically applied.

There may be cases in which you prefer to exclude particular mailboxes from suffering this fate. For these users' mailboxes, you can accomplish this by excluding the user's mailbox from being subject to automatic e-mail address updates based on e-mail address policies. Both Active Directory Users and Computers (legacy Exchange servers) and the Exchange Management Shell (command line) are suited to this task.

From Active Directory Users and Computers, open a user's account properties page and click the E-mail Addresses tab.

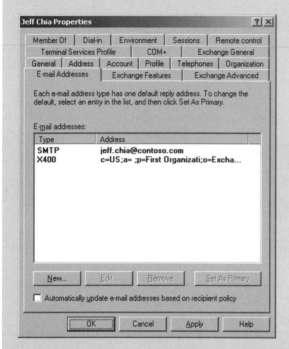

Figure 8-12   Exclude this account from the recipient policy.

From the Exchange Server 2007 Exchange Management Shell:

```
Set-Mailbox -identity garth.fort-EmailAddressPolicyEnabled:$false
```

The Decommissioning Process

You just completed the process of moving your mailboxes from your legacy Exchange servers to Exchange Server 2007. In Chapter 7, you learned how to replicate your public folder infrastructure to your new Exchange server as well. At this point, you can begin the process of tearing down your legacy infrastructure and removing legacy Exchange servers from your organization. By the time you finish with this section, you won't have any legacy Exchange servers left to deal with, and the coexistence phase of your transition will be over.

Re-Home Client Services

Some changes have taken place between Exchange versions with regard to client-based services. These services include Outlook Web Access, and RPC-over-HTTP, now called Outlook Anywhere in Exchange Server 2007. If you have clients pointing at your old Exchange server, they will continue to work; however, users may have to enter credentials twice to gain access to resources that have moved to new servers. To correct this, take steps in your organization to point clients to your new servers. There are some considerations to note. For example, Outlook Web Access on your legacy Exchange servers resides at https://server/exchange. In Exchange Server 2007, this location changes to https://server/owa. In many cases, client redirection is best handled at the firewall level by rewriting rules on which these client services depend. That way, you can make changes in one place.

Note   Manual configuration changes are not required for full Outlook clients. Outlook clients will automatically reconfigure themselves to point at a new server once an associated mailbox is moved from your legacy Exchange server to Exchange Server 2007.

Important   If you currently use Outlook Mobile Access in your legacy Exchange environment, be aware that this service is no longer available in Exchange Server 2007. If you have clients that depend on this legacy service, begin considering alternatives, such as the new Outlook Web Access (if possible) and ActiveSync/DirectPush. As a last resort, consider purchasing new devices that support these newer technologies.

Remove SMTP Connectors from Your Legacy Exchange Organization

After you create the new Internet-facing SMTP Send connector in your Exchange Server 2007 organization and move your mailboxes to the new organization, remove the complementary connector from your legacy Exchange organization. Once you do so, and assuming you have no other legacy SMTP connectors with overlapping scope, the default SMTP virtual server in your legacy Exchange organization again takes over for the now-deleted SMTP connector. As you read earlier, this means that all outgoing mail sent through your legacy Exchange organization goes through the routing group connector created during your installation of Exchange Server 2007. Of course, by this point, all mailboxes should be moved out of your legacy Exchange organization, so there should be no mail using this connector anyway. For completeness, here's how you remove the appropriate connector from your legacy Exchange organization:

1. From one of your legacy Exchange servers, start the Exchange System Manager.

2. Expand First Organization (Your Org Name), then Administrative Groups, then First Administration Group, and then Connectors.Right-click the connector that

handles outbound Internet e-mail and, from the shortcut menu, choose Delete. You will be prompted to verify this action.

When complete, if you do happen to send mail from an account that resides in your legacy Exchange organization, the headers on the message reflect the fact that it took a route through your Exchange Server 2007 organization before heading out to the Internet. Figure 8-13 gives you a look at the headers for a message that took this route.

Received: from E2003-1.contoso.com (192.168.0.21) by E2007-4.contoso.com (192.168.0.22) with Microsoft SMTP Server id 8.0.685.24

Figure 8-13   This message originated in the legacy Exchange organization and went through the Exchange Server 2007 organization.

Re-Home Public Folders

As a part of the coexistence phase discussed in Chapter 7, you learned how to replicate your public folders between a legacy Exchange organization and a new Exchange Server 2007 organization. With your coexistence phase quickly coming to an end, you no longer have to replicate content to the soon-to-be-discontinued legacy Exchange organization. Therefore, you should re-home your public folder into the new Exchange Server 2007 organization.

Note   If you have upgraded all of your clients to Microsoft Office Outlook 2007 and otherwise do not use public folders in your company, you can skip this section.

The easiest way to re-home a public folder is by using the Exchange System Manager from one of your legacy Exchange servers. Follow these steps:

1. From an Exchange Server 2003 server, start the Exchange System Manager.

2. Expand First Administrative Group, then Servers, then (Server Name with Public Store instance), then First Storage Group, and then Public Folder Store (servername).

3. Right-click Public Folder Store (servername).

4. From the shortcut menu, choose Move All Replicas.

5. From the Move All Replicas window (see Figure 8-14), choose the Exchange Server 2007 server to which you want to move the public folder replicas.

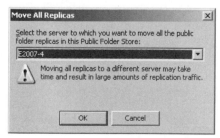

Figure 8-14   Move all public folder replicas to an Exchange Server 2007 server.

6. The tool provides you with some information about the move, indicating that the process can take quite some time to complete. To minimize the risk for data loss, do not forcibly remove the public folder database until this process is complete.

You're not done yet. Now, in order to make sure that your new Exchange Server 2007-based public folder database mounts after you eventually remove the legacy Exchange administrative group, move the public folder tree from your legacy Exchange server to an Exchange Server 2007 server. Follow these steps:

1. From one of your legacy Exchange servers, start the Exchange System Manager.

2. Expand Administrative Groups.

3. Right-click Exchange Administrative Group (FYDIBOHF23SPDLT) and, from the shortcut menu, choose New, and then choose Public Folders Container. Leave the Exchange Server 2007 administrative group expanded. This process creates a new entry called Folders that resides in your Exchange Server 2007 administrative group.

4. Expand First Administrative Group, and then expand Folders.

5. Click and drag the Public Folders entry to the Folders group to the Folders container in your Exchange Server 2007 administrative group (see Figure 8-15).

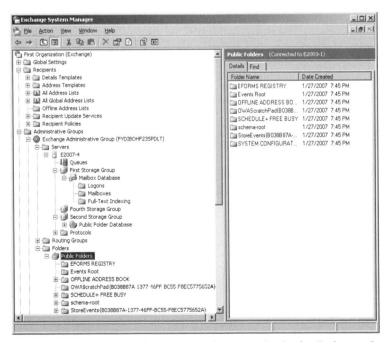

Figure 8-15   The public folder hierarchy now exists in the Exchange Server 2007 administrative group.

Move the Offline Address Book to Exchange Server 2007

Until you take steps to change the server that generates offline address books, one of your legacy Exchange servers continues to handle this task. In order to continue to support your clients after a transition is complete, you need to move this functionality to an Exchange Server 2007 server. Using the Exchange Server 2007 Exchange Management Console:

1. From one of your Exchange Server 2007 servers, start the Exchange Management Console.

2. Expand Organization Configuration and choose Mailbox.

3. In the Work pane, click the Offline Address Book tab.

4. Right-click the Default Offline Address List option and choose Move to start the Move Offline Address Book Wizard.

5. The only page of the wizard is shown in Figure 8-16, and on that page you provide the name of a server that will generate the Offline Address Book. Click Browse to choose an Exchange Server 2007 server for this task.

6. Click Move when ready.

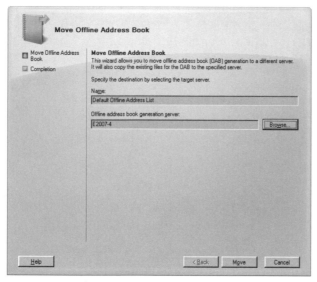

Figure 8-16   Which organizational Exchange Server 2007 server should handle Offline Address Book generation?

Management Shell

The Offline Address Book continues to be an integral part of the Exchange topology. Even after you install Exchange Server 2007 into your organization, and until you take steps to change this fact, the offline address book continues to be generated on one of your legacy Exchange servers. Because the goal of this chapter is to eliminate all vestiges of legacy Exchange servers from your environment, it stands to reason that the offline address book needs to be generated by one of your Exchange Server 2007 servers. The following command shows you how to move one address list—the default offline address list—to an Exchange Server 2007 computer. Note that E2007-4 is just the name of the server used in this example. Make sure to change this reference for your use.

```
move-OfflineAddressBook -Identity 'Default Offline Address List'
-Server 'E2007-4'
```

The Server parameter specifies the Exchange Server 2007 server to which you want to move generation responsibilities for the list specified in the Identity parameter. Repeat this command for each offline address list in your organization.

Move the Recipient Update Service to Exchange Server 2007

In order to eventually remove legacy Exchange software from your old servers, you must move the Recipient Update Services to one of your Exchange Server 2007 servers. Until you take this step, your legacy Exchange server removal process will not proceed. From one of your legacy Exchange servers, move the Recipient Update Services to your new environment using Exchange System Manager by following these steps:

1. Expand First Organization (Your org name), and then expand Recipients.

2. Select Recipient Update Services. At least two recipient update service policies appear in the right-hand portion of the window.

3. Right-click the first Recipient Update Services policy and, from the shortcut menu, choose Properties.

4. From the Properties page (see Figure 8-17), click Browse located next to the Exchange Server field.

5. In the Select Exchange Server window, type the name of the Exchange Server 2007 server to which you want to move the policy.

6. Click OK until you're back at the Exchange System Manager window.

7. Repeat steps 3 through 6 for each Recipient Update Services entry.

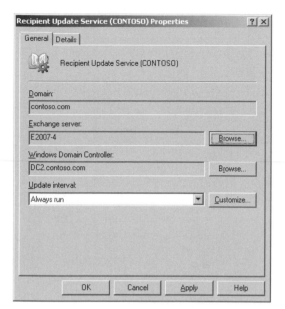

Figure 8-17   The Properties page for a Recipient Update Service policy

Important   If you have not enabled the viewing of routing groups in Exchange System Manager, do so at this point. From the Exchange System Manager, right-click First Organization (Your Org Name). Select the check box next to Display Routing Groups and then click OK.

What does this change? In short, it takes a little longer to get deeper into the organization, but it's necessary in order to accomplish some of the goals in the following sections.

The Exchange Server 2003 end is located at First Organization (Your Org Name), then Administrative Groups, then First Administrative Group, then Routing Groups, then First Routing Group, and then Connectors. For the Exchange Server 2007 end of the connector, browse to Expand First Organization (Exchange), then Administrative Groups, then Exchange Administrative Group (FYDIBOHF23SPDLT), then Routing Groups, then Exchange Routing Group (DWBGZMFD01QNBJR), and then Connectors. This goes for the next sections as well.

Remove Legacy Connectors

At this point in your transition, you definitely have at least one SMTP connector in your legacy Exchange organization—the connector that was created during the installation of Exchange Server 2003 in order to facilitate communication between your legacy and new Exchange organizations. Before you remove Exchange software from your old servers, remove this connector.

Even though this connector cannot be managed with the Exchange System Manager, it can be deleted with this tool as well as with the Exchange Server 2007 Exchange Management Shell. Note that there are two ends to this connector. In order to completely delete the connector, both ends must be deleted. Follow these steps:

1. From the Exchange System Manager, expand First Organization (Your Org Name), then Administrative Groups, then First Administrative Group, and then Connectors.

2. Right-click the connector created during Exchange Server 2007 installation. The connector is usually named with the name of both Exchange servers. For example, "e2003-1 e2007-4" or similar.

3. From the shortcut menu, choose Delete.

4. Expand First Organization (Your Org Name), then Administrative Groups, then Exchange Administrative Group (FYDIBOHF23SPDLT), and then Connectors.

5. Right-click the connector created during Exchange Server 2007 installation. The connector is usually named with the name of both Exchange servers. The name will be the reverse of the one you deleted earlier. For example, "e2007-4 e2003-1" or similar.

6. From the shortcut menu, choose Delete.

7. Repeat these steps for other routing group connectors that may exist in your legacy Exchange organization.

Management Shell

It's important to make sure you clean up your Exchange organization as fully as possible before declaring victory in your Exchange transition goals. If you fail to remove legacy items, these items stick around in your directory and may cause problems later on and make troubleshooting considerably more difficult.

Among items that should be removed are routing group connectors that exist in your legacy Exchange organization. Remove legacy routing group connectors through the use of the `Remove-RoutingGroupConnector` command.

In particular, if you installed Exchange Server 2007 into an existing Exchange environment, the installer created a bidirectional routing group connector to enable mail flow between your Exchange organizations. You must remove both ends of this routing group connector. Use the following commands. The first command removes the Exchange Server 2003 end of the connector while the second handles the Exchange Server 2007 end.

```
Remove-RoutingGroupConnector
-Identity "First Administrative Group\First Routing Group\e2003-1-e2007-4"
-confirm:$false
```

```
Remove-RoutingGroupConnector -Identity
"Exchange Administrative Group (FYDIBOHF23SPDLT)\Exchange Routing Group (DWB
GZMFD01QNBJR)\e2007-4-e2003-1" -confirm:$false
```

Repeat these commands for any other routing group connectors that may still exist in your legacy Exchange organization.

Uninstall Exchange from Legacy Exchange Servers

Removing Exchange server from legacy servers is probably the most consternating part of a transition to Exchange Server 2007. You've done everything you can to make sure that your new Exchange organization gets off to a good start but, until you actually see it operate without the support of your legacy Exchange organization, you won't be comfortable. However, it's probably the easiest step of all, with the exception of removing the first-installed legacy Exchange server. Follow these steps:

1. From the legacy Exchange server, go to Control Panel and then to Add Or Remove Programs.

2. Choose Microsoft Exchange and then click Change/Remove.

3. On the component installation screen, use the drop-down box to choose Remove.

4. Repeat these steps for each legacy Exchange server in your organization.

Remove Legacy Exchange Routing Groups

One of the final steps you must complete before the transition process is complete is the deletion of your legacy Exchange routing groups. After all, with all of your users moved to Exchange Server 2007 and that system's ability to use your Active Directory topology in place of routing groups, there is no more need for routing groups. In fact, in a pure Exchange Server 2007 organization, routing groups are obsolete.

Before you can delete a routing group from a legacy Exchange server, no servers can exist in a routing group. As such, make sure that Exchange Server is fully removed from your legacy servers before continuing.

Important   You might be asking yourself exactly how you should go about deleting routing groups now that Exchange is a thing of the past on most of your servers. Simple: Install the Exchange management tools on one of your decommissioned Exchange servers. Make sure to also install the latest service pack for your version of Exchange before you continue.

---

1. From the Exchange System Manager, expand First Organization (Your Org Name), then Administrative Groups, then First Administrative Group, then Routing Groups, and then First Routing Group.

2. Right-click First Routing Group from the shortcut menu and then choose Delete.

3. When the Exchange System Manager asks whether you really want to delete the routing group, click Yes (see Figure 8-18).

Figure 8-18   Do you really want to delete the routing group?

Real World   Removal of Legacy Administrative Groups

You might be tempted to remove every last vestige of legacy Exchange from your organization, but think carefully before taking this ultimate step. In fact, you should not delete any legacy administrative groups that once held user mailboxes. Why? The user account's LegacyExchangeDNs property continues to reference old administrative groups. As long as clients are using versions of Outlook earlier than Outlook 2007, this property is used to find free/busy information. If the administrative group is removed, the free/busy folder for users that have the matching LegacyExchangeDN may not be able to be located, resulting in difficulty for those users with regard to finding or publishing free/busy information.

Important   Consider leaving Exchange System Manager in place on one of your servers. With this legacy tool, you can use a GUI to manage any public folders that may reside on your Exchange Server 2007 servers—a feat not currently possible with the Exchange Management Console in Exchange Server 2007.

Summary

Even though it's easier to make the transition from an earlier Exchange environment to Exchange Server 2007 than it was to upgrade from Exchange Server 5.5 to Exchange 2000 Server, the process is still relatively involved. There are a number of steps that must be taken in the right order in order to make sure that the risk of data loss remains as close to zero as possible. In this chapter, you completed the process you began in Chapter 6, "Installing Exchange Server 2007," at which point you took the plunge by installing the initial Exchange Server 2007 server into your environment. Throughout the rest of this book, you learn how to capitalize on your Exchange investment.

Chapter 9

High Availability in Exchange Server 2007

In all situations that require high availability, it's best to establish more than one point of failure. Case in point—a parachute. If one chute fails to open, there is a secondary chute. The same thinking holds true in airplanes, whether it is redundant engines, fuel lines, even pilots that are required to eat different types of meals—no single point of failure.

Within your Exchange organization, the key to high availability extends to more than just your Exchange servers. Your Exchange servers may function perfectly, but you might lose availability to them if a dependent system such as Active Directory or DNS has a problem. It is not your job as an administrator (or even your ability) to offer perfect availability. However, perfect availability is a good target to work toward. You can offer redundancy, failover plans, and minimal downtime. In a sense, you can reach near perfection if you eliminate as many single-point failures as possible and constantly focus on recovery methodologies.

This chapter focuses on three high-availability features in Microsoft Exchange Server 2007 that are used to protect your mailbox servers:

- Local continuous replication (LCR)
- Cluster continuous replication (CCR)
- Single copy clusters (SCC)

Note   Other Exchange server roles may require high-availability planning that this chapter doesn't cover. Consider researching the following possibilities to ensure a higher level of availability from each of the following servers. Note that a good starting point is Microsoft TechNet article *http://technet.microsoft.com /en-us/library/bb124721.aspx*.

- Hub Transport and Unified Messaging servers: Deploy redundant servers to increase availability.
- Client Access: Use Network Load Balancing (NLB).
- Edge Transport: Work with DNS round-robin techniques.

Real World   Service Level Agreements

While many organizations demand that high availability solutions be implemented, there is a cost factor they often ignore. The cost of new hardware and software, possible training for your IT staff, and a variety of other costs can be quite high.

Microsoft TechNet discusses the complex issues involved in balancing your organizations need for availability in the following article: *http://technet.microsoft.com /en-us/library/bb123523.aspx*.

Typically, in larger companies, achieving high availability means relying on outside help from third-party vendors. If you do require the need for assistance, make sure you establish Service Level Agreements (SLAs), which are guidelines and standards for ensuring expectations in writing. A good SLA should have clear terms for both parties—the service provider and the customer.

Microsoft explains further the need to plan ahead for SLA conditions in the following TechNet article: *http://technet.microsoft.com/en-us/library/bb124694.aspx*.

Continuous Replication and Transaction Logs

Clustering scenarios for previous versions of Exchange Server were criticized because the servers within the cluster were required to share the same physical data, so the cluster provided redundancy for the Exchange system resources but not for the data storage (which would either have an alternative fault tolerance solution and/or be backed up for disaster recovery). This led to the data being considered a single point of failure. Depending on the size of a database, restoration could take an extensive amount of time unless you sought out costly third-party solutions or were very creative in your disaster recovery planning.

Another criticism of Exchange clustering solutions was the previously supported active/active cluster scenario where both servers (only two were allowed with active/active clustering) were active at the same time. Due to performance issues, active/active clustering has been discontinued in Exchange Server 2007. The more common Exchange cluster in previous versions is the active/passive cluster, in which one server remains active until a failure occurs and then the passive server takes over activity. This cluster mode has been enhanced and carried forward into Exchange Server 2007 with one big improvement being redundancy of the storage database, removing that point of failure.

The concept of continuous replication is new for Exchange Server 2007. In continuous replication, a storage group's database and log files are copied to a secondary location (either on a second server, as in the case of CCR, or onto a secondary storage location, as in the case of LCR). The accessible storage group holds the active copy of the database, and the secondary location contains a passive copy of the database. The replication between the clustered servers is asynchronous and performed with a technique called *log shipping* of the transaction logs combined with replay technology. The fact that the replication in CCR and LCR is asynchronous means the passive node is not 100 percent in sync with the active node. The reason for this is that the transaction logs are not copied over until they are no longer in use and have been closed.

Transaction logs have been, and continue to be, an essential part of the operation of an Exchange server. When a message is sent to a mail server, the message resides in system memory to begin with and is then written to a transaction log before being committed to the Exchange database as the system load permits. If there is a server failure before the transactions have been committed to the database, you want those transaction logs to be in a safe location. The best practice with these logs is to keep them on a disk that doesn't contain the operating system or the mailbox databases. You should also make the location of the transaction logs fault tolerant for redundancy (or, in the case of Exchange Server 2007, replicated through one of the high-availability solutions provided).

Exchange maintains a single set of logs for the databases in a storage group. Transaction logs are created in a sequential manner (called a *log stream*). These log files are now 1 MB in size (as opposed to 5-MB log files in Exchange Server 2003). The reduction in file size was one of the changes made to support continuous replication. There can be up to 2,147,483,647 log files in a log stream. This is not due to the amount of disk space on the server but to the number of log file names that can be created.

In Exchange Server 2003, log files are named with the following format: E*nnfffff*.log (with *nn* being the prefix that changes from one storage group to the next and *fffff* allowing about one million logs) under the larger, 5-MB size.

In Exchange Server 2007, however, the naming convention is increased to E*nnfffffff*.log, offering the ability to handle more than 400 times more data. This is per storage group—not per server.

> **Note**   Exchange Server 2007 (Standard Edition) enables you to create up to five storage groups and to mount up to five databases. Exchange Server 2007 (Enterprise Edition) enables you to create up to 50 storage groups and mount up to 50 databases.

Transaction logs were made smaller in Exchange Server 2007 to minimize the data that might be out of synchronization between the original log and its replicated copy. It is possible—if the server crashes and a transaction log isn't replicated—that you will lose only the 1 MB that hasn't been written to the database.

Transaction logs do not completely commit until the entire set of logs is complete. The logs are not restorable if the last portion of the data is missing. If an e-mail is sent that has about 3 MB of data, three transaction logs are created. However, if the server crashes before the final portion of the data and commit transaction is completed, you would lose the entire message in the restore process. The reason you should be aware of that fact is that, ultimately, you have to make the decision whether you or your company can handle that level of data loss. It's a small amount, but it is a loss. Note that there is a difference in the amount of possible loss between an LCR and a CCR availability solution. If this is unacceptable, you need to seek out other forms of data protection that provide you up-to-the-second services.

> **More Info**   The list of Exchange Server 2007 partners with Microsoft includes EMC Corporation, CommVault, and NSI Software Inc. (Double-Take). You can find the complete list of partners at *http://www.microsoft.com/exchange/partners/2007 /backup.mspx*.

The following list provides some recommendations for how you should structure your Exchange disks before you even consider replication and clusters:

- Keep your operating system files and Exchange Server binaries on one disk.

- Place your database files on a separate physical disk from your OS and transaction logs. You might consider a striped set for performance.

- Place your transaction logs on a separate set of physical disks from your database. In the event the disk fails with the database and transaction logs together, your nearest point of recovery is the latest backups. But if the logs and database files are separated, even if the database disk fails, the log files can be used to recover data to a closer point in time to the failure.

Log shipping is the process in which logs are copied over to their secondary location and replayed into a copy of the database. The end result is a failover backup (either an entire server ready to step in as an active server, or simply a failover set of data to be used in the event of a single server LCR) that is prepared with nearly all the transaction log data and ready to go.

Continuous replication comes in two forms: local continuous replication and cluster continuous replication. Now that you understand the underlying database/transaction log structure, the next section provides you with a deeper understanding of these two types of high-availability solutions.

Local Continuous Replication

Local continuous replication (LCR) allows you to take a single Exchange server and replicate a copy of a storage group onto a secondary disk set using the concepts explained previously. The database is copied over the secondary passive storage group; the logs are shipped over as they complete their transactions with the primary database; and they are replayed for the passive copy (as shown in Figure 9-1). In the event of a disk failure, a manual switch will have you up and running in no time with a secondary copy of the data.

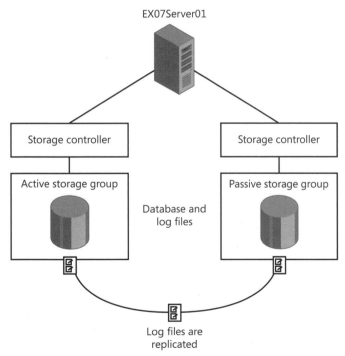

Figure 9-1   Local continuous replication

LCR offers a quick recovery from a corrupted database, disk failure, or controller failure. In addition, you can perform a backup of the Exchange server from the passive copy of the database and logs, extending the backup window. All in all, this provides you with peace of mind and a lower TCO.

Preparing for LCR

The biggest design concern in implementing LCR involves configuring the storage group and database properly and providing an adequate storage solution for LCR to occur.

One recommendation is that the storage medium for the passive copy of the data be similar in capacity and performance to the medium for the active copy. Here are some additional points:

- You can only have one database per storage group. When you create a storage group and then include a database (either a mailbox or public folder database), it is important in your planning to remember that LCR works only if the storage group contains just one database. In fact, if you try to enable LCR on a storage group that has additional databases, LCR cannot be enabled.

- LCR will not function on a storage group with a public folder database if the organization contains more than one public folder database. Replication occurs automatically in an organization with more than one public folder database. This is important to remember if you decide that it is important to have additional public folder databases for your organization. You must discontinue LCR on the storage group first.

- Volume mount points are recommended for Exchange data and will help recover quickly from a crash because you can use a volume mount to quickly change where database files and transaction logs are located.

- Disk space, CPU, and memory considerations need to be evaluated before enabling LCR. Microsoft recommends that the disks containing both the active and passive copies should be relatively equal in both size and performance, with plenty of disk space for your mail database to grow. In addition, you will be looking at a processing cost of about 20 percent (due mostly to the copying and replaying of logs to the passive copy of the database), and it's recommended that you add more physical RAM to your systems (1 GB minimum) to ensure efficiency from your ESE database cache while using LCR.

- Although the redundancy of your data may give you a greater sense of confidence and allow you to grow your databases larger than usual, don't become careless in this regard. Microsoft recommends that the database on an LCR-enabled mail server not exceed 200 GB (whereas the limit recommendation for a non–LCR-enabled mail server is 100 GB). This recommendation is not absolute, however. Each company works differently, and the limitations for your databases should be determined by backup and restore factors for your team. These are recommendations for maximums. When the active copy goes down, switch to your passive copy. Remember that this means you have no further redundancy. If your passive copy (which is now your active database) also fails, your next step is to restore from backups, and data will be lost. Move quickly to establish a new passive copy, and (depending on the size of your database) this could take a long time. So, caution is required in allowing your database size from growing too large, and immediate action is necessary in the event your active disks fail.

Enabling Local Continuous Replication

There are two ways to enable LCR for a storage group. The first way is to enable LCR for an existing storage group. The second way is to enable LCR during the creation of a storage group. You can use either the Exchange Management Console or the Exchange Management Shell to enable LCR. To enable LCR, make sure the server with the mailbox role has your account configured as a member of the local Administrators group and Exchange Server Administrator role.

Enabling LCR for an Existing Storage Group

To enable LCR for an existing storage group, follow these steps:

1. Open the Exchange Management Console.

2. Expand Microsoft Exchange and then expand Server Configuration and select Mailbox.

3. From the Result pane, select the mailbox server with the storage group you want to replicate with LCR. You'll see within your Database Management tab for that mailbox server a listing of your storage groups and corresponding databases. (Remember the requirements mentioned previously regarding the number of databases allowed and public folder limitations). You might also note the status of the mailbox Database as "Mounted."

4. Select the storage group you want to enable with LCR.

5. The Action pane displays options specific to your storage group. Click Enable Local Continuous Replication, which starts the Enable Storage Group Local Continuous Replication wizard.

6. On the Introduction page, verify the Storage group and Database name and click Next.

7. On the Set Paths page, the replication system file's path and the log file's path is set to your local drive. While this is possible, and for testing you might allow it, you really want to click Browse and select another location for your replication, as shown in Figure 9-2. Then click Next.

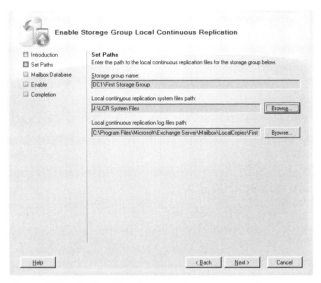

Figure 9-2   Redirecting log files to another disk.

8. On the Mailbox Database page, click Browse to determine the path for your Mailbox Database.edb database file. Click Next to continue.

9. On the Enable page, you can review the Configuration Summary before clicking Enable. If anything needs to be corrected, click Back. If all your settings look proper, click Enable.

Note   What is going to occur here is a process called *seeding* of your database. Seeding is the creation of the starting point for the LCR version of the database file. This starting point can be an offline copy of the production database or a new empty database into which existing transaction logs are replayed. Before LCR will work, database seeding must occur.

---

10. On the Completion page, shown in Figure 9-3, click Finish. Note, you can select Ctrl+C to copy the commands used to create these paths. This can be helpful if you decide to use the Exchange Management Shell to perform the configuration of your server.

After the LCR setup is complete, you should notice a change in the icon next to your storage group from within the Exchange Management Console. If you right-click an LCR-enabled storage group, you will notice the options to Disable or Suspend the LCR, as shown in Figure 9-4.

Note   One great way to confirm the functionality of your LCR setup is to open the folder for the active location of your transaction logs and place another open folder next to it on your desktop that shows the passive copy of the logs. Then, either through Outlook Web Access or an Outlook client, send some larger-sized e-mail to generate some transaction logs. Watch the logs increase on the active server first and then watch as they slowly trickle into the passive copy. It's a good feeling to know your replication works.

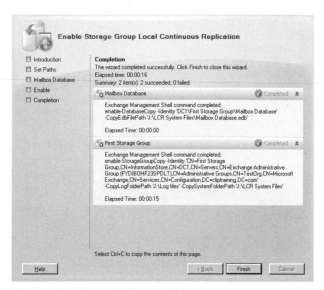

Figure 9-3   Your LCR is complete.

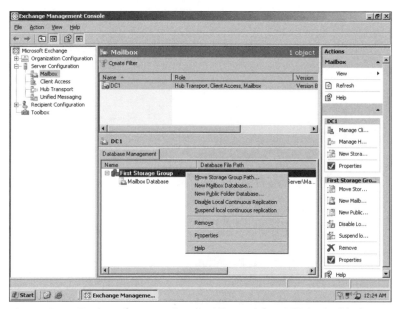

Figure 9-4   Options for your Storage Group after LCR is enabled.

Management Shell

You can also enable LCR from the Exchange Management Shell using the `Enable-DatabaseCopy` and `Enable-StorageGroupCopy` cmdlets. The syntax for using these commands is:

```
Enable-DatabaseCopy -Identity <Server>\<StorageGroup>\<Database>
-CopyEDBFilePath:<FullPathIncludingDatabaseFileName>

Enable-StorageGroupCopy -Identity <Server>\<StorageGroup>
-CopyLogFolderPath:<FullPath> -CopySystemFolderPath:<FullPath>
```

To follow the example from the previous scenario, you might use the commands:

```
Enable-DatabaseCopy -Identity 'DC1\First Storage Group\Mailbox Database'
-CopyEdbFilePath 'E:\LCR Database\Mailbox Database.edb'

Enable-StorageGroupCopy -Identity 'DC1\First Storage Group\
Mailbox Database' -CopyLogFolderPath 'E:\LCR Log Files'
-CopySystemFolderPath 'E:\LCR System Files'
```

Note   When using the Exchange Management Shell to enable LCR, you may not notice any immediate indication that the process succeeded from within the Exchange Management Console. If this is the case, manually refresh the console from the Action pane, and the storage group icon should change.

Enabling LCR for a New Storage Group and Mailbox Database

To enable LCR during the creation of a new storage group and mailbox database, follow these steps:

1. Open the Exchange Management Console.

2. Expand Microsoft Exchange, then expand Server Configuration, and click Mailbox.

3. Select the server to which you want to add the new storage group. From the Action pane, click New Storage Group.

4. From the New Storage Group page (see Figure 9-5), type a name in the Storage Group Name: field.

5. Click the Browse buttons to specify the location of your log and system files.

6. Then select Enable Local Continuous Replication For This Storage Group.

7. Click the Browse buttons to specify the location of the LCR system files and log files.

8. Check your information to make sure it is correct. Click New.

9. After you create the storage group, click Finish.

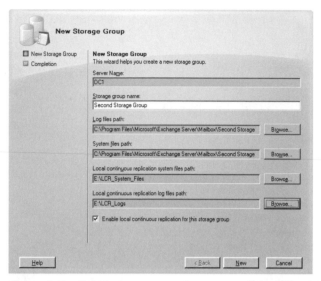

Figure 9-5   Creating a new storage group and enabling LCR at the same time

10.   Add the database. If you select the new storage group and then click New Mailbox Database from the Action pane, you have the option to determine the location of your database and your LCR database, as shown in Figure 9-6.

11.   Create a Mailbox Database Name and determine the paths for your database and LCR replication database. Click New.

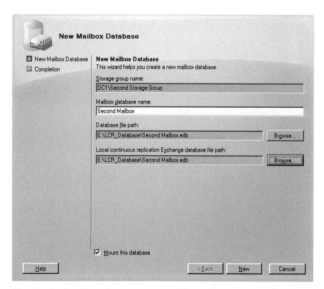

Figure 9-6   Creating a new mailbox database within your storage group with LCR configurations

Management Shell

Once again, the Exchange Management Shell can make life easier with the command-line approach. To create a new LCR-enabled storage group with the management shell, use the following command syntax:

```
New-StorageGroup -server <Server> -name <StorageGroupName>
  -HasLocalCopy:$true -CopyLogFolderPath <PathforLCRLogFiles>
  -CopySystemFolderPath <PathforLCRSystemFiles>
```

The following is an example of the syntax involved for a new storage group called Second Storage Group that has replication enabled toward the E drive.

```
new-StorageGroup -Server 'DC1' -Name 'Second Storage Group'
  -LogFolderPath 'C:\Program Files\Microsoft\Exchange Server\Mailbox'
  -SystemFolderPath 'C:\Program Files\Microsoft\Exchange Server\
  Mailbox\Second Storage Group' -HasLocalCopy $true -CopyLogFolderPath
  'E:\LCR Log Files' -CopySystemFolderPath 'E:\LCR System Files'
```

In addition to creating the storage group, create and replicate the mailbox and then mount the mailbox. This is all done automatically through the wizard, but through the command line you need to remember to do this. Here is the syntax necessary for creating a new mailbox:

```
New-MailboxDatabase -Name <NameofDatabase> -StorageGroup:
  <NameofStorageGroup> -HasLocalCopy:$true
  -EdbFilePath:<FullPathIncludingDatabaseFileName>
  -CopyEdbFilePath:<FullPathIncludingDatabaseFileName>
```

Here is an example of creating the mailbox database in the Second Storage Group, establishing the LCR copy on the E drive, and then mounting the database. These commands are recorded using the Ctrl+C option from within the wizard.

```
new-mailboxdatabase -StorageGroup 'CN=Second Storage
  Group,CN=InformationStore,CN=DC1,CN=Servers,
  CN=Exchange Administrative Group (FYDIBOHF23SPDLT),
  CN=Administrative Groups,CN=TestOrg,CN=Microsoft
  Exchange,CN=Services,CN=Configuration,DC=cliptraining,DC=com'
  -Name 'Second Mailbox' -EdbFilePath 'C:\Program Files\
  Microsoft\Exchange Server\Mailbox\Second Mailbox.edb'
  -HasLocalCopy $true -CopyEdbFilePath 'E:\LCR Database\
  Second Mailbox.edb'

mount-database -
Identity 'CN=Second Mailbox,CN=Second Storage Group,CN=InformationStore,
  CN=DC1,CN=Servers,CN=Exchange Administrative Group (FYDIBOHF23SPDLT),
  CN=Administrative Groups,CN=TestOrg,CN=Microsoft Exchange,CN=Services,
  CN=Configuration,DC=cliptraining,DC=com'
```

Verifying that the LCR Is Functional

The Exchange Management Console provides a basic Copy Status column when looking at your LCR-enabled storage groups. The reported status might be Broken, Disabled, Healthy, or Failed (certainly not a verbose method of technical communication). There are other ways to view the status of your LCR copy that may prove more helpful should you discover a Failed status. From within the Exchange Management Console, you can perform the following steps:

1. From the Server Configuration options, select Mailbox and then select the server you want to investigate further.

2. Right-click the LCR-enabled storage group and choose Properties.

3. Click the Local Continuous Replication tab (shown in Figure 9-7), and you notice some basic information that will prove helpful in determining the cause of any given problem.

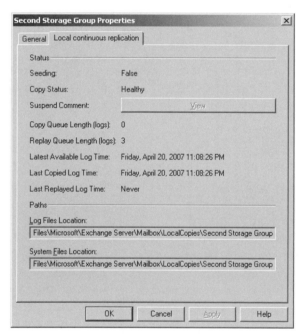

Figure 9-7   Viewing the status of your LCR through the Exchange Management Console

Note   To discover similar information from within the Exchange Management Shell, type the following at the command prompt:

```
Get-StorageGroupCopyStatus -Identity <Server>\<StorageGroup>
```

Some of the possible responses that indicate trouble with the LCR are long queues for either copying or replaying logs or a failed copy status. Make sure all the paths are correct for your configuration and that those paths are accessible. If you find an error, make the correction and then suspend and restart LCR on the storage group. You may also find that a missing transaction log is delaying your replication, in which case you need to search for it, and if you cannot find it, use the `Update-StorageGroupCopy` cmdlet to reseed.

More Info   To find more information on troubleshooting your LCR configuration, see the following TechNet information at *http://technet.microsoft.com/en-us /library/aa996038.aspx*.

Using Performance Monitor to View Replication Activity

If you want to view the progress of your replication between your active and passive copies, it's actually quite easy through Performance Monitor, which is covered in Chapter 17, "Tuning Exchange Server 2007 Performance." All of the counters you want to view are found under one object called MSExchange Replication. Notice that only the storage groups that have LCR enabled are available to monitor.

You can enable all the counters at once or simply choose a few that can give you a reasonable view of your activity. Two very interesting counters that you might consider include the following:

- CopyGenerationNumber: which is the number of the log file currently being generated

- ReplayQueueLength: which is the outstanding number of transaction logs that have yet to be replayed into the database

Recovery from Your Active Copy Failure

In the event the disk containing the active copy of your data fails (through corruption of the database or a disk failure) you can recover your data quickly (albeit manually) from your passive copy. The process requires three actions: dismount the database, change the pointer for the database toward the passive copy of the data, and remount the database. To recover your data through the passive copy, follow these steps:

1. Assess the usability of the passive copy. Hopefully, the status of your copy is healthy so that you can recover as much of the data as possible.

2. Dismount the corrupt database by either selecting the database and selecting the Dismount option from the Action pane (or by right-clicking the database and selecting the Dismount Database option). From within the Exchange Management Shell, you can also use the `Dismount-Database` cmdlet.

3. At this point, you can try to move the passive copy files into the production locations so that the paths are not altered. This is possible if the disk itself is still available and the data only becomes corrupted. If you are able to do this (able, both physically, and within a reasonable time frame so as to have the high availability you are seeking) then move the files and run the following command to restore activation of the database:

```
Restore-StorageGroupCopy -Identity:<Server>\<StorageGroupName>
```

4. If you want to quickly move to your passive copy and activate the storage group with a new database path, run the following command:

```
Restore-StorageGroupCopy -Identity:<Server>\<StorageGroupName>
-ReplaceLocations:$true
```

5. Remount the database again. This can be done quickly through the Exchange Management Console by selecting the mailbox database and clicking Mount Database from the Action pane.

Note   At this point, your mail server may be up and running, and everything may seem wonderful, but you are now vulnerable to a single point of failure. You are no longer LCR protected. There are several possibilities to consider. If the disk with your active database crashed, schedule a time to replace the disk. In the meantime, you might choose to LCR your storage group to another disk for now. If the database simply becomes corrupted, you might want to delete those files and then LCR your passive copy (currently serving as the active copy) with your active copy (newly restored). Once the two are synchronized, and if time allows, switch them back the way you originally had things planned. This will ensure that your Exchange structure remains organized.

Cluster Continuous Replication

Cluster continuous replication (CCR) uses the same concept as LCR with seeding of the database and transaction log shipping; however, instead of simply having two locations for the databases (the active and passive), two separate nodes exist that run in an active/ passive configuration so that recovery from any failure on the active node is immediate through the passive node.

Once again, you see the asynchronous log shipping and replaying that you saw in LCR combined now with the automatic failover features found in a cluster. An Exchange Server 2007 cluster continuous replication topology (see Figure 9-8) can support only two systems, one as the active node and one as the passive, but this is enough to ensure no single point of failure (not the server itself, nor the data storage location). In addition, a CCR cluster can assist with routine maintenance that occurs from time to time within your Exchange organization because you can move the production side to the passive node while maintenance occurs on the active side and then restore the connection. And, like LCR, you can also perform your backups using the passive side of your cluster.

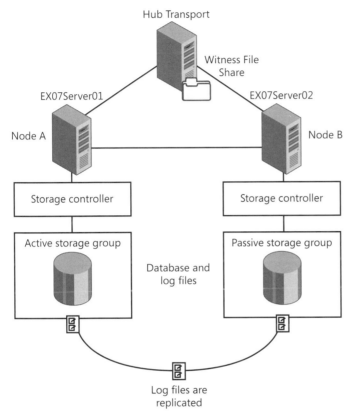

Figure 9-8   Cluster continuous replication

CCR requires a bit more understanding of the technology and a bit more planning in order to implement this correctly within your organization. First, review some of the important new terminology.

CCR Terminology

You may notice in the previous figure that there are pieces to a CCR structure that do not exist in the LCR structure. For example, there is more than one server, each of which is called a node. In addition, the Hub Transport server is carrying a witness file share.

The way a CCR cluster is formed involves the standard Cluster Service in Windows 2003 Server. Before even installing Exchange Server 2007 on the servers—your nodes (which should be member servers in your domain)—you configure a two-node cluster through the Cluster Administrator. What makes this setup different is that a third computer is needed to form a new type of cluster quorum model. This is called the Majority Node Set (MNS) quorum with file share witness.

Note   It's assumed that you will want to form a two-node cluster using the MNS quorum with file share witness. However, it is possible to create a cluster with three nodes in a traditional MNS quorum. This chapter refers to the two-node cluster with the file share witness.

A quorum is the cluster's configuration database that resides in a file named \MSCS\quolog.log, and it performs two very important functions: first, it informs the cluster which node is active (so that each node knows their particular role in the cluster); second, it intervenes when there is a communication failure between nodes. Under normal circumstances, the nodes of a cluster use a private network to communicate with one another so that all the cluster nodes are up to date and aware that the active node is on the job. To communicate, the systems send *heartbeats* to each other. In the event communication fails between two cluster nodes (for whatever reason) the passive node begins to think that it should switch to active. This is known as *split brain syndrome* (or *world chaos*, at times). The quorum helps to prevent this from happening by being a secondary point of failure. If two servers cannot communicate with each other, it could be for any number of reasons, but the quorum (which resides on a third server) makes the determination if it cannot communicate as well with a server and then authorizes the cluster failover.

You need to install the new MNS quorum with file share witness by either installing Windows Server 2003 Service Pack 2 (which includes the needed hotfix) on each of the nodes in your cluster or by downloading a hotfix and installing the fix on each of the nodes in your CCR cluster before you form your cluster. The hotfix and details regarding its features can be found at the Microsoft Knowledge Base article at *http://support.microsoft.com/kb/921181*. The article explains in greater detail the two important features that are being added to your cluster:

- **File Share Witness**   This feature allows you to configure and use a file share that is external to your cluster and separate from the two nodes as an added vote of determining whether the connection between nodes has been truly broken, to prevent unnecessary failover. The file share for the file share witness can technically be hosted on any Windows Server, but it is recommended that it be configured on the Hub Transport server in the Active Directory site where the cluster nodes are located.

- **Configurable Cluster Heartbeats**   It was mentioned that heartbeats are sent back and forth between nodes. The current default algorithm for a heartbeat is every 1.2 seconds from each interface of a cluster node. In the event two heartbeats are consecutively missed by a node, the Cluster service suspects that there is a problem and begins to investigate. This feature of the hotfix doesn't allow you to change the timing of the cluster heartbeats, but you can configure tolerance levels to allow for more missed heartbeats before worrying. You can learn how to configure cluster heartbeats from the Knowledge Base article 921181.

The Transport Dumpster

The transport dumpster is a required component for CCR and is located on your Hub Transport servers. It is not enabled by default; it is enabled only for CCR. This is another feature that helps to ensure a clean failover between your two nodes. Here is how it works. When a node goes down and fails over to the secondary passive node, there is a loss of some data. The most recent mail may not have been entered into the logs and shipped between the nodes. In an LCR configuration, there isn't much you can do to prevent this loss. Hub Transport servers, however, maintain a queue of recently delivered mail to a CCR mailbox cluster in an area called the *transport dumpster*.

When a failover occurs that is not lossless, the CCR requests every Hub Transport server to resubmit all its mail from the transport dumpster queue. Duplicates are automatically weeded out. This helps prevent against data loss in the event of an unscheduled failover.

Preparing for CCR

The following is a list of requirements to consider before enabling your cluster:

- On each of the servers running in the cluster (node A and B), make sure you have Windows Server 2003 Enterprise Edition installed (on the same boot and system drive letters) and either Windows Server 2003 Service Pack 2 or the hotfix from the Knowledge Base article 921181. Only the Mailbox server role will be installed on the nodes within the cluster.

- Create a separate account for the cluster service; that account must be placed as a member of the Exchange Server Administrators group or Exchange Organization Administrators group. In addition, place the account in the local Administrators group for each node.

- You do not want to install Exchange Server 2007 until after the cluster is in place, and you cannot have earlier versions of Exchange on the servers within the cluster, or SQL Server. When you install Exchange Server 2007, make sure it is in the same physical location on both nodes in your cluster.

- The file share witness role can be created on any Windows Server, although it is recommended you install this on the Hub Transport server.

- Each node in the cluster requires two network adapters configured with static IP addresses, one for your public network and one for your private network. The public network is used to communicate with Active Directory, other Exchange servers, and so forth. Transaction logs are also replicated on your public network. The private network is used for intracluster communications to exchange heartbeats between the clusters.

■ Remember that the high-availability options in Exchange Server 2007 have limitations regarding storage groups. You can have only one database per storage group on a clustered server. However, you can have quite a number of storage groups (up to 50 on the Enterprise version of Exchange Server 2007).

More Info   Additional requirements and planning checklists can be found through the TechNet library at *http://technet.microsoft.com/en-us/library /bb124521.aspx*.

Enabling Continuous Cluster Replication

There is a process involved with installing CCR. You need to configure your file share witness, configure your network adapters with public and private addresses (ensure your nodes have either Windows Server 2003 Service Pack 2 installed or KB 921181), establish the cluster, install Exchange Server 2007 on the active node, and then install Exchange Server 2007 on the passive node. This path is pursued one section at a time.

Configure Your File Share Witness

Your file share witness for the MNS Quorum can be installed on any Windows server; however, it is recommended that you install it on the Hub Transport server located in the same site as the clustered nodes. The following steps for creating, sharing, and securing the directory can be done through the GUI or command-line interface (CLI):

1. Create the directory. Give it any name you want, but to make life easier for you and easier for others who might need to find the directory without your assistance, try to name it something logical. You might place the directory right at the root drive of your system and call it something like MNS_FS_ExCluster (for Majority Node Set_File Share_ Exchange Cluster) or something else along those lines.

2. Share the folder and configure the permissions to allow the domain Administrator (or Cluster Service Account) and local Administrator to have Full Control.

Note   If you want to perform the same tasks from a CLI you use the commands, `mkdir` (to create the directory), **net share** (to share out the directory and establish share permissions), and `cacls` (to establish the permissions on the shared-out directory).

Later on, from within the cluster, you point the cluster toward this share.

Configure Your Network Adapters

It is important to configure your network adapters with static IP addresses that are on different subnets: one for the private network and one for the public network. You may decide to rename the connection names for each adapter. Remember to do this on both servers so that you can keep track of which connection goes with which static IP address and subnet.

> **Note** It's not a requirement, but it is recommended that you name your node servers something logical like ExNode1 and ExNode2 or Ex2K7NodeA and Ex2K7NodeB.

In configuring your Public and Private addressing, remember that your public address has to be a static address that functions on your standard network. It is an address that will be connected to the adapter that contacts the other servers, including the DC, and the other Exchange servers. In addition, the public address is going to be in the same network as the virtual address you provide to your cluster later on.

The private address must be on a completely different network from the public. Microsoft recommends an address of 10.10.10.10 and 10.10.10.11 for the two nodes with a subnet mask of 255.255.255.0. That might make life easier for you because you don't have to worry too much about what addresses to choose. In addition, the private network doesn't have to be configured with a default gateway or DNS settings. Those settings are only configured on the public network.

When configuring network addresses, you also want to alter the binding order between your two networks. To open your Advanced Settings, go to Control Panel, double-click Network Connections, and in the menu selections choose Advanced and then Advanced Settings. On the Adapters and Bindings tab you see Connections Are Listed In The Order In Which They Are Accessed By Network Services. Move the public connection to the top of the binding order. What this means is your pubic network connection is always the first one your servers use. The private network is purely for heartbeats, so that comes second in the list. Note that any remote access connections go last. For your private network, you also want to deselect File and Printer Sharing for Microsoft Networks (because this network is not for any form of file/print sharing).

> **Note** Some additional steps to complete on your network adapters include going to the WINS tab for each adapter and making sure that Disable NetBIOS over TCP/IP is not selected on the public network, but it is selected on the private network. In addition, on the public network you want to ensure your DNS settings include server addresses in order of use and DNS suffixes are correct. However, on the private side, these settings are unnecessary and should be left blank.

After your network adapters are configured with a public and private address, you are ready to move on to the next step. Remember to install either Windows Server 2003 Service Pack 2 or the hotfix from KB article 921181 before establishing the cluster between your nodes.

Establishing the Cluster

When your systems are ready, you can begin the process of forming your two-node cluster. Follow these steps:

1. Begin with the first node in your cluster (for your purposes NodeA) by starting the New Server Cluster Wizard from a CLI by typing **cluster.exe /create /wizard**, or you can click Start, click Administrative Tools, click Cluster Administrator, and select Create New Cluster in the drop-down box. Click OK, and you will be in the same place as if you typed the command. Read the first page of the wizard and click Next.

2. From the Cluster Name And Domain page, shown in Figure 9-9, note that the Domain is already filled in for you, but you must give your cluster a name that is unique to the domain. Using a term like "ExchangeCluster" or "Ex2K7Cluster" may work for you. Click Next.

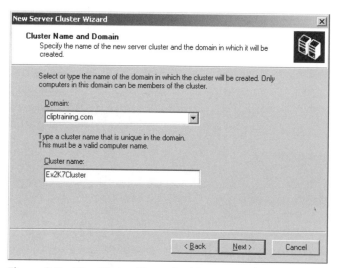

Figure 9-9   The Cluster Name And Domain page

3. Type the name of the server that will be the first node of the cluster. (You may name your servers Node1 and Node2, or NodeA and NodeB, and so forth). Click Next.

4. The Cluster Wizard analyzes the configuration, as shown in Figure 9-10. When it is complete, even if there are a few warnings, click Next to continue.

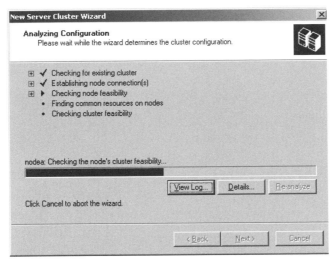

Figure 9-10   Analyzing cluster configuration

5. You are asked for the IP address that the cluster management tools will use to connect to the cluster. Make sure you include an IP address from your public network that is not in use by another system. After putting in the IP address, click Next.

6. You are asked for the Cluster Service Account. In a real-world setting, you should have a specific account created for the cluster service to run off of. Click Next.

7. You are shown the settings for your Proposed Cluster Configuration and you can verify this is what you want, or you can click Back to make changes. One change you are going to have to make is a change in Quorum. To do that, select the Quorum button, click the down arrow from the Cluster Configuration Quorum dialog box, and choose Majority Node Set, as shown in Figure 9-11. Click OK, and then click Next.

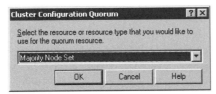

Figure 9-11   Configure the Quorum as a Majority Node Set.

8. You are now on the Creating the Cluster page where the first node for your cluster is established for you. After all tasks are complete, click Next.

9. On the completion screen, you can view the log of the entire procedure. Click Finish, and your cluster is in place.

10. To confirm the first node is online and functioning, open Cluster Administrator, as shown in Figure 9-12. Expand the name of your cluster. Under Groups and then Cluster Groups, you should see your cluster settings as Online.

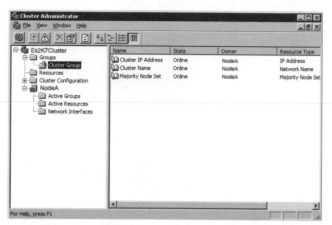

Figure 9-12   Confirming your first node is online through your Cluster Administrator

What you have done so far is create a cluster with only one node in it. That is obviously not going to be very helpful in the event of a problem. Your goal now is to add your secondary node, which you can do from within the Cluster Administrator. To add a second node, follow these steps:

1. Open Cluster Administrator. You see the name of your cluster, and underneath that you see the actual name of the first server in your node. Right-click the server name, hover your mouse over the New option, and select Node. This begins the Add Nodes Wizard. Click Next to move forward. Note that if you wanted to start this wizard from the command line, type: **cluster.exe /cluster:<ClusterName> /add / wizard**.

2. Select a computer. Type the name of your second node and click Add. You may notice that there is room for more than one in the Selected Computers section (see Figure 9-13). This is because the cluster services in Windows Server 2003 allow you to cluster more than two nodes together; however, in your case, with a CCR cluster, you are only using two. Click Next.

3. The wizard checks the cluster configuration to ensure that everything is ready for the formation of additional nodes into the cluster. When analysis is complete, click Next.

4. You are asked for an account under which the cluster service will run. If you have a specific account for the cluster service established, use that account. Click Next.

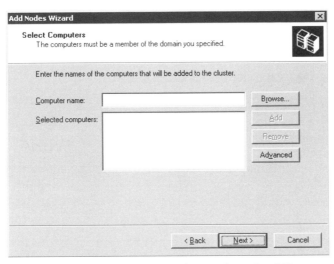

Figure 9-13   Adding your secondary node to the CCR

5. The Proposed Cluster Configuration page appears with all your settings. If something appears out of order, click Back to revise it. If things appear correct, click Next to initiate the adding of the node to the cluster.

6. After the cluster configures itself, click Next. If the wizard encounters some difficulties, you can view the log or the details to see what problems have arisen.

7. Once the cluster completes successfully, click Finish.

To confirm the formation of your two-node cluster, open Cluster Administrator, and you should see your cluster and the two servers that are your nodes. The State column should indicate that they are Up, as shown in Figure 9-14.

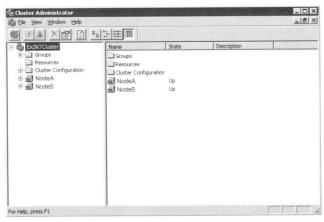

Figure 9-14   Confirm your two-node cluster is operational through the Cluster Administrator tool.

> **Note**   You can also confirm the cluster is functioning by going to a command prompt on one of the nodes (either one) and using cluster.exe to administer your cluster. Confirm the cluster by typing **cluster group**. The response should be a listing of all available resource groups and their status. You can also type **cluster node** and this should respond with a list of all available nodes and their status. If the responses you receive are positive, your cluster is functional.

Configure the MNS Quorum to Use the File Share Witness

Now that the cluster is established, tell your MNS Quorum to use the file share you created earlier on the Hub Transport server. Do this from a CLI by first setting the private property for the MNS resource to point to the share. The resource needs to go offline and then come back online.

From a command line, type the following:

```
Cluster res "Majority Node Set" /priv MNSFileShare=\\servername\sharename
```

In the previous command line, remember to use the shared-out UNC path for the location of the folder you created earlier. Note that this command only works if you install either Windows Server 2003 Service Pack 2 or the hotfix.

You will get a warning that tells you that the changes will not take effect until the next time the resource is brought online. The fastest way for this to occur is to take the resource offline and bring it back online. One way to do this is by moving the cluster group (which takes the group offline and online). You can do this by using the following command:

```
Cluster group "cluster group" /move
```

You should see the following result from the previous command:

```
Moving resource group 'Cluster Group'
Group              Node          Status
Cluster Group      <NodeName>    Online
```

This moves your cluster group off to the secondary node. You can move it back if you want. To confirm the value for the MNSFileShare has been configured properly, you can run the following command:

```
Cluster res "Majority Node Set" /priv
```

This is the same command you ran earlier, but this time you aren't looking to make changes; you are simply looking to confirm that your file share is pointing in the right direction.

Installing Exchange Server 2007 on Your Cluster

Once you confirm your MNS Quorum cluster is functional, you are ready to install Exchange Server 2007. As you learned in an earlier chapter, installation requires certain installed prerequisites, including .NET Framework 2.0, MMC 3.0, and PowerShell. In addition, make sure that IIS is installed and the following subcomponents are also included:

- Common Files
- Internet Information Services Manager
- The World Wide Web Service

Installing Exchange Server 2007 on Your Active Node

The installation begins just like a standard install. Go through the License Agreement and Error Reporting sections first and then follow these steps:

1. On the Installation Type page,, select the Custom Exchange Server Installation option because you can only install a mailbox server on the cluster. Click Next.

2. You are shown a number of individual role options, but in this case, select the Active Clustered Mailbox Role, as shown in Figure 9-15. Note that, by default, the Management Tools are selected for installation as well. Click Next.

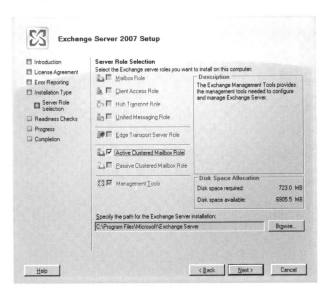

Figure 9-15   Selecting the Active Clustered Mailbox Role

Note   In Step 3 you will be asked to specify a Clustered Mailbox Server Name and IP address. The Clustered Mailbox Server (CMS), which was previously referred to as the Exchange Virtual Server (EVS), is a unique name that your Outlook clients will use when they connect to their Exchange Server.

3. You are shown the Cluster Settings, as shown in Figure 9-16. You are being asked the name of your virtual server (which is the name you will configure your Outlook clients to use when they connect). You are also asked for an IP address for the clustered mailbox, which should be a unique address for your network, not one of the addresses you already have configured for your individual nodes. And you can specify the path of the clustered mailbox server database files. The default is fine, as shown in the figure. When ready, click Next.

4. Your setup wizard performs a readiness check to see whether Exchange can be installed. If all is ready, click Install.

5. When the Completion page appears, click Finish.

Figure 9-16   Configure your cluster settings for a virtual mailbox name, an IP address, and a database location.

After your active node is installed with Exchange Server 2007, you are ready to install it on the passive node.

Installing Exchange Server 2007 on the Passive Node

The installation on the passive node requires all the same preinstallation tasks as the active node does. The only difference in the process is the selection once you decide to install a Custom server role. In this case, select the Passive Clustered Mailbox Role. Note that you can configure the location of the database from within this dialog box for the passive node.

Verifying the Status of Your CCR

To begin, you might check Cluster Administrator to verify that you have a new cluster group with a number of resources that are online. You can also check the location of your database and transaction logs for both NodeA and NodeB to verify the data is duplicated. You can perform a similar test to what you did with LCR in sending a large e-mail file out and watching the logs from NodeA increase, and then watch as NodeB catches the log shipping.

Another way to verify your cluster status is through the Exchange Management Shell. After you open the PowerShell, type the following to get a report on the status of the clustered mailbox server:

```
Get-ClusteredMailboxServerStatus -Identity <name of cluster>
```

Note from the response, as shown in Figure 9-17, that the status of the server is Online and the second node, NodeB, is currently the Active node, making it the owner of the cluster.

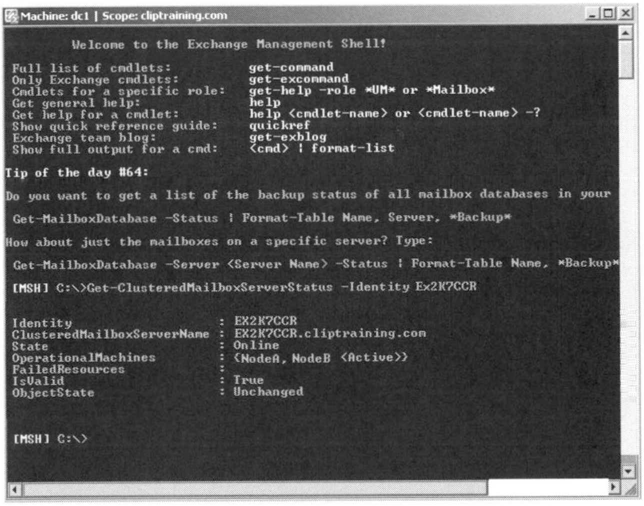

Figure 9-17   Verifying the status of your cluster using the `Get-ClusteredMailboxServerStatus` command

Verifying That a Server Can Handle a Failover

Now that you are confident of the status of your mailbox cluster, test them to see how they handle a test failover. You do this by moving the Exchange resources from the active node to the passive from within the Exchange Management Shell. When this is done manually by an administrator, this is not called failover, but rather it's called a handoff, and this type of purposeful shift is lossless. Type the following command:

```
Move-ClusteredMailboxServer -Identity:<name of cluster>
-TargetMachine:<passive node>
```

In the previous command, the **<passive node>** is whichever node is passive at the time. In addition, at the end of the command you could have included a comment with the **-MoveComment** tag, for example: **-MoveComment:"Practice Failover Drill"**.

Note When you worked with clusters in previous versions of Exchange, to simulate the failure you used Cluster Administrator. This is still possible; however, one of the goals of the Exchange Development Team was to minimize the need to use the Cluster Administrator.

When you perform the handoff of the cluster to the passive node, one way to confirm the process visually is by opening the Cluster Administrator and selecting the Exchange CCR group. When you perform the move, you should see the process happen in real time from one node to another.

When a real failure occurs, the process of failover can take up to a minute. This is such a short period of time that even if users are aware of the connection break, it is restored before they can react. In the perspective of the user, nothing has changed.

Configuring the Transport Dumpster

Earlier in this chapter, you learned the purpose of the transport dumpster. The Hub Transport server(s) has a queue with recent e-mails. In the event of a crash (that is, not a lossless failover, because some of the data has not been replicated between the nodes), the transport dumpster can minimize data loss by providing the active server with any e-mails still within the queue. In order for the transport dumpster to be of any assistance, you need to configure the settings for it. You can configure the settings from within the Exchange Management Shell.

To see the current configuration settings for your transport dumpster, as shown in Figure 9-18, type **get-transportconfig**.

In Figure 9-18, there are two settings (which currently hold no values) that you must configure:

- **MaxDumpsterSizePerStorageGroup** This setting shows the maximum size of the transport dumpster queue for each storage group. The recommended setting here is 1.5 times the amount of the largest message that can be sent. So, if your largest message can be 10 MB, set this to 15 MB. To determine how much disk space you need for a transport dumpster to function, simply count the amount of space required under the MaxDumpsterSizePerStorageGroup setting and multiply this by the number of storage groups that you have on the Mailbox server.

■ **MaxDumpsterTime** This setting indicates the maximum time messages can remain in the transport dumpster. The recommendation is seven days, which is plenty of time for systems to be brought back online to avoid any loss of data.

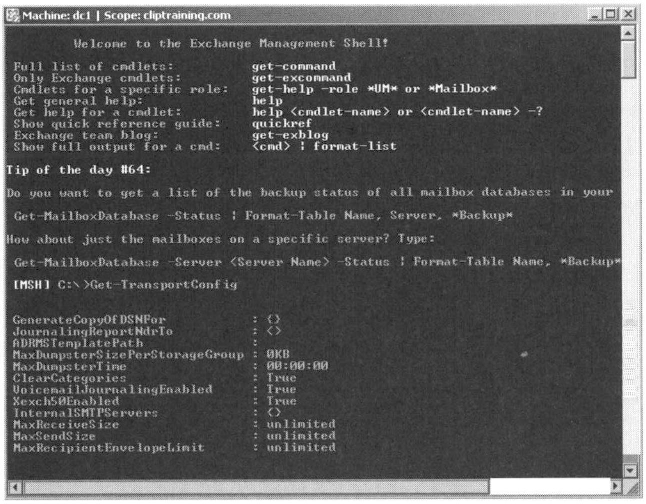

Figure 9-18   Viewing the current configuration settings for your transport dumpster

To configure these settings, use the `Set-TransportConfig` command. If you used the examples of 15 MB and seven days, type the following in the Exchange Management Shell:

```
Set-TransportConfig -MaxDumpsterSizePerStorageGroup 15MB
-MaxDumpsterTime 07.00:00:00
```

Closing Thoughts on CCR

This chapter discussed the underlying theory behind CCR, the planning necessary to implement within your Exchange organization (including various caveats to your setup), a step-by-step on how to configure the cluster, and methods to test its functionality and failover ability, with some final points on enabling the transport dumpster.

More Info There is more to learn and know about CCR, including more command-line options for your Exchange Management Shell, failover settings, and tuning your cluster. The Exchange Server 2007 Product Documentation is an excellent resource that can be found in the following locations:

For the Online Web Help, visit *http://technet.microsoft.com/en-us/library /cb24ddb7-0659-4d9d-9057-52843f861ba8.aspx*.

For a downloadable set of help files, visit *http://www.microsoft.com/downloads /details.aspx?FamilyID=555f5974-9258-475a-b150-0399b133fede&DisplayLang=en*.

Single Copy Clusters

Single copy clusters (SCC) are a carry-over from the cluster solutions available under Exchange Server 2003 with some enhancements in 2007. Single copy clusters, as shown in Figure 9-19, have multiple nodes within the cluster that use only one copy of the Mailbox database located on a shared set of storage. Exchange Server 2007 doesn't support active/active clusters (as in previous Exchange versions), only the active/passive configuration.

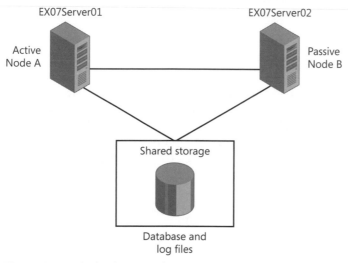

Figure 9-19   A single copy cluster (SCC)

Much of what you learned in the CCR portion of this chapter applies to SCC implementations. The cluster has its own identity that Outlook clients use to connect, but behind the scenes there are multiple nodes with one being active. In the event the active node fails, the passive node takes over the workload using the same shared storage to which all nodes have connectivity. The shared storage is typically an SAN or NAS that has its own fault-tolerant solution implemented. Your cluster makes the Exchange server's resources redundant, but not the data itself.

Shared data storage is a single point of failure that you need to worry about. Obviously, with an expensive disk solution like an SAN/NAS, you should be prepared for a disk failure. But if you are simply using an array of disks without some form of redundancy other than backup, you are susceptible to data loss, even with a cluster. CCR uses the strengths of a cluster for your system resources, with the new log file shipping mechanisms that allow you to have redundant storage.

The preparation, implementation, and testing of your SCC is almost exactly the same as for your CCR. Each node for your cluster must have Windows 2003 Enterprise Edition, with two network adapters that are configured to use static IP addresses for a public network and a private network. Note that in the case of an SCC cluster, you do not need to install Windows Server 2003 Service Pack 2 or the Knowledge Base article hotfix 921181, although it is always recommended that you keep your server as up-to-date as possible so you may choose to install SP2.

Prior to forming the cluster, configure all of your shared storage. The quorum disk will be located on the shared storage array so all nodes in the cluster need to be able to access the shared storage array. The cluster will fail if the quorum is not available to all the nodes in the cluster.

After you configure your network adapters and your shared storage array is accessible by all nodes, proceed with the installation. The steps are exactly the same for the installation of the first and second nodes of your cluster for SCC as they are for CCR, so you can use the previous steps to install your cluster. There is one notable difference between the steps: when you reach the Proposed Cluster Configuration page in the New Server Cluster Wizard (located under the heading "Establish the Cluster," Step 7) you do not need to change the Quorum to a Majority Node Set (because this is not a CCR cluster). Leave the defaults and continue to establish the primary and secondary nodes of the cluster.

After you configure your cluster, you can use Cluster Administrator to verify that it is functional and configured properly. Your Cluster Administrator also shows you the networks used (the recommendation is to name them Public and Private on each node to keep them clear in your mind), and you can configure the networks to use the Private network for Internal Cluster Communications Only (Private Network) for the heartbeat, and the Public network for All Communications (Mixed Network).

Another way to confirm the operational status of your cluster is to open a command prompt and use the `cluster group` and the `cluster node` commands to verify the status of both your group and your node.

***

Note If you aren't sure what type of cluster a company is using (either SCC or CCR), open your Exchange Management Shell and type `get-mailboxserver` from the shell. In the results, look for the value called `ClusteredStorageType`. It will say `Disabled` (if this is a nonclustered server), `NonShared` (for CCR), and `Shared` (for SCC).

***

Installing Exchange Server 2007 is also the same as for the CCR with one exception: once your member servers have met all the prerequisites for the Exchange installation (including .NET 2.0, MMC 3.0, and the PowerShell), along with necessary components required for an Exchange Mailbox server (which, again, is the only server role you can install in a SCC cluster), you can proceed with the installation of your active node. Follow the same steps until you reach the part where the Exchange Server 2007 Setup asks you to select a cluster type. Select the Single Copy Cluster.

The rest of the process for both the active and passive nodes is the same as CCR. In addition, to confirm your Exchange cluster, do one of the following things:

- Open Cluster Administrator and confirm that both nodes are created. Expand one of your nodes and select Active Resources to see whether the resources have been created and whether they are online.

- Open the Exchange Management Shell and use the `Get-ClusteredMailbox-ServerStatus` command to see whether the state of your cluster is online and which node is active; that is, which node takes responsibility for the Quorum.

- To test the failover ability of your cluster, you can perform a scheduled handoff by using the `Move-ClusteredMailboxServer` cmdlet as you did earlier for CCR.

Note In a single copy cluster (SCC), there is no need to install SP2 or the Knowledge Base hotfix 921181, nor do you need to establish a file share witness on your Hub Transport server or make any changes to the transport dumpster because these aspects to the cluster do not apply.

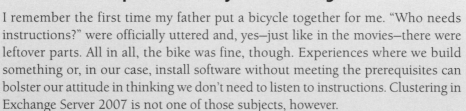

Real World Preparation Is Key to Clustering

I remember the first time my father put a bicycle together for me. "Who needs instructions?" were officially uttered and, yes—just like in the movies—there were leftover parts. All in all, the bike was fine, though. Experiences where we build something or, in our case, install software without meeting the prerequisites can bolster our attitude in thinking we don't need to listen to instructions. Clustering in Exchange Server 2007 is not one of those subjects, however.

One admin configured everything perfectly. He configured his network adapters (even renamed them Public and Private) and installed the KB hotfix needed for the CCR cluster. All prerequisites were even installed ahead of time for the Exchange Server 2007 installation. But when it came time to create the first node of the cluster, it failed. During the determination of feasibility, the cluster continued to fail. The administrator rechecked his settings, rechecked documentation, and finally read the log files for the failure. Apparently, this version wouldn't allow the cluster. The reason? CCR requires Windows 2003 Server Enterprise Edition. He had installed Standard Edition. Not the end of the world, but a loss of a couple of hours work. Lesson learned for the next time.

There is a ton of great information about real-world success and failure of Exchange Server 2007 clusters (among other topics) provided by MSExchange.org at *http://forums.msexchange.org*. In addition, troubleshooting clusters can be a real challenge, but Microsoft TechNet provides some assistance a the following link: *http://technet.microsoft.com/en-us/library/aa998567.aspx*.

Summary

As mentioned at the beginning of this chapter, Exchange Server 2007 offers high availability of server resources (using a single copy cluster), disk resources (using local continuous replication), or both (using cluster continuous replication). Your goal with high availability is to eliminate single points of failure for your Exchange mailboxes, protecting your data, and offering you more peace of mind. The new techniques and mechanisms in Exchange Server 2007, as well as the new Exchange Management Shell (based on Power-Shell) make the implementation, configuration, and monitoring of your high-availability solution much easier.

Part IV
Management

Chapter 10
Managing Exchange Server 2007

Now that you've installed Microsoft Exchange Server 2007, you're probably eager to start working with it. You'll want to begin creating mailboxes, groups, and other recipients, but first you need to know some basics of managing the Exchange system.

Exchange Server 2007 introduces a radical shift in the way you manage an Exchange server or organization. Exchange Server 2007 is built entirely upon a new command-line interface named Exchange Management Shell—a modified version of the new Windows PowerShell. You can perform just about every imaginable administrative function with Exchange Server 2007 by using shell commands called cmdlets.

The graphical management interface for Exchange Server 2007 is Exchange Management Console. It is essentially a Microsoft Management Console (MMC) snap-in that is built to run commands from the Exchange Management Shell. Whenever you configure an object in the console or run a wizard, the interface actually is using the underlying Exchange Management Shell to issue the appropriate commands. In fact, when you issue a command in the console, it even provides information about how to issue those same commands from the Exchange Management Shell, providing a friendly way to get to know the shell interface and command structure.

This chapter introduces you to the Microsoft Management Console, the Exchange Management Console, and the Exchange Management Shell. Throughout this book, you learn about ways to perform administrative functions in both interfaces. This chapter is meant to give you grounding in the two interfaces you'll be using to manage Exchange Server 2007.

Microsoft Management Console

Microsoft Management Console (MMC) provides a common environment for the management of various system and network resources. MMC is actually a framework that hosts modules called snap-ins, which provide the actual tools for managing a resource. For example, you manage Exchange Server 2007 using the Microsoft Exchange snap-in.

Note   The Start menu icon that loads the Exchange Management Console essentially creates an MMC and loads the Microsoft Exchange snap-in, and you can do nearly all your administration by selecting this shortcut. However, you may find it useful to add the Microsoft Exchange snap-in to an MMC console you create along with other snap-ins representing common tasks you perform.

MMC itself does not provide any management functionality. Rather, the MMC environment provides for seamless integration between snap-ins. This allows administrators and other users to create custom management tools from snap-ins created by various vendors. Administrators can save the tools they have created for later use and share them with other administrators and users. This model gives administrators the ability to delegate administrative tasks by creating different tools of varying levels of complexity and giving them to the users who will perform the tasks.

The MMC User Interface

When you first load MMC, you might notice that it looks a lot like Microsoft Windows Explorer. MMC uses a multiple-document interface, meaning that you can load and display multiple console windows in the MMC parent window simultaneously. Figure 10-1 shows the MMC parent window with the Microsoft Exchange snap-in loaded. The next few sections discuss the main parts of this window.

MMC Toolbar

The main MMC toolbar holds six menus: File, Action, View, Favorites, Window, and Help. The View, Favorites, Window, and Help menus are pretty much what you would expect. The View menu lets you customize the columns you see in the display and turn on or off visual effects. The Favorites menu lets you add items to a list of favorites and organize that list into categories. The Favorites list can include shortcuts to tools, items in the console, or tasks. The Window menu lets you manage console windows if you have more than one window open in MMC. The Help menu lets you access general MMC Help as well as Help for the snap-ins that are currently loaded.

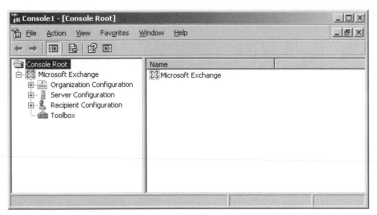

Figure 10-1   MMC window with the Microsoft Exchange snap-in loaded

The Action menu provides access to commands pertinent to the object you have selected in the console. The commands on the Action menu change depending on what snap-in is loaded and what object within that snap-in is currently selected.

The File menu is where most of the action is. From this menu, you can open and save consoles and even create new ones. You can also add snap-ins to and remove them from open consoles and set general MMC options. Options you can set include the following:

- **Console Title**   Specifies the console name as it appears in the MMC title bar.

- **Console Mode**   Author mode grants the user full access to all MMC functionality. User mode comes in three flavors: Full Access lets the user access all MMC commands but not add or remove snap-ins or change console properties; Limited Access Multiple Window allows the user to access only the areas of the console tree that were visible when the console was saved and to open new windows; Limited Access Single Window works the same as Limited Access Multiple Window, except that users cannot open new windows.

Other options define whether users can access context menus on taskpads, save changes to the console, and customize views.

Scope Pane

The Scope pane contains a hierarchy of containers referred to as a console tree. Some containers are displayed as unique icons that graphically represent the type of items they contain. Others are displayed as folders, simply indicating that they hold other objects. Click the plus sign next to a container to expand it and display the objects inside. Click the minus sign to collapse the container.

Details Pane

The Details pane changes to show the contents of the container selected in the Scope pane. In other words, the Details pane shows the results of the currently selected scope. The Details pane can display information in a number of ways, referred to as *views*.

Note   The View menu also lets you customize the columns that are shown in the scope and details panes. In the Details pane itself, you can rearrange columns and click a column heading to reorder rows alphabetically or chronologically.

In addition to the standard views, for some snap-ins you can also create a taskpad view to show in the Details pane. A taskpad view is a dynamic HTML (DHTML) page that presents shortcuts to commands available for a selected item in the Scope pane. Each command is represented as a task that consists of an image, a label, a description, and a mechanism for instructing the snap-in to run that command. Users can run the commands by clicking a task.

You can use taskpad views to do the following things:

- Include shortcuts to all the tasks a specific user might need to perform.

- Group tasks by function or user by creating multiple taskpad views in a console.

- Create simplified lists of tasks. For example, you can add tasks to a taskpad view and then hide the console tree.

- Simplify complex tasks. For example, if a user frequently performs a given task involving several snap-ins and other tools, you can organize, in a single location, shortcuts to those tasks that run the appropriate property sheets, command lines, dialog boxes, or scripts.

Snap-in Root Container

The snap-in root container is the uppermost container in the snap-in; it is usually named based on the product or task with which it is associated. MMC supports stand-alone and extension snap-ins. A stand-alone snap-in, such as Microsoft Exchange, provides management functionality without requiring support from another snap-in. Only one snap-in root container exists for each stand-alone snap-in. An extension snap-in requires a parent snap-in above it in the console tree. Extension snap-ins extend the functionality provided by other snap-ins.

Containers and Objects

Exchange Server 2007 is a great example of an object-based, hierarchical directory environment. All the little bits and pieces that make up Exchange are objects that interact with one another to some degree. The objects you see in the scope and details panes can be divided into two types:

- **Containers**   Containers can contain both other containers and noncontainer objects. Container objects can also appear in the Details pane. They are used to logically group all the objects that make up a management environment. An administrator uses the container objects to organize the tree and then to navigate through it.

- **Leaf Objects**   A leaf object is simply an object that cannot contain other objects. Some common leaf objects with which an administrator works daily include servers and connectors.

You manage all the objects in an MMC console through the use of property sheets. A *property sheet* is a dialog box you open by selecting an object and then choosing Properties from the Action menu. It consists of one or more tabs that contain controls for setting a group of related properties. Figure 10-2 shows the property sheet for a server object in the Microsoft Exchange snap-in.

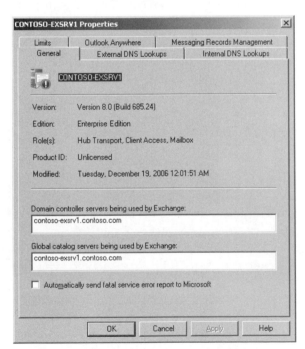

Figure 10-2   Property sheet for a server object

How MMC Works

The MMC interface permits snap-ins to integrate within a common management console. This gives all snap-ins a similar look and feel, although they might perform their tasks in different ways. The console itself offers no management functions; it merely acts as a host to the snap-ins. Snap-ins always reside in a console; they do not run by themselves.

Snap-ins

Each MMC tool is built of a collection of instances of smaller tools called MMC snap-ins. A snap-in is the smallest unit of console extension and represents one unit of management behavior. The snap-in might call on other supporting controls and dynamic-link libraries (DLLs) to accomplish its task.

Snap-ins extend MMC by adding and enabling management behavior. They can provide this behavior in a number of ways. For example, a snap-in might add elements to the container tree, or it might extend a particular tool by adding shortcut menu items, toolbars, property sheet tabs, wizards, or Help to an existing snap-in. There are two basic types of snap-ins:

- **Stand-alone Snap-ins**   Provide management functionality even if they are alone in a console with no other supporting snap-ins. They do not rely on any other snap-ins being present. The Exchange System snap-in is an example of a stand-alone snap-in.

- **Extension Snap-ins**   Provide a variety of functionality, but only when used in conjunction with a parent snap-in. Some extend the console namespace, while others simply extend context menus or specific wizards.

Note   Many snap-ins support both modes of operation, offering some stand-alone functionality and also extending the functionality of other snap-ins.

Packages

Snap-ins are usually shipped in groups called *packages*. For example, the Microsoft Windows operating system itself includes one or more packages of snap-ins. Additionally, other vendors might ship products composed entirely of packages of snap-ins. Grouping snap-ins into packages provides convenience for downloading and installation. It also permits several snap-ins to share core DLLs so that these DLLs do not have to be placed in every snap-in.

Custom Tools

MMC provides functionality for creating custom management tools. It allows administrators to create, save, and then delegate a customized console of multiple snap-ins tailored for specific tasks. Administrators can assemble these specific snap-ins into a tool (also called a *document*) that runs in one instance of MMC. For example, you can create a tool that manages many different aspects of the network—Active Directory, replication topology, file sharing, and so on. After assembling a tool, the administrator can save it in an .msc file and then reload the file later to instantly re-create the tool. The .msc file can also be e-mailed to another administrator, who can then load the file and use the tool.

Custom Consoles

One of the primary benefits of MMC is its support for customization of tools. You can build custom MMC consoles tailored for specific management tasks and then delegate those consoles to other administrators. These tools can focus on the particular management requirements of various administrator groups.

For example, you could create a custom console, as shown in Figure 10-3, that includes the Microsoft Exchange, Active Directory Users and Computers, Disk Management, and Event Viewer snap-ins—several tools that are important to any Exchange administrator.

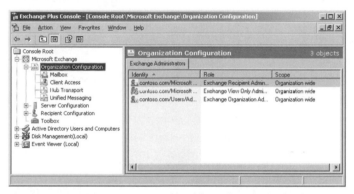

Figure 10-3   A custom console with various snap-ins

More Info   Obviously, there is a lot more to MMC than can be covered in a single chapter, especially when the chapter is really about using the Microsoft Exchange System snap-in. For more information about MMC, start with the Help file available from any console window.

Using the Exchange Management Console

The Exchange Management Console provides a graphical view of all the resources and components of an Exchange organization. No matter how many servers you have set up, you can manage them all from a single Exchange Management Console window. Use this window, and the property sheets of all the objects in it, to navigate the Exchange organizational hierarchy and perform the various tasks associated with Exchange administration.

You use both container and leaf objects to administer an Exchange organization. Most objects in the Exchange System console window—both container and leaf—have a property sheet that allows you to configure various parameters for that object and make it act in the way that best serves the organization's needs. You can open an object's property sheet by selecting the object and choosing Properties from the Action menu. You can also right-click an object and choose Properties from its shortcut menu. You use property sheets to both configure and administer Exchange Server 2007.

Major Areas of the Exchange Management Console

You can start the Exchange Management Console by clicking Start, pointing to All Programs, then to Microsoft Exchange Server 2007, and then clicking Exchange Management Console. The Exchange Management Console is divided into the major areas shown in Figure 10-4. These areas include:

- **Console tree** The console tree is located on the left side of the console and is organized by containers that represent the hierarchy of the Exchange organization. The specific containers that are displayed are based on the server roles that are installed. When you select a container in the console tree, the results of that container are shown in the Result pane.

- **Results pane** The Results pane is located in the center of the console. This pane displays objects that reflect the container you have selected in the console tree. For example, if you select the Mailbox object inside the Recipient Configuration container, the Results pane shows individual mailboxes.

- **Work pane** The Work pane is located at the bottom of the Result pane. The Work pane is shown only when you select objects under the Server Configuration container, such as Mailbox, Client Access, or Unified Messaging. This pane displays objects based on the server role that is selected in the Server Configuration container. For example, if you select the Mailbox object in the Server Configuration container, the Results pane shows a list of Mailbox servers. When you select a server in the Results pane, storage groups on that server are shown in the Work pane.

- **Actions pane** The Actions pane is located on the right side of the console. This pane lists actions you can perform based on the object that is selected in the console tree, Results pane, or Work pane. These actions are the same actions you can take by displaying the Action menu or by right-clicking the object. For this reason, you might find it more useful to hide the Actions pane. You can do this by clicking the Show/Hide Action Pane button on the Exchange Management Console toolbar.

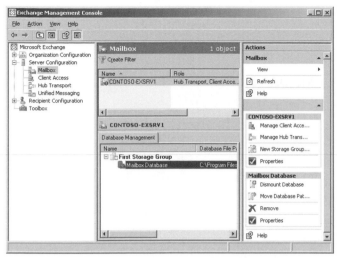

Figure 10-4   Areas of the Exchange Management Console

Real World   Explore!

The sheer number of property sheets you encounter when administering Exchange Server 2007 can seem daunting, but don't let them intimidate you. Take the time to play with the program. You probably won't be able to remember exactly where to go to accomplish every administrative task in Exchange Server 2007, but it helps to think about what the task involves. If you need to manage the way all mailboxes on a server are handled, find the Mailbox container inside the Server Configuration container. If you need to manage a single mailbox, find the Mailbox container inside the Recipient Configuration container. Each component handles a different aspect of the configuration, so multiple components might be involved with a single configuration or administrative task. As you use the program and get used to the Exchange environment, it becomes easier to navigate the program and find exactly the object or objects you need to administer.

Learning the contents and layout of the various property sheets in the Exchange Management Console is a key to learning how Exchange Server 2007 works. After you know how to organize tasks that match the way Exchange Server 2007 is structured, your administrative tasks flow more easily.

To administer an Exchange environment with the Exchange Management Console, you must log on to Active Directory under a domain user account that has administrative privileges for administering the Exchange organization.

Examining the Exchange Hierarchy

The top of the hierarchy in the console tree of the Exchange Management Console is the snap-in root container that represents the Exchange organization, as shown in Figure 10-5. The snap-in root container is named Microsoft Exchange. All the Exchange containers are held within this container. Additionally, selecting the root container shows two tabbed screens in the Results pane: Finalize Deployment, which shows you tasks to perform after installation (and which is discussed in Chapter 6, "Installing Exchange Server 2007"); and End-to-End Scenario, which allows you to configure end-to-end solutions in Exchange, such as implementing best practices for disaster recovery.

There are four primary containers directly within the snap-in root container. The following sections describe each of these containers.

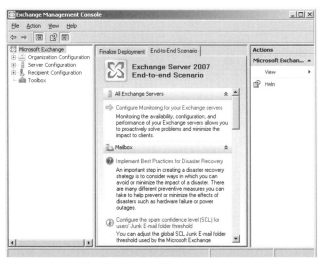

Figure 10-5   The Exchange hierarchy

Organization Configuration

Selecting the Organization Configuration container itself displays all users configured as Exchange administrators and allows you to configure administrative access roles for users or groups, as shown in Figure 10-6. You must be a member of the Exchange Server Administrators group in order to view the Organization Configuration container or change the roles assigned to users.

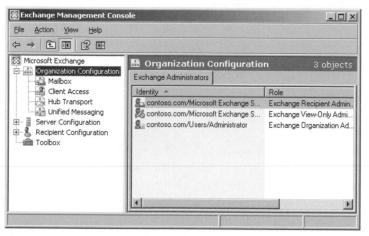

Figure 10-6 Viewing Exchange administrative roles with the Organization Configuration container

Exchange administrator roles are similar in function to Windows Server security groups. Administrator roles allow you to easily assign sets of permissions to users for the most common administrative functions in Exchange Server. Exchange administrative roles include the following:

- **Exchange Server Administrators** This role provides access to only local server Exchange configuration data, either in the Active Directory or on the physical computer on which Exchange Server 2007 is installed. Users who are members of the Exchange Server Administrators role have permissions to administer a particular server, but do not have permissions to perform operations that have global impact in the Exchange organization. Members assigned to this role are granted the following:

  ❑ They are made owners of all local server configuration data. As owners, members of the role have full control over the local server configuration data.

  ❑ They are made local administrators on the computer on which Exchange is installed.

  ❑ They are made members of the Exchange View-Only Administrators role.

- **Exchange Organization Administrators Role** The Exchange Organization Administrators role provides administrators with full access to all Exchange properties and objects in the Exchange organization. Additionally, members assigned this role are granted the following:

  ❑ They are made owners of the Exchange organization in the configuration container of Active Directory. As owners, members of the role have control over the Exchange organization data in the configuration container in Active Directory and the local Exchange server Administrator group.

❑ They are given Read access to all domain user containers in Active Directory. Exchange grants this permission during setup of the first Exchange Server 2007 server in the domain, for each domain in the organization. These permissions are also granted by being a member of the Exchange Recipient Administrator role.

❑ They are given Write access to all Exchange-specific attributes in all domain user containers in Active Directory. Exchange Server 2007 grants this permission during setup of the first Exchange Server 2007 server in the domain, for each domain in the organization. These permissions are also granted by being a member of the Exchange Recipient Administrator role.

❑ They are made owners of all local server configuration data. As owners, members have full control over the local Exchange server. Exchange Server 2007 grants this permission during setup of each Exchange server.

■ **Exchange Recipient Administrators Role**   The Exchange Recipient Administrators role has permissions to modify any Exchange property on an Active Directory user, contact, group, dynamic distribution list, or public folder object. Members are granted the following:

❑ They are given Read access to all the Domain User containers in Active Directory that have had Setup /PrepareDomain run in those domains.

❑ They are given Write access to all the Exchange-specific attributes on the Domain User containers in Active Directory that have had Setup /PrepareDomain run in those domains.

❑ They are automatically granted membership in the Exchange View-Only Administrator role.

■ **Exchange View-Only Administrators Role**   The Exchange View-Only Administrators role has read-only access to the entire Exchange organization tree in the Active Directory configuration container and read-only access to all the Windows domain containers that have Exchange recipients.

The Organization Configuration container contains the following containers:

■ **Mailbox**   At the organization level, the Mailbox container allows you to manage Mailbox server role settings that apply to the entire Exchange organization. You can create and manage address lists, managed custom folders, messaging records management (MRM) mailbox policies, and offline address books (OABs). You learn more about this in Chapter 11, "Creating and Managing Recipients."

- **Client Access**   At the organization level, the Client Access container allows you to create and manage Exchange ActiveSync mailbox policies for mobile users. These policies apply common sets of security settings or policies to collections of users.

- **Hub Transport**   At the organization level, the Hub Transport container allows you to configure features of the Hub Transport server role. The Hub Transport server role handles all internal mail flow, applies organizational message routing policies, and is responsible for delivering messages to a recipient's mailbox.

- **Unified Messaging**   At the organization level, the Unified Messaging container allows you to manage Unified Messaging (UM) server role settings that apply to your entire Exchange Server 2007 organization. You can maintain existing or create new UM dial plans, UM IP gateways, UM mailbox policies, and UM auto attendants. For more information on Unified Messaging, see Chapter 14, "Unified Messaging."

Server Configuration

Use the Server Configuration container, shown in Figure 10-7, to view a list of all the servers in your Exchange organization and perform tasks specific to server roles. When you select the Server Configuration container itself, you can view the role, version, edition, product ID, cluster status, last modified time, and site for each server in the Results pane. For more information about how to view these columns in the Results pane, see the section, "Custom Consoles," earlier in this chapter.

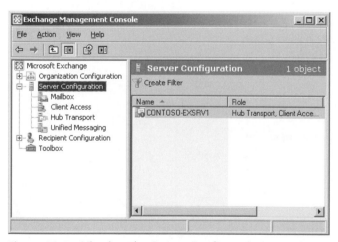

Figure 10-7   Viewing the Server Configuration container

The containers that appear under Server Configuration show only the Exchange servers that have a particular server role installed. The Server Configuration container contains the following containers:

- **Mailbox**   At the server level, the Mailbox container allows you to display a list of all servers in the organization that have the Mailbox server role installed and to perform actions specific to that server role. The Database Management tab in the Work pane lists all the storage groups and databases that exist on the selected server.

- **Client Access**   At the server level, the Client Access container allows you to view and maintain the settings for Microsoft Outlook Web Access (OWA), Exchange ActiveSync, and the offline address book (OAB).

- **Hub Transport**   At the server level, the Hub Transport container allows you to display a list of all servers in the organization that have the Hub Transport server role installed and to perform actions specific to that server role.

- **Unified Messaging**   At the server level, the Unified Messaging container allows you to configure voice messaging, fax, and e-mail messaging into one store that users can access from a telephone and a computer. Exchange Server 2007 Unified Messaging integrates Microsoft Exchange with telephony networks and brings the Unified Messaging features to the core of Microsoft Exchange.

Recipient Configuration

The Recipient Configuration container, shown in Figure 10-8, allows you to perform a variety of recipient management tasks. You can view all the recipients in your organization, create new recipients, and manage existing mailboxes, mail contacts, mail users, and distribution groups.

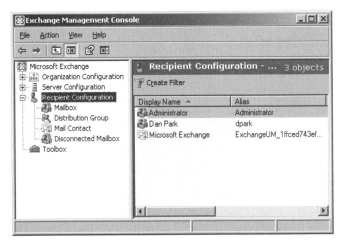

Figure 10-8   Viewing the Recipient Configuration container

The Recipient Configuration container contains the following containers:

- **Mailbox**   At the recipient level, the Mailbox container allows you to manage mailbox users and resource mailboxes. Resource mailboxes include room and equipment mailboxes. You can create new mailboxes and remove, disable, or move existing mailboxes. You can also configure mailbox properties, enable and disable Unified Messaging (UM), and manage mobile devices.

■ **Distribution Group**   The Distribution Group container allows you to manage mail-enabled distribution groups (which include security groups) and dynamic distribution groups. You can create new distribution groups and remove, disable, or configure existing distribution groups.

■ **Mail Contact**   The Mail Contact container allows you to manage mail contacts. You can create new mail contacts and delete or configure existing mail contacts.

■ **Disconnected Mailbox**   The Disconnected Mailbox container allows you to view and connect disabled mailboxes. Disconnected mailboxes are retained based on the configured mailbox database limits. You will see only the mailboxes that have been disconnected within the retention period that is specified for the mailbox database.

Toolbox

The Toolbox is a collection of tools that are installed with Microsoft Exchange Server 2007. The Toolbox provides a central location for diagnostic, troubleshooting, and recovery activities using various Exchange tools.

The tools in the toolbox are divided into the following categories:

■ **Configuration Management Tools**   This category contains only the Exchange Server Best Practices Analyzer, which automatically examines an Exchange Server 2007 deployment and determines whether the configuration is in line with Microsoft best practices. Run the Exchange Server Best Practices Analyzer after installing a new Exchange server or after making any configuration changes. You learn more about this tool in Chapter 15, "Troubleshooting Exchange Server 2007."

■ **Disaster Recovery Tools**   This category contains two tools: Database Recovery Management Tool and Database Troubleshooter. Both tools work through a set of troubleshooting steps to help identify and resolve database issues.

■ **Mail Flow Tools**   This category contains the following three tools:

❑ **Mail Flow Troubleshooter** This tool allows you to troubleshoot common mail flow problems. After selecting a symptom of the mail flow problems you are experiencing (such as delays or non-delivery reports), the tool attempts to find a solution and then provides advice to walk you through the correct troubleshooting path. It shows an analysis of possible root causes and provides suggestions for corrective actions.

❑ **Message Tracking Tool** This tool lets you view a detailed log of all message activity as messages are transferred to and from an Exchange Server 2007 server that has the Hub Transport server role, the Mailbox server role, or the Edge Transport server role installed. You can use message tracking logs for mail flow analysis, reporting, and troubleshooting.

- ❑ **Queue Viewer** This tool allows you to monitor mail flow and inspect queues and messages. You can also perform actions to the queuing databases such as suspending or resuming a queue, or removing messages

- ■ **Performance Tools**   This category contains two tools: Performance Monitor and Performance Troubleshooter. Performance Monitor is a tool you can configure to collect information about the performance of your messaging system. Specifically, you can use it to monitor, create graphs, and log performance metrics for core system functions. Performance Monitor is covered in detail in Chapter 17, "Tuning Exchange Server 2007 Performance." Performance Troubleshooter helps you to locate and identify performance-related issues that could affect an Exchange server. You diagnose a problem by selecting the symptoms observed. Based on the symptoms, the tool walks you through the correct troubleshooting path. This tool is covered in Chapter 15.

Using the Exchange Management Shell

The Exchange Management Shell, shown in Figure 10-9, is based on Microsoft Windows PowerShell, which provides a powerful command-line interface for executing and automating administrative tasks. With the Exchange Management Shell, you can manage every aspect of Exchange Server 2007, including enabling new e-mail accounts, configuring store database properties, and just about every other management task associated with Exchange Server 2007.

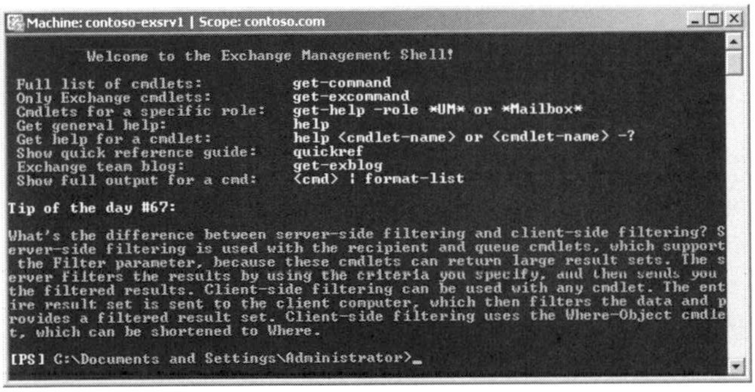

Figure 10-9   The Exchange Management Shell

In fact, you can use the Exchange Management Shell to perform every task available in the Exchange Management Console and a number of tasks that cannot be performed in the Exchange Management Console. It helps to think of it this way: the Exchange Management Console provides a graphical interface for most of the functionality of the Exchange Management Shell. When you run a command in the Exchange Management Console, the Exchange Management Shell is actually called to perform the command. When you perform a command in the Exchange Management Console, the graphic interface often even shows you the associated shell command, as shown in Figure 10-10.

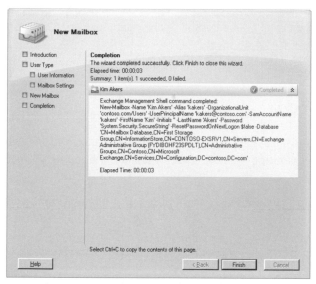

Figure 10-10   Viewing shell commands from the Exchange Management Console

So why use the shell instead of the console? Aside from the fact that some commands (such as those used to manage public folders) are only available as shell commands, the shell also offers a flexibility that can speed up and simplify common operations. For example, with a single shell command, you can get a list of recipients, filter that list according to a set of criteria, and then perform a function on only the filtered list of recipients.

Note   The Exchange Management Shell also provides a robust and flexible scripting platform that can reduce the complexity of current Microsoft Visual Basic scripts. Tasks that previously required many lines in Visual Basic scripts can now be done by using as little as one line of code in the Exchange Management Shell. The Exchange Management Shell provides this flexibility because it does not use text as the basis for interaction with the system, but uses an object model that is based on the Microsoft .NET platform. This object model enables the Exchange Management Shell cmdlets to apply the output from one command to subsequent commands when they are run.

To open the Exchange Management Shell, follow these steps:

1. Click Start, point to All Programs, and then point to Microsoft Exchange Server 2007.

2. Click Exchange Management Shell.

More Info This section is intended to introduce you to the basics of using the Exchange Management Shell. Throughout this book, you find specific examples of using shell commands to complete administrative tasks. For more information on using the Exchange Management Shell, please consult the Exchange Server 2007 Help files. Help includes detailed advice on using advanced options such as `WhatIf` and comparison parameters, command output, shell variables, structured data, and scripting.

Understanding Cmdlets

At first glance, the shell may seem similar to other command-line interfaces with which you may be familiar. However, after working with the shell for just a few minutes, you see that there are dramatic differences.

In the Exchange Management Shell, a cmdlet is the smallest unit of functionality. A cmdlet is roughly analogous to a built-in command in other types of shells. You type cmdlets directly into the shell interface.

All cmdlets consist of at least two parts:

- **A verb** The verb represents the action of the command. An example of a verb is `get`, which is used to retrieve information about an object. Table 10-1 lists the most common verbs used in the Exchange Management Shell.

- **A noun** The noun represents the recipient of the verb's action. An example of a noun would be an object in the Exchange organization such as a mailbox server. The noun in this case would be `MailboxServer`.

Cmdlets always contain a verb and a noun separated by a hyphen. To continue the previous example, the cmdlet for getting information about a mailbox server would be:

```
Get-MailboxServer
```

Table 10-1 Common Verbs in the Exchange Management Shell

Verb	Function
Disable	Disables the specified Exchange object
Enable	Enables the specified Exchange object
Get	Retrieves information about an object

Table 10-1 Common Verbs in the Exchange Management Shell (Continued)

Verb	Function
Move	Moves an object from one container to another
New	Creates a new object
Remove	Deletes an object
Set	Modifies the properties of an object

Obviously, you can't do too much with just a verb and a noun. For example, the cmdlet `Get-MailboxServer` doesn't provide enough information for the shell to do anything. You need to specify which mailbox server and likely what information you want to get. You provide this extra information through parameters. Parameters provide information to the cmdlet, either identifying an object and its attributes to act on, or controlling how the cmdlet performs its task.

To use a parameter, type a space following the verb-noun pair and then type the parameters you need. The name of the parameter is always preceded by a hyphen (-) and the use of parameters follows this syntax:

```
Verb-Noun –ParameterName <ParameterValue>
```

For example, to get information about a specific mailbox server (say, a server named contoso-exsrv1), add the identity parameter to the cmdlet, like this:

```
Get-MailboxServer –Identity contoso-exsrv1
```

> **Note** You can find a complete reference of cmdlets including parameters available in the Exchange Management Shell in the Exchange Server 2007 Help files. The cmdlets used to perform various activities are included throughout this book.

Getting Help

Obviously, it is difficult to remember all the verbs, nouns, and parameters available in the Exchange Management Shell. Fortunately, there are several ways to get help right within the shell.

Help Cmdlets

Three help cmdlets are available in the shell to help you find the information you need to perform tasks: `Get-Help`, `Get-Command`, and `Get-ExCommand`.

When you use the `Get-Help` command by itself (that is, when you type no parameters with it), the shell provides basic information about using the shell, as shown in Figure 10-11.

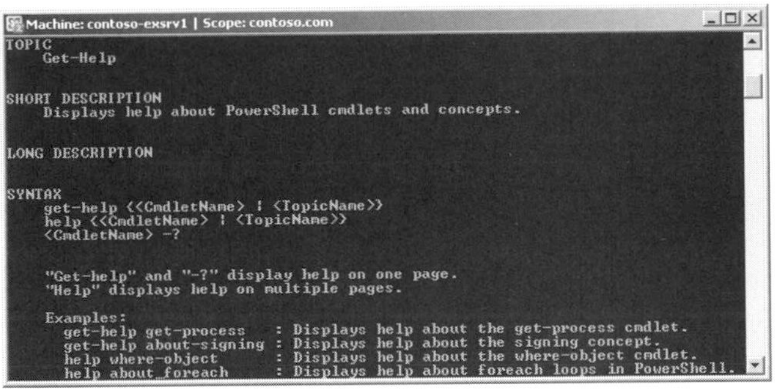

Figure 10-11   Getting help in the Exchange Management Shell

You can also use several parameters along with the `Get-Help` cmdlet to get more focused help on the task you're trying to perform. For example, you can use the name of a cmdlet as a parameter to get help on using that cmdlet. Typing the following gives you help on using the `Get-MailboxServer` cmdlet:

```
Get-Help Get-MailboxServer
```

You can even go a step further by adding parameters to further narrow the help you receive. Following the `Get-Help <cmdlet>` syntax, you can add the following parameters:

- `Get-Help <cmdlet> -Full`   Provides full help on the specified cmdlet.

- `Get-Help <cmdlet> -Parameter <parametername>`   Provides just the help view for the specific parameter of the cmdlet you name.

- `Get-Help <cmdlet> -Examples`   Provides just the examples portion of the help view for the cmdlet you name.

You can use the `Get-Command` cmdlet by itself (no parameters) to view a list of all commands available in the shell. You can also add **–noun** and **–verb** parameters to the `Get-Command <commandname>` syntax to view all cmdlets with the specified noun or verb.

Also, you can use the `Get-ExCommand` cmdlet to return all the cmdlets that are specific to Exchange Server 2007. Otherwise, the `Get-Excommand` cmdlet works just like the `Get-Command` cmdlet.

Tab Completion

Tab completion helps reduce typing when using the shell. When you have typed a partial cmdlet name, just press Tab, and the Exchange Management Shell completes the cmdlet name if it finds a matching cmdlet. If it finds multiple matching cmdlets, the shell cycles through each cmdlet name as you keep pressing Tab. When you use tab completion with cmdlet names, you must supply at least the verb and the hyphen (-).

For example, you can use Tab completion to quickly view the nouns associated with the get verb. Just type `Get-` at the prompt and then keep pressing Tab to cycle through the available nouns you can use with `get`.

For another example, if you cannot remember (or just didn't want to type) a full cmdlet such as `Get-MailboxServer`, you can type `Get-Mail` and press Tab to find the correct cmdlet without having to type the full name.

Summary

This chapter provided a basic introduction to the tools used to administer an Exchange Server 2007 organization. The primary tool you use to administer Microsoft Exchange Server 2007 is the Exchange Management Console, which provides a graphical environment for configuring the various services and components of an Exchange organization. Exchange Server 2007 also features the new Exchange Management Shell, a powerful command-line interface for managing an Exchange organization. Chapter 11 begins a series of chapters that look at specific aspects of Exchange administration. In it, you learn how to create and manage the basic Exchange recipients.

Creating and Managing Recipients

Sending and receiving information is the foundation of messaging, groupware, and, of course, Microsoft Exchange Server 2007. In this chapter, you start looking at the message transfer process within an Exchange system. Exchange Server 2007 is based on a multitude of messaging components, but with some analysis it becomes apparent how these components interact to create an enterprise-wide messaging system.

Recipients are objects in the Active Directory directory service. These objects in turn reference resources that can receive messages through interaction with Exchange Server 2007. Such a resource might be a mailbox in the mailbox store in which one of your users gets e-mail or a public folder in which information is shared among many users.

No matter where a resource resides, however, a recipient object for that resource is always created within Active Directory on your network. One of your main tasks as an administrator is to create and maintain these recipient objects. Therefore, in addition to discussing mailboxes and message transfer, this chapter explains how to create and manage various types of messaging recipients.

Understanding Recipient Types

Thinking of a recipient as a mailbox or simply as an object that can receive a message is tempting, and as you administer your organization, it might be convenient to take that view. But it is important to understand the ways in which the underlying architecture affects how you work with recipients in Exchange Server.

In Exchange Server, a recipient object does not receive messages. Instead, it is a reference to a resource that can receive messages. This is a subtle but important distinction. Recipient objects are contained in and maintained by Active Directory. The resources that those objects reference could be anywhere. One resource might be a mailbox for a user in your organization. A mailbox resource would be contained in the mailbox store of a particular Exchange server and maintained by that server. Another resource might be a user on the Internet. In this case, the recipient object would contain a reference to that resource, along with rules governing the transfer of messages to the Internet.

Five types of recipient objects are available in Exchange:

- **User**   A user is any individual with logon privileges on the network. With regard to Exchange Server, each user in Active Directory can be a mailbox user, a mail-enabled user, or neither. As you recall from earlier chapters, a mailbox user has an associated mailbox on an Exchange server. Each user mailbox is a private storage area that allows an individual user to send, receive, and store messages. A mail-enabled user has an e-mail address and can receive, but not send, messages.

- **Resource mailbox**   A resource mailbox is a mailbox that represents a conference room or a piece of shared equipment. Users can include resource mailboxes as resources in meeting requests, providing a simple way to schedule resource availability for an organization. There are two types of resource mailboxes in Microsoft Exchange Server 2007: room and equipment. Room mailboxes are assigned to a meeting location, such as a conference room. Equipment mailboxes are assigned to a resource that is not location specific, such as a projector or company car.

- **Mail contact**   A mail contact is essentially a pointer to a mailbox in an external messaging system and is most likely used by a person outside the organization. This type of recipient points both to an address that will be used to deliver messages sent to that person and to the properties that govern how those messages are delivered. Contacts are most often used for connecting your organization to foreign messaging systems, such as Lotus Notes or the Internet. An administrator creates contacts so that frequently used e-mail addresses are available in the Global Address List as real names. This makes it easier to send e-mail because users do not need to guess cryptic e-mail addresses.

- **Distribution group**   A distribution group is a mail-enabled group object in Active Directory. Messages sent to a group are redirected and distributed to each member of that group. Groups can contain any combination of the other types of recipients, including other groups. Distribution groups allow users to send messages to multiple recipients without having to address each recipient individually. A typical group is the one named Everyone. All Exchange recipients are made members of the Everyone group. When a public announcement is made, the sender of the announcement simply selects the Everyone group and is not forced to select every user's mailbox from the Global Address List.

- **Public folder**   A public folder is a public storage area, typically open to all users in an organization. Users can post new messages or reply to existing messages in a public folder, creating an ongoing forum for discussion of topics. Public folders can also be used to store and provide access to just about any type of document. The concept of a public folder as a recipient is sometimes difficult to grasp because the repository for information is shared.

Although a public folder is a type of recipient, it performs many more functions than just transferring or receiving messages. For that reason, this chapter focuses on the other recipient types: users, resource mailboxes, mail contacts, and distribution groups. Chapter 12, "Using Public Folders," is devoted to a full review of the features, functions, and administration requirements of public folders.

Users

Users can have two possible e-mail configurations: the mailbox user and the mail-enabled user. Each of these configurations is detailed in the sections that follow.

Mailbox Users

Mailboxes—the mainstay of any messaging system—are private, server-based storage areas in which user e-mail is kept. Every user in your organization must have access to a mailbox to send and receive messages because it is one of the primary methods of communication. In Exchange Server 2007, a user with a mailbox is referred to as a mailbox user. Mailbox users can send and receive messages as well as store messages on an Exchange server. One of your principal tasks as an administrator is to create and configure mailboxes for users.

In previous versions of Exchange Server, many of the features of mailboxes (including creating new mailboxes) were managed within the Active Directory Users and Computers tool. In Exchange Server 2007, all mailbox management happens within the Exchange

Management Console. You can create a new mailbox and create a new Active Directory user at the same time, or you can create a new mailbox for an existing user. You also use the Exchange Management Console to configure all mailbox-related properties.

Creating a New Mailbox for a New User

You can use the Exchange Management Console to create a new user in Active Directory and to create a new mailbox for that user at the same time. After you create the new user and mailbox, the user can immediately begin sending and receiving messages.

To create a new mailbox for a new user, follow these steps:

1. Click Start, point to All Programs, point to Microsoft Exchange Server 2007, and then click Exchange Management Console.

2. In the console tree, expand the Recipient Configuration node and then click the Mailbox subnode.

3. In the Action pane, click New Mailbox to start the New Mailbox Wizard, as shown in Figure 11-1.

> **Note**   You can also right-click the Recipient Configuration node or the Mailbox subnode and click New Mailbox on the shortcut menu to start the New Mailbox Wizard.

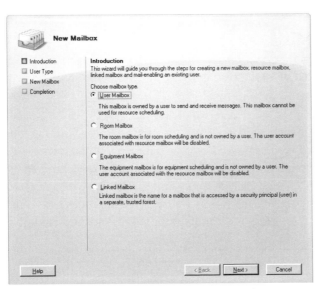

Figure 11-1   Starting the New Mailbox Wizard

4. On the Introduction page, click User Mailbox and then click Next.

5. On the User Type page, select the New User option and then click Next.

6. On the User Information page, as shown in Figure 11-2, configure the information for the new Active Directory user. Type the First Name, Initials, and Last Name. The Name field is filled in for you as you type. Type a User Logon Name that conforms to your organization's naming standards. Type and confirm a password, select whether the user must change the password the first time the user logs on with the new account, and then click Next.

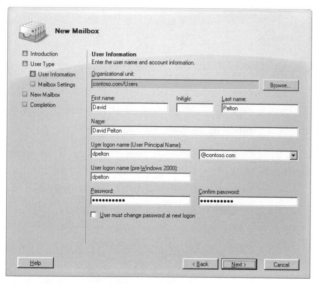

Figure 11-2   Creating the new Active Directory user in the New Mailbox Wizard

7. On the Mailbox Settings page, as shown in Figure 11-3, configure the information for the new mailbox. You can configure the following options and then click Next:

❑ **Alias**   An alias provides an alternate means of addressing the user. By default, the alias is whatever you use on the User Information page for the User Principal Name, but you can modify the alias according to your needs.

❑ **Server**   Choose the Exchange Mailbox server on which the mailbox should be created.

❑ **Storage Group**   Choose the storage group in which the mailbox should be created.

❑ **Mailbox Database**   Choose the mailbox database in which the mailbox should be created.

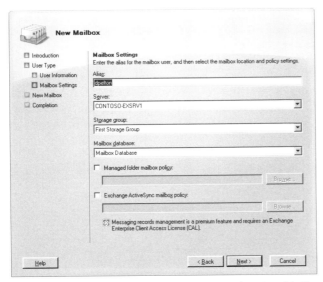

Figure 11-3   Creating the new mailbox in the New Mailbox Wizard

❑   Managed Folder Mailbox Policy. Optionally, you can specify a messaging records management (MRM) policy, to be associated with this mailbox. For example, use this option if you want this mailbox to adhere to an MRM policy such as the retention period for the mailbox data.

More Info   For more information about MRM, visit *http://technet.microsoft.com/en-us/bb123507.aspx*.

❑   Exchange ActiveSync Mailbox Policy. Optionally, you can specify an Exchange ActiveSync mailbox policy to be associated with this mailbox.

8.   On the New Mailbox page, review the settings you have configured for the new user and mailbox. You can click Back to return through the wizard pages to make changes. If the configuration looks good, click New to create the new user and mailbox.

9.   On the Completion page, click Finish to exit the New Mailbox Wizard.

Management Shell

You can also create a new user and mailbox using the Exchange Management Shell. The cmdlet you use is named `New-Mailbox`. You also need to supply a number of parameters that identify the name of the user, as well as the Exchange storage group and database in which the mailbox will be created.

The syntax for creating a new user and mailbox is

```
New-Mailbox -Alias <aliasname> -Database <"StorageGroup\MailboxDatabase">
    -Name <FirstLast> -OrganizationalUnit <OUName> -FirstName <First>
    -LastName <Last> -DisplayName <"DisplayName"> -UserPrincipalName
    <userprincipalname>
```

For example, to create a user named Dan Jump with the alias Dan in the first mailbox database of the first storage group in an organization named contoso.com, you could use the cmdlet:

```
New-Mailbox -Alias dan -Database "Storage Group 1\Mailbox Database 1"
    -Name DanJump -OrganizationalUnit Users -FirstName Dan
    -LastName Jump -DisplayName "Dan Jump" -UserPrincipalName
    djump@contoso.com
```

Creating a New Mailbox for an Existing User

Creating a new mailbox for an existing user is even easier than creating a new user and mailbox at the same time. You use the same wizard and same basic procedure, except that instead of having to configure information about the Active Directory user, you just select the user you want to create the mailbox for.

To create a new mailbox for an existing user, follow these steps:

1. Click Start, point to All Programs, point to Exchange Server 2007, and then click Exchange Management Console.

2. In the console tree, expand the Recipient Configuration node and click the Mailbox subnode.

3. In the Action pane, click New Mailbox to start the New Mailbox Wizard.

4. On the Introduction page, click User Mailbox and then click Next.

5. On the User Type page, click Existing User. Click Browse, click the name of the user for whom you want to create a new mailbox, and then click OK. Click Next.

6. On the Mailbox Settings page, configure the information for the new mailbox (as described in the previous section) and then click Next.

7. On the New Mailbox page, review the settings you have configured for the new mailbox. You can click Back to return through the wizard pages to make changes. If the configuration looks good, click New to create the new mailbox.

8. On the Completion page, click Finish to exit the New Mailbox Wizard.

Management Shell

You can also create a new mailbox for an existing user using the Exchange Management Shell. The cmdlet you use is named `Enable-Mailbox`. You also need to supply parameters that identify the Exchange storage group and database in which the mailbox will be created.

The syntax for creating a new user and mailbox is:

```
Enable-Mailbox <userprincipalname>
-Database <"StorageGroup\MailboxDatabase">
```

For example, to create a mailbox for a user named Brad Joseph, you use the following cmdlet:

```
Enable-Mailbox bjoseph@contoso.com -Database "MyServer\First Storage
    Group\Mailbox Database"
```

Configuring Mailbox Properties

No matter which method you use to create mailboxes, you configure them in the same way—with the mailbox's property sheet. To do so, select any mailbox in the Exchange Management Console and then choose Properties from the Action pane (or right-click the Mailbox and choose Properties from the shortcut menu). The property sheet for a mailbox has quite a few tabs. The next several sections cover the tabs for mailbox configuration.

General Tab

The General tab, shown in Figure 11-4, lets you view general information about the mailbox, including the size of the mailbox and the total items it contains. This tab also shows the location of the mailbox, including the server and database on which the mailbox resides, along with some administrative information such as when the user last logged on and when the mailbox was last modified.

You can change the alias for the mailbox. The alias is an alternate e-mail alias that can be used when sending a message to the recipient (especially from an outside system like the Internet). The alias can be a combination of characters separated by a period but can contain no spaces. For example, the user Dan Park in the organization contoso.com might have the alias dan.park, making his e-mail address dan.park@contoso.com.

You can also specify whether to hide the mailbox from Exchange address lists. By default, all recipients except public folders are visible to users via the Global Address List. You can select the Hide From Exchange Address Lists option to hide the mailbox from that list or from other lists created in the Exchange Management Console. The mailbox can still receive e-mail; it simply is not included in address lists.

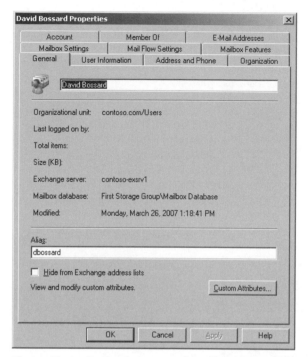

Figure 11-4   Reviewing general mailbox usage information on the General tab

Clicking Custom Attributes displays the Exchange Custom Attributes dialog box, as shown in Figure 11-5. This dialog box lets you type information about a mailbox in 15 custom fields. These fields can be used for any information you need to include that isn't available on the other tabs. Most of these fields are available to users in the Global Address List. By default, these fields are labeled Custom Attribute 1 through Custom Attribute 15.

User Information Tab

The User Information tab, shown in Figure 11-6, is where you configure basic user information. The first name, middle initial, and last name that you type here are used to generate a display name, which is the name of the recipient as it appears in the Exchange Management Console.

The Simple Display Name is an alternate name for the mailbox. It appears when the full display name cannot be shown for some reason. This situation often occurs when multiple language versions of the Exchange Management Console are used on the same network.

You can also enter the Web page for the user and any notes you might find useful. Most of this information is available to users when they browse the Global Address List.

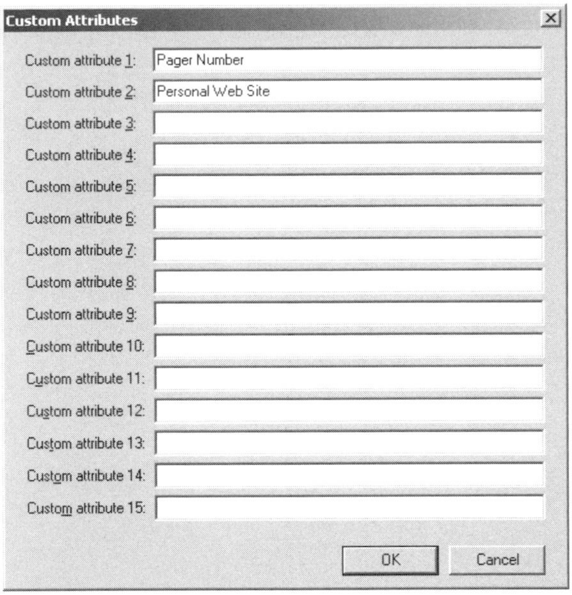

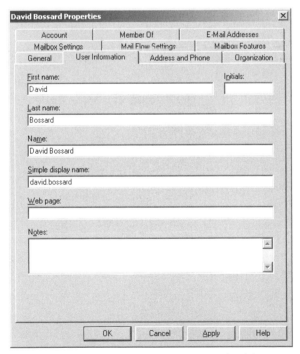

Figure 11-5   Typing additional recipient information by using custom attribute fields

David Bossard Properties

Account	Member Of	E-Mail Addresses
Mailbox Settings	Mail Flow Settings	Mailbox Features
General	User Information	Address and Phone	Organization

First name:
David

Initials:

Last name:
Bossard

Name:
David Bossard

Simple display name:
david.bossard

Web page:

Notes:

OK   Cancel   Apply   Help

Figure 11-6   Reviewing user names and addresses on the User Information tab

Address and Phone Tab

The Address And Phone tab, shown in Figure 11-7, allows you to configure further information about a user, including a street address and different phone numbers. This information is also available to users when they browse the Global Address List.

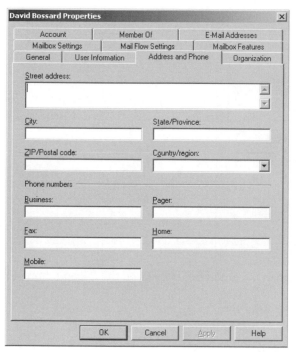

Figure 11-7   Reviewing user names and addresses on the Address And Phone tab

Organization Tab

The Organization tab, shown in Figure 11-8, is used to configure additional information about the user's position in the company. You can use this tab to specify a user's manager and also view a list of people who report directly to the user. Click Browse to display a list of recipients in the organization. All information configured on this tab is made available in the Global Address List.

Account Tab

The Account tab, shown in Figure 11-9, shows information about the user's Active Directory account. You can view or change the logon names for the Active Directory user account associated with the mailbox.

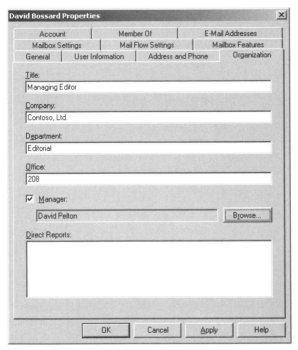

Figure 11-8 Describing a user's position in the organization by using the Organization tab

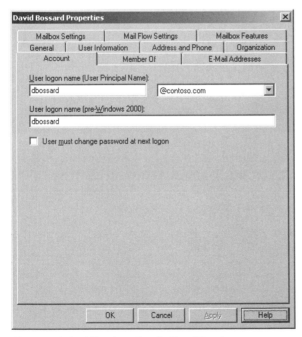

Figure 11-9 Viewing the Active Directory user account associated with the mailbox

Member Of Tab

The Member Of tab, shown in Figure 11-10, lists the groups to which the user currently belongs. You cannot manage group membership from this tab, however. To manage group membership, you must use Active Directory Users and Computers. For more information, see the section titled "Distribution Groups" later in this chapter.

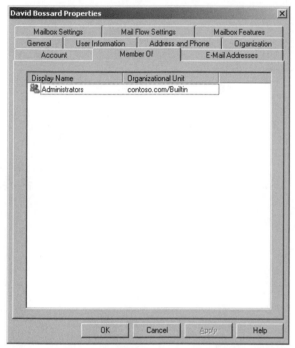

Figure 11-10 Viewing the groups to which a mailbox belongs

E-Mail Addresses Tab

The E-Mail Addresses tab, shown in Figure 11-11, lets you configure the e-mail addresses for the mailbox. You can modify the existing addresses or create additional addresses. Each mailbox must have at least one primary Simple Mail Transfer Protocol (SMTP) address. By default, each recipient will have e-mail addresses based on the e-mail address policies that are defined in your Exchange organization.

Click Add to add a new e-mail address for the mailbox. You can add either another SMTP address or a custom address for connecting with other messaging systems, such as Lotus Notes or X.400 systems.

Mailbox Settings Tab

The Mailbox Settings tab, shown in Figure 11-12, allows you to configure Messaging Records Management (MRM) and Storage Quotas for the mailbox. Click either setting and then click Properties to display a property sheet for those settings.

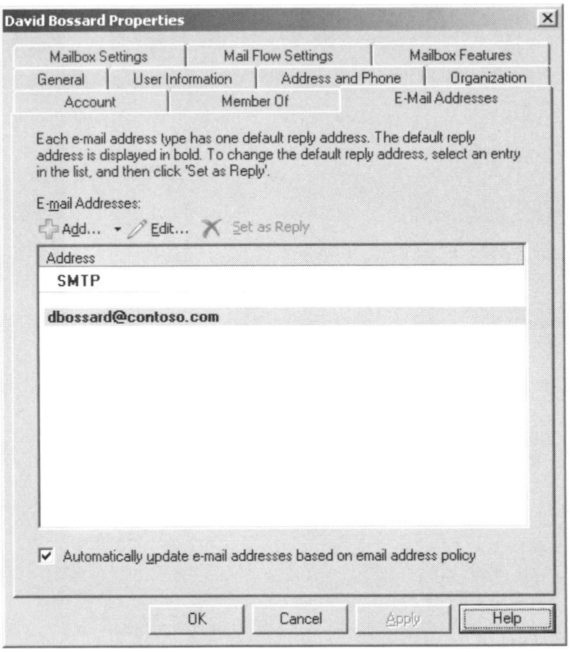

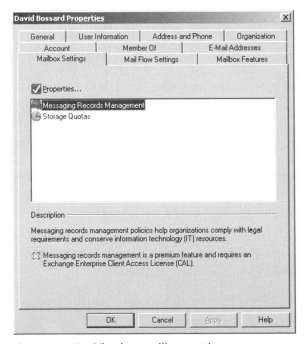

Figure 11-11   Viewing e-mail addresses for a mailbox

Figure 11-12   Viewing mailbox settings

MRM polices help your organization comply with legal requirements, such as retention and deletion policies for messages. The Messaging Records Management property sheet, shown in Figure 11-13, allows you to configure the following properties:

- **Managed Folder Mailbox Policy**   Select this check box and then click Browse to locate the policy for managed folders.

- **Enable Retention Hold For Items In This Mailbox**   Select this check box to configure dates for retaining items in the mailbox, regardless of whether users delete those items. This setting is useful if your organization needs to maintain records for a set period of time.

Figure 11-13   Configuring Messaging Records Management properties

Storage Quotas let you govern the size of a user's mailbox. The Storage Quotas dialog box, shown in Figure 11-14, lets you set parameters for storage limits and deleted item retention time. By default, these values are inherited from settings made at the server level for all mailboxes. You can use the settings on this tab to override the database defaults and configure settings for the individual mailbox.

Often, users send and save huge attachments or are simply negligent about cleaning out their mailboxes. Either of these situations can cause a great deal of disk space to be consumed on your server. Fortunately, administrators can set any of three storage limits on a mailbox:

- **Issue Warning At (KB)**   Specifies the mailbox size, in kilobytes, at which a warning is issued to the user to clean out the mailbox.

- **Prohibit Send At (KB)**   Specifies the mailbox size, in kilobytes, at which the user is prohibited from sending any new e-mail. This prohibition ends as soon as the user clears enough space to fall back under the limit.

- **Prohibit Send And Receive At (KB)**   Specifies the mailbox size, in kilobytes, at which the user is prohibited from sending, receiving, or even editing any e-mail. All the user can do is delete messages. This prohibition ends as soon as the user clears enough space to fall back under the limit. To do this, a user must delete items from his or her mailbox and then empty the Deleted Items folder. When a user sends a message to a recipient who is prohibited from receiving any new messages, a non-delivery report is generated and returned to the sending user. Prohibiting the sending and receiving of e-mail is a pretty strong measure for an administrator to take. It is recommended that you implement this solution only if you experience continued problems that you cannot otherwise resolve.

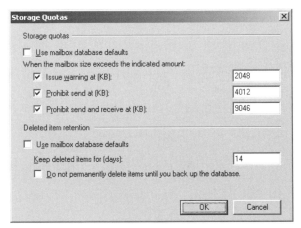

Figure 11-14   Setting storage quotas for a mailbox

Exchange Server 2007 also includes a feature that gives users a certain amount of time to recover items that have been deleted from their Deleted Items folder. When a user deletes a message using a client application such as Microsoft Outlook, that message is placed in the user's Deleted Items folder. Only when the user deletes the item from the Deleted Items folder is it actually removed from the user's personal folders. However, the deleted item is still not actually deleted from the mailbox store. Instead, it is marked as hidden and is kept for a specified amount of time. During that period, the user can recover the item with the client application.

The Deleted Item Retention area of the Storage Quotas dialog box specifies the retention time for deleted items in that particular mailbox, overriding any default settings inherited from the server level. You can either use the default value that is configured for the entire mailbox store or override it with a different value for the selected mailbox. If you choose to override the value, you can also specify that deleted messages not be permanently removed until the mailbox store has been backed up.

Mail Flow Settings Tab

The Mail Flow Settings tab, shown in Figure 11-15, provides access to features that govern mail flow, including features for Delivery Options, Message Size Restrictions, and Message

Delivery Restrictions. As with the settings on the Mailbox Settings tab, the settings on the Mail Flow Settings tab are used to override properties that are by default inherited by settings made at the server level. You use settings on this tab to change settings for the particular mailbox.

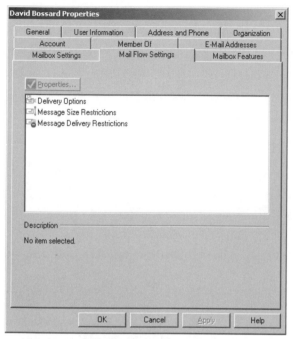

Figure 11-15   Changing mail flow settings for a mailbox

The Delivery Options property sheet, shown in Figure 11-16, governs several different additional actions that can be taken when messages are sent to or from the mailbox. Granting the Send On Behalf permission allows another user to send messages on behalf of the user of the mailbox you are configuring. Users included in this list can send messages that appear as though they came from the selected mailbox. Any messages sent include the names of both the primary mailbox user and the user who actually sent the message. This permission might be used by an assistant who needs to send a message from a manager who is out of the office.

Note   The Send On Behalf permission can also be helpful in troubleshooting. If you assign this permission to yourself, as administrator, you can send test messages from any recipient in the organization. This practice can be a great way to test connections from remote servers. It is recommended that you use test mailboxes created for this purpose and not actual user mailboxes. Many users would consider this type of extended access to their e-mail an intrusion.

Figure 11-16   Setting delivery options for a mailbox

You can also use the Delivery Options property sheet to assign a forwarding address for a mailbox. Any messages sent to the mailbox are routed to the mailbox of the designated alternate recipient. You can also specify that messages be sent both to the primary mailbox and to the alternate recipient. Exchange Server will deliver to each mailbox a separate reference to the message, so deleting the message from one mailbox does not cause it to be deleted from another. Finally, you can specify the maximum number of recipients to which a user can send a single message. By default, there is no limit.

The Message Size Restrictions property sheet, shown in Figure 11-17, allows you to set limits on the size of messages that can be transferred out of or into a particular mailbox. If an incoming or outgoing message exceeds its respective limit, it is not sent or received, and the sender of the message receives a nondelivery report.

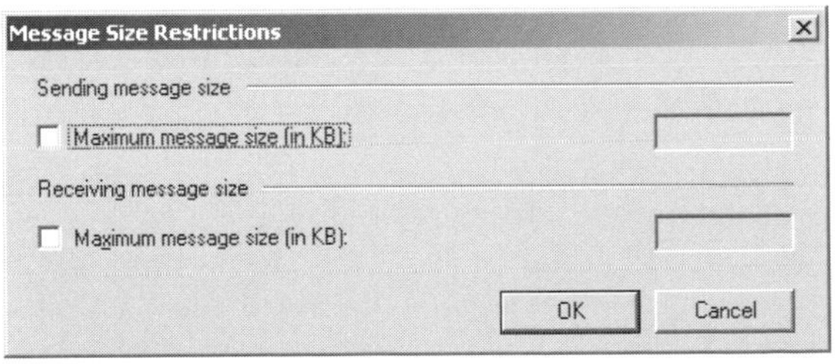

Figure 11-17   Setting message size restrictions for a mailbox

The Message Delivery Restrictions property sheet, shown in Figure 11-18, allows you to restrict the messages coming into the selected mailbox. The default is to accept messages from all senders. You can specify that messages be accepted only from designated senders or that messages be accepted from everyone except a list of specific users. Select the option you want and click Add to select from recipients listed in Active Directory. You can also specify that messages be accepted only from authenticated users (that is, users with valid logon credentials for the network). This option works in conjunction with the other message restrictions you set.

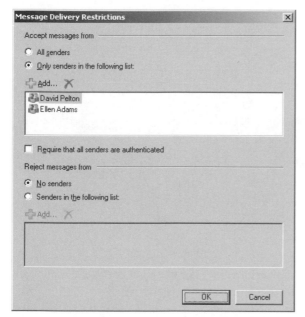

Figure 11-18   Setting restrictions on a mailbox

Note   Setting general limits for an entire site or server at the same time is much more efficient than setting them for each individual user. Setting limits for a particular mailbox is one way of dealing with users who need to send large messages or who simply let messages accumulate.

Mailbox Features Tab

The Mailbox Features tab lets you enable and disable extra features for a user's mailbox, including the following:

- Outlook Web Access
- Exchange ActiveSync

- Unified Messaging
- MAPI

Again, these features are usually enabled or disabled for all users at the organization or server level, and it is better to leave management at those levels. However, this tab provides a way to override settings from higher levels and enable or disable features for a specific user.

Management Shell

All of the properties you can set for a mailbox using the Exchange Management Console can also be set using the Exchange Management Shell. You can use the `Set-User` and `Set-Mailbox` cmdlets to configure the properties discussed in the previous sections. `Set-User` modifies properties of the user object in Active Directory. `Set-Mailbox` modifies mailbox-specific properties. You can use these cmdlets to modify the properties of one user or mailbox at a time or you can pipeline the output of a `Get` cmdlet to modify multiple users.

For more information on the `Set-User` and `Set-Mailbox` commands, see the Exchange Server 2007 help files. For more information on getting help with the parameters for these commands, see Chapter 10, "Managing Exchange Server 2007."

Mail-Enabled Users

As you know, a mail-enabled user is simply a user that has an e-mail address but no mailbox on an Exchange server. This means that the user can receive e-mail through its custom address but cannot send e-mail using the Exchange system. As with mailboxes, you can create a new mail user while you create the Active Directory user or you can mail-enable an existing user.

To create a new mail-enabled user, follow these steps:

1. In the Exchange Management Console, click the Recipient Configuration node.

2. In the Action pane, click New Mail User (you can also right-click the Recipient Configuration node and then click New Mail User on the shortcut menu).

3. On the Introduction page of the New Mail User Wizard, click New User and then click Next. (If you are mail-enabling an existing user, click Existing User at this point and locate the user.)

4. On the User Information page, shown in Figure 11-19, type the name of the user, the user logon name, and the user's password, and then click Next.

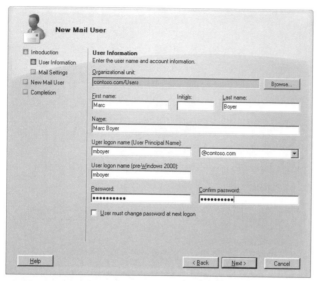

Figure 11-19   Creating a mail-enabled user

5. On the Mail Settings page, supply an alias if you do not want to use the default value. You must also create an external address, such as an SMTP address or address for an external mail system. Click Next.

6. On the New Mail User page, review the settings you have configured for the new mail user. You can click Back to return through the wizard pages to make changes. If the configuration looks good, click New to create the new mail user.

7. On the Completion page, click Finish.

Management Shell

You can also create a new mail user by using the Exchange Management Shell. The cmdlet you use is `New-MailUser`. You also need to supply a number of parameters that identify the name of the user and the external mail address.

The syntax for creating a new mail user is:

```
New-MailUser -Name <name> -FirstName <First> -LastName <Last>
-ExternalEmailAddress <externalmailaddress> -UserPrincipalName
<userprincipalname> -OrganizationalUnit <OU>
```

For example, to create a user named Marc Boyer with the external address marc.boyer@adventureworks.com, you could use the cmdlet:

```
New-MailUser -Name Marc -FirstName Marc -LastName Boyer -ExternalEmailAddress
marc.boyer@adventureworks.com -UserPrincipalName marc@contoso.com
-OrganizationalUnit contoso.com
```

Mailbox Resources

Resource mailboxes are mailboxes that are not designed to receive messages, but instead to represent resources in an organization that users can schedule—resources like conference rooms, projectors, or company cars. Users can include resource mailboxes in meeting requests the same way they would include any mailbox. This provides users with a simple way to schedule the use of resources in your organization.

Exchange Server 2007 supports two types of resource mailboxes:

- **Room Mailbox**   This type of resource mailbox is assigned to a meeting location, such as a meeting room or auditorium.

- **Equipment Mailbox**   This type of resource mailbox is assigned to a resource that does not have a location.

You can create both types of resource mailboxes using the same New Mailbox Wizard that you use when you create a new mailbox for a user. In the Exchange Management Console, with the Recipient Configuration node selected, click New Mailbox in the Action pane. On the Introduction page of the New Mailbox Wizard, shown in Figure 11-20, choose whether you want to create a Room Mailbox or an Equipment Mailbox.

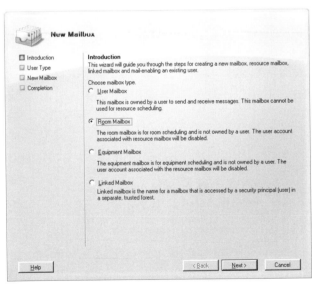

Figure 11-20 Creating a resource mailbox

The steps of the wizard are much like creating a mailbox for a user. You select whether to associate the resource mailbox with a new or existing user, select the user or create the user details in Active Directory, configure the mailbox settings, and you're done. Users can immediately begin including the resource in their meeting requests.

Management Shell

You can also create a new mailbox resource by using the Exchange Management Shell. The cmdlet you use is `New-MailBox`. You also need to supply a number of parameters that identify the resource.

The syntax for creating a new mailbox resource is:

```
New-Mailbox -database <"StorageGroup\MailboxDatabase"> -Name <Name>
-OrganizationalUnit <"OU"> -DisplayName <"DisplayName"> -UserPrincipalName
<userprincipalname> -Type
```

The **type** parameter will be either **room** or **equipment**. For example, to create a room mailbox named Train1 in an organizational unit named Training Rooms, you could use the cmdlet:

```
New-Mailbox -database "Storage Group 1\Mailbox Database 1" -Name Train1
-OrganizationalUnit "Training Rooms" -DisplayName "Train1"
-UserPrincipalName train1@contoso.com -Room
```

Mail Contacts

Mail contacts are objects that serve as pointers to resources outside an Exchange organization. You can think of a contact as a pointer that contains an address for that outside resource and rules for handling the transmission of messages. Whenever a user sends a message to a mail contact, Exchange Server forwards the message to the appropriate foreign messaging system. Contacts have many of the same attributes as mailboxes and can be viewed in the Global Address List.

Creating a Mail Contact

To create a new mail contact, follow these steps:

1. In the console tree of Exchange Management Console, expand the Recipient Configuration node and then click the Mail Contact subnode.

2. In the Action pane, click New Mail Contact.

3. On the Introduction page of the New Mail Contact Wizard, click New Contact and then click Next. (You can also create a Mail Contact for an existing user by clicking Browse.)

4. On the Contact Information page, shown in Figure 11-21, type the name of the mail contact and the alias (if you want it to be different from the default value), create the external e-mail address for the contact, and then click Next.

5. On the New Mail Contact page, review the configuration summary, which contains information about the options that you selected for the new mail contact. To make changes, click Back. To create the new mail contact, click New.

6. On the New Mail Contact page, review the settings you have configured for the new mail user. You can click Back to return through the wizard pages to make changes. If the configuration looks good, click New to create the new mail user.

7. On the Completion page, click Finish.

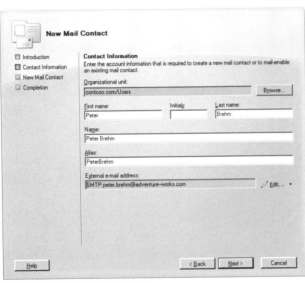

Figure 11-21 Creating a new mail contact

Management Shell

You can also create a new mail contact by using the Exchange Management Shell. The cmdlet you use is **New-MailContact**. You also need to supply a number of parameters that identify the name of the contact and the external mail address.

The syntax for creating a new mail contact is:

```
New-MailContact -Name <"name"> -ExternalEmailAddress <address>
-OrganizationalUnit <OU>
```

For example, to create a user named Peter Brehm with the external address peter.brehm@adventure-works.com, you could use the cmdlet:

```
New-MailContact -Name "Peter Brehm" -ExternalEmailAddress
peter.brehm@adventure-works.com -OrganizationalUnit contoso.com
```

Configuring a Mail Contact

Like all other objects, mail contacts are configured by means of a property sheet. The tabs for a mail contact are identical to those for a mailbox user, except that only a subset of tabs is available. You will, of course, encounter a couple of differences:

- On the General tab of a mail contact's property sheet, you choose whether to use MAPI rich text format (RTF) for the mail contact. You can set this property to always use MAPI RTF, never use it, or rely on the settings configured in the client's messaging software.

- On the Mail Flow Settings tab, you cannot configure storage quotas because the user has no mailbox in the Exchange organization.

Distribution Groups

In Active Directory, a *group* is a container of sorts that can hold users and other groups. You can assign permissions to a group that are inherited by all the objects that are members of that group. This makes the group a valuable security construct. Exchange Server 2007 also uses groups for another purpose. A group can be mail-enabled and then populated with other mail-enabled or mailbox recipients to make a distribution list—a term you might be familiar with from earlier versions of Exchange Server. A group can contain users, mail contacts, public folders, and even other distribution groups. When you send a message to a distribution group, the message is sent to each member of the list individually. Distribution groups are visible in the Global Address List.

You can create three types of distribution groups in Exchange Server 2007:

- **Mail-Enabled Universal Distribution Group**   This is the primary type of distribution group you will use for sending e-mail messages to large groups of recipients. You cannot assign permissions to a mail-enabled universal distribution group.

- **Mail-Enabled Universal Security Group**   You can use this type of group to assign permissions to a group of recipients to access permissions to resources in Active Directory, as well as to send e-mail messages to all recipients in the group.

- **Dynamic Distribution Group**   This type of group does not have a static list of recipients, but instead uses recipient filters to generate its membership when a message is sent to the group. For example, you might use a dynamic distribution group to send messages to all recipients outside the organization that are in a particular company, or to all users that are in a particular department or located on a particular floor of a building. When someone sends a message to this dynamic distribution group, Exchange queries Active Directory for all recipients that match the filter and condition specified.

Creating a Distribution Group

Creating a new distribution group is easy and follows largely the same procedure as creating a mailbox. To create a new distribution group, follow these steps:

1. In the console tree of the Exchange Management Console, expand the Recipient Configuration node, and then click the Distribution Group subnode.

2. In the Action pane, click New Distribution Group.

3. On the Introduction page of the New Distribution Group Wizard, click New Group and then click Next. (You can also click Existing Group to mail-enable a security group that already exists in Active Directory.)

4. On the Group Information page, shown in Figure 11-22, choose whether you want to create a new distribution group or security group. Select the organizational unit, type a name for the group, change the alias if you want it to be different from the default, and then click Next.

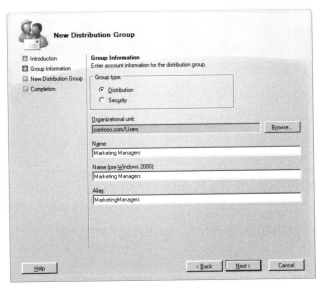

Figure 11-22   Creating a new distribution group

5. On the New Distribution Group page, review the settings you configured for the new distribution group. You can click Back to return through the wizard pages to make changes. If the configuration looks good, click New to create the new distribution group.

6. On the Completion page, click Finish.

Management Shell

You can also create a new distribution group by using the Exchange Management Shell. The cmdlet you use is `New-DistributionGroup`. You also need to supply a number of parameters that identify the group.

The syntax for creating a new distribution group is:

```
New-DistributionGroup -Name <"Name"> -OrganizationalUnit <"OU">
-SAMAccountName <"SAMAccountName"> -Type <"Type">
```

For example, to create a distribution group named Marketing Managers, you could use the cmdlet:

```
New-DistributionGroup -Name "Marketing Managers" -OrganizationalUnit
"Contoso.com/Users" -SAMAccountName "Marketing Managers" -Type "Distribution"
```

To create a new security distribution group instead of a normal distribution group, you would use the type parameter `Security` instead of `Distribution`.

Configuring a Group

You configure a group in the same way that you configure other recipients—with a property sheet. Many of the tabs are identical to those of the same name for user objects; refer to the "Users" section earlier in this chapter for details on those tabs. Some of the tabs found on a user's property sheet simply don't exist for a group. This section covers the three tabs that do differ for a group.

Group Information Tab

The Group Information tab allows you to change the name of the group and to assign the group a manager. The manager of the group controls the group's membership. By default, the administrator who creates the group is the manager, but you can designate as manager any user, group, or contact in the Global Address List. If you give management to another user, that user can use Outlook to modify the group's membership and does not need access to the Exchange Management Console. You can relieve yourself of a great deal of work by specifying managers for the groups you create. As groups grow larger, they can consume a considerable amount of management time.

Members Tab

The Members tab lists every member of the group. Click Add to access the Active Directory list, from which you can add new members to the group. You can click Remove to remove selected members. As mentioned earlier, groups can hold any other type of object, including users, contacts, public folders, and even other groups.

Advanced Tab

The Advanced tab, shown in Figure 11-23, allows you to create a simple display name for the group.

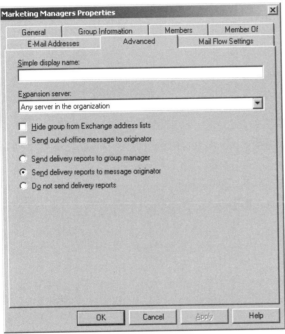

Figure 11-23 Setting advanced properties for a group

You can also configure several options that govern how the distribution group works:

- **Expansion Server** Whenever a message is sent to a group, the group must be expanded so that the message can be sent to each member of the group. A single Exchange server performs this expansion. The default choice is Any Server In The Organization. This setting means that the home server of the user sending the message always expands the group. You can also designate a specific server to handle expanding the group, which is a good choice if you have a large group. In this case, expansion could consume a large amount of server resources, which can compromise performance of busy servers.

- **Hide Group From Exchange Address Lists**   If you select this option, the group is not visible in the Global Address List.

- **Send Out-Of-Office Message To Originator**   If you select this option, users can configure Exchange clients to reply automatically to any messages received while they are away from their offices. When this option is selected, users who send messages to the group can receive these automatic messages. For particularly large groups, it's best not to allow out-of-office messages to be delivered because of the excess network traffic they generate.

- **Send Delivery Reports To Group Manager**   If you select this option, the owner of the group is notified whenever an error occurs during the delivery of a message to the group or to one of its members. This option is not available when the group has not been assigned an owner.

- **Send Delivery Reports To Message Originator**   If you select this option, any error notifications are sent to the user who sent a message to the group. If the Send Delivery Reports To Group Owner option is also selected, both the sender and the owner are notified.

- **Do Not Send Delivery Reports**   If you select this option, no delivery reports are sent.

Real World   Using Message Restrictions on Groups

The Message Size Restrictions and Message Delivery Restrictions options on the Mail Flow Settings tab of a group's property sheet are often much more useful for groups than for individual users. In large organizations, groups can grow quite large, sometimes holding thousands of users. Because of the possibility of misuse, providing general access to groups this large is usually not a good idea. Imagine the increase in traffic if your users sent messages to thousands of users every time their kids had candy bars to sell or they found a good joke. Placing delivery restrictions on large groups allows you to limit access to the groups to a few select, responsible users.

Another potential risk is that someone from the Internet could e-mail everyone in your company, using a group's SMTP address. Imagine what your job would be like on the day that an anonymous person e-mailed malicious information to the entire company. Limiting access to the group also helps prevent this type of unwanted e-mail from occurring.

Creating Dynamic Distribution Groups

Exchange Server 2007 introduces the dynamic distribution group (which is modeled after the query-based distribution groups of Exchange Server 2003). This type of group is dynamic because instead of making specific objects members of the group, the membership is generated at the time a message is sent based on general filters that you create. For example, you can create a dynamic distribution group that includes all mailbox-enabled Exchange users. No one has to manually update the membership of the group because whenever a message is sent to the list, the membership is generated on the fly.

Although dynamic distribution groups are an exciting and useful addition to Exchange Server 2007, you need to take a few limitations and costs into consideration:

■ The on-the-fly generation of members for a query-based distribution group generates additional overhead on the server that performs that generation—the expansion server. Expect the server to show increased CPU time and disk activity each time a message is sent to the group.

■ The generation also causes increased network traffic and Active Directory utilization because the expansion server must send a query to Active Directory to resolve the current membership each time a message is sent to the group.

Because of the additional overhead generated by query-based distribution groups, they are best used for making periodic announcements to important groups of users and are not intended as a replacement for standard distribution groups.

Creating a dynamic distribution group is straightforward. In the Exchange Management Console, expand the Recipient Configuration node, select the Distribution Group subnode and, in the Action pane, click New Dynamic Distribution Group. Name the group, give it an alias, and click Next. On the Filter Settings page, shown in Figure 11-24, you can choose from a number of predefined filters. On the next page, the Conditions page, you have the option of customizing the filtering of recipients. If you do not want to customize the filter, you can just leave this page alone and click Next, finish the wizard, and create the group.

Custom filtering works much like setting up a messaging rule in Outlook. First, select a condition. Conditions relate to attributes of the mailbox such as state, department, company, or any of the custom attributes your organization uses. After selecting a condition, edit the condition. For example, you can specify a particular state or department and create a dynamic distribution group that includes all mailbox users who are in the Marketing department.

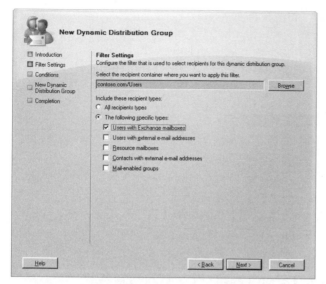

Figure 11-24   Setting a filter for a dynamic distribution group

Filtering Recipients

When you have relatively few recipients, it is easy to find specific recipients or groups of recipients by simply ordering your list using the column headers in the Exchange Management Console. However, when you have hundreds or thousands of recipients in an organization, you need more powerful tools for isolating the recipients you want to work with. The Exchange Management Console offers a filtering tool for recipients so that only selected types of recipients are shown. For example, you can choose to view only mailbox users or only contacts, or you can create more complex filters that let you view only recipients for which a certain attribute is true.

To apply a filter, in any recipient view in the Exchange Management Console, click the Create Filter button at the top of the view to open the filter commands, as shown in Figure 11-25. Build an expression by selecting an attribute from the left-most drop-down menu, choosing an operator (such as Equals, Does Not Equal, Contains, Does Not Contain, Starts With, Ends with, Is Present, or Is Not Present), and type a value. For example, you might build an expression by selecting City in the left drop-down menu, choosing the operator Equals, and then typing Dallas for the value. This creates a filter that shows only recipients for whom the City attribute is Dallas. After you create a filter, click Apply Filter to view the filtered recipient list. You can also create more complicated filters by clicking Add Expression to build multiple expressions. For example, you might create three expressions: one that filters by a particular city, one that filters by a particular department, and one that filters by office numbers starting with a particular digit. The combined filtering effect of these expressions would return a list of recipients that are in a specified department, in a particular range of offices, and in a particular city.

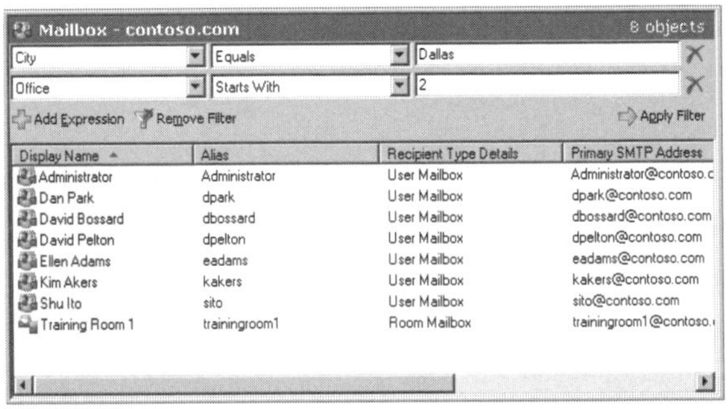

Figure 11-25   Filtering a view in the Exchange Management Console

Templates

A *template* is a recipient object that is used as a model for creating other recipient objects of that type. Every recipient type except public folders can serve as a template. To create a template, create a recipient object as you normally would. Enter any information that you want to use in the model. If, for example, you are creating a mailbox user template for new employees, you might type all the organizational, phone, and address information for your company.

Note   When you create a recipient to use as a template, you will probably want to hide the recipient from the address book. That way, users won't be able to view the template in the Global Address List. You will always be able to see it in Active Directory Users and Computers or the Exchange Management Console. Also name your template in such a way that it is both easy to find and easy to distinguish from regular recipients. You can prefix the name with "template" so that all templates are grouped together, or even with "ztemplate" so that they are shown at the end of the list.

Creating a new mailbox from a template requires using the Exchange Management Shell. To create a new mailbox, you use two commands. The first command retrieves the template information and stores it in a temporary variable named $Template:

```
$Template = Get-Mailbox <"TemplateName">
```

The second command uses the information you retrieved to create the mailbox:

```
New-Mailbox -Name <"Name"> -UserPrincipalName <"userprincipalname">
-Database <"ServerName\MailboxDatabase"> -OrganizationalUnit <"OU">
-TemplateInstance $Template
```

> **Note**   For more information about using templates to create recipients, includ-
> ing how to create multiple recipients at one time from a single template, consult
> the Exchange Server 2007 help files.

Address Lists

Address lists are collections of recipients that make it easier for users to find particular
recipients in your organization. Address lists are automatically populated, so you don't
have to add recipients manually. Exchange Server 2007 features six default address lists,
as shown in Figure 11-26.

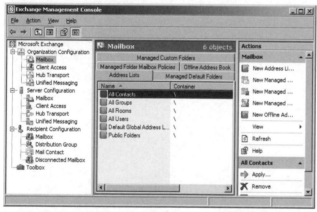

Figure 11-26   Viewing address lists in the Exchange Management Console

- **All Contacts**   This address list contains all mail-enabled contacts in your organization. Mail-enabled contacts are those recipients who have an external e-mail address.

- **All Groups**   This address list contains all distribution groups in your organization.

- **All Rooms**   This address list contains all mailbox resources that have been designated as a room in your organization.

- **All Users**   This address list contains all mail-enabled users in your organization. A
  mail-enabled user represents a user outside your Exchange organization. Each mail-
  enabled user has an external e-mail address.

■ **Default Global Address List**   This address list contains all mail-enabled users, contacts, groups, or rooms in the organization.

■ **Public Folders**   This address list contains all public folders in your organization.

In large organizations, finding recipients in the default address lists can be cumbersome for users. You can create custom address lists to further organize recipients. For example, you might create a custom address list that includes only mailbox users from a particular department. You can also create subcategories in a custom address list, which allow you to add a hierarchical structure to the otherwise flat view provided by the address list. For example, you might create a custom address list for all users in a particular country and then create a category within that address list that groups users by cities within that country.

To create a custom address list in the Exchange Management Console, follow these steps:

1. In the console tree of the Exchange Management Console, expand the Organization Configuration node, and then click the Mailbox subnode.

2. In the Action pane, click New Address List.

3. On the Introduction page of the New Address List Wizard, shown in Figure 11-27, type a name for the address list. By default, the address list is created in the main address list container, but you can click Browse to select a different container. Choose which types of recipients to include in the address list, and then click Next.

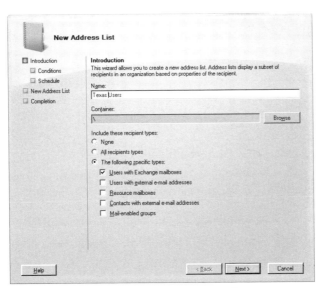

Figure 11-27   Creating a custom address list

4. On the Conditions page, shown in Figure 11-28, you can select a condition to further customize your address list by recipient attribute. This page is optional. If you don't want to further customize the address list, just click Next. If you do want to set conditions, first select the condition. Conditions relate to attributes of the mailbox such as state, department, company, or any of the custom attributes your organization uses. After selecting a condition, edit the condition in the lower window—specifying a particular state or department, for example. At any point while setting conditions, you can click Preview to view a list of recipients that appear in the address list. When you finish setting conditions, click Next.

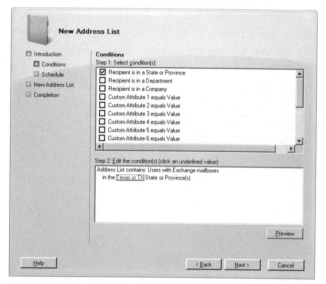

Figure 11-28   Creating conditions for a custom address list

Note   The values that you enter for conditions need to exactly match those that appear in the recipient's attributes.

5. On the Schedule page, you can specify whether Exchange should generate the address list immediately or at a scheduled time. In large organizations, address lists can take some time to generate and to avoid consuming system resources, you can schedule the list to be compiled during hours of low usage.

6. On the New Address List page, review your settings. Click New to create the address list.

7. On the Completion page, confirm whether the address list was created successfully. A status of Completed indicates that the wizard completed the task successfully. A

status of Failed indicates that the task was not completed. If the task fails, review the summary for an explanation, and then click Back to make any changes. Click Finish to complete the New Address List Wizard.

Address lists can be quite useful in large or complex organizations. Users can open these lists in client applications and find information about recipients quickly. Administrators can use the lists in the Exchange Management Console to help organize recipients.

Summary

This chapter discussed how to create and work with recipients, the destination of all Exchange interactions. You learned about several of the basic types of recipients in Exchange Server 2007—mailbox users, resource mailboxes, mail contacts, and distribution groups—including how to create and configure each. You also learned how to filter recipients and change the recipient scope in Exchange Management Console to make finding recipients easier in large organizations. You learned how to create a template that can serve as a model for creating recipients and create address lists that group recipients in different ways. The next chapter looks at another type of recipient available in an Exchange organization—the public folder.

Chapter 12

Using Public Folders

Sharing information is a powerful means of facilitating workgroups and teams. When members of a team are located in geographically distant locations, the ability to share information is even more important. Microsoft Exchange Server 2007 offers that powerful groupware foundation through its implementation of public folders.

In Chapter 11, "Creating and Managing Recipients," you learned how to create and manage the basic types of Exchange recipients: mailbox users, resource mailboxes, distribution groups, and mail contacts. This chapter covers the other type of recipient—the public folder. To begin your look at the shared storage architecture of an Exchange Server system, this chapter explores how a user views shared storage and describes how to create and manage public folders in an Exchange organization.

In Exchange Server 2007, public folders are de-emphasized compared to previous versions of Exchange Server. While you can create and manage public folders using the Exchange Management Shell, there is no provision for doing so in the Exchange Management Console—at least, not in the release version of the product. It is likely that this de-emphasis is due to the growing popularity and power of Microsoft SharePoint Server, which like the public folder feature of Exchange Server offers centralized document storage. However, SharePoint Server also offers sophisticated document management, versioning, and tracking features that public folders lack.

If all users in your organization are using Microsoft Office Outlook 2007, there is no need for public folders unless you just want to use them for centralized storage. If users in your organization are still using previous versions of Outlook, public folders are required, as they provide offline address book distribution, free/busy information, and Outlook security settings. In fact, during installation of Exchange Server 2007, you are asked whether you have any users running Outlook 2003 or previous versions of Outlook. If you answer yes, Exchange Server 2007 enables public folders during installation. If you answer no, public folders are disabled by default, and you must add a public folder database later.

Understanding Public Folder Storage

Public folders can be wonderful things, providing centralized storage of virtually any type of document or message and allowing controlled access by any user in the organization. To perform the primary management of public folders, you will use the Exchange Management Shell. You can use the Exchange Management Console to perform a few database-related tasks. You can also use the Microsoft Outlook client to create and access public folders, and to perform limited administrative duties.

A public folder is essentially a special kind of mailbox. Like other mailboxes, public folders can be mail-enabled or mail-disabled. Also like other mailboxes, public folders can contain a hierarchy of folders inside the top-level folder. Where public folders differ is that they are publically available to the users in the organization.

When you create a public folder, that folder is placed in the public folder database of a particular Exchange server. Any Exchange server that has a public folder database can host a public folder. A public folder is created in the public folder database of one server but can then be replicated to the public folder databases of multiple additional servers. In a typical organization, the public folders do not all exist on one server; rather, they are distributed across several servers.

Within a public folder tree, the folders at the first level are referred to as top-level public folders. When a user creates a top-level public folder, it is placed in the public folder store on that user's home server. When a user creates a lower-level public folder, it is placed in the public folder store containing the parent folder in which the new folder is created. In addition, each public folder can be replicated to other servers in the organization. As you can see, this situation can get complicated. Public folders exist on different servers, and some public folders have instances on multiple servers.

Real World   Keeping Exchange Server 2003 if You Have an Entrenched Public Folder Structure

If your existing organization uses a large public folder structure and you have no plans to migrate to something like SharePoint Server, you might consider keeping a server running Exchange Server 2003 in your organization and using it as a dedicated public folder server. The System Management console in Exchange Server 2003 provides a nice graphical interface for creating and managing a public folder structure. You can learn more about coexistence with Exchange Server 2003 in Chapter 7, "Coexisting with Previous Versions of Exchange Server."

Using Public Folders in Outlook 2007

Your users—and you—can use the Outlook 2007 client both to create public folders and to manage certain public folder properties. This section covers both of these topics. You can also create and manage public folders using previous versions of the Outlook clients. Although this section focuses on the use of Outlook 2007, most of the techniques described work with these other clients as well.

Creating a Public Folder in Outlook

Creating a public folder using Microsoft Outlook is quite easy. To create a public folder, ensure that the Public Folders object (or the folder inside which you want to create the new folder) is selected and choose New Folder from the File menu. In the Create New Folder dialog box, type the name of the public folder that you want to create, choose the type of items that folder should contain, select the folder in which it should be created, and click OK. You can set the types of messages that can be posted in a new folder, including calendar items, notes, tasks, contacts, and e-mail items. The default is the type of item that can be posted in the parent folder.

Managing Public Folders in Outlook

After you create a public folder, you can configure it in several ways. The management of a public folder occurs in two places: the Outlook client and the Exchange Management Shell. Because users can create public folders, it is advantageous to allow them certain managerial responsibilities, which is why some management can occur in the client.

When a user creates a public folder, that user automatically becomes the folder's owner. The owner is responsible for the folder's basic design, which includes its access permissions, rules, and association of electronic forms. To perform this management, the user can simply open the property sheet for a particular public folder in Outlook.

Administration Tab

You use the Administration tab to set various options governing a public folder's use. The settings on this tab include the following:

- **Initial View On Folder**   Specifies the initial Outlook view that is used whenever the public folder is opened. Available views include the default Normal threaded view as well as views grouped by discussion subject, topic, and poster.

- **Drag/Drop Posting Is A**   Defines what happens when an item is dragged into a public folder. Options include Move/Copy and Forward.

- **Add Folder Address To**   Adds the address of the folder as a contact to the Outlook Contacts folder.

- **This Folder Is Available To**   Specifies whether the folder is accessible by anyone who has appropriate permissions or only by the folder owners.

- **Folder Assistant**   Lets you create rules that apply to new items placed in the folder. Rules include such actions as automatically replying to or rejecting messages based on the posting user or subject.

- **Moderated Folder**   Allows you to establish one or more moderators for the folder. A *moderated folder* is one in which a moderator must approve all newly posted items before they are made available to the public. Click this button to configure the folder's moderators. Keep in mind that users' posts to the folders do not appear immediately in a moderated folder. For this reason, you might want to configure an automatic reply to messages posted to moderated folders, letting users know that the moderator has received their message. You can do so by using the Reply To New Items With area and configuring either a standard or custom response.

Forms Tab

The Forms tab allows you to specify the forms that can be used in conjunction with the public folder. The forms specified on this tab appear as the choices in the drop-down list for the When Posting To This Folder option. You can also manage any associated form from this tab.

Permissions Tab

The Permissions tab allows you to assign permissions to users on the current public folder. Each user can be assigned one of several roles, and each role has a set of permissions associated with it. The available permissions are as follows:

- **Create Items**   Allows the user to post items in the folder.

- **Read Items**   Allows the user to open any item in the folder.

- **Create Subfolders**   Allows the user to create subfolders within the folder.

- **Edit Items**   Specifies which items in the folder the user can edit. The None option indicates that a user cannot edit items. The Own option indicates that the user can edit only items that he or she created. The All option indicates that a user can edit any item in the folder.

■ **Folder Owner**   Grants the user all permissions in the folder, including the ability to assign permissions.

■ **Folder Contact**   Specifies that the user is to receive copies of any status messages regarding the folder, including nondelivery reports.

■ **Folder Visible**   Permits the user to see the folder in the public folder hierarchy.

■ **Delete Items**   Specifies which items in the folder the user can delete. The None option indicates that a user cannot delete items. The Own option indicates that the user can delete only items that he or she created. The All option indicates that a user can delete any item in the folder.

You can modify the permissions associated with any given role. Table 12-1 shows the available roles and the default permissions granted for each role.

Table 12-1   Default Permissions for Public Folder Roles

Role	Create	Read	Edit	Delete	Subfolders	Owner	Contact	Visible
Owner	Yes	Yes	All	All	Yes	Yes	Yes	Yes
Publishing editor	Yes	Yes	All	All	Yes	No	No	Yes
Editor	Yes	Yes	All	All	No	No	No	Yes
Publishing author	Yes	Yes	Own	Own	Yes	No	No	Yes
Author	Yes	Yes	Own	Own	No	No	No	Yes
Nonediting author	Yes	Yes	None	Own	No	No	No	Yes
Reviewer	No	Yes	None	None	No	No	No	Yes
Contributor	Yes	No	None	None	No	No	No	Yes
None	No	No	None	None	No	No	No	Yes

Managing Public Folder Databases in the Exchange Management Console

If during Exchange Server 2007 installation, you indicated that your organization did not contain versions of Outlook previous to Outlook 2007, then public folders are not enabled by default. You need to create a new public folder database in order to use public folders. Depending on the size of your public folder infrastructure, you may also want to create multiple public folder databases.

Creating a New Public Folder Database

You can create a new public folder database using either the Exchange Management Console or the Exchange Management Shell. To create a new public folder database using Exchange Management Console, follow these steps:

1. In the console tree of the Exchange Management Console, expand the Server Configuration node and then click the Mailbox subnode.

2. In the Result pane, click the server on which you want to create the new public folder database, as shown in Figure 12-1.

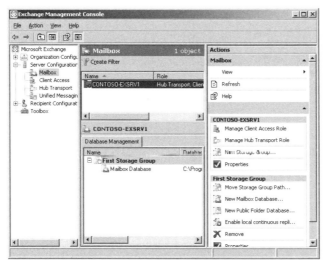

Figure 12-1   Choosing the server on which to create a new public folder database

3. In the Work pane, click the storage group in which you want to create the new public folder database.

4. In the Actions pane, click New Public Folder Database.

5. On the New Public Folder Database page of the New Public Folder Database Wizard, shown in Figure 12-2, type the name of the new public folder database. If you want to specify the location of the public folder database files, click Browse, and then type the name and location of the new Exchange database file (.edb) for the public folder. By default, the new database is mounted right after creation. If you want to mount it manually later, clear the Mount This Database check box. When you finish, click New.

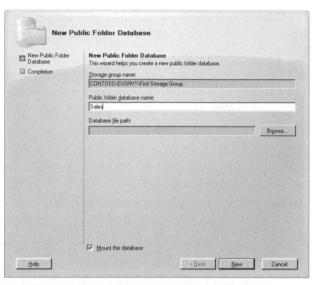

Figure 12-2   Creating a new public folder database

6. On the Completion page, click Finish.

Management Shell

You can also create a new public folder database by using the Exchange Management Shell. The command you use to do this is `New-PublicFolderDatabase`, and you need to supply some parameters to identify the location and name of the database. The syntax for the `New-PublicFolderDatabase` command is:

```
New-PublicFolderDatabase -Name <"DatabaseName">
-StorageGroup <"StorageGroup">
```

For example, to create a new public folder database named Sales in the storage group named First Storage Group, you use the command:

```
New-PublicFolderDatabase -Name <"Sales">
-StorageGroup <"First Storage Group">
```

Removing a Public Folder Database

You can remove a public folder database that is no longer in use. However, before you can remove a public folder database, be aware of the following:

- You cannot remove a public folder database that contains data. You must delete or move the public folders in the database to another database.

- You cannot remove a public folder database if any mailbox databases are associated with it. If any mailbox database uses the public folder as its default database, assign another default database to those mailbox databases.

- When you remove a public folder database, the database file is not deleted from the disk; you must delete the file manually. The default location for a public folder database file is C:\Program Files\Microsoft\ExchangeServer\Mailbox\<storage group name>\<public folder database name>.

- You cannot remove the last public folder database in an organization if there are any previous versions of Exchange Server running in the organization. You must also use a special command in the Exchange Management Shell to remove the last public folder database. Also, when the last public folder database is removed, only users of Outlook 2007 or Outlook Web Access can to connect to the organization.

To remove a public folder database using the Exchange Management Console, follow these steps:

1. In the console tree of the Exchange Management Console, expand the Server Configuration node and then click the Mailbox subnode.

2. In the Result pane, click the server from which you want to remove the public folder database.

3. In the Work pane, expand the storage group from which you want to remove the public folder database and then click the public folder database that you want to remove.

4. In the Action pane, click Remove. A message appears asking whether you are sure that you want to remove the database. Click Yes.

5. A Microsoft Exchange Warning page appears, indicating that the database was successfully removed and reminding you to manually remove the database file.

Management Shell

You can also remove a public folder database by using the Exchange Management Shell. The command you use to do this is **Remove-PublicFolderDatabase**, and you need to supply some parameters to identify the location and name of the database. The syntax for the **Remove-PublicFolderDatabase** command is:

```
Remove-PublicFolderDatabase -Identity "<servername>\
<storage group>\<public folder database>"
```

For example, to remove a public folder database named Sales in the storage group named First Storage Group on a server named contoso-exsrv1, use the command:

```
Remove-PublicFolderDatabase -Identity "<contoso-exsrv1>\
<First Storage Group>\<sales>"
```

Note that if you are removing the last public folder database in an organization, you need to answer yes to prompts that ask you to confirm the action and that warn you that only users of Outlook 2007 will be able to connect to the organization.

Creating and Managing Public Folders in the Exchange Management Shell

In Exchange Server 2007, creating and managing public folders all happens within the Exchange Management Shell. The following sections describe the creating and management commands for working with public folders.

Creating a Public Folder

To create a new public folder in the root of the public folder tree on the closest mailbox server that has a public folder database, you use the New-PublicFolder cmdlet. To determine the closest server, Exchange Server 2007 first checks to see whether the local server is a mailbox server with a public folder database. If it is not, site costs are used to determine the closest mailbox server with a public folder database.

The syntax for this cmdlet is:

```
New-PublicFolder -Name <"PublicFolderName">
```

You can also specify a mailbox server on which to create the new public folder and that folder's place in the public folder hierarchy by using the following syntax:

```
New-PublicFolder -Name <"foldername"> -Path <path>
-Server <"ServerName">
```

For example, to create a new public folder named Brochures inside an existing top-level folder named Sales on the server contoso-exsrv1, you use the command:

```
New-PublicFolder -Name "Brochures" -Path \Sales
-Server "contoso-exsrv1"
```

Removing a Public Folder

To remove an existing public folder, use the Remove-PublicFolder cmdlet. To remove a public folder, use the syntax:

```
Remove-PublicFolder -Identity <"path\foldername">
```

For example, to remove the Brochures folder inside the Sales folder, use the command:

```
Remove-PublicFolder -Identity <"\Sales\Brochures">
```

To specify the server from which you want to remove the public folder, use the syntax:

```
Remove-PublicFolder -Identity <"path\foldername">
-Server <"Servername>"
```

To remove a public folder and also remove all of its subfolders, use the following syntax:

```
Remove-PublicFolder -Identity <"path\foldername">
-Recurse: $True
```

> **Note** Remember that with many cmdlets, including the **Remove-Public-Folder** cmdlet, you can use the **–WhatIf** parameter to make no actual changes, but test how the command will perform.

Getting Information about a Public Folder

To retrieve information about a public folder or even a hierarchy of public folders, you can use variations of the **Get-PublicFolder** cmdlet. In fact, to get information about the root public folder, simply use the **Get-PublicFolder** cmdlet by itself.

To get the names of the root public folder and all of the folders below it in the hierarchy, use the cmdlet:

```
Get-PublicFolder -Recurse | Format-List Name
```

To get information about a particular public folder in the hierarchy, use the following syntax:

```
Get-PublicFolder -Identity <"path \foldername">
```

For example, to get information about the Brochures folder, which is inside the Sales top-level folder, use the cmdlet:

```
Get-PublicFolder -Identity "\Sales\Brochures"
```

You can also get information about a particular folder in the hierarchy and all the children folder of that folder by adding the parameter **–GetChildren**.

> **More Info** For more information about the parameters you can use with the **Get-PublicFolder** cmdlet, consult the Exchange Server 2007 help files.

Managing Settings for a Public Folder

There are a number of settings for public folders that you can modify using the **Set-PublicFolder** cmdlet. Typically, you will use the cmdlet and the **–Identity** switch to identify the path to the public folder, along with the parameters you want to use to modify particular settings for the folder.

Table 12-2 lists some of the parameters used with the `Set-PublicFolder` cmdlet. For any of these parameters, you can get help with using the parameter by using the following syntax:

```
Get-Help Set-PublicFolder –Parameter <parametername>
```

Note   The contents of public folders are not replicated to other mailbox servers in your organization automatically. If you want replication to occur, set it up manually on a per-folder basis. You can configure each public folder individually to have replicas on multiple mailbox servers. When you set up replication for a parent folder, its child folders are also replicated by default, although you can change this for individual child folders. You can set up replication using the replication parameters for the `Set-PublicFolder` cmdlet.

Table 12-2   Parameters Used with the `Set-PublicFolder` cmdlet

Parameter	Description
AgeLimit	Specifies the overall age limit on the folder. This parameter cannot be used along with the UseDatabaseAgeDefaults parameter.
DomainController	Specifies the domain controller to use to write this configuration change to Active Directory. Use the fully qualified domain name (FQDN) of the domain controller that you want to use.
HiddenFromAddressListsEnabled	Specifies whether to hide the public folder from address lists.
LocalReplicaAgeLimit	Specifies the age limit of the replica on the connected server, if there is a replica on it.
MaxItemSize	Specifies the maximum item size in kilobytes (KB) that can be posted. This parameter is mutually exclusive with the UseDatabaseQuotaDefaults parameter.
Name	Specifies the name for the public folder.
PerUserReadStateEnabled	Specifies to maintain read and unread data on a per-user basis.
PostStorageQuota	Specifies the size (in KB) when a public folder doesn't allow posting. This parameter cannot be used with the UseDatabaseQuotaDefaults parameter.
Replicas	Specifies a list of Mailbox servers with which to replicate this public folder.

Table 12-2 Parameters Used with the `Set-PublicFolder` cmdlet (Continued)

Parameter	Description
ReplicationSchedule	Specifies the replication schedule for the folder in the following format: `Weekday.Hour:Minute [AM/PM]-Weekday.Hour:Minute [AM/PM]`.
RetainDeletedItemsFor	Specifies the retention time for deleted items. This parameter cannot be used with the `UseDatabaseRetentionDefaults` parameter.
Server	Specifies the server on which to perform the selected operations.
StorageQuota	Specifies the size (in KB) when the public folder will start issuing warnings. This parameter cannot be used with the `UseDatabaseQuotaDefaults` parameter.
UseDatabaseAgeDefaults	Specifies to use the database age limit.
UseDatabaseQuotaDefaults	Specifies to use the public store quota limits.
UseDatabaseReplicationSchedule	Specifies the public folder replication schedule.
UseDatabaseRetentionDefaults	Specifies to use the database retention defaults.

Summary

Public folders provide centralized storage of virtually any type of document or message and allow controlled access by any user in the organization. In this chapter, you learned what you need to know to create and manage a public folder system in your Exchange organization. Now it's time to turn to another aspect of the Exchange storage architecture. In Chapter 13, "Creating and Managing Storage Groups," you will learn how to configure and manage Exchange Server 2007 storage groups.

Chapter 13
Creating and Managing Storage Groups

In the previous three chapters, you've learned how to manage Microsoft Exchange Server 2007, as well as how to manage recipients and public folders, if you still use them in your organization. One item that has not been covered yet is one of the most important aspects of Exchange Server 2007—storage group administration.

In this chapter, you turn your attention to these basic Exchange building blocks and get some insight regarding the issues involved in creating and managing storage groups in your Exchange Server 2007 organization. The topics you review in this chapter include:

- Planning multiple databases
- Planning multiple storage groups
- Discussing if and when you should use circular logging
- Creating, managing, and deleting storage groups and stores
- Mounting and dismounting stores

Review of Exchange Server 2007 Storage Architecture

This chapter includes a review of some information from Part I, "Introduction," and Part II, "Planning Your Deployment," but focuses solely on helping you make the best storage archictecture decisions for your Exchange environment. Exchange Server 2007 makes massive improvements over previous versions of Exchange when it comes to storage.

Before you get too deep into this discussion, it's important that you understand what is meant by the terms "store" and "storage group." In Exchange, a *store* is the entity in which user mailboxes are located. A store also has its own associated database file in which mailbox contents are saved. *Storage groups*, first introduced in Exchange 2000 Server as a means to achieve more reasonable scalabilty, are collections of individual stores. The version and edition of Exchange Server in use at your organization dictates the level to which you can utilize stores and storage groups. Table 13-1 shows you the significant changes that have taken place in Exchange's inner workings when it comes to store and storage group support in Exchange Server 2007.

Table 13-1   Exchange Server Stores and Storage Groups

	2000 Std.	2000 Ent.	2003 Std.	2003 Ent.	2007 Std.	2007 Ent.
Storage groups	1	4	1	4	5	50
Stores per group	2	5	2	5	5	50
Stores per server	2 (one is for the public folder store)	20	2	20	5	50
Database size limit	16 GB	16 TB	75 GB	16 TB	16 TB	16 TB
Recovery group	No	No	Yes	Yes	Yes	Yes

Note   In this chapter, the terms store, information store, and database are more or less interchangeable.

Take special notice of the *stores per server* values in the two editions of Exchange Server 2007. Under Exchange Server 2003, the value for the maximum stores allowed on a single server was a simple mathematical operation that multiplied the maximum number of storage groups and the maximum stores per storage group. Partially due to the 64-bit architecture of Exchange Server 2007, the allowed number of stores and storage groups have been significantly increased in both editions of Exchange Server 2007. However, the maximum stores per server is no longer a function of stores and storage groups per server. Instead, the Standard Edition of Exchange Server 2007 supports a maximum of five stores on a server while the enterprise edition supports up to 50 stores on a single server.

Under Exchange Server 2007, you have a variety of options when it comes to designing your storage layout. A storage group in an Exchange Server 2007 system resides on a Mailbox server and consists of a set of up to 50 databases (stores) for the Enterprise

Edition and five for the Standard Edition. Stored in each separate store is a single database file and other information, including data definitions, indices, and other information associated with user mailboxes or public folders.

As was the case in older versions of Exchange, log files belong to the storage group and not to each individual store. All the databases in a storage group use the same transaction log files. Each database in Exchange Server 2007 consist of a single file, the database, sometimes referred to as the EDB file after the name of the actual file's extension. This file is managed by the Information Store service.

Note   For those of you who have made the leap from Exchange 2000 Server or Exchange Server 2003, note that the streaming file (STM file) that used to be associated with each information store has been eliminated. All content is now stored in the database, resulting in a smaller overall I/O footprint for Exchange, which was one of the Exchange Server 2007 design considerations. In addition, the Exchange Installable File System (ExIFS) has been removed.

Benefits of Using Storage Groups

These days, it is not uncommon to find Exchange databases that are massive—approaching 100 GB or more. The time necessary to back up these databases can exceed several hours. The problem with this is not the time it takes to back up the database, but the time it takes to *restore* such a large database. During the restoration, of course, your users' productivity with regard to e-mail approaches zero. In Exchange database planning, the old cliché is a good one: *Always plan for failure so that you can succeed.* You'll find that prudent use of storage groups helps you succeed during disaster recovery.

As you read earlier, in implementing storage groups and allowing multiple databases per Mailbox server, Microsoft has made some tremendous changes to the Extensible Storage Engine (ESE) database architecture since Exchange Server 2003. These changes are even more dramatic when you go back as far as Exchange Server 5.5 (see Table 13-1). These changes significantly enhance recoverability and maximize productivity if an Exchange database becomes corrupted. In addition, storage groups offer several key benefits, which are listed here and discussed in the sections that follow:

- Each server can host more users than before.

- Each database can be backed up and restored individually.

- Each server can host multiple businesses.

- A separate store can be used for special mailboxes that may require different limits than users in other stores.

Increased User Support

Probably the largest benefit of storage groups is that they allow you to spread users across databases and storage groups on the same Exchange Server 2007 server. This scenario provides three distinct advantages:

- **You can support more users on a single server than was possible in earlier versions of Exchange.**   This is particularly true when you look at the way Exchange Server 2007 is architected. The 64-bit capability of the product makes significantly more memory available, thus increasing the number of potential users per server.

- **You have less downtime if a database becomes corrupted.**   By breaking up your users into separately managed groups, you keep the overall database size lower for each individual group, thereby reducing the amount of time it takes to restore after a failure.

- **You can host more users on an Exchange server because you can keep your databases to a manageable size.**   As you create more storage groups, they become separately managed entities and are backed up and restored separately. If a database becomes corrupt, you affect fewer users.

As mentioned earlier, within a storage group, you can have up to 50 databases. Each server can house up to 50 storage groups. However, each server can have a maximum of 50 databases in total, no matter how many storage groups you create. Bear in mind that this is just for Exchange Server 2007 Enterprise Edition. The Standard Edition has lower limits, which were detailed in Table 13-1.

There are some good reasons to refrain from creating the maximum number of databases possible in a single storage group. First, a log file problem could bring down all of the databases in that storage group, resulting in an ugly situation for your help desk. Further, when you run the Information Store Integrity Checker (Isinteg.exe) on a database, you must dismount that individual database's information store. In addition, Isinteg.exe needs a second database for temporary use while the tool works its magic. Therefore, if you have five databases operating in a given storage group on a Standed Edition server, you will have to dismount a second database so that Isinteg.exe can run properly. If you limit the number of operating databases to less than the maximum for a storage group, you will always have room to run Isinteg.exe without having to dismount a second store.

Having your users spread out across multiple databases means that only a subset of your users is affected if one of your databases goes offline for some reason. The other users can continue to work because their databases are up and running. A database that is offline is considered to be *dismounted*. Its icon appears with a down arrow in the Exchange Management Console, as shown in Figure 13-1. Further, the database's status is listed as Dismounted.

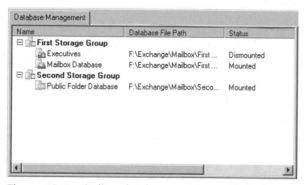

Figure 13-1   Online databases and an offline database (Executive) in a single storage group

Individual Backup and Restore

Because each individual database can be mounted or dismounted, you can back up and restore databases individually while other databases in the same storage group are mounted and running. Consider a scenario in which you have created four mailbox stores in the same storage group—one for each of four departments. If one of those stores becomes corrupted, the other three can remain mounted while you restore the fourth store from backup and then mount it again. You are not required to dismount all the stores in a storage group in order to restore one of them. And if one store becomes corrupted and cannot be mounted, it does not stop other stores in the same storage group from being mounted and available to users.

> **Note**   Exchange Server 2007 continues to offer the Recovery Storage Groups, which were first introduced in Exchange Server 2003. A Recovery storage Group is intended as a temporary group that you can bring online for use in performing recovery operations. For example, you could bring the recovery storage group online, restore mailboxes to it, and allow users to access it while you create a new blank store or repair the original database. You could then merge the mailboxes of the storage recovery group back into the original storage group. The use of the recovery storage group is detailed in Chapter 16, "Disaster Recovery."

Hosting of Multiple Businesses

If you manage e-mail for multiple businesses, you can host them on a single server. You can create an individual store for each business or even devote a storage group to a business, if needed. In either case, Exchange Server 2007 keeps the information for each business completely separate in its respective store.

Separate, distinct stores allow you to set up different administrative schedules for the businesses. For example, some administrators might want to have full backups performed every day, while others might need only weekly full backups. Some might want to have each department hosted in a separate store, while others might want to house all their users in the same store. This flexibility makes it easier to meet your customer's needs.

Support for Special Mailboxes

Through creative use of storage groups and stores, you can segregate special mailboxes and house them in their own store. One instance when this might be useful would be for a journalizing recipient who receives copies of all appropriate e-mails in your organization to ensure they comply with local laws or industry-specific regulations. Another instance might be for a project team that is working with highly sensitive and mission-critical company information. Their work might warrant the use of a separate store.

Planning Storage Groups

In most new implementations, whether they are transitions or new installations, proper planning will benefit both your short-term and long-term goals and will result in less downtime later on. It's not possible to place enough emphasis on the fact that poor planning leads to poor implementation and increased administration over the long term. If you were to record the types of support activities you perform each day for a month and then review them, you might find that 50 percent or more of them could have been avoided with better planning and implementation. Although most IT pros are simply overwhelmed when it comes to workload, spending a little extra time planning your Exchange Server 2007 storage needs will reap huge rewards down the line.

Real World   Service Level Management

In many organizations, service level management is paramount when it comes to measuring the effectiveness of the IT organization. After all, downtime in any IT-managed system can cost a company untold amounts of money. Further, service level management analysis can help an organization make decisions about investments in IT that need to be made in order to advance the organization or reduce risk. Microsoft has a wide variety of literature regarding service level management. The most comprehensive guide, the *Microsoft Operations Framework Service Management Functions* guide, is available for download from *http://www.microsoft.com /downloads/details.aspx?displaylang=en&familyid=1952dffb-f132-4e96-90ae-06bb9a077c2c*. This document can be invaluable when it comes to planning any service in your organization, including the introduction of Exchange Server 2007 to the environment.

Also consider the Microsoft System Center, a solution that plays a central role in the Microsoft vision to help IT organizations benefit from self-managing, dynamic systems. Microsoft Systems Center includes such tools as System Center Operations Manager (formerly Microsoft Operations Manager) and System Center Configuration Manager (formerly SMS). For more information regarding Microsoft System Center, visit *http://www.microsoft.com/systemcenter/about/default.aspx*.

Planning for Disk Space

Because this chapter focuses on storage groups, the discussion is confined to planning for disk space, multiple databases, and multiple storage groups. (For a broader look at how to plan for Exchange Server 2007, refer to Chapter 4, "Assessing Needs," and Chapter 5, "Planning for Deployment.") When planning disk space capacities for your Exchange Server 2007 infrastructure, consider several key factors:

- The number of users to be housed on a given Exchange server

- The average workload of users to be housed on a given Exchange server

- The amount of time it takes to recover from a failure (recovery time objective)

- The average size of an e-mail and an attachment and the number of attachments that users will need to send and receive

- The number and size of public folders

The next two sections describe how to calculate the disk space needs of your Exchange server.

Calculating Required Mailbox Disk Space

Messaging activity by your users can be difficult to forecast. Some users send and receive only a few e-mails each day, while others send and receive dozens of e-mails each day, some with large attachments. Obviously, given the same hardware specifications, you can house more light-usage users in a single mailbox store than you can heavy-usage users. Although it might seem trivial to do so, it's best to develop some type of classification system for your environment and then perform calculations to determine the best number of users per store, per storage group, and finally, per server. If you can get a somewhat accurate picture of your current messaging usage, you are better able to predict hardware and storage group needs.

A good way to do this is to pick a random sample of your users—at least 15 percent—and then conduct an audit of their current e-mail usage. Be sure they are saving copies of their sent e-mails in the Sent Items folder so that you can get an idea as to how many e-mails they are sending each day and the size of their emails. You can also see how many e-mails had attachments and, by opening the e-mails, you can see the sizes of the attachments. Security concerns might keep you from getting the information you need from some users, and in those cases you can give them a short survey to fill out.

More Info   Microsoft has released a tool that can help you gather this data in a much more organized fashion and includes all of your user mailboxes in the results so you can perform Exchange Server 2007 storage calculations with much more information on hand. This tool, called the Profile Analyzer, is available for download from Microsoft's Web site at *http://www.microsoft.com/technet /prodtechnol/exchange/downloads/2003/tools-name.mspx.*

After you collect your data, you need to analyze it. This part simply involves performing some calculations based on the data that you have captured. Consider this example: assume that you conducted your analysis on 300 users over a 60-day period, and you find that the average number of e-mails per day for each user is 20, with an average size of 1 K, with two attachments, each averaging 200 KB in size. The numbers would look like this:

- 20 e-mails × 10 KB = 200 KB per day in e-mail.

- 2 attachments × 200 KB = 400 KB per day in attachments.

- Total average disk space usage per day: 600 KB.

- Total average disk space usage: 1.2 MB per day (600 KB for the store, 600 KB for the transaction logs).

- 1.2 MB × 300 users = 360 MB of disk space per day for all 300 users. Over a 60-day period, there will be 44 working days, so 15,840 MB, or 15.8 GB of disk space is required to house all of the data.

This final figure of 15.8 GB is somewhat misleading because the transaction logs will not be retained forever and users will likely delete some of the messages they receive. Eventually, Exchange deletes the old logs, freeing up disk space to be used again by the transaction logs. Therefore, assume that Exchange keeps only a week's worth of logs, or 5 × 600 KB = 3 MB. Thus, after two months of activity, you need only about 7.74 GB (44 days × 600 KB average usage × 300 users, plus 3 MB for the logs) of disk space to run Exchange Server 2007.

Note that this figure does not take into consideration any of the advanced opportunities offered by Exchange Server 2007. Use of such advanced features as replication and content indexing, the use of a dedicated restore disk, your deleted item retention period (default is 14 days in Exchange Server 2007), and other factors play a significant part in your storage design. Further, decisions regarding the type of storage, such as Fibre Channel, iSCSI storage, or directly attached disks, as well as your backup window, backup methodology, hardware backup speed, and more, go into planning your storage architecture. After all, if you can't reliably back up your stores in the time allotted for your backup window, you don't have a good plan.

In addition to all of these facts, you still need to consider how much storage space is necessary for public folders if you plan to continue using them in Exchange Server 2007.

Part of this planning process involves measuring the overall performance, in Input/Output Operations Per Seconds (IOPS), of your storage infrastructure. Exchange Server 2007 is a disk-intensive application that requires storage that can stay up with the demands placed on it. Exchange Server 2007 has significantly modified I/O characteristics when compared with older versions of the product, so new baseline measurements should be made to make sure that your storage architecture is up to Exchange Server 2007 standards.

More Info   Use the iometer tool to measure the overall effectiveness of your Exchange storage architecture to make sure that it is capable of sustaining the number of users you need to support in your Exchange organization. For more information about iometer, visit *http://www.iometer.org*.

Determining the number of IOPS that your storage supports isn't too difficult with the iometer tool. However, figuring out how much performance you *need* from your storage can be a little trickier. In this section, you learn two tricks to make this calculation very simple.

First, Microsoft provides a list of standard IOPS based on the type of user in your environment. Table 13-2 provides this list, which outlines four classes of users.

Table 13-2   IOPS Estimate Per User

User type (usage profile)	Send/receive per day approximately 50-KB message size	Estimated IOPS per user
Light	5 sent/20 received	0.11
Average	10 sent/40 received	0.18
Heavy	20 sent/80 received	0.32
Very heavy	30 sent/120 received	0.48

To use this table, figure out the approximate number of users for each user type and then multiply that number by the figure in the Estimated IOPS Per User column for that user type. Then, add up the IOPS for all user types to come up with an overall IOPS figure for your Exchnage Server 2007 organization. Table 13-3 shows you a sample worksheet.

Table 13-3   IOPS Calculation Worksheet

User type (usage profile)	Number of Users	Estimated IOPS per user	IOPS/Class
Light	100	0.11	11
Average	600	0.18	108
Heavy	300	0.32	96
Very heavy	100	0.48	48
		Total IOPS	263

The calculation in Table 13-3 indicates that the storage infrastructure needs to support 263 IOPS. However, this is just a simple calculation that provides you with a rough estimate of your storage performance needs. There are a number of other factors that you must consider in your calculations. For example, if your Outlook clients run in cached mode as opposed to online mode, your Exchange Server 2007 server doesn't have to do as much work since much of the disk processing takes place locally. Therefore, your IOPS estimates can be lowered.

This leads to the second way to determine IOPS for your organization, which is much more exacting. The Microsoft Exchange team has developed an absolutely fantastic calculator that can help you take the guesswork out of storage planning and performance. Besides helping you figure out how much disk space your Exchange infrastructure requires, the tool helps you to determine how many stores your intended configuration requires and will even calculate your IOPS based on the input your provide. It even goes so far as to provide a recommended physical storage layout. Finally, the tool uses all the information you provide and figures out how much RAM you need for your server. You can download the tool from *http://msexchangeteam.com/archive/2007/01/15/432207.aspx*.

Planning for Multiple Storage Groups

After you understand your disk space needs, consider how many storage groups you need. One factor you must consider is the varying priorities of the work your users do. Assume that 20 of your 300 users perform work that is absolutely mission critical. Perhaps they are sales staff who take orders over the phone or who process customer orders that are placed in a public folder that is exposed on your Web site. Assume that if these users are down for even 15 minutes, your company loses in excess of $50,000. In this type of situation, you should consider splitting these users into two groups and hosting each group in its own mailbox and public folder store. Hosting them in their own storage group would not be necessary. However, given two factors—Microsoft's recommendation that you maintain a 1:1 ratio between stores and storage groups whenever possible, and the fact that you have 50 storage groups to work with—you should seriously consider doing so.

The reasoning behind this recommendation is that if the other databases become corrupted, these users can continue to operate without disruption because you can dismount and restore one or any combination of stores while another store runs in the same storage group. And if one group's database needs to be restored, it would be a fast restore because it would be much smaller than the company-wide database in which the other 280 users are hosted. In addition, because these users are spread over two databases, the other half of the group can continue to work and remain productive. Hence, plan your storage groups with disaster recovery in mind more than disk space usage considerations.

Planning for Backup and Restore Throughput

Many different backup and restore are methods available to the administrator. The key metric with backup and restore is the throughput, or the number of megabytes per second that can be copied to and from your production disks. After you determine the throughput, you need to decide whether it is sufficient to meet your backup and restore service level agreement. For example, if you need to be able to complete the backup within 4 hours, you may have to add more hardware to achieve it. Depending on your hardware configuration, there may be gains that can be achieved by changing the allocation unit size. This can help with both streaming online backups and the Eseutil integrity check that occurs during a VSS backup.

With 2,000 users on a server, moving from a 200 MB to a 2 GB mailbox increases the database size tenfold. Many administrators are not accustomed to having to deal with very large amounts of data on a single server. Consider a server with two thousand 2-GB mailboxes. With the overhead described previously, this is more than 4 TB of data. Assuming you can achieve a backup rate of 175 GB/hour (48 MB/min), it would take at least 23 hours to backup the server. An alternative for servers that don't use LCR or CCR might be to perform a full backup of 1/7th of the databases each day and an incremental backup on the remainder, as illustrated in Table 13-4.

Table 13-4 Sample Backup Methodology

	Day 1	Day 2	Day 3	Day 4	Day 5	Day 6	Day 7
Full	DB 1-2	DB 3-4	DB 5-6	DB 7-8	DB 9-10	DB 11-12	DB 13-14
Incremental	DB 3-14	DB 1-2	DB 1-4	DB 1-6	DB 1-8	DB 1-10	DB 1-12
		DB 5-14	DB 7-14	DB 9-14	DB 11-14	DB 13-14	

However, backup time is only one half of the equation. Restore time is just as, if not more, important. Suppose that as a result of these discussions you determine that no one is to be without Exchange services for more than 30 minutes. To plan how to stay within this maximum downtime, take the restore time you calculated in the previous section and divide it by the maximum downtime allowed by management policy. This calculation determines the number of stores you need to create on your Exchange server.

During the planning process, keep in mind that Exchange servers use one set of transaction logs per storage group. Using a greater number of storage groups prevents the buildup of a large number of transaction logs per storage group, although it would cause an overall increase in the number of transaction logs for the entire system.

Managing Storage Groups

As was the case with previous versions of Exchange, Exchange Server 2007 provides full management capability for dealing with storage groups, including creating, modifying, and deleting these store containers. In Exchange Server 2007, storage groups are a function of the Mailbox Role Server and managed using either the Exchange Management Console or the Exchange Management Shell. In this section, you learn how to manage storage groups.

Creating Storage Groups

Before you create a new storage group, make sure you have physical disk space available that corresponds to your Exchange storage master plan. To create a storage group, follow these steps:

1. From the Mailbox server on which you intend to install the new storage group, start the Exchange Management Console. You can actually do this from any server. One option is to work directly on the server you intend to manage.

2. Expand the Server Configuration container.

3. Select the Mailbox server on which you want to create the new storage group.

4. From the Action pane, choose New Storage Group. This starts a wizard that helps you to complete the procedure.

5. The wizard consists of a single screen (see Figure 13-2) asking you to provide a little information. Specifically, you need to name the new storage group. The rest is optional, unless you want to change the location of the the log and database files. Further, if you want to enable local continuous replication for your new storage group, select the check box next to Enable Local Continuous Replication For This Storage Group. Click Browse to direct each item into a particular location. It is recommended that you always create a specific subdirectory for each storage group.

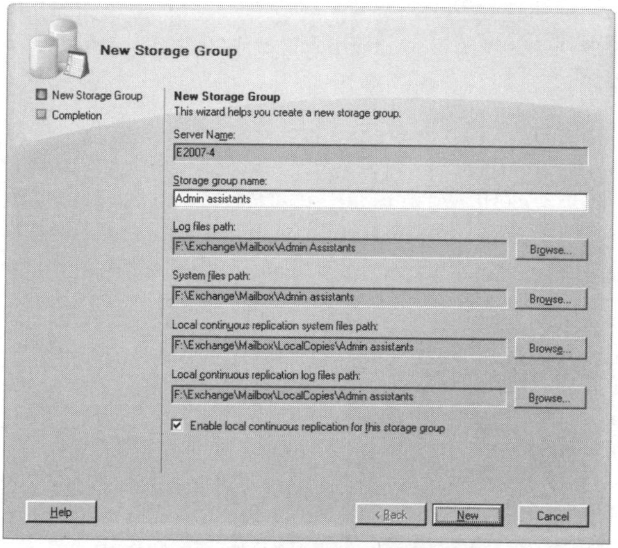

Figure 13-2   Creating a storage group

Management Shell

Exchange Server 2007, like its predecessors, relies on combinations of storage groups and database stores in order to house e-mail and function effectively. Supporting up to 50 individual storage groups per server, Exchange Server 2007 servers are far more scalable than older versions of the product. Creating a new storage group from the command line is as simple as using the **new-StorageGroup** command and deciding which options you want to enable, such as saving the storage group files to a different folder or enabling local continuous replication. The following command creates a new storage group on the server named E2007-4. The name of the new storage group is Purchasing Managers, and the files (log files, and so on) associated with the storage group are saved in the Mailbox folder in a subdirectory with the same name by way of the **LogFolderPath** and **SystemFolderPath** parameters. Using the **HasLocalCopy** parameter enables local continuous replication for this new storage group. The **CopyLogFolderPath** and **CopySystemFolderPath** parameters indicate the location to which the replicated copy of the data is written.

```
new-StorageGroup -Server 'E2007-4' -Name 'Purchasing Managers'
-LogFolderPath 'F:\Exchange\Mailbox\Purchasing managers'
-SystemFolderPath 'F:\Exchange\Mailbox\Purchasing managers'
-HasLocalCopy $true -
CopyLogFolderPath 'F:\Exchange\Mailbox\LocalCopies\Purchasing managers'
-CopySystemFolderPath
'F:\Exchange\Mailbox\LocalCopies\Purchasing managers'
```

> Note that you do not have to create the new storage group directories ahead of time. The `new-StorageGroup` cmdlet takes care of that task for you.

Regardless of the method you use to create the new storage group, it appears in the Exchange Management Console window, as shown in Figure 13-3. Note that the icons for the two new storage groups (Admin assistants and Purchasing Managers) look a little different than the others. This difference indicates that local continuous replication is enabled for these storage groups.

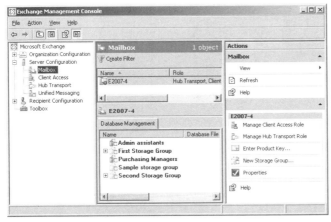

Figure 13-3   The new storage groups in the Exchange Management Console

Management Shell

Getting a list of storage groups from the command line allows you to quickly determine what storage groups are on which server, and also gives you a look at other high-level options, including whether or not local continuous replication is enabled or whether a storage group is a recovery storage group. Use the `get-StorageGroup` command to get a list of storage groups in use in your organization. This graphic shows you the results of this command.

Modifying Storage Group Configuration

After you create your storage group, the time may come when you want to make modifications to the new object. For example, you may want to enable circular logging (discussed below) for a particular storage group. As with most things Exchange, the Storage Group Properties page gives you the opportunity to make changes. Storage group configuration changes are handled in a couple of different ways, depending on what you're trying to modify.

Here's a quick look at what is modifiable from the Sample Storage Group Properties page, which is accessed by right-clicking an exsiting storage group and choosing Properties.

- **Rename The Storage Group**   At the top of the properties page lies the name of the storage group. If you want to rename this storage group, just overwrite the contents of this field with the desired name.

- **Enable Circular Logging**   The Enable Circular Logging option enables circular logging for the storage group, which basically reduces the number of transaction logs that are stored on the disk, but at a cost. Consider enabling this feature only for those storage groups that do not hold mission-critical data. With circular logging enabled, you can recover only to the last full backup. Consider carefully the full implications of losing the most recent data in your Exchange databases before selecting this option (see Figure 13-4).

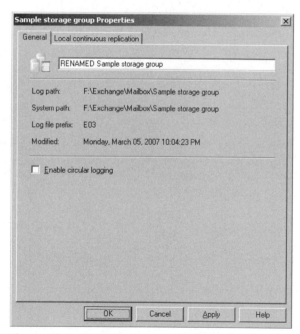

Figure 13-4   Modify some parameters related to the storage group configuration.

- **Local Continuous Replication** If you enable local continuous replication, a tab by the same name is available on the properties page. This tab's contents contain no configurable information, but is a status update instead (see Figure 13-5).

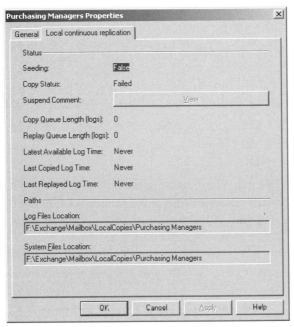

Figure 13-5 The contents of the Local Continuous Replication tab

Management Shell

With your new storage group up and running, all is probably going well...until you realize that you need to rename the storage group or enable circular logging. Circular logging makes your storage group use less disk space, but at a potential database recovery cost. These two options are configurable from the Exchange Management Shell through the use of the **set-StorageGroup** cmdlet. The following example command renames the Admin assistants storage group to Administrative Assistants and enables circular logging.

```
Set-StorageGroup -Identity "Admin assistants"-Name
"Administrative Assistants" -CircularLoggingEnabled:$true
```

And that's all that you can configure from the properties page of a storage group. There are, however, more configurable options that are available by simply right-clicking a storage group. This menu of options is shown in Figure 13-6.

Figure 13-6   There are a few more options you can use to configure your storage group.

Included in these options are

- **Move Storage Group Path**   Until you invoke this option, your storage group log files are stored in the path you specify when you initially create a storage group. If you choose this option, you are given the opportunity to change the paths you defined when you created the storage group. Figure 13-7 gives you a look at the familiar screen. Before you can move an entire storage group, suspend local continuous replication for the storage group using the Suspend Local Continuous Replication command from the storage group's shortcut menu. During this process, all of the mailbox databases in the storage group are dismounted, making them inaccessible for the duration of the move, after which they are remounted. Note that this command does not move the actual mailbox database (.edb file). It does move all of the storage group's log and system files as well as the full-text index associated with the storage group. If you want to move an individual database inside the storage group, use the `Move Database Path` command, which is described later in this chapter.

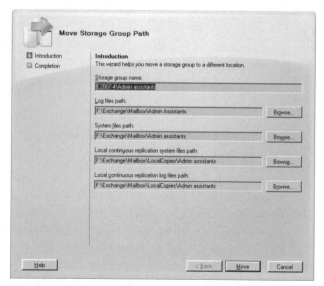

Figure 13-7   Provide the wizard with the necessary information to move the storage group.

- **New Mailbox Database**   This option is discussed later in this chapter.

- **New Public Folder Database**   Public folders were discussed in Chapter 12, "Creating and Managing Public Folders."

- **Local Continuous Replication options**   If you have not enabled local continuous replication for a storage group, the only option on the shortcut menu is one that lets you enable this feature. If you do opt to enable local continuous replication on an existing storage group, it's important to understand that you must maintain a 1:1 ratio between stores and storage groups. In other words, local continuous replication does not support housing multiple stores in a storage group. It's a one-database affair. If you have already enabled local continuous replication for a storage group, the shortcut menu gives you the opportunity to either disable this availability feature or temporarily suspend its operation.

Management Shell

If you want to move a storage group to a new disk location, use the `move-StorageGroupPath` command. The following command moves the storage group log files, system files, and full-text index to the locations specified by the `LogFolderPath` and `SystemFolderPath` parameters. The `CopyLogFolderPath` and `CopySystemFolderPath` parameters do the same thing for the replicated version.

```
move-StorageGroupPath -Identity 'E2007-4\Administrative Assistants'
-LogFolderPath 'F:\Exchange\Mailbox\New Storage Group Location'
-SystemFolderPath 'F:\Exchange\Mailbox\New Storage Group Location'
-CopyLogFolderPath 'F:\Exchange\Mailbox\LocalCopies\
New Storage Group Location' -CopySystemFolderPath
'F:\Exchange\Mailbox\LocalCopies\New Storage Group Location'
```

Removing Storage Groups

Perhaps you decide to jettison a division, or you just move mailboxes to stores in other storage groups. The time may come when it's time to purge a storage group from your Exchange system. This is an easy step, but there is one strict requirement: you cannot have any stores/databases residing within the storage group you intend to delete. If you try to do so, Exchange Server 2007 will kick back an error.

When there are no longer any stores associated with a particular storage group, delete it from within the Exchange Management Console by right-clicking the group choosing Remove. Exchange Server 2007 asks whether you really want to take this step. If you approve, the storage group is removed from the Exchange Management Console window. However, you need to manually clean up any log files that may still exist in the directory location of the former storage group.

> **Management Shell**
>
> You can also use the Exchange Management Shell to remove a storage group that is no longer needed. Removing a storage group is an easy process committed by using the `Remove-StorageGroup` command, as shown here.
>
> ```
> Remove-StorageGroup -Identity "Division 3"
> ```

With storage groups out of the way, you can turn your attention to the database side of the equation—stores.

Managing Stores

Exchange supports two kinds of stores, or individual mailbox (or public folder) databases in a storage group: a *mailbox* store for messages and a *public folder* store for public folder use. Each store is associated with its own database file but shares the storage group's log files. You can't create a store until you create a storage group. When you first install Exchange Server 2007, it creates a storage group named First Storage Group as well as a mailbox store and, if you indicated that you need to support legacy Outlook clients, a public folder store inside that storage group.

Beyond this, you can also create your own additional stores, change a number of parameters associated with a store, and, eventually, delete a store. All three of these management topics are discussed in this section.

Creating a Mailbox Store

Both the Exchange Management Console and the Exchange Management Shell are capable when it comes to the task of creating stores to house mailboxes. To create a new mailbox store from the Exchange Management Console, follow these steps:

1. From the Mailbox server on which you intend to install the new store, start the Exchange Management Console. You can actually do this from any server. One option is to work directly on the server you intend to manage.

2. Expand Server Configuration.

3. Select the Mailbox server on which you want to create the new storage group.

4. Select the storage group in which you want to create the new mailbox store/database.

5. From the Action pane, choose New Mailbox Database. This starts a wizard that helps you to complete the procedure.

6. The wizard consists of a single screen, shown in Figure 13-8. On this screen, name the new storage group, and, if you like, you can also change the location of the database file and, if you are using the feature, the path in which the replicated database copy is saved. If you want the database to mount immediately after it is created, select the check box next to Mount This Database. Click New to continue.

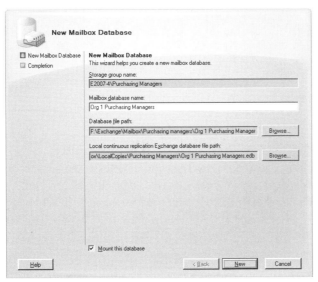

Figure 13-8   Provide information for the new database store.

After you complete these steps, the new database appears in the Exchange Management Console inside the storage group you selected.

Management Shell

A mailbox store is a pretty critical piece of the overall Exchange picture. Without it, your Exchange organization wouldn't serve much use to the company. A mailbox store is created inside one of your existing storage groups, and it's considered a best practice to create only a single mailbox store in a storage group. To create a mailbox store, use the **new-MailboxDatabase** command with the **StorageGroup** parameter to specify in which storage group the new mailbox database should reside. Optionally, you can also use the **EdbFilePath** and **CopyEdbFilePath** parameters to specify the location in which the database and the replica, respectively, should be written.

```
new-MailboxDatabase -StorageGroup 'CN=Administrative
Assistants,CN=InformationStore,CN=E2007-4,CN=Servers,
CN=Exchange Administrative Group (FYDIBOHF23SPDLT),
CN=Administrative Groups,CN=First Organization,
```

```
CN=Microsoft Exchange,CN=Services,CN=Configuration,
DC=contoso,DC=com' -Name 'Org 1 Administrative Assistants'
-EdbFilePath 'F:\Exchange\Mailbox\Administrative Assistants\
Org 1 Administrative Assistants.edb' -HasLocalCopy $true
-CopyEdbFilePath 'F:\Exchange\Mailbox\LocalCopies\
Administrative Assistants\Org 1 Administrative Assistants.edb'
```

After you create the new database, you need to mount it in order for it to be accessible for mailbox population. Accomplish this task using the mount-Database command, as shown here:

```
mount-database -Identity 'CN=Org 1 Administrative Assistants,
CN=Administrative Assistants,CN=InformationStore,CN=E2007
-4,CN=Servers,CN=Exchange Administrative Group (FYDIBOHF23SPDLT),
CN=Administrative Groups,CN=First Organization,
CN=Microsoft Exchange,CN=Services,CN=Configuration,DC=contoso,
DC=com'
```

Modifying Mailbox Database Configuration

Initially creating your mailbox store is only the first step in managing your new mailbox store. With the store created, you can now change some of the configuration options associated with it, such as whether or not to mount the database on startup, setting send and receive limits, and defining client settings. To access mailbox database settings, from the Exchange Management Console, right-click the mailbox database you want to configure and, from the shortcut menu, choose Properties.

Changing Mailbox Database General Options

There are a few options on the mailbox database's General tab, shown in Figure 13-9, that you can use to define how the mailbox database operates.

Here's an overview of what each of these options can do for you:

- **The name field**   Note that this field is changeable. You can overwrite the contents of this field and rename the mailbox database.

- **Journal Recipient**   In today's regulation-heavy world, organizations need to take steps to comply with a wide variety of burdensome laws. Exchange Server 2007 assists in these efforts by providing the ability to automatically copy every sent message to a safe storage space. As a part of this feature, you can configure a mailbox database so that all mail is copied to a separate mailbox. Select the check box next to Journal Recipient and then click Browse to locate the user mailbox to which you want to copy mail.

- **Maintenance Schedule**   Specify the time at which you want the store maintenance utilities to run for this particular store.

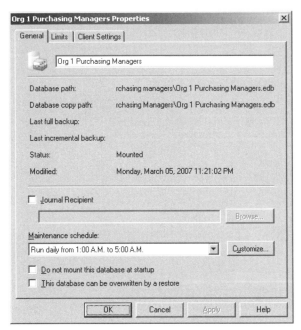

Figure 13-9   Mailbox database general options

- **Do Not Mount This Database At Startup**   Select the check box next to this option in order to prevent this mailbox database from being mounted at system startup. This can be useful if you need to perform maintenance on a store right after a reboot.

- **This Database Can Be Overwritten By A Restore**   Exchange protects its mailbox databases by making it difficult to accidentally overwrite them by mistake during a restore. When you need to restore a database from backup, you need to first select this check box.

Real World   Database Overwrites

Each database has a GUID. This GUID is stored in the database in one of the general purpose tables. The database GUID, along with its physical path on the hard drive, is also stored in Active Directory. When the Store.exe process starts, one of its tasks is to attempt to mount the database. Before mounting the database, however, the Store.exe process compares the database GUID it finds in the database to the database GUID for that database in Active Directory. The directory paths are also compared.

If everything matches, the database is mounted. If there is a mismatch in any of the information, the Store.exe process refuses to start up the database. This failure can occur if the database files are moved from a different server or directory to their present location. The reason the Store.exe process requires the GUID to match is to prevent a database from being accidentally moved to a different location and having it start up under a different storage group with different transaction logs.

If the This Database Can Be Overwritten By A Restore option is selected, the Store.exe process assumes you really want to move the database to this present location. So at startup, the Store.exe process will "fix" the database by changing the GUID in the database to the GUID that is in Active Directory; then at the next mounting, the GUIDs will match, and the database will mount. Finally, the option is cleared as part of this process.

If no database is found in the path when the Store.exe process is trying to mount the database, the process prompts you with an option to create a new database. The This Database Can Be Overwritten By A Restore option is really only invoked when the Store.exe process finds a database in the path it is instructed to look in and finds what it believes is the *wrong* database because the GUID is different.

The This Database Can Be Overwritten By A Restore option functions similarly during a restore. During the *process*, Windows Backup Utility passes in the GUID, database name, and storage group name to the Store.exe process. If these match, the Store.exe process passes back the locations where the files should be restored. If the GUID doesn't match, the Store.exe process looks at this check box, and if selected, it passes the database back to the backup process where the database files should be written.

By moving databases around and selecting the This Database Can Be Overwritten By A Restore check box, you can create multiple, different databases with the same GUID on your Exchange Server. If you try to mount both databases, only one will mount because of the conflicting GUIDs. Under no circumstances does Microsoft recommend keeping two databases with the same GUID or "swapping" databases for any reason. Unexpected and undesirable results can occur.

Management Shell

Mailbox databases are manipulated from the Exchange Management Shell through the use of the `set-MailboxDatabase` command. The items on the General tab are no exception. The following command uses the **MountAtStartup** parameter to indicate that the Mailbox Database should be mounted when the system starts.

```
Set-MailboxDatabase "Org 1 Purchasing Managers" -MountAtStartup:$true
```

Likewise, use the same command, but with the **JournalRecipient** parameter to determine the mailbox that should receive journal copies of messages.

```
Set-MailboxDatabase "Org 1 Purchasing Managers"
-JournalRecipient contoso\tony.allen
```

You can even rename a mailbox database from the command line, using the **Name** parameter, as shown here:

```
Set-MailboxDatabase "Org 1 Purchasing Managers" -Name "PMs"
```

To allow a database to be overwritten by a restore operation, use the following command:

```
Set-MailboxDatabase "Org 1 Purchasing Managers"
-AllowFileRestore:$true
```

Settings Limits on Mailbox Databases

Now, move on over to the Limits tab, shown in Figure 13-10.

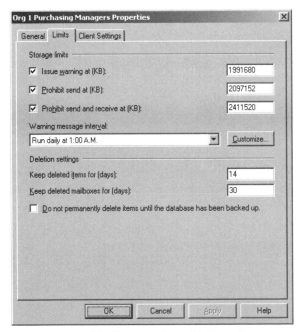

Figure 13-10   Mailbox database Limits tab

On this tab, you can determine the limits that will be imposed upon mailboxes that reside in the mailbox database. Most of the items shown in the figure are pretty self-explanatory, but a couple of items are especially important:

- **Storage Limits**   Use the options in this section to determine the point at which a user's mailbox size results in received warnings or an inability to send and receive mail. Note that all values are represented in KB.

- **Warning Message Interval**   This parameter determines the time of day at which messages go out to users that have exceeded one of the limits you set on the mailbox database.

- **Do Not Permanently Delete Mailboxes And Items Until The Database Has Been Backed Up.**   As was the case with journaling, this option can be useful in a regulated environment. Regardless of the values in the Deletion settings area, if this check box is selected, items are not deleted until they have been backed up.

Management Shell

There are a number of storage-related limits that you can set on an Exchange Server 2007 mailbox store, such as the point at which a user is notified that his or her mailbox has exceeded a warning limit, and that point at which the user is no longer allowed to send or receive mail. These kinds of controls can help you to maintain some semblance of control over a burgeoning mailbox database.

Use the `Set-MailboxDatabase` command to set various limits on your mailbox store. The following command sets the following limits:

- Send a warning to the user: 500 MB (512,000,000 bytes)

- Disable the user's ability to send mail: 550 MB (563,200,000 bytes)

- Disable the user's ability to send or receive mail: 600 MB (614,400,000 bytes)

```
Set-MailboxDatabase "Org 1 Purchasing Managers"
-IssueWarningQuota 512000000 -ProhibitSendQuota 563200000
-ProhibitSendReceiveQuota 614400000
```

Note that, when you use the command line to set quotas, you must provide the values in bytes. This is in contrast to the GUI that uses KB values. If you want to set even numbers, like 500 MB, using the command line, multiply the megabyte value by 1,024.

Defining Mailbox Database Client Settings

The last mailbox configuration tab, Client Settings (see Figure 13-11), provides a place for you to determine which public folder database and offline address book will be associated with this mailbox database. If you support legacy clients in your organization, specify these options in order for those clients to function properly. Selecting a public folder store to associate with the new mailbox is required because each legacy Exchange client must have a default public folder store for public folder access. Selecting a public folder store here does not limit the user's ability to access other public folder stores or public folder trees. Instead, it provides an entry point into the whole public folder area.

After selecting a public folder store to associate with your mailbox store, click Browse next to the Default Offline Address Book field to choose a default offline address list for users homed in this store. Users will still be able to download other offline address lists; this option simply specifies the default.

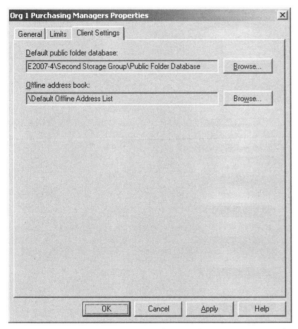

Figure 13-11 Mailbox database Client Settings tab

Management Shell

If you continue to use legacy clients, define which public folder store will be the default for clients with mailboxes housed in this database. Also determine which offline address book will be the default for the same clients. The

`PublicFolderDatabase` and `OfflineAddressList` parameters, used with the `Set-MailboxDatabase` command help you out here.

```
Set-MailboxDatabase "PMs" -PublicFolderDatabase
"Public Folder Database"
-OfflineAddressBook "Default Offline Address List"
```

Mounting and Dismounting a Mailbox Database

In order for a user to access a database, it must be mounted in order to be made available. Conversely, if you need to perform maintenance on a database, you might want to dismount it. To mount or dismount a database, right-click the database and, from the shortcut menu, choose either Mount Database or Dismount Database.

Management Shell

To mount and dismount a specific mailbox database using the Exchange Management shell, use the **mount-Database** and **dismount-Database** commands, respectively.

```
mount-Database "PMs"

dismount-Database "PMs" -confirm:$false
```

Moving a Mailbox Database

Moving a mailbox database is a matter of right-clicking the mailbox database entry in the Exchange Management Console and choosing Move Database Files from the shortcut menu. Once you do so, a wizard starts that consists of a single screen, shown in Figure 13-12, on which you can choose the location at which the database, and its locally replicated copy, should be stored.

Management Shell

Moving a mailbox database is a very real possibility when it comes to managing an Exchange server. At some point, your database may outgrow the storage you initially provided, forcing you to move the database to a new location. The command **move-DatabasePath** takes care of this work for you.

```
move-DatabasePath -Identity 'E2007-4\Administrative Assistants\
Org 1 Administrative Assistants' -EdbFilePath
'F:\Exchange\Mailbox\Administrative Assistants\
Org 1 Administrative Assistants.edb' -CopyEdbFilePath
'F:\Exchange\Mailbox\LocalCopies\Administrative Assistants\
Org 1 Administrative Assistants.edb'
```

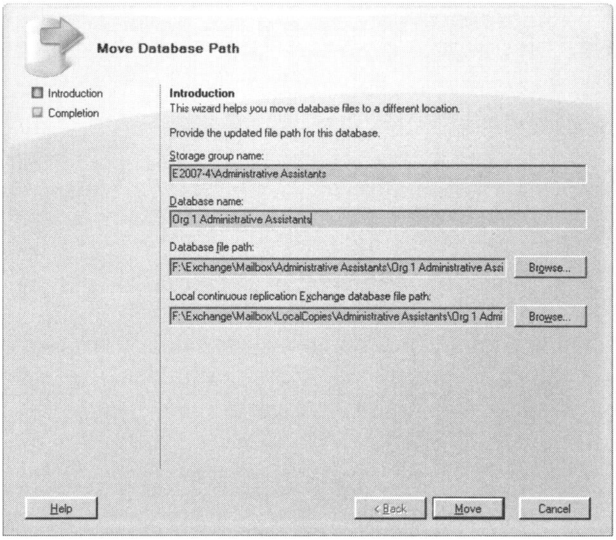

Figure 13-12   The Move Database Path Wizard

Removing a Mailbox Database

At times, it might be necessary to completely remove a mailbox database from your organization. Before you remove the mailbox database, be sure to move all of the mailboxes inside the database to other mailbox databases in your organization.

If you have created a copy of the database managed by local continuous replication, that copy is also removed from Active Directory when you delete the main database.

When there are no longer any mailboxes associated with a particular mailbox database, delete it by, from within the Exchange Management Console, right-clicking the database and choosing Remove. Exchange Server 2007 asks whether you really want to take this step. If you approve, the database is removed from the Exchange Management Console window. Note that this action only removes the object from Active Directory. If you want to reclaim the disk space in use by the database, you must manually remove the files.

Management Shell

Over time, you might find it necessary to remove a mailbox database from your Exchange organization. Use the `Remove-MailboxDatabase` command to perform this function, as shown here:

```
Remove-MailboxDatabase -Identity "Org 1 Administrative Assistants"
```

Summary

This chapter has given you the information you need to administer storage groups and mailbox databases in your Exchange organization. You should now understand the storage group architecture and be able to create and manage storage groups and stores. In the next chapter, you learn how to implement the new Unified Messaging features of Exchange Server 2007.

Chapter 14
Unified Messaging

In other chapters of this book, you learned that Microsoft Exchange Server 2007 sports a brand-new architecture and a number of new features that make the product a great upgrade for many organizations. From a new functionality standpoint, Unified Messaging services of Exchange Server 2007 rate high on the list of things that administrators need to learn. In this chapter, you learn about the Unified Messaging role in Exchange Server 2007 and how to manage this new service.

With the wide variety of telephony hardware available on the market and the number of options you have for making your particular equipment work with Exchange Server 2007, it's not possible to cover a single real-world deployment scenario that would apply to any significant group. Therefore, this chapter includes enough information to get the Unified Messaging server role deployed and goes over the tasks involved in administering Unified Messaging. Private Branch Exchange (PBX) and other kinds of integration instructions are not included.

In this chapter, you learn how to create dial plans, mailbox policies, and IP gateways. You also learn how to associate dial plans with a Unified Messaging server, which essentially enables the Unified Messaging service on that server. Finally, you learn how to enable the Unified Messaging features on a user's account.

More Info   Microsoft understands that before taking the Unified Messaging plunge, many organizations will want to test the new services to make sure that they meet the needs of the organization. To address this need, Microsoft makes available the Unified Messaging Test Phone, an application that installs on a workstation and allows you to test the functionality of specific Unified Messaging features such as call answering, subscriber access, and auto attendants. As a part of this application, Microsoft provides instructions for configuring all of the necessary Unified Messaging objects on your test server to work with the Test Phone. For more information about deploying this test environment, visit *http://technet.microsoft.com/en-us/library/aa997146.aspx.*

Unified Messaging Overview

Historically, voice mail administration has been the purview of the person or group responsible for managing an organization's telephony systems. However, in recent years, the distinction between voice and data communications has blurred as many PBX vendors have made available unified messaging products designed to integrate multiple forms of electronic communication, including e-mail, voice mail, and fax communications. Exchange administrators who have not had responsibility for communication beyond e-mail will find that Unified Messaging itself adds a level of complexity to daily tasks. Further, because all of the traditional voice mail functionality is moved into Exchange Server, Exchange administrators have a steep learning curve to undertake when it comes to deploying Unified Messaging. In this section, you're introduced to the features in the Unified Messaging services of Exchange Server 2007. You are also introduced to the various components—software and hardware—that make up Unified Messaging in Exchange Server 2007.

Unified Messaging Features

Exchange Server 2007 includes all of the features that you have come to expect from traditional voice mail systems, including voice mail inboxes and automated attendants. Exchange Server 2007 builds on these traditional features and includes much more. In this chapter, you learn how to create and manage these objects. Some objects have both physical and logical components. For example, in the case of an IP gateway, there is a physical device that actually handles a workload and then there is an associated logical Active Directory object.

- **Voice Messaging** Exchange Server 2007 replaces an organization's existing voice mail system and integrates the user's voice mail inbox with his or her e-mail inbox. With this integration come the benefits of Outlook-accessible e-mail, a single point of administration, and reduced hardware costs. Messages are accessible through Outlook, Outlook Web Access, Outlook Voice Access, Office Outlook Mobile, ActiveSync, and through other clients by way of attachments.

- **Fax Messaging** The Unified Messaging Fax Messaging feature in Exchange Server 2007 adds fax server capabilities to an organization, making faxes accessible in all of the ways described in the Voice Messaging feature.

- **Active Directory integration**   Managing two disparate messaging environments—voice mail and Exchange e-mail—often means managing two completely separate user databases. By implementing Exchange Server 2007 with Unified Messaging, you decrease the amount of administration required as all users' configuration information is stored in Active Directory.

- **Speech-Enabled Automated Attendant**   Many companies have implemented automated attendants as a way to reduce costs and handle an ever-increasing number of calls. An automated attendant is used to direct callers to their desired department or person in the most efficient way possible. Automated attendants in Exchange Server 2007 can work either through dual-tone multifrequency (DTMF)—also called touch tones—or through speech-enabled commands. In short, Exchange Server 2007 supports speech recognition capabilities so callers have a choice in how they respond to your menu system.

- **Flexible PBX integration**   Although not all PBX vendors directly support Session Initiation Protocol (SIP)—the communications protocol employed by Exchange Server 2007—on all versions of their PBX hardware and software, just about any PBX that does support this VoIP standard can integrate with the Unified Messaging server in Exchange Server 2007. For PBXs that do not or cannot support SIP, Exchange Server 2007 supports the use of third-party IP/PBX gateway devices. These gateway devices sit between the Exchange server and the PBX and handle communication between the two devices.

- **Voice-based Inbox access**   Unified Messaging in Exchange Server 2007 provides a number of ways beyond the traditional client to access information, including e-mail, calendars, and voice mail. In fact, most Exchange-based information is available to users using nothing more than a telephone. With Outlook Voice Access, users can access their Exchange mailbox using a standard telephone, available anywhere. Through touch-tone or speech-enabled menus, they can hear and act on their calendar, listen to e-mail messages (translated from text to speech), listen to voice mail messages, call their personal contacts, or call any user listed in the company directory.

- **Play on Phone**   There is a great convenience in having all communications delivered to a single inbox and available through Outlook. A user can read an e-mail on the screen or listen to voice mail on the computer's speakers. However, in crowded environments, or in security-conscious places, this public broadcast of voice mail may not be desirable. Therefore, the Unified Messaging in Exchange Server 2007 provides a feature that allows you to click an icon in Outlook and request that Exchange Server call you at any phone number and play your messages to you over the phone.

Exchange Server 2007 Unified Messaging Objects

With an understanding of some of the functionality provided by Unified Messaging, you also need to understand what is involved in making Unified Messaging work in your environment. In fact, there are a number of objects required to make Unified Messaging work.

Dial Plans

A Dial Plan is an Active Directory container object that represents sets or groupings of PBXs that share common user extension numbers. Users can dial one another's telephone extensions without appending a special number to the extension or dialing a full telephone number. A Dial Plan represents a PBX's extensions and ensures that a user's extension uniquely identifies his or her Exchange mailbox.

IP Gateways

Unified Messaging services in Exchange Server 2007 rely on VoIP and IP protocols, such as Session Initiation Protocol (SIP), Realtime Transport Protocol (RTP), or T.38 for real-time facsimile transport. Unless a PBX is IP-enabled and can communicate natively with the Exchange server using one of these protocols, a device that can translate time division multiplex (TDM) signals to one of the supported protocols is necessary. A physical IP gateway is such a device and handles the PBX-to-IP conversion that needs to take place. A Unified Messaging IP gateway *object* establishes a logical link between the IP/VoIP gateway, a dial plan, and single or multiple hunt groups.

Hunt Groups

A hunt group is a group of PBX resources or extension numbers that are shared by users. Hunt groups are used to efficiently distribute calls into or out of a given business unit. For example, a PBX might be configured to have 10 extension numbers for the sales department. These 10 sales extension numbers would be configured as one hunt group. In a PBX, hunt groups are used to efficiently locate an open line, extension, or channel when an incoming call is received. In a telephone network, a hunt group is defined as a set of extension numbers that are grouped as a single logical unit. When an incoming call is received, the PBX uses the hunt group that is defined to "hunt" for an available or open line, extension, or channel that can be used to receive the call.

Following are some terms that are important to understand when it comes to managing hunt groups:

- **Pilot number**   Because a PBX can have multiple hunt groups, the system needs a way to identify where a particular hunt group starts in order to route calls to the appropriate location. This is the function of the pilot number. Every hunt group has an associated pilot number. A pilot number is often the first telephone extension assigned to a hunt group. For example, if you have a hunt group with the telephone number 9000, 9001, 9002, 9003, 9004, and 9005, you might use 9000 as the pilot number. When a call is received at extension 9000, the PBX looks for the next available extension in the hunt group in order to send the call to the right phone.

■ **Unified Messaging hunt groups**   Exchange Server 2007 relies heavily on Unified Messaging hunt groups, which are logical representations of PBX hunt groups. A Unified Messaging hunt group is used to locate the PBX hunt group from which an incoming call was received. Failure to correctly configure a Unified Messaging hunt group will result in call failures since the server will not know how to handle incoming calls. Unified Messaging hunt groups are links between Unified Messaging IP gateways and Unified Messaging dial plans. Therefore, a single Unified Messaging hunt group must be associated with at least one Unified Messaging IP gateway and one Unified Messaging dial plan.

Mailbox Policies

Unified Messaging mailbox policies are required when you enable users for Unified Messaging and are useful for applying and standardizing Unified Messaging configuration settings for Unified Messaging–enabled users. Among the policies you can set are the following:

■ **PIN policies**   Every Unified Messaging–enabled user gets a PIN that allows that person to access his or her mailbox over the phone. PIN policies allow you to define settings such as the minimum number of digits in a PIN or the maximum number of logon attempts allowed.

■ **Dialing restrictions**   Dialing Restrictions govern how, and if, people are allowed to call outside the organization.

Automated Attendants

In telephony or Unified Messaging environments, an automated attendant transfers callers to the extension of a user or department without the intervention of a receptionist or an operator. In many auto attendant systems, a receptionist or operator can be reached by pressing or saying zero. The automated attendant is a feature on most modern PBX and Unified Messaging solutions.

Exchange Server 2007 Unified Messaging enables you to create one or more Unified Messaging auto attendants depending on the needs of your organization. Unified Messaging auto attendants can be used to create a voice menu system for an organization that lets external and internal callers move through the UM auto attendant menu system to locate and place or transfer calls to company users or departments in an organization.

Automated attendants can be configured for business hours and after-hours support. During these times, you might want different welcome messages to be played or different menus to be presented so that users can be directed to live after-hours resources instead of to the voice mailboxes of daytime employees.

Creating and Managing Unified Messaging Objects

At this point, it's assumed that you have installed the Unified Messaging server role on one of your Exchange Server 2007 servers. The Unified Messaging server role installs just like most of the other server roles through the use of the Exchange Server 2007 installer.

In order for Unified Messaging to work, you need to create a number of Active Directory objects and associate one of your Unified Messaging servers with a particular Unified Messaging dial plan. This section explains how to create the necessary objects and perform required associations. Note that this information is extremely dependent on the PBX or gateway hardware in use in your organization, and it's suggested that you work very closely with your telephony vendor when implementing Exchange Server 2007 Unified Messaging.

Unified Messaging Dial Plans

A dial plan is the foundational object for the Unified Messaging server role in Exchange Server 2007 and represents a logical connection between a PBX dial plan and Active Directory.

Creating a New Dial Plan

To create a new dial plan in your organization, follow these steps:

1. Open the Exchange Management Console.

2. Choose Organization Configuration and then choose Unified Messaging.

3. Click the UM Dial Plans tab, as shown in Figure 14-1.

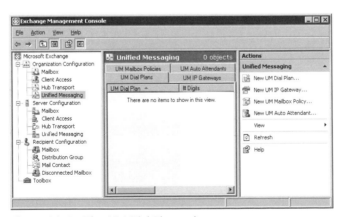

Figure 14-1 The UM Dial Plans tab

4. From the Action pane, choose New UM Dial Plan.

5. The New UM Dial Plan Wizard is a single-page wizard that asks for just two pieces of information: the UM Dial Plan Name and the number of digits in extensions at your organization (see Figure 14-2).

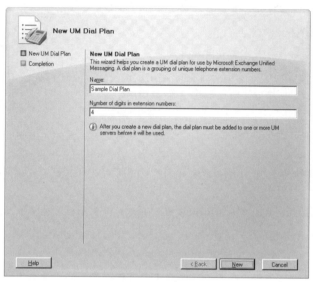

Figure 14-2   The New UM Dial Plan Wizard

6. Click New to create the new dial plan.

When you create a new dial plan using the Exchange Management Console, a default mailbox policy is also created with the name "*dial plan name* Default Policy." If you want to suppress the automatic creation of a mailbox policy, use the Exchange Management Shell to create the dial plan.

Management Shell

A dial plan is the foundational element in the Unified Messaging service in Exchange Server 2007 and links all other Unified Messaging elements together. When using the Exchange Management Console to create a new dial plan, you can only specify the name of the dial plan and the number of digits in the extensions used in your organization. The following command replicates this limited functionality.

```
new-UMDialPlan -Name 'Sample Dial Plan' -NumberOfDigitsInExtension '4'
```

The Exchange Management Shell `new-UMDialPlan` command gives you the ability to specify a number of other parameters, including whether or not the signaling channel should be encrypted, whether or not a default mailbox policy will be created, a list of pilot ID numbers, and more. For example, the command below does the following:

- Creates a new dial plan named Sample Dial Plan

- Indicates that the organization's extensions contain four digits

- Disables VoIP security

- Disables the creation of a default mailbox policy

```
New-UMDialplan -Name "Sample Dial Plan" -NumberofDigits 4
-VOIPSecurity Unsecured -GenerateUMMailboxPolicy:$false
```

Managing Dial Plans

After you create a new dial plan, there are a number of ways in which you can configure the dial plan to meet the needs of your organization. For example, you can configure the following:

- **Welcome Greeting**   Decide which welcome greeting should be played to users.

- **Informational Announcement**   Configure an informational announcement to be sent out to users. You can configure this announcement as uninterruptable so that users are required to listen to it.

- **Associated Subscriber Access Numbers**   Use this field to add telephone numbers or extensions that a user will call to access the Unified Messaging system by using Outlook Voice Access. In most cases, you will enter an extension number or an external telephone number, as shown in Figure 14-3.

- **Dial Codes**   When incoming or outgoing calls are placed to or from the Unified Messaging server, you can determine codes that will be used to support this access, as shown in Figure 14-4. For example, if your PBX configuration requires that you dial 9 for an outside line or that you dial 011 to dial internationally, you can configure this information as a part of the dial plan.

- **Allow Callers To Transfer To Users**   By default, allows users associated with the dial plan to transfer calls to other users in the same dial plan. Change the Callers Can Contact option to broaden or limit the scope of this transfer capability, as shown in Figure 14-5.

- **Allow Callers To Send Voice Message**   By default, allows users who are associated with the dial plan to send voice messages to users in the same dial plan. Change the Callers Can Contact option to broaden or limit the scope of this transfer capability.

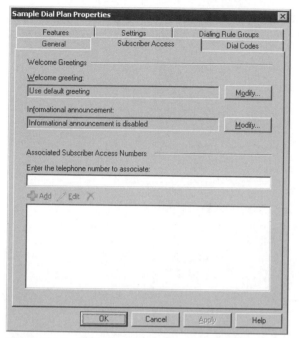

Figure 14-3   Dial Plan Properties Subscriber Access tab

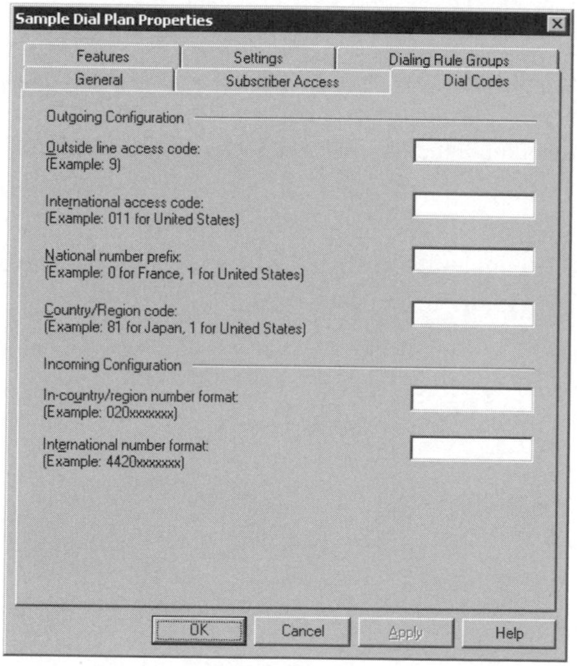

Figure 14-4   Dial Plan Properties Dial Codes tab

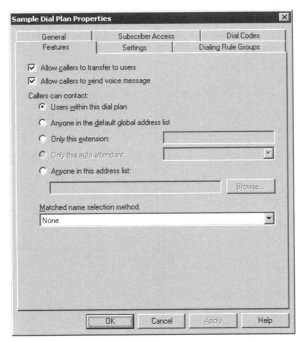

Figure 14-5 Dial Plan Properties Features tab

- **Callers Can Contact** Allows callers to transfer calls to a broader or more limited group of users. You can choose the default Users Within This Dial Plan, or you can expand the option to include all of the users in your Global Address List. If desired, you can allow transfers only to a specific extension or, if you have an auto attendant created, to a specific auto attendant. Finally, you can select a different address list to use for this purpose.

- **Matched Name Selection Method** If you have users with similar names, how should the dial plan differentiate between them? You can allow differentiation based on job title, department, location, or a user's alias.

- **Dial By Name Primary Method** When using the Dial By Name feature, what will callers use to locate a name? The default is last name followed by first name, as shown in Figure 14-6. The available options are last-first, first-last, and SMTP address.

- **Dial By Name Secondary Method** Provides a second way for callers to locate users. The default secondary method is SMTP address. You do not have to have a secondary method.

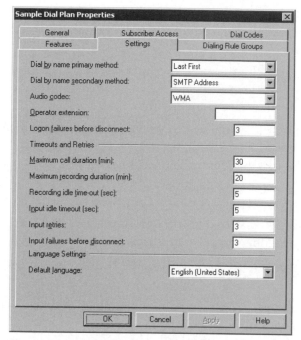

Figure 14-6   Dial Plan Properties Settings tab

- **Audio Codec**   Unified Messaging provides three formats in which messages can be recorded: Windows Media Audio (WMA), G.711 Pulse Code Modulation (PCM) Linear, and Group System Mobile 06.10 Global System for Mobile Communications (GSM). The default and recommended choice is WMA due to its high quality and high level of compression.

- **Operator Extension**   What is the extension for the operator for this dial plan? When a caller presses the # key, says "operator" or "receptionist," or exceeds your retry threshold, he or she is transferred to this extension for help. If you leave this field blank, callers are disconnected if they try to get to an operator.

- **Logon Failures Before Disconnect**   Indicates how many sequential unsuccessful logon attempts are allowed before a caller is disconnected. The default is 3 attempts but can range from 1 to 20.

- **Maximum Call Duration (Min)**   Specifies how long (in minutes) an incoming call can stay connected to the system without being transferred to a valid extension number. The default is 30 minutes and can range from 10 to 120 minutes.

- **Maximum Recording Duration (Min)**   Specifies the maximum number of minutes allowed for each voice recording when a caller leaves a voice mail message. The default is 20 minutes and can range from 5 to 100 minutes.

- **Recording Idle Time-out (Sec)** Specifies the number of seconds of silence that can elapse when a message is being recorded before the call is ended. The default is 5 seconds but can range from 2 to 16 seconds.

- **Input Idle Timeout (Sec)** Specifies the number of seconds that the system will wait for a caller to provide some kind of input before a voice command is issued. The default is 5 seconds, and this value can range from 3 to 32 seconds.

- **Input Retries** Indicates to the system how many times a caller is prompted for input before the call is transferred to the extension specified in the Operator Extension field. The default is 3 retries, but this field provides a range of 1 to 16 times.

- **Input Failures Before Disconnect** Specifies how many times a caller can provide incorrect data before the call is disconnected. This parameter takes effect when, for example, a caller wants to be transferred to an extension that doesn't exist. The default value is 3 attempts, but this can be set to any number between 1 and 20.

- **Default Language** Specifies the language that should be used by the Unified Messaging server.

- **In-Country/Region Rule Groups** Create dialed number masks that match local standards, as shown in Figure 14-7.

- **International Rule Groups** Create dialed number masks that allow international calling.

Management Shell

After you create a new dial plan, there are a number of ways in which you can configure the dial plan to meet the needs of your organization. The Exchange Management Shell `Set-UMDialPlan` command allows you to modify the configuration for an existing dial plan. Here are some sample commands that can be used to configure a dial plan.

This example configures a dial plan named Sample Dial Plan to use 9 for the outside line access code:

```
Set-UMDialPlan -Identity "Sample Dial Plan" -OutsideLineAccessCode 9
```

This example configures the same dial plan and limits the call duration to 15 minutes and the maximum recording duration to 10 minutes. It also sets the Operator extension to 1234 and sets the audio codec to WMA.

```
Set-UMDialPlan -Identity "Sample Dial Plan" -MaxCallDuration 15
-MaxRecordingDuration 10 -OperatorExtension 1234 -AudioCodec WMA
```

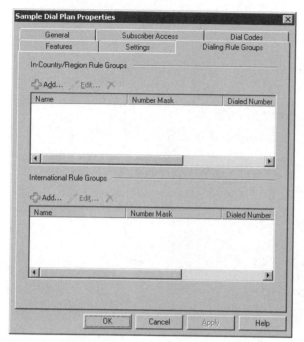

Figure 14-7   Dial Plan Properties Dialing Rule Groups tab

Unified Messaging Mailbox Policy

Earlier in this chapter, you learned that you can configure mailbox policies that, among other things, limit the greeting duration and specify the minimum number of digits in a user's PIN.

Creating Mailbox Policies

There are a number of ways to create mailbox policies in Exchange Server 2007. If you create a dial plan using the Exchange Management Console, a default mailbox policy is created for you and automatically associated with the dial plan. Or you can create your own mailbox policy. Before you can create a mailbox policy, you must create a dial plan with which to associate the mailbox policy. To do so, follow these steps:

1. Open the Exchange Management Console.

2. Choose Organization Configuration and then choose Unified Messaging.

3. Click the UM Mailbox Polices tab (refer back to Figure 14-1).

4. From the Action pane, choose New UM Mailbox Policy.

5. The New UM Mailbox Policy Wizard is a single-page wizard that asks for just two pieces of information—the UM Mailbox Policy Name and the name of the dial plan

with which the new mailbox policy should be associated. You must associate the mailbox policy with an existing dial plan (see Figure 14-8).

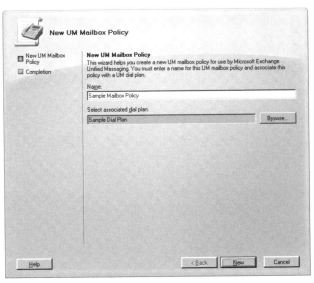

Figure 14-8 The New UM Mailbox Policy Wizard

6. Click New to create the new mailbox policy. The new mailbox policy is created and associated with the specified dial plan.

Management Shell

A mailbox policy provides an Exchange administrator with the capability to protect the messaging environment by requiring a minimum PIN length and determining the number of entry errors allowed after which a PIN is automatically reset. The Exchange Management Shell `New-UMMailboxPolicy` command is used to create a new mailbox policy.

```
New-UMMailboxPolicy -Name "Sample Mailbox Policy"
-UMDialPlan "Sample Dial Plan"
```

This command does not support any other configuration-related parameters.

Managing Mailbox Policies

After you create a new mailbox policy, additional configuration parameters become available and are configurable through the Exchange Management Console. For example, on the General tab of the Mailbox Policy Properties dialog box (shown in Figure 14-9), you can configure the following:

- **Name field**   If desired, change the name of the mailbox policy.

- **Maximum Greeting Duration (Minutes)**   Specify the maximum number of minutes allowed for each user's greeting. The default is 5 minutes, and the value can range from 1 to 10 minutes.

- **Allow Missed Call Notifications**   Select this check box to set a policy that sends an e-mail message to users each time they miss a call. If the caller also records a voice mail message, users receive two e-mail messages.

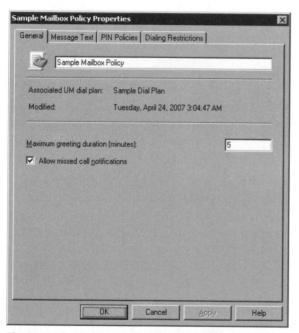

Figure 14-9   Mailbox Policy Properties General tab

On the Message Text tab of the Mailbox Policy Properties dialog box (shown in Figure 14-10), you can configure the following settings:

- **Fax Identity**   The identity sent to a receiving fax machine along with the fax.

- **Text Sent When A UM Mailbox Is Enabled**   When a user's mailbox is enabled for Unified Messaging, that user is sent an e-mail message that includes welcome text and the user's access PIN. In this field, you can type up to 512 characters of text that are included in the welcome message.

■ **Text Sent When A PIN Is Reset**   If a user tries too many times to access the Unified Messaging server, the user's access PIN is automatically reset. In this field, you can include a 512-character message that accompanies the reset notification e-mail that the user receives.

■ **Text Included With A Voice Message**   For each voice mail message that a user receives in his or her inbox, you can include a 512-character message. For example, you may want to include a warning that forwarding a voice mail outside an organization could be prohibited by company policy.

■ **Text Included With A Fax Message**   For each fax message that a user receives, you can include a 512-character message that accompanies the fax message.

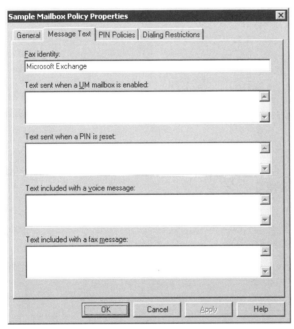

Figure 14-10   Mailbox Policy Properties Message Text tab

On the PIN Policies tab of the Mailbox Policy Properties dialog box (shown in Figure 14-11), you can configure the following settings:

■ **Minimum PIN Length**   Specifies the minimum number of digits allowed in a PIN. The default setting is 6 digits, but can be as low as 4 digits or as high as 24 digits.

■ **PIN Lifetime (Days)**   Like network passwords, you can require users to change their Unified Messaging PINs on a regular basis. The default setting requires users to change their PINs every 60 days. Specify a value of 0 to disable PIN expiration. This value can be as high as 999 days.

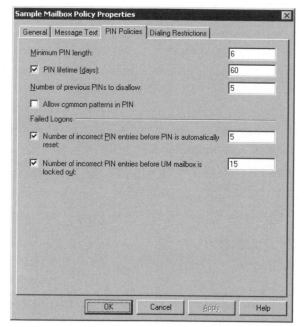

Figure 14-11   Mailbox Policy Properties PIN Policies tab

- **Number Of Previous PINs To Disallow**   If you allow users to reuse old PINs, you can reduce the overall security of your messaging system. By providing a value in this field, you can decide how many old PINs are not usable. The default is 5 PINs, and this value can range from 1 to 20 old PINs.

- **Allow Common Patterns In PIN**   For ease of access, some users set their PINs to things like 123456 or 111111 or 222222 or their extension. These kinds of patterns are easy to guess and can reduce the overall security of your messaging system. If you want to allow this ease of use and understand the security implications, enable this setting. Leave the setting disabled for the highest level of protection. Note that, even if you select this check box, users cannot use their extension number as a PIN.

- **Number Of Incorrect PIN Entries Before PIN Is Automatically Reset**   With a default of 5 attempts and a range of 0 to 999 attempts, this entry determines how many tries a user gets to enter his or her PIN correctly. If you provide a value of 0, the system will never reset a user's PIN. You must set this value lower than the **Lockout** parameter.

- **Number Of Incorrect PIN Entries Before UM Mailbox Is Locked Out**   At some point, your security policy might dictate that a user is to be completely denied access to a resource after a number of access attempts. In this case, the default value is 15 attempts with values between 1 and 999 allowed.

On the Dialing Restrictions tab of the Mailbox Policy Properties dialog box (shown in Figure 14-12), you can configure the following settings:

- **Allow Calls To Users Within The Same Dial Plan**   Allows Unified Messaging–enabled users to place calls to other Unified Messaging–enabled users that are in the same dial plan. By default, this option is enabled.

- **Allow Calls To Extensions**   Allows Unified Messaging–enabled users to place calls directly to the extensions serviced by the dial plan. By default, this option is disabled.

- **Select Allowed In-Country/Region Rule Groups From Dial Plan**   Choose the regional groups from the dial plan that are to be covered under this policy.

- **Select Allowed International Rule Groups From Dial Plan**   Choose the international groups from the dial plan that are to be covered under this policy.

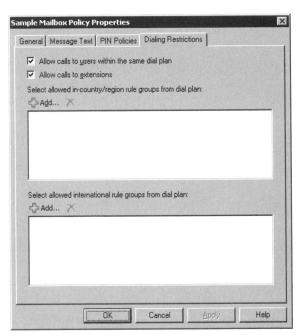

Figure 14-12   Mailbox Policy Properties Dialing Restrictions tab

Management Shell

The mailbox policy creation process does not provide any configuration parameters from the Exchange Management Console or from the Exchange Management Shell. Therefore, if you want to change any of the items associated with a mailbox policy, first create the policy and then make the desired changes.

After you create a new mailbox policy, use the Exchange Management Shell `Set-UMMailboxPolicy` command to modify the configuration for an existing mailbox policy. Here is a sample command that can be used to configure a mailbox policy.

```
Set-UMMailboxPolicy -Identity "Sample Mailbox Policy"
-AllowCommonPatterns:$true -AllowMissedCallNotifications:$true
```

This example configures a mailbox policy named Sample Mailbox Policy to allow the use of repeating patterns in PINs and to enable missed call notifications.

Unified Messaging IP Gateways

In order to work, your Exchange Server 2007 Unified Messaging server needs to have something to talk to. A Unified Messaging IP gateway is used to connect Unified Messaging servers to an IP/VoIP gateway or an SIP-enabled IP/PBX. Bear in mind that the steps outlined in this section cover the creation and management of the logical representation for a physical gateway device. This section does not cover the configuration of the physical IP/VoIP gateway or SIP-enabled IP/PBX.

Creating IP Gateways

Unified Messaging IP gateways are simple to create using the Exchange Management Console and require only a few parameters, including a name, the IP address for the physical gateway or SIP-enabled PBX, and the name of a dialing plan with which to associate the IP gateway. To create a Unified Messaging IP gateway, follow these steps:

1. Open the Exchange Management Console.

2. Choose Organization Configuration and then choose Unified Messaging.

3. Click the UM IP Gateways tab (refer back to Figure 14-1).

4. From the Actions pane, choose New UM IP Gateway.

5. The New UM IP Gateway Wizard is a single-page wizard that asks for just three pieces of information—the UM IP Gateway Name, the IP address or fully qualified domain name of the physical gateway or SIP-enabled PBX, and the name of the dial plan with which the new IP gateway should be associated. You don't have to associate the IP gateway with an existing dial plan in this step. When you do, however, a hunt group is automatically created (see Figure 14-13).

6. Click New to create the new UM IP gateway. The new IP gateway is created and, if provided, associated with the specified dial plan.

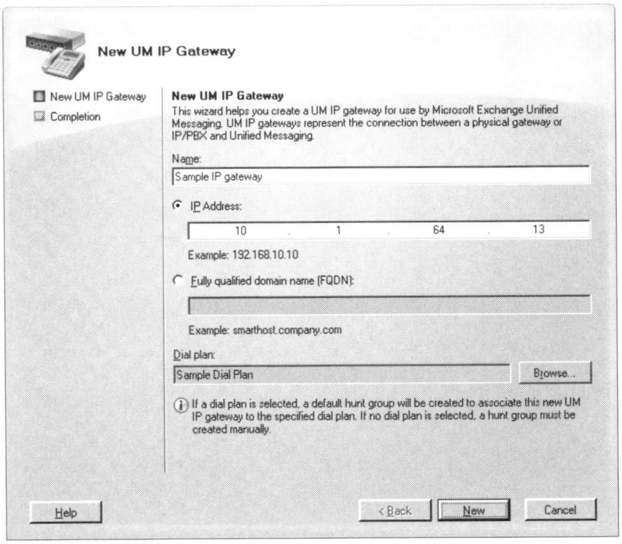

Figure 14-13 The New UM IP Gateway Wizard

Management Shell

A Unified Messaging IP gateway is used to provide a logical connection between a Unified Messaging server and an IP/VoIP gateway or an SIP-enabled IP/PBX.

The Exchange Management Shell **New-UMIPGateway** command is used to create a new IP gateway object on a Unified Messaging server.

```
New-UMIPGateway -Name "Sample IP Gateway" -Address "10.1.64.13"
-UMDialPlan "Sample Dial Plan"
```

This command does not support any other configuration-related parameters. Upon completion of this command, if you specified a dial plan, the Exchange Management Shell also creates an associated hunt group.

Managing IP Gateways

There are very few parameters associated with the IP gateway object. They are shown in Figure 14-14 and in the following list.

- **Name field** If desired, change the display name of the IP gateway.

- **IP Address** Optionally, provide the IP address of the gateway or SIP-enabled PBX.

- **Fully Qualified Domain Name** Optionally, provide the full DNS name for the physical gateway device.

■ **Allow Outgoing Calls Through This UM IP Gateway**   Allow the Unified Messaging IP gateway to accept and process outgoing calls. By default, this option is enabled.

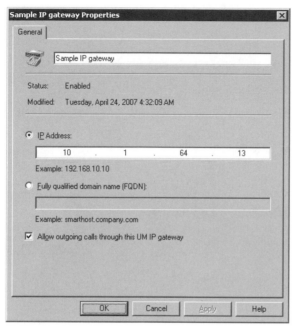

Figure 14-14   The IP Gateway Properties General tab

Management Shell

With a lot of the commands in the Exchange Management Shell, there are a number of parameters available that are inaccessible via the Exchange Management Console. However, in the case of the command that manages existing IP gateway objects, `Set-UMIPGateway`, only a few parameters are not accessible through the GUI.

After you create a new IP gateway object, use the Exchange Management Shell to modify the object's configuration. This example configures an IP gateway object named Sample IP Gateway to allow outbound calls and to use a nonstandard VoIP TCP port for communication:

```
Set-UMIPGateway -Identity "Sample IP Gateway"
-OutcallsAllowed:$true -Port:65535
```

For a complete list of parameters allowed by the **Set-UMIPGateway** command, visit *http://technet.microsoft.com/en-us/library/aa996577.aspx*.

Associating Servers with Dial Plans

Even if you create a number of Unified Messaging objects, such as a dial plan, mailbox policy, and IP gateway, in order for Unified Messaging services to operate, you need to enable the services on each of the servers on which you installed the Unified Messaging server role. Follow these steps to accomplish this goal:

1. Open the Exchange Management Console.

2. Choose Server Configuration and then choose Unified Messaging.

3. Select the server on which you have installed the Unified Messaging server role.

4. In the Actions pane, click the Properties option. The Properties page for the server opens.

5. Click the UM Settings tab, as shown in Figure 14-15.

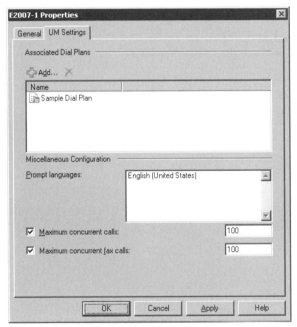

Figure 14-15 The Server Properties UM Settings tab

6. In the Associated Dial Plans section, click Add. The Select Dial Plan window opens, as shown in Figure 14-16.

7. From this window, select the dial plan you want to associate with this server and click OK.

8. Back on the UM Settings tab, click OK.

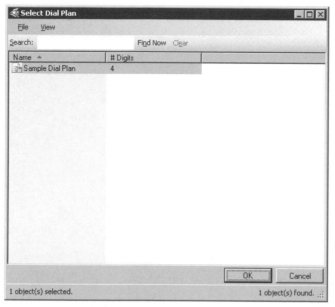

Figure 14-16   The Select Dial Plan window

Management Shell

When you install the Unified Messaging server role on an Exchange Server 2007 computer, the service is enabled by default. However, before the server can accommodate incoming calls, you must add the Unified Messaging server to one of your Unified Messaging dial plans. Use the `Set-UMServer` command to accomplish this, as per the following example. Make sure to replace the `identity` parameter and `DialPlans` parameter with the name of your Unified Messaging server and the name of one of your own dial plans, respectively.

```
Set-UMServer -Identity e2007-1 -DialPlans "Sample Dial Plan"
```

Enabling Unified Messaging for Individual Mailboxes

After you create the necessary Unified Messaging objects and associate a Unified Messaging server with a dial plan, and use your vendor's instructions to make sure that connectivity is working, you can start enabling Unified Messaging on individual mailboxes. To do so, follow these steps:

1. Open the Exchange Management Console.

2. Choose Recipient Configuration and then choose Mailbox.

3. In the Action pane, select the user you want to enable for Unified Messaging.

4. From the Actions pane, select the Enable Unified Messaging option. This starts a one-page wizard (see Figure 14-17) on which you must configure user-related messaging options.

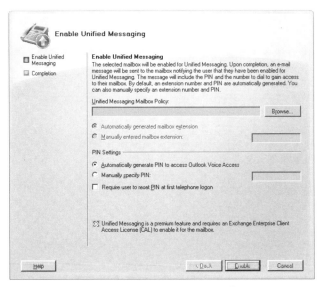

Figure 14-17   Enable Unified Messaging features on a user's mailbox

5. On the Enable Unified Messaging page of the wizard, select a previously created Unified Messaging mailbox policy that will apply to this user. Click Browse to locate a policy.

6. If the user has a phone extension in Active Directory, the Automatically Generate Mailbox Extension option is available and pulls the user's extension from Active Directory. Otherwise, select the Manually Entered Mailbox Extension option and provide the extension number.

7. Under PIN Settings, either allow Exchange to generate a PIN to the user by selecting the Automatically Generate PIN To Access Outlook Voice Access option. Or, if you want to manually specify a PIN for the user, select Manually Specify PIN and provide the PIN. For added security, select the check box next to Require User To Reset PIN At First Telephone Login.

8. Click Enable.

When you enable a user for Unified Messaging, the user receives an e-mail message that includes his or her newly assigned PIN (see Figure 14-18).

Figure 14-18   The e-mail message that is sent after enabling Unified Messaging

Management Shell

After you create the necessary Unified Messaging objects and associated a Unified Messaging server with a dial plan, and used your vendor's instructions to make sure that connectivity is working, you can start enabling Unified Messaging on individual mailboxes.

Use the `Enable-UMMailbox` command to enable Unified Messaging on a user's mailbox. The `PinExpired:$false` parameter indicates that the user does not have to change his or her PIN on the first login to the system. The `Extensions` and `UMMailbox` policy parameters indicate the telephone extension the user will use and the mailbox policy that will apply to this user, respectively.

```
Enable-UMMailbox -identity kim.akers@contoso.com
-PinExpired:$false -UMMailboxPolicy "Sample Mailbox Policy"
-Extensions "1002"
```

Summary

One of the most noticeable enhancements to Exchange Server 2007, the Unified Messaging server role takes a lot of up-front work and planning with your PBX vendor in order to determine the best way to handle the deployment. On the Exchange side, in this chapter you learned how to create the basics—dial plan, mailbox policy, and IP gateway objects—learned how to associate a server with a dial plan, and learned how to enable a user's mailbox for Unified Messaging.

Part V
Maintenance

Chapter 15

Troubleshooting Exchange Server 2007

Nothing is perfect—not your car, your house, or even Microsoft Exchange Server 2007. It's no wonder, then, that stores selling car parts and building supplies are successful. Even a stable system like Exchange Server 2007 can break down once in a while. Troubleshooting Exchange Server 2007 is a skill that you will develop as you solve real problems on your network. One chapter cannot prepare you for all the possibilities you could face as an Exchange administrator. However, this chapter introduces some of the troubleshooting tools that are available in Exchange Server 2007 and discusses some places to find more information and help with specific types of Exchange problems.

Using Troubleshooting Tools

When you troubleshoot a system as complex as Exchange Server 2007, your most valuable tool is your understanding of the system itself. This understanding includes knowledge of how Exchange Server 2007 works in general and how your organization is set up in particular. Ideally, this book gives you a good understanding of Exchange Server 2007 and, if you take the advice in Chapter 4, "Assessing Needs," you have completely documented your network. With this knowledge in hand, you are ready to find and repair whatever might go wrong in your organization. This section introduces some of the tools you will use in the process.

Using Event Viewer

As you might know, Microsoft Windows Server 2003 records many events in its own event logs. You can view the logs of both local and remote servers by using the Event

Viewer utility, which you can find in the Administrative Tools folder on the Programs menu. Windows maintains three distinct logs:

- **Application**   The application log is a record of events generated by applications. All Exchange Server 2007 services write their status information to this log. If you enable diagnostics logging for any Exchange components, that information is also recorded in the application log. This log is the most valuable one for monitoring the general health of an Exchange server. Figure 15-1 shows an entry made in the application log following an error in obtaining DNS records from a domain controller.

- **Security**   The security log is a record of events based on the auditing settings specified in the local policy of a machine or by group policy that applies to the machine.

- **System**   The system log is a record of events that concern components of the system itself, including such events as device driver and network failures.

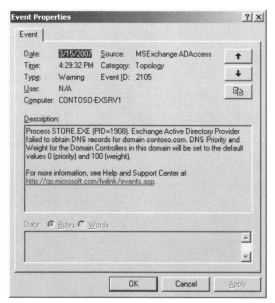

Figure 15-1   Reviewing an application event created by Exchange Server 2007

Note   You will also see additional event logs in Event Viewer based upon the services installed on your server. For example, a server running Domain Name System (DNS) will show a DNS Service log. Domain controllers also show a File Replication Service and Directory Service log. Exchange servers also show a PowerShell and Windows PowerShell log for events related to the new command shell.

If you have a particular log file that you want to save, you have at your disposal three formats in which to save it. You can save it as a binary event log file with the .evt extension, as a text file with the .txt extension, or as a comma-delimited text file with the .csv extension. Binary files with the .evt extension can be read only with Event Viewer; the two text files can be read with your favorite ASCII editor/viewer or even imported into a spreadsheet or database.

Note The Event ID associated with an event can be useful in troubleshooting. You can use the Event ID as the keyword in a search of the Microsoft Knowledge Base and often find good descriptions and solutions to problems. You can search the Knowledge Base from the Microsoft Support site at *http://support.microsoft.com*.

You encounter five types of events in the three logs, and a unique icon identifies each event type so that you can easily distinguish between the information entries and the error entries. Table 15-1 shows these icons and describes each of them. Normally, you will encounter only the first three icons in the table in relation to Exchange Server. The classification of events is controlled by the applications and system and cannot be configured by the administrators.

Table 15-1 Event Types Displayed in Event Viewer

Icon	Event	Description
⊗	Error	A significant problem has occurred, such as an Exchange Server service that may not have started properly.
⚠	Warning	An event has occurred that is not currently detrimental to the system but might indicate a possible future problem.
ⓘ	Information	A successful operation has occurred. For example, an Exchange Server service starting successfully might trigger this type of event.
🗝	Audit success	An audited security access attempt—for example, a successful logon to the system—was successful.
🔒	Audit failure	An audited security access attempt—for example, a failed access to an audited file or directory—was not successful.

Using Diagnostics Logging

All Exchange Server 2007 services log certain critical events to the Windows Server 2003 application log. For some services, however, you can configure additional levels of diagnostics logging. Diagnostics logging is one of the most useful tools for troubleshooting problems in Exchange Server 2007.

You can only modify the levels of diagnostics logging on a particular Exchange server by using the Exchange Management Shell; there is no provision for configuring diagnostic logging in the Exchange Management Console.

Modifying the Logging Level for a Process

The first step in modifying the logging level of an Exchange process is to determine whether the logging level of a process is configurable and its current logging level. To see the logging levels of all configurable processes (and while you're at it, to see the processes for which you can modify the logging levels), use the following cmdlet in the Exchange Management Shell:

```
get-eventloglevel
```

Figure 15-2 shows a partial listing of the results of this command, indicating the identity of processes for which the logging level is modifiable and the current logging level of each process.

Figure 15-2   Viewing diagnostics logging levels for available processes

If you are unsure of the name of the process or just want to see what processes can be modified, the `get-eventloglevel` cmdlet by itself is useful. However, if you already know the name of the processes you want to check on, you can append that process name to the cmdlet in the following manner:

```
get-eventloglevel <processname>
```

This command returns only the named process and its logging level, which can sometimes be more useful (and quicker) than browsing through the whole list of processes.

After you determine that the diagnostic logging can be changed for a particular process, you can change the level by typing the following cmdlet:

```
set-eventloglevel <process> -level <level>
```

For example, to set the logging level of the MSExchange OWA\Core process to level 5 (Maximum), type the following command:

```
set-eventloglevel MSExchange OWA\Core -level 5
```

Note   When you set the logging level of a process to anything other than Lowest, you can use the number for the –level parameter to indicate the level you want to set. However, when setting a process to Lowest logging level, you must use the word "Lowest" instead of the number 1.

Logging Levels

For each process, you can enable five distinct levels of logging. All events that occur in Exchange Server 2007 are given an event level of Lowest (0), Low (1), Medium (3), Maximum (5), or Expert (7). The logging level you set determines which levels of events are logged. Those levels are:

- **Lowest**   Only critical events, errors, and other events with a logging level of 0 are logged. These events include application and system failures. This level is the default level of logging for all Exchange processes except for two (which are set to the Low level): MSExchange ASAccess\Validation and MSExchange ADAccess\Topology. Table 15-1 shows the processes for which you can configure diagnostic logging and their default logging levels.

- **Low**   All events with a logging level of 1 or lower are logged.

- **Medium**   All events with a logging level of 3 or lower are logged.

- **Maximum**   All events with a logging level of 5 or lower are logged.

- **Expert**   All events with a logging level of 7 or lower are logged

For a list of all processes for which you can change diagnostic logging levels, along with their default levels, see Appendix D, "Default Diagnostic Logging Levels for Exchange Processes."

Note   In the Exchange Management Shell, a logging level 5 is named "High." However, in the Exchange Server 2007 help files and other documentation, logging level 5 is named "Maximum." You should be aware of this discrepancy.

Real World   Size of the Event Viewer Application Log

Diagnostics logging of Exchange Server 2007 components generates many entries in the Event Viewer application log, especially if you set the diagnostics logging level to Maximum or Expert level. Use diagnostics logging only when you troubleshoot potential problems in specific components and disable it when you finish. By default, the application log file is set to a maximum size of 16,384 KB, which is a fine size for most situations. Setting this size to at least 4 MB (4096 KB) when using diagnostics logging is recommended. By default, each log file overwrites events as needed, meaning that when the log has reached its maximum size the oldest events are removed to accommodate the newest events.

You can configure the default settings for size and overwriting by changing the Maximum Log Size and Event Log Wrapping options on the property sheet for the log. To see this property sheet, in Event Viewer, right-click the log in question and then click Properties. The options are in the Log Size area of the General tab. The Maximum Log Size option can be adjusted in 64-KB increments.

You can choose from among three Event Log Wrapping options: Overwrite Events As Needed, Overwrite Events Older Than X Days, and Do Not Overwrite Events. (If you select the last option you must clear the log manually.) Make sure that you set the wrapping option correctly for what you are trying to accomplish. For example, if you set it to Overwrite Events As Needed, you could lose critical information that might have helped you solve the problem you had when you turned diagnostics on in the first place.

Real World   Using High Levels of Diagnostics Logging

Although diagnostics logging can be a very useful tool in some circumstances, at other times it can be more of a hindrance than a help. Enabling high levels of diagnostics logging, such as Medium or higher, can fill up your event log quickly, often hiding important level 0 events in a flood of trivial events. In addition, many events are logged that might seem like errors but actually are not. These events include the routine errors and timeouts that occur in normal Exchange Server 2007 operation.

Finally, many events are logged that are really not documented anywhere in the product literature. Exchange developers often use these undocumented events to perform diagnostics.

It is recommended that diagnostics logging be set to Lowest for general purposes. If you need to troubleshoot malfunctions of particular services, raise the diagnostics logging level for related processes to Low or Medium for brief periods.

Inbox Repair Tool

Not all problems in an Exchange organization occur on an Exchange server. Many users keep personal folders and offline folders on their client computers. A set of personal folders is stored as a single file with the extension .pst. The name and location of the PST file is shown in the Personal Folders property sheet in Outlook, as shown in Figure 15-3. Multiple sets of personal folders can be stored on a single client. Like any other type of file, personal folder files can become corrupt. Fortunately, Microsoft Outlook provides the Inbox Repair Tool, which helps you repair corrupt personal folder files.

Figure 15-3   Personal folders stored in a .pst file

The Inbox Repair Tool (Scanpst.exe) is installed during a typical installation of Microsoft Outlook, but no shortcut is created on the Start menu. You can find the file Scanpst.exe in the \Program Files\Microsoft Office\Office12 directory for Microsoft Office Outlook 2007. Note that these are default paths that can be changed during client installation. When you launch the Inbox Repair Tool, a dialog box appears in which you can type the path and file name of the corrupt file and then click Start (see Figure 15-4).

After you start the scanning process, the Inbox Repair Tool examines the entire contents of the specified file and shows you what it finds, as shown in Figure 15-5. The Inbox Repair Tool gives you a chance to back up the file before you perform repairs on it, and you should always use this option. The Inbox Repair Tool usually moves messages that it cannot repair to a special Lost And Found folder, but it often discards messages that it cannot repair. Without a backup, these messages are permanently lost. When the Inbox Repair Tool finishes running, launch Outlook to access this Lost And Found folder. Create a new set of personal folders and move any recovered items to these new folders.

Often, however, the Inbox Repair Tool simply fixes problems you are having in Outlook and should always be given a chance.

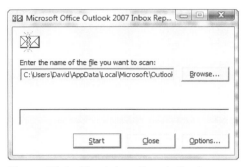

Figure 15-4   The Inbox Repair Tool

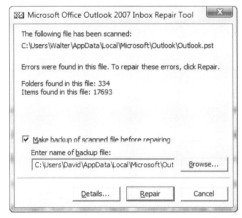

Figure 15-5   The Inbox Repair Tool after scanning a .pst file

> **Note**   The OST Integrity Check Tool (scanost.exe—also in the \Program Files\Microsoft Office\Office12 directory for Outlook 2007) does for offline folder files (.ost files) what scanpst.exe does for personal folder files, scanning .ost files for any signs of corruption and then fixing that corruption if it can.

RPing Utility

Many of the connections among computers in an Exchange organization rely on remote procedure calls (RPCs). As you know, an RPC calls a protocol that allows a program on one computer to execute a program on another computer. Exchange servers in a routing group rely on RPCs to communicate with one another. Exchange clients connect to Exchange servers by using RPCs. Likewise, the Exchange Management Console connects to remote Exchange servers via RPCs. Often, connectivity problems in an Exchange organization are the result of bad RPC connectivity.

You can use the RPing utility to confirm the RPC connectivity between two systems as well as to make sure that Exchange services are responding to requests from clients and other servers. RPing has two components: a server component (rpings.exe) and a client component (rpingc.exe). You can find both of these components in the Windows Server 2003 Resource Kit tools directory following installation of the Resource Kit tools, which are available at *http://www.microsoft.com/downloads/details.aspx?familyid=9d467a69-57ff-4ae7-96ee-b18c4790cffd&displaylang=en*.

RPing Server

The server component of RPing is a file named rpings.exe, which you must start on the server before using the client component. To run the server component, type **rpings.exe** at the command prompt. This command runs the server component using all available protocol sequences, as shown in Figure 15-6. A *protocol sequence* is a routine that allows the return of a ping for a given networking protocol, such as TCP/IP or IPX/SPX. You can also restrict the server component to any single protocol sequence by using the following switches:

- -p ipx/spx
- -p namedpipes
- -p netbios
- -p tcpip
- -p vines

To exit the RPing server, type the string **@q** at the RPC server command prompt.

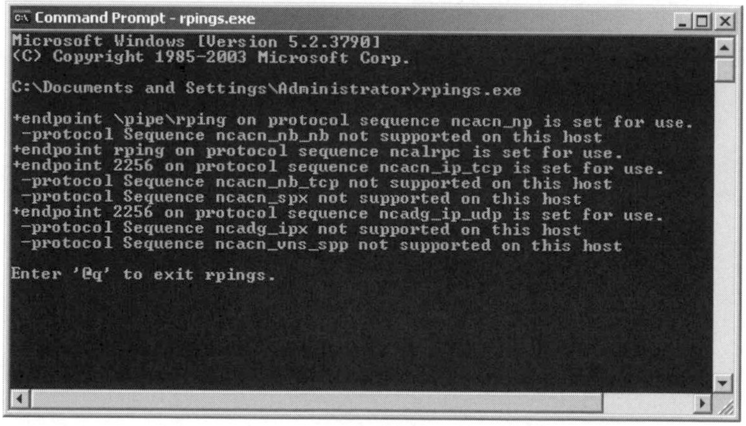

Figure 15-6   RPing running on an Exchange server

RPing Client

After you launch the RPing server on the Exchange server, you use the RPing client, shown in Figure 15-7, on another computer to test RPC connectivity to that server.

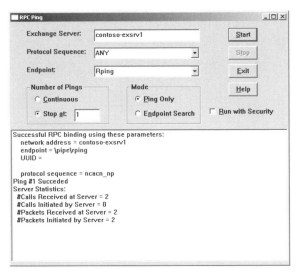

Figure 15-7   Checking RCP connectivity with Rpingc.exe

The options are straightforward, and the information you provide is rather simple:

- **Exchange Server**   Specifies the NetBIOS name or IP address (if TCP/IP is used on the network) of the server running the RPing server.

- **Protocol Sequence**   Specifies the RPC mechanism that will be used in the test. Options include Any (all protocol sequences are tested), Named Pipes, IPX/SPX, TCP/IP, NetBIOS, and VINES. Set the protocol sequence to correspond to the protocol sequence setting on the RPC server.

- **Endpoint**   Specifies protocol-specific ports that the RPC client uses to communicate with the server. Choose Rping to collect information about RPing client-to-server communication itself. Choose Store to simulate communications with the Information Store service on the Exchange server and choose Admin to simulate communications with the Exchange server.

- **Number Of Pings**   Specifies whether to ping the server continuously or a certain number of times. This option is available only if you choose Ping Only mode.

- **Mode**   Specifies the mode. Ping Only means that the ping is returned directly by the RPC Ping server. Endpoint Search returns Pings from detected endpoints.

- **Run With Security**   Verifies authenticated RPCs.

If the RPing from the client is successful with a particular protocol, you'll want to move that protocol to first in the binding order so that the client system doesn't have any problems connecting to the Exchange server. If the RPC Ping is not successful over any protocols, check for a corrupted RPC.DLL file on the client. There are nine RPC.DLL files used to support RPC for Windows clients. All these files are included in the Windows Server 2003 operating system, just as they are for Microsoft Windows XP and Microsoft Windows Vista. If replacing these .dll files does not fix the problem, trace the packets between the client system and the Exchange server. A packet analyzer such as Network Monitor, a Windows utility, can be handy in this situation.

The Microsoft Windows Server 2003 Resource Kit Tools, available for download at *http://www.microsoft.com/downloads/details.aspx?familyid=9d467a69-57ff-4ae7-96ee-b18c4790cffd&displaylang=en*, also supplies a utility named RPCPing, which is a simpler command-line tool that tests RPC connectivity for a computer. Open the command prompt, navigate to the Resource Kit tools directory, and type **rpcping /?** for a list of options to use with this command.

Eseutil.exe Offline Tool

The public folder store and the mailbox store on an Exchange server begin as empty database files. As messages accumulate, these databases grow. Unfortunately, they do not shrink when messages are deleted. Instead, the emptied space is simply marked as available for use during routine garbage collection performed by the Information Store service. When new messages are stored in the databases, they are written in any available free space before the database enlarges to hold them. This method of using free space can result in single items actually being broken up and stored in several physical places within the database—a process known as *fragmentation*.

During their scheduled maintenance cycles, the Information Store service defragments the databases. It also checks for database inconsistencies every time the server shuts down or starts. Because of this routine maintenance, fragmentation itself is not much of a problem on an Exchange server. However, online defragmentation routines do nothing about the size of the databases themselves. To compact the databases, you must turn to an offline utility. Exchange Server 2007 provides an offline defragmentation tool named Eseutil.exe, which you can use to perform database defragmentation while the Information Store service is stopped.

Note   Eseutil.exe is not meant to be used as a regular tool for maintenance of your Exchange servers. Use it only when you are in contact with Microsoft Technical Support.

You can launch this tool by typing **eseutil.exe** at the command prompt from the Program Files\ Microsoft\Exchange Server\bin directory. The eseutil.exe command allows you to perform eight distinct functions:

- **Defragmentation (/d)** Defragments the database by moving the used pages in the database into contiguous blocks in a new database. Unused pages are discarded, which is the only way to recover empty space inside the database for other uses. By default, eseutil.exe writes the contents of the database file to a temporary file, temp-dfrg.edb. When this process is complete, the temporary database becomes the new database and replaces the original database.

- **Recovery (/r)** Performs a soft recovery, bringing all databases into a consistent state. This function is carried out automatically before defragmentation begins.

- **Integrity (/g)** Checks the integrity of a database. The main purpose of this switch is to provide feedback to the development team for debugging purposes. This is a read-only command and does not make any changes to the database. It checks the database index, builds a second index in a temporary database (integ.edb), and compares the two.

- **File Dump (/m)** Displays information about the database files, log files, and checkpoint files of a particular log file.

- **Repair (/p)** Examines the structure of the database and attempts to restore broken links. This process is slow and uncertain and should be used only as a last resort. If the repair finds a physical corruption, which is seen as a -1018, -1019, or -1022 error in Event Viewer, the injured page is removed, resulting in a loss of data for that page. After the repair is completed, you are instructed to delete all your current transaction logs. This step is necessary because the page numbers in the database will not correspond to the page numbers referenced in the transaction log files. Running a repair also rewrites the database signature.

- **Restore (/c)** Used to bring a store into a consistent state. This function is performed automatically before a defragmentation.

- **Checksum (/k)** Calculates a checksum value and compares it to the data page's checksum value. This function is performed automatically during the repair process.

- **Copy File (/y)** Makes a copy of the checkpoint file.

Best Practices Analyzer

The Best Practices Analyzer is a new tool to Exchange Server 2007 and is available in the Toolbox of the Exchange Management Console. The Best Practices Analyzer automatically examines an Exchange Server 2007 deployment and determines whether the configuration is set according to Microsoft best practices.

Run the Best Practices Analyzer right after you first install Exchange Server 2007 and also after you make any configuration changes to a server. However, the Best Practices Analyzer can also be a useful troubleshooting tool, because it can help you determine the overall health of your Exchange servers and organization topology.

To run the Best Practices Analyzer, follow these steps:

1. In the Exchange Management Console, in the Console Tree, click Toolbox.

2. In the Result pane, double-click Best Practices Analyzer.

3. On the Welcome To The Exchange Best Practices Analyzer page, shown in Figure 15-8, click Select Options For A New Scan. If you want to review a previous scan, you can also click Select A Best Practices Scan To View.

Figure 15-8   Using the Best Practices Analyzer

386 Part V Maintenance

4. On the Connect To Active Directory page, you log on to the Active Directory Server. If you are currently logged on to the server with an account that has read access to Active Directory, go ahead and click Connect To The Active Directory Server. If you are logged on with an account that does not have this privilege, click Show Advanced Login Options, type the credentials of an account that does have read access to Active Directory, and then click Connect To The Active Directory Server.

5. On the Start A New Best Practices Scan page, shown in Figure 15-9, you set up the scan. Type an identifying label that describes the scan well enough that you'll know what the scan was for when you come back to review it later—usually, the date and the type of scan will suffice. Specify the scope for the scan. You can limit the scope to a single Exchange server or expand it to scan the entire organization. Next, select the type of scan to perform from the following:

❑ **Health Check** A health check performs a full scan. It checks for errors, warnings, nondefault configurations, recent changes, and other configuration information. Run a Health Check scan if you want to check the health of your Exchange Server organization or if you want to troubleshoot a particular problem.

❑ **Permission Check** This scan checks permissions on each Exchange server included in the scope of the scan. Run this scan if you are experiencing problems with permissions access.

❑ **Connectivity Test** This scan tests network connections on each Exchange server included in the scope of the scan. Run this scan if you suspect a problem with connectivity or if you have firewalls in your network.

❑ **Baseline** The baseline scan compares the configuration of servers to parameters that you configure. The baseline scan report identifies as baseline mismatches all properties on the selected servers whose values are different from the properties you select.

❑ **Exchange Server 2007 Readiness Check** This scan checks a server's readiness for running Exchange Server 2007. This scan is performed automatically during setup of Exchange Server 2007. For more information on what this scan does, see Chapter 6, "Installing Exchange Server 2007."

Finally, configure the speed of the network. You can select Fast LAN, LAN, Fast WAN, or WAN. After you configure the scanning options, click Start Scanning (or Baseline Options if you choose a Baseline scan).

6. If you select any type of scan other than Baseline, the scan starts running immediately and when the scan is finished, you can view or save the results. If you run a

Baseline scan, supply the configuration parameters against which the scan will compare other servers.

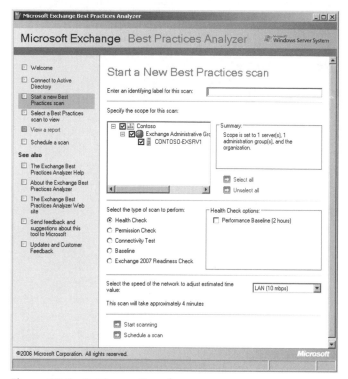

Figure 15-9   Setting options for a scan

Mail Flow Troubleshooter

The Mail Flow Troubleshooter, shown in Figure 15-10, helps you diagnose common mail flow problems, such as when users' messages are not being delivered or received, or when there are long delays in message delivery. The troubleshooter collects data from Exchange servers and then provides advice for fixing any problems that it finds.

When you run the Mail Flow Troubleshooter, you can select from six common symptoms that you or your users are experiencing:

■ **Users Are Receiving Unexpected NonDelivery Reports When Sending Messages.** Select this symptom if users are having messages bounced or receiving nondelivery reports (NDRs) when they try to send messages to certain senders. Typically, NDRs are seen when deliveries to recipients outside the Exchange organization fail. While it is rare to see NDRs generated from failed deliveries between users in the same organization, it is possible. If possible, The Mail Flow Troubleshooter analyzes the problem and provides recommendations for solutions. Be aware though, that because most NDRs come from outside an organization, the causes of the delivery problems may also lie outside the organization and may therefore be beyond your control. See Appendix B, "Delivery Status Notification Codes," for more help on interpreting NDRs.

Figure 15-10   Using the Mail Flow Troubleshooter

■ **Expected Messages From Senders Are Delayed Or Are Not Received By Some Recipients.**   Select this symptom if the messages from senders outside the Exchange organization are not being received or are experiencing delays.

■ **Messages Destined To Recipients Are Delayed Or Are Not Received To Some Recipients.**   Select this symptom if the messages that are supposed to be delivered outside the Exchange organization are not being properly delivered or if messages are being blocked at a non-Exchange gateway server at your network boundary.

■ **Messages Are Backing Up In One Or More Queues On A Server.**   Select this symptom if messages are staying in Exchange Server queues, especially the Remote Delivery Queue, the Awaiting Directory Lookup Queue, or the Local Delivery queue.

■ **Messages Sent By Users Are Pending Submission On The Mailbox Servers (For Exchange Server 2007 Only).**   Select this symptom if messages are staying on the user's mailbox server and are not being transferred to other servers.

- **Problems With Edge Server Synchronization With Active Directory (For Exchange Server 2007 Only).**   Select this symptom if messages are experiencing delivery problems because an Edge Server is not being properly synchronized with Active Directory.

Note   Some of the symptoms you can select in the Mail Flow Troubleshooter overlap or can have similar causes. For example, if messages are backing up in one or more queues, this could also cause message delays or nondelivery both within and outside the organization. You may need to run the Mail Flow Troubleshooter multiple times, selecting different symptoms in order to fully resolve a problem.

Performance Troubleshooter

The Exchange Performance Troubleshooter, shown in Figure 15-11, is another tool available in the Toolbox in the Microsoft Management Console. It is useful for diagnosing performance problems related to RPC connectivity. The Performance Troubleshooter collects data from different sources, analyzes the data, and then offers advice for fixing any problems it finds.

Figure 15-11   Running the Exchange Performance Troubleshooter

When you run the Performance Troubleshooter, you can select from three common symptoms for the tool to diagnose:

- **Multiple Users Are Complaining Of Delays While Using Outlook, Or Are Seeing The Outlook Cancellable RPC Dialog Box.**   This option helps diagnose problems when users are complaining about delays when using Outlook. This includes delays when logging on to the Exchange server, retrieving messages, or switching folders. Some versions of Outlook also show a Requesting Data message if a server does not respond quickly enough. These issues are typically caused by a high server load or a performance problem on the server.

- **The Number Of RPC Operations Per Second Is Higher Than Expected.**   This option helps diagnose problems when you think that a server is running slower than you expect it to. The Performance Troubleshooter helps to diagnose the problem on the server. As part of the scan, the Microsoft Exchange User Monitor (ExMon) tool also tracks the RPCs from Outlook and other MAPI clients. If it detects an abnormally high user load, the tool isolates the source of the problem, such as the individual user, that is causing the server performance problem.

- **The Number Of Outstanding RPC Requests Is High.**   This option helps diagnose problems when too many RPC requests are queued and the server seems slow in responding to them. These problems are typically caused by performance problems on the server.

Other Useful Utilities

You can use many other tools to troubleshoot Exchange Server 2007. Table 15-2 lists some of these tools and briefly describes their purpose as well as where to find them.

Table 15-2   Some Utilities for Troubleshooting Exchange Server 2007

Filename	Purpose	Location
Dnsdiag.exe	Verifies DNS connectivity for a computer	Available as one of the Windows Support Tools on the Windows Server 2003 CD-ROM.
Filever.ex	Displays versions of .exe and .dll files	Available in Windows Server 2003 at the command line.
Isinteg.exe	Checks the integrity of the information stores	\Exchange Server\Bin in your Exchange installation.

Finding Help

As an administrator, you sometimes have problems that you cannot solve by yourself. In these circumstances, knowing where to go for help can save your day. Many sources of information about Exchange Server 2007 are available.

Product Documentation

The product documentation for Exchange Server 2007 is actually quite good. (Many administrators have never even looked at the product documentation, primarily because they have grown accustomed to shoddy documentation in other products.) This documentation is available from the Help menu of Exchange Management Console.

Microsoft TechNet

TechNet is an online resource from Microsoft that provides a wealth of technical resources for IT professionals, including articles, white papers, webcasts, newsletters, and access to the Microsoft Knowledge Base. If you're not already familiar with TechNet, check it out right away. You can find TechNet at *http://technet.microsoft.com /en-us/default.aspx*. TechNet also maintains an Exchange Server TechCenter at *http:// www.microsoft.com/technet/prodtechnol/exchange/default.mspx*, where you'll find all the resources you could ask for about Exchange Server 2007.

TechNet is also available in a subscription version, which is a DVD subscription that delivers current information about the evaluation, deployment, and support of all Microsoft products. It consists of hundreds of thousands of pages of information, including the full text of all Microsoft resource kits and the entire Microsoft Knowledge Base. Each month, subscribers also receive other DVDs and CD-ROMs that include useful items, such as all published service packs for all Microsoft products, server and client utilities, and Microsoft Seminar Online.

Further support mechanisms include contacting the local Microsoft office or using Microsoft Support through *http://support.microsoft.com*.

Internet Newsgroups

Newsgroups, which Microsoft also calls Communities, offer the chance to interact with other administrators and to get opinions and ideas about your specific problems. Many newsgroups are available on the Internet. Microsoft maintains a public Usenet server that hosts hundreds of newsgroups on many Microsoft products. If you are setting up a newsreader client, the address of the news server to use is *msnews.microsoft.com*. You can also view these communities on the Web along with blogs by Microsoft employees and Most Valuable Professionals (MVPs) at *http://www.microsoft.com/communities/newsgroups /default.mspx*.

Following are a few of the Exchange-specific newsgroups available on this server:

- Exchange Server Administration—*microsoft.public.exchange.admin*
- Exchange Server Clients—*microsoft.public.exchange.clients*

- Exchange Server Clustering—*microsoft.public.exchange.clustering*
- Exchange Server Design—*microsoft.public.exchange.design*
- Exchange Server Development—*microsoft.public.exchange.development*
- Exchange Server Miscellaneous—*microsoft.public.exchange.misc*
- Exchange Server Setup—*microsoft.public.exchange.setup*
- Exchange Server Tools—*microsoft.public.exchange.tools*

Hundreds of people, including Microsoft personnel and Exchange MVPs, read and post to these newsgroups daily. These newsgroups are also replicated by many other Usenet servers and might be available through your own Internet service provider's news server.

Summary

This chapter discussed some tools you can use to troubleshoot problems with Exchange Server 2007, including the Inbox Repair tool, OST Integrity Checker, Exchange Best Practices Analyzer, RPC Ping utility, and the Microsoft Exchange Server Performance Troubleshooting Analyzer Tool. It also described other sources of troubleshooting information, such as TechNet and the Microsoft newsgroup communities. The next chapter continues the discussion of maintaining Exchange Server 2007, with a look at disaster recovery scenarios.

Chapter 16
Disaster Recovery

Backing up and restoring Microsoft Exchange Server 2007 databases are critically important aspects of Exchange planning and configuration. Unfortunately, many organizations overlook the importance of backing up and restoring Exchange servers, and even when they do perform regular backups, they may not test those backups appropriately.

This chapter focuses on the backup and recovery of your Exchange Server 2007 databases. The first part of the chapter details the Exchange database architecture, the types of backups, and the types of restores. The second part of the chapter discusses methods for implementing common backup and restore strategies. You also become familiar with the tools required to help implement and troubleshoot backup and restore issues in most situations.

Backup and Restore Technologies

This section introduces the Exchange database architecture and the types of backups and restores that are possible within that architecture. Several Exchange Server 2007 features are mentioned, such as Local Continuous Replication (LCR) and Clustered Continuous Replication (CCR). These are log shipping features implemented by seeding a replica copy of the database on separate storage (LCR uses separate storage on the same server, while CCR uses separate storage on a additional cluster node) and replaying the closed transaction logs from the production copy into the seeded replica to keep it up to date.

The Exchange Database

The core component of the Exchange Mailbox server role is the Exchange Information Store. Understanding the Information Store and the underlying Microsoft Extensible Storage Engine (ESE) database is an important first step to understanding how backups and restores work in Exchange Server 2007.

Note   The ESE database has previously been referred to as Jet Blue (which is a different version than the Jet Red database used by Microsoft Office Access).

Basic Architecture

The ESE database in use by Exchange Server 2007 is the same version of the B+-Tree database used by Exchange Server 2003 SP1 and Active Directory. Exchange Server 2007 implements this database with an updated set of attributes including:

- The log file size changes from 5 MB to 1 MB.

- The database page size changes from 4 KB to 8 KB.

These attributes are necessary to support the built-in log shipping capabilities and support a lower I/O profile. The log shipping capabilities (Local Continuous Replication and Clustered Continuous Replication) require the lower log file size to break up the data loss potential into smaller chunks. The lower I/O profile is achieved by a number of features in Exchange Server 2007 and allows more users per server then previous versions. The attributes are important to configuration and performance, and in gaining an understanding of what happens during a backup or restore.

Transactions

The database transactions are an ACID operation. ACID database transactions ensure integrity by being Atomic, Consistent, Isolated, and Durable.

- **Atomic**   Indicates that a transaction state change is all or none, which means the entire transaction must be completed before any one part of the transaction can be recognized as completed. Atomic state changes include database page rearrangements, mailbox folder view additions, and e-mail message submissions. Without an Atomic nature, it is impossible to assure complete transactions.

- **Consistent**   Indicates that a transaction is a correct transformation of the current state of the database. The actions taken as a group do not violate any one of the integrity constraints associated with the current state of the database. Without Consistent properties, it would be possible for corrupt e-mail messages to enter the database during regular operation.

- **Isolated**   This term indicates that even though transactions run at the same time, it appears to each transaction (T) that others executed either before T or after T, but not both. Without Isolated properties, an item could be marked as read before the item is delivered to the mailbox.

- **Durable**   This term indicates that as soon as a transaction is completed success-fully (the commit operation enters the database), its changes survive failures. This also means that if a transaction does not complete in its entirety (no commit oper-ation is specified for the transaction), the entire transaction is rolled back. Without Durable properties, the database would not be recoverable to the last e-mail mes-sage delivered to a mailbox through power failures, server outages, or other incon-sistent states.

These properties are critical to backup and restore operations. Without them, an Exchange administrator would not enjoy the feeling of safety that comes with the infre-quent corruption of ESE databases. These properties help guarantee the following rules:

- Exchange rolls back any changes (or e-mail messages) that are not received by the database in their entirety.

- Exchange disregards all pages that are not in order to prevent corruption.

- Exchange does not accept any operations that do not allow the database to easily become consistent.

- Exchange allows only one transaction at a time to be entered into the database, even though multiple transactions are accepted at once to allow for increased performance.

- Exchange guarantees that once a transaction is committed, the transaction is fully recoverable within the database file itself.

These guarantees are important to keep in mind when evaluating any backup/restore and disaster recovery strategy.

Logging

So where do all of the log files come in? The basic principle behind the ESE database is that writing to memory is a cheaper operation than writing to disk. It has been this way since the inception of Exchange Server and is extended even further in Exchange Server 2007 with the move to a 64-bit architecture. The problem with writing to memory and later flushing those writes to disk is the information stored in memory is stateless; for Exchange, this means the e-mail message state is not guaranteed to be committed and recoverable while it is in memory. To ensure that the statelessness is not a problem, the log files were built to ensure that all transactions are in the log file at the same time they are posted to memory. This is called a *dual-phase commit* and is illustrated in Figure 16-1.

- Phase 0: commit the user transaction in fast way

    Sequential write of page changes (modification, deletion, insertion)

- Phase 1: update the database in an atomic way

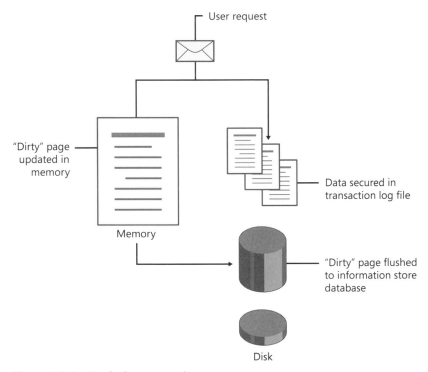

Figure 16-1   Dual-phase commit

To illustrate the process, assume that User1 sends a 2500-KB (2.4-MB) message to User2, another user on the same message store:

- User1 sends a 2500-KB (2.4-MB) message.

- 312.5 8-KB pages are consumed in memory.

- 2.44 log files are written to disk.

- User1's message is registered in User1's Outlook client as Sent.

- User2 receives a message with a pointer to the record in memory for the 312.5 pages that contain the message.

At this point, the message is sent; it is in memory and has been written sequentially to a log file. With the message in the log files, it is in a semirecoverable state. It is only semi-recoverable because the last part of the message (the .44 MB) is in an open log file. Additionally, the message is not stored or indexed in a way that the message is easily retrievable at a later date. For that to happen, the message must be written to the database. The ESE database has several ways to write data from memory to the database. Those methods are as follows:

- **Anomalous writes**   This is the most common write that ESE performs. This is the scenario in which there is a page that has been entered into memory and not been requested lately. Such a page is often referred to as a dirty page.

- **Idle writes**   This is the least common write that ESE performs. This is the scenario in which no other activity is happening on the server and there are many extra cycles to write data from memory to disk.

- **Opportune writes**   In Exchange Server 2007, this is more common than in previous versions. The opportune writes are writes of pages that may not be ready to be written but are destined for database pages that are next to a write that is ready to be written. This could consist of several separate e-mails destined for a single B+-Tree, or two attachments destined for an attachment table, and so on.

- **Normal writes**   Oddly enough, these are not normal. The normal write occurs when the checkpoint depth has reached its limit (which defaults to 20 MB per storage group). This scenario occurs only in a heavily loaded system and should be watched for. It also means that backups slow down during this time as the database must be in a recoverable state prior to taking a backup copy.

- **Repeatedly written**   This does not commonly occur. It is only in heavily loaded systems that a page is repeatedly written. Repeatedly written means that a page has been entered into memory. That page is then written to disk via one of the four previous methods. After the page is written, the checkpoint location moves past that page. At this point, if the page is rediscovered, which would require a user to have immediately changed (edited, deleted, and so on) a message, it is recognized as a repeatedly written page.

It is important to understand these concepts to know how the ACID properties are implemented in the database and how different technologies may conflict with the nature of the ESE database. For example, a technology that backs up data in memory is not a good technology as those pages may be updated, removed, or rejected before they ever make it into the database.

Circular Logging

Circular logging is intended to reduce storage requirements for the transaction logs after the transactions in the logs are committed to the databases. Circular logging is generally not recommended on production mail systems. Circular logging is used by default in ESE implementations where recoverability of a single database is not absolutely critical (for example, Active Directory or Exchange Hub Transport). This is due to the way circular logging treats the log files after they are committed. When circular logging is enabled, logs are removed from the system after they are committed to the database. This means there are only a few logs left on the system at any given time. This also means that during a restore, there is no way to roll forward the database as all logs are not backed up during a full backup. Fortunately, circular logging is disabled by default except on Edge and Hub Transport server roles. These server roles contain mostly transient data and under most circumstances do not require the databases to have backups performed on them.

Checksum

The *checksum* (also called a message hash) is a string that is calculated and then added to each page in the database to verify page's integrity. The checksum itself does not guarantee data integrity; instead, the recalculation of the checksum when the page is read into RAM ensures that the data being read from the database is identical to the data that was written to the database.

When a page is loaded into RAM, the checksum is calculated and the page number is verified. If the checksum doesn't match the one that was written to the page when the page was written to the database, you can be sure that the page is damaged or corrupted. ESE ignores and/or corrects simple *bit flip* errors; these are errors where a single bit is written as a 1 instead of a 0. ESE ignores the error when it is found in conjunction with manual checksum verification (as in a checksum initiated during a Volume Shadow Copy Service [VSS] backup).

Note that ESE does not cause the damage to the page—it merely reports the damage to you. In nearly all instances, corruption to the database is the result of a hardware device or a device driver malfunctioning. ESE cannot cause page-level corruptions. These corruptions occur when the data is written to the disk and are caused by your hardware or device drivers. This is why it is imperative that you ensure all your firmware and device drivers are using the latest patches and updates and all hardware you are using is on the WHQL. Microsoft Customer Service and Support (CSS) will work with your hardware manufacturer to resolve any problems that might exist between your hardware and your Exchange Server 2007 database.

Volume Shadow Copy Service

The Volume Shadow Copy Service (VSS) is a common method in use to back up and restore Exchange Server 2007. All VSS-based backups are considered online backups as they require the Exchange Information Store to be started during the process. VSS backups rely heavily on the Virtual Disk Service (VDS) and the Windows VSS framework. The premise behind the VSS framework is

- Windows provides a framework that governs how applications are backed up. Windows can do this because it understands all components that work under the Windows operating system.

- Applications provide writers that regulate when the application is ready to have a backup copy taken. The Application writer can do this because it understands the application.

- Microsoft and third-party vendors provide requestors that interact with an overall backup application. The requestor can do this because it understands how the backup application functions and it knows what data the backup application requires to be successful.

- Microsoft and third-party vendors provide hardware and software that understand how storage arrays can synchronize and subsequentially split the volumes.

The end result of these four components is a solution where a requestor asks Windows to set up an environment that supports a VSS snapshot to be taken. Once this is done, the requestor asks the application writer to set up a snapshot of the application. The writer then asks the provider to set up a snapshot based on whatever technology the provider supports. When all of the puzzle pieces are in place, the writer lets the requestor know when it has decided the application is ready for a snapshot to be taken. For Exchange, this means that the pages that are in the process of being written to disk have completed, and no new transactions are started in the database. This pause in activity is allowed to last for only 10 seconds while the provider takes its snapshot of the data. When the snapshot is complete, the requester informs the writer that everything went well and that the transaction processing can continue. At this point, the provider has obtained a copy of the database and log files. The provider then works with the requestor to ensure the database is checked for consistency and the logs on the production volume are truncated. To help visualize this, Figure 16-2 is a diagram of the process.

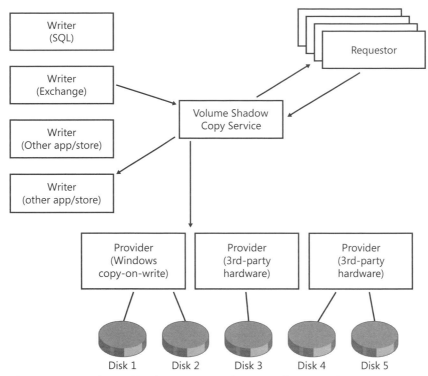

Figure 16-2 Volume Shadow Copy Service (VSS) framework

Types of VSS Backups Supported

The requestors available vary in functionality and in what VSS features are supported. For example, the VSS framework supports all of the standard backup methods: full, differential, incremental, and copy; however, most vendors implement only full and differential backups. This section describes what happens during each of these events.

Full Backup

The database volume or file is mirrored to an alternate location via a hardware or software mechanism.

1. The Exchange writer informs the requestor when it is ready for a snapshot to be taken.

2. The requestor has 10 seconds to complete the snapshot. This includes mirroring the remaining blocks in the database or database volume that are not in sync and severing the relationship.

3. The requestor is then responsible for mounting the mirror to an alternate location to perform a checksum of the database. The checksum is run through a checksum

API or through the `eseutil.exe /k` command. Depending on the size of the database, the checksum process can be lengthy and demanding on the storage subsystem with a series of sequential reads. This process can be throttled to relieve the demand on the system; however, it still must complete prior to truncating the log files.

Incremental Backup

The log volume or file is mirrored to an alternate location via a hardware or software mechanism.

1. The Exchange writer informs the requestor when it is ready for a snapshot to be taken.

2. The requestor has 10 seconds to complete the snapshot. This includes mirroring the remaining log file or blocks in the log file disk that are not in sync and severing the relationship.

3. The database files are left alone to be backed up during the next full backup. This means that each incremental backup that is taken contains all of the log files since the last full or incremental backup. To restore, only the last full backup and the last incremental are required.

Differential Backup

The log volume or file is mirrored to an alternate location via a hardware or software mechanism.

1. The Exchange writer informs the requestor when it is ready for a snapshot to be taken.

2. The requestor has 10 seconds to complete the snapshot. This includes mirroring the remaining log file or blocks in the log file disk that are not in sync and severing the relationship.

The difference is that the differential backup does not truncate the log files generated since the last backup. This means that each differential backup that is taken contains only the log files since the last full or incremental backup. To restore, the last full backup and each of the subsequent differential backups are required.

Copy Backup

A copy backup follows a similar process to the full backup. The difference is that the copy backup does not truncate the log files.

Exchange Streaming Backup API

The Exchange Streaming Backup API has been in existence since Exchange Server 5.5. It has been slightly updated, but for the most part left alone to support the array of backup applications that use the API. The Exchange Streaming Backup API's backups are referred to as streaming backups and are also an online backup process as they require the Exchange Information Store to be running. In Exchange Server 2007, the mature streaming API did not require any updates. To use the API, begin the backup process by starting the backup application. The backup application informs the ESE that it is entering a backup mode, and then a patch file (.pat) is generated for each database in the backup (assuming this is a full backup). During an online, full backup, the database is open for business, and transactions can be entered into the databases. If a transaction causes a split operation across the backup boundary (the location in the EDB file that designates what has and has not been backed up), the affected page before the boundary is recorded in the .pat file. A separate .pat file is used for each database that is backed up, such as Priv1.pat or Pub1.pat. These files are seen only during the backup and restore processes. During differential or incremental backups, a patch file is not created.

When the ESE enters a backup mode, a new log file opens. For example, if Edb.log is the current open log file, Edb.log closes and is renamed to the latest generation, and a new Edb.log is opened. This indicates the point when the ESE can truncate the logs, after the backup is complete.

When the backup begins, backup requests that ESE read the database and sequence the pages. After sequencing, the pages are grouped into 64-KB chunks (eight pages) and loaded into RAM. ESE then verifies the checksum on each individual page to ensure data integrity. If any page has a calculated checksum that does not match the checksum recorded in the page when the page was written to disk, the Information Store evaluates whether it is a single bit flip error (meaning the single bit is a 1 when it is supposed to be a 0 or vice versa). If the error is a single bit flip, an attempt to correct the error is made. If the error is not a single bit flip, the backup process stops and records an error message in the event logs. Backup does this to prevent the storage of damaged data.

The backup API also takes this opportunity to scrub the pages if the "zero out deleted pages" flag is set. It is only during an online streaming backup that this occurs and only after the original data has been moved to alternative storage that the streaming API overwrites pages that contain zero references from other pages (including indexes and mail items) with a set of alphanumeric characters. The nice thing about all this is that when you get a successful full, online backup of your Exchange databases using the Exchange agent from your software vendor, you can be certain that the database on your disk library or tape has complete integrity, because every page was read into RAM, its checksum calculated, and then copied to disk or tape. This is also different than a VSS backup which each database page's checksum is not verified. As an administrator, this is something to consider when planning a backup strategy.

Once the backup is successfully completed and all the pages are read, backup copies the logs and patch files to the backup set. The log files are then truncated or deleted at the point when the new generation started at the beginning of the backup. The backup set closes, the ESE enters normal mode, and the backup is complete.

In an incremental or differential backup, only the log files are affected. Operations that involve patch files, checksums, or reading pages sequentially are not executed.

To recap, here are the steps of the full backup process:

1. The backup starts, a synchronization point is fixed, and an empty patch file is created.

2. Edb.log is renamed to the next log number regardless of whether it is full, and a new Edb.log is created.

3. The backup for the current storage group begins.

4. A .pat file is created for each database that is being backed up in the storage group, and the database header is written into the .pat file.

5. During backup, split operations across the backup boundary are written into the .pat file.

6. During backup, Windows Server 2003 Backup Utility copies 64 KB of data at a time. Additional transactions are created and saved as normal. Each page's checksum is calculated and compared to the checksum recorded for that page in the page. The checksums are compared to ensure data integrity on each page.

7. If the database is configured to overwrite deleted pages, they are overwritten with an alphanumeric character set.

8. Logs used during the backup process (those from the checkpoint forward) and the patch files are copied to disk or tape.

9. If the database is configured to overwrite deleted pages, the overwritten pages are written to disk.

10. The old logs on the disk are deleted.

11. The old patch files on the disk are deleted.

12. Backup finishes.

Types of Streaming Backups Supported

The streaming backup programs have a standard set of methods they can use to back up Exchange databases. The Windows Backup Utility takes advantage of all the features and can be used in a recovery strategy. Other streaming backup applications add feature sets that are specific to each vendor. This section describes what happens during each of these events.

Full Backups

1. The backup application starts and informs the ESE of the backup; a patch file is created for each database in the backup. A new log generation is opened to receive incoming database requests.

2. The backup application reads the database file into memory page by page. As the database is read into memory, the checksum is verified and the Zero Out Deleted Pages flag is checked.

3. If there are any uncorrectable -1018 or -1022 errors, the database stops on those pages, and the backup does not continue.

4. If there are any pages that are marked for deletion and the Zero Out Deleted Pages flag is enabled, these pages are overwritten with an alphanumeric set of characters and written back to disk.

5. Once the entire database passes through steps 1 through 4, the database, patch file, and logs are copied to the backup media, the logs are truncated to the log generation opened in step 1, and the database header is updated with a current timestamp under the backup complete heading.

Incremental

1. The backup application starts and informs the ESE of the backup. A new log generation is opened to receive incoming database requests.

2. The backup application reads the log files on disk and copies them to the backup media.

3. Once all of the logs up to the log generation opened in step 1 are copied to media, the logs are truncated and the backup is complete.

Differential

1. The backup application starts and informs the ESE of the backup. A new log generation is opened to receive incoming database requests.

2. The backup application reads the log files on disk and copies them to the backup media.

3. Once all of the logs up to the log generation opened in step 1 are copied to media, the backup is complete.

Copy

A copy backup follows a similar process to the full backup. The difference is that the copy backup does not truncate the log files.

Restore Process

Before you begin the restore process, you must dismount the databases to make them inaccessible to users. You can do this by using the Exchange Management Console (EMC) or the Exchange Management Shell (EMS).

When a restore operation begins, the store informs the ESE that a restore process is starting and ESE enters restore mode. The backup agent copies the database from the tape directly to the database target path. The associated log and patch files are copied to the server in a temporary location specified by you so that they aren't saved to the same location as current files in the production environment. If you happen to select the production path as your temporary path, you can overwrite log files and cause a logical corruption of the current production database. So, ensure that your temporary path is not your production path.

After the log and patch files are restored to the temporary location, a new restore storage group needs to be created for the purpose of restoring the database. The database is then copied from tape to the temporary location (and into the restore storage group). Then the patch file data and the log files from the tape backup are copied into the database by the restore database engine.

ESE processes the current logs, bringing you back to the point in time of your database backup (assuming you have all the transaction logs available from the last full, online, successful backup to the point of the disaster). After this is complete, ESE performs some cleanup by deleting log and patch files from the temporary location and deleting the restore storage instance. Then the storage group is mounted into the production environment, and your database is mounted, too.

Other Exchange Server Components

In addition to the Exchange database, several other items must be included in backup planning. Some of these items are common among different roles and can be backed up and restored in a similar fashion. For example, a system state backup is useful to have on all server roles. Some of the items are unique per server role and are useful only on those specific server roles. Refer to Table 16-1 for additional server components to back up.

Table 16-1   Additional Server Components to Back Up

Server role	Data to back up	Location/method
Mailbox	Mailbox or public folder database and logs	Streaming Backup or VSS Backup
	Content Index	No backup necessary, rebuild index during recovery
	System settings	System state backup

Table 16-1   Additional Server Components to Back Up (Continued)

Server role	Data to back up	Location/method
Hub Transport	System settings	System state backup
Client Access	Client Access configuration (IMAP settings, availability services, etc)	\ClientAccess*.*
	Exchange ActiveSync configuration	System state backup
	Web services configuration	
	Autodiscover services configuration	
	System settings	
Edge Transport	ADAM Customizations	Clone Config (ExportEdgeConfig.ps1)
	System settings	System state backup

Additional information is available on Microsoft's Web site at *http://technet.microsoft.com /en-us/library/bb124780.aspx.*

Backup and Restore Strategies

Your restore strategy determines your backup strategy. These operations cannot be planned separately. When you plan what backup strategy is best for your environment, first think about how and where the backups will be restored. This first step leads your planning down a path that will suit your environment and overall requirements better than thinking about backups first.

For example, how will you need the database backup to be available in the event of a restore? It could be in the form of a file on a tape that can be copied to a production location. It could be in the form of a disk that can be mirrored to a production location. It could be in the form of several backup files on a disk, or on several disks. The point is that consideration must be given to what types of restores are possible in most of the recovery scenarios that may arise.

You need to ensure you have enough hard drive space to restore both the database and the log files. If you generate 2000 log files in a single week, you have 2 GB of information to (potentially) restore. Add to that your database sizes, and you begin to see why you need to plan your restore strategy along with your backup strategy.

In addition to the backup and restore technology considerations, consideration of Service Level Agreements (SLAs) for backup times, restore times, and mail availability is important. These business level requirements are critical to consider when planning what methods to use for recovery. The SLAs need to meet the requirements of all consumers of the Exchange system. This includes individual users, applications, and business processes. With this wide array of consumers in the Exchange environment, SLAs are difficult to agree upon, and the complexity of the system will increase. As a point of reference, look at the SLA scorecard shown in Table 16-2.

Table 16-2   SLA Scorecard

SLA	Standard maximum time*	Premium maximum time**	Actual observed
Exchange Service availability	99.999%	99.999%	99.99875%
	M-F 0700-1800	S-S 0000-2400	
Mobile Service availability	99.999%	99.999%	99.997%
	M-F 0700-1800	S-S 0000-2400	
Application relay availability	99.999%	99.999%	100%
	M-F 0700-1800	S-S 0000-2400	
Outlook client availability	99.999%	99.999%	100%
	M-F 0700-1800	S-S 0000-2400	
Outlook Web Access availability	99.999%	99.999%	99.98%
	Business Hours	S-S 0000-2400	
Single mailbox restoration	4 hours	1 hour	2 hours
Mailbox database restoration	4 hours	1 hour	2 hours
Mailbox server restoration	5 hours	2 hours	7 hours
Per mailbox e-discovery	5 days	2 days	3 days
Mailbox item recovery	1 week	1 week	5 days

*Standard is defined as all users that pay the default chargeback rate per user
**Premium is defined as all users that pay above the default chargeback rate for a higher level of service

When evaluating the restoration and availability requirements, it becomes easy to draw the line in terms of the technical architecture to support those requirements. One critical area to look at is mailbox and database sizing. Notice that a single mailbox restoration and a mailbox database restoration are separate. This is normal and is due to the size of the mailbox and the number of users on a single mailbox database. There are several ways to leverage the Exchange configuration to support different SLAs. The most common is to leverage the size of mailboxes and number of users per database. These two components are what define the database size and the related backup and restore times per server. An example of this would be to look at the average restore time for an existing server. If we assume there are several servers that contain five databases (one per storage group) each, have 100 users per database, and each user has a mailbox limit of 400 MB. Each database would be about 47 GB. If the concern is the time it takes to restore the entire server, reducing the number of users per server or reducing the size of the mailbox per user are good options. In either case, you need to perform an offline defragmentation to reduce the physical size of the database. On the other hand, if the number of servers was the concern, a consolidation could occur to bring all users onto a single server by growing the number of storage groups and databases for a single server. This would affect the time it would take to restore the entire server, yet the individual mailbox database restoration time would remain the same. This is an important concept to understand when planning the underlying plan for server sizing.

You can find additional information on storage planning at *http://technet.microsoft.com /en-us/library/c5a9c0ed-e43e-4bc7-99fe-7d1a9cb967f8.aspx.*

Testing Restore Capabilities

Testing the restoration of backups on a regular basis solves three critical problems for organizations. The first problem it solves is keeping technical staff current with restoration techniques and skills that are normally only used during a disaster. The second problem it solves is fully validating the backup that was taken from the system. The third problem it solves is finding issues that exist in the backup process that otherwise would be found only during a real disaster.

All three of these problems are addressed with a single restore that occurs on a regular basis. It is recommended that a full restoration be tested at least once a quarter. This restoration can be done by different staff members each quarter, or a different service can be tested each quarter (such as testing a stand-alone mailbox restoration one quarter and a cluster failover the next). This way the restoration tests are not intrusive on other projects or daily operations yet remain an important component of regular activities.

The most common of these restores is the Mailbox server restore. This is the core component of Microsoft Exchange Server 2007 and will be the most important server to restore in the event of a site failure or a single server motherboard failure. For this reason, you will walk through a common scenario to test this type of restore.

There are two methods that are generally recommended to restore Exchange Server 2007; the first is to restore all databases of a failed server to a similar server, and the second is to restore the databases from the failed server across the remaining Mailbox servers in the environment. The first option is similar to the restoration technique in earlier versions of Exchange. The second option is new to Exchange Server 2007. The first option is reviewed; however, the same techniques are applicable to the second option as well.

It is important to understand a feature in Exchange Server 2007 referred to as Database Portability. This feature provides the ability of databases in Exchange Server

2007 to be portable between Exchange servers in the same Exchange organization. What this means is that an Exchange database that resides in Storage Group 1 named DB1 on a server named Exch1 can be shut down (or otherwise made consistent), moved to Storage Group 2 on a server named Exch2, and mounted with no further actions or modifications. To make this work, you must first create a placeholder database in Storage Group 2 on the Exch2 server and then enable the This Database Can Be Overwritten By Restore option.

To test a full server restore and validate the mailbox contents, a new Active Directory forest should be installed on a spare server in a lab environment. This server can be a virtual server, workstation-class computer, or other underpowered computer that is available. With the new Active Directory forest, a new Exchange server must be installed. This Exchange Server can be installed into an Exchange Organization with the same or a different name. The Exchange server itself can be installed with any name you choose, as well. With a new server installed and configured similarly to the production server, the storage groups and placeholder databases must be created. At this point, the databases from the production server must be restored by whatever means your backup strategy allows. Remember, it is important to follow real restoration procedures here. After the databases are restored, they should be mounted, and mailboxes can be connected to the databases to validate the contents of the mailboxes. Should you perform these actions in a production environment instead of a lab environment, ensure that test mailboxes are connected to the restored mailboxes and not the user mailboxes.

During a real disaster, or in a test Exchange organization that is left available, it is easy to repoint the users' Active Directory settings to the restored databases. Simply run the following command from the Exchange Management Shell:

```
move-mailbox -configurationonly -targetdatabase <new_database_name>
```

You can't perform a restore without knowing that your backups are working. Verify your backup jobs complete every day and test a restore quarterly. Failure to verify backups is a common mistake because it is easy to assume that backup tapes are swapped and that data is backed up properly. Make it part of your regular routine to review all backup logs and perform a restore to ensure that restoration and recovery is feasible.

Note   Verifying backups does not have to be difficult; it can be monitored through an automatic system like Microsoft Systems Center Operations Manager or through custom scripts that parse the event logs looking for backup success events. It is important to look for the backup success events instead of just the backup failure events; this is so that you know the backup did not run too long without reporting a failure.

Testing restoration procedures of the features other then the mailbox databases and Mailbox servers is also important. In many cases, this will be a rebuild operation. In other cases, this will be an intricate process. For more information on these procedures, refer to *http://technet.microsoft.com/en-us/library/aa998890.aspx*.

Recovering an Exchange Mailbox Server

Planning for recovery of an entire Exchange Mailbox server can be a lengthy process. It is the core server in the Exchange infrastructure. It is the reason all of the other components exist. Consider the following three things when planning the type of recovery strategy you will use:

1. **The Active Directory location of the restore.**   Is the Active Directory site intact, and are all Active Directory objects that were previously there intact?

2. **The supporting Exchange Server infrastructure.**   Are the Client Access server and Hub Transport server roles in existence in the site where the Mailbox server is being recovered? If there are Unified Messaging, Edge, SharePoint, or Rights Management services in use, will the recovered Mailbox server be able to interact with them?

3. **The server that is being restored.**   Is the server a clustered Mailbox server, a stand-alone server, or a stand-alone server that is functioning as a single-node cluster?

The most common recovery strategies for the full Mailbox server are full server restores and Exchange application rebuilds. These two strategies are typically used with warm (also known as stand-by) servers, and using dial-tone servers is the first step.

Full Server Restores

Full server restores occur when a backup of the Exchange databases is maintained somewhere in addition to a backup of the Windows Server data. These are not commonly used with Exchange installations because Exchange does not rely heavily on the Windows Server system state during its operation. The steps involved in this restore process are as follows:

1. Obtain replacement hardware with components that match the original server's hardware components. This can include RAID controllers, network interface cards, and so on.

2. Rebuild Windows Server to the same version, service pack, and driver versions as the original server.

3. Restore the Windows Server system state and file system backup.

4. Re-install Exchange Server and service packs.

5. Restore the Exchange Server 2007 databases.

At the end of this process, users can access their mailboxes with no reconfiguration. No database recovery is needed, and the server is expected to last as long as the components allow. The Active Directory and Exchange considerations previously discussed need to be considered in this strategy. One exception to this is where Exchange Server 2007 resides on the Active Directory server and is combined with the Hub and CAS roles. In this case, all components are restored during the steps outlined.

This is a reliable solution; however, it is costly and carries a high amount of administrative overhead. Ensuring the exact same components can be obtained usually requires keeping them on hand as hardware components have a shorter cycle then software components. The time it takes to rebuild and restore a Windows Server 2003 computer is more than the time it takes to only rebuild the server and reinstall the applications. These limitations make this option a difficult choice in situations in which e-mail is in the least bit critical.

The solution is limited by the Recovery Point Objective (RPO) and the Recovery Time Objective (RTO) it supports. The RPO can be increased with third-party technologies that replicate the database to the recovery site. The most common technologies are VSS copies/log shipping the data over the network or replicating the changed tracks on the disks. The RTO is very high; this is first due to the large amount of work that must be done to prepare the environment and is secondly due to the large amount of time required to restore the data from backups.

Exchange Application Rebuilds

Exchange application rebuilds is a broad term. It refers to a rebuild of the Exchange Server application followed by a recovery or restoration of the data. To rebuild the Exchange application on a server, the application can simply be installed from scratch on a new Windows server, or the application can be installed on a stand-by server using the `/m:RecoverServer` switch or the `/RecoverCMS` switch. The first thing an administrator needs to know before walking through the steps is what type of Exchange server will be reinstalled. If it is a clustered server, use the `/RecoverCMS` switch; if it is not clustered, use the `/m:RecoverServer` switch.

To use the `/m:RecoverServer` switch, complete the following steps:

1. Using Active Directory Users and Computers, reset the computer account for the server name that you are attempting to recover.

2. Verify all server names, volume configuration, and directory paths are the same as the previous server.

3. From a command prompt, change into the Exchange Server source directory and run the following command:

```
Setup.exe /m:RecoverServer
```

At this point, the Exchange Setup program queries Active Directory to obtain the configuration information for the server name you are attempting to recover. The server roles previously installed and the locations of the data are used to configure how Exchange Server is installed. Users should not need to change any information, and administrators should not have to move user configuration.

To use the `/RecoverCMS` option, complete the following steps:

1. Using Active Directory Users and Computers, reset the computer account for the server name that you are attempting to recover.

2. Verify all server names, volume configuration, and directory paths are the same as the previous server.

3. Build the cluster server with the same configuration as the previous cluster. Single copy clusters cannot be restored to clustered continuous replication clusters and vice versa.

4. Install the passive Exchange Server Mailbox server role on the node of the cluster you are recovering to.

5. From a command prompt, change into the Exchange Server source directory and run:

   ```
   Setup.exe /RecoverCMS /CMSName:<CMSName> CMSIPAddress:<CMSIPAddress>
   ```

6. If you are recovering an SCC cluster with several Exchange Clustered Mailbox Servers (CMSs), perform steps 4 and 5 until all Exchange CMSs are installed on active nodes.

7. Recover Exchange Mailbox databases. This can be from backup, from a disk-based replication, or from a log shipping–based replication.

8. Install one or more passive nodes in the cluster.

At this point, the Exchange CMS is recovered and operational. Users should not need to change any information, and administrators should not have to move user configuration.

For both Exchange recovery strategies, the Active Directory and Exchange considerations need to be considered. No other Exchange roles can reside on a clustered Exchange server, which introduces a requirement for these to already exist in the site. These should have already been rebuilt, already exist, or be the next item on the list to rebuild.

These are reliable solutions; the cost and administrative overhead can vary depending on what configuration is used. The servers used do not have to match exactly, although for SCC, the servers do have to be on the Windows Hardware Quality Labs (WHQL). The Exchange CMS name must match the CMS name that was previously used; however, the server names, IP addresses, and so on, do not have to match. The time it takes to use a recovery option is much less then the time it would take to manually re-create the configuration and validate that the configuration was entered correctly.

The solution is limited by the RPO/RTO it supports. The RPO can be increased with third-party technologies that replicate the database to the recovery site. The most common technologies are VSS copies/log shipping the data over the network or replicating the changed tracks on the disks. The RTO is still higher than a high availability strategy as some amount of work still needs to be done. The RTO is lower than a restore strategy as more of the data that already exists and is necessary for the application to run is used during the process.

Dial-Tone Servers

Dial-tone servers are similar to dial-tone databases and are simply empty configurations that are used in an effort to restore service to end users. Dial-tone servers or databases do not meet any of the requirements of a clustered, stand-by, or highly available service. This is because the messaging data is not readily available during a dial-tone recovery. Basic e-mail functionality is enabled immediately; however, e-mail data, rules, calendar data, UM settings, mobile device configuration, and so on, are not recovered. The advantage to this solution is that users are able to operate in a limited form until the rest of the data can be recovered or re-created.

To implement a dial-tone recovery, complete the following steps:

1. Fully install an Exchange Mailbox server and create all of the necessary storage groups, databases, and other environmental configurations.

2. If this is a database dial tone, create storage groups and databases on existing servers that are managerially designated for use in a dial-tone recovery strategy.

3. If dial-tone recovery is needed—for example, if the server or site suffered a failure—use the `Move-Mailbox -ConfigurationOnly` cmdlet and point the all mailboxes that must be moved to the dial-tone databases.

4. If the messaging data becomes available, it can either be recovered to the dial-tone server and imported to the mailboxes, or it can be prepared on a replacement Exchange server and the users can be moved to the replacement hardware.

This solution has a very low RTO for the service and a low RPO; however, the RTO for the data is usually higher. This has some advantages for organizations that require e-mail services to process business functions but do not require historical data to process those same business functions.

Recovering an Exchange Mailbox Database

Exchange Server 2007 mailbox database recovery is usually more complex than recovering the Mailbox server itself. Mailbox database recovery can involve simple tools such as the Exchange Disaster Recover Analyzer, or it can involve complex tools such as the Exchange ESE Utility or the Exchange Information Store Integrity tool.

There are times when a clean backup of a mailbox database cannot be obtained, and some form of database recovery must be performed. For the most part, Exchange Server 2007 has simplified the recovery process by enabling database portability. This is a feature built into the database that allows a database to move to and be mounted on any server regardless of the server name. This is important to recovery strategies as once a database is in a consistent state and mountable, it can be placed almost anywhere to be used.

The trick is getting the database into a consistent state. There are several ways to accomplish this task. If you perform a restore of your database and find that it is corrupted or unmountable, a good first step is to go into the Exchange Disaster Recovery Analyzer in the toolbox and point it at the database. This wizard walks you through finding the database and running Eseutil.exe in recovery mode in an attempt to make the database mountable.

If this is unsuccessful, two options exist. The first is to manually run a soft recovery on the database with Eseutil.exe by running the `Eseutil.exe /r` switch against the database. The second is to run an `Isinteg.exe -fix` to fix any errors that are in the database pages from an application perspective.

Recovering a Single Exchange Mailbox

Events have been covered where your site, server, and database have all failed. In these scenarios, entire servers have been restored to working order, and mailbox databases have been recovered. However, the most common recovery situation Exchange administrators experience is mailbox recovery. It is more common that a mistake occurs against a single mailbox level than on an entire database or server level. Because of this, the ability to recover a single mailbox is a crucial part of your overall planning.

Recovering a single mailbox in Exchange Server 2007 is relatively simple; in fact, once you have the database in an RSG waiting for the restore, it is as simple as running the following command:

```
Restore-mailbox -identity <DisplayName> -RSGDatabase <RSG\MailboxDatabase>
```

This command is the simplest method of recovering a single mailbox database and restores the mailbox data to the mailbox associated with the <DisplayName> specified. This is good and it is useful. In fact, it is probably the most common scenario for deleted mailbox recovery; however, there are other options to accomplish this task.

If you are in a situation in which an employee has left the company and the previous manager wants to see the state of the mailbox prior to departure, a restore of an old mailbox database backup would be restored to the RSG. You would then need to put the employee's mailbox into the manager's mailbox. You would run the following command:

```
Restore-Mailbox -RSGMailbox 'Ex-Employee Name' -
RSGDatabase 'RSG\Mailbox Database' -id 'Manager Mailbox' -TargetFolder 'Ex-
Employee's OldEmail'
```

It is important to build in the capability to restore a single database to an RSG to support this capability. Without it, restoring a single mailbox will be available only with third-party tools.

Real World   Planning a Deleted Item Retention Strategy

All of these recovery strategies are great; however, it is well known amongst seasoned administrators that e-mail has a tendency to be accidently deleted. This presents a problem for e-mail users and administrators. The need to quickly recover e-mail that has been deleted is usually of the utmost importance and without proper planning can be cause for a stressful situation. I have been in this position several times. A senior executive was working late on a proposal or project and, of course, I was working late updating server patches. Suddenly an Instant Message pops up from the senior executive asking for a way to recover one of her e-mail items. I dropped everything I was doing to respond to the request (after all it was late, and this could make a good impression). After some brief discussion over IM, I discover that during the course of the evening the executive had been referencing several e-mails from her employees to generate a report for her boss. To use the e-mails, the executive was opening and closing each message and then closing it with a familiar keystroke. When she completed her work, she printed and reviewed her report only to find an error in some of her data. She went back to her inbox to find the e-mail that contained the correction only to discover the e-mail was gone. She searched the folder and the deleted items folder to no avail.

After some testing on my own client, I found that the keystroke she was using was common for a separate application; however, it caused our corporate e-mail client to permanently delete the e-mail item. This is when I was glad that our deleted item retention policy was still using the default 14 days. I could confidently respond that I could recover any of the items that she needed to complete her work for the evening without the process of database restores and item restores from the Exchange Management Shell.

It is important to plan an appropriate deleted item retention strategy and ensure that the amount of time specified can be stored within the database space planned for. A general rule of thumb is 10 percent of the database for the default 14-day deleted item retention. Of course, should you go over the 14-day deleted item retention and need to recover specific items from a database restore, the `Restore-Mailbox` command does the trick. To use the command, simply restore the database to an RSG then run the cmdlet and specify which messages you want to restore to which mailbox in production.

Backing up an Exchange Mailbox Server

Now that you have an understanding of what is required to recover Exchange servers, there is enough context to talk about how to back up Exchange servers. There are several ways to implement the two technologies discussed previously to accommodate the recovery strategies. These include streaming or VSS-based full, differential, incremental, and copy backups in conjunction with ensuring certain information is available in Active Directory or in a transportable copy of the server.

For server backups, ensure the system state, the registry, and the applications that support the server installation are included in the backup definition. These backups do not need to be taken every night; however, they should be taken before and after all patching and software upgrade processes.

For server rebuilds, make sure you keep thorough documentation. This could be in the form of meticulously written configuration documentation, a standard automated installation for Exchange servers, or by using a third-party configuration management system. In any of these cases, the backup should be simple and it should be tested every time a new server is built.

For server recovery, there are more options for Exchange Server. In the case of using the information in Active Directory, the operating system needs to be rebuilt to a state that supports Exchange, but not to the same state it was in previously. This removes the need to maintain a backup or copy of the system. You can also recover from a storage area network (SAN). In this scenario, logical unit numbers (LUNs) are maintained on the storage area network storage array and can be reused in the event of a physical server failure. The server itself must be rebuilt to match the previous configuration (including HBAs, drivers, SAN connections, and so on) as in the first scenario; however, the data is not restored from a backup. To recover, the rebuilt server is simply plugged into the SAN, given access to the LUNs, and powered on. This scenario also gives you the flexibility of replicating operating system boot LUNs to other storage arrays or storage array volumes.

Backing up an Exchange Mailbox Database

Backing up an Exchange mailbox database can be difficult to plan. There are many things using the database throughout the day that should not be interrupted for backups. User access, content index rebuilds, and online maintenance are the most common things using the database during the day. It is best to schedule the backup operations to take place during a time that will not conflict with these things and still complete every night.

The following two methods are commonly used; they are well-tested methods that meet certain recovery point and recovery time objectives:

- A weekly full backup plus a daily incremental backup
- A daily full backup

Note   As an alternative to these technologies, some third-party vendors enable non-VSS and non-streaming backups through custom disk mirroring and/or file system drivers. A careful evaluation of these third-party technologies is necessary to ensure supportability and technical soundness prior to any production implementation. Often Microsoft will not support these technologies, leaving the first level support to third-party vendors.

Using a Combination of Weekly and Daily Backup Methods

The first method is a weekly full backup plus a daily incremental backup. This method can be done using a streaming-based backup or a VSS-based backup. This method generally keeps backup times lower due to the speed of the incremental backups. With a lower backup window, databases can be larger, which in turn allows for higher mailbox sizes while still allowing user consolidation. This is important in many environments, which has made this a popular method. The lower backup window also does not bump into the critical online maintenance, which should complete once per week and should not bump into index rebuilds or general user activity. All of these attributes are good for backups; however, there are downsides to this method.

The most obvious downside is the number of backups that need to be restored to accomplish a full recovery. Another downside is that the potential corruption of any one of the incremental backups could be detrimental to the overall backup strategy; however, using only full backups would allow a recovery of any one of the latest full backups.

Using a Daily Full Backup Method

The second method is a daily full backup. This method can be done using a streaming-based backup or a VSS-based backup. This method generally has longer backup times every night due to the amount of data that is backed up. Thankfully, disk mirroring VSS backups are able to drastically reduce the time and impact to the hosts. If you are unable to use one of these solutions, a software VSS provider or a streaming backup program will suffice. Regardless of the technology in use, a longer backup window should be planned for to ensure that a successful completion of the backup is obtainable. Often issues such as long-running consistency checks, media mounting errors, and midbackup failures are not planned for and backup windows are overrun.

During the planning stages of a VSS-based full backup solution, there are several things you need to understand:

- The time it takes to complete a consistency check
- The time it takes to synchronize the VSS media with production spindles
- The behavior of media mounting failures, including disk and tape media
- The behavior of midbackup failures, including the ending state of the disks

During the planning stages of a streaming-based full backup solution, there are several things you need to understand, as well:

- The impact to the host if the Zero Out Deleted Pages flag is enabled
- The time it takes to perform a full backup
- The behavior of media mounting failures, including disk and tape media
- The behavior of midbackup failures, including the ending state of the disks

These are all important to understand and plan for to ensure a smooth operational state of your backups. Far too often, these are overlooked and managing backup operations becomes a long-running task that is never resolved. This can result in backups that are incomplete or nonrestorable in the event of a failure.

Backing up a Single Exchange Mailbox

Backups of single Exchange mailboxes is the simplest topic discussed in this chapter. To put it simply, Microsoft does not natively support this feature. The two backup technologies, streaming and VSS, allow for only full database backups and restores. However; this does not mean that single mailbox or brick-level backups are not possible. In Exchange Server, it is feasible that a third party could create a backup product that would back up each mailbox individually. This is usually done through the MAPI interface in the same manner that an Outlook client logs into a mailbox and is able to read all of the items in a mailbox. This has been accomplished in previous versions, and vendors have added and dropped this capability frequently. Some vendors have implemented this strategy to the level of backing up at an item level, so that individual messages can be restored from an actual backup file.

These third-party applications can add a lot of value to your environment, but performance and timelines of these solutions introduce some serious problems. If you are looking at putting one of these solutions into place, seriously consider moving that backup from the production copy of the database to a replica copy of the database. That replica could be a CCR, LCR, or other replication technology replica, as long as it is not taking up time on the production volume.

An alternative to using a brick-level backup solution would be to go with an application that allows for a hands-off backup/restore strategy of a mailbox using a full database backup/restore through the recovery storage group. This strategy would not impact performance on the production system to the same degree a brick-level backup solution to the same degree as a brick-level backup solution would.

Planning for Corruption

Corruption is a fact of life. At some point in time, a database under your control will become corrupted. This is something that you should plan for and be well prepared for, with knowledge of the tools, procedures, and calmness required to deal with this critical situation.

You should be familiar with the following tools:

- Eseutil
- Isinteg
- MfcMAPI

Familiarity with these tools allows you to manage the ESE database engine (eseutil), find and fix errors in the Information Store layer (isinteg), and look into specific mailboxes through the MAPI protocol (mfcMAPI). It is important to know the basic difference between the three components so that you understand where a particular problem might lie. In Figure 16-3, the database instances (ESE) are at the bottom; this is where the data is actually stored. The Information Store sits on top of the databases and is a single process that manages access to all of the individual databases; this process controls how all information gets into and out of the databases. The MAPI interface connects to the Information Store; this controls how Outlook clients view and communicate with the Information Store and ultimately the database. Outlook uses the MAPI interface to communicate with Exchange. You see that each tool can affect a separate portion of the stack: Eseutil.exe can interact with the ESE database directly; Isinteg.exe can interact with the databases in the context of the Information Store; and MfcMAPI.exe can interact with the Information Store through the MAPI interface in the same way that Outlook can (however, it can do this without any restrictions).

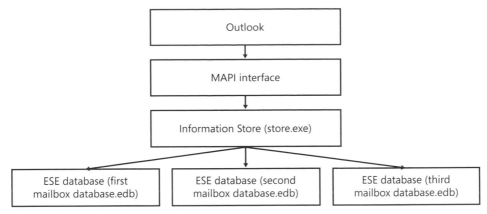

Figure 16-3 Layers between Outlook and the database

Implementing Backup Strategies

The three major requirements that need to be considered when implementing any of the previous strategies are RPO/RTO, financial, and environmental. These requirements define how the strategies are implemented and how they operate.

RPO and RTO are the most commonly discussed of these requirements. The RPO is the Recovery Point Objective and is the desired point in time the system is recovered to. This means that if you back up the system once a week on Wednesday at 10 a.m., your recovery point objective for the rest of the week is Wednesday at 10 a.m. as that is the only point in time that you can recover to. The RTO is the Recovery Time Objective and is the desired amount of time it takes to recover the system. This means that if your backup methodology allows you to plug in a USB cable, click a button, and wait 10 minutes to have the system fully recovered, your backup time is about 11 minutes (assuming the cable and button work take about one minute to complete). Combining these two is common. Usually systems with high RPOs come with high RTOs, and the same is true for the reverse. The problem is that the financial cost of these usually increases and decreases together as well: low RPO/RTO scenarios usually cost more, and high RPO/RTO scenarios usually cost less.

This leads to the second of the major requirements: financial cost. Financial cost is an important consideration and is likely one that heavily influences what strategies are used. For example, a fully geographically dispersed cluster with replicated storage arrays has the lowest RPO and RTO for e-mail database environments and is usually an expensive solution. On the other hand, an encrypted backup tape mailed to the recovery site where it is restored to new servers has a very high RPO and RTO and is about as inexpensive as you can get.

The environmental consideration is the last major requirement and one that requires significant planning. This consideration includes what Exchange Server roles are on the server that needs to be recovered, to what Active Directory site the server is recovered, and what infrastructure is in place between those two sites. If the server that needs to be recovered contains only the Mailbox server role, then a clustering solution may be an option; however, the Client Access server and Hub Transport server must already reside in the Active Directory site where the Mailbox server is recovered to. If the only network connection between the two sites is a high-latency T-1, disk replication or cluster continuous replication may not be a feasible solution to get the mailbox database copies to the recovery site.

The next section presents some common scenarios in which the previous requirements have been considered in devising strategies for services and data recoverability. These scenarios meet specific requirements and are for illustration purposes only.

Clustered Continuous Replication with VSS

The first scenario is Clustered Continuous Replication (CCR) with Volume Shadow Copy Service (VSS) backups. This scenario combines the new CCR technology with the standard VSS framework. Using CCR and VSS in your environment provides several advantages to other data replication solutions; cost, supportability, and the restart rate are the primary advantages. Combining these into a scenario means your environment consists of the following hardware:

- One Microsoft Cluster Service cluster consisting of two Exchange Server 2007 Mailbox servers and one quorum device.

  - The Exchange Server 2007 Mailbox servers do not have to have matching hardware, although you should plan to run your production workload from either system at any given time.

  - The quorum device can be any supported quorum device in a Microsoft cluster. This includes a quorum disk, a quorum server in a Majority Node Set (MNS) cluster or a file share witness in an MNS cluster.

- One server to perform backups. This server can also act as the file share witness host for your MNS cluster. This server's hardware can be 32-bit or 64-bit and does not have to match the other server configurations. The VSS Requestor resides on the server performing backups. If the server uses a shared storage array, disk replicas are mounted on the backup server in order to perform a checksum verification.

This scenario is usually set up so that the cluster can operate on either node and can be failed over to either node for server maintenance or emergencies (planned or unplanned). The backup server can talk to both nodes over the network and has the ability to talk to the VSS provider that is used. The schedule of backups depends primarily on the amount of data that is on each CCR group and the allowed backup window in the organization. The most common is a scenario in which full backups are taken on the weekends during an extended backup window and differential backups are taken during the week during a shorter backup window.

Two critical things to consider when implementing a scenario like this are

- What is the amount of data loss your environment can sustain (RPO)?

- What is the amount of time your environment needs to be restarted within (RTO)?

In the event of a planned failover, CCR ensures the last log file is closed and pulled over to the passive node in the CCR cluster. Once the log file is pulled over, the passive node can restart the clustered Mailbox server and the underlying database. On restart, the database should already be consistent due to the log replay mechanism on the remote side. This allows the restart to happen almost instantaneously and begin to serve client requests immediately after the failover is initiated.

In the event of an emergency failover, the process is similar. The passive node attempts to copy any log files from the active node that are closed or have not yet been closed. Once copied over, the passive node immediately attempts a replay of those log files to get any remaining data into the passive database. At this point the lost log resiliency feature kicks in to ensure the logs that were copied contain complete data. If the data is incomplete, the logs are not played into the database; instead, a new log generation is created, and any incoming data is processed through the new log generation while the incomplete data is disregarded. This allows the clustered Mailbox server to come online quickly and recall any data from the Hub Transport server's dumpster that may be available.

In both planned and unplanned scenarios, data loss is a possibility. If the last log cannot be copied to the passive node for any reason and the data cannot be resent through the transport dumpster mechanism for any reason, an amount of data equal to the number of messages that were partially available in those logs will be lost. This means the RPO for the failover portion can be variable; however, it is complemented in the scenario with a VSS backup, which provides a high-speed backup/restore mechanism to enable a more recent point-in-time copy on the VSS backup. The RTO is still relatively low for the failover and is also relatively low for the VSS restore (provided the VSS vendor in use allows for a fast restore).

Some of the drawbacks to this scenario are as follows:

- Failovers can cause data loss.

- If backups are taken from the replica, they are not easily moved between the production and replica nodes.

- Extending the solution between disparate sites can be difficult.

The data-loss component is hard to avoid with any scenario where the production copy of the database is not shared with, or synchronously replicated to, the passive copy. The amount of data loss is configurable through transport dumpster settings and investments in network infrastructure; however, the risk of data loss cannot be entirely removed. Additionally, if the VSS backup application takes backups from the replication writer, those backups can be restored only to the production writer. This means that a backup taken on the replica cannot be restored to the replica unless the Clustered Mailbox Server is failed over to the replica prior to performing the restore. In the event the backup is taken from the replica and the site where the passive cluster node becomes unavailable, there would not be a backup to restore.

Single Copy Clustering with Streaming Backups

The second scenario is single copy clustering (SCC) with streaming backups. This scenario combines the traditional SCC technology with the legacy streaming backup API. Using SCC and streaming backups in your environment provides several advantages to the data replication solutions: minimal data loss, highest RTO, and minimal chances of database corruption. Combining these into a scenario means your environment would consist of the following hardware:

- One Microsoft Cluster Service cluster consisting of two or more Exchange Server 2007 Mailbox servers and one quorum drive.
    - The servers in the cluster should all contain the same components and be on the cluster WHQL.
    - The quorum drive must be accessible by all of the servers in the cluster.
- One server to perform backups. This server is responsible only for controlling the backups. The Mailbox servers themselves do most of the work to move the data in the database to an external location.

Two critical things to consider when implementing a scenario like this are:

- What is the amount of data loss your environment can sustain (RPO)?
- What is the amount of time your environment needs to be restarted within (RTO)?

In the event of a planned failover, SCC performs a restart of the clustered Mailbox server on the preferred passive node of the cluster. The active node shuts down the database of the clustered Mailbox server and starts the database on the passive node. Once all services start and the databases are mounted, the clustered Mailbox server is again ready for use.

In the event of an unplanned failover, SCC first attempts to restart on the active node hosting the clustered Mailbox server. If there are any limiting factors, like the active node's motherboard failing, SCC attempts to restart the clustered Mailbox server on the preferred passive node with the database in whatever state it is in. This means that if there are any logs that have not been committed, any complete transactions are replayed into the database and any partial transactions are rolled back.

In both planned and unplanned failovers, this process ensures there is no data loss, which puts the RPO at zero. It also ensures the restart time is similar to that of restarting the services on the same node, which puts RTO at near zero.

The last component is the streaming backups. With streaming backups, the restoration of the data can take longer than the amount of time required for a VSS-based restore. However, because this scenario has such a highly available service, restoration for recovery purposes can be removed from the procedures. Doing this enables a lower-cost backup solution to coincide with a higher-cost availability solution.

Some of the drawbacks to this scenario are: server hardware costs, backup times are long, and database restores are lengthy. The hardware costs are unavoidable with a single copy cluster; it is the financial price that is paid for a high RPO and RTO. The length of the backup and restore times are also inherent in the solution. An alternative to this would be to make an environmental and financial investment in a VSS-based solution.

Single Multi-Role Mailbox Server with VSS

The third scenario is a single multi-role Mailbox server with VSS backups. This scenario combines several roles onto a single server to provide a consolidated entity to manage in a recovery scenario. The roles that typically exist on a consolidated server are the Mailbox role, the Hub Transport role, and the Client Access server role. Combining this consolidated entity with VSS backups reduces the overall RTO and potentially reduces the RPO. This consolidation of roles means that the environment consists of the following hardware:

- One Microsoft Windows Server 2003 computer running two or more Exchange Server 2007 roles.

- One server to perform backups. This server is responsible only for controlling the backups.

This scenario is usually set up so recovery of the server to a hot, warm, or cold standby server in an alternate site is possible. The primary method of recovering the server is to perform a VSS restore to the same or to a new physical server. Consider these two critical things when implementing a scenario like this:

- What is the amount of data loss your environment can sustain (RPO)?

- What is the amount of time your environment needs to be recovered within (RTO)?

The unique thing about this scenario is that planned failovers are not possible; any downtime results in a service outage. This is also an indication of the amount of time required to recover the roles to a new server during an unplanned failover. The procedure involves bringing up a new server as described earlier in the section "Recovering an Exchange Mailbox Server."

In both planned and unplanned recoveries of the system, data loss is a real possibility if the database is not shut down properly prior to the recovery.

The drawbacks of this scenario should be more obvious then the first two; there is no automatic failover of the Exchange server roles, and the recovery time can be lengthy depending on the state of the standby server.

Review of Sample Scenarios

The three scenarios presented here are certainly not the only configurations. They are illustrated to show you the breadth of solutions available and help to guide you to what configuration items will affect the three major requirements in your environment.

The first scenario uses a lower-cost, high-availability solution with a higher-cost backup/restore solution. This enables a customer to maintain a reliable failover mechanism that allows a minimal amount of data loss accompanied by a fast backup/restore mechanism to maintain more frequent point-in-time copies that can be quickly restored if necessary.

The second scenario uses a lower-cost backup/restore mechanism with a higher-cost, high-availability solution. This allows a customer to suffer zero to minimal data loss and downtime while only allowing long backup and restore times.

The third scenario does not use a high-availability solution, yet uses a fast backup/restore mechanism to allow for a quick recovery in the event of a failure. This solution is more common among small and medium enterprises as well as large enterprises that are using some other form of high availability.

Note   A common extension to the third scenario is to use LCR in conjunction with the multi-role Exchange server. LCR is implemented at the storage group level, so it can be configured more granularly, which is important to organizations that are on a tight budget.

Operational Best Practices

To successfully back up or restore an operation, follow some best practices:

- Document your backup and restore procedures.
- Ensure copies of the backups are stored in an alternate location.

ing system every day to ensure thesuccessful from the previous night.
- Perform a trial backup and restore on a monthly or quarterly basis to ensure your solution is working and to keep your restore skills up to snuff.

- De-duplication technologies will benefit your backup media space consumption.

- If you use tape storage for your backups:

  ❑ Routinely clean the tape drives according to manufacturer specifications.

  ❑ Do not overuse tapes. Discard them after they reach the maximum number of cycles specified by the manufacturer.

  ❑ Ensure that the raw storage capacity of your tape exceeds the compressed storage capacity of your database by a comfortable safety margin. If it does not, plan for tape changes when doing backups.

- If you use disk storage for your backups:

  ❑ Routinely verify data integrity on the disk.

  ❑ Ensure the raw storage capacity of your backup LUNs exceeds the storage capacity of your database by a comfortable safety margin. If it does not, plan for future growth.

Summary

This chapter covered a lot of ground pertaining to backup and restore operations. It outlined how to perform restores of your Exchange databases, the general steps to follow to recover an entire server, and a brief overview of how the VSS feature in Windows Server 2003 can be used to keep your restore times to a minimum. If your databases become corrupted or something goes awry, be sure to use the techniques presented in this chapter to recover your databases and restore your Exchange information.

Chapter 17
Tuning Exchange Server 2007 Performance

The Performance snap-in is a valuable tool included with Microsoft Windows Server 2003 and is available in the Administrative Tools folder on the Programs menu. It graphically charts the performance of hundreds of individual system parameters on a computer running the Windows operating system. When you install Microsoft Exchange Server 2007 on a computer running Windows Server 2003, several Exchange-specific counters are installed for you to track with the Performance snap-in. This chapter provides an overview of how to use the Performance snap-in to better understand your Exchange system.

Understanding How the Performance Snap-in Works

Although a full discussion of the Performance snap-in is beyond the scope of this chapter, this section covers some of its basic concepts and briefly describes how the Performance snap-in works. Because the bulk of your performance-tuning activities will involve the Windows operating system, this discussion focuses on monitoring Windows Server 2003.

More Info For more detailed information on monitoring performance in Windows Server 2003, refer to *Microsoft Windows Server 2003 Administrator's Companion*, Second Edition, by Charlie Russel, Sharon Crawford, and Jason Gerend (Microsoft Press, 2006).

Performance Monitoring Concepts

Before beginning the discussion, some basic concepts and terms are briefly covered. One thing you notice right away is the use of the terms performance monitoring and Performance snap-in. *Performance monitoring* is the activity of gathering measurements and data from individual counters that show how a server is performing its activities. *Performance snap-in* is the snap-in utility in Microsoft Management Console (MMC) that is used to gather this data.

Note   In some previous versions of Windows, the Performance snap-in was named System Monitor—a much less confusing name. You still see it referred to as System Monitor in some documentation, but this chapter uses the official name, Performance.

More specifically, performance monitoring looks at how the Windows operating system and installed applications use the resources of the system. The four main subsystems that are monitored are the disks, memory, processors, and network components. Later in this chapter, you look at each of these components, and some important counters and measurements for them are highlighted. In connection with performance monitoring, four concepts are discussed: throughput, queue, bottleneck, and response time.

Throughput

Throughput is a measurement of the amount of work done in a given unit of time. Most often, throughput is thought of as the amount of data that can be transmitted from one point to another in a given time period. However, the concept of throughput is also applied to data movement within a computer. Throughput can either decrease or increase. When it increases, the load, which represents the amount of data that the system is attempting to transmit, can increase to the point that no more additional data can be transmitted. This is called the *peak* level. If the load begins to decrease, which means that less and less data needs to be transmitted, the throughput also falls.

When data is being sent from one point to another, or in any end-to-end system, the throughput depends on how each component along the path performs. The slowest point in the overall data path sets the throughput for the entire path. If the slowest point is too slow (which is defined differently in each situation) and a queue begins to develop, that point is referred to as a *bottleneck*, a concept that is discussed in more detail in just a moment. Often the resource that shows the highest use is the bottleneck, and a bottleneck is often the result of an overconsumption of that resource.

Generally, you do not define a heavily used resource in data transmission as a bottleneck unless a queue is also developing for the resource. For example, if a router is being heavily used but shows little or no queue length, it is not thought of as a bottleneck. On the other hand, if that router develops a long queue (which is defined differently in each situation for each router), it could be said to be a bottleneck.

Queue

A *queue* is a place where a request for a service sits until it can be processed. For example, when a file needs to be written to a disk, the request to write that file is first placed in the queue for the disk. The driver for the disk then reads the information out of the queue and writes that information to the disk. Long queues are rarely considered a good thing.

Queues develop under various circumstances. When requests for a service arrive at a rate faster than the resource's throughput, or if certain requests take a long time to fulfill, queues can develop. When a queue becomes long, the work is not being handled efficiently. Windows Server 2003 reports queue development on disks, processors, server work queues, and server message block (SMB) calls of the server service.

Response Time

Response time is the amount of time required to perform a unit of work from start to finish. Generally speaking, response time increases as stress on the resource increases. It can be measured by dividing the queue length for a given resource by the resource throughput. By using the trace log feature in Windows, you can track a unit of work from start to finish to determine its response time.

Bottleneck

As mentioned earlier, a *bottleneck* represents overconsumption of a resource. You experience this as a slow response time, but think of it as overconsumption. Finding bottlenecks is a key goal in performance tuning because eliminating bottlenecks makes your system run more efficiently. Moreover, if you can predict when a bottleneck will occur, you can do much to proactively solve a problem before it affects your users. Factors that contribute to bottlenecks are the number of requests for the services of a resource, the frequency with which those requests occur, and the duration of each request.

Collecting Data with the Performance Snap-In

Before you can properly tune an Exchange server, you must first collect data that shows how the server is presently running. Data collection involves three distinct elements: objects, counters, and instances. An *object* is any resource, application, or service that can be monitored and measured. You will select various objects for which you want to collect data.

Each object has multiple *counters* that measure various aspects of the object. Examples include the number of packets that a network card has sent or received in a given time period or the amount of time the processor has spent processing kernel-mode threads. The counters are where the data is actually measured and collected.

Finally, a counter might have multiple *instances*. The most common use of multiple instances is to monitor multiple processors on a server or multiple network cards. For example, if a server has two processors, you can either measure the amount of time each processor is spending processing nonidle threads or you can measure the two processors as one unit and look at the average. Instances allow greater granularity in measuring performance. It is important to note that not all object types support multiple instances.

Each counter is assigned a *counter type*, which determines how the counter data is calculated, averaged, and displayed. In general, counters can be categorized according to their *generic type*, as outlined in Table 17-1. The Performance snap-in supports more than 30 counter types. However, many of these types are not implemented in Windows Server 2003 and so are not listed in the table.

Table 17-1   Generic Counter Types

Counter type	Description
Average	Measures a value over time and displays the average of the last two measurements.
Difference	Subtracts the last measurement from the previous measurement and displays the difference, if the result is a positive number. If the result is negative, the display is zero.
Instantaneous	Displays the most recent measurement.
Percentage	Displays the result as a percentage.
Rate	Samples an increasing count of events over time and divides the cache in count values by the change in time to display a rate of activity.

More Info   For more information about each counter type—its name, its description, and how the formulas are calculated—see the Windows Server 2003 Performance Counters Reference at *http://technet2.microsoft.com/WindowsServer /en/library/3fb01419-b1ab-4f52-a9f8-09d5ebeb9ef21033.mspx?mfr=true*.

Viewing Collected Data

When you first open the Performance snap-in (from the Administrative Tools folder on the Start menu), you see a blank screen called a *chart view*, which displays selected counters in real time as a graph (see Figure 17-1). To see data displayed in the chart, you have to add some counters. Choose Add from the toolbar to open the Add Counters dialog box (see Figure 17-2).

By default, the computer that you monitor is the computer on which you launched the Performance snap-in, but you can monitor remote computers as well. In fact, you can select different counters from multiple computers at the same time. You might do so, for example, to monitor how a distributed application is running. You can also choose to monitor the same counter on multiple computers for comparative purposes.

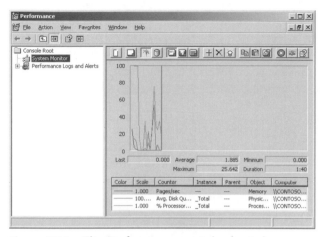

Figure 17-1   The Performance snap-in chart view

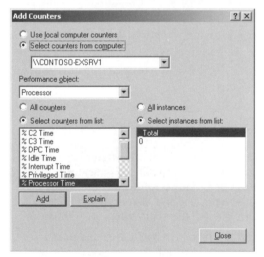

Figure 17-2   Add Counters dialog box

Evaluating the Four Main Subsystems in Windows

Earlier the four subsystems that you should always monitor were mentioned: memory, processor, disk, and network. In this section, each element is briefly discussed, and some advice is offered on tuning these parts of Windows to optimize their work with Exchange Server 2007.

One point that applies to all four of these areas is this: current data is not that helpful unless you have a baseline against which to compare it. This argues in favor of setting up regular monitoring schedules for *all* your servers and then regularly compiling that data to form a baseline of how your servers operate at off-peak, normal, and peak periods of usage. As an example, if one server is averaging 53 pages per minute, that number won't mean much unless you know the period of time that the average represents and whether it depicts abnormal behavior or is an expected result. The only way to understand this comparative information is to conduct regular monitoring of the server.

Evaluating Memory Usage

Use the counters listed in Table 17-2 to set up a baseline for your system's memory. When you monitor these counters, you will see occasional spikes that you can exclude from your baseline because these short-term values are not representative of your servers. However, do not ignore these spikes if they are occurring with increasing frequency. This increase could indicate that a resource is becoming too heavily utilized.

Recall from Chapter 3, "Exchange Server 2007 Architecture," that the Extensible Storage Engine (ESE) automatically checks the system's performance and allocates to itself all available memory that it anticipates it will need. This allocation means that when you monitor the Memory\Available Bytes counter, the counter might hover around 4000 KB, even if there isn't much activity on the server. In addition, you'll find that the Store.exe process allocates a large amount of memory to itself. This action is by design and does not represent a memory leak or a memory bottleneck.

Table 17-2   Essential Memory Counters

Counter name	Description
Memory\Pages/Sec	Shows the rate at which pages are read from or written to the disk to resolve hard page faults. This counter is a primary indicator of the type of page faults that can significantly slow down your system. It is the sum of Memory\Pages Input/Sec and Memory\Page Faults/Sec. Microsoft recommends keeping this value below 20.
Memory\Available Bytes	Shows the amount of physical memory, in bytes, available to processes running on the computers. Microsoft recommends keeping this value above 4000 KB.
Paging File(_Total)\ % Usage	Shows the amount of the paging file in use during the sample interval, as a percentage. A high value indicates that you might need to increase the size of your Pagefile.sys file or add more RAM. Microsoft recommends keeping this value below 75 percent.

To see memory allocations on a per-process basis, use the Memsnap tool, which is part of the Support Tools on your Windows Server 2003 CD-ROM. The Memsnap tool records system memory usage to a log file for later review. It gives just a snapshot of your memory usage, not an ongoing logging of how each process is using memory. Figure 17-3 illustrates what the log file looks like.

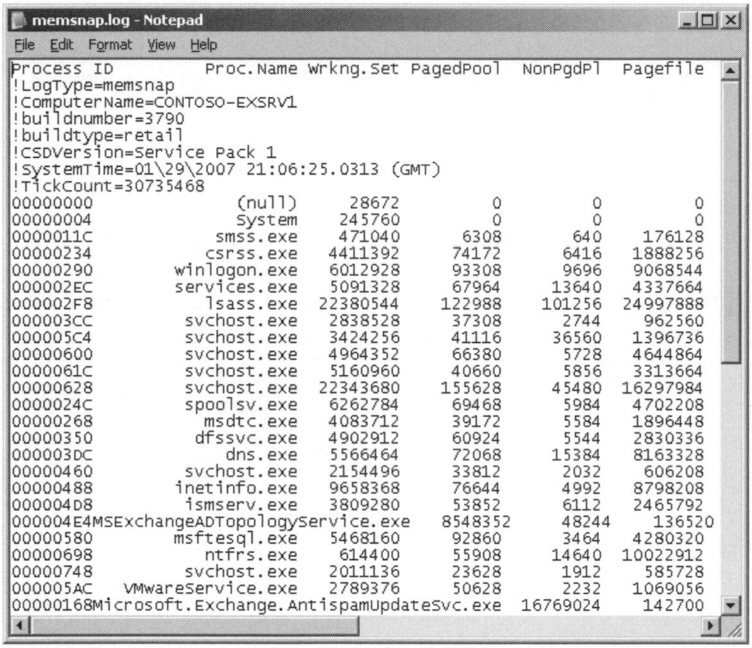

```
memsnap.log - Notepad                                              _ □ ×
File  Edit  Format  View  Help
Process ID        Proc.Name  Wrkng.Set  PagedPool  NonPgdPl   Pagefile  ▲
!LogType=memsnap
!ComputerName=CONTOSO-EXSRV1
!buildnumber=3790
!buildtype=retail
!CSDVersion=Service Pack 1
!SystemTime=01\29\2007 21:06:25.0313 (GMT)
!TickCount=30735468
00000000         (null)      28672          0          0          0
00000004         System     245760          0          0          0
0000011C       smss.exe     471040       6308        640     176128
00000234       csrss.exe   4411392      74172       6416    1888256
00000290    winlogon.exe   6012928      93308       9696    9068544
000002EC    services.exe   5091328      67964      13640    4337664
000002F8       lsass.exe  22380544     122988     101256   24997888
000003CC     svchost.exe   2838528      37308       2744     962560
000005C4     svchost.exe   3424256      41116      36560    1396736
00000600     svchost.exe   4964352      66380       5728    4644864
0000061C     svchost.exe   5160960      40660       5856    3313664
00000628     svchost.exe  22343680     155628      45480   16297984
0000024C     spoolsv.exe   6262784      69468       5984    4702208
00000268       msdtc.exe   4083712      39172       5584    1896448
00000350      dfssvc.exe   4902912      60924       5544    2830336
000003DC         dns.exe   5566464      72068      15384    8163328
00000460     svchost.exe   2154496      33812       2032     606208
00000488    inetinfo.exe   9658368      76644       4992    8798208
000004D8     ismserv.exe   3809280      53852       6112    2465792
000004E4MSExchangeADTopologyService.exe   8548352      48244     136520
00000580     msftesql.exe   5468160      92860       3464    4280320
00000698       ntfrs.exe    614400      55908      14640   10022912
00000748     svchost.exe   2011136      23628       1912     585728
000005AC  VMwareService.exe   2789376      50628       2232    1069056
00000168Microsoft.Exchange.AntispamUpdateSvc.exe  16769024     142700 ▼
◄                                                                ► ◢
```

Figure 17-3   Memsnap log file

Evaluating Processor Usage

Use the counters listed in Table 17-3 to set up a baseline for your processor usage. The processor always has a thread to process. Most often, the system supplies an idle thread for the processor to process while it is waiting to process an active thread. The Processor\% Processor Time counter does not factor in the idle thread when calculating its value.

The most common causes of processor bottlenecks are insufficient memory and excessive numbers of interrupts from disk or network I/O components. During periods of low activity, the only source of processor interrupts might be the processor's timer ticks. Timer ticks increment the processor's timer. These interrupts occur every 10 to 15 milliseconds, or about 70 to 100 times per second. Use the Processor(_Total)\Interrupts/Sec counter to measure this value. The normal range is in the thousands of interrupts per second for a Windows server and can vary from processor to processor. Installing a new application might cause a dramatic rise in this value.

Table 17-3   Essential Processor Counters

Counter name	Description
Processor\% Processor Time	Shows the percentage of elapsed time that all the threads of this process used to execute instructions. An *instruction* is the basic unit of execution in a computer; a *thread* is the object that executes instructions; and a *process* is the object created when a program is run. Microsoft recommends keeping this value to 80 or below (sustained).
System\Processor Queue Length	Shows the number of threads in the processor queue. There is a single queue for processor time, even on computers with multiple processors. This counter shows ready threads only, not threads that are currently running. Microsoft recommends keeping this value to 2 or less.

If you want to improve processor response time or throughput, you can schedule processor-intensive applications to run at a time when system stress is usually low. Use the Scheduled Tasks tool in the Control Panel to do this. You can also upgrade to a faster 64-bit processor with a dual or quad core. This upgrade always increases your system's performance, and you can use multiple processors instead of a single processor to balance the processing load.

Evaluating Disk Usage

Windows Server 2003 includes counters that monitor the activity of the physical disk and logical volumes. The PhysicalDisk object provides counters that report physical-disk activity, whereas the LogicalDisk object provides counters that report statistics for logical disks and storage volumes. By default, the Windows operating system activates only the PhysicalDisk performance counters. To activate the LogicalDisk counters, go to the command prompt and type **diskperf –yv**. The counters activate when you reboot your server.

Table 17-4 lists the counters for evaluating disk performance. They are the same for both the LogicalDisk and PhysicalDisk objects. The PhysicalDisk object has been selected to use in the table.

Table 17-4   Essential Disk Counters

Counter name	Description
PhysicalDisk\Avg. Disk Sec/Transfer	Indicates, in seconds, how fast data is being moved. A high value might mean that the system is retrying requests due to lengthy queuing or, less commonly, a disk failure. There are no benchmark recommendations from Microsoft. Watch for significant variances from baseline data.

Table 17-4   Essential Disk Counters (Continued)

Counter name	Description
PhysicalDisk\Avg. Disk Queue Length	Shows the number of requests that are queued and waiting for the disk to process. Microsoft recommends that this value be 2 or less.
PhysicalDisk\Disk Bytes/Sec	Indicates the rate at which bytes are transferred. It is the primary measurement of disk throughput.
PhysicalDisk\Disk Transfers/Sec	Shows the number of completed read and write operations per second. This counter measures disk utilization and is expressed as a percentage. Values over 50 percent might indicate that the disk is becoming a bottleneck.

Diagnosing a disk as a bottleneck is a tricky process that requires both time and experience. Some helpful tips are provided here, but for a more complete discussion of this topic, see the works cited earlier in this chapter.

What you want to see so that you can diagnose a disk as a bottleneck in your system is either a sustained rate of disk activity that is well above your baseline or an increasing rate of disk activity that represents a dramatic departure from your baseline statistics. In addition, you'll want to see persistent disk queues that are either steadily increasing or that are significantly above your baseline statistics, coupled with *the absence of a significant amount of paging* (less than 20 pages per second). If these factors combine in any other way than those described here, it is unlikely that your disk is a bottleneck. For example, if your system doesn't have enough RAM to accommodate its load, you will find that paging occurs more frequently, creating unnecessary disk activity. If you monitor only the PhysicalDisk object, you might see this activity as evidence that your disk is a bottleneck. Therefore, you must also monitor memory counters to determine the real source of this type of problem.

If you do determine that your disk is too slow, consider following one or more of these strategies:

- Rule out a memory shortage, for the reasons just discussed.

- Defragment the disk, using Disk Defragmenter. For information about using Disk Defragmenter, see the online help for Windows Server 2003.

- Consider implementing a stripe set to process I/O requests concurrently over multiple disks. If you need data integrity, implement a stripe set with parity.

- Place multiple drives on different I/O buses.

- Be sure you're using the best and fastest controller, disk, and I/O bus that you can afford.

Evaluating Network Usage

Windows Server 2003 provides two utilities for monitoring network performance: the Performance snap-in and Network Monitor. Network Monitor is not discussed here. For more information on Network Monitor, see your system documentation and the Windows Server 2003 Resource Kit.

You should monitor other resources, such as disk, memory, and processor objects, along with network objects to obtain an overall perspective on the network objects' results. In addition, you can select which layer of the Open Systems Interconnection (OSI) model you want to monitor. Table 17-5 summarizes each counter and its corresponding OSI layer.

> **More Info**   For more information about the OSI model, see "OSI Model in the Microsoft Windows 2000 Server Resource Kit" at *http://www.microsoft.com/technet /prodtechnol/windows2000serv/reskit/cnet/cnfh_osi_owsv.mspx?mfr=true*.

Table 17-5   Essential Network Counters and Their OSI Layer

Counter name	Description	OSI layer
Network Interface\Output Queue Length	Indicates the length of the output packet queue. A queue length of 1 or 2 is often satisfactory. Longer queues indicate that the adapter is waiting for the network and thus cannot keep pace with the server.	Physical
Network Interface\Packets Outbound Discarded	A high value indicates that the network segment is saturated. An increasing value means that the network buffers cannot keep pace with the outbound flow of packets.	Physical
Network Interface\Bytes Total/Sec	A high value indicates a large number of successful transmissions.	Physical
IP\Datagrams/Sec	Shows the rate at which datagrams are received from or sent to each interface.	Network
TCP\Segments Received/Sec	Shows the rate at which segments are received, including those received in error. This count includes segments received on currently established connections. A low value means that you have too much broadcast traffic.	Transport
TCPv4\Segments Retransmitted/Sec	For TCP version 4, gives the rate at which segments containing one or more previously transmitted bytes are retransmitted. A high value might indicate either a saturated network or a hardware problem.	Transport

Table 17-5 Essential Network Counters and Their OSI Layer (Continued)

Counter name	Description	OSI layer
TCPv4\Segments Retransmitted/Sec	For TCP version 6, gives the rate at which segments containing one or more previously transmitted bytes are retransmitted. A high value might indicate either a saturated network or a hardware problem.	Transport
Redirector\Network Errors/Sec	Measures serious network errors that indicate the Redirector and one or more servers are having serious communication problems.	Application
Server\Pool Paged Failures	Indicates the number of times that allocations from the paged pool have failed. If this number is high, either the amount of RAM is too little or the page file is too small or both. If this number is consistently increasing, increase the physical RAM and the size of the page file.	Application

The Network Interface object is installed when you install TCP/IP. The Network Segment object is installed when you install Network Monitor. To monitor the TCP/IP protocol, use the TCP/IP, UDP, and ICMP objects. (You no longer need to install SNMP to get the IP counters as you did with Microsoft Windows NT.) Use the NBT Connection object to track session-layer packets between computers. You can also use this object to monitor routed servers that use NETBIOS name resolution.

Application-layer objects include the Browser, Redirector, Server, and Server Work Queue on computers running Windows Server 2003. These objects will help you understand how your file and print services are performing, using the server message block (SMB) protocol.

Using the Performance Snap-in to Tune Exchange Server 2007

It would take an entire book to discuss in depth all the extra counters installed with Exchange Server 2007 and how they can be combined to give you a particular type of report. Instead, the focus here is on the more important counters and with a few suggestions for using them. The SMTP, Microsoft Outlook Web Access (OWA), and Unified Messaging counters are covered. If some of the discussion of the SMTP protocols is unfamiliar to you, refer to Chapter 25, "Supporting Other Clients," where this protocol is discussed in depth. Unified Messaging is covered in Chapter 14, "Unified Messaging."

SMTP System Monitor Counters

The SMTP server receives messages, categorizes them, places them in queues created for the intended destination, and then delivers them to that destination. Messages can be received from port 25, through Exchange transport, or from a local store submission. Table 17-6 lists the counters that are most important with the SMTP service. The main objects you are looking at here are the MSExchangeTransport SmtpReceived and the MSExchangeTransport SmtpSent objects. Some counters originate in different objects; these are noted in the Counter column.

Table 17-6   Counters for Monitoring SMTP

Messages Received Total	MSExchangeTransport SmtpReceived	Total number of messages received.
Connections Current	MSExchangeTransport SmtpReceived	Number of simultaneous inbound connections over port 25.
Messages Submitted	MSExchangeTransport Pickup	Number of messages submitted to the mail pickup directory. An unusually high number could indicate the use of a large distribution list with many mail-enabled contacts.
Messages Badmailed	MSExchangeTransport Pickup	Number of messages that are malformed, such as having a nonexistent destination domain. These messages are delivered to the Badmail directory. A high number here could indicate that some addresses for mail-enabled contacts were entered incorrectly.
Messages Submitted Total	MSExchangeTransport Queues	Total number of messages submitted to queuing for delivery.
Active Remote Delivery Queue Length	MSExchangeTransport Queues	Number of messages going to other servers that are waiting to be sent. An increasing number in this queue could indicate a problem with the physical connection to the Internet or between two Exchange servers. If one queue in particular has a steadily increasing number, you may want to see if the remote SMTP server is available.
Messages Queued for Delivery	MSExchangeTransport Queues	Number of messages going to local recipients, to the MTA, or to other gateways.

Outlook Web Access

Outlook Web Access (OWA) allows users to access their mailboxes over the Internet through a browser, such as Microsoft Internet Explorer or Netscape Navigator. OWA is measured in Performance Monitor using two different objects: MSExchange OWA and MSExchange Web Mail. Due to differences in code paths between IE4 level (Internet Explorer 4 and Netscape Navigator) and IE 5.x-level browsers, performance counters in the MSExchange Web Mail object exist in three instances: non-IE5, IE5 and above, and

_Total (which sums the former two counters). Table 17-7 shows important counters for monitoring OWA.

Table 17-7   Counters for Monitoring OWA

Counter	Object	Description
Average Response Time	MSExchange OWA	Average time (in milliseconds) that elapsed between the beginning and end of an OEH or ASPX request
Average Search Time	MSExchange OWA	Average time elapsed while waiting for a search to complete.
Current Proxy Users	MSExchange OWA	Number of users who are logged on whose mailbox access is being proxied to another server.
Current Unique Users	MSExchange OWA	Number of unique users currently logged on to OWA. This value monitors the number of unique active user sessions.
Logons/sec	MSExchange OWA	Number of OWA user sessions that are created per second.
Messages Sent	MSExchange OWA	Total number of messages sent by users since the process was started.
Peak User Count	MSExchange OWA	Largest number of users simultaneously connected to OWA since the process was started.
Store Logon Failure %	MSExchange OWA	Percentage of the last 100 OWA user logons to Exchange servers that have failed.
Authentications (total)	MSExchange Web Mail	Total number of authentications. This is the total number of times authentication is needed.
Message opens (total)	MSExchange Web Mail	Total number of message opens.
Message sends (total)	MSExchange Web Mail	Total number of message sends. After OWA submits a message, the message is handled by SMTP, and the applicable SMTP counters are affected.

Unified Messaging Counters

There are several performance objects that monitor Unified Messaging. Depending on the features that you implement, you may be able to monitor the following UM performance objects:

■ **MSExchangeUMGeneral**   This object includes counters for measuring general Unified Messaging statistics. Table 17-8 shows the counters for monitoring general Unified Messaging performance.

- **MSExchangeUMCallAnswering** This object includes counters for measuring Call Answering statistics.

- **MSExchangeUMFax** This object includes counters for measuring Fax statistics.

- **MSExchangeUMSubscriberAccess** This object includes counters for measuring Subscriber Access statistics.

- **MSExchangeUMAutoAttendant** This object includes counters for measuring Unified Messaging AutoAttendant statistics.

- **MSExchangeAvailability** This object includes counters for measuring Exchange availability related to Unified Messaging.

- **MSExchangeUMPerformance** This object includes counters for measuring Unified Messaging Performance statistics.

Table 17-8 Counters for Monitoring General Unified Messaging Performance

Counter	Object	Description
Average Call Duration	MSExchangeUMGeneral	Average Call Duration is the average duration, in seconds, of calls since the service was started.
Average Recent Call Duration	MSExchangeUMGeneral	Average Recent Call Duration is the average duration, in seconds, of the last 50 calls.
Call Duration Exceeded	MSExchangeUMGeneral	Call Duration Exceeded is the number of calls that were disconnected because they exceeded the UM maximum call length. This number includes all types of calls, including fax calls.
Calls Disconnected by User Failure	MSExchangeUMGeneral	Calls Disconnected by User Failure is the total number of calls disconnected after too many user entry failures.
Calls Rejected	MSExchangeUMGeneral	Calls Rejected is the total number of new call invitations that have been rejected.
Calls Rejected per Second	MSExchangeUMGeneral	Calls Rejected per Second is the number of new call invitations that have been rejected in the last second.
Current Auto Attendant Calls	MSExchangeUMGeneral	Current Auto Attendant Calls is the number of auto attendant calls that are currently connected to the UM server.
Current Calls	MSExchangeUMGeneral	Current Calls is the number of calls that are currently connected to the UM server.

Table 17-8   Counters for Monitoring General Unified
Messaging Performance (Continued)

Counter	Object	Description
Current CAS Connections	MSExchangeUMGeneral	Current CAS Connections is the number of connections that are currently open between the Unified Messaging server and Client Access servers.
Current Fax Calls	MSExchangeUMGeneral	Current Fax Calls is the number of fax calls that are currently connected to the UM server. Voice calls become fax calls after a fax tone is detected.
Current Play on Phone Calls	MSExchangeUMGeneral	Current Play on Phone Calls is the number of outbound calls initiated to play back messages.
Current Prompt Editing Calls	MSExchangeUMGeneral	Current Prompt Editing Calls is the number of logged on users who are editing custom prompts.
Current Subscriber Access Calls	MSExchangeUMGeneral	Current Subscriber Access Calls is the number of logged on subscribers who are currently connected to the UM server.
Current Unauthenticated Pilot Number Calls	MSExchangeUMGeneral	Current Unauthenticated Pilot Number Calls is the number of voice calls to the pilot number that have not yet been authenticated.
Current Voice Calls	MSExchangeUMGeneral	Current Voice Calls is the number of voice calls that are currently connected to the UM server.
Delayed Calls	MSExchangeUMGeneral	Delayed Calls is the number of calls that experienced one or more delays longer than 2 seconds.
Total Calls	MSExchangeUMGeneral	Total Calls is the number of calls since the service was started.
Total Calls per Second	MSExchangeUMGeneral	Total Calls per Second is the number of new calls that arrived in the last second.
Total Play on Phone Calls	MSExchangeUMGeneral	Total Play on Phone Calls is the total number of Play on Phone calls that have been initiated since the service was started.
User Response Latency	MSExchangeUMGeneral	User Response Latency is the average response time, in milliseconds, for the system to respond to a user request. This average is calculated over the last 25 calls. This counter is limited to calls that require significant processing.

Real World   System Center Operations Manager 2007

Microsoft System Center Operations Manager 2007 is an end-to-end management solution for monitoring the health of an entire Microsoft network, including servers, clients, applications, and server solutions like Exchange Server 2007. It helps automate routine administration, as well as identifying and resolving issues involving network health.

You can use System Center Operations Manager 2007 to monitor an entire messaging system, including servers, hardware performance, connectivity, and clients. It is likely, especially on larger networks, that System Center Operations Manager is used for network maintenance. If so, you can relegate many of the regular performance monitoring tasks to System Center Operations Manager, since it provides not only tools for measuring performance of Exchange servers themselves, but of the entire messaging system.

Using Other Exchange Performance Tools

Microsoft makes tools available to help test the performance of a server before putting Exchange Server 2007 into production. While these tools are not designed to monitor or tune ongoing performance of an existing Exchange server, they are useful for gauging the performance of an Exchange server before it is put into production by simulating loads on the server. You can then make configuration and hardware adjustments before putting the server into production.

This section discusses the following tools:

- Microsoft Exchange Server Jetstress Tool
- Exchange Load Generator

Microsoft Exchange Server Jetstress Tool

The Microsoft Exchange Server Jetstress Tool verifies the performance and stability of a disk subsystem prior to putting an Exchange server into production. Jetstress, shown in Figure 17-4, simulates Exchange disk Input/Output (I/O) load to help verify that the disk subsystem can handle the load generated by Exchange Server 2007. Specifically, Jetstress simulates the Exchange database and log file loads produced by a specific number of users. You use Performance Monitor, Event Viewer, and ESEUTIL in conjunction with Jetstress to verify that your disk subsystem meets or exceeds the performance criteria you establish. After a successful completion of the Jetstress Disk Performance and Stress

Tests, you will have ensured that your Exchange disk subsystem is adequately sized (in terms of performance criteria you establish) for the user count and user profiles you have established.

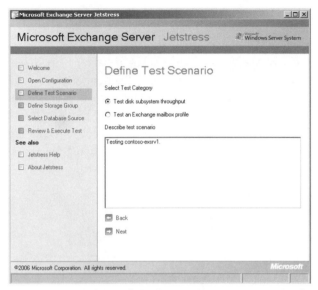

Figure 17-4   Microsoft Exchange Server Jetstress Tool

You can download Jetstress from the following location: *www.microsoft.com/downloads /details.aspx?FamilyID=94B9810B-670E-433A-B5EF-B47054595E9C&displaylang=en.*

Important   You should only use Jetstress on a nonproduction server. Further, the server should not be connected via network to any production servers in your organization.

Jetstress enables you to do three types of tests:

- **Disk Performance Test**   This test runs for 2 to 24 hours and enables you to verify the performance and sizing of your storage solution.

- **Disk Subsystem Stress Test**   This test runs for 24 hours and enables you to test the server storage reliability over a longer time.

- **Streaming Backup Test**   This test measures the database throughput and end-to-end streaming backup (both read and write) performance.

The Disk Performance Test and the Streaming Backup Test are the most useful tests for verifying the performance of your disk subsystem.

More Info   For more information, including how to interpret the results of a Jetstress test, see the documentation that comes with the Jetstress tool.

Exchange Load Generator

The Microsoft Exchange Load Generator tool (LoadGen) simulates the delivery of messaging requests to measure the impact of MAPI clients on Exchange servers. LoadGen, shown in Figure 17-5, allows you to test how a computer running Exchange Server 2007 responds to e-mail loads. To simulate the delivery of these messaging requests, you run LoadGen tests on client computers. These tests send multiple messaging requests to the Exchange server, thereby causing a mail load. LoadGen is a useful tool for determining the necessary size of servers and for validating a deployment plan. LoadGen helps you determine if each of your servers can handle the load that they are intended to carry.

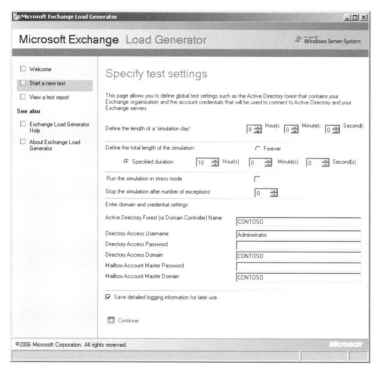

Figure 17-5   Exchange Load Generator

You can download LoadGen from the following location: *www.microsoft.com/downloads /details.aspx?familyid=DDEC1642-F6E3-4D66-A82F-8D3062C6FA98&displaylang=en.*

Important You should only use LoadGen to test a nonproduction server. Further, the server should not be connected via network to any production servers in your organization.

LoadGen is designed to run from a client computer and not from the Exchange server itself in order to accurately simulate the load on the server. The client computer should be a member of the same Active Directory domain as the Exchange server. LoadGen requires Windows Enterprise Administrator permissions because it must create users, Organizational units, and query-based distribution groups in the Active Directory forest.

When creating accounts using the Load Generator graphical user interface, the Master Password and Master Domain parameters are not used. Instead, the domain and password of the directory access account are used for this purpose, so the created accounts will have the same password and domain as the directory access account.

Note If you use the recipient management features of this release to create users or other recipient objects and you have one or more Exchange Server 2007 servers in your test topology, you must run the Load Generator application with user credentials that have permission to manage Exchange recipients. The directory access account specified in the application configuration is not used for this purpose.

Summary

This chapter described the counters that are important in measuring the performance of the four primary subsystems of a Windows server: disks, memory, network, and processor. It also examined the more important counters for the SMTP, OWA, and Unified Messaging activities. Regular monitoring of your Exchange servers can give you advance warning so that you can fix problems before they grow too big. This chapter also looked at two important tools for helping ensure that an Exchange server is ready to provide the kind of performance necessary for an intended user load—Jetstress and Load Generator. Use the information in this chapter to devise a regular monitoring strategy for your system.

Part VI
Security

Security Policies and Exchange Server 2007

You might be wondering why a chapter on security policies is in a technical book. The reason is simple: you can't effectively implement security for your Microsoft Exchange Server 2007 infrastructure until you implement security policies that communicate to your organization goals and priorities with regard to protection and management of all information held by the organization. By defining what you are trying to secure and why, you can write information security policies that form the foundation for the security technology you purchase and the electronic policies (e-policies) you create and implement. Figure 18-1 illustrates how information security policies lead to electronic policies. Figure 18-2 shows an example of how this would work.

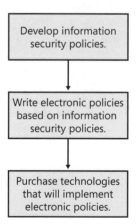

Figure 18-1 How information security policies ultimately translate into electronic policies

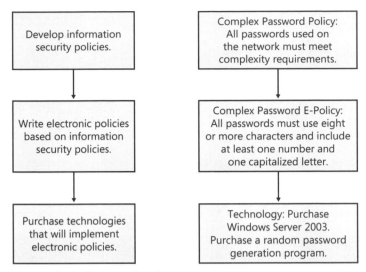

Figure 18-2   Password policy example

More Info   If you want an outstanding book on writing information security policies, please reference *Information Security Policies Made Easy*, by Charles Cresson Wood (Information Shield, 2005).

In most environments, the implementation of a security technology is the result of conversations between the IT department and other interested parties. What is often lacking in the initial planning stages is an explicit rationale for the security technology in the form of a written policy. Writing down your policy objectives and strategies and justifying them against business priorities goes a long way toward garnering support for your information security plan. This chapter helps you accomplish this by outlining the issues you need to consider when creating your information security policies and explaining why these issues are important.

Why Are Information Security Policies Important?

Your greatest risk is not your security technology—it is the people you work with every day. Each member of your organization is a hacker's potential access point to sensitive information in your company. And, conversely, each member of your organization could potentially become a disgruntled internal hacker. Information security policies define acceptable and unacceptable behavior for handling information and thus help ensure that information is not accidentally leaked, compromised, or destroyed.

You might find this assertion to be a bit paranoid because you likely know and trust many people in your organization. However, abuse of company resources does occur, even in smaller firms. Take, for example, an individual who is a consultant for a small company with roughly 35 employees. One employee was discovered to be running his own online used car sales company from his workstation as well as his own Web site, using the firm's e-mail address for his own purposes. Security policies can curtail this type of activity. By the way, this firm implemented a new security policy stating that use of the company's computers for personal or side businesses was strictly prohibited. This action stopped one other employee from engaging in an online trading business over the lunch hour.

The process of outlining security policies forces management to define how much risk it is willing to accept relative to its most critical information assets. Specifically, it answers these questions:

- What is the most critical information?

- Where does this critical information reside?

- Who will be able to access this information?

- What are the costs to the organization if the information is compromised or destroyed?

- What measures will the company take to ensure the information's privacy and integrity?

Important Do not underestimate the importance of protecting your organization's information, particularly if you handle people's personal information. These days, identity theft is rampant, organizations are failing to protect customer data, and those same organizations are being sued for significant damages, seriously hitting the bottom line, not to mention tarnishing the company's reputation.

Explicit information security policies ensure the purchase and implementation of the proper security technologies. Failure to establish an adequate organizational infrastructure for information security can lead to costly mistakes—in terms of money, time, and unexpected vulnerability. Your organization must thoroughly document who assumes responsibility for a number of areas, including the following:

- Actions

- Policies

- Standards

- Operational procedures

- Enforcement mechanisms

- Risk analysis

- The security incident response team

- The information security budget

- The planning team

One other very important reason to implement information security policies is the growing regulation that essentially says management and sometimes technical staff can be held liable for inadequately addressing information security matters. The basis of such liability can be negligence, breach of fiduciary duty, failing to use the same security measures found in other organizations in the same industry, failing to exercise due care, or failure to act after a real breach has occurred. Be sure to speak with your legal counsel about the level of exposure you currently have regarding the security in your organization.

Information Security Policies and Electronic Policies

In the previous section, it is suggested that more than one document is necessary to communicate and implement security in your organization. One of those documents is an e-policy document. *E-policies* translate information security policies into specific, measurable objectives for your IT staff. Table 18-1 provides some examples.

Table 18-1   E-Policy Examples

Information security policy	Electronic policy
Administrative and service account passwords must never be in a readable form outside the servers or a physically secure environment.	Administrative and service account passwords can never be written down unless such documentation is secured in the IT vault. Passwords can be read and communicated only to members of the administration team.
Unless specifically authorized, users cannot acquire, possess, or use hardware or software tools that could be used to compromise information systems security.	Only members of the administrative team are authorized to acquire, possess, and use hardware or software tools that can be used to compromise information systems security. These tools will not be used without the approval of the director of technology, and the approval must be in writing. The tools will be used only for specific, time-limited functions and then their use must be stopped.
Users will not use company computers for personal use.	IT personnel are authorized to uninstall unsupported programs or programs installed for personal use. IT personnel are authorized to delete any data files—without warning to the owner of those files—that are clearly created and used for noncompany activities.

After the information security policies are written, you must write the e-policies. Only then are you ready to implement security technologies, which are covered in Chapter 19, "Exchange Server Security Basics," and Chapter 21, "Securing Exchange Server 2007 Messages."

Information Security Policies for Exchange Server 2007

The next few sections outline policies that relate to messaging and that should be a part of your overall information security policies. Several examples are listed to help illustrate the points.

Password Policies

Because users need to authenticate to an Exchange Server 2007 server, and because they need to be authenticated in the Active Directory environment, you need password policies. Such policies could include the following topics:

- Minimum password length
- Password complexity
- Reuse of old passwords prohibited
- User-selected passwords prohibited
- Storage of passwords
- Anonymous user IDs prohibited (consider Microsoft Outlook Web Access)
- Displaying and printing of passwords
- Periodic password changes
- Transmission of passwords to remote users
- Limits on consecutive attempts to log on using a bad password
- Help desk password resets
- Encryption of passwords
- Use of passwords in scripts, code, and other electronic forms
- Use of duress passwords
- Disclosing passwords to consultants and contractors
- Password sharing prohibitions
- Forced change of all passwords after system compromise

This list isn't comprehensive—some topics might or might not be in your password information security policies—but it should get you started. Here are two examples of the way these topics can be expanded into information security policies:

- **Password sharing prohibited**   Users are prohibited from sharing their passwords in any form with other users in this company or anyone outside this company. If a member of the IT department needs to log on under your user account, that member must obtain a password reset on your user account before logging on.

- **Use of duress password**   The information about Server X is highly sensitive and, if leaked to unauthorized personnel, would irrevocably and significantly damage the purpose and work of your organization. Therefore, only the director of technology is allowed to log on to this server and perform administrative functions. Should the director of technology be logging on to the server under a situation of duress, the director must type the duress password. This password must execute code that immediately destroys all data on the server.

The second example is a bit extreme and would be implemented only in environments requiring extremely high security. However, the policy illustrates what must occur in a given scenario. An electronic policy would stipulate how the information was to be deleted. The information security policy dictates only that the information must be deleted.

Logon Policies

Because each user needs to authenticate to Active Directory before using any of the Exchange Server 2007 services, you need to focus on your logon policies as part of the Exchange Server 2007 information security policy development. Here are some ideas for what your policies can cover:

- Requirement of a user ID and password to access services on your network

- No sharing of user IDs and passwords

- A security notice in the system logon banner indicating who is authorized to log on to your network

- The displaying of the last user name that was used to log on

- Limitation on the daily number of logons to prevent unauthorized use of the system

- Restriction against multiple logon sessions at multiple nodes

- Restriction against automatic logon processes

- Automatic logoff process

- Requirement to log off when you have left your desk (as opposed to locking the workstation)

Here is an example of an information security policy for the network logon banner in the preceding list:

■ This system is for the exclusive use of authorized personnel only. If you are not an authorized user, you are instructed to not attempt to log on and to leave this terminal. All activities on this terminal will be monitored and recorded by system personnel. Improper use of this system is strictly prohibited and could result in termination of employment. Criminal activity will be prosecuted to the fullest extent of the law.

Many locations don't employ such a banner, but it can be invaluable in court when an unauthorized user logs on to your system and commits criminal activity.

Acceptable Use Policies

Some acceptable use policies directly affect the use of Exchange services. This section lists policies that you should consider implementing, with your Exchange Server 2007 server in mind:

■ Prohibition of storage of personal e-mail on company servers

■ Use of e-mail system for business purposes only

■ Incidental use of company e-mail system for personal use

■ Prohibition of using e-mail system for unapproved activities

■ Permissible uses of company e-mail system

■ Nonemployee use of company e-mail system

■ Termination of employee and mailbox retention

■ Voluntary leaving of employee and mailbox retention

■ Access to e-mail via Outlook Web Access

■ Use of company e-mail address in e-mail lists

■ Transference of e-mail to portable devices

■ Requirement of digital signatures for sensitive e-mails

■ Requirement of encryption of e-mails for sensitive data

■ Requirement of SSL for browser-based access to e-mail

As you can see, you have much to consider when writing security policies for e-mail. You won't end up including every item in this list in your security policies, but you should consider and discuss each one. There might also be other policy items not included here that would be suitable for your environment.

As security becomes more and more important in business transactions, you might need to clarify when e-mails should be encrypted and signed. Saying that all e-mails should be encrypted and signed is the easy answer but might not be warranted. In many scenarios, specifying that only some types of content should be encrypted and/or signed when sent is more appropriate treatment. You might even need to specify a policy regarding which third-party certification authorities (CA) can be trusted.

Computer Viruses, Trojans, and Worms

Because computer viruses, Trojans, and worms (all of which are referred to generically as *viruses* in this discussion) are spread through the use of e-mail, you must write information security policies about the viruses. Simply installing antivirus software is often not enough protection. Users should be told how to treat suspicious e-mails, what and what not to do when they suspect they have been infected, and how to avoid committing actions that introduce viruses on your network. Here is a list of items to consider when writing security policies about viruses and e-mail:

- Users must not attempt to clean viruses on their own.

- Duty to report suspicious e-mail.

- Antivirus software must be installed and working on all network nodes.

- Prohibition against downloading software from third-party sources.

- Prohibition against using unapproved antivirus software.

- All outbound e-mail and attachments must be virus-free.

- Virus checking at firewalls, servers, workstations, and other network devices.

- Use of multiple antivirus software packages from different vendors.

- Virus checking of all software downloaded from third-party sources.

- Updating of virus definitions on firewalls, servers, desktops, laptops, and other network devices.

- Prohibition against use of personal floppy disks without virus checking.

- Antivirus software must be current.

- Prohibition against scanning of Exchange databases and transaction logs with virus-checking software.

- Content must be decrypted before checking for viruses.

- Backup or imaging of servers before cleaning for viruses.

- All user involvement with computer viruses prohibited.

Important   Use antivirus software written specifically for Exchange Server to avoid database and transaction log corruption. Use this software to scan the databases and use the normal file-based scanning software to scan everything on your Exchange server except the database (.edb) files and their supporting transaction logs (E*******.log).

Schema Extensions by Exchange Server 2007

Because the installation of Exchange Server 2007 extends the schema in your organization, you should include a few security policies about this extension. Consider the following requirements:

- The schema extension by Exchange Server 2007 should be tested in a laboratory environment first.

- All "home-grown" applications must be tested for quality assurance and compatibility with the schema extensions introduced by Exchange Server 2007.

- Installing Exchange Server 2007 in your production environment before all quality assurance and compatibility tests have been successfully passed is strictly prohibited.

Because Exchange Server is also a development environment, here are some issues that should be discussed regarding ongoing development for Exchange Server 2007:

- Separation between testing and production environments

- Development staff has administrative access to testing environment but not to production environment

- No testing by developers in production environment

- Use of images or backups of production servers on test servers

- Formal change control procedure required for all production servers

- Production system changes must be consistent with security policies and architecture

- Requirement to document all changes to production system

- Requirement to test all production system changes for security vulnerabilities in test environment first

- Movement of software from test environment to production environment

Third-party applications will be installed on your Exchange Server 2007 server, so consider the following issues when writing your information security policies:

- Test third-party applications in the test environment first.

- Assess third-party applications for security vulnerabilities.

- Installing third-party applications if known security vulnerabilities cannot be fixed is prohibited.

- Running nonessential services on servers and workstations is prohibited.

- Conduct periodic operating system and application audit on all servers.

- Implement security patches and fixes promptly.

- Test all security updates and fixes in test environment before installing in production environment.

- Run the same service pack levels and same security fixes on all Exchange servers.

- Management approval is required for installation of service packs and security fixes on all Exchange servers after the software has been successfully tested in the test environment.

- Set the timing of changes to production systems that cause a reboot of production servers.

- Back up or image Exchange production servers before installing new software.

- Third-party software vendors must supply a written integrity statement.

As you can see, overall change management processes are important. Also, most of these policy items assume the company has invested in a development environment in which new software can be tested. Creating a list of standards against which new software can be measured is difficult, but you can use the following standards as a starting point for developing your own quality and compatibility measurements:

- Ability to send and receive e-mail

- Ability to send and receive signed e-mail

- Ability to send and receive encrypted e-mail

- Ability to send and receive signed and encrypted e-mail

- Ability to access public folders

- Ability to post to a public folder

- Ability to run custom applications presented via a public folder

- Ability to perform all mailbox functions, such as calendaring, tasks, and journals

- Ability to enforce Inbox rules

- Ability to use Out Of Office Assistant

- Ability to recover a mailbox

Test the more common functions and check the various forums and blogs (*http://www.microsoft.com/technet/community/en-us/exchange/default.mspx*) for any complaints or bugs that were found in the new software. If the new software is from a third-party source, find out from the company whether there are any known issues with this software and Exchange Server 2007.

Data Security

Because Exchange will host critical and sensitive information, consider the following for Exchange Server 2007:

- Statement that information is an important company asset
- Legal ownership of e-mail and messages
- Requirement of disclaimer notices on all e-mail
- Prohibition of downloading company e-mail to personal home computers
- Use of company information for nonbusiness uses
- Using e-mail to transfer company information to third parties
- Right of company to examine e-mail content at any time
- Right of company to monitor use of e-mail
- All e-mail activity monitored and reported to management
- Prohibition of disclosure of confidential information via e-mail
- Prohibition of responding to e-mail receipts
- Acceptable use of e-mail receipts
- Prohibition of stationary in e-mails
- Use of signatures in e-mail
- Confidentiality e-mail agreements required for all employees
- New confidentiality e-mail agreement required for change in employment status
- Prohibition against giving nonemployees e-mail accounts on production systems
- Data classification scheme
- Acceptable retention of hardcopy e-mails
- Removal of sensitive information from the company's network via e-mail
- Permission required to take secret information off company's premises

- Scrubbing Exchange databases that hold secret information after backup

- Shredders required to dispose of hardcopies of e-mail

- Dissemination of confidential or secret information prohibited via distribution lists or e-mail server lists

Data security encompasses many issues. A few of them are discussed here. First, if you can define a data classification scheme such as public, private, confidential, or secret, you can tie the encryption and signing of e-mail to certain levels of content. For example, you could require that all e-mail containing confidential information be signed, and all e-mail containing secret information be both signed and encrypted. Spelling this requirement out in a set of policies will help your users know when to use these advanced methods of sending and receiving messages and protect your company.

Second, check with your legal counsel regarding ownership and monitoring of e-mail. A user can assert a right of privacy for his or her company-given e-mail account unless the company clearly informs the user that e-mail hosted on a company server is company property.

Finally, if your users send out confidential or sensitive content in their e-mails, it may be a good idea to add a disclaimer to all outgoing e-mails to protect the user and the company in the event the e-mail is accidentally sent to the wrong recipient. Check with your legal counsel.

Legal Exposure to Unwanted E-Mail Content

A significant percentage of spam is related to pornography or other adult content, including advertisements for adult-related pharmaceuticals and medical procedures. This adult or offensive content that is received by employees in your company has the potential to land you in court unless you take active and reasonable steps to prevent it. Further, some of this kind of spam attracts the reader with promises that are fulfilled once the reader clicks on a link in the message and visits a Web site. Unfortunately, this Web site contains code that takes advantages of a newly discovered exploit, thus, infecting the user's computer. A set of information security policies should be developed with these security and legal issues in mind:

- No company endorsement of unwanted, received e-mail content

- Requirement to make reasonable efforts to block all offensive e-mail

- Requirement of user to notify management of received offensive e-mail

- Prohibition of sending or forwarding offensive content, such as jokes, in e-mail

- Right of company to remove offensive material and e-mail without warning

- Disclaimer of responsibility or liability for message contents

- Requirement of disclaimer that personal statements do not necessarily reflect the company's views, positions, and opinions

- Prohibition of using e-mail to engage in sexual, ethnic, or racial harassment

Every element of this list should be included in your security policies because, for example, adult-related spam likely violates your sexual harassment policies, and jokes innocently passed among co-workers might leave your company exposed to unnecessary sexual harassment liability.

Backing Up and Archiving Exchange Databases

Surprisingly, some organizations do not guard their backup tapes and media very well. Most organizations view the backup of databases as a routine software procedure. However, more thought needs to be given to the backing up and storage of Exchange databases. Here are some elements to consider when writing security policies in this area:

- Acceptable archival storage media

- Regular testing of archival storage media

- Backup media stored in separate fire zones from Exchange servers

- Backup media rooms must be fire-proofed

- Backup media rooms must be physically secure

- Offsite storage of backup media required

- Specification of backup process and frequency

- Users notified that Exchange Server data is routinely backed up

- Requirement to encrypt backup media

- Two copies of backup media required for confidential or secret information

- Two copies of backup media stored offsite for confidential or secret information

- Monthly trial backup and restore required to test backup processes and media

- Quarterly audit of backup processes required

- Minimum information retention period for mailboxes

- Minimum backup media retention period

- Regular purging of old e-mails or outdated information for all users' mailboxes

- Requirement to retain a copy of all e-mail

You can move a user's mailbox between databases, so you can place those users who send and receive the most sensitive e-mails in a single database and then require multiple backups of that database along with message journaling, increasing the chance that information can be recovered in the event of a disaster.

In certain industries, laws and rules might stipulate that you implement a certain backup and retention policy. Some of this work might have been done for you already in industry standards. Be sure to pay attention to those standards.

E-Mail Integrity

This section outlines some issues that you should consider regarding e-mail integrity:

- E-mail address changes confirmed via previous address.

- E-mail originator must be clearly identified.

- E-mail system must reject all e-mail that does not have a verifiable originator.

- Employees must make truthful statements in their messages.

- Prohibition against misrepresentation of identity in e-mail system.

- Employee contact information must be consistently represented.

- Right to free speech does not apply to company's e-mail system.

- Contracts cannot be signed using digital signatures.

- Only designated employees can form contracts via e-mail and digital signatures.

- Prohibition of use of encryption technologies that cannot be decrypted by system personnel.

- No trusting of unapproved certificate authorities.

- Maximum life for all encryption keys.

- Process for generating encryption keys.

- Requirement of minimum key length.

- Protection of private keys.

There is positive case law regarding contracts that can be formed and signed using a digital signature. However, check with your legal counsel on whether you want to allow this to occur.

Also, check with your legal counsel regarding whether a person's First Amendment rights can be curbed by the company. This free speech issue could potentially be controversial, so clarify it and be proactive.

Finally, because more and more encryption is taking place, specifying which CAs can be trusted is important. Also, specify which encryption methods are acceptable in your organization and prohibit the encryption of data that can't be decrypted by your company.

Miscellaneous Elements to Consider

The information security issues listed in the preceding lists aren't comprehensive, so one last list of items is provided that doesn't quite fit in these categories. Although the items in the following list are called miscellaneous, these items are critical for you to consider when writing information security policies for your organization:

- Prohibiting the use of e-mail addresses other than official company addresses for company use
- Forwarding company e-mail to noncompany addresses prohibited
- No use of the e-mail system as an electronic database
- Periodic destruction of archived e-mail databases employed without warning
- Owner authorization required to read e-mail messages of other workers
- Prohibiting the altering of e-mail message headers
- Prohibiting the sending of unsolicited bulk e-mail
- User must stop sending e-mail messages after request to stop has been received
- Authorization to send e-mail to distribution lists required
- Prohibition against opening attachments unless they are expected
- Use of e-mail system requires attendance at authorized training sessions

Some of you are going to love the element in this list about not using the e-mail system as an electronic database. More than a few Exchange Server administrators complain about users filing and saving every e-mail forever. Perhaps this element alone piques your interest in writing these information security policies!

Several of these elements ensure users don't use your company system for spam. If your marketing department or sales department sends out bulk e-mail, word the policy such that authorization is required and that all bulk e-mail is not inherently prohibited.

Forwarding company e-mail to personal e-mail accounts is often prohibited. This policy ensures that those who work with sensitive information cannot send that information to their own e-mail account and then sell the information to your company's competitors. Auditing the mailboxes of these users ensures that they follow the policy. A written policy, in and of itself, can't keep someone from doing anything prohibited, but it can give you authority to monitor user activities and expose the user if a policy is being violated.

Related Resources

Microsoft makes available software and other resources designed to help organizations implement effective security policies and practices. Among these resources are the following:

- **Microsoft Operations Framework**   The Microsoft Operations Framework is a collection of best practices from which you can design the procedures, controls, and roles required for the efficient operation of your IT infrastructure. MOF is based on the IT Infrastructure Library (ITIL), and it adds specificity for the Microsoft platform. Well-documented, thorough operational processes and procedures help make sure that all components in an organization's environment on which Exchange relies are managed efficiently and effectively. By using MOF-based processes to help make sure that there is documentation of these service interdependencies, an organization can help minimize the possibility for preventable outages and reduce the impact of scheduled changes.

  More Info   For more information about the Microsoft Operations Framework and how it can support security efforts in your Exchange Server 2007 implementation, visit *http://technet.microsoft.com/en-us/library/bb232042.aspx*.

- **Windows Rights Management Service**   Microsoft Windows Rights Management Services (RMS) for Windows Server 2003 is information protection technology that works with RMS-enabled applications to help safeguard digital information from unauthorized use—both online and offline, inside and outside of the firewall. RMS augments an organization's security policies and strategy by protecting information through persistent usage policies, which remain with the information, no matter where it goes. Organizations can use RMS to help prevent sensitive information—such as financial reports, product specifications, customer data, and confidential e-mail messages—from intentionally or accidentally getting into the wrong hands.

  More Info   For more information about Windows Rights Management Services, visit *http://www.microsoft.com/windowsserver2003/technologies/rightsmgmt/default.mspx*.

Summary

This chapter outlined some security policy elements that relate to e-mail and Exchange Server that should be included in your overall security policy manual. The creation of such policies forms the foundation for creating electronic policies that, in turn, inform security technology decisions and purchases. In reality, a great security implementation starts with information security policies that are comprehensive in nature and that specify acceptable and unacceptable behavior in a number of areas, including messaging.

In Chapters 19, "Exchange Server Security Basics," Chapter 20, "Antivirus and Anti-Spam," and Chapter 21, "Securing Exchange Server 2007 Messages," you learn how to implement specific security policies and technologies to support a secure Exchange messaging infrastructure in your organization.

Chapter 19
Exchange Server Security Basics

Security incidents, including hacking, virus attacks, spyware outbreaks, and identity theft, have rocked the computing world. Due to the e-mail server's reliance on access to the outside world, e-mail has become a target for miscreants everywhere, who try to use this medium to gain access to an organization. As such, security has become so central to the administrator's role that a large portion of this book is devoted to a discussion of it.

This chapter offers ideas about how to add complexity and create hindrances to those who wish to attack your network over port 25. It is never fool-proof, but the more you invest in security, the more secure your e-mail server will be. However, if you have good strategies in place and adequate tools to assist you, you can anticipate and thwart most attacks.

Think Globally When Diagnosing a Security Problem

Recently, a United States firm with national visibility in its industry was attacked by a group based outside of the U.S. The attacking group used its Exchange server to send out spam messages (in its own language) to addresses all over the world. At first, this problem looked like a virus, but then the company realized the attackers had planted a program on the Exchange server that was launching the outgoing e-mails.

By the time the firm figured out the problem, outbound SMTP queues had nearly 100,000 messages sitting in them, ready to be sent. Besides the obvious concern that the people receiving the spam would be unhappy, there were also a multitude of other negative possible consequences that could have occurred as a result of this problem:

- **A tarnished reputation**   By "allowing" this activity to take place, the company proved to those that received the spam that inadequate security measures were being taken. Whether this statement actually reflected reality would be a moot point to those who's perceptions of this company changed.

- **Lawsuits**   By sending out spam, the company opened itself up to lawsuit that could prove to be costly and further harm the company's reputation.

The Scope of Security

Everyone has heard the old phrase "a chain is only as strong as its weakest link." You can easily apply that thinking to security: a network is only as secure as its least secured component. Always consider e-mail to be one of those weak links on your network because it is an obvious entry point. Attackers use e-mail to wreak havoc because it's easy: no matter how well you secure your network, chances are good that you have port 25 open on your firewall and that a Simple Mail Transport Protocol (SMTP) server is ready to work with e-mail when it comes in.

When you begin thinking about security strategies, always answer the following question: What am I securing Exchange Server 2007 against? The answers to this question are varied and can be grouped into four categories:

1. Social engineering attempts

2. Physical security

3. Administrative security

4. SMTP security

You learned about social engineering in depth in Chapter 18, "Security Policies and Exchange Server 2007." In this chapter, the other three security categories are covered.

Motivations of a Criminal Hacker

Although a lot of literature has been written about the technical aspects of securing a network, not much is available about who your enemies are and what motivates them to attack. Before you can determine how to protect your organization, you must learn to think like a hacker, figure out where you're vulnerable, and then develop a game plan to reduce your exposure. If you can understand who would want to do you harm and what can be gained from such harm, you can better protect your company and your information. Make the following assumptions:

- You do have professional adversaries.

- You are on their target list.

- You will be attacked some day.

- You cannot afford to be complacent.

One of the most difficult realities for an organization to accept is the presence of adversaries who might attempt to harm it by using technology. It's also possible that you really do not have adversaries in this traditional sense. Today, attackers look for any system that has an exploitable weakness that they can turn to their advantage. Often, attackers look at weakly secured systems as bases from which to launch more sophisticated attacks.

The motivations of attackers can be varied and complex. Hackers are often motivated, in part, by their invisibleness. Today's more sophisticated hackers are often also motivated by the prospect of a big payday. On the Internet, a hacker can "peek" into a company's private world—its network—and learn a lot while remaining anonymous.

Some individuals are just curious to see what they can learn about your company or individuals within your company. These hackers often don't have any malicious intent and are unaware that their actions violate security policy or criminal codes. That does not mean that these casual hackers are any less dangerous, however.

Other hackers are simply trying to help. You've probably been in this category once or twice yourself. In your zeal to be helpful, you bypass security policies to fix problems or accomplish emergency assignments. You might even believe that your efforts are more efficient than following established guidelines and policies. Nevertheless, the bypassing of known security policies is one element of hacking a network.

Some individuals act with malicious intent, engaging in acts of sabotage, espionage, or other criminal activities. They can become moles, stealing information to sell to competitors or foreign groups. Some simply enjoy destroying the work of others as well as their own work. Others act out of revenge for a real or perceived wrong committed against them, or believe they are acting in line with a strongly held belief system. Still others are more methodical and hardened and turn hacking into a career; they might even take employment just to do your company harm.

How Hackers Work

Hackers start by learning that an e-mail server exists, which generic scanning tools can tell them. Coupled with the public information of your Domain Name System (DNS) records, hackers can quickly know a lot about your network.

Finding company information is easy for anyone. You can do it. Simply open a command prompt and type **nslookup**. Set the type of the record you're looking for to a mail exchanger (MX) record by typing **set type=mx**. Type a domain name. This example uses Microsoft.com. Figure 19-1 shows the results.

Figure 19-1   Using the NSLookup tool to find the public MX records for Microsoft.com

Next, the hacker determines the platform of your SMTP server in one of two ways. In the first approach, the hacker can use Telnet to open a session to your server over port 25 and then read the banner. Under Exchange Server 2007, the banner no longer identifies the version of Exchange Server being run, but does still indicate that the server is running the Microsoft ESMTP service. By removing the version number, Microsoft makes it harder for hackers to determine the exact version of Exchange that you are using. Note, of course, that because Exchange Server 2007 is the only version that, by default, lacks this identifying information, there are methods to achieve the same goal in older versions. However, a hacker can still figure out what he wants to know. It will take a couple of service packs and another major version of Exchange before this default omission really begins to bear fruit. Figure 19-2 gives you a look at an ESMTP conversation that takes place with an Exchange Server 2007 server.

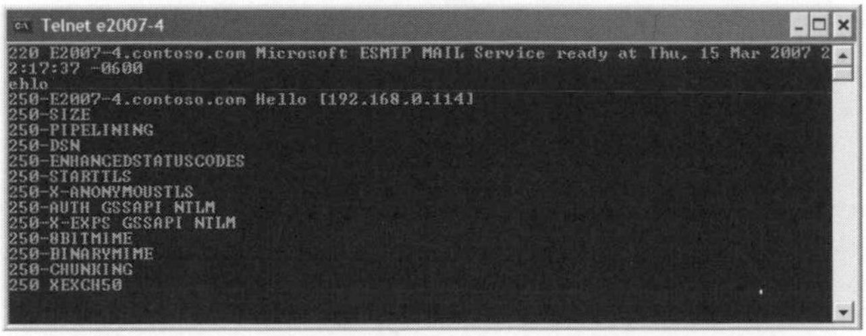

Figure 19-2   Opening a Telnet session to a server running Exchange Server 2003

Under older versions of Exchange Server, the exact version of the Exchange server being run is displayed (see Figure 19-3). The main version number, 6.0, means Exchange Server 2003. An Exchange 2000 Server registers with a main version number of 5.0. A SendMail server has its name and the version of SendMail software used by the company displayed in the header as well as the operating system (OS). Using this kind of information, a hacker can target his efforts by looking for exploits that will work for your specific system.

Figure 19-3   Opening a Telnet session to a server running Exchange Server 2007

> **More Info**   Although Exchange Server 2007 is the first version of Exchange Server that, by default, does not display versioning information in a telnet window, you can manually configure older versions of Exchange Server to act the same way. Refer to *http://support.microsoft.com/kb/281224/en-us* for more information..

The second way to determine your e-mail server platform is to send a bogus e-mail to your server. This is accomplished by sending a message to an unlikely e-mail address such as pancake@contoso.com. The nondelivery report (NDR) that is returned has the e-mail server information located somewhere in the NDR. The following sample is a message header sent to the lab Exchange server at contoso.com. Notice that the Exchange server version is included right in the Sent by line:

```
Delivery has failed to these recipients or distribution lists:

pancake@contoso.com
This recipient e-mail address was not found in the recipient e-mail system.
Microsoft Exchange will not try to redeliver this message for you. Please
check the recipient e-mail address and try resending this message, or provide
the following diagnostic text to your system administrator.
---------------------------------------------------------------------------
Sent by Microsoft Exchange Server 2007
Diagnostic information for administrators:
Generating server: E2007-4.contoso.com
pancake@contoso.com
#550 5.1.1 RESOLVER.ADR.RecipNotFound; not found ##
Original message headers:
Received: from E2007-4.contoso.com ([192.168.0.22]) by E2007-4.contoso.com
  ([192.168.0.22]) with mapi; Thu, 15 Mar 2007 22:31:42 -0600
Content-Type: application/ms-tnef; name="winmail.dat"
Content-Transfer-Encoding: binary
From: Francis Cat <cat.francis@contoso.com>
To: "pancake@contoso.com" <pancake@contoso.com>
Date: Thu, 15 Mar 2007 22:31:37 -0600
Subject: Test message
Thread-Topic: Test message
Thread-Index: AQHHZ4P8FQkU6/4hJka2OY89GGOrfg==
Message-ID: <48B260B970217342AAFBCD9BD19B2E5D20A39D1C1B@E2007-4.contoso.com>
Accept-Language: en-US
Content-Language: en-US
X-MS-Has-Attach:
X-MS-TNEF-Correlator: <48B260B970217342AAFBCD9BD19B2E5D20A39D1C1B@E2007-4
      .contoso.com>
MIME-Version: 1.0
```

Now that the hacker knows which e-mail server software you run, he or she checks known databases to find vulnerabilities to exploit. The known vulnerabilities for Exchange Server 2007 are listed in Microsoft's Security Bulletins and can be found at www.microsoft.com/security/ default.mspx. On older versions of Exchange, some of the vulnerabilities could involve Microsoft Internet Information Services (IIS) because IIS managed the SMTP service for Exchange. In Exchange Server 2007, SMTP is a core part of Exchange itself, which helps to reduce the attack potential on your server. Other vulnerabilities may involve Microsoft Outlook Web Access (OWA), again because of the involvement of IIS managing the HTTP connectivity to the Exchange server. At a minimum, be aware of any vulnerabilities that exist for Exchange Server 2007 and test and install the patches when they are released.

Generally speaking, the e-mail administrator can expect the following kinds of attacks:

■ **Buffer overflows**   Buffer overflows send a larger quantity of data to the server than is anticipated. Depending on how the overflow is executed, it could cause the server to stop working or it might run malicious code from the attacker.

- **Data processing errors**   These are not common currently, but the concept is that a small program is sent directly to the server, and the server runs it. More common today is sending these programs to a network though e-mail as attachments. Depending on their function and purpose, these programs can be viruses, Trojans, or worms (discussed at length later in this chapter).

- **HTML viruses**   These do not require user intervention to run unattended scripts.

- **Custom programs written to run against port 25 (SMTP)**   The more common types of programs that attack port 25 include e-mail–flooding programs or programs that contain their own SMTP engine that use the port for their own malicious purposes.

- **Denial of Service (DoS)**   A Denial of Service attack is an attack on a network that is undertaken in an effort to disrupt the services provided by a network or server.

- **Cross-site scripting**   Cross-site scripting is a vulnerability whereby an attacker places malicious code into a link that appears to be from a trusted source.

- **Spam and phishing expeditions**   Spam, or junk mail, is a well-known e-mail malady and affects just about everyone that uses the communication medium. A particular type of spam, called a phishing e-mail, attempts to lure unsuspecting users into clicking on unsafe web links. These links point to web forms that ask the user to provide sensitive personal information.

Here are some broad actions you can take to guard against the attacks just described, plus others:

- **Physical access to the server**   Lock the doors and use some type of biotech authentication.

- **Viruses, Trojans, and worms**   Use antivirus software and regularly scan your servers and workstations. Use the Exchange Server 2007 Edge Transport server role on at least one Exchange server.

- **Loss of data**   Perform regular backups.

- **Unauthorized use of user accounts**   Conduct user training on information security policies and require complex passwords.

- **Denial of service attack**   Harden the TCP/IP stack and the router.

- **Platform vulnerabilities**   Install all software patches and engage in service that offers minimization. Microsoft has released excellent free software for updating its patches on your servers. This software is called Windows Server Update Services (WSUS).

More Info   A discussion of WSUS is outside the scope of this chapter, but you can learn more about WSUS on Microsoft's Web site at *http://www.microsoft.com/windowsserversystem/updateservices/default.mspx.*

The rest of this chapter is intended to help you secure Exchange Server 2007 against these types of attacks. However, a brief discussion of physical security of your Exchange server is in order.

Physical Security

Physical security is a topic not often mentioned in many security books, particularly in books only about Exchange, but it is a topic worth mentioning. Servers can be left on desks running in a corner cubicle or in an unlocked server room. However, it is always best practice to store your servers in a secure location using door locks and, in some instances, motion detectors and/or other physical security measures.

When you limit physical access to a server, you limit who can log on locally to the server, who can use portable storage to introduce a new virus or malicious program on your network, and who can retrieve information directly from the server. Limiting physical access is one of the easiest and most elementary methods of securing your server against internal attacks that exist.

Most administrators reading this book already have these physical security measures in place. Those who haven't physically secured your servers should do so at their earliest opportunity. Limiting physical access to a server can go a long way toward protecting your information from would-be attackers.

Administrative Security

In previous versions of this book, this section talked extensively about the use of administrative groups as a way to achieve some semblance of administrative security for your Exchange organization. In Exchange Server 2007, however, Microsoft has mostly done away with administrative groups, leaving only a single administrative group named Exchange Administrative Group (FYDIBOHF23SPDLT) in which only Exchange Server 2007 servers reside. This administrative group is present only to support coexistence with legacy Exchange servers.

> **Note** The name of the Exchange administrative group, Exchange Administrative Group (FYDIBOHF23SPDLT), is pretty convoluted. Likewise, Exchange Server 2007's legacy routing group, named Exchange Routing Group (DWBGZMFD01QNBJR), is also fairly convoluted. Have you wondered at all why Microsoft chose these particular names? First, Microsoft had to be careful that it didn't choose a name that already exists in a customer's legacy Exchange organization. Second, the Exchange team decided that a little creativity was in order. Look carefully at the two names. Both have the same number of characters with each letter and number occupying the same positions. To make a long story short, if you look at the administrative

group's name, you find you can go to the previous letter (or number) in the alphabet for each character in the name and spell "EXCHANGE12ROCKS." Likewise, for the routing group, go to the next letter of the alphabet for each letter in the routing group name and you also get "EXCHANGE12ROCKS." It's really nice to see the product team having so much fun with a product that is generally considered all business!

Why did the Exchange team eliminate administrative groups from the Exchange equation? With the complete overhaul of the management interface and its new "area of responsibility" focus, administrative groups simply aren't necessary and can add to the overall complexity of managing Exchange. Figure 19-4 gives you a side-by-side look at the legacy Exchange System Manager and the Exchange Server 2007 Exchange Management Console. With their absence in Exchange Server 2007, you need to use a way other than administrative groups to achieve administrative security. In this section, you learn two methods by which you can add users to act in various Exchange administrative capacities.

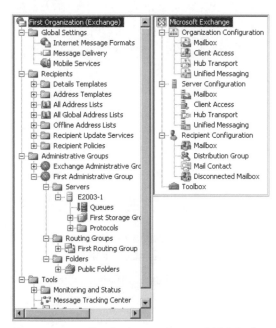

Figure 19-4   The Exchange Server 2003 Exchange System Manager is on the left and the Exchange Server 2007 Exchange Management Console is on the right.

The Built-in Exchange Administrative Groups

When you run the initial installation of Exchange Server 2007, five Active Directory universal security groups are created, each with specific rights to various parts of the Exchange organization. Four of the five groups, shown in Figure 19-5 inside Active Directory Users and Computers, pertain directly to management of the Exchange organization and are as follows:

- **Exchange View-Only Administrators** This role allows you to view configurations on all Exchange objects, but not to make any changes to those configurations.

- **Exchange Servers** This role provides the following rights:

  ❑ Members of this group have all of the rights of Exchange View-Only Administrators.

  ❑ Members of this group have access to server-based Exchange configuration information and to the Active Directory objects that are server-related.

  ❑ Members of this group may perform server-based administration but cannot perform operations at the global Exchange organization level.

  ❑ Members of this group are also members of the local Administrators group on each server on which Exchange Server 2007 is installed.

- **Exchange Recipient Administrators** This role provides the following rights:

  ❑ Members of this group have all of the rights of Exchange View-Only Administrators.

  ❑ Members of the group are also allowed to configure any object related to recipients and public folders, including contacts, groups, public folder objects, Unified Messaging mailbox settings, Client Access mailbox settings, and any other recipient Exchange property found in Active Directory.

- **Exchange Organization Administrators** This role provides the following rights:

  ❑ Members of this group have all of the rights of Exchange Recipient Administrators, plus more.

  ❑ Users assigned to this group are allowed to view and administer all aspects of the Exchange organization, including servers, and organizational configuration.

  ❑ Members of the role are considered the owners of all Exchange-related Active Directory objects.

  ❑ During Exchange Server 2007 installation, this group is added to the membership of the server's local Administrators group. If you install Exchange Server 2007 on a domain controller, which is not recommended, Exchange Organization Administrators have additional rights by virtue of the local Administrators group having more rights on a domain controller.

If you want to add a full Exchange administrator to your organization, all you have to do is add the appropriate user account to the Exchange Organization Administrators group. The same holds true for the other security groups.

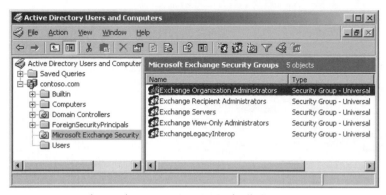

Figure 19-5   The Exchange Server 2007 built-in security group

The Add Exchange Administrator Wizard

Exchange Server 2007 also provides an easy way to add Exchange administrators with each administrator role having responsibility for only a specific part of the Exchange organization, such as a single server, a group of servers, or only able to manage recipients. You will find that this administrative delegation method is far more flexible and effective than administrative groups were in the past.

The best way to demonstrate how the Add Exchange Administrator operation works is to see it in action. To start the process, open the Exchange Management Console and select the Organization Configuration option, as shown in Figure 19-6.

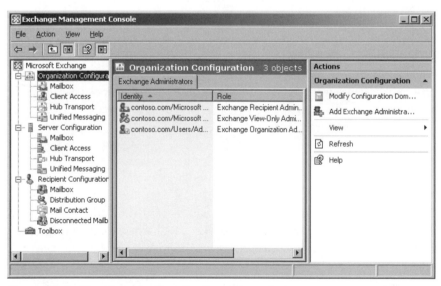

Figure 19-6   The Organization Configuration window

Note that the work pane shown in Figure 19-6 shows you the groups that already have some level of permission to the Exchange organization. To add Exchange administrators, from the Action pane, choose Add Exchange Administrator. This selection displays a one-page wizard, shown in Figure 19-7.

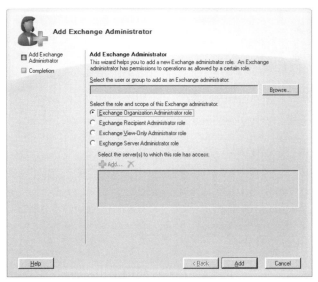

Figure 19-7   The Add Exchange Administrator Wizard

There are three selections that you must make in order to complete this wizard.

First, select the user or group to which you want to grant Exchange administrative rights. Next, select the role and scope that should apply to the new Exchange administrator. Finally, if you've selected the Exchange Server Administrator role, select at least one server to which this new user or group has access. Click Add, and from the Select Exchange Server window, choose the desired servers. Figure 19-8 shows what the screen looks like after you select the Exchange Server Administrator role and add a managed server.

Note   When you add someone to the Exchange Server Administrator role, you must manually add that user or group to each managed server's local Administrators group.

In reality, when you run the Add Exchange Administrator wizard, the resulting command simply adds the selected users to one of the groups that you learned about in the section "The Built-in Exchange Administrative Groups." The only role for which this does not hold true is for the Exchange Server Administrator role. When users or groups are assigned to this role, the user or group is assigned Full Control permission on the specified server object and all child objects.

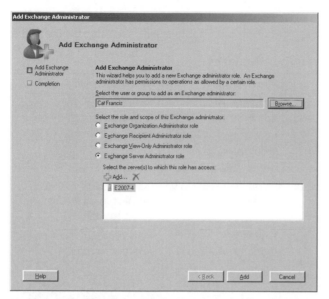

Figure 19-8   Selecting the Exchange Server Administrator role

Management Shell

You can also manage administrative roles through the Exchange Management Shell.

The following command adds a user account that can manage the Exchange Server 2007 server named E2007-4:

```
Add-ExchangeAdministrator -Identity 'contoso.com/Users/David So'
  -Role 'ServerAdmin' -Scope 'E2007-4'
```

If you add someone using Exchange Server Administrator role, you need to manually add the selected user or group to the built-in local administrators group on the target server.

This command adds a user to the Exchange Recipient Administrators role:

```
Add-ExchangeAdministrator -Identity 'contoso.com/Users/David So'
  -Role 'RecipientAdmin'
```

This command adds a user to the Exchange View-Only Administrators role:

```
Add-ExchangeAdministrator -Identity 'contoso.com/Users/David So'
  -Role 'ViewOnlyAdmin'
```

This command adds a user to the Exchange OrganizationAdministrators role:

```
Add-ExchangeAdministrator -Identity 'contoso.com/Users/David So'
  -Role 'OrgAdmin'
```

Table 19-1 comes from Microsoft's documentation on the role of roles in Exchange Server 2007 and provides a concise look at exactly what each administrative role accomplishes.

Table 19-1 Exchange Server Administrative Roles

Role	Members	Member of	Exchange permissions
Exchange Organization Administrators	Administrator, or the account that was used to install the first Exchange 2007 server	Exchange Recipient Administrator, Administrators local group of *<Server Name>*	Full control of the Microsoft Exchange container in Active Directory
Exchange Recipient Administrators	Exchange Organization Administrators	Exchange View-Only Administrators	Full control of Exchange properties on Active Directory user object
Exchange Server Administrators	Exchange Organization Administrators	Exchange View-Only Administrators, Administrators local group of *<Server Name>*	Full control of Exchange *<Server Name>*
Exchange View-Only Administrators	Exchange Recipient Administrators, Exchange Server Administrators (*<Server Name>*)	Exchange Recipient Administrators, Exchange Server Administrators	Read access to the Microsoft Exchange container in Active Directory. Read access to all the Windows domains that have Exchange recipients.

SMTP Security

By default, an SMTP server attempts to make a TCP port 25 connection to your Exchange server via an anonymous connection. Anonymous does not mean that a user account set up in your Active Directory proxies the connection request, as is the case with the IIS Anonymous user account, IUSR_<machinename>. In the SMTP world, anonymous means that no user name or password is required for the remote SMTP service to make a port 25 connection. Hence, any SMTP server on the Internet can make, by default, a port 25 connection to your Exchange server.

To make SMTP more secure, you could require either Basic or Integrated Windows Authentication (IWA) before the SMTP Virtual Server (VS) could accept an inbound connection. But this configuration isn't practical on the Internet because you can't predict who will be connecting to your Exchange server in the future and thus can't assume that the user has an appropriate user name and password to make a connection. Moreover, not many messaging administrators are interested in implementing such a security measure at their end. So even though an anonymous connection to port 25 on your Exchange server represents a vulnerability, it is one that must be managed using a different approach than removing anonymous connections.

How do you protect against these kinds of attacks? With Exchange Server 2007, you can use an Edge Transport server that offloads the security burden from your primary Exchange servers. You learn about implementing the Edge Transport server in Chapter 20, "Antivirus and Anti-Spam." This chapter also discusses how the Edge Transport server can help improve the overall security of your Exchange infrastructure. However, more traditional ways of protecting Exchange also apply even when Edge Transport servers are used.

Perhaps the most common way to protect an Exchange infrastructure is through the use two firewalls. A dual firewall topology allows you to protect your internal Exchange servers while also filtering incoming e-mail against potential attacks. The area between the two firewalls is called the *perimeter network* (also known as DMZ or demilitarized zone). The philosophy is to put up a line of defense against potential attacks. Hence, you're willing to sacrifice your Exchange servers in the perimeter network, but not willing to sacrifice your Exchange servers on the internal network. Because the Exchange servers in the perimeter network do not host any important information—no mailboxes or public folders—they can be both sacrificed during an attack and easily rebuilt. And because they act only as relay servers, they can be used to sanitize incoming e-mail over port 25.

Take a look at Figure 19-9. Note that there are three network levels. Starting from the top, each network becomes more trusted, with the External, or Internet, zone being completely untrusted. The perimeter network is more trusted as it resides behind at least one organizational firewall and generally houses servers that can be considered "expendable." In this diagram, the external firewall has port 25 open in order to facilitate incoming SMTP traffic. Mail is routed to the Exchange Server 2007 Edge Transport server where it is processed for viruses, checked using various spam filters, and run through various incoming transport rules. Your external MX records must point to this Edge Transport server. There is another important note in this diagram. Note that the external firewall also provides the ability to scan incoming content for viruses and spyware. When possible, always run your e-mail through a similarly configured firewall even before that mail hits the Edge Transport server's content-scanning engines. Many of today's security appliances, such as the Cisco ASA and Sonicwall's family of firewalls, provide this additional protection.

From a software perspective, also consider running Microsoft Forefront Security for Exchange Server. Forefront has the ability to scan every incoming message with up to five completely separate virus scanners. By instituting this multilayer security infrastructure, all incoming mail is scanned by many different virus scanning engines, some hardware-based and some software-based, which results in a much higher likelihood you will be protected against even the newest viruses.

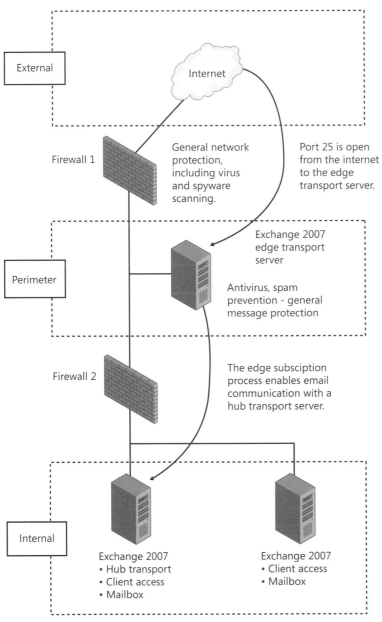

Figure 19-9   One way to secure your Exchange infrastructure

However, even the best virus-scanning infrastructure on the planet does not always protect you. Think back to some of the major viruses in the last few years, which were able to spread worldwide very quickly, usually in a matter of hours. It is almost impossible for any antivirus company to get the virus, study it, write a definition for it, and then push out the new definition for that virus before it spreads worldwide. You can tell an Edge Transport server, however, to quarantine or delete any message that contains certain types of attachments and, in effect, block most viruses based on their type of content rather than on a comparison to a virus definition file.essent.

Note   Be aware of two issues regarding traditional antivirus servers. First, many products offered by the major antivirus vendors perform content scanning at the same time as the virus scanning. While there may be no problem with this method of scanning e-mail, be aware of a distinction between content scanning and antivirus scanning, which highlights the need to perform both types of scanning in the perimeter network, a capability enabled through the use of Exchange Server 2007's Edge Transport server. Second, everyone may not be able afford to purchase everything required in order to achieve the configuration outlined in this chapter—namely, a separate Exchange server running Edge Transport as well as firewalls/security appliances that perform virus scanning functions. These ideas are presented to highlight the concepts being discussed. Other, less expensive (and potentially less secure) options include:

- Using a single firewall with multiple interfaces and creating a perimeter network using firewall rules

- Using a single firewall and running the Edge Transport server on the internal interface alongside your other Exchange servers

- Skipping the installation of the Edge Transport server and delivering mail directly to an internal Hub Transport server

---

Once scanned and approved, the e-mail is sent to an internal Hub Transport server. The internal Exchange Server 2007 Hub Transport server should be configured to accept inbound e-mail only from the perimeter network's Edge Transport server. Inbound mail that has been approved by the Edge Transport server also rides on the standard SMTP TCP port 25, so you need to open this port on your internal firewall as well. To do this in the most secure way possible, create a firewall rule that only allows port 25 traffic specifically between the Edge Transport server and one of your internal Hub Transport servers. Then, secure the communication tunnel using IPsec, which is discussed further in Chapter 21. The internal Exchange server should also be running its own antivirus software, preferably from a vendor that is different from the one the servers are using in the perimeter network. The whole point of implementing this model is to ensure that port 25 traffic is as well protected as possible.

In order to use an Edge Transport server, subscribe the Edge Transport server to the Active Directory domain. The subscription process establishes one-way replication of recipient and configuration information from your Active Directory into an Active Directory Application Mode (ADAM) instance running on your Edge Transport server. Further, the Edge Subscription process creates the SMTP Send connectors required to enable mail flow from your Exchange servers to the Internet through an Edge Transport server. If you are using the recipient lookup or safe list aggregation features of the Edge Transport server, subscribe the Edge Transport server to the organization.

More Info   The complete process for installing, configuring, and subscribing the Edge Transport services is covered in Chapter 20, "Antivirus and Anti-Spam."

No system is foolproof, but this dual firewall topology has multiple advantages:

- By passing incoming e-mail through the Edge Transport servers content filtering services, you filter for code types that virus scanners don't.

- By passing your e-mail through a virus scanner, you do your best to ensure that all known viruses are cleaned out. Not passing your e-mail through an updated antivirus scanner after running it through a content scanner is unwise because older viruses might not be caught by the content scanner.

- By passing all of your outgoing e-mail through the Exchange Server 2007 Edge Transport server, the IP address (private or public) of the internal Exchange Server 2007 server does not need to be published in the public DNS records. This means that an attacker attempting to Telnet into your server is never able to reach it directly. Also, if you configure the internal Exchange Server 2007 server to accept e-mail only from DMZ-based Exchange servers, any attempts to make port 25 connections to the internal Exchange server from any other IP address will fail.

If a hacker decides to bring down your perimeter Exchange servers, you've really lost nothing of value other than your time in getting the servers functioning again. Your company might lose some money due to the inability to communicate via e-mail, but it hasn't lost any current data. This is an important point. The server that hosts your data is the one most protected. And the ones most exposed do not host important data. If those servers are lost, at least all the business-critical data is saved on the internal Exchange Server 2007 server. For many companies, this is an acceptable level of risk to assume. This is the beginning stage of a defense that provides multiple layer of protection, starting with expendable services with the really important data protected in a variety of different ways.

As explained throughout this chapter, no answer is perfect, and this security scenario does have a few major holes, such as doing nothing to protect against messages sent to the Exchange server via Outlook Web Access. Port 25 is well protected, but port 80 access to your Exchange server is wide open. If you want to learn more about OWA, refer to Chapter 24, "Supporting Outlook Web Access."

The second major hole in this model is one that cannot be plugged: messages are continuing to flow to your internal Exchange server. As long as a packet can reach your internal Exchange server, there is always the potential for harm. So remember the 80-percent rule: you can make your data only about 80-percent secure. But don't let that discourage you from implementing appropriate security strategies.

Computer Viruses

This section expands on computer viruses in general and discusses some implications for viruses on Exchange Server 2007.

What Is a Virus?

A *virus* is a piece of code that attaches itself to other programs or files. When these files run, the code is invoked and begins replicating itself. The replication occurs over the network. Viruses can now exploit the vulnerabilities of nearly every platform.

Some viruses reside in memory after the original program is shut down. When other programs are executed, the virus attaches itself to these new programs until the computer is shut down or turned off. Some viruses have a "dormant" phase and appear only at certain times or when certain actions are performed.

There are many types of viruses. Some overwrite existing code or data. Others include the ability to recognize whether an executable file is already infected. *Self-recognition* is required if the virus is to avoid multiple infections of a single executable, which can cause excessive growth in size of infected executables and corresponding excessive storage space, contributing to the detection of the virus.

Resident viruses install themselves as part of the operating system upon execution of an infected host program. The virus remains resident until the system is shut down. Once installed in memory, a resident virus is available to infect all suitable hosts that are accessed.

A *stealth virus* is a resident virus that attempts to evade detection by concealing its presence in infected files. For example, a stealth virus might remove the virus code from an executable when it is read (rather than executed) so that an antivirus software package sees only the noncompromised form of the executable.

Computer viruses can spread by the use of e-mail and usually appear in e-mail attachments. If the virus can find its way into the messaging stream, it uses the client capability to send and receive e-mail to replicate itself quickly and do its damage as fast as possible.

An essential aspect of protecting your messaging system against viruses is user education. Users should learn to be guarded about which attachments they are allowed to open.

Your information security policies should also outline the types of e-mails and attachments that users are allowed to open. For example, users should be forbidden to open attachments in two instances: when they were not expecting the attachments, and when the attachments arrive from unrecognizable aliases.

Finally, whenever possible, consider a centralized antivirus service that updates the distributed clients from a centrally managed server. Most such solutions provide you with ways to more granularly manage each client and proactively fix problems that may take place.

Trojans

A *Trojan* (also known as a Trojan horse) is a malicious program embedded inside a normal, safe-looking program. The difference between a virus and a Trojan is that the Trojan is embedded and the virus is attached to the file or executable.

When the normal program runs, the malicious code runs as well and can cause damage or steal critical information. An example of a Trojan is a word-processing program that, when executed, allows the user to compose a document while, in the background, malicious code is running that deletes files or destroys other programs.

Trojans generally are spread through e-mail or *worms*, which are programs that run by themselves. The damage that Trojans can cause is similar to that of a virus: from nominal to critical. Trojans are particularly frightening because in most cases, users are unaware of the damage the Trojan is causing. The malicious work is being masked by the Trojan effect of the program.

Worms

As just mentioned, worms are programs that run by themselves. They do not embed or attach themselves to other programs nor do they need to do this to replicate. They can travel from computer to computer across network connections and are self-replicating. Worms might have portions of themselves running on many different computers, or the entire program might run on a single computer. Typically, worms do not change other programs, although they might carry other code that does.

The first network worms were intended to perform useful network management functions by taking advantage of operating system properties. Malicious worms exploit system vulnerabilities for their own purposes. Release of a worm usually results in brief outbreaks, shutting down entire networks.

The damage that worms can cause, like Trojans and viruses, ranges from the nominal to the critical. The type and extent of damage must be assessed individually for each worm. However, worms can install viruses and Trojans that then run their own code.

An attack that combines a worm, Trojan, and/or virus can be a very difficult attack to survive without significant damage. The impact of viruses, Trojans, and worms on your messaging system and network should not be underestimated. Because they use e-mail to exploit system vulnerabilities, installing antivirus software is simply not enough. You must also ensure that known vulnerabilities in all your operating systems are patched. Don't focus only on your servers. Every device should be updated with the most recent patches from each vendor as soon as possible. Most environments will want to test these patches before installing them. But after they have been tested, install them.

Junk E-Mail

Junk e-mail is a huge issue. One client with whom this author recently worked installed its first e-mail filtering software and found that it had 46 percent fewer inbound e-mails.

Exchange Server 2007's new Edge Transport role has new capabilities that can help to significantly reduce the amount of junk e-mail that enters your environment. The Edge Transport Role server has the following agents that help to protect your e-mail infrastructure. The information in Table 19-2 is right from Microsoft's Edge Transport server documentation.

Table 19-2   Edge Transport Agents

Agent name	Description
Connection Filtering Agent	Performs host IP address filtering based on IP Allow Lists, IP Allow List providers, IP Block Lists, and IP Block List providers.
Address Rewriting Inbound Agent	Modifies recipient SMTP addresses in inbound messages based on predefined address alias information. Address rewriting can be useful in scenarios which an organization wants to hide internal domains.
Edge Rule Agent	Processes all messages received over SMTP to enforce transport rules defined on the Edge Transport server.
Sender ID Agent	Determines whether the sending SMTP host is authorized to send messages for the SMTP domain of the message originator.
Recipient Filter Agent	Verifies that the recipients specified during the SMTP session through the RCPT TO: command are valid and not on the list of blocked SMTP addresses and domains.
Sender Filter Agent	Verifies that the sender specified in the MAIL FROM: command and in the message header is valid and not on the list of blocked SMTP addresses and domains.
Content Filter Agent	Uses Microsoft SmartScreen technology to assess the contents of inbound messages in order to assign an SCL rating for junk e-mail processing based on transport and store thresholds.
Protocol Analysis Agent	Interacts with Connection Filtering, Sender Filtering, Recipient Filtering, and Sender ID agents to determine Sender Reputation Level (SRL) rating and to take action based on rating thresholds.

Table 19-2   Edge Transport Agents   (Continued)

Agent name	Description
Attachment Filtering Agent	Filters messages based on attachment file name, file name extension, or MIME content type to block potentially harmful messages or remove critical attachments.
Address Rewriting Outbound Agent	Modifies sender SMTP addresses in outbound messages based on predefined address alias information. Address rewriting can be useful in scenarios where an organization wants to hide internal domains.
Forefront Security for Exchange Routing Agent	Responsible for connecting into the Transport stack to ensure that the scanning process scans messages prior to delivery to Hub Transport servers.

Many of these features are discussed in the next Chapter 20, "Antivirus and Anti-Spam," and Chapter 21, "Messaging Security."

Security Tools Provided by Microsoft

In order to help you deploy and maintain the most secure Exchange infrastructure possible, Microsoft provides a number of tools designed to remove malware, make sure that your environment is properly configured, and to help you configured a multitude of security settings.

- **Malicious Software Removal Tool**   The Microsoft Windows Malicious Software Removal Tool checks computers running Windows XP, Windows 2000, and Windows Server 2003 for infections by specific, prevalent malicious software—including Blaster, Sasser, and Mydoom—and helps remove any infection found. When the detection and removal process is complete, the tool displays a report describing the outcome, including which, if any, malicious software was detected and removed. Microsoft releases an updated version of this tool on the second Tuesday of each month, and as needed to respond to security incidents. On a regular basis, run the Malicious Software Removal Tool on your Exchange server to make sure your system is free of threats.

> **More Info**   To download the Microsoft Software Removal Tool, visit *http://www.microsoft.com/security/malwareremove/default.mspx.*

- **Microsoft Baseline Security Analyzer**   The Microsoft Baseline Security Analyzer (MBSA) is a tool that analyzes your existing environment and, in particular, analyzes how you have configured a number of Microsoft products, including Windows 2000 SP3; Windows XP and Windows Server 2003; Office XP, 2003 and 2007; Exchange 2000, 2003 and 2007; SQL Server 2000 SP4; and SQL Server 2005. With this information, Microsoft compares your configuration against a list of best practices and provides you with a report of action items that you can take to improve the security of your environment.

More Info   To download the Microsoft Baseline Security Analyzer, visit *http://www.microsoft.com/technet/security/tools/mbsa2/default.mspx.*

- **Security Configuration Wizard**   Windows Server 2003 Service Pack 1 includes the Security Configuration Wizard (SCW), a tool designed to reduce the attack surface of your Windows servers. SCW helps administrators to create security policies that are consistent with the practice of least privilege. In this case, that means running the fewest possible services on a server in order to reduce the number of services that can be used to attack the computer.

Summary

This chapter discussed how hackers think, how to secure incoming SMTP e-mail, and how to secure Administrator access to your Exchange server. Also discussed were the differences between a virus, a Trojan, and a worm, and a method was outlined for securing inbound SMTP traffic. Two other areas in this book were also referenced that discuss sender filtering and securing OWA. The next chapter discusses how to secure e-mail messages using encryption and certificates.

Chapter 20
Antivirus and Anti-Spam

Viruses and spam are the bane of every Exchange Server administrator's existence. Between the costs associated with protecting against these threats and users actually being subjected to the threats that become reality when they slip by your forces, the bottom lines for almost every organization suffer.

In this chapter, you learn how to protect your messaging environment from succumbing to these maladies. Specifically, you learn how to deploy one of the new roles for Microsoft Exchange Server 2007—the Edge Transport server role. You also learn how to battle spam and viruses using only a Hub Transport server.

The Edge Transport Server at a Glance

The Edge Transport server was described in Chapter 3, "Exchange Server 2007 Architecture." However, this section provides a short recap of some of that information to bring you up to speed on what this new role is all about. In short, the Edge Transport server provides the following services:

- Connection filtering
- Content filtering
- Sender filtering

- Recipient lookup
- Recipient filtering
- Sender ID lookup
- Header filtering
- Rules processing
- Attachment filtering
- Virus scanning

Many of these services are discussed in this chapter.

The Edge Transport server has some unique requirements and recommendations. First, the Edge Transport server is a stand-alone role. That is, you can't deploy the Edge Transport server on an Exchange Server 2007 server on which you've installed other roles or intend to install other roles. The reason: the Edge Transport server is intended to protect your Exchange environment by running either outside your firewall or in your perimeter network. By segregating this role on its own hardware outside your network, you run less risk of an infected message wreaking havoc in your organization.

Furthering its isolation, Microsoft recommends that you install the Edge Transport server onto a computer that is not a part of your Active Directory domain. You may be wondering just how this server can communicate with your other Exchange servers because the Edge Transport server isn't a part of your Active Directory infrastructure. As a server designed to handle mail coming into (and out of) the organization, it makes sense that this server needs pretty tight communication with the rest of your network.

It probably appears that your Edge Transport server sits alone and isolated from everything else on the network. While mostly true, the Edge Transport server needs some kind of lifeline to your Active Directory in order to achieve some of its goals. After all, you wouldn't want the Edge Transport server sitting in your perimeter network forwarding mail to users that don't exist in Active Directory. Therefore, the Edge Transport server uses an Active Directory tool, Active Directory Application Mode (ADAM), along with a component called EdgeSync. EdgeSync runs on a separate server that has the Hub Transport role installed and performs regular one-way synchronization of recipient and configuration information from Active Directory to the ADAM instance running on the Edge Transport server.

The Edge Transport server sees every message that comes into and goes out of your organization. This server is the one to which your domain's external DNS Mail Exchange (MX) record should point, and Exchange automatically routes outgoing mail through this service as well after you take the necessary steps to install the Edge Transport server.

Edge Transport Server Deployment

The short version is this: the Edge Transport server is fully deployed once you install ADAM and the Edge Transport server role on its own server, and also install at least one Hub Transport server from which you then subscribe the Edge Transport server. This subscription process automatically creates all of the SMTP connectors that are necessary in order for end-to-end mail flow to be operational in your environment.

To deploy an Edge Transport server into your organization, follow these steps:

1. Using the information from the other chapters in this book, get the other Exchange Server 2007 roles deployed on other servers in your organization.

2. On a server that is not a member of your Active Directory domain, install the Exchange Server 2007 prerequisites. These include the .NET Framework 2.0, Microsoft Management Console (MMC) 3.0, and PowerShell 1.0. If you need more information about installing prerequisites, refer to Chapter 6, "Installing Exchange Server 2007." Ideally, this server will reside in your company's perimeter network or outside the firewall. It's highly recommended that you deploy the Edge Transport server in a perimeter network so that it has at least some protection.

3. Make sure the new server has an appropriate DNS suffix.

4. Make sure any firewalls between the Exchange Server 2007 organization and the Edge Transport server are configured to pass appropriate traffic. Necessary configurations are discussed in the following section.

5. Install ADAM, which is available for download from *http://www.microsoft.com/downloads/details.aspx?familyid=9688f8b9-1034-4ef6-a3e5-2a2a57b5c8e4&displaylang=en.*

6. Install the Exchange Server 2007 Edge Transport server role.

7. Subscribe the Edge Transport server to the Exchange Server 2007 organization.

8. Change external DNS MX records to point to the Edge Transport server.

Because steps 1 and 2 are covered in other areas of this book or are self-explanatory, instructions in this chapter start with step 3.

Verify the Edge Transport Server's DNS Suffix

Unless you join a Windows Server 2003 computer to a domain or assign a DNS suffix via DHCP, the default primary DNS suffix of the server is normally blank. The Edge

Transport server services in Exchange Server 2007 cannot be installed on a server on which the primary DNS suffix has been left blank. Before you continue, make sure that your server's primary DNS suffix is configured by following these steps:

1. From the server's desktop, right-click My Computer.

2. From the shortcut menu, choose Properties to open the System Properties window.

3. Click the Computer Name tab.

4. Click Change to open the Computer Name Changes window.

5. Click More to open the DNS Suffix And NetBIOS Computer Name window.

6. Type the DNS suffix for your domain. The examples in this chapter use "contoso.com."

7. Click OK until you're asked whether you want to restart the computer.

8. Restart the computer for the computer name changes to take effect. Figure 20-1 shows what the DNS Suffix And NetBIOS Computer Name window looks like after the system is rebooted.

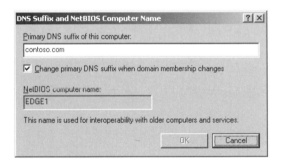

Figure 20-1   The DNS Suffix And NetBIOS Computer Name window

Configure Firewalls to Pass Edge Traffic

It's highly recommended that you place a firewall between your Edge Transport server and your Hub Transport server. Doing so limits the potential breadth and depth of the damage that can be caused by a successful attack on your Edge Transport server. Doing so, however, requires that you make sure that certain traffic can pass unfettered between the two servers.

Table 20-1, from Microsoft's Edge Transport server deployment documentation, outlines the communications ports on your firewall that must be open in order for necessary traffic to flow between your Edge Transport server and your Hub Transport server.

Before you continue, make sure that the Edge Transport and Hub Transport servers can use DNS to see one another. Use the **nslookup** command from both servers to make sure that DNS is working as expected.

Table 20-1 Edge Server Communication Settings

Network interface	Open port	Protocol	Note
Inbound from and outbound to the Internet	25/TCP	SMTP	This port must be open for mail flow to and from the Internet.
Inbound from and outbound to the internal network	25/TCP	SMTP	This port must be open for mail flow to and from the Exchange organization.
Inbound from the internal network	50636/TCP	Secure LDAP	This port must be open for EdgeSync synchronization.
Inbound from the internal network	3389/TCP	RDP	Opening this port is optional. It provides more flexibility in managing the Edge Transport servers from inside the internal network by letting you use a remote desktop connection to manage the Edge Transport server.

Install Active Directory Application Mode

The Edge Transport server role uses ADAM to store configuration and recipient information. Make sure you install ADAM on the intended server before you install the Edge Transport server role. During the ADAM installation, accept all of the default settings. The Exchange Server 2007 installer configures ADAM during the installation of the Edge Transport server role. ADAM is available for download from *http://www.microsoft.com/downloads /details.aspx?familyid=9688f8b9-1034-4ef6-a3e5-2a2a57b5c8e4&displaylang=en.*

More than likely, you'll find that the ADAM installation is very fast and straightforward.

Install the Exchange Server 2007 Edge Transport Server Role

Before you install the Exchange Server 2007 Edge Transport server role, make sure that you have installed the Exchange Server 2007 prerequisites, including the .NET Framework 2.0, Microsoft Management Console (MMC) 3.0, and PowerShell 1.0. If you need more information about installing prerequisites, refer to Chapter 6.

The Edge Transport server role installation starts just like the installation of any other Exchange Server 2007 role. Run the setup program and choose options that pertain to your goal. In this case, after you get to the Installation Type page (see Figure 20-2), choose Custom Exchange Server Installation and click Next.

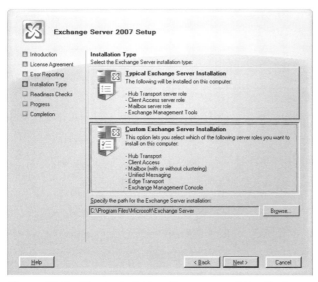

Figure 20-2   The Installation Type page of the Exchange Server 2007 Setup Wizard

Choosing the custom installation option affords you the chance to pick and choose which roles you want on the new server. On the Server Role Selection page, shown in Figure 20-3, select the Edge Transport Server Role option. When you select this option, all of the other options become unavailable because the Edge Transport server role cannot be combined with any other role. Click Next to proceed with the installation.

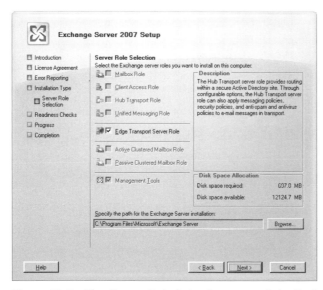

Figure 20-3   The Server Role Selection page of the Exchange Server 2007 Setup Wizard

Unless you failed to install a prerequisite or forgot to add a primary DNS suffix on the server, the installation of the Edge Transport server role should proceed without incident, after which your server is ready for the next part of the deployment process.

Subscribe the Edge Transport Server to the Exchange Server 2007 Organization

Before you continue, review exactly where you are at this point. You now have an Exchange Server 2007 organization that is sitting on its own island. On a separate island lies the Edge Transport server that you just installed. Until you take active steps, there is no communication between these two islands of information. There are two ways that you can enable communication between your Exchange Server 2007 organization and the Edge Transport server:

- Manually create SMTP send and receive connectors on a Hub Transport server in your organization and on the new Edge Transport server. Remember, the only servers in your organization that can pass mail are Hub and Edge Transport servers. The primary drawback to this method is that you are unable to take advantage of powerful edge services, such as recipient lookup features or safe-list aggregation. Recipient lookup is a feature that verifies that a user exists in your Active Directory organization before a message is sent to that user. Safe-list aggregation collects data from each user's Safe Recipients Lists, Safe Senders Lists, and Outlook contacts, and makes this information available to the Edge Transport server. This helps to reduce the likelihood of false positives because incoming mail destined for these safe addresses is not subjected to spam tests. Because both of these services rely on the Edge Transport server's ability to have an understanding of your Active Directory organization, you must establish some way for the Edge Transport server to be able to query Active Directory. This method is discussed in the Real World sidebar later in this chapter.

- The subscription process, which is the preferred process and the one discussed at length in this chapter, is actually a multistep process that provides one-way recipient synchronization from the Active Directory domain to the Edge Transport server. Using this synchronized information allows the Edge Transport server's power and efficient recipient lookup feature and safe-list aggregation features. By using the subscription method, you can also perform configuration tasks on the Hub Transport server and push them out to the Edge Transport server, thus reducing the amount of administrative overhead required to manage your infrastructure. There are a number of steps that you need to take in order for the subscription method to be successful:

  1. Export an Edge Subscription file on the Edge Transport server.

  2. Copy this Edge Subscription file to the Hub Transport server.

3. Import the Edge Subscription file on the Hub Transport server.

4. Verify that synchronization is completed successfully.

During the subscription process, the following actions take place, thus providing end-to-end mail flow for your Exchange organization:

- An implicit Send connector is created from the Hub Transport servers that are in the same forest to the new Edge Transport server.

- A Send connector is created from the Edge Transport server to the Hub Transport servers in the Active Directory site to which the Edge Transport server is subscribed.

- A Send connector from the Edge Transport server to the Internet is created.

Export an Edge Subscription File on the Edge Transport Server

In the subscription process, recipient and configuration information is replicated to the Edge Transport server from Active Directory to the Edge Transport server's ADAM instance. EdgeSync—the service that handles this synchronization—copies the information that is required for the Edge Transport server to perform anti-spam and message security tasks and information about the connector configuration that is required to enable end-to-end mail flow.

The first step in the subscription process is performed on the Edge Transport server and involves exporting an .xml file from your Edge Transport server for use on the Hub Transport server. Called the Edge Subscription file, this file contains the authentication and authorization credentials used for LDAP communication between the ADAM instance on the Edge Transport server and the Active Directory directory service. Note that the export process can be accomplished only from the Exchange Management Shell. The GUI-based Exchange Management Console does not support this feature. Follow these steps to complete the export process:

1. Log on to the Edge Transport server using an account that is a member of the local administrators group.

2. Start the Exchange Management Shell.

3. Issue the following command:

```
new-edgesubscription -filename "c:\newedgesubscription.xml"
```

You must include the path information. Figure 20-4 shows the results of this command. Note the warnings that indicate that all manually created accepted domains, message classifications, remote domains, and Send connectors will be deleted. After the subscription process finishes, all of these items are managed from Hub Transport servers, which then synchronize the information out to the Edge Transport server.

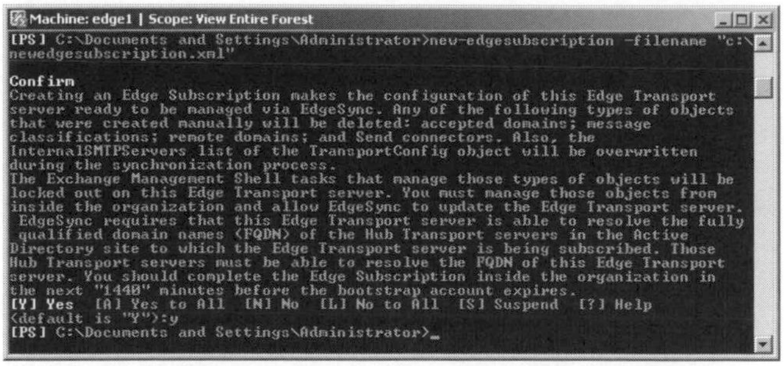

Figure 20-4   The `new-edgesubscription` command

Copy the Edge Subscription File to a Hub Transport Server

This step is pretty self-explanatory. Copy the file you created in the previous step to your Hub Transport server. After the copy is finished, Microsoft recommends that you delete the .xml file from the Edge Transport server. In this example, the file has been copied to the root of the C drive on the Hub Transport server.

Import the Edge Subscription File on a Hub Transport Server

With the Edge Subscription file copied to a Hub Transport server, you must indicate to the Hub Transport server that the new subscription should be initiated. This is accomplished by importing the .xml file you copied from the Edge Transport server into the Exchange organization. During the import process, necessary SMTP Send and Receive connectors are silently created on the Hub Transport server, enabling end-to-end mail flow from your clients to the Internet and vice versa.

Follow these steps to import the Edge Subscription file:

1. Log on to the Hub Transport server with an account that has Exchange Organization Administrator rights.

2. Start the Exchange Management Console.

3. Expand Organization Configuration.

4. Select the Hub Transport option.

5. From the Actions pane, click the Edge Subscriptions tab. Figure 20-5 shows this screen.

6. In the Actions pane, choose New Edge Subscription. This action starts the New Edge Subscription Wizard (see Figure 20-6).

7. On the first page of the wizard, choose the Active Directory site for which this edge subscription will apply.

8. Also on the first page, click Browse to locate the .xml file you copied to the Hub Transport server earlier.

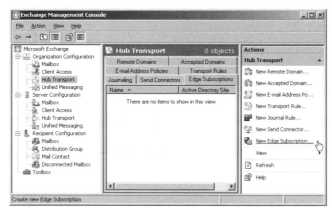

Figure 20-5   Creating a new edge subscription using the Exchange Management Console

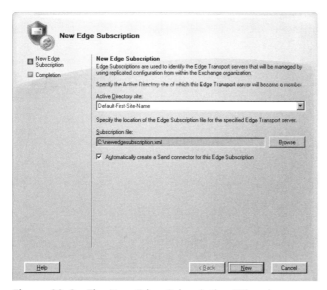

Figure 20-6   The New Edge Subscription Wizard

Note   You should also select the Automatically Create A Send Connector For This Edge Subscription check box. Doing so instructs the process to create a Send connector on your Edge Transport server. This Send connector is configured to send mail to the Internet and is necessary for end-to-end mail flow.

9. Click New.

10. After the process is complete, click Finish.

Management Shell

You must take proactive steps to complete the Edge subscription process, which creates and enables SMTP Send and Receive connectors on both the Hub Transport and Edge Transport servers. Further, this subscription process makes it possible to completely manage the environment from the Hub Transport server. Configuration changes made on the Hub Transport server are automatically synchronized to the Edge Transport server. From the Exchange Management Shell, use the **new-edge-subscription** command to complete the subscription process.

```
new-edgesubscription -filename "c:\newedgesubscription.xml"
  -site "Default-First-Site-Name"  -createinternetsendconnector $true
  -createinboundsendconnector $true
```

Verify Synchronization Success

When you finish with the subscription process on the Edge Transport server, open the Exchange Management Console and, under Organization Configuration, choose Hub Transport. In the Work pane, choose Edge Subscriptions. You should see a result similar to the one shown in Figure 20-7, which shows the Edge Subscription.

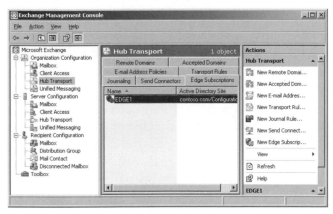

Figure 20-7   The New Edge Subscription process is successful.

You can also verify on the Edge Transport server that the process is successful. From the Exchange Management Console on the Edge Transport server, select Edge Transport and, from the Work pane, click the Send Connectors tab. Figure 20-8 shows you the SMTP Send connectors that were automatically created as a part of the subscription process.

Figure 20-8   SMTP Send connectors created by the subscription process.

Force Synchronization

In some cases, you may want to force the EdgeSync synchronization process to take place immediately. For example, if you create a number of new users en masse, or if you want the initial synchronization process to start immediately. To force synchronization to take place, from the Exchange Management Shell on the Edge Transport server, issue the command `start-edgesynchronization`. This command does not require any parameters.

Managing Anti-Spam Features

The Edge Transport server is the foundation on which the messaging protection features of Exchange Server 2007 rest. Most e-mail administrators look forward to the day when spam no longer exists, but until that utopia arrives, Exchange Server 2007 provides a number of ways that an administrator can combat spam. It should be noted that although the examples in this chapter use the Edge Transport server, most of these examples also work on a Hub Transport server and accomplish the same goals. Microsoft recommends, but does not require, that you use an Edge Transport server in order to maintain the highest level of security in the organization.

Content Filtering

Microsoft introduced the first version of the Content Filter in Exchange Server 2003 under the name Exchange Intelligent Message Filter. Now renamed Content Filter, the service evaluates inbound messages and determines the likelihood of whether a message is spam. Content filtering uses a statistically significant sample of messages to make its determination, thus decreasing the chance for mistakes. Based on the results of the Content Filter's analysis, a spam confidence level—a number between 0 and 9—is assigned to each message. The higher the spam confidence level, the more likely it is that a message is spam.

There are four actions that the Content Filter can take, based on the spam confidence level assigned to a message:

- Allow the message.

- Delete the message. No notification is sent back to the sender.

- Reject the message. The sender is notified that the message was rejected.

- Quarantine the message.

You might decide that messages with a particularly high spam confidence level should be immediately deleted while messages with a lower level are quarantined until further review.

To change the action taken, follow these steps:

1. From the Edge Transport server, open the Exchange Management Console.

2. Choose the Edge Transport option.

3. From the Work pane, choose the Anti-spam tab.

4. From the Work pane's lower window, right-click Content Filtering and, from the shortcut menu, choose Properties.

5. In the Content Filtering Properties dialog box, click the Action tab, as shown in Figure 20-9.

6. On this page, make selections that make sense based on your organization's policies. Select the spam confidence level at which messages should be deleted, rejected, or quarantined. If you choose to quarantine messages, provide a mailbox address to which quarantined messages can be sent.

7. Click OK.

There are two other ways that you can manage how content filtering works in your organization. There might be some users for whom content filtering is not a desirable way to combat spam. In these instances, exclude the user from content filtering by clicking the Exceptions tab. On the Exceptions tab, shown in Figure 20-10, provide the e-mail address that should be excluded from the service and then click Add.

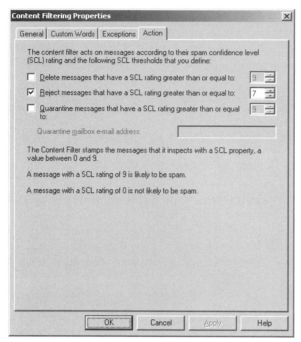

Figure 20-9 The Action tab of the Content Filtering Properties dialog box

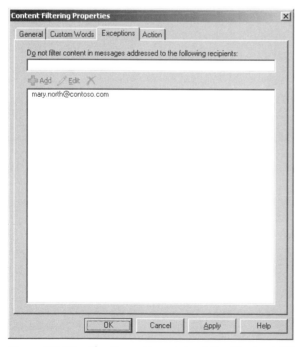

Figure 20-10 The Exceptions tab of the Content Filtering Properties dialog box

The Custom Words tab gives you a way to filter messages based on specific words or phrases in the message. For example, suppose that there is a huge new virus outbreak and one of the attack vectors is via an e-mail message with the phrase "I love you" embedded in the message. Click the Custom Words tab, shown in Figure 20-11, on the Content Filtering Properties dialog box to automatically filter messages with this phrase. Conversely, you can also indicate that messages with a particular phrase should not be filtered.

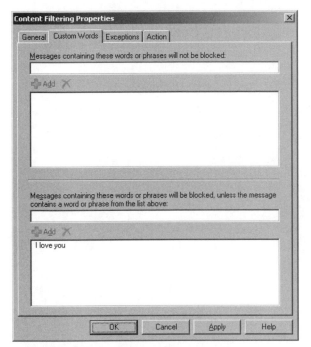

Figure 20-11   The Custom Words tab of the Content Filtering Properties dialog box

Finally, you can altogether disable content filtering by right-clicking Content Filtering in the Work pane of the Exchange Management Console and choosing Disable from the shortcut menu.

Management Shell

Content Filtering also can be managed from the Exchange Management Shell. Run the Exchange Management Shell from the Edge Transport server.

To enable Content Filtering:

```
Set-ContentFilterConfig -Enabled $true
```

To disable Content Filtering:

```
Set-ContentFilterConfig -Enabled $false
```

To reject messages with an SCL rating of 7 or more:

```
Set-ContentFilterConfig -SCLRejectEnabled $true -SCLRejectThreshold 7
```

To delete messages that have an SCL rating of 8 or higher:

```
Set-ContentFilterConfig -SCLDeleteEnabled $true -SCLDeleteThreshold 8
```

You can also send spam to a quarantine mailbox for later processing. Before you do so, you need to tell the Content Filter which mailbox should be used for this purpose. To do so, use the following command, replacing *spammail@contoso.com* with a mailbox in your organization:

```
Set-ContentFilterConfig -QuarantineMailbox spammail@contoso.com
```

To send messages that have an SCL rating of 6 or more to a spam quarantine mailbox:

```
Set-ContentFilterConfig -SCLQuarantineEnabled $true
  -SCLQuarantineThreshold 6
```

If you have recipients in your organization that you want to exclude from content filtering, use the same command, but with different parameters. This example excludes the users named Neil Black and Arno Bost from the service:

```
Set-ContentFilterConfig -BypassedRecipients neil.black@contoso.com,
  arno.bost@contoso.com
```

Likewise, there are a number of ways that you can exclude specific senders from being subjected to content filtering. Use the **BypassedSenders** parameter to provide a list of individual SMTP addresses that should be excluded. Use the **ByPassedSenderDomains** parameter to exclude an entire domain from filtering:

```
Set-ContentFilterConfig -BypassedSenders sender@example.com,
  sender2@example.com
```

```
Set-ContentFilterConfig -ByPassedSenderDomains example.com
```

To exclude a domain plus all of its subdomains, use a wildcard, as shown here:

```
Set-ContentFilterConfig -ByPassedSenderDomains *.example.com
```

Connection Filtering: IP Allow List

One feature of connection filtering allows you to use the IP Allow List feature to specify IP addresses that are always allowed to send mail to your organization. To add addresses to the IP Allow List, follow these steps:

1. From the Edge Transport server, open the Exchange Management Console.

2. Select the Edge Transport option.

3. From the Work pane, click the Anti-Spam tab.

4. From the Work pane's lower window, right-click IP Allow List and, from the short-cut menu, choose Properties.

5. In the IP Allow List Properties dialog box, click the Allowed Addresses tab, as shown in Figure 20-12.

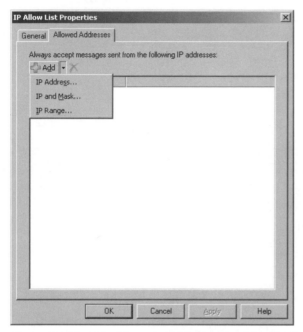

Figure 20-12   The Allowed Addresses tab of the IP Allow List Properties dialog box

6. Click the Add button to add an IP Address with a (Classless Inter-Domain Routing) CIDR identifier. Alternatively, click the down arrow next to the Add button to determine how to add IP addresses and ranges. Figure 20-12 shows you the choices you have with regard to IP address entry.

7. Click OK when you finish.

Management Shell

By using the Exchange Management Shell, you can add entries to the allowed IP address list. And, using the management shell, you can accomplish one task not possible from the GUI—assigning an expiration date for each entry after which the IP address will no longer be on the allow list. To do this, use the `Add-IPAllowListEntry` command in the Exchange Management Shell, as shown in the following code. The first example adds just a single IP address. The second adds an IP address range along with an expiration date. The third example adds an IP address range. Note that the first example uses the `IPAddress` parameter while the others use the `IPRange` parameter.

```
Add-IPAllowListEntry -IPAddress 192.168.0.1

Add-IPAllowListEntry -IPRange 192.168.0.1/24 -ExpirationTime
  "2/3/2009 00:00"

Add-IPAllowListEntry -IPRange 192.168.0.1-192.168.0.100
```

Connection Filtering: IP Allow List Providers

IP Allow List Providers gives you a way to specifically indicate a sender that should be considered a safe sender. In this case, the safe list includes the names of domains you trust to send only legitimate mail to your organization. Follow these steps to add a new organization to the IP Allow List Provider list:

1. From the Edge Transport server, open the Exchange Management Console.

2. Select the Edge Transport option.

3. From the Work pane, click the Anti-spam tab.

4. From the Work pane's lower window, right-click IP Allow List Provider and, from the shortcut menu, choose Properties.

5. In the Add IP Allow List Provider window, click the Providers tab, shown in Figure 20-13.

6. Click the Add button to add a new entry to the list.

There are a number of options on this screen. Here are the explanations for each of the options:

■ **Provider Name**   Type a name that identifies the provider. This is for your use.

■ **Lookup Domain**   Type the domain name that the Connection Filter agent will use for queries to the provider's information.

■ **Match Any Return Code**   When this option is selected, the agent treats any IP Address status code that is returned by the IP Allow List Provider service as a match.

■ **Match Specific Mask and Responses**   Granularly manage the match parameters by choosing from the options listed below in the window.

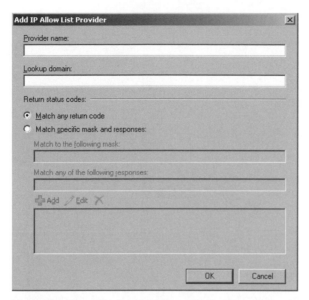

Figure 20-13   The Add IP Allow List Provider dialog box

■ **Match To the Following Mask**   When this option is selected, the agent acts only on messages that match particular return status codes:

1. 127.0.0.1. The IP address is on an IP Allow list.

2. 127.0.0.2. The SMTP server is configured to act as an open relay.

3. 127.0.0.4. The IP address supports a dial-up IP address.

■ **Match Any of the Following Responses**   When you select this option, the agent acts only on messages that match the same IP address status code that is returned by the IP Allow List Provider service.

> ## Management Shell
>
> You can also use the `Add-IpAllowListProvider` command in Exchange Management Shell to add an entry to IP Allow List Providers. For this command, you need to provide `Name` and `LookupDomain` parameters.
>
> ```
> Add-IPAllowListProvider -Name:Contoso -LookupDomain:contoso.com
> ```

Connection Filtering: IP Block List

Use the IP Block List feature to specify IP addresses that are never allowed to send mail to your organization. To add addresses to the IP Block List, follow these steps:

1. From the Edge Transport server, open the Exchange Management Console.

2. Select the Edge Transport option.

3. From the Work pane, click the Anti-Spam tab.

4. From the Work pane's lower window, right-click IP Block List and, from the short-cut menu, choose Properties.

5. In the IP Block List Properties dialog box, click the Blocked Addresses tab, as shown in Figure 20-14.

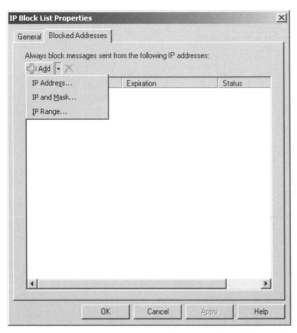

Figure 20-14   The Blocked Addresses tab of the IP Block List Properties dialog box

6. Click the Add button to add an IP Address with a (Classless Inter-Domain Routing) CIDR identifier. Alternatively, click the down arrow next to the Add button to determine how to add IP addresses and ranges. Figure 20-14 shows you the choices you have with regard to IP address entry.

7. Click OK when you finish.

Management Shell

By using the Exchange Management Shell, you can add entries to the blocked IP address list. And, using the management shell, you can accomplish one task not possible from the GUI—assigning an expiration date for each entry after which the IP address will no longer be on the block list. To do this, use the Exchange Management Shell's `Add-IPBlockListEntry command`, as shown here. The first example adds just a single IP address. The second adds an IP address range along with an expiration date. The third example adds an IP address range. Note that the first example uses the `IPAddress` parameter while the others use the `IPRange` parameter.

```
Add-IPBlockListEntry -IPAddress 192.168.0.1

Add-IPBlockListEntry -IPRange 192.168.0.1/24 -ExpirationTime "1/3/2009"

Add-IPBlockListEntry -IPRange 192.168.0.1-192.168.0.100
```

Connection Filtering: IP Block List Providers

IP Block List Providers, providers of real-time block lists (RBLs), give you a way to build on the work of others in determining whether or not mail coming from a particular sender should be regarded as spam. Organizations that provide these block list services use three main methods to help you determine whether or not to trust a message.

- **Known Past Spammers on an IP Block List**   The provider compiles a list of IP addresses that are known to have originated spam in the past.

- **Open Relay Check**   The provider looks for SMTP servers that are configured as open relays. Open relays can be easily exploited by spammers to send mail from unwitting organizations.

- **Dial-up Services Check**   Some Internet service providers and providers of SMTP services continue to provide dial-up access for their clients. Using these accounts, a client receives a dynamic IP address for the duration of the dial-up session, making it difficult to trace the client. Further, these providers allow clients to send mail via SMTP over these dial-up connections.

Important   Be careful when you select an RBL vendor or service. If you choose a vendor or service that is too aggressive in blocklisting addresses, you could negatively impact mail flow into your organization by having too much mail blocked.

Follow these steps to add a new organization to the IP Block List Provider list:

1. From the Edge Transport server, open the Exchange Management Console.

2. Select the Edge Transport container.

3. From the Work pane, click the Anti-Spam tab.

4. From the Work pane's lower window, right-click IP Block List Provider and, from the shortcut menu, choose Properties.

5. In the IP Block List Providers dialog box, on the Providers tab, click the Add button. This opens the Add IP Block List Provider dialog box shown in Figure 20-15.

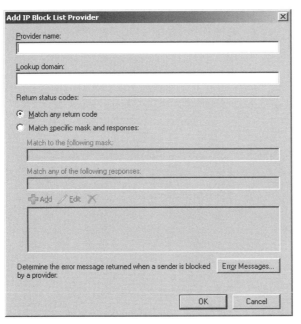

Figure 20-15   The Add IP Block List Provider window

There are a number of options on this screen. Here are the explanations for each of the options:

■ **Provider Name**   Type a name that identifies the provider. This is for your use.

■ **Lookup Domain**   Type the domain name that the Connection Filter agent will use for queries to the provider's information.

■ **Match Any Return Code**   When this option is selected, the agent treats any IP Address status code that is returned by the IP Block List Provider service as a match.

■ **Match Specific Mask And Responses**   Granularly manage the match parameters by selecting from the options listed below in the window. For example, you can determine that only entries on the block list that are configured to act as open relays should be blocked.

■ **Match To The Following Mask**   When this option is selected, the agent acts on only messages that match particular return status codes:

    1. 127.1.0.1. The IP address is on an IP Block list.

2. 127.1.0.2. The SMTP server is configured to act as an open relay.

3. 127.1.0.4. The IP address supports dial-up services.

■ **Match Any Of The Following Responses** When you select this option, the agent acts only on messages that match the same IP address status code that is returned by the IP Block List Provider service.

There may be situations in which you want mail sent to a particular address to get through regardless of the results returned by the block list. In these cases, click the Exceptions tab, shown in Figure 20-16, in the IP Block List Providers Properties dialog box.

Figure 20-16 The Exceptions tab of the IP Block List Providers Properties dialog box

Management Shell

To manage the list of IP Block List Providers in Exchange Management Shell, use the **Add-IPBlockListProvider** command. The following example adds an entry by the name of **Example** with a lookup domain of **Example.com**. In this example, the service is used to check whether the originating SMTP server is on a list of open relay servers, in which case the message will be affected.

```
Add-IPBlockListProvider –Name Example –LookupDomain Example.com
   –BitmaskMatch 127.1.0.2
```

Recipient Filtering

Do you have users that should not ever receive mail from the Internet? The Edge Transport server's Recipient Filtering feature lets you effectively block incoming mail from the Internet for up to 800 users in your organization. Add new users to this list using these steps:

1. From the Edge Transport server, open the Exchange Management Console.

2. Select the Edge Transport option.

3. From the Work pane, click the Anti-Spam tab.

4. From the Work pane's lower window, right-click Recipient Filtering and, from the shortcut menu, choose Properties.

5. In the Recipient Filtering Properties window, click the Blocked Recipients tab, as shown in Figure 20-17.

6. Select the check box next to Block The Following Recipients.

7. Click the Add button to add a new entry to the list.

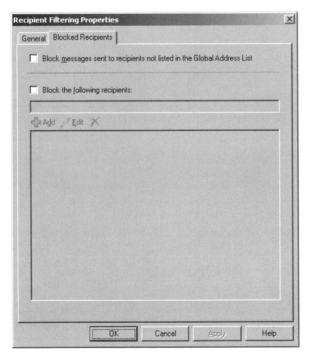

Figure 20-17   The Blocked Recipients tab on the Recipient Filtering Properties window

Unless you have a good reason to avoid this, it's also recommended that you select the check box next to Block Messages Sent To Recipients Not Listed In The Global Address List. Doing so reduces some of the workload on your internal Exchange servers because they do not need to process bad mail.

> **Management Shell**
>
> Use the `Set-RecipientFilterConfig` command in Exchange Management Shell to manage the Recipient Filtering service. Using the `BlockListEnabled` parameter in conjunction with the `BlockedRecipients` parameter, you can indicate which specific users should be included on this list.
>
> ```
> Set-RecipientFilterConfig -BlockListEnabled:$true
>   -BlockedRecipients jun.cao@contoso.com, jane.dow@contoso.com
> ```
>
> You can also use the Recipient Filter to reject messages addressed to users that do not exist in your organization. Use the `RecipientValidationEnabled` parameter, as shown here:
>
> ```
> Set-RecipientFilterConfig -RecipientValidationEnabled:$true
> ```

Sender Filtering

The Sender Filter services take action on messages from specific addresses outside your organization. The Sender Filter service lets you block addresses in a number of different ways:

- A single e-mail address at a time (neil.black@contoso.com)
- A whole domain (*@contoso.com)
- A whole domain plus all subdomains (*@contoso.com, *@sales.contoso.com, *@engineering.contoso.com, and so on.)

You can also configure what action is taken when a message arrives from a sender on the blocked list:

- Reject the message and return an SMTP "554 5.1.0 Sender Denied" error to the sender.
- Accept the message, but tag it to indicate that it came from a sender on the block list. The fact that the message originated from a blocked sender is taken into consideration when the Content Filter calculates the spam confidence level.

To add an entry to the sender filter list, follow these steps:

1. From the Edge Transport server, open the Exchange Management Console.

2. Select the Edge Transport option.

3. From the Work pane, click the Anti-Spam tab.

4. From the Work pane's lower window, right-click Sender Filtering and, from the shortcut menu, choose Properties.

5. In the Sender Filtering Properties window, click the Blocked Senders tab.

6. Click the Add button to add a new entry to the list. This window is shown in the context of the Blocked Senders tab in Figure 20-18.

7. To add a single e-mail address, select the Individual E-mail Address option and type the e-mail address. To provide a whole domain, select the Domain option, provide the name of the domain and, if desired, select Include All Subdomains to prevent mail from all incarnations of a company's domain.

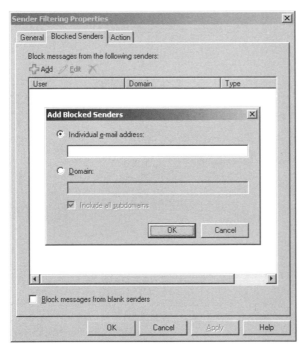

Figure 20-18   The Blocked Senders tab on the Sender Filtering Properties window

Management Shell

You can manage the Sender Filter services from the Exchange Management Shell using the `Set-SenderFilterConfig` command. The following parameters are pertinent with regard to this command:

- **BlankSenderBlockingEnabled**   If a message is sent into your organization without an entry in the From line, the message is rejected. The valid values for this command are `$true` and `$false`, with `$false` being the default.

- **BlockedSenders**   Provide a list of specific e-mail addresses from which e-mail should not be accepted. When a message arrives that has been sent from an address on this list, the Sender Filter agent takes the action that is specified in the `Action` parameter.

- **BlockedDomains**   Provide a list of domains from which mail should not be accepted. When a message arrives that has been sent from a domain on this list, the Sender Filter agent takes the action that is specified in the `Action` parameter. You can include up to 800 entries on this list.

- **BlockedDomainsAndSubdomains**   Provide a list of domains and subdomains from which mail should not be accepted. When a message arrives that has been sent from a domain or subdomain on this list, the Sender Filter agent takes the action that is specified in the `Action` parameter. You can include up to 800 entries on this list.

- **Action**   This parameter indicates what action the Edge Transport server takes when a message is sent from a blocked domain or sender. Valid actions are `StampStatus` or `Reject`, with the default being `Reject`.

The following example enables blank sender blocking, bars all incoming e-mail from example.com plus all of its subdomains, and blocks messages originating from jan.dryml@example.com and dan.jump@example.com.

```
Set-SenderFilterConfig -BlankSenderBlockingEnabled:$true
  -BlockedDomainsAndSubdomains example.com
  -BlockedSenders jan.dryml@example.com, dan.jump@example.com
  -Action reject
```

Sender ID

One method that spammers use to bypass even the best spam filters is spoofing. In a spoofed message, the From indicator on the message indicates that the message comes from a particular organization when, in reality, the message originates on a mail server used by the spammer. By spoofing the From information, and without further intervention, a message can land in a user's inbox, especially if the spoofed From address happens to be on an allow list.

Sender ID makes spoofing much more difficult and makes it more likely that spam will be classified as such. With Sender ID in place, when an e-mail message is received by the Edge Transport server, the Edge Transport server queries the originating DNS server to verify that the sending SMTP server is allowed to send mail for the domain specified in the message's header. This IP address for the originating server is called the purported responsible address (PRA).

In situations in which the From IP address property value on a message is not set, Exchange Server continues to process the message without the Sender ID information, and an event is logged in the Edge Transport server's event log.

There are three possible options for handling spoofed mail and unreachable DNS servers:

- **Reject the message**   The message is rejected by the Edge Transport server and a corresponding error report is sent back to the originating SMTP server.

- **Delete the message**   The message is deleted without an error report being returned to the sending server. Instead, the Edge Transport server returns an SMTP "OK" message back to the sending server to prevent the originating server from retrying the send operation.

- **Stamp the message with a status**   The default action, the Sender ID status is added to the message metadata and message processing continues.

More Info   Configuring Sender ID goes beyond just your Exchange server. You must create an overall environment that is conducive to the Sender ID framework, which includes modifications to your public-facing DNS server. For more information about implementing Sender ID in your organization, visit Microsoft's extensive information site located at *http://www.microsoft.com/mscorp/safety /technologies/senderid/default.mspx.*

To make Sender ID configuration changes on your Edge Transport server, follow these steps:

1. From the Edge Transport server, open the Exchange Management Console.

2. Select the Edge Transport option.

3. From the Work pane, click the Anti-spam tab.

4. From the Work pane's lower window, right-click Sender ID and, from the shortcut menu, choose Properties.

5. In the Sender ID Properties window, click the Action tab, as shown in Figure 20-19.

6. On the Action tab, select the action to take when a message fails Sender ID checks.
    The three possible actions were described earlier.

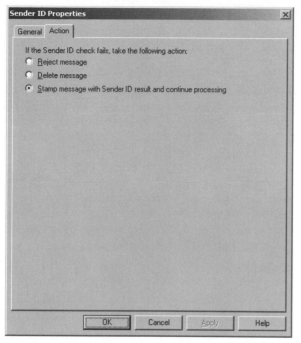

Figure 20-19   The Action tab on the Sender ID Properties window

Management Shell

To manage Sender ID actions on the Edge Transport server using Exchange Management Shell, use the `Set-SenderIDConfig` command. The following parameters are important to keep in mind when configuring Sender ID:

- **Enabled**   With a value of either `$true` or `$false`, indicates whether the Sender ID service should be enabled.

- **SpoofedDomainAction**   Values for this parameter include `StampStatus`, `Reject`, or `Delete` and indicate what action Sender ID will take when a message is deemed spoofed.

- **BypassedRecipients**   Allows you to exclude certain addresses from `SenderID` processing. You can include up to 100 addresses.

- **BypassedSenderDomains**   Allows you to exclude certain sending domains from `SenderID` processing. You can include up to 100 domains in this list.

To enable Sender ID, use the following command:

```
Set-SenderIDConfig -Enabled $true
```

To disable Sender ID, use the following command:

```
Set-SenderIDConfig -Enabled $false
```

The following example configures `SenderID` to delete messages when they have been deemed spoofed, indicates that messages to two users should not subjected to Sender ID filtering, and excludes the example.com domain from Sender ID filtering.

```
Set-SenderIdConfig -SpoofedDomainAction Delete
  -BypassedRecipients yale.li@contoso.com, peter.waxman@contoso.com
  -BypassedSenderDomains example.com
```

Attachment Filtering

With the Edge Transport server role in Exchange Server 2007, you can use attachment filtering to decide which kinds of attachments your users receive from outside the Exchange organization. With some file types being more susceptible than others to viruses or harmful scripts, dangerous attachments may cause significant damage to your organization. A virus or harmful script can damage a user's work by deleting important documents or can expose private information to the public, which can cost your company money both directly and, possibly, through litigation. To protect your company, filter dangerous attachment types at the Edge Transport server. By default, this service is installed and enabled when you install the Edge Transport server role.

Exchange Server 2007 provides two ways to filter attachments:

- **File name or extension**   Exchange Server 2007 can filter attachments based on the name of the attachment or on the file extension of the attachment. This can be incredibly useful.

- **MIME type**   The Edge Transport server attachment filter can also filter by Multipurpose Internet Mail Extensions (MIME) type. The MIME type of an attachment determines the kind of information held in the attachment. For example, .jpg picture files, Word documents, and even text are MIME types.

A default Edge Transport server role includes a number of blocked attachment types. When the Attachment Filter receives an attachment that matches either a file name or MIME type, there are three actions that can be taken:

- **Block The Message And The Attachment**   Prevents the whole message along with the attachment from being delivered to a user's mailbox. In this instance, the sender receives a delivery status notification indicating that the message was refused as a result of an inappropriate attachment.

- **(Default setting) Allow The Message, But Strip The attachment** Allows the message to make its way into a user's inbox, but replaces the attachment with a text file that explains why the attachment was removed.

- **Silently Delete The Message And The Attachment** Prevents the whole message along with the attachment from being delivered to a user's mailbox. Neither the sender nor the recipient is notified that the delivery was prohibited.

Important Once a message or attachment is blocked, you are not able to retrieve the contents of either. Be careful when you configure attachment filtering to prevent false positives that result in lost mail.

At present, attachment filtering is managed from the Exchange Management Shell. There is no corresponding GUI-based management tool available in the Exchange Management Console.

To verify that attachment filtering is enabled on your Edge Transport server, issue the command **Get-TransportAgent**. This command provides you with a list of agents that are enabled and running on your Edge Transport server. Figure 20-20 shows you such a list along with the order in which each agent processes an incoming message. In Figure 20-20, note that the Attachment Filtering Agent is enabled.

Figure 20-20 The results of the Get-TransportAgent command

If the Attachment Filter is not enabled, issue the command **Enable-TransportAgent -Identity "Attachment Filter agent"**. This command can also be used to enable any of the other agents on the Edge Transport server. Just replace "Attachment Filter agent" with the name of the agent you want to enable. Conversely, if you want to disable the Attachment Filter agent, issue the command **Disable-TransportAgent -Identity "Attachment Filter agent"**.

Enabling and disabling the Attachment Filter agent is only part of the administration effort that goes into managing this service, though. As you probably expect, you can add filter entries on which the Attachment Filter agent can act. You can also remove existing filters from the list. The first step is to look at the entries that are already on the filter list. Use the `Get-AttachmentFilterEntry` command to do so. This command, with results shown in Figure 20-21, does not require any parameters.

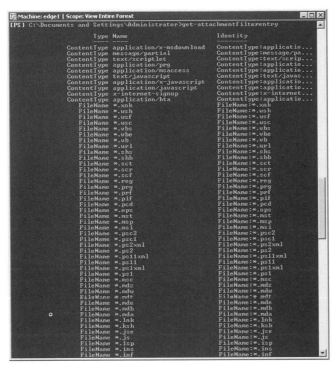

Figure 20-21   The results of the Get-AttachmentFilterEntry command

To add and remove entries to and from the list, use the `Add-AttachmentFilterEntry` and `Remove-AttachmentFilterEntry` commands, respectively.

The `Add-AttachmentFilterEntry` command takes two parameters:

- **Name**   Specify the file name, file extension, or MIME type of the attachment you want to block. A file name can be an exact file name, while an extension entry takes the form of *.ext.

- **Type**   The allowed values here are `FileName` or `ContentType`.

The first command here adds an entry to the filter list for attachments named virusemail.txt while the second entry keeps messages with .jpg attachments from entering the message system.

```
Add-AttachmentFilterEntry -name virusemail.txt -type FileName
```

```
Add-AttachmentFilterEntry -name image/jpeg -type ContentType
```

To remove an entry from the list, use the **Remove-AttachmentFilterEntry** command. This command takes only a single parameter, **Identity**. The **Identity** parameter is created by concatenating the Type and Name of an entry on the list. For example, the two sample commands here would remove the entries added above by the **Add-AttachmentFilterEntry** commands:

```
Remove-AttachmentFilterEntry -identity filename:virusemail.txt -confirm:$false
```

```
Remove-AttachmentFilterEntry -identity contenttype:image/jpeg -confirm:$false
```

The **confirm:$false** parameter in these commands indicates that the Exchange Management Shell should not prompt you for approval before removing these items from the Attachment Filter list.

Finally, you should learn how to modify the configuration of the Attachment Filter agent. For example, you read earlier that the Attachment Filter's default action is to allow a message with a forbidden attachment to pass through the filter, but to strip the attachment. If you want to change this behavior to, for example, simply block the message altogether, use the **Set-AttachmentFilterListConfig** command. This command has a number of parameters, including:

- **Action**   What action do you want to take when a message arrives with a prohibited attachment? The choices here are **Reject**, **Strip**, and **SilentDelete**. These three options are explained in detail earlier in this chapter.

- **AdminMessage**   If you choose the **Strip** action, the contents of the **AdminMessage** parameter are placed into a text file that replaces the attachment. The message and the text file are then sent to the original recipient. The default **AdminMessage** is "This attachment was removed."

- **RejectResponse**   If you choose the **Reject** action, the contents of the **RejectResponse** parameter are sent back to the original sender. The default **RejectResponse** is "Message rejected due to unacceptable attachments."

- **ExceptionConnectors**   This parameter specifies a list of connectors that should be excluded from the Attachment Filter agent. You must use a connector's GUID in this parameter. To get a list of connectors with each connector's GUID, use the following commands, with the results of these commands shown in Figure 20-22. The **fl identity,guid** pipe command filters the results from each of the commands to show you just the connector name and GUID.

```
Get-SendConnector | fl identity,guid
Get-ReceiveConnector | fl identity,guid
```

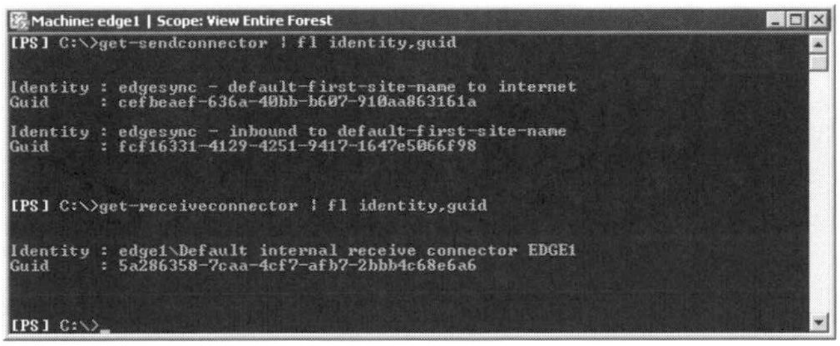

Figure 20-22   The results of the Get-SendConnector and Get-ReceiveConnector commands

The following example configures the Attachment Filter agent to reject messages with bad attachments and excludes one connector from this service:

```
Set-AttachmentFilterListConfig -Action Reject
  -ExceptionConnectors fcf16331-4129-4251-9417-1647e5066f98
```

Managing Antivirus with Microsoft Forefront Security for Exchange Server

Besides combating spam, the other major message protection task for e-mail administrators involves preventing viruses from using the messaging system as a vector for intrusion into an organization. Exchange Server 2007 provides a number of options when it comes to choosing an antivirus solution:

- **Use Third-Party Antivirus**   If you've run Exchange Server for a while, you've probably become comfortable with a third-party antivirus software vendor. If you choose to continue down this path, understand that antivirus vendors must write Exchange Server 2007–aware software. Without an upgrade, your old antivirus software will not work under Exchange Server 2007. Whenever possible, choose antivirus software that runs on the Hub Transport or Edge Transport servers and that acts on transport events, which are similar to the event sinks used in older versions of Exchange.

- **Use Microsoft Forefront Security for Exchange Server**   Microsoft Forefront Security for Exchange Server includes a transport-based antivirus agent for Exchange Server 2007.

- **Use Microsoft Exchange Hosted Services**   Microsoft Exchange Hosted Services is composed of four distinct services that help organizations protect themselves from e-mail–borne malware, satisfy retention requirements for compliance, encrypt data to preserve confidentiality, and preserve access to e-mail during and after emergency situations.

More Info   For more information regarding Microsoft Exchange Hosted Services, visit *http://technet.microsoft.com/en-us/exchange/bb288501.aspx*.

This chapter focuses solely on Microsoft Forefront for Exchange Server.

About Microsoft Forefront Security for Exchange Server

Forefront Security for Exchange provides you with a number of capabilities that help to protect your messaging environment. Some of Forefront's antivirus capabilities include:

- Virus scanning using as many as five antivirus engines. Multiple scanning engines make it much less likely that a virus will be able to get past your defenses.

- Protection on all storage and transport Exchange Server roles including Edge Transport servers, Mailbox servers, and Hub Transport servers.

- Comprehensive administrative reporting and notification.

- Automatic hourly updates to the scanning engine to ensure that the latest protection is in place.

Installing Microsoft Forefront Security for Exchange Server

The Microsoft Forefront Security for Exchange installation is very straightforward. In the examples in this chapter, and for demonstration, the software is installed to an Edge Transport server. However, in your environment, you can install the software to any Exchange Server 2007 computer in your organization. If you install the product to multiple servers, you won't necessarily have a situation in which a single message is scanned every single time it passes through one of your servers. When a message passes through a Forefront scanner, it is tagged as having been scanned, and subsequent servers on which Forefront is installed will simply pass the message.

To install Microsoft Forefront Security for Exchange, execute the setup.exe program and follow the instructions in the installation wizard. When asked whether you want a full or a client installation, choose Full Installation. The Client – Admin Console Only option does what the name indicates and installs only a console.

The Quarantine Security Settings page (see Figure 20-23) presents you with two options:

- **Secure Mode**   Content filters will be applied to messages that exit quarantine.

- **Compatibility Mode**   Content filters will not be applied to messages that exit quarantine.

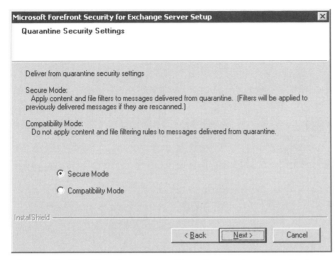

Figure 20-23   The Quarantine Security Settings installation page

On the Engines page of the installer, shown in Figure 20-24, choose up to five virus-scanning engines to install along with the Microsoft Antimalware Engine. For this example, only the Microsoft engine is being used. In a real-world environment, you should purchase at least one additional scanning engine.

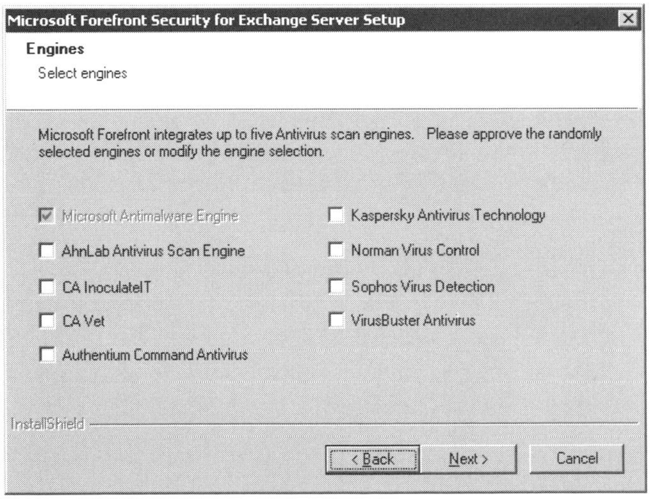

Figure 20-24   The Quarantine Security Settings Engines page

After making these decisions, continue with the installer, choosing the defaults. If you are installing the product to a transport server, the installation process will stop and you must restart the Microsoft Exchange Transport Service. This briefly disrupts organizational mail flow.

The installer notifies you when installation is complete after which you can verify that the services installed are running. Open the Services Control Panel applet on the server and look for the services that start with "FSC."

Managing Microsoft Forefront Security for Exchange Server

Microsoft Forefront Security for Exchange Server is managed through the use of the Forefront Server Security Administrator, which is accessible from Start menu by choosing All Programs, Microsoft Forefront Server Security, Exchange Server, and then Forefront Server Security Administrator. Figure 20-25 provides a look at the Antivirus option in the Forefront Administrator. Notice that, by default, the Transport Scan Job is enabled and is performing virus scanning as evidenced by the On tag in the Virus Scanning column. The settings in Figure 20-25 indicate that only the Microsoft Malware Engine is being used with a bias that favors virus certainty over system performance. When a virus is detected in an attachment, Forefront attempts to repair the attachment and sends notifications regarding the action.

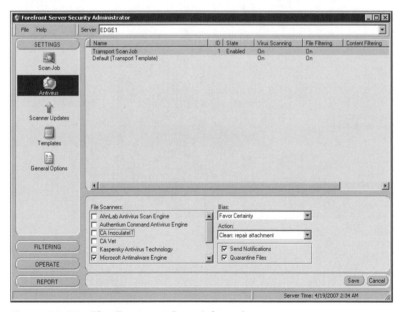

Figure 20-25   The Transport Scan Job settings page

> **More Info** The bias setting controls how many engines are needed to provide an acceptable probability that your system is protected. The more engines used, the greater the probability that all viruses will be caught, but the trade-off for this protection is system performance.

If you want to make changes to this default job, make them in the Work pane and click Save at the bottom of the window when you finish.

On the Scanner Updates page, shown in Figure 20-26, you can determine which engine and signature versions are being used for each scanner in your organization. You can also indicate the path from which updates should be downloaded and specify the update frequency, which defaults to 1 hour. To change the update frequency, modify the value next to the Repeat and Every values on the screen shown in Figure 20-26. If you want to update scanners immediately, click Update Now. This feature can be useful if there is a new virus outbreak and you want to get the latest definition file as quickly as possible.

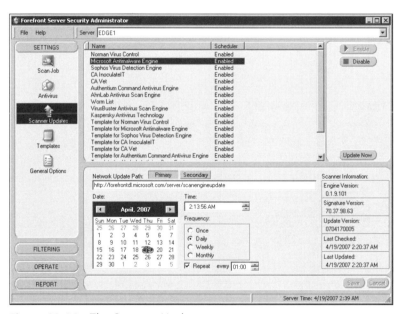

Figure 20-26 The Scanner Updates page

The final figure presented in this chapter—Figure 20-27—shows the Scanning portion of the General Options window.

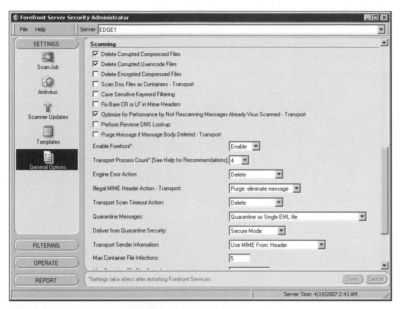

Figure 20-27   The General Options Scanning page

Other Microsoft Forefront Security for Exchange Server Benefits

Microsoft Forefront Security for Exchange Server also provides the following premium spam protection features:

- **Exchange Server 2007 IP Reputation Filter**   An IP Block list that is offered exclusively to Exchange Server 2007 customers. Premium anti-spam services include automatic updates for this filter.

- **Automated Content Filtering Updates**   Automated content filtering updates for Microsoft Smartscreen spam heuristics, phishing Web sites, and other content filtering updates.

- **Targeted Signature Data**   Targeted spam signature data and automatic updates to identify the latest spam campaigns.

More Info   For more information about Microsoft Forefront Security for Exchange Server, including full deployment details and other benefits, visit *http://www.microsoft.com/forefront/serversecurity/exchange/default.mspx*.

Summary

In recent years, messaging protection has become a massive industry and is a critical part of any organization's messaging infrastructure. In this chapter, you learned how to deploy the Edge Transport server role in Exchange Server 2007. You also learned how to manage the spam-busting features in Exchange Server 2007, which include content filtering, recipient filtering, sender filtering, attachment filtering, and much more. Finally, you received an overview and basic installation notes regarding Microsoft Forefront Security for Exchange Server. Microsoft Forefront Security for Exchange Server is a powerful new tool from Microsoft that gives you the ability to scan every incoming message with up to five different scanning engines.

Chapter 21

Securing Exchange Server 2007 Messages

The previous three chapters discussed how to secure Microsoft Exchange Server 2007, how to implement antivirus and anti-spam protection, and what to consider when developing a comprehensive information security policy for your e-mail users. This chapter focuses on securing messages. Exchange Server 2007 is tightly integrated with Microsoft Windows Server 2003, and you learn how Windows Server 2003 supports a comprehensive public key infrastructure (PKI) to ensure that the messaging component for Exchange Server 2007 is secure. Microsoft Certificate Services and the PKI are the two foundations upon which you design, deploy, and maintain your public-key security needs.

Windows Server 2003 Security Protocols

Windows Server 2003 provides security via the following security protocols:

- **Kerberos version 5**   The default protocol for authentication and logon.

- **NTLM (Windows Challenge/Response)**   Provided for backward compatibility with Microsoft Windows NT 4.

- **Digital Certificates**   Used with a PKI deployment. Especially useful for authenticating parties outside your organization. The use of digital certificates is becoming more frequent as companies attempt to secure their communications more fully.

- **SSL/TLS (Secure Sockets Layer/Transport Layer Security)**   Appropriate for connection-oriented security, such as access to Web-based resources on the Internet.

In this chapter, you examine the use of digital certificates and public and private keys to secure messages in Exchange Server 2007. You start by looking at the public-key infrastructure in Windows Server 2003.

Understanding the Public Key Infrastructure in Windows Server 2003

A PKI deployment involves several basic components. A solid understanding of how these components work is essential to setting up good, basic network security. You can think of the PKI as a collection of resources that work together to provide a secure messaging authentication system. The major components of a PKI are as follows:

- Certificate Services

- Digital certificates

- Policies to manage the certificates

- Microsoft CryptoAPI and cryptographic service providers (CSPs)

- Certificate stores for storing certificates

Encryption and Keys

Basic security starts with *encryption*, which is the process of scrambling data before sending it over a medium. A key is input into a mathematical function, which is then used to scramble the data into an unreadable form. Hence, plain text becomes encrypted, or *cipher*, text. Encrypted data is much more difficult for an interceptor to read than plain text data. Encryption technology uses two types of keys: symmetric keys and asymmetric keys.

Symmetric keys, also known as shared keys, are identical: both the sender and the recipient use the same key to encrypt and decrypt the data. *Asymmetric keys* are not identical: one key is used to encrypt the data, and a different key is used to decrypt it. With asymmetric keys, one key is known as the *public* key, and the other is known as the *private* key. Exchange Server 2007 uses a combination of symmetric and asymmetric encryption.

The public key is often made public by being published in some central place, such as a public folder or the Active Directory directory service. The private key must be secured so that no one but the owner of that key has access to it. A pair of public and private asymmetric keys is generally referred to in cryptography as a *key pair*.

With key pairs, either key can encrypt or decrypt the data, but the corresponding key is required to perform the opposite function, whether that is encrypting or decrypting. If the key that decrypts the data is not available, the encrypted data remains encrypted and is, essentially, useless unless the key can be found and employed. Although in theory either key can perform either function (for example, a private key can be used to encrypt and the public key used to decrypt), Windows Server 2003 and Exchange Server 2007 implement this technology by having the public key perform the encryption while the private key is used for decryption. When a user digitally signs a message, the signing happens with the user's private key and the signature is verified with the user's public key.

In Exchange Server 2007, someone having your public key is not a concern, because that individual can only encrypt data with it. However, the private key must be kept secure, because the private key decrypts the data. The best way to keep a private key secure is to never send it over a medium where a would-be hacker can capture it and use it.

The use of one key to encrypt (the public key) and a different key to decrypt (the private key) forms the foundation of Certificate Services. Table 21-1 summarizes the key types and when they are used.

Table 21-1   Private and Public Key Usage

Action	Encryption/decryption	Electronic signatures
Sending a message	Recipient's public key is used to encrypt message contents.	Sender's private signing key is used to apply the signature.
Reading a message	Recipient's private key is used to decrypt the message contents.	Sender's public signing key is used to interpret the applied signature.

Encryption Schemes

Encryption helps to safely send a message via an insecure channel, such as the Internet, safely. The message subject and body (but not the headers), as well as attachments, are encrypted. The *strength* of an encryption describes how difficult the encryption is to break, or decrypt. The length of the key determines the encryption strength. Here are some numbers to consider:

8-bit key = 28 keys = 256 keys

56-bit key = 256 keys= 72,057,594,037,927,936 keys

128-bit key = 2128 keys= 3.4 x 1038 keys

Attempting to break a 128-bit encryption and trying one trillion keys per second would take 10,819,926,705,615,920,821 years to test every possible key. Needless to say, 128-bit encryption is currently very strong. Table 21-2 lists some common encryption schemes.

Table 21-2   Common Encryption Algorithms

Encryption type	Description
CAST	A 64-bit symmetric block cipher (which encrypts one *block*, or set length, of data at a time, rather than one byte) developed by Carlisle Adams and Stafford Tavares. It is similar to DES and supports key strengths of 40 bits and 128 bits.
DES	Data Encryption Standard. Developed by IBM for the government for use by the National Institute of Standards and Technology (NIST). This standard uses 56-bit keys with a 64-bit symmetric block cipher. It is the most commonly used encryption algorithm.
3DES	Triple DES; encrypts the data structure three separate times.
DH	The Diffie-Hellman approach for passing symmetric keys.
KEA	Key Exchange Algorithm. An improved version of Diffie-Hellman.
MD2	Message Digest. An algorithm that creates a 128-bit hash value. It was developed by Ron Rivest of RSA (Rivest, Shamir, and Adleman).
MD4	Another RSA algorithm that creates a 128-bit hash value.
MD5	A better version of MD4.
RC2	Rivest's Cipher, a 64-bit symmetric block cipher.
RC4	An RSA stream cipher (which encrypts one byte or bit at a time) that can use variable-length keys. Microsoft's implementation of RC4 uses either a 40-bit or 128-bit key.
RSA	A commonly used public/private key encryption scheme developed at RSA.
SHA	Secure Hash Algorithm, developed at NIST. It produces a 160-bit hash value and is similar to MD5, but more secure and thus slower.

Certificate Services in Windows Server 2003

Public and private keys are not enough to guard your sensitive data. For example, it is not too difficult for someone to impersonate a server with which you are communicating. An impersonator can easily do this if he or she is in your organization. In this scenario, you might believe that you're communicating with Server1 when in fact you're communicating with a different server. Certificate Services is designed to protect against this type of attack.

Windows Server 2003 certificates form the core of the Windows Server 2003 public key infrastructure. You can install Windows Server 2003 Certificate Services to create a *certificate authority* (CA) that issues and manages digital certificates. Active Directory can maintain information that a CA needs, such as user account names, group memberships, and certificate templates, as well as information about each CA installed in the domain. Active Directory also maintains certificate mappings to user accounts for authenticating clients and controlling access to network resources.

Digital Certificates and the X.509 Standard

Digital certificates verify a user's identity and are issued by the CA (discussed later in the section "Certificate Authority"). You can trust digital certificates because you trust the source of the certificate—the CA. In addition to issuing the certificate itself, the CA by default creates the public key/private key pair, which is the basis of security in any digital certificate.

Digital certificates generally follow the X.509 standard, which means that they meet the standard criteria for electronic certificates outlined in it. Typically, an X.509 certificate incorporates the following fields:

- Version number
- Serial number of the certificate
- Signature algorithm ID
- Name of the person to whom the certificate was issued
- Expiration date of the certificate
- Subject user name
- Subject public-key information
- Issuer unique ID
- Subject unique ID
- Extensions
- Digital signature of the authority that issued the certificate

SSL/TLS also conforms to the X.509 standard. In Windows Server 2003, external users' digital certificates can be mapped to one or more Windows Server 2003 user accounts for permissions to network resources. Windows Server 2003 then uses the Subject field (the subject user name in the list of fields just given) to identify the user associated with the certificate. In this way, Windows Server 2003 and Certificate Services can map an external user to a user account stored in Active Directory.

The X.509 Standard

The X.509 standard describes two levels of authentication: *simple authentication*, using a password as the only verification of a claimed identity; and *strong authentication*, using credentials generated by cryptographic technologies. The standard recommends that only strong authentication be used as a basis for providing secure services.

The strong authentication method specified in the X.509 standard is based upon public-key technologies. The one huge advantage of this standard, and the reason why it is so popular today, is that user certificates can be held within Active Directory as attributes and can be communicated within the directory systems like any other attribute of a user account.

Although the X.509 standard does not require the use of a particular algorithm to produce the certificates, it notes that for two users to communicate, they must use the same algorithms during authentication.

Certificate Authority

As mentioned earlier, a certificate authority issues certificates and enables parties to trust each other. The private key is used to sign the certificate, and the certificate is needed to verify the signatures. Because certificates originate from a verified authority, the receiving party can explicitly trust them. For example, a client application can import a certificate to be trusted by a user who is reading data from the application.

Clients and CAs can maintain a list of explicitly trusted certificates. Certificates can also be placed on a certificate revocation list (CRL), which lists certificates that are explicitly distrusted. In addition, they can be set to expire after a predetermined amount of time.

Certificate Services Architecture in Windows Server 2003

Figure 21-1 illustrates the components of Windows Server 2003 Certificate Services. These components work together, in cooperation with CryptoAPI and the cryptographic service providers, to perform all the tasks necessary to generate, store, and apply certificates in the enterprise. You can manipulate these objects and modules in the Certification

Authority snap-in. (For information about how to install this snap-in, see the section "Installing and Configuring Certificate Services" later in this chapter.)

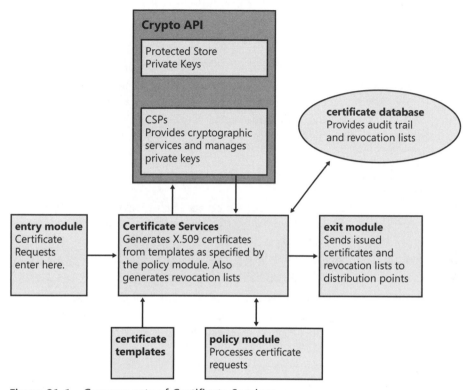

Figure 21-1   Components of Certificate Services

Entry Module

Certificate requests—such as those a user submits via the Web enrollment support page—enter the entry module of Certificate Services, either through remote procedure calls (RPCs) or HTTP. The requests are placed in a pending queue until they are approved or rejected by the policy module.

Policy Module

The policy module determines whether a certificate request should be approved, denied, or left pending for an administrator to review. When the certificate is approved, the policy module can verify information in the request against various sources, such as Active Directory or an external database. Additional attributes or extensions can be inserted into the policy module if a customized client application requires them. For example, a signing limit can be inserted into certificates and used by an online purchasing form to determine whether the user can sign for the amount requested.

Certificate Templates

Certificate templates define the attributes for certificate types. You can configure enterprise CAs to issue specific types of certificates to authorized users and computers. When the CA issues a certificate, a certificate template is used to specify its attributes, such as the authorized uses for the certificate, the cryptographic algorithms that are to be used with it, the public-key length, and its lifetime. Certificate templates are stored in Active Directory. Table 21-3 lists the standard certificate types.

Table 21-3   Certificate Types

Certificate type	Description
Administrator	Used for authenticating clients and for Encrypting File System (EFS), secure e-mail, certificate trust list (CTL) signing, and code signing.
Authenticated Session	Used for authenticating clients.
Basic EFS	Used for EFS operations.
CA Exchange	Used to store keys that are configured for private key archival.
CEP Encryption	Used to enroll Cisco Systems, Inc., routers for Internet Protocol Security (IPSec) authentication certificates from a Windows Server 2003 CA.
Code Signing	Used for code signing operations.
Computer	Used for authenticating clients and servers.
Directory Email Replication	Used to replicate e-mail within Active Directory.
Domain Controller	Used for authenticating domain controllers. When an enterprise CA is installed, this certificate type is installed automatically on domain controllers to support the public-key operations that are required when domain controllers are supporting Certificate Services.
Domain Controller Authentication	Used to authenticate Active Directory computers and users.
EFS Recovery Agent	Used for EFS encrypted-data recovery operations.
Enrollment Agent	Used for authenticating administrators who request certificates on behalf of smart-card users.
Enrollment Agent (Computer)	Used for authenticating services that request certificates on behalf of other computers.

Table 21-3 Certificate Types (Continued)

Certificate type	Description
Exchange Enrollment Agent (offline request)	Used for authenticating Microsoft Exchange Server administrators who request certificates on behalf of secure e-mail users.
Exchange Signature Only	Used by Exchange Server for client authentication and secure e-mail (used for signing only).
Exchange User (offline request)	Used by Exchange Server for client authentication and secure e-mail (used for both signing and confidentiality of e-mail).
IPSec	Used for IPSec authentication.
IPSec (offline request)	Used for IPSec authentication.
Key Recovery Agent	Recovers private keys that are archived on the certification authority.
RAS And IAS Server	Enables RAS and IAS servers to authenticate their identity to other computers.
Root Certification Authority	Used for root CA installation operations. (This certificate template cannot be issued from a CA and is used only when installing root CAs.)
Router (offline request)	Used for authentication of routers.
Smart Card Logon	Used for client authentication and logging on with a smart card.
Smart Card User	Used for client authentication, secure e-mail, and logging on with a smart card.
Subordinate Certification Authority (offline request)	Used to issue certificates for subordinate CAs.
Trust List Signing	Used to sign CTLs.
User	Used for client authentication, EFS, and secure e-mail (used for both signing and confidentiality of e-mail).
User Signature Only	Used for client authentication and secure e-mail (used for signing only).
Web Server (offline request)	Used for Web server authentication.
Workstation Authentication	Enables client computers to authenticate their identity to servers.

Online certificate templates are used to issue certificates to requestors that have Windows Server 2003 accounts and that support obtaining certificates directly from an enterprise CA. Offline templates are used to issue certificates to requestors that don't have Windows Server 2003 accounts or that don't support obtaining a certificate from an enterprise CA.

When a CA issues an online certificate, it obtains information about the requestor from the requestor's Windows Server 2003 account for inclusion in the certificate. When it issues an offline certificate, it includes in the certificate the information that the requestor entered as part of the request into a Web form, such as a user name, an e-mail address, and a department.

Certificate Database

The certificate database records all certificate transactions, such as certificate requests. It records whether requests were granted or denied, and it also holds information about the certificate, such as its serial number and expiration date. Revoked certificates are flagged and tracked in this database as well. You'll use the Certification Authority snap-in to manage the audit trail.

Exit Modules

Exit modules send the certificate to the location specified in the request. Acceptable destinations include LDAP directory services, file systems, and URLs. You can create customized exit modules so that new certificates are sent in e-mail messages or to a public folder on the network. There can be many or few exit modules, depending on your needs. Modules can be written in the Component Object Model (COM) interface to allow any entity or directory to be notified when a certificate is issued. In fact, you could write an exit module to notify a database of a new certificate, for billing purposes.

Managing the Public Key Infrastructure

Now that you understand the Windows Server 2003 public key infrastructure and are familiar with how Certificate Services works, you need to learn how to install and manage the Certification Authority snap-in. You can use this Microsoft Management Console snap-in to manage one or more CAs. For more information about how to create a customized snap-in, see Chapter 10, "Managing Exchange Server 2007."

Installing and Configuring Certificate Services

If you do not include Certificate Services as an optional component during the installation of Windows Server 2003, you can install it at any time by selecting the Certificate Services component on the Windows Components page of the Windows Components Wizard (see Figure 21-2). Immediately upon selecting Certificate Services, a message box appears indicating that once Certificate Services is installed, you can't rename this server or move it from the domain.

On the CA Type selection page in the Windows Component Wizard (see Figure 21-3), you can choose the type of CA server you want to install. Select the appropriate type for your installation.

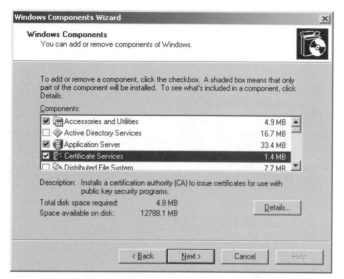

Figure 21-2   Selecting Certificate Services in Add/Remove Programs

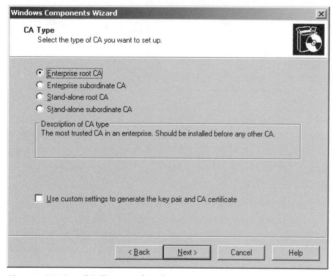

Figure 21-3   CA Type selection page

If you want to configure advanced options for the public and private keys, select the Use Custom Settings To Generate The Key Pair And CA Certificate check box and click Next. The Public And Private Key Pair page shown in Figure 21-4 appears. Table 21-4 describes the choices you have on this page.

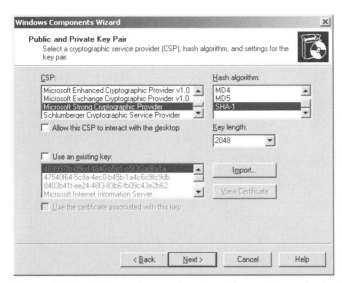

Figure 21-4   Setting advanced options for public and private key pairs

---

> **Note**   Installing an enterprise CA requires Active Directory services, so the CA computer must already be joined to the Windows Server 2003 domain.

Table 21-4   **Advanced Options for Public and Private Key Pairs**

Option	Description
CSP	Select the Cryptographic Service Provider (CSP) to be used to generate the public key and private key set for the CA certificate. The default CSP is the Microsoft Strong Cryptographic Provider.
Hash Algorithms	The default is SHA-1, which provides the strongest cryptographic security.
Allow This CSP To Interact With The Desktop	Be sure to select this check box. Unless you do so, system services will not interact with the desktop of the user who is currently logged on. If you're logging on using a smart card or some other hardware device, allow the CSP to interact with the desktop to allow the user to log on.
Key Length	The default key length is 2048 bits for the Strong Cryptographic Provider and 1024 bits for the Basic Cryptographic Provider. The minimum key length is 512 bits, and the maximum is 4096 bits. Generally, the longer the key, the longer the safe lifetime of the private key.
Use An Existing Key	Allows you to choose an existing private key from the list. The existing private key is used for the CA. You might need to use this option to restore a failed CA.

Table 21-4   Advanced Options for Public and Private Key Pairs (Continued)

Option	Description
Use The Certificate Associated With This Key	Enables the selection of the certificate that is associated with the existing private key that is used for the CA. You might need to use this option to restore a failed CA.
Import	Gives you the ability to import a private key that is not in the Use An Existing Key list. For example, you might import a private key from an archive for a failed CA.
View Certificate	Displays the certificate associated with the private key in the Use An Existing Key list.

After selecting Custom Settings and choosing options from the Public And Private Key Pair page, click next. Type the CA identifying information, as illustrated in Figure 21-5. You can also enter a Validity Period that indicates the valid lifetime of a certificate. This helps ensure that clients participating in autoenrollment are governed by a set certificate lifetime. Click Next again.

A quick screen appears indicating that the key pair is being generated. It will appear for fewer than 2 seconds in most cases. After the key is generated, Setup needs to know where to put the database. Type or browse to the appropriate path. As Figure 21-6 shows, you can also select the Store Configuration Information In A Shared Folder check box. This option creates a folder that makes information about CAs available to users. It is useful only if you are installing a stand-alone CA and do not have Active Directory.

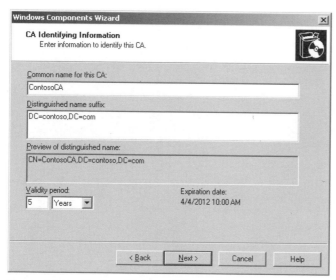

Figure 21-5   Typing CA identifying information

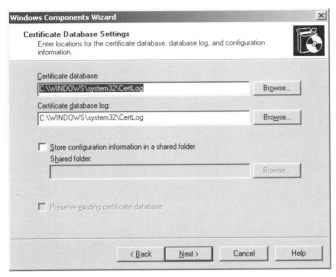

Figure 21-6 Specifying data storage locations

When you click Next, a message box appears indicating that Microsoft Internet Information Services (IIS) services must be stopped. Click Yes, and the wizard configures the components. When it is finished, installation of Certificate Services is complete. A shortcut to the Certification Authority snap-in appears in the Administrative Tools menu. Figure 21-7 illustrates the basic Certification Authority snap-in.

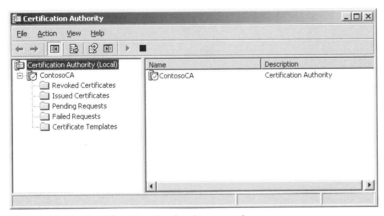

Figure 21-7 Certification Authority snap-in

Installing Web Enrollment Support

By default, when Windows Server 2003 Certificate Services is installed, the same server also installs Web enrollment support (see Figure 21-8). You can also choose to install the Web enrollment form on another Windows Server 2003–based computer. You might do so if the traffic volume for Certificate Services is high and you need to spread the enrollment traffic load over more than one server.

Figure 21-8 Web enrollment home page

The default location for the Web enrollment pages is <drive:>\%windir%\System32\Certsrv, where <drive:> is the letter of the disk drive on which the pages are installed. To install the Web enrollment pages on a server other than the one housing Certificate Services, start the Add Or Remove Programs tool in Control Panel, open the Add/Remove Windows Components window, and select Certificate Services, as though you were installing it. Then click Details and clear the Certificate Services CA check box (see Figure 21-9). Verify that the Certificate Services Web Enrollment Support check box is selected and click OK. Follow the wizard to completion.

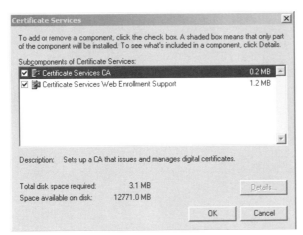

Figure 21-9   Installing Web enrollment support on a separate server

Using the Web Enrollment Pages

Users can access the Web enrollment pages via the default URL *http://servername/certsrv*. On the welcome screen, you have several options. Clicking the Download A CA Certificate, Certificate Chain, Or CRL option retrieves the certificate or the most current CRL and displays a screen allowing you to perform a couple of different tasks, including establish a trust for the CA certificate chain, which involves installing the certification chain for the certificate in the certificate store of the local computer (see Figure 21-10). Selecting this option is most useful when you need to trust a subordinate CA but do not have the certificate of the root CA in your local certificate store.

More often, you use this Web site to obtain a new user certificate. To begin the process, on the Welcome page (refer to Figure 21-8), click the Request A Certificate link. On the next page that appears (see Figure 21-11), you can either request a User Certificate or submit an Advanced Certificate Request. For information about the advanced options, see the next section, "Making an Advanced Request."

To request a new basic user certificate, click the User Certificate link. The User Certificate-Identifying Information page appears (see Figure 21-12). Here, you are informed that no more information is needed for the CA to generate a certificate. Clicking Submit initiates the certificate generation process. Clicking the More Options link allows you to specify the cryptographic service provider and the request format for the certificate. In most circumstances, you will want to click Submit; the More Options area is only for advanced users.

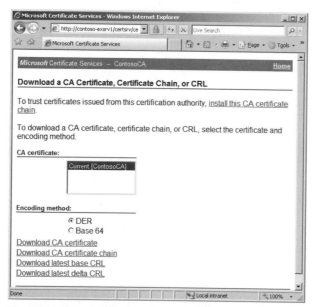

Figure 21-10 Retrieving the certificate

Figure 21-11 Requesting a new certificate

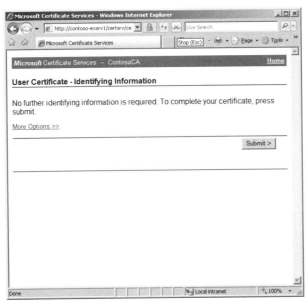

Figure 21-12 Message indicating system is ready to submit a certificate request

After you click Submit, the certificate is generated. Click Yes when the message box finishes the submission request. The next support page gives you the opportunity to install the certificate (see Figure 21-13).

Figure 21-13 Message indicating system is ready to install the certificate

Clicking the Install This Certificate link installs the certificate on the local computer. The certificate is available only to the user for whom the certificate is generated. If other users log on to the computer, they are not able to use this certificate. The final enrollment page then appears, indicating that the certificate has been installed properly. To verify that the certificate has been created, open the Certification Authority snap-in and open the Issued Certificates folder. The user's certificate is displayed in the Details pane (see Figure 21-14).

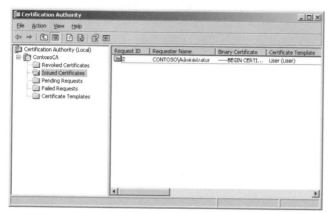

Figure 21-14   Verifying that a user certificate has been created

You can also verify that the user certificate has been installed by opening the Microsoft Office Outlook 2007 client, choosing Trust Center from the Tools menu, and then clicking the E-Mail Security category (see Figure 21-15). In the Encrypted E-Mail area, click Settings to reveal the Change Security Settings dialog box (see Figure 21-16).

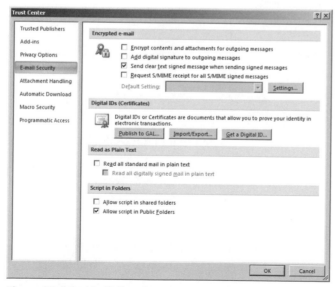

Figure 21-15   Verifying that a user certificate has been installed

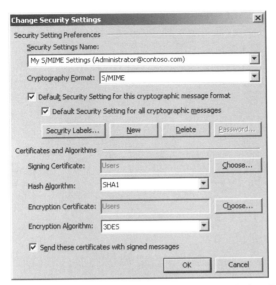

Figure 21-16   Change Security Settings dialog box

Click Choose for both the signing and encryption certificate to view the certificate, as shown in Figure 21-17. Note that the hash algorithm and encryption algorithm can be changed, but not the certificate itself.

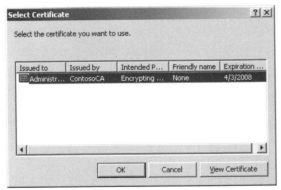

Figure 21-17   Selecting the Users Certificate for assignment in the Outlook client

If different certificates are installed, you can specify a particular certificate by clicking Choose and making a selection. Although the items in the list look like multiple copies of the same certificate, they are not. Each item is a unique certificate.

Making an Advanced Request

The Advanced Request option allows you to specify additional options while making a certificate request. Figure 21-18 shows the three types of requests available. The first choice, Create And Submit A Request To This CA, walks you through an advanced form. You can use this advanced form to request any certificate types supported by the enterprise CA. You also use this form to configure the key, format, and hash options for the certificate request. Generally, only administrators use this form because it is likely to be too complicated for the average user.

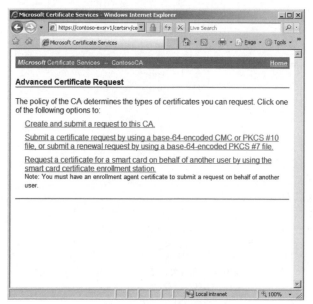

Figure 21-18   The three options available for an advanced certificate request

The second choice, Submit A Certificate Request Using A Base-64-Encoded CMC Or PKCS #10 File, Or Submit A Renewal Request By Using A Base-64-Encoded PKCS #7 File, allows you to submit a certificate request using a file rather than a form. The file must already exist in base 64, using either the #10 or #7 PKCS encoding format. Select which type of certificate is being requested in the Certificate Template section as well.

The last choice, Request A Certificate For A Smart Card On Behalf Of Another User By Using The Smart Card Enrollment Station, allows an administrator to create a certificate for a smart-card user that can then be installed onto the physical card.

Viewing Information About Certificates

You can view specific information about certificates by navigating to the Issued Certificates folder in the Certificate Authority snap-in and opening an individual certificate. To open a certificate, right-click it and choose Open. Figure 21-19 shows the General tab of the property sheet for a user certificate. This tab lists the purpose of the certificate, the issuer, to whom the certificate is issued, and the dates the certificate is valid.

Figure 21-19   General tab of the property sheet for a user certificate

The Issuer Statement button is unavailable in Figure 21-19 because in this case, the issuing CA does not provide a statement. If the issuing CA for a given certificate provides a statement, you can click this button to read additional information about the certificate from the issuing CA's Web site.

The Details tab shows the information contained in the certificate. When you select an item in the Field column, the contents of that field are revealed in the Value column. Figure 21-20 shows the Public Key field selected. The Value column indicates that it is a 1024-bit key.

The Certification Path tab (see Figure 21-21) shows the trust status of the certificate. If there is a problem with either the certificate or the path, a warning appears in this tab with information explaining the problem.

On the client side, you can use Outlook 2007 to edit certain certificate properties. With the certificate open in Outlook 2007, click Edit Properties at the bottom of the certificate's properties Details tab to see the sheet shown in Figure 21-22. Here, you can change the friendly name and description for the certificate. You can also restrict the purposes for which the certificate can be used. By default, all purposes are enabled, but you can manually disable certain purposes or disable all purposes, which would make the certificate invalid.

The Cross-Certificates tab (see Figure 21-23) allows you to specify cross-certificates for this certificate. *Cross-certificates* are special certificates that are used to establish complete or qualified one-way trusts between otherwise unrelated CAs. If your organization has multiple, distributed IT departments, you might not be able to establish a single, trusted root. In this situation, you can implement a network hierarchy trust model in which all CAs are self-signed and trust relationships between CAs are based on cross-certificates.

Figure 21-20 Details tab of a certificate's property sheet

Figure 21-21 Certification Path tab of a certificate's property sheet

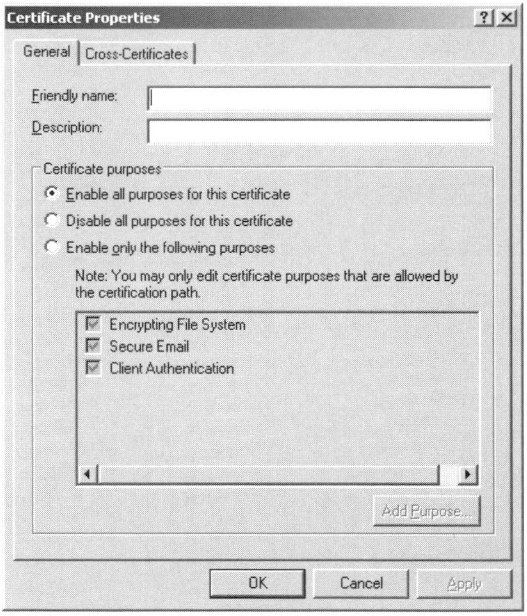

Figure 21-22   Editing certificate properties in Outlook 2007

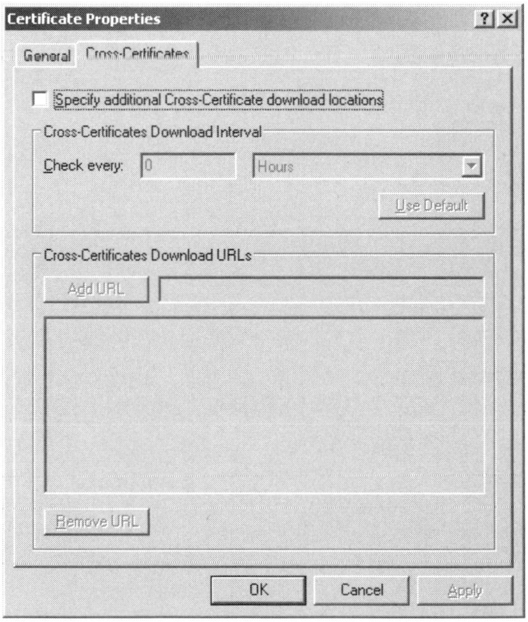

Figure 21-23   Cross-Certificates tab in the certificate properties

Securing Messaging in Outlook 2007

From the client perspective, one question that must be answered is how the Outlook 2007 client knows which certificates to trust. The answer is found in the properties of Microsoft Internet Explorer. When Internet Explorer is installed, a large number of root certificates are embedded in the installation. Outlook uses the Internet Explorer cryptographic service provider to read these certificates and then determine whether the CA is trusted. To see which CAs are trusted, in Internet Explorer, choose Internet Options from the Tools menu and then display the Content tab and click Certificates. In the Certificates window, click the Trusted Root Certification Authorities tab. Figure 21-24 shows a partial list of the default trusted root certificate authorities that ship with Outlook 2007 and Internet Explorer 7.

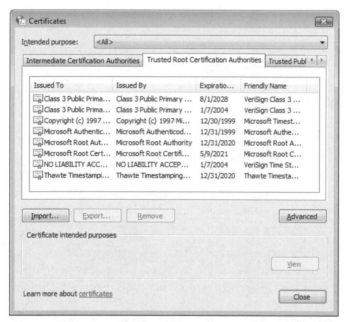

Figure 21-24 Partial list of trusted root certificate authorities in Internet Explorer

> **Note** A cryptographic service provider is the actual code that has the algorithms for encrypting data and creating signatures.

Both root CAs and individual users can be imported at this location. Assume, for example, that a user needs to add a certificate you have been given by an administrator. In the

Certificates dialog box, you display the Trusted Root Certification Authorities tab and then click Import. The Certificate Import Wizard will walk the user through the steps.

Initially Trusting a Certificate

If your company implements its own CA or if you need to trust specific CAs that are not embedded by default in IE, you can import their certificates by clicking Import.

You need to think carefully about whether to initially trust a certificate. For example, if the certificate is included on an installation CD-ROM from Microsoft, you can be sure it's trustworthy. However, if you download software from the Internet, someone might have slipped in a certificate that you don't want to trust. To prevent this, Microsoft uses Authenticode certificates for its software. With these certificates, if any bits have changed, you are notified during installation that the signature is invalid and that you shouldn't install the software.

You can also verify certificates independently by contacting the root CA directly to see whether the certificate's serial number is valid. Some CAs include serial numbers on their Web sites, or you can contact the system administrator of a corporate CA.

Encryption and Outlook 2007

When both the sender and receiver use Outlook 2007 along with certificates, their messages are encrypted end to end, meaning that the Outlook 2007 client encrypts them when it sends them, and they are not decrypted until opened by the recipient. Encrypted messages in the store remain encrypted. Hence, if someone is able to obtain access to a mailbox on an Exchange server, the messages are still unreadable because that person does not have the private key to decrypt the message. Only the intended recipient holding the correct private key can decrypt the message.

Here is how Outlook 2007 provides message privacy. First, the sender composes and addresses the message. Outlook then locates the recipient in Active Directory by doing an address book lookup. If the sender has chosen to encrypt outbound messages, Outlook retrieves the recipient's certificate. To see the encryption options, choose Trust Center from the Tools menu in Outlook 2007 and display the E-mail Security category (see Figure 21-25).

Outlook extracts the recipient's public key from his or her certificate and generates a one-time *lockbox*, encrypting all the data with a one-time, symmetric key and placing it inside this box. The lockbox, along with its contents, is encrypted with the recipient's public key and sent to the recipient. When the recipient opens the message, the recipient's client decrypts the lockbox, using the recipient's private key, extracts the symmetric key, and decrypts the message with the symmetric key. Then the recipient can read the message.

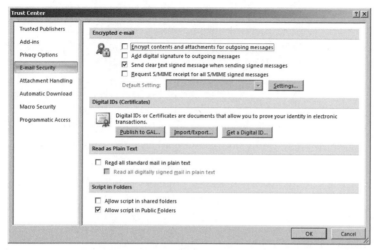

Figure 21-25   The Trust Center, showing options to encrypt outbound messages

Digital Signatures and Outlook 2007

Digital signatures are as binding as a signature on paper. Digital signatures provide origin authentication, because only the sender holds the private key used to generate the signature. The signature also provides data integrity because the signature is a protected hash of the message, meaning that the document is hashed and then encrypted with the signer's private encryption key and, after verification, it is decrypted with the signer's public key. If even one bit changes during message transmission, the hash will not be the same at the receiving end, and the message will be considered invalid. A given signature is generated for only a single message and is never used again. Digital signatures work because embedded into each signature is an indicator that explains what hash functions the sender used. The recipient can use the same function and compute the same hash when the message is received. If the hashes match, the signature is considered valid. If the message is encrypted, it must be decrypted before the algorithm can be run to compare the hashes.

S/MIME and Outlook 2007

Secure/Multipurpose Internet Mail Extensions, or S/MIME, was designed by an RSA-led vendor consortium in 1995. S/MIME allows recipients using non-Microsoft software to see and understand encrypted, secure messages sent from Outlook 2007 users.

> **More Info**   For more information about S/MIME, visit the RSA Web site at
> *http://www.rsasecurity.com.*

When a message is signed, the content of the message is converted to a MIME format. The message headers and body use the algorithm from the user's private key to produce a message integrity check (MIC). The result is the digital signature. The message is then sent with a copy of the sender's public key embedded in the message.

When the message is read, the MIC is generated at the recipient's end, and the results are compared to the sender's digital signature. If they match, the signature is considered valid.

When it comes to encryption, the recipient's public key is used to encrypt the data. To send an encrypted message, the sender must be able to retrieve the recipient's public key. The recipient can then decrypt the message using his or her private key. By default, the Outlook client looks to either Active Directory or the recipient's own personal certificate store for the recipient's public key.

For all of this to work, there must be a common CA trusted between the sender and recipient. *Trust verification*, which is the act of determining whether a given public certificate comes from a trusted source, is performed by the Outlook client (and Windows Mail) on the desktop.

Configuring Outlook 2007 for Secure Messaging

Certificate Services is integrated with Active Directory, and you can specify whether you want the certificates to be published in a file system in addition to Active Directory. To configure this setting, open the property sheet for the CA in the Certification Authority snap-in, display the Exit Module tab, and click Properties (see Figure 21-26).

The advantage of publishing a certificate in Active Directory is that the certificate becomes an attribute of the user's account, as shown in Figure 21-27. Before a user sends an encrypted message to another user, the client can look up the recipient's account in Active Directory to see whether that recipient has a certificate. If one exists, the message is sent as described previously. In addition, every 24 hours the client picks up certificate trust and revocation lists that are published by Certificate Services and applies them as needed. In the absence of a hierarchical CA structure, the client can build a linear trust network of different CAs.

In the Outlook client, use the Trust Center (refer to Figure 21-25) to select whether you want e-mail to be sent signed, encrypted, or both.

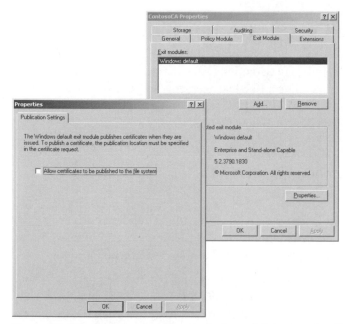

Figure 21-26   Allowing certificates to be published to the file system option

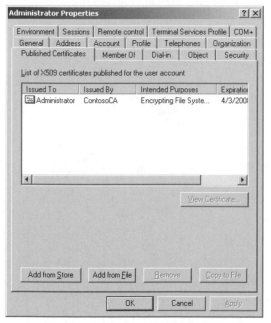

Figure 21-27   Published Certificates tab of a user's property sheet

Installing Exchange Certificate Templates

In Microsoft Exchange 2000 Server and previous versions, you had to manually add the certificate templates of Enrollment Agent (Computer), Exchange User, and Exchange Signature Only certificates before installing a Key Management Server (KMS). In Exchange Server 2003 and now Exchange Server 2007, KMS is no longer used, and the Users certificate that is installed by default has the following functions:

- Encrypting File System

- Secure E-Mail (both signature and encryption)

- Client Authentication

Because the "generic" users certificate now has these functions bundled into a single certificate, you find that the default installation of Certificate Services in Windows Server 2003 should meet most of your needs as far as your users are concerned.

However, at some point you might need to install additional certificate templates to issue certificates for other needs. You can easily accomplish this in the CA snap-in. To add another certificate template to those already there by default, right-click the Certificate Templates folder in the Certification Authority snap-in, point to New, and select Certificate Template To Issue. The dialog box shown in Figure 21-28 appears. In this dialog box, you can choose, by default, from the following templates (list is not exhaustive):

- Authenticated Session

- CEP Encryption

- Code Signing

- Enrollment Agent

- Enrollment Agent (Computer)

- Exchange Enrollment Agent (offline request)

- Exchange Signature Only

- Exchange User

- IPSec

- IPSec (offline request)

- Router (offline request)

- Smartcard Logon

- Smartcard User

- Trust List Signing

- User Signature Only

These are default certificate templates installed with Certificate Services (list is not exhaustive):

- EFS Recovery Agent

- Basic EFS

- Domain Controller

- Web Server

- Computer

- User

- Subordinate Certification Authority

- Administrator

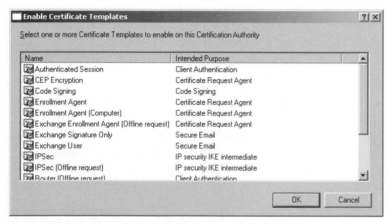

Figure 21-28   Choosing a certificate template

Understanding How Exchange Server 2007 Integrates with Windows Server 2003 Security

This section focuses on how Exchange Server 2007 uses the Windows Server 2003 security features. The Windows Server 2003 security features can be divided into two broad areas: core operating system features and additional features.

The core operating system features form the basis of a secure implementation of Windows Server 2003. Those features include the following:

■ **Active Directory Services**   Unifies Exchange Server 2007 and Windows Server 2003 objects into one directory

■ **Kerberos Authentication**   Performs authentication for access to domain and local services

■ **Access Control Model**   Gives granular control over Active Directory entries and Exchange objects

■ **Microsoft Certificate Services**   Can be used by other applications to provide security across different layers

Additional applications that enhance the features of the core operating system include the following:

■ **IP Security**   Used for network, remote access, and virtual private networks

■ **Security Configuration Analyzer**   Ensures adherence to security policies

Active Directory

Active Directory in Windows Server 2003 replaces the Security Accounts Manager (SAM) in Windows NT Server 4 as the security database. However, like an object in the SAM, most Active Directory objects are given a 96-digit, pseudorandom security identifier (SID) that is globally unique.

Not all objects in Active Directory are assigned a security identifier (SID). For example, a security group has an SID, but a distribution group does not. Likewise, mail-enabled users have SIDs, but mail-enabled contacts do not. Only those objects that have SIDs can be added to the access control list (ACL) of a resource. If an object does not have an SID, it cannot be placed in the ACL. Therefore, non-SID objects cannot access resources guarded by an ACL.

Kerberos Authentication

When a client needs to contact an Exchange server, the client first requests an Exchange service ticket from the key distribution center (KDC). The ticket is then used for authentication to the Exchange server.

The Exchange services also use Kerberos to make a service account log on to a domain controller through the local system account. This account uses computer identification that changes every seven days. The user name of Exchange Server 2007 is added to the Exchange Servers group, which is added to the ACL for the core objects.

More Info   It is beyond the scope of this book to cover Kerberos authentication in detail. To learn more about Kerberos authentication, what a ticket is, and how this protocol works, consult "Kerberos Authentication in Windows Server 2003" at *http://www.microsoft.com/windowsserver2003/technologies/security/kerberos /default.mspx*.

Access Control Model

The access control model in Exchange Server 2007 follows that of Windows Server 2003, giving you greater granularity of control for Exchange Server 2007 objects than for objects in previous versions of Exchange Server. For example, you can grant or deny access by container, by item, and at the property level. In addition, Exchange Server 2007 objects are based on the Windows Server 2003 NTFS file system and Active Directory objects. By way of illustration, if a user has access to only 5 out of the 10 items in a public folder, the user sees only those 5 items. Moreover, when a user who does not have access rights to certain attributes performs a search, the user has only the results that he or she can see.

IP Security

Although S/MIME provides security on the application layer, IP Security provides security on the IP transport layer; hence, IPSec provides a different type of security than S/MIME. In a highly secure environment, IPSec can be used to encrypt information from client to server and from server to server. IPSec works in tandem with Layer 2 Tunneling Protocol (L2TP).

With all these different security features available, you need to consider which types of security you want to implement. Table 21-5 summarizes some of the encryption and authentication methods commonly used today.

Table 21-5   Common Encryption and Authentication Methods

Services	Method used	Keys
IPSec	Encryption	DES 128-bit
	Authentication	MD5 128-bit
	Integrity	SHA 160-bit
		Kerberos
S/MIME	Encryption	DES, 3DES 128-bit
	Digital signature	RSA 512-bit
EFS	Encryption	DESX 128-bit

Table 21-5   Common Encryption and Authentication Methods (Continued)

Services	Method used	Keys
Rights Management Services (RMS)	Encryption	AES 128-bit
		RSA 1024-bit
		XrML Certificates
		Granular rights
	Authentication	Authenticates to RMS server

> **More Info**   For more information on RMS, visit Windows Rights Management Services at *http://www.microsoft.com/windowsserver2003/technologies/rightsmgmt /default.mspx*.

Summary

This chapter provided an overview of approaches to securing messages in Exchange Server 2007. As security technologies become increasingly important and common, you will find that many companies are hiring teams of people who focus only on security. In this chapter, you learned how to install and use Certificate Services, as well as how to perform some of the more common administrative tasks associated with certificates. The next chapter turns your attention away from security to learn how to connect Exchange Server 2007 to client software used within an Exchange organization.

Part VII
Clients

Chapter 22
Overview of Exchange Clients

Up to this point, the focus of this book has primarily been on the server aspect of the Exchange environment, because this book is primarily about administering Microsoft Exchange Server 2007. However, a server does not operate in a void; clients must connect to it to complete the picture.

This is the first of four chapters that examine the deployment of clients in an Exchange organization. This chapter introduces you to the main types of clients that you might find in your Exchange environment:

- Microsoft Outlook
- Windows Mail or Microsoft Outlook Express
- Microsoft Outlook Web Access
- Standard Internet e-mail clients
- Non-Windows platforms including UNIX and Apple Macintosh clients

Each of these can be used as a client in an Exchange organization. Because the focus of this book is Exchange Server 2007, and because each of these clients has a wide range of functionality and features, each client is not described in depth. Instead, this chapter simply introduces the major types of Exchange client software. Chapter 23, "Deploying Microsoft Office Outlook 2007," covers the deployment of the standard desktop client,

Outlook 2007, in more detail. Chapter 24, "Supporting Outlook Web Access," focuses on Outlook Web Access; and Chapter 25, "Supporting Other Clients," looks at using other types of Internet protocols to access Exchange Server 2007.

Microsoft Office Outlook 2007

Microsoft Office Outlook 2007 is the latest version of Microsoft's premier messaging client. Originally introduced with Exchange Server 5, Outlook delivers a complete messaging, scheduling, and contact-management solution. As you learned in Chapter 12, "Using Public Folders," Outlook clients can also work with public folders to share information.

Outlook also supports *add-ins*—program modules that, as their name implies, can be seamlessly added to the Outlook environment to extend the functionality of the product. The ability to use add-ins makes Outlook a strategic product for Microsoft because third-party developers can use Outlook as an application development platform. One example of a third-party add-in is a product named Pretty Good Privacy (PGP), which allows a user to send encrypted and signed messages using the PGP protocol. PGP is used mainly for Internet e-mail.

Outlook 2007 is a component of some versions of Microsoft Office 2007 and will become widely used as organizations upgrade to this newest version of the popular Office suite. It is included in most of the 2007 Microsoft Office suites: Office Basic 2007, Office Standard 2007, Office Small Business 2007, Office Professional 2007, Office Professional Plus 2007, and Office Enterprise 2007. Outlook 2007 is also shipped with Exchange Server 2007. As shown in Figure 22-1, Outlook 2007 looks similar to previous versions of Outlook. However, it includes several new features, including the ability to do the following:

- Use a new messaging interface that features the new Ribbon found in other Office 2007 products

- Take advantage of better integration with Exchange Server 2007, including the following:

    ❑ Improved Out of Office Assistant options

    ❑ A new AutoDiscover feature for easily configuring Outlook to connect to an Exchange server

    ❑ Instant Search

- Access to e-mail, voice mail, and faxes in one inbox using the new Unified Messaging feature in Exchange Server 2007

- Organize and find information quickly with color categories and attachment previewing

- Collaborate more easily with improved scheduling capabilities

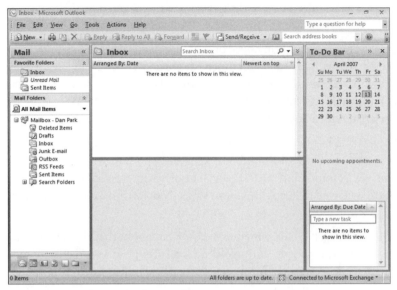

Figure 22-1   The Outlook 2007 client

Although this book focuses on using Outlook 2007 with Exchange Server 2007, take a look at all the features that Outlook provides on its own:

- **Messaging**   E-mail has become a way of life. Outlook provides a single, universal Inbox for all the user's messaging needs. Users can send and receive messages using a variety of servers. The servers supported are Exchange Server; Microsoft Mail; Internet-based HTTP, SMTP, POP3, and IMAP4; and a variety of third-party messaging servers. Messages can be created in three formats: plain text, rich text, and HTML.

- **Scheduling**   Life today is so fast-paced that most people use some kind of calendar or planner. Most businesses rely on electronic calendars to coordinate employee activities. Outlook's Calendar feature allows you to manage appointments and recurring events for yourself or another user on an Exchange server. You can schedule meetings for anyone in your organization or across the Internet through the use of iCalendar group scheduling.

- **Contact management**   Too many people keep track of their contact information for friends, relatives, and co-workers in a paper-based phone book that has scratched-out entries and entries with arrows pointing to other entries with more updated information. In essence, it is an inefficient and messy method. You can keep track of clients, staff, or any other category of people and their contact information within Outlook. This information can include phone numbers, addresses, birthdays, anniversaries, and anything else you might need to make note of for a contact.

■ **Journaling**   There's an old business quip that is often used to settle business disputes: the person with the most documentation wins. Having a record of every type of contact with a co-worker, a client, or anyone else could come in handy later on. Outlook's Journal feature can keep track of every phone call, fax, and e-mail sent and associate it with a specific contact.

■ **Notes**   Everyone has been in situations in which it was necessary to jot down an address or phone number but had no paper and pen handy. The Notes feature of Outlook gives you the electronic equivalent of sticky notes. Use Notes to record information you need to keep that doesn't exactly belong in a contact, a calendar, or an e-mail item.

■ **Tasks**   Did you forget to call someone back? What about that report you promised your boss—it was due today! Outlook's Tasks feature gives you the ability to create tasks, assign them to yourself or others, and establish due dates. You'll never miss that important deadline again.

More Info   For more details about installing, using, and supporting Outlook 2007, see *Microsoft Office Outlook 2007 Inside Out* by Jim Boyce, Beth Sheresh, and Doug Sheresh (Microsoft Press, 2007).

Windows Mail and Microsoft Outlook Express

In versions of Windows prior to Windows Vista, Outlook Express, shown in Figure 22-2, provides a subset of the standard Outlook product. In Windows Vista, Outlook Express is replaced by Windows Mail (which is essentially an updated and renamed Outlook Express). This section discusses Windows Mail, but the discussion applies equally to Outlook Express.

Windows Mail comes built in to Windows Vista. It is the default e-mail reader for Windows Vista unless Outlook or another e-mail client is installed. Windows Mail allows users to retrieve and send e-mail messages, participate in Internet newsgroups, and access directory information over standard Internet-based protocols. Windows Mail cannot take advantage of most of the collaboration features that Exchange Server 2007 provides, such as native access to public folders and calendaring.

Figure 22-2 Windows Mail

E-mail support within Windows Mail is similar to that of the Internet mail options in Outlook: only messaging over the POP3, IMAP4, and SMTP protocols is supported. When Windows Mail interacts with Exchange Server 2007 for retrieving messages, it does so over either the POP3 or IMAP4 protocol. This means that although Windows Mail can use Exchange Server 2007 as its messaging server, Windows Mail is not a native Exchange Server 2007 client. In addition, using Windows Mail to access an Exchange Server 2007 mailbox does not provide the groupware messaging present in Outlook, such as native access to public folders and Outlook forms.

Windows Mail provides support for multiple e-mail accounts, letting users retrieve messages from multiple servers and view them all in a single inbox. It also allows multiple users to have their own individual identities for messages, contacts, and tasks. Some basic rules functionality (Figure 22-3) is available through the Message Rules command on the Tools menu. Windows Mail can impose some client-side rules for handling incoming e-mail, but you cannot use it to create server-side rules, as you can with the Rules Wizard in the full Outlook 2007 product.

Figure 22-3   Creating a rule in Windows Mail

Outlook Web Access

Outlook Web Access (OWA) is a way of accessing e-mail and scheduling information from an Exchange server, just as you would from Outlook, through a standard Web browser such as Microsoft Internet Explorer. OWA is present in two versions:

- Outlook Web Access Premium, which takes advantage of features in Internet Explorer 6 (or later) to provide features such as secure messaging, rules, spell-checking, and reminders

- Outlook Web Access Light, which can be used with any Web browser but does not support all the features of Outlook Web Access Premium

OWA is really just a way to access e-mail over port 80 from a browser (or whatever port your browser and network are set to use), although you can also use OWA for remote document access, RSS feeds, and to search the Global Access List for an Exchange organization. OWA support is configured when you install Exchange Server 2007. Thereafter, a user can use a browser to access many of the functions ordinarily available through Outlook. Users have access to basic e-mail, calendar and group scheduling, basic public folders, and collaborative applications. OWA is more powerful than it ever has been and could certainly be used as a primary Exchange client by someone who didn't need access to advanced features. However, some features are not available when using either version of OWA, including the following:

- Offline use; you must be connected to an Exchange server to use OWA
- Personal address books (because they are stored on your workstation)
- WordMail and Microsoft Office integration
- Outlook forms
- Access to a local PST file

The universality of the browser client makes OWA an attractive choice in environments with diverse clients (such as Windows, Macintosh, and UNIX) that require a shared messaging client, as well as to remote users that need to connect to the Exchange server over the Internet. OWA is also beneficial for users, such as information systems staff, who move around to different workstations frequently during the day. They can simply check their e-mail using OWA instead of creating an e-mail profile on each workstation. You learn more about supporting and using OWA in Chapter 24.

Standard Internet E-Mail Clients

One of the goals of Exchange Server 2007 is to continue to comply with the standards being used by the Internet community. Because Exchange Server 2007 is compliant with several popular Internet protocols, it can be used as the messaging server for third-party e-mail clients, provided that the clients are also compliant with those protocols.

If you run third-party Internet e-mail client software as either a POP3 client or an IMAP4 client, you can use Exchange Server 2007 as your messaging server. Although Windows Mail is a Microsoft product, it is a good example of the type of software being discussed here. Windows Mail really has nothing specifically to do with Exchange Server; you could use it to get your e-mail from your local ISP and to read newsgroup messages from a UNIX-based news server somewhere on the Internet. In the case of Windows Mail, Exchange Server might never even enter the picture.

Non-Windows Platforms

In the discussions of clients using Exchange Server 2007, it is usually assumed that the clients are running on a Windows operating system. How do non-Windows operating systems connect with Exchange 2007 Server? Look at two other popular operating systems: UNIX and Macintosh.

UNIX Clients

No Outlook client exists for the UNIX operating system, so UNIX users have one of two choices for connecting to Exchange Server 2007:

■ **Internet e-mail client**   A UNIX-based, third-party Internet e-mail client can be used to access messages from Exchange Server 2007 over either the POP3 or IMAP4 protocols.

■ **Outlook Web Access**   Because the light version of OWA runs in a standard browser, UNIX users can access their e-mail using their own Web browsers.

Macintosh Clients

Macintosh clients have several choices for accessing Exchange Server 2007:

■ **Microsoft Entourage**   Microsoft's Entourage X client for Apple Mac OSX (part of Microsoft Office for Macintosh) provides functionality very similar to that of Microsoft Outlook, including the ability to connect to an Exchange server.

■ **Internet e-mail client**   Like UNIX users, Macintosh users can access Exchange Server 2007 with their own POP3 or IMAP4 e-mail clients.

■ **Outlook Web Access**   OWA is also accessible from a Macintosh-based Web browser.

As you can see, the client choices for the UNIX and Macintosh operating systems are extensive, mainly due to Exchange's support for industry-standard protocols. Exchange Server 2007 gives the user a variety of ways to access messages, regardless of the operating system.

Choosing a Client for Exchange Server

Philosophically, choosing a client for Exchange Server is easy. Outlook 2007 is the most current version of the Outlook client; it provides the greatest amount of functionality, and it is designated by Microsoft as the official client for Exchange Server 2007. Outlook 2007 is bundled with some versions of Microsoft Office 2007 and with Exchange Server 2007. Standard Internet e-mail clients miss a great deal of the functionality that Exchange offers, but they are fast enough to be used efficiently over the Internet.

As they say, however, your mileage may vary. You might have a large installed base of users that have other e-mail readers, and upgrading them can be a significant administrative task. Some or all of the people in your organization might already have an e-mail program that they like and, rather than going through the pain of change, they might choose to forgo the advanced features available with Outlook. Any of these factors might contribute to a decision to support non-Outlook clients as part of your Exchange environment or to use Outlook Web Access.

You might also have such a widespread mix of client platforms that you need to use the most generic client possible: the Outlook Web Access client. Or you might need to use OWA to service the messaging needs of some of your users and use the complete Outlook product for other users. Client machines can also use standard Internet POP3 and OWA clients to access your Exchange Inbox over the Internet.

The bottom line is that Outlook 2007 allows you to take advantage of all that Exchange Server 2007 has to offer, but other preexisting clients, although potentially missing some newer features, are supported and work with Exchange Server 2007 as well.

Summary

Exchange Server 2007 supports a wide variety of clients, including Outlook, Windows Mail (and Outlook Express), Outlook Web Access, Exchange Client, Schedule+, and standard Internet e-mail clients. Outlook 2007 is the current standard client for Exchange Server 2007 because it provides the most functionality and is the clear upgrade path for forthcoming Exchange clients.

Windows Mail is a capable client for Exchange Server 2007 as long as the server is configured for POP3 or IMAP4 access. Outlook Web Access is a good client to use when your organization supports non-Windows–based clients such as UNIX and Macintosh, or when your users need to access the server over the Internet. The new version of Outlook Web Access makes great strides in becoming more like Outlook than ever before. Exchange Client and Schedule+ are still functional alternatives in the Exchange environment, although upgrading to Outlook gives you considerably more functionality. The next chapter takes a more in-depth look at deploying and using Outlook 2007.

Chapter 23

Deploying Microsoft Office Outlook 2007

Microsoft Office Outlook 2007 is the latest version of Outlook. Because it is a component of some versions of Microsoft Office 2007, Outlook 2007 will be widely used as organizations upgrade to this newest version of the popular Office suite. It is included in most Office 2007 editions and ships with Microsoft Exchange Server 2007. This chapter looks at some of the issues an administrator faces when deploying Outlook 2007, including installation, using Outlook 2007 offline, and enabling multiple users.

Installing Outlook 2007

Installing client software is among the more repetitive tasks you face as an administrator. However, it's one that you must perform because a client/server system such as Exchange Server 2007 will not work unless both sides of the equation are in place.

Because this book focuses on Exchange Server, this chapter does not provide detailed instructions for installing Outlook 2007. However, it does provide an overview of the installation methods available, explaining some of the options you or your users have when performing a standard Outlook installation on an individual machine. It also introduces the Office Customization Tool, which allows you to create customized installations for your users.

> **More Info** This chapter provides an overview of the concerns regarding Outlook 2007 from an administrator's view, but Outlook is a complex program. If you want to learn more about using Outlook 2007, read *Microsoft Office Outlook 2007 Inside Out* by Jim Boyce, Beth Sheresh, and Doug Sheresh (Microsoft Press, 2007). To learn more about Office 2007 deployment, check out the 2007 Office Resource Kit at *http://technet2.microsoft.com/Office/en-us/library/9df1c7d2-30a9-47bb-a3b2-5166b394fbf51033.mspx?mfr=true*.

Standard Outlook Installation

Like most Microsoft programs, Outlook 2007 installs with a setup wizard regardless of whether you install Outlook as part of Office 2007 or as a standalone installation. You can customize just about every aspect of an installation, including adding and removing components during or after an installation. Figure 23-1 shows the component selection process for Outlook 2007 during a custom installation of Office 2007. (The list of Outlook components is the same when installing only Outlook.) For each component of Outlook 2007, you can elect to perform one of the following actions:

- **Run From My Computer** If hard drive space is abundant, many administrators choose to install every available component to run in this way.

- **Run All From My Computer** This essentially chooses the previous option for an entire group of components.

- **Installed On First Use** If a user never uses a certain component of Outlook, the component is never installed and doesn't waste space. On the other hand, constantly used components are installed locally. This option also saves time during the initial install.

- **Not Available** This simply means that the user must run the installer again to install the component. You can also use this option to prevent the user from installing certain components, as long as you don't make the installation files available.

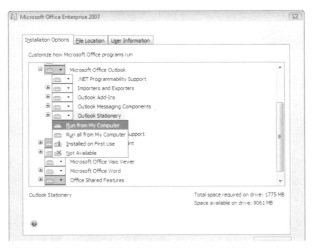

Figure 23-1 Specifying which Outlook 2007 components to install

After you select the components to install, Windows Installer takes care of the rest of the installation with little or no intervention on your part.

The first time a user runs Outlook 2007 following a standard installation, Outlook starts and prompts the user to configure the user's e-mail account. In an Exchange organization,

Outlook 2007 can usually detect the appropriate Exchange server and mailbox for the user. If it does not, this configuration may involve the user providing the name of the Exchange server and the user name.

Installing Outlook 2007 by Using the Office Customization Tool

As an administrator, you can customize the setup of Outlook 2007 by using the Office Customization Tool. The Office Customization Tool lets you create a Setup customization file that includes custom settings and Outlook profile configuration. The Setup customization file is then applied when you install Outlook 2007 from a network installation point.

Using the Office Customization Tool, you can perform the following actions:

- Define the path where Outlook 2007 is installed on client computers.

- Set the installation states (Run From My Computer, Installed On First Use, Not Available, Hidden, or Locked) for individual components of Outlook 2007.

- Specify Outlook 2007 user settings.

- Customize profiles by specifying Exchange server connections and defining account information. This information is saved in an Outlook 2007 profile file (a PRF file).

- Configure Send/Receive settings for Exchange mailboxes, including creating multiple Send/Receive groups and configuring different options for when Outlook is online and offline.

To accomplish all this, the Office Customization Tool creates a Setup customization file (an MSP file). When you install Office 2007 on a client computer, Setup looks for this customization file and applies the customizations the file contains.

More Info To use the Office Customization Tool, start an Office installation by typing **setup.exe /admin** at the command line. You can find detailed information about using the Office Customization Tool in the 2007 Office Resource Kit at *http://technet2.microsoft.com/Office/en-us/library/fff8197f-284d-4837-8086-47cf2cb410ed1033.mspx?mfr=true*.

Supporting Outlook 2007

Many features of Outlook 2007 are especially relevant in a book about Exchange Server 2007 because they involve interaction between the Outlook 2007 client and Exchange

Server. These features include the ability to work while disconnected from the Exchange server and to let more than one user work with a specific computer.

Using Cached Exchange Mode

Exchange Server and Outlook form the two ends of a powerful communications system. Most of the time, people communicate while the programs are in direct contact with each other so that the give and take of the process can proceed freely.

However, recall from Chapter 1, "Overview of Microsoft Exchange Server 2007," that communication with messaging systems such as Exchange Server is *asynchronous*, which means that one party can send a message without the other party being available to receive the message. Even though messages and replies might fly through your Exchange Server environment as rapidly as a conversation transpires on the telephone, the recipient is not required to be available when a message is sent, and the sender does not have to be online when the message is received.

This simple fact means that you can also use the Outlook 2007 client without being connected to the Exchange server. You can read messages in the local folders or create messages that are stored in your Outbox and sent when you reconnect to Exchange Server. This powerful feature makes users more productive in many situations that are typically thought of as downtime. (For example, you've probably seen people sitting on planes answering their e-mail without network connectivity.)

You can work offline with Outlook 2007 without modifying the software in any way. In fact, if you start Outlook 2007 when you are disconnected from the network, the environment looks almost the same as it does when you are connected to an Exchange server. The folder list displays all the folders for your mailbox, and you can create messages as though you were connected. Of course, the Outlook 2007 client must previously have been connected to the Exchange server at some point.

All this is accomplished through a feature called *Cached Exchange Mode*, which, when enabled, stores a copy of your Exchange mailbox on the local computer. This copy is stored in a file called an offline storage (OST) file. When a client computer is offline (either deliberately or due to a network error), Outlook 2007 automatically switches over to a disconnected mode, during which it periodically attempts to restore the connection. While the connection is unavailable, all the data inside the OST file is available to the user.

By default, however, public folders are not displayed in the folder list when you work offline. The main reason for this is that public folders tend to be both numerous and large. Synchronizing public folders by default would cause a lot of undue network traffic. As such, you must manually select public folders to be synchronized by first placing them in your Public Folder Favorites folder and then setting up Outlook to download Public Folder Favorites. You see how to configure all this in the upcoming sections.

Configuring Cached Exchange Mode

Cached Exchange Mode is enabled by default when you install Outlook 2007 and set up an Exchange Server mailbox, and little configuration is necessary. However, you can change the connection setting used in this mode and also disable Cached Exchange Mode.

Changing Cached Exchange Mode Connection Settings

To change the connection settings used by Outlook 2007 for Cached Exchange Mode, use the commands on the Cached Exchange Mode submenu on Outlook's File menu. The following connection settings are available:

- **Download Full Items**   This setting causes Outlook to download the header, body, and attachments of all messages at once. The presentation of messages is a bit slower when using this setting because each message is displayed in the client only when the previous message finishes downloading.

- **Download Headers And Then Full Items**   This setting causes Outlook to download all the headers of messages first and then download the complete items. The result is that the user sees the full list of messages more quickly in the Outlook client.

- **Download Headers**   This setting causes Outlook to download only the headers of new messages. The body of the message and any attachments are downloaded only when you open the item.

- **On Slow Connections Download Only Headers**   This setting differs in that you can select it in addition to one of the three previous settings. Outlook 2007 has the ability to detect a slow network connection state. When the setting is enabled, Outlook switches to downloading only headers when it detects a slow link—no matter which of the previous three settings is selected.

Disabling Cached Exchange Mode

Whenever you enable your Outlook 2007 client for offline use, you automatically enable the standard folders in your mailbox for offline use. The only way to disable offline use of your mailbox folders is to disable Cached Exchange Mode for your Outlook client. You can disable offline use by selecting the Account Settings option from the Tools menu in Outlook 2007. On the E-Mail tab of the Account Settings dialog box, select the Exchange account and click Change. On the Change E-Mail Account window that opens, click More Settings, switch to the Advanced tab, and clear the Use Cached Exchange Mode check box.

Note   Outlook 2007 and Exchange Server 2007 support the use of offline folders without using Cached Exchange Mode. Just deselect the Cached Exchange Mode option and make sure an offline folder file is configured. The only reason you might want offline folder access is to limit the synchronization of particular Exchange folders—something most users won't need to deal with. You can learn more about this in *Microsoft Office Outlook 2007 Inside Out* by Jim Boyce, Beth Sheresh, and Dan Sheresh (Microsoft Press, 2007).

After you disable Cached Exchange Mode, you no longer are able to use Outlook 2007 with the contents of any of your Exchange-based folders if you are not connected to an Exchange server. If you open Outlook with offline access disabled when you are not connected to an Exchange server, you receive a message that Outlook could not open your default e-mail folders, and Outlook opens with your default file system instead.

Note   Disabling offline access after you create an offline folder does not delete the offline folder. It is not deleted until you explicitly delete it.

Synchronizing a Mailbox

Synchronizing a mailbox is a simple process from the user's perspective, but the system must perform several complex tasks to accomplish it. When you start Outlook 2007, the system determines whether the client computer is connected to an Exchange server. You can create messages, delete messages, and perform other standard functions while offline. The next time you start Outlook and connect to an Exchange server, Outlook and Exchange Server automatically synchronize the contents of your offline folder. When Exchange Server synchronizes the contents of a folder on an Outlook 2007 client machine with the contents of the matching folder on the Exchange server, the system makes a copy of any messages that exist in only one location and places them in the other location. Exchange also synchronizes messages that have been deleted in one location but not in the other location.

The standard, default folders in your Outlook mailbox (Inbox, Outbox, Deleted Items, and Sent Items) are synchronized automatically, as long as you set up a location in which to store their contents.

Real World   When Synchronization Doesn't Work

Even though you configure everything correctly on your Outlook 2007 client, at times your folders might not synchronize automatically when you reconnect. If Outlook determines that you have a slow connection, it automatically stops synchronization from occurring. You can still synchronize either all folders or a specific folder by using any of the synchronize commands on the Tools menu.

Other errors might also prevent synchronization. Synchronization messages are stored in a Sync Issues folder in each user's mailbox. Check this log for error codes that can help you solve synchronization problems.

Synchronizing Public Folders

As mentioned earlier in this chapter, the standard mailbox folders are automatically enabled for offline access. You can verify this capability by displaying the property sheet for one of the folders in the mailbox, such as your Inbox. One of the tabs in the property sheet is labeled Synchronization. (This tab is discussed in the "Shaping Synchronization" section of this chapter.) However, if you display the property sheet for a public folder, you do not see the Synchronization tab because public folders, by default, are not enabled for offline access. Public folders typically contain large amounts of information that would clog your client machine. In addition, the contents of public folders are often subject to change, making synchronization difficult.

You can, however, easily enable a public folder for offline access. Simply move the public folder to the Favorites list in the Public Folders container of the Folder list. You can make this change by dragging the folder into the Favorites folder or by pointing to Folder on the File menu and choosing Add To Public Folder Favorites. When you drag a public folder to the Favorites folder, the folder has the same name as the original public folder.

When you designate a public folder as a Favorite, you do not move it from its established place in the public folder hierarchy; you simply add the folder to your list of Favorites. When a public folder is in the Favorites list, the property sheet for the folder contains a Synchronization tab. You can remove a folder from the Favorites list by selecting and then deleting it.

Real World   Public Folder Synchronization Conflicts

Conflicts can arise when more than one person is using and modifying the items in a public folder offline. If you change an item in a public folder while you are offline, when you synchronize that folder, Exchange Server checks the timestamp for the existing version of the item. If the timestamp for the existing version is later than the original timestamp for the item you changed, someone changed the contents of the folder item since you last downloaded it. If this type of conflict occurs, you receive a message that includes copies of all conflicting versions of the item. It is up to you to resolve the conflict, either by combining all versions of an item into a single version and then clicking Keep This Item or by clicking Keep All to keep all versions of the message.

This procedure is more complicated than it sounds. A user might find it difficult to decide whether to keep an existing item or overwrite it, and the wrong decision could have negative results. For this reason, you should use the standard Exchange security system to place controls on who is allowed to download and modify public folders.

Shaping Synchronization

After you enable offline access for your Outlook client, you can shape the way that each folder synchronizes with Exchange. If a folder is enabled for offline use, the property sheet for the folder contains a Synchronization tab, as shown in Figure 23-2.

Figure 23-2 Synchronization tab of a folder's property sheet

Click Filter to display a dialog box that allows you to define filtering conditions (see Figure 23-3). This dialog box has several tabs that allow you to define a complex condition. After you set up a filter, Outlook uses the conditions described in the filter to control which messages are synchronized between the Outlook client and the corresponding folders in Exchange Server. Keep in mind that these limits are imposed on all future synchronization attempts but have no effect on any messages that currently reside in the offline message store.

Filtering is an enormously useful tool for getting all the benefits of offline access without incurring the excessive overhead caused by synchronizing less important messages. For example, you could create a filter that disables synchronization for any messages that have large file attachments or that synchronizes only messages from your boss. Be careful to remember when you have synchronization filters on. In an offline folder, there is no indication that the messages presented in the folder are not the complete set of messages stored in the matching Exchange folder.

Figure 23-3   Filtering messages to be synchronized

Deciding Whether to Copy or Synchronize Public Folders

Synchronization is no more than a sophisticated way to copy messages automatically between folders on the Exchange server and the offline folder on an Outlook 2007 client. For your Inbox, Outbox, and other mailbox folders, synchronization works well. But should you use the process for public folders?

Public folders can serve a wide variety of purposes. A public folder can be a simple repository of static information, such as a library, or it can be a dynamically changing discussion group. You can copy the contents of a public folder to your mailbox simply by dragging the folder into the Mailbox container in your Outlook folder list. When should you copy, and when should you synchronize the contents of a public folder?

The longer the contents of a public folder are away from the Exchange server, the more likely it is that you will have a conflict when you reconnect—that is, you might make changes to your offline copy while others are changing the version on the Exchange server. Although public folders have a way to detect conflicts, as described earlier, you must resolve those conflicts manually, which can be time consuming.

When deciding whether to copy or synchronize a public folder, carefully analyze how the folder is intended to be used offline. If its contents are meant only to be read, you probably will find that a simple copy operation works well. If you change the contents of the folder, seriously consider preventing later conflicts by applying filters to the synchronization process so that you modify only the messages that are unlikely to be modified by other users.

Enabling Multiple Users in Outlook 2007

The capabilities of Outlook 2007 and the capabilities of Exchange Server 2007 work in conjunction with each other. Outlook is a client, and Exchange is a server. When an Outlook client is connected to an Exchange server, the client is representing a single user. In some situations, however, the same Outlook client can be used to support multiple users at different times. This section explores the scenarios in which this situation can occur.

Understanding Outlook Profiles, Exchange Mailboxes, and User Accounts

Before you learn how to implement multiple users with Outlook, you need to understand the differences between an Outlook profile and an Exchange mailbox, as well as how both of these entities interact with user accounts.

A *profile* is a client-side configuration. An Outlook profile is a set of information services configured for a particular user or purpose. The Exchange Server information service in a profile includes a reference to an associated Exchange server and mailbox. When a user starts Outlook, he or she uses the information in an Outlook profile to establish a connection with a particular Exchange server.

Normally, each client machine has a single default Outlook 2007 profile. When a user starts Outlook on that machine, the default profile is used to determine which Exchange mailbox is used on the server side of the environment. A user who starts Outlook for the first time or is using a machine that does not have a profile is prompted to create a profile before fully logging on to the associated Exchange server. To see the profile that your Outlook client is currently using, choose Account Settings from the Tools menu of Outlook 2007 and then select View or Change Existing E-mail Accounts. The dialog box is shown in Figure 23-4.

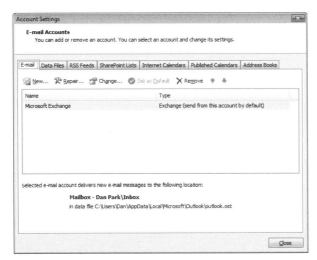

Figure 23-4   Viewing the current profile from Outlook 2007

Creating Multiple Profiles with Outlook 2007

Sometimes a single profile on an Outlook client is not enough. You might want to use more than one Outlook profile for any of several reasons. Perhaps you use Outlook on a machine that you share with others. Having separate profiles allows each profile to reflect the various mailboxes and configuration information for a given user. You might also be using a machine under different circumstances (such as in the office and on the road), making it desirable to be able to select a profile based on your current situation.

When you first log on to Outlook 2007, you are prompted to create a profile, which is used as the default profile. To create an additional profile, open Control Panel, double-click the Mail icon, and click Show Profiles. Clicking this button displays a list of the profiles on the machine, as shown in Figure 23-5.

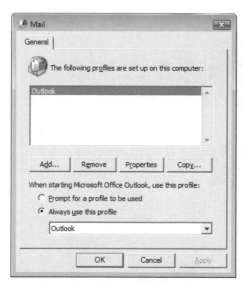

Figure 23-5   A list of e-mail profiles

To add a new profile, click Add, which starts the New Profile Wizard. This wizard prompts you for the values needed for a profile, much as when you create the first account after installing Outlook.

At the bottom of the Mail dialog box, you can specify a user profile to be used as the default profile for this client machine. Outlook uses this default profile to connect to an Exchange server unless you specify otherwise. The use of a default profile can be somewhat cumbersome, however, because it requires you to display the Outlook property sheet when you want to use a different profile. Alternately, you can have Outlook prompt you for a profile every time you start Outlook. If you select this option, a dialog box appears every time you start Outlook, allowing you to select the profile to use.

Accessing the Exchange Server

The Outlook profile described in the preceding section includes client-side configuration information. But remember that Outlook is the client portion of a client/server system. You still need the appropriate user privileges to access the server side of the equation in Exchange Server.

Exchange security is based on the Windows Server 2003 security model. Each Exchange object has an access control list (ACL) consisting of a discretionary access control list (DACL) and a system access control list (SACL). These lists are used in conjunction with the user's access token to either grant or deny access. For example, before an Outlook client can access an Exchange server, the user must log on to a network and receive a ticket from the domain controller. This ticket is used to gain entrance to the Exchange server. Figure 23-6 illustrates this process.

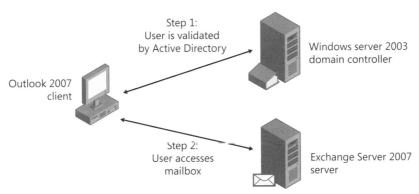

Figure 23-6   Using the Outlook client to connect to an Exchange Server 2007 server

Using Outlook to Delegate Mailbox Access

A mailbox in Exchange is really just a storage place in an Exchange server's private store provided for a mailbox-enabled user. An Outlook user can also allow other users to see any folder in your mailbox by granting them permission through the standard property sheet for a folder in Outlook. If users have permission for a specific folder or their user accounts have been granted permissions on the mailbox, they can open the folder by choosing Other User's Folders from the Open submenu of the main File menu.

Using Outlook, users can grant privileges to other users without contacting the administrator. They can grant these privileges by right-clicking the folder (such as Inbox), choosing Properties, and then adding the appropriate user on the Permissions tab, as shown in Figure 23-7. These permissions are similar in nature to ACLs, except that they are Exchange-specific and can be assigned only to certain mail-enabled Active Directory objects. There is no one-to-one correlation between the permissions you see here and the Windows permissions.

In addition, a user can use the Delegates tab of the Options dialog box (available from the Tools menu) to delegate access to the folders in his or her mailbox. The user can also assign different levels of permissions for each folder. The person being granted delegate access receives e-mail indicating that permissions are granted and detailing what level those permissions are.

After the privileges are assigned to another user, that user can access the folders by pointing to Open on the File menu and choosing Other User's Folder. This option is commonly used by administrative assistants checking their bosses' schedules or in other situations in which more than one person needs access to folders.

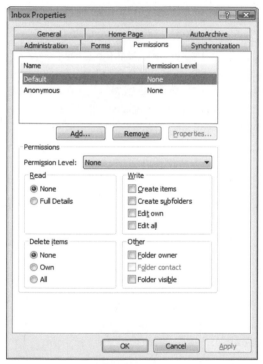

Figure 23-7   Granting access to a folder using Outlook

Setting Up Roaming Users

A *roaming user* is a user who does not have a fixed physical location and might consequently log on to many different machines. To accommodate such a user, you could set up a user profile on each of the machines he or she might use, but this solution might be impractical. Another way to address this situation is by creating a roaming user profile.

The configuration information for a roaming user is stored on a shared drive on a network server, allowing this information to be accessed from any machine that can connect to the network. When you set up a roaming user profile on a machine running Windows Server 2003, client machines that log on to the network with that profile look on the shared drive for configuration information. The common access to the storage of a roaming profile eliminates the need to have this profile stored on many machines. When you enable roaming users in Windows, that's all you have to do. Outlook 2007 automatically supports roaming Exchange users. For more information about setting up a shared user profile on Windows Server 2003 and various clients, refer to the documentation for those products.

You can also accommodate roaming users through Microsoft Outlook Web Access and the Web Store. These features are discussed in Chapter 24, "Supporting Outlook Web Access."

Outlook Anywhere

The Outlook Anywhere feature for Exchange Server 2007 allows Outlook 2007 (and Outlook 2003) clients to connect to an Exchange server over the Internet by using remote procedure calls (RPC) over HTTP. To deploy Outlook Anywhere in an organization, use the Outlook Anywhere Wizard to enable Outlook Anywhere on at least one Client Access server in each Active Directory site in the organization.

Benefits of Outlook Anywhere

Outlook Anywhere provides the following benefits:

- Outlook 2007 (and Outlook 2003) clients can remotely access Exchange servers from the Internet.

- You can use the same URL and namespace that you use for Microsoft Exchange ActiveSync and Outlook Web Access.

- You can use the same Secure Sockets Layer (SSL) server certificate that you use for both Outlook Web Access and Exchange ActiveSync.

- You only need to open port 443 on your firewall because the RPCs are encapsulated within an HTTP layer. Thus, you do not also need to open specific RPC ports.

- Unauthenticated requests from Outlook cannot access Exchange servers.

- Clients must trust the certification authority that issues the certificate.

- You do not have to use a virtual private network (VPN) to access Exchange servers across the Internet.

Outlook Anywhere Requirements

To use Outlook Anywhere, ensure that the following steps are taken:

1. Install a valid Secure Sockets Layer (SSL) certificate from a trusted certification authority (CA) that the client trusts. You learn more about this in Chapter 19, "Exchange Server 2007 Security Basics."

2. Install the Windows RPC over HTTP Proxy component.

3. Enable Outlook Anywhere

Installing the RPC over HTTP Windows Proxy Component

To install the RPC over HTTP Windows Proxy component, complete the following steps:

1. Click Start, point to Settings, click Control Panel, and then double-click Add Or Remove Programs.

2. Click Add/Remove Windows Components.

3. On the Windows Components page, in the Components window, select Networking Services and then click Details.

4. On the Networking Services page, in the Subcomponents Of Networking Services window, select the RPC Over HTTP Proxy check box (shown in Figure 23-8) and click OK.

5. On the Windows Components page, click Next.

6. Click Finish to close the Windows Components Wizard.

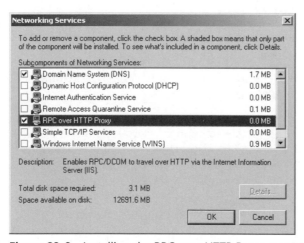

Figure 23-8   Installing the RPC over HTTP Proxy component

How to Enable Outlook Anywhere

To enable Outlook Anywhere using the Exchange Management Console, complete the following steps:

1. In the console tree, expand Server Configuration and click Client Access.

2. In the Action pane, click Enable Outlook Anywhere.

3. In the Enable Outlook Anywhere Wizard, in the box under External Host Name, type the external host name for your organization, as shown in Figure 23-9.

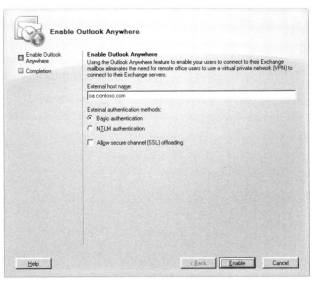

Figure 23-9   Enabling Outlook Anywhere

4. Select an available external authentication method. You can select Basic Authentication or NTLM Authentication.

5. If you are using an SSL accelerator and you want to do SSL offloading, select the Allow Secure Channel (SSL) Offloading check box.

> **Note**   Do not use the SSL accelerator option unless you are sure that you have an SSL accelerator that can handle SSL offloading. If you do not have an SSL accelerator that can handle SSL offloading and you select this option, Outlook Anywhere will not function correctly.

6. Click Enable to apply these settings and enable Outlook Anywhere.

7. Click Finish to close the Enable Outlook Anywhere Wizard.

Management Shell

You can also enable Outlook Anywhere using the Exchange Management Shell with the following command:

```
enable-OutlookAnywhere -Server:'ServerName' -
ExternalHostName:'ExternalHostName'-ExternalAuthenticationMethod:'method' -
SSLOffloading:$condition
```

Just set **ServerName** to the name of the server, **ExternalHostName** to the name of the external host, **method** to either Basic or NTLM, and **condition** to either True or False.

Summary

Outlook 2007 is the preferred client for Exchange Server 2007. This chapter covered how to deploy Outlook 2007 in your organization, describing the various installation options, how to support offline use of Outlook 2007, and how to set up profiles and provide access to other users' mailboxes. Outlook is a full-featured client that can be used in conjunction with Exchange Server, even when the client machine is not directly connected to an Exchange server. A single Outlook client can support many users, and a single user can roam to different machines and use Outlook on each of those machines to check his or her e-mail.

Chapter 24, "Supporting Outlook Web Access," looks at how to access e-mail, public folders, and calendars over the Web.

Chapter 24

Supporting Outlook Web Access

This chapter focuses on Microsoft Outlook Web Access (OWA). Because the need for remote access to e-mail has greatly increased, use of OWA has increased and will continue to increase. Understanding the advantages and limitations of OWA will benefit your planning, implementation, and troubleshooting efforts. In the following sections, you examine the new OWA features in Microsoft Exchange Server 2007. You also examine OWA deployment and management tasks and then take a quick look at the new interface and document management feature.

Features of OWA

OWA provides an environment for users to access both public folder store data and mailbox store data using a browser. With OWA, clients based on UNIX, Macintosh, and Microsoft Windows can view and work with any public folder, mailbox, Global Address List (GAL), and calendar. (For UNIX users, OWA is the primary Exchange-based solution for e-mail, calendar, and collaboration functionality.) With OWA 2007, Windows users running Internet Explorer can also access any file or folder to which they have access on network resources.

Following are some of the many navigation, view, and workflow improvements that have an impact on performance and functionality of OWA in Exchange Server 2007:

- Two different versions of OWA: OWA Premium version for Internet Explorer users and an OWA Light version for users of other browsers. In Exchange Server 2007, both versions have undergone tremendous improvement; the Light version is an all-new experience.

- Ability to access files housed in a SharePoint-based repository or located on a Windows file share directly from within OWA.

- A customizable logon page.

- Ability to implement two-factor authentication for improved security.

- HTML-only viewing to prevent caching of sensitive information on kiosk-type machines.

- Cookie-based validation in which the OWA cookie is invalid after the user logs out or becomes inactive for a configured period of time.

- Clearing of the credentials cache after logout.

- User-configured window size that persists during an OWA session.

- Preview pane can be to the right of messages and attachments that open directly in the pane.

- Spell check is provided for e-mail messages.

- Server-based e-mail handling rules that are created and managed by the user.

In spite of all these new features, OWA does retain some limitations. Therefore, before you deploy OWA, consider what is not accommodated:

- Offline use. A user must connect to an Exchange server to view information.

- No access to offline folders. There is no synchronization of local offline folders with server folders.

Deploying OWA

Two basic deployment scenarios are covered: the single-server scenario and a multiserver scenario.

Single-Server Scenario

In the single-server scenario, there is only one Exchange server. Users connect directly to Internet Information Services (IIS) on the single Exchange server and access their mailboxes on the Exchange server. In this configuration, the Mailbox server role and the Client Access server role are both installed on a single server. Many smaller environments will use this topology. This is also the most simple and straightforward approach to implementing OWA.

There are no limitations inherent in this scenario. All protocols, including POP3 (Post Office Protocol version 3), IMAP4 (Internet Messaging Application Protocol version 4), and HTTP (Hypertext Transfer Protocol), are available for users and, with appropriate firewall rules, can be made available to users.

Multiserver Scenario

In a multiple-server scenario, at least one publicly accessible server running the Client Access server role hosts the Exchange protocols in a bank of IIS servers. Behind them, and usually behind an organization's firewall, at least one Exchange database server is running the Mailbox server role. The Client Access server role servers handle client calls, which are then passed on to the Mailbox server role computers to give users access to their mailboxes or public folders.

The protocols that can be offered using this scenario include POP3, IMAP4, and HTTP.

Both the enterprise and standard editions of Exchange Server 2007 support this multiple-server scenario. The servers onto which you install the Client Access server role and that you place in a location accessible from the Internet should not have the Mailbox server role installed. These Client Access server role–based servers forward client requests to the better-protected Mailbox server role servers that are also running Exchange Server 2007. Remember that a Mailbox server role computer maintains at least one mailbox or public folder store. Note that you can use an Exchange Server 2007 Client Access server to access mailboxes housed on Exchange 2000 Server or Exchange Server 2003 servers.

This multiple-server configuration gives you several advantages:

- **Single namespace**   If you have a lot of OWA users, you can install them with network load balancing (NLB) services supporting the Client Access servers, all accessible with a single Domain Name System (DNS) name and Internet Protocol (IP) address. This ability provides additional availability for your OWA users.

- **Offload processing**   If you choose to implement Secure Sockets Layer (SSL) encryption, the Client Access server role servers will handle all the encryption and decryption processing, thus offloading this work from the Mailbox server role servers.

- **Better security**   You can select where you want your Client Access server role servers to reside—inside a firewall, outside a firewall, or perhaps in a perimeter network. Client Access server role servers can be configured to authenticate users before proxying their requests to Mailbox server role servers.

- **Scalability**   Because you can add new servers to the Client Access server load-balancing cluster, each added server represents additional capacity to manage new and existing client requests. And because clients do not need to know which Mailbox server hosts their mailboxes, you can move a client's mailbox to a new server, and that move will be transparent to the client. This architecture is very scalable and can accommodate millions of users.

NLB is a server that ships with Windows Server 2003 that dynamically distributes client calls for services between multiple Client Access server role servers. Notice that this refers to the client request level, not the client session level. Sessions aren't load-balanced; all the individual client calls are. Load balancing is achieved through the virtualization of the Media Access Control (MAC) and IP addresses on each Network Interface Card (NIC) on each server in the cluster. Hence, as each call comes into the servers, that call has the same host name, IP address, and MAC card combination as the other calls, making it much easier to load-balance the traffic load, not just session load, between servers.

More Info   To learn more about network load balancing, refer to the Network Load Balancing Overview white paper, which can be found on the TechNet site at *http://technet.microsoft.com/ en-us/default.aspx* or in the MSDN Library at *http:// msdn2.microsoft.com/en-us/default.aspx.*

You can always use a third-party hardware solution for load balancing, or you can implement the Domain Name System (DNS) round-robin scheme.

Microsoft has some other guidelines for implementing this multiple-server architecture. First, place at least two servers in the NLB cluster for each protocol you want to offer using this architecture. Each Client Access server determines where the user's mailbox resides by using the user's directory information from Active Directory.

Second, if you need broad availability for your Exchange databases, implement a clustering solution for these databases. Doing so ensures you achieve as much up-time as possible. Exchange Server 2007 introduces significantly enhanced clustering capabilities. Look to Chapter 9, "High Availability in Exchange Server 2007," for more information about this high availability feature.

Finally, do not allow direct access to Mailbox servers. In other words, don't install the Client Access server role on your mailbox servers. It defeats your purpose in creating Client Access servers in the first place, and it places unnecessary load on those mailbox servers. Bear in mind that the Mailbox server also serves up the MAPI-based Outlook client requests, so you can't completely separate client access, but, for OWA purposes and access from the Internet, the Client Access server is critical. Outlook Anywhere, formerly known as RCP over HTTP, however, is served by the Client Access server.

Multiple-Server Scenario: Firewalls and Client Access Servers

Consider your firewall topology when you plan the placement of your Client Access servers. You have only three placement choices: place the Client Access server inside your firewall, place the Client Access server outside your firewall, or place the Client Access server between two firewalls. Each configuration has pros and cons. Each one is discussed individually in the following sections.

Placing a Client Access Server inside a Single Firewall

When you place a Client Access server inside your firewall, you have a single firewall separating your Client Access server and the network from the Internet. The positive aspect of this topology is the cost savings as well as the offering of some security to your Client Access server and network. You need to open the client access ports to the Client Access server, such as port 110 for POP3, 143 for IMAP4, 119 for NNTP, and 80 for HTTP.

The downside to this topology is that once the firewall is compromised or traversed, your entire network is exposed. This isn't just an issue with the Client Access server—it is an issue of having only one firewall. Many smaller organizations choose a single firewall because of the financial savings. However, if at all possible, implement two firewalls and a perimeter network.

Of course, you can also implement a single firewall with one interface dedicated as a perimeter network (also know as a demilitarized zone or DMZ). This configuration provides much of the security benefit of two firewalls, but requires only a single hardware device to protect the network. This option is dicussed in the section "Placing the Client Access Server between Two Firewalls" because the concepts carry over.

Placing the Client Server outside Your Firewall

Placing your Client Access server (or any server, for that matter) outside of a single firewall is probably the least desirable configuration because your Client Access server is entirely exposed, and the number of ports you must open on your firewall to allow the Client Access server to talk with the Mailbox server makes the firewall look like Swiss cheese. The risks of opening some ports can be mitigated by using Hosts file entries on each Client Access server.

Placing the Client Access Server between Two Firewalls

Placing the Client Access server between two firewalls is the preferred method of implementing the multiple-server topology. The other option here is to use a single firewall with at least three interfaces. One port faces the Internet; another port faces your internal network; and a third port creates a place for you to place servers that need to be accessible from the Internet. Where necessary in this section, differences between the two methods are pointed out, but in most cases where "Internet firewall" is referred to you can substitute "Internet facing port" if you use a single firewall. The same holds true for the protected network-facing port.

In this scenario, the Client Access server is protected by the Internet firewall, and only the client access ports are open on the Internet firewall. If you place a Client Access server in a perimeter network to service HTTP requests, then on the Internet firewall, open only port 80. On the firewall between your Client Access and Mailbox servers, open all of the necessary communications ports.

Also consider implementing Internet Protocol Security (IPSec) at the network layer between Client Access and Mailbox servers. IPSec can be configured to either require the security or simply to ask for the security.

ISA Server 2006 and OWA

Beyond simply deploying a single server or multiple servers and firewall layers, Microsoft also provides well-supported and secure OWA deployment scenarios. Used in conjunction with Microsoft Internet Security and Acceleration (ISA) Server 2006, you can deploy OWA and provide an increased level of security for your messaging environment. ISA Server 2006 and Exchange Server 2007 were developed to coexist; ISA Server 2006 includes a new Exchange Publishing Rule Wizard that configures your ISA Server 2006 computer to allow client access to the OWA server and all of the new features available in OWA 2007.

Table 24-1 outlines the ISA Server 2006 features that can be used to help secure your Outlook Web Access environment. This table is from Microsoft's ISA Server 2006 documentation.

Table 24-1   ISA Server 2006 Security Features

Feature	Description
Link Translation	ISA Server 2006 redirects Outlook Web Access requests for internal URLs that are contained in the body of any object in Outlook Web Access, such as an e-mail message or calendar entry. Users no longer have to remember the external namespaces for internal corporate information that is mapped to an external namespace. For example, if a user sends a link in an e-mail message to an internal namespace such as *http://contoso*, and this internal URL is mapped to an external namespace such as *http://www.contoso.com*, the internal URL is automatically translated into the external URL when the user clicks the internal URL.
Web Publishing Load Balancing	ISA Server 2006 can load balance client requests and send them to an array of Client Access servers. When ISA Server 2006 receives a request for a connection to Outlook Web Access, it selects a Client Access server and then sends the name of the Client Access server back to the Web browser in a cookie.
HTTP Compression	In the past, if you used forms-based authentication on the ISA Server computer that had Exchange Server 2003 and ISA Server 2004 or ISA Server 2000 installed, it was not possible to use Gzip compression. This was because ISA Server could not decompress and recompress the information correctly. ISA Server 2006 can decompress, inspect, and then recompress data before it sends the data to your Exchange servers.

Table 24-1   ISA Server 2006 Security Features (Continued)

Feature	Description
Exchange Server Locations Are Hidden	When you publish an application through ISA Server, you are protecting the server from direct external access because the name and IP address of the server cannot be viewed by the user. The user accesses the ISA Server computer. The ISA Server computer then creates a connection to the Client Access server according to the conditions of the server publishing rule.
SSL Bridging and Inspection	Secure Sockets Layer (SSL) bridging protects against attacks that are hidden in SSL-encrypted connections. For SSL-enabled Web applications, after ISA Server receives the client's request, ISA Server decrypts the request, inspects it, and acts as the endpoint for the SSL connection with the client computer. The Web publishing rules determine how ISA Server communicates the request for the object to the published Web server. When you use SSL bridging, the secure Web publishing rule is configured to forward the request by using Secure HTTP (HTTPS). ISA Server then initiates a new SSL connection with the published server. Because the ISA Server computer has become an SSL client, it requires the published Web server to respond with a certificate. An additional advantage of SSL bridging is that an organization has to buy SSL certificates from an external certification authority only for the ISA Server computers. Servers that use ISA Server as a reverse proxy can either not require SSL or use SSL certificates that are generated internally.
Single Sign-On	Single sign-on enables users to access a group of published Web sites without being required to authenticate with each Web site. When you use ISA Server 2006 as a reverse proxy server for Outlook Web Access, ISA Server 2006 can be configured to obtain the user's credentials and pass them to the Client Access server, so that users are prompted for their credentials only one time.

More Info ISA Server 2006 deployment is beyond the scope of this book. See *http://technet.microsoft.com/en-us/library/aa996545.aspx* for more information about deploying ISA Server 2006 with Outlook Web Access.

Authentication Options

You have two choices when it comes to authenticating users that attempt to log in to OWA. By default, when you install a Client Access server, OWA is configured for Basic Authentication, meaning that, upon browsing to your OWA site, a user is greeted with a pop-up window asking for credentials. These credentials are then sent back in clear text to the OWA server for verification. You can see where this might lead to problems. Clear text is not generally acceptable for secure environments. This is covered more in the next section. Your other option is to use forms-based authentication, which has been around since the feature was introduced in Exchange Server 2003.

Securing Default Authentication

To secure the transmission of messages between Exchange Server 2007 OWA and a client, you must decide how to authenticate the client and whether you want client traffic encrypted or signed. Figure 24-1 gives you a look at all of OWA's authentication options.

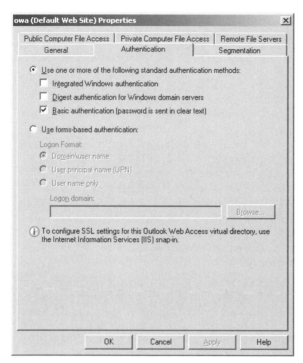

Figure 24-1   Enabling logon authentication

You can authenticate your client in one of three ways: Anonymous, Basic, and Integrated Windows. The *Anonymous* setting is the least secure authentication scheme, providing limited access for specific public folders and directory information. Anonymous authentication is supported by all clients and is the preferred method of allowing general public access to specific public folders.

Basic authentication uses clear text to authenticate the client with a domain controller. Basic authentication requires the user to type the user name, the domain name, and the password. Because the user name and password are sent in clear text between the server and the client, using SSL to encrypt the user name and password is recommended to ensure safer communication.

Integrated Windows Authentication (IWA) is meant for clients running Internet Explorer 5 or later. IWA uses Kerberos to perform authentication and offers the highest level of security. In

IWA, the user's password is not sent on the line in clear text. Instead, it is encrypted so that even when the password's packets are sniffed, the attacker cannot read the password.

Forms-based Authentication

OWA's forms-based authentication method stores the user's user name and password in a cookie instead of in the browser. When the user leaves his OWA session or after a configured period of inactivity, the cookie is cleared. In either scenario, a user must reauthenticate to use OWA again. Forms-based authentication is not enabled by default. To enable an OWA logon page, follow these steps:

1. Open the Exchange Management Console.

2. Under Server Configuration, choose Client Access.

3. Click the OWA (Default Web Site) entry and, from the Action pane, click Properties.

4. From the OWA (Default Web Site) Properties page, click the Authentication tab.

5. Under the Use Forms-Based Authentication option there are three options for enforcing a particular logon format. The Domain\User Name option is self-explanatory and is particularly useful if you have multiple domains. The User Principal Name (UPN) option, or e-mail address format, is probably the easiest for users to remember in a multiple domain environment. The User Name Only option is the last option, which is also self explanatory. If you choose the User Name Only format, you also need to choose a Logon Domain. See Figure 24-1.

6. Click OK.

7. Because this change affects Internet Information Services (IIS), you must restart IIS. From a command line on the OWA server, issue the command iisreset /noforce.

Security Alert   OWA sessions do not timeout during the creation of a message.

Management Shell

If you want to enable forms-based authentication from the command line, issue the following command from the Exchange Management Shell:

```
Set-owavirtualdirectory -identity "owa (default web site)"
  -FormsAuthentication:$true
```

This command enables forms-based authentication for the default Outlook Web Access instance.

Before you use this feature, you should have Secure Sockets Layer (SSL) configured in IIS. To configure SSL, you must either install Certificate Services on your Windows Server 2003 server and generate a certificate for the OWA Web site, or purchase an SSL certificate from a third-party source. After you install the SSL certificate and require SSL on your Web site that is hosting OWA, you will be presented with the new logon screen shown in Figure 24-2. Note that the default URL to access OWA 2007 is *https://server/owa*.

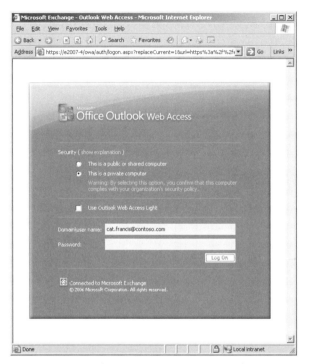

Figure 24-2 Exchange Server 2007 OWA logon screen

The OWA logon screen sports three other features. First, users cannot accidentally choose to cache their OWA password. Second, when users log off, they have no way to access thier inboxes unless they reauthenticate. Finally, the OWA toolbars and graphics are downloaded in a hidden frame during the logon process to give a peppier logon experience to the user.

During the logon process, the user has the option to use OWA Light. This light version does not include all of the bells and whistles available in the default premium version. The premium experience includes all OWA features. The light experience does not include everything and is meant for users who are connecting over a slow wide area network (WAN) link and need only the essentials of OWA. For users with faster connection speeds, the premium experience is preferred. Only users running Internet Explorer can use the premium version of OWA. All other browsers must use the light version.

Now, take note of the options in the Security section of the OWA logon screen shown in Figure 24-2. The two options—This Is A Public Or Shared Computer and This Is A Private Computer—are important in that the choice dictates the period of time that can elapse before an OWA user is automatically logged out of OWA.

As an administrator, you can configure the registry of the Client Access server—which hosts OWA—for timeout settings. Think also in terms of a public computer and a private, or trusted, computer. A *public computer* is one that is available to the general public—for instance, a kiosk in a public area that supplies OWA. If the Public setting is selected, the timeout is set to 15 minutes by default. If this is not appropriate for your organization, this timeout setting can be overridden by a server-side registry setting:

```
Location: HKEY_LOCAL_MACHINE\SYSTEM\CurrentControlSet
\Services\MSExchange OWA
Parameter: PublicClientTimeout
Type: REG_DWORD
Value: <number of minutes>
```

This registry key assumes a 15-minute timeout setting. The minimum value is 1 minute, and the maximum value is 43,200 minutes, which equates to 30 days. This registry parameter does not exist until you create it. To do so, follow these steps:

1. On each Client Access server, start the Registry Editor (regedit).

2. In the Registry Editor, browse to the following registry key: HKEY_LOCAL_MACHINE \SYSTEM\CurrentControlSet\Services\MSExchange OWA.

3. Choose Edit, then choose New, and then choose DWORD Value.

4. Name the new value PublicClientTimeout.

5. Right-click the new PublicClientTimeout DWORD value and choose Modify.

6. In the Edit DWORD Value window, under the Base option, choose Decimal.

7. In the Value Data box, provide a value in minutes between 1 and 43,200 (30 days).

8. Click OK.

9. Restart IIS. You can do this from the command line by issuing the `iisreset` command.

Management Shell

If you have a lot of Exchange servers, or you just don't want to fool with the registry on each of your Client Access servers, use Exchange Server 2007's management shell to set the cookie timeout value for public computers that log in to OWA using forms-based authentication. Issue the following command:

```
set-ItemProperty 'HKLM:\SYSTEM\CurrentControlSet\Services\MSExchange OWA'
  -name PublicClientTimeout -value <amount of time> -type dword
```

Replace the <amount of time> parameter with a number between 1 and 43200. This number represents the numbers of minutes that will pass before an OWA user on a public kiosk is automatically logged out of OWA. Don't include the quotes or <> characters in your command.

After you issue this command, restart IIS by issuing the command iisreset /noforce.

If you're curious as to whether or not the shell command actually worked, open the registry editor and take a look.

The *trusted computer* setting is meant for those computers that sit on your internal network. The default value for this setting is assumed to be 1440 minutes, or 24 hours. If you want to change this setting, use the same registry key you would for the Public computer but use the parameter TrustedClientTimeout. The minimum and maximum values for PublicClientTimeout and TrustedClientTimeout are the same. The instructions given previously, both the registry editor method and the Management Shell method, work for this parameter as well. Simply substitute TrustedClientTimeout for PublicComputerTimeout.

You need to know about some issues with the timeout setting. First, the cookie-based timeout setting is not absolute—it triggers between the value of the setting and $1.5 \times$ <setting>. In other words, if you set the timeout value as 10 minutes, the timeout actually triggers between 10 and 15 minutes ($10 \times 1.5 = 15$). Because the default setting for the trusted computer is 1440 minutes, the actual timeout triggers somewhere between 1440 and 2160 minutes, or 24 to 36 hours. Such a wide window for a timeout trigger might not be compatible with your security policies. Unfortunately, the formula is not configurable, so you might be forced to lower the default value on trusted computers if your information security policies so dictate.

The second issue you need to be aware of is that the TrustedClientTimeout setting cannot be lower than the PublicClientTimeout setting. Even when you set the trusted value lower than the public value, Exchange Server 2007 automatically adjusts the trusted value to be equal to the public setting. This automatic configuration change kicks in regardless of which value you incorrectly set. So whether you set the trusted value too low or the public value too high, you end up with the trusted value being automatically set to be equal to the public value.

Disabling User Access to OWA

In addition to deciding on an authentication mechanism for OWA and configuring timeout information, you can further secure OWA by disallowing OWA access on a per-user basis. Exchange Server 2007 removes the Exchange-specific tabs and values from the user account information available in Active Directory Users and Computer, so you are left with the Exchange Management Console or the Management Shell as your sole user configuration tool. You can easily disable a user's privilege to OWA using either tool. Bear in mind that, by default, all users start out as OWA-enabled.

Disabling a user's OWA privileges isn't a complex task. Use the Exchange Management Console and follow these steps, which correspond to the screen shown in Figure 24-3:

1. Open the Exchange Management Console.

2. Under Recipient Configuration, choose Mailbox.

3. Right-click the display name of the user for whom you want to disable OWA rights.

4. Click Properties.

5. On the Properties page, click the Mailbox Features tab.

6. In the Features pane, choose Outlook Web Access.

7. Click Disable.

8. Click OK.

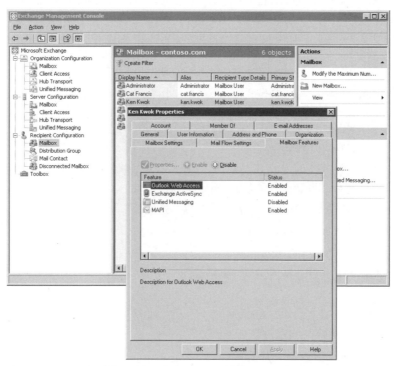

Figure 24-3   Disabling OWA in a user's mailbox properties

Management Shell

Using the Exchange Management Shell, you can enable and disable a user's rights to use Outlook Web Access. This is useful if, for example, you're in a very security-conscious environment and want OWA only for specific users or if you charge for services and want to charge more for OWA. In any case, use the following commands to enable and disable access to OWA:

```
Set-CASMailbox -Identity cat.francis@contoso.com
  -OWAEnabled:$true

Set-CASMailbox -Identity cat.francis@contoso.com
  -OWAEnabled:$false
```

To manage the OWA server, you use two administrative tools: the Exchange Management Console and the Internet Services Manager.

Creating Additional OWA Instances

Another way to help to secure OWA is to create additional OWA instances, each with a different configuration. You will create more than one virtual server when you have users with different authentication needs in OWA–for example, when only certain users need to read their e-mail using SSL; or when you host e-mail for more than one domain name and you want to ensure that each domain name has its own OWA configurations.

With the Exchange Management Shell, you can create new virtual directories that will ultimately appear in, and be configurable from, the Exchange Management Console. Each virtual server (virtual directory in the IIS manager) requires its own unique IP address and port number combination.

When you install the Exchange Server 2007 Client Access server role, the installer automatically creates four Outlook Web Access virtual directories. All four virtual directories are created in the default IIS Web site on the Exchange server:

- **OWA**   Exchange Server 2007 Outlook Web Access virtual directory.

- **Exchange (legacy)**   The Outlook Web Access virtual directory accessible by users whose mailboxes are housed on Exchange Server 2003 or Exchange 2000 Server servers.

- **Public (legacy)**   The Outlook Web Access virtual directory that points to public folders housed on Exchange Server 2003 or Exchange 2000 Server computers.

- **Exchweb (legacy)**   An Outlook Web Access virtual directory used by users to access the Outlook Web Access virtual directories. Requests to this virtual directory are sent to the user's Mailbox server.

IIS Virtual Directories in Exchange Server 2007

A number of other virtual directories are created in IIS as well. They are not directly related to OWA but are critical to Exchange's operation.

- **Autodiscover**   This virtual directory is used by the Exchange Server 2007 AutoDiscover service, which automatically configures e-mail settings for Microsoft Office Outlook 2007 clients and compatible mobile devices.

- **EWS**   The EWS virtual directory is used to access the Exchange Server 2007 Web Services components. Web Services are an integral component to the Exchange Server 2007 and Outlook 2007 experience and enable significant functionality, such as the Exchange Server 2007 Availability Service.

- **Exadmin** (*http://server/exadmin*)   This root is for administration of public folders.

- **Exchange** (*http://server/exchange*)   This is a legacy root that points to Exchange mailboxes for users whose mailboxes remain housed on Exchange Server 2003 or Exchange 2000 Server computers.

- **Public** (*http://server/public*)   This is a legacy root that points to public folders housed on Exchange Server 2003 or Exchange 2000 Server computers.

- **Microsoft-Server-ActiveSync**   This root is used to synchronize information with mobile clients and their devices.

- **OAB**   The OAB directory is the Exchange Server 2007 distribution point for the Offline Address Book.

- **UnifiedMessaging**   This directory is used for access to Exchange Server 2007 Unified Messaging services.

A Web site in IIS can have only one OWA site, but you can run multiple Web sites on a single IIS server. You can create a few different kinds of virtual directories, including the types listed above. Only the most common type of virtual directory—an Exchange Server 2007 OWA site—is looked at here. To create an additional virtual directory, follow these steps:

1. Add an IP address to your Exchange server.

2. On your DNS server, create an entry that points to the new IP address.

3. In the Internet Information Services manager, create a new Web site and bind the new IP address to this new Web site.

4. Using the Exchange Management Shell, create the new OWA virtual directory.

Accomplish the task of creating a new OWA 2007 virtual directory by using the `new-owavirtualdirectory` command. You need to specify the name of the new directory along with the IIS Web site name that you created. Additional parameters are necessary if you want to create different kinds of virtual directories or if you want to create an OWA directory that supports Exchange 2000 Server or Exchange Server 2003 mailboxes.

To create a new OWA directory that connects to Exchange Server 2007–based mailboxes, use the following command:

```
new-owavirtualdirectory -Name "owa" -website "contoso.com"
```

The results are shown in Figure 24-4. After you create the new directory, browse to it using the /owa suffix.

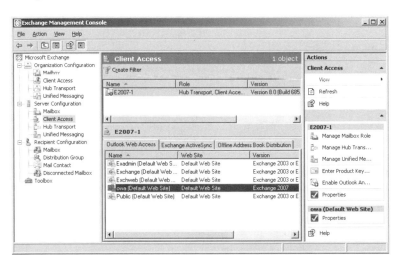

Figure 24-4   The new OWA site in the Exchange Management Console

Configuring OWA Properties and Features

By default, Exchange Server 2007 OWA does not require any further configuration to be able to serve clients. However, there are a number of configurable parameters you can use to enhance or control the OWA experience for your users. In this section, you learn how to control how users use OWA's new document sharing features and how to use Segmentation to limit what OWA features users can access.

Managing Access to UNC Shares and SharePoint Document Repositories

Perhaps the most significant functionality addition to OWA in Exchange Server 2007 is the ability for a user to access files and documents stored on your organization's Share-Point servers and other file servers. Later in this chapter, you see what this feature looks like from the user's perspective. For now, consider what this type of access means for you and your users.

The Good

Providing an easy way to remotely access server-based files and documents has some significant benefits:

- Maintaining collaborative ability for mobile users is significantly improved because all users can access all files at any time.

- Less e-mailing of documents between users helps to maintain a single instance of a document and keep the size of your information store at a reasonable level.

The Bad

With the increase in accessibility to your organization's electronic assets come some drawbacks:

- When users were able to remotely access only what was e-mailed to them, it was much less likely that your entire document repository could be leaked to the outside world.

- You have fewer controls over who is accessing organization files and when they are accessing files. While NTFS permissions are still used to protect files, users can access them in the middle of the night from a public computer at the local copy shop.

Exchange Server 2007 provides several means by which you can limit what users can do with this functionality. Among them are options to disallow access to both Windows file servers and SharePoint servers. Further, you can selectively disable access to these resources dependent on what type—public or private—of remote computer a user is using. By default, all access is enabled for all users, regardless of remote computer type. You can modify this behavior on a per-server basis.

To change this access, do the following:

1. From the Exchange server, open the Exchange Management Console.

2. Under Server Configuration, choose Client Access.

3. In the middle pane, choose OWA (Default Web Site).

4. From the Action pane, under OWA (Default Web Site), choose Properties.

5. On the Properties page are a number of tabs, with three of them related to remote file access. Adjust the selections accordingly, depending on what you want to accomplish.

     ❑ **Public Computer File Access**   The options on this tab (shown in Figure 24-5) allow you to control what users logging in from public computers are allowed to access. These settings are in effect when the users select This Is A Public Computer during the logon process.

     ❑ **Private Computer File Access**   The options on this tab allow you to control what users logging on from private computers are allowed to access. These settings are in effect when the users choose This Is A Private Computer during the logon process.

     ❑ **Remote File Servers**   The options on this tab allow you to specify file servers you want users to be able to access remotely or to which you want to disallow this type of access.

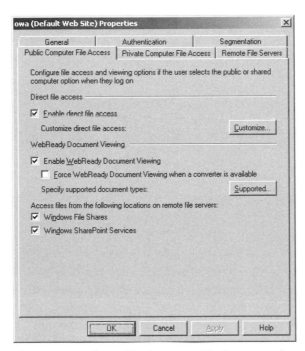

Figure 24-5   The Public Computer File Access configuration tab

The following options are on each tab:

■ **Enable Direct File Access**   When this check box is selected, users are allowed to open files that are located on Windows file servers and that are stored in Windows

SharePoint Services repositories. The Customize button next to this option opens a window (see Figure 24-6) that lets you granularly specify what types of files OWA users are allowed to remotely access (see Figure 24-7). Specify the allowed and blocked file types by clicking the appropriate button. Click Force Save to decide that users must save certain files locally before being allowed to open.

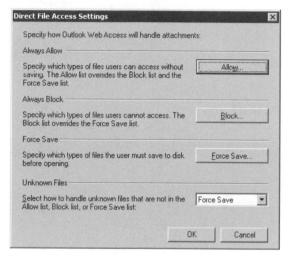

Figure 24-6   Direct File Access Settings

- **Enable WebReady Document Viewing**   WebReady Document Viewing is new to OWA 2007 and lets users view documents, including Word documents and Excel spreadsheets, inside the OWA window. WebReady Document Viewing is also used for attachments read inside OWA. WebReady Document Viewing lets users view any supported document, even if the creating application is not installed on the client computer.

- **Force WebReady Document Viewing When A Converter Is Available**   This option forces users to view attachments and other files and documents using WebReady Document Viewing before the user is allowed to open the file or document in the native application. After viewing in this way, the user is then allowed to download and open the document.

- **(Access Files From) Windows File Shares**   Select this check box to allow OWA users to access files location on Windows File Shares.

- **(Access Files From) Windows SharePoint Services**   Select this check box to allow OWA users to access files location in Windows SharePoint Services repositories.

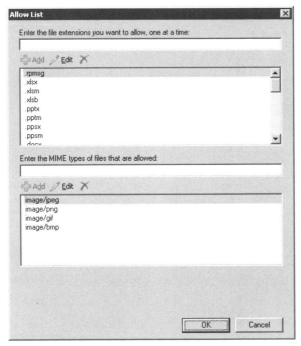

Figure 24-7   The Allow List screen

For example, if you want to disable OWA access to your file servers and SharePoint Services repositories, but only for users logging in from public terminals, clear the Enable Direct File Access check box on the Public Computer File Access tab.

Management Shell

As you probably expect, you can also manipulate these OWA file access options using the Exchange Management Shell. To disable OWA access to file servers and SharePoint Services repositories for users logging in from public terminals, use this command:

```
Set-OwaVirtualDirectory -identity "owa (Default Web Site)"
  -WebReadyDocumentViewingPublicComputersEnabled $false
```

Replace `"owa (Default Web Site)"` with the name of your OWA directory, although the listed name is the default applied during the installation of the Client Access Server role.

Other configurable parameters include:

- `DirectFileAccessOnPrivateComputersEnabled`: Determines whether you support direct file access at all for users logging on from private computers

- **DirectFileAccessOnPublicComputersEnabled**: Determines whether you support direct file access at all for users logging on from public computers

- **ForceWebReadyDocumentViewingFirstOnPrivateComputers**: Controls whether you require initial WebReady Document Viewing on public computers

- **ForceWebReadyDocumentViewingFirstOnPublicComputers**: Controls whether you require initial WebReady Document Viewing on public computers

- **UNCAccessOnPrivateComputersEnabled**: Controls whether you allow access to Windows file server from OWA when users log on from private terminals

- **UNCAccessOnPublicComputersEnabled**: Controls whether you allow access to Windows file server from OWA when users log on from public terminals

- **WebReadyDocumentViewingPrivateComputersEnabled**: Controls whether you allow WebReady Document Viewing on private computers

The last main tab, Remote File Servers (see Figure 24-8), gives you a way to control which servers are accessible by users logging on via OWA. You might have a server that contains particularly sensitive documents that you want to keep accessible only to users inside your network, for example.

These four options are available on this tab:

- **Block List** Click Block to add servers that should not be accessible from OWA. For a look at the Block List window, see Figure 24-9.

- **Allow List** Click Allow to add servers that should be accessible from OWA.

- **Unknown Servers** The Unknown Servers option lets you decide how you want to handle requests to servers that have not been added to either of the Block or Allow lists. By default, OWA is configured to allow access to all unknown servers. You can use the drop-down selector to change this behavior. If you decide to block access to unknown servers, make sure you add servers to the Allow list, or OWA remote file access is effectively disabled.

- **Configure** The Configure button sits next to the Enter The Domain Suffixes That Should Be Treated As Internal option and gives you a place to specify a list of domain suffixes. Fully qualified domain names (FQDNs) can also be added to this list and are treated as internal.

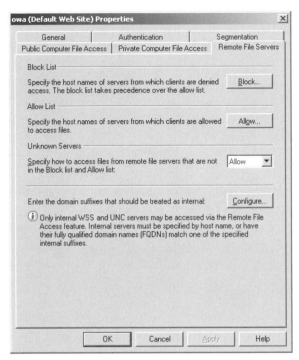

Figure 24-8   The Remote File Servers tab

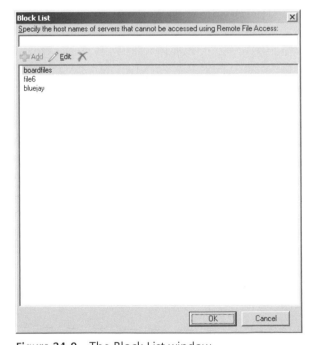

Figure 24-9   The Block List window

OWA Segmentation

OWA segmentation provides the ability to selectively enable or disable OWA features in the user's browser interface. For example, you can enable or disable calendaring, contacts, and public folders. Segmentation can occur on either a per-user or a per-server basis. User settings override server settings when a conflict arises.

Segmentation is useful when you want to limit client functionality due to training constraints or other organization-specific policies; charge a premium for certain functionalities; or lessen the performance impact of certain features on the server, the network, or a slow WAN connection from the client.

In earlier versions of Exchange, segmentation is available, but requires either modification of the registry or installation of additional administrative software. A matrix of possible segmentation values is used, with each value representing a subset of possible OWA features. In Exchange Server 2007, segmentation management has been changed. That's not to say that it's necessarily easier, though. However, no longer do you need a registry editor or additional administrative tools. You can do everything from within the Exchange Management Console and the Exchange Management Shell.

Changing segmentation settings on an OWA virtual directory basis is the easy part. However, changing segmentation settings on a per-user basis is still rather cumbersome. Start with the easy topic. To change segmentation settings for a virtual directory, follow these steps:

1. Start the Exchange Management Console.

2. From under Server Configuration, choose Client Access.

3. Select the Client Access server with the OWA instance you want to modify.

4. Right-click OWA (Default Web Site) and, from the shortcut menu, choose Properties.

5. From the Properties page, click the Segmentation tab (see Figure 24-10).

6. Select the feature you want to modify and select either Enable or Disable.

7. Click OK when you finish.

After you modify global OWA segmentation settings, the features you disable are no longer available in OWA. In Figure 24-11, you can see the effect of disabling features using the Segmentation tab. The user's default folder set for OWA is now vastly different because only the Inbox, Calendar, Contacts, and Documents options are available; Tasks, Journal, Notes, and other folders do not appear as they were disabled in the Exchange Management Console. Even the Options section is limited when you apply segmentation. Options for features that you disable no longer appear on the Options window, either.

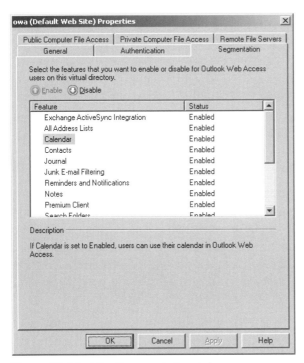

Figure 24-10   The Segmentation tab

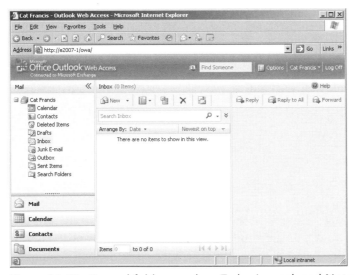

Figure 24-11   Several folders, such as Tasks, Journal, and Notes, do not appear after being disabled.

Management Shell

If you need to enable these interface limitations on a per-user basis, your only option is to use the Exchange Management Shell. The Exchange Management Console still does not provide a GUI-based way to handle per-user segmentation. From the Exchange Management Shell, the `Set-CASMailbox` command is used to handle segmentation on a per-user basis. Note that, while you can enable or disable multiple features with a single command, the command is limited to managing one user at a time.

The following command disables the calendar for the user named Cat Francis and also disables the OWA Premium client, forcing her to use the Light client.

```
Set-CASMailbox -identity cat.francis@contoso.com
  -OWACalendarEnabled:$false -OWAPremiumClientEnabled:$false
```

You're not left to hoping your command was successful, though. Use the `Get-CASMailbox` command to see which users have, for example, the OWA Calendar disabled. Accomplish this by using a filter, as shown in the example below. The results are shown in the figure.

```
get-CASmailbox | fl identity, OWACalendarEnabled,
  OWAPremiumClientEnabled
```

Where you see a blank after a colon, OWA is using the default value because a value has not been explicitly defined. After you provide a value for a user, such as `$false` or `$true`, the output from the `get-CASmailbox` command reflects that value.

Table 24-2 provides a complete list of OWA Segmentation parameters.

Table 24-2   OWA Segmentation Options

Feature	Command name (for set-CASmailbox command)	Behavior when enabled	Behavior when disabled
Exchange ActiveSync Integration	`OWAActiveSync-IntegrationEnabled`	Lets users manage mobile devices from OWA's Options window.	ActiveSync options do not appear on the Options tab.
All Address Lists	`OWAAllAddress-ListsEnabled`	User is able to see all address lists available in the Exchange organization.	User is able to see only the Global Address list.
Calendar	`OWACalendarEnabled`	The user can see and can manage his or her calendar.	The user's calendar is not accessible from Outlook Web Access.
Contacts	`OWAContactsEnabled`	The user can see and can manage his or her list of contacts.	The user's contacts are not accessible from Outlook Web Access.
Journal	`OWAJournalEnabled`	The user can see and can manage journal entries.	The user cannot see or maintain journal entries.
Junk E-mail Filtering	`OWAJunkEmailEnabled`	Users are able to manage junk e-mail settings from within OWA.	Only administrator or Outlook-enforced junk e-mail settings will be used. These settings will not be modifiable from within OWA.
Reminders and Notifications (OWA Premium only)	`OWARemindersAnd-NotificationsEnabled`	The user will receive reminders and alerts for appointments and notification of new messages.	The user will receive no automatic notifications.
Notes (View-only access)	`OWANotesEnabled`	The contents of the Notes folder are available for viewing in OWA.	The contents of the Notes folder are not made available for viewing in OWA.

Table 24-2 OWA Segmentation Options (Continued)

Feature	Command name (for set-CASmailbox command)	Behavior when enabled	Behavior when disabled
Premium Client	OWAPremiumClient-Enabled	Allows the user to make use of the enhanced functionality offered by the OWA Premium client.	Only the OWA Light client will be made available to the user.
Search Folders	OWASearchFolders-Enabled	Users can see the Search Folders icon and make use of this timesaving resource.	The Search Folders icon is visible to the user, but the search folders themselves are not available.
E-mail Signature	OWASignatures-Enabled	The user can use the Options window to manage e-mail signatures.	The user is unable to manage e-mail signatures.
Spelling Checker (OWA Premium only)	OWASpellChecker-Enabled	Makes the spell checker available for OWA users.	Users are not allowed to spell check their outgoing messages.
Tasks (OWA Premium only)	OWATasksEnabled	The user can see and can manage his or her list of tasks.	The user's tasks are not accessible from Outlook Web Access.
Theme Selection (OWA Premium only)	OWAThemeSelection-Enabled	Allows the user to select an OWA theme.	The user is forced to use the default OWA theme.
Unified Messaging Integration	OWAUMIntegration-Enabled	Allows the user to manage his or her Unified Messaging settings from within OWA.	The user is not able to manage Unified Messaging settings from OWA.
Change Password	OWAChangePassword-Enabled	The user is allowed to change his or her Active Directory password from within OWA.	Active Directory password changes are not allowed.

Real World   Important Segmentation Change in Exchange Server 2007

In previous versions of Exchange, you need to modify an Active Directory field (msExchMailboxFolderSet) to manage per-user segmentation. This requires the use of ADSI Edit or a third-party tool. By setting the msExchMailboxFolderSet field to a particular value, you can make the segmentation changes that have been discussed in this section. With the introduction of the Exchange Management Shell and the `set-CASmailbox` command, ADSI Edit is no longer necessary, but can still be used.

OWA User Features

In this section, you take a quick look at the OWA user interface. When the user opens OWA, the default interface is very similar to Outlook 2007 (see Figure 24-12), in which the panes have a vertical format. The user who wants a more traditional view of Outlook can change this default presentation by clicking the Show/Hide Preview Pane button.

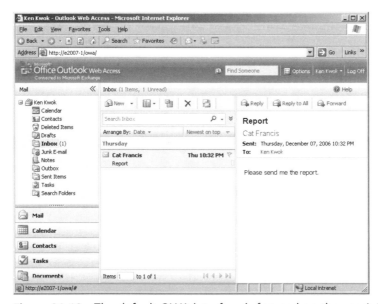

Figure 24-12   The default OWA interface is focused on the user's Inbox.

Through the OWA interface, users can also set configuration options for the following:

- Out of Office Assistant

- Messaging

- Spelling

- Secure messaging

- Privacy and junk e-mail prevention

- Date and time formats

- Calendar

- Reminders

- Contacts

- Changing the password (if enabled on the server)

- Recovering deleted items

OWA 2007 includes some impressive new functionality for the user. In this section, you learn about the most significant new feature—remote document access. This section won't cover more simple functionality, such as sending or receiving e-mail.

The Documents button in the lower-left corner of the OWA 2007 window (see Figure 24-12) provides users with ways to access documents that are stored on a Windows SharePoint Server or on a regular Windows file server.

Once a user clicks Documents, the Open Location option becomes available, as shown in Figure 24-13. Clicking this option opens a window asking the user to provide the Share-Point or Windows Server address to which the user wants to connect. In this address box, the user types the name of the resource. For Windows file shares, UNC convention works just fine. If the user doesn't know the full path to the document location, a browsing mechanism is provided.

After the user locates the document location, a list of the documents available at that location appears (see Figure 24-14). The user can open the document in the native application, but only if that native application is installed on the user's computer. Otherwise, the document can still be viewed using OWA's new WebReady Viewer application.

Note Additional details are not presented here about the OWA user experience, but OWA's new document viewing capability is significant and worthy of mention.

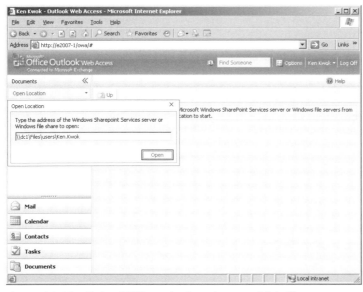

Figure 24-13   Point OWA to the location at which files are stored.

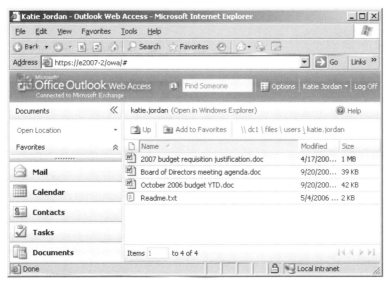

Figure 24-14   The files located at the specified location

Summary

In this chapter, you learned about the features of OWA, how to implement OWA, and how to secure client transactions. You also learned how to limit the OWA interface both at the server and user account levels. In the next chapter, you look at the various Exchange protocols, such as POP3, IMAP4, and SMTP.

Chapter 25
Supporting Other Clients

This chapter covers Post Office Protocol version 3 (POP3) and Internet Message Access Protocol version 4 (IMAP4), both of which provide alternate ways for an e-mail client to retrieve messages from an e-mail server. At first glance, talk of Internet mail foundational protocols may seem like a dry topic. However, in reality, a good understanding of the basic Internet protocols will greatly assist you in your efforts to troubleshoot and understand the Microsoft Exchange Server 2007 architecture.

POP3 and IMAP4 are different ways to access mailboxes housed on Mailbox servers (or to access other mail servers outside your organization, for that matter). Understanding the advantages and limitations of each protocol will benefit your planning, implementation, and troubleshooting efforts.

Post Office Protocol Version 3

Post Office Protocol version 3 (POP3) was developed in response to Simple Mail Transfer Protocol (SMTP) and is designed for workstations that don't have the resources to maintain both SMTP services and a message transfer system. In addition, continuous connectivity to the network for each workstation, which is necessary for an SMTP host to operate correctly, is impractical in many instances.

POP3 permits a workstation to periodically access a server that is holding e-mail for it but does not allow extensive manipulation of e-mail on the server. Instead, it is used to download e-mail from the server and into a client mail program such as Microsoft Office Outlook 2007, Outlook Express, Windows Mail, or Eudora. After the e-mail is downloaded, the server deletes its copy of the messages unless you configure your POP3 client to keep a copy of the message on the server. POP3 is a very small, fast, lean protocol that is really for e-mail retrieval only. To send e-mail, a POP3 client uses a normal SMTP connection to the destination e-mail server or a local SMTP relay server. POP3 is simply the message retrieval mechanism.

POP3 has both a client side and a server side. The server starts the POP3 service by listening on TCP port 110. When a POP3 client wants to use this service, the client establishes a TCP connection with the server and, in return, receives a greeting from the server. The client and server then exchange commands and responses until the connection is either closed or aborted. Like SMTP commands, POP3 commands are not case sensitive and can contain one or more arguments. A POP3 session between the server and the client progresses through several stages:

1. After the TCP connection is open and the POP3 server sends a greeting, the session enters the Authorization state. In this state, the client must identify itself to the POP3 server.

2. When the client is successfully authenticated, the session enters the Transaction state. During this phase, the server gathers the client's e-mail and, in response to requests from the client, sends e-mail to the client. The client's mailbox is locked to prevent messages from being modified or removed until the session enters the Update state. A series of commands and responses usually passes between the client and server during this phase.

When the client issues a QUIT command, the session enters the Update state. In this state, the POP3 server releases any resources it is holding on behalf of the client and sends a good-bye message. Messages are then deleted from the server, and the TCP session is terminated.

Table 25-1 summarizes the POP3 commands.

Table 25-1   Summary of POP3 Commands

Command	Description
USER	Supplies user name for mailbox
PASS	Supplies password for mailbox
STAT	Requests the number of messages and total size of message
LIST	Lists the index and size of all messages
RETR	Retrieves the specified messages
DELE	Deletes the specified message
NOOP	No action required
RSET	Rolls back message deletion
QUIT	Updates (commit) message deletion and terminates connection

Administering POP3 in Exchange Server 2007 can be accomplished only with the Exchange Management Shell. There is no GUI method to configure POP3. Moreover, the POP3 service is, by default, disabled after you first install Exchange Server 2007. Therefore, your tasks are to enable POP3 and then to decide which users should and should not have the ability to retrieve their mail from your servers.

Enabling POP3

Making the POP3 service available for your users is actually pretty easy and can be accomplished in one of two ways. First, you can use the Exchange Management Shell, which you have been exposed to throughout this book. Second, simply start the Microsoft Exchange POP3 service from the Services control panel. Remember, if you decide to use the control panel option, change the Microsoft Exchange POP3 service to start up automatically, too.

Management Shell

Because POP3 cannot be managed using the Exchange Management Console, Microsoft provides an administration mechanism via the Exchange Management Shell. To start the POP3 service from the Exchange Management Shell, use the following commands:

```
set-service msExchangePOP3 -startuptype automatic
start-service -service msExchangePOP3
```

Note that you need to execute these commands from the Client Access server role server to which you want your clients to connect. By default, the POP3 service starts on TCP port 110 for unencrypted communication and on port 995 for encrypted traffic.

Administering POP3

After you enable POP3 on your Client Access server role server, all users can use POP3 to retrieve their mail from the server. However, be aware of some things before you proceed.

First, by default, the Exchange Server 2007 POP3 service is configured to accept only secure connections. If you set up a POP3 client like you always have, the chances are good that you'll be greeted with an error message that reads something like "Command is not valid in this state." Basically, this cryptic message is telling you that you can't submit plain text credentials to the POP3 server because it expected an SSL-secure logon.

You can fix this in one of two ways:

1. Change the Exchange Server 2007 POP3 server to accept plain text logons.

2. If possible, reconfigure your POP3 client to use an SSL-secured authentication method. This is the preferred method as it maintains the highest level of security.

Management Shell

Managing the POP3 service is, at the present time, accomplished solely through the Exchange Management Shell. If you have a client that cannot be configured to provide a secure logon, you can change the POP3 server's settings to accept a plain text logon. Use the `Set-PopSetting` command, as shown here.

```
Set-PopSettings -LoginType PlainTextLogin
```

After you make any configuration change to the POP3 service, restart the service for the change to take effect.

```
restart-service -service msExchangePOP3
```

Note No matter how hard you try, you can't use POP3 on the Administrator's mailbox. For security reasons, Microsoft does not enable this accessibility feature for this most important administrative account. So, if you are frustrated by trying to make POP3 work, and you have already allowed plain text logons, make sure you're testing with an account other than Administrator.

Limiting POP3 Access

In this day of careful e-mail tracking and in our litigious society, you may not want to allow certain individuals—top executives, for example—to be able to pop their mail off your servers.

To accomplish your goals, you can disable POP3 access to mailboxes on a user-by-user basis. Again, you can do this only from the Exchange Management Console. There is no GUI tool to manage POP3 access (yet).

Management Shell

Like the POP3 service itself, managing access to the POP3 service is accomplished through the Exchange Management Shell. By default, all users are allowed to use POP3. Use the `set-CASMailbox` command to manage user access to the POP3 protocol. The following command is used to disable a user's access to POP3.

```
set-CASMailbox -identity cat.francis@contoso.com -POPEnabled:$false
```

Conversely, the next command reenables a user's access to POP3.

```
set-CASMailbox -identity cat.francis@contoso.com -POPEnabled:$true
```

You can verify that Exchange accepted your configuration change by issuing the following command:

```
get-CASMailbox -identity cat.francis@contoso.com
```

The following screen shows you the output from the **get-CASMailbox** command for the user that has had POP3 access disabled.

In these examples, the name "cat.francis@contoso.com" is used for examples only. In your work, make sure to use the name of a user in your own organization. After you make configuration changes to the POP3 server, restart the server or your changes may not take effect. To restart the server using the management shell, use the following command:

```
restart-service -service msExchangePOP3
```

Other POP3 Parameters

Exchange Server 2007 provides a number of configurable parameters that relate to the POP3 service. Get a complete look at how your POP3 service is configured by issuing the **get-PopSettings** command from the Exchange Management Shell. Figure 25-1 gives you a sample of what this output looks like.

Figure 25-1   Exchange Server 2007 POP3 settings

The partner command to **get-popsettings**, **set-popsettings** (which you also saw earlier in this chapter) is the vehicle through which you, as the administrator, make changes to how POP3 works in your environment. For example, to increase the maximum number of connections allowed to your POP3 server from the default of 2,000 to 5,000, use the command `set-popsettings -maxconnections 5000`. As usual, the Exchange Management Shell will not respond indicating that your command was successful, but the shell lets you know whether you made a mistake. Table 25-2 provides you with a complete look at the configurable parameters included with the Exchange Server 2007 POP3 server.

Table 25-2   Set-PopSettings Parameters List

Parameter	Default	Possible values	Description
Authenticated-ConnectionTimeout *value*	1,800 seconds	30 to 86,400 seconds	Specifies the time to wait before closing an idle authenticated connection.
Banner *string*			This parameter specifies the banner string that is displayed after a connection to a Client Access server has been established.
CalendarItem-RetrievalOption	iCalendar	iCalendar, intranetUrl, InternetUrl, Custom	This parameter specifies the type of calendar item that is returned when the calendar is accessed by using POP3.
DomainController *String*			To specify the fully qualified domain name (FQDN) of the domain controller that retrieves data from the Active Directory directory service, include the `DomainController` parameter in the command.
Instance Pop3AdConfiguration			The `Instance` parameter enables you to pass an entire object to the command to be processed. It is mainly used in scripts where an entire object must be passed to the command.
LoginType	SecureLogin	PlainTextLogin, PlainTextAuthentication, SecureLogin	This parameter specifies the authentication setting that is used for the Client Access server that is running the POP3 service.
MaxCommandSize *value*	40 bytes	40 to 1,024 bytes	This parameter specifies the maximum size of a single command.

Table 25-2 Set-PopSettings Parameters List (Continued)

Parameter	Default	Possible values	Description
MaxConnection-FromSingleIP *Value*	20 connec-tions	1 to 1,000 connections	This parameter specifies the number of connections that the specified server will accept from a single IP address.
MaxConnections *value*	2000 connections	1 to 25,000 connections	Top of Form Specifies the total number of connections the specified server will accept. This includes authenticated and unauthenticated connections.
MaxConnections-PerUser *value*	10 connec-tions	1 to 1,000 connections	Bottom of Form This parameter specifies the maximum number of con-nections that the Client Access server will accept from a particular user.
MessageRetrieval-MimeFormat	BestBody-Format	TextOnly, HtmlOnly, Htm-lAndTextAlternative, Tex-tEnrichedOnly, TextEnrichedAndText-Alternative, BestBodyFormat>	This parameter specifies the format of the messages that are retrieved from the server.
MessageRetrieval-SortOrder	Descending	Ascending, Descending	This parameter specifies the order in which the retrieved messages are sorted.
OwaServerUrl *string*			This parameter specifies the Client Access server from which to retrieve calendar information for instances of custom Outlook Web Access calendar items.
preAuthenticated-ConnectionTimeout *value*	60 seconds	10 to 3,600 seconds	This parameter specifies the period of time to wait before closing an idle connection that is not authenticated.

Table 25-2   Set-PopSettings Parameters List (Continued)

Parameter	Default	Possible values	Description
ProxyTargetPort *value*	110		This parameter specifies the port on the Exchange Server 2003 back-end server to which the POP3 service on a Client Access server will relay commands.
Server <ServerId-Parameter>			This parameter specifies an individual Client Access server in your organization for which you are specifying POP3 settings.
SSLBindings *MultipleValues*	995		If this parameter is specified, the cmdlet returns the IP port to use f or a Secure Sockets Layer (SSL) session.
UnencryptedOrTLS-Bindings *MultipleValues*	110		This parameter specifies the IP port for communication over the Transport Layer Security (TLS)–encrypted connection or the connection that is not encrypted.
X509CertificateName <String>	Server name		This parameter specifies the host name in the SSL certificate from the Associated Subject field.

Even though Exchange Server 2007 does not include a GUI to manage POP3 settings, there is really very little that needs to be done besides initially enabling the POP3 server and making sure that your clients can connect via a POP3 client. The hard part is determining who is allowed to use the service.

Internet Messaging Access Protocol 4

In POP3, once a message has been downloaded from the server, it is, by default, deleted from the server unless the user proactively configures his e-mail client to act otherwise. This deletion is a real disadvantage for users who move from workstation to workstation because e-mail they have already downloaded remains on the workstation to which they downloaded it. IMAP4 was developed to allow users to leave their e-mail on the server and to allow remote access to messages. Thus, IMAP4 extends the functionality of POP3 to allow both offline and online storage of messages.

In addition, IMAP4 allows user-initiated storage of messages and nonmail messages, permits users to manage their own configurations, and allows the sharing of mailboxes. This protocol allows a client to manipulate e-mail messages on a server as though it were a local mailbox, unlike POP3, which can do little more than copy a message from a POP3 server to a local mailbox.

Table 25-3 lists the more common IMAP4 commands.

Table 25-3   IMAP4 Commands

Command	Description
CAPABILITY	Requests a listing of the functionality of the server
AUTHENTICATE	Indicates an authentication mechanism
LOGIN	Identifies a client with user name and password
SELECT	Selects the mailbox to use
EXAMINE	Selects a mailbox in read-only mode
CREATE	Creates a mailbox
DELETE	Deletes a mailbox
RENAME	Renames a mailbox
SUBSCRIBE	Adds a mailbox to the server's set of active mailboxes
UNSUBSCRIBE	Removes a mailbox from the server's set of active mailboxes
LIST	Lists a set or subset of mailboxes
LSUB	Lists subscribed mailboxes
STATUS	Requests the status of a mailbox
APPEND	Adds a message to a mailbox
CLOSE	Effects pending deletions and closes a mailbox
EXPUNGE	Effects pending deletions
SEARCH	Searches a mailbox for messages satisfying a given criterion
FETCH	Fetches specified body parts for a given message
STORE	Changes the data of specified messages in a mailbox
COPY	Copies a message to another mailbox
NOOP	No action required
LOGOUT	Closes the connection

Enabling IMAP4

Like POP3, Exchange Server 2007's IMAP server does not come in a running state. However, it's easy to start the service—a task accomplished either via the Services control panel or through the Exchange Management Shell. Remember, if you decide to use the Services control panel option, you should change the Microsoft Exchange IMAP4 service to start up automatically, too. The full name of the service is Microsoft Exchange IMAP4.

Management Shell

Because you cannot manage IMAP4 using the Exchange Management Console, Microsoft provides an administration mechanism via the Exchange Management Shell. To start the IMAP4 service from the Exchange Management Shell, use the following commands:

```
set-service msExchangeImap4 -startuptype automatic
start-service -service msExchangeImap4
```

Note that you need to execute this command from the Client Access server role server to which you want your clients to connect. By default, the IMAP4 service starts on TCP port 143 for unencrypted communication and on port 993 for encrypted traffic.

Administering IMAP4

After enabling IMAP4 on your Client Access server role server, all users—unless you specify otherwise—can use IMAP4 to manage their server-based e-mail. However, be aware of some things before you proceed.

First, by default, Exchange Server 2007's IMAP4 service is configured to accept only secure connections. If you initially set up an IMAP4 client, the chances are pretty good that you'll be greeted with an error message indicating that the logon to the IMAP server failed. This error message is telling you that you can't submit plan text credentials to the IMAP server because it expected an SSL-secure logon.

You can fix this in one of two ways:

1. Change the Exchange Server 2007 IMAP4 server to accept plain-text logons.

2. If possible, reconfigure your IMAP4 client to use an SSL-secured authentication method. This is definitely the preferred, more secure method, but not all IMAP4 clients support SSL.

Management Shell

Managing the IMAP4 service also happens solely through the Exchange Management Shell. If you have a client that cannot be configured to provide a secure logon, you can change the IMAP4 server's settings to accept a plain-text logon. Use the `Set-IMAPSetting` command, as shown here.

```
Set-IMAPSettings -LoginType PlainTextLogin
```

After you make any configuration change to the POP3 service, restart the service for the change to take effect.

```
restart-service -service msExchangeIMAP4
```

Note   As is the case with POP3, you cannot use IMAP4 with the Administrator's mailbox. Microsoft considers this a security weakness and disabled this behavior. So, if you are frustrated by trying to make IMAP4 work, and you have already allowed plain text logons, make sure you test with an account other than Administrator.

Limiting IMAP4 Access

For the most part, IMAP4 requires little administration with the exception of starting the service. After you enable POP3 on your Client Access server role server, all users can use the service to retrieve their mail from the server. Like POP3, IMAP4's initial configuration allows all users to use the service. Through the use of the `set-CASMailbox` command, you can enable and disable a user's ability to use IMAP4. can disable IMAP4 access to mailboxes on a user-by-user basis.

Management Shell

Manage access to the IMAP4 service through the Exchange Management Shell. By default, all users are allowed to use IMAP4. Use the `set-CASMailbox` command to manage user access to the IMAP4 protocol. The following command is used to disable a user's access to IMAP4.

```
set-CASMailbox -identity cat.francis@contoso.com -ImapEnabled:$false
```

Conversely, the next command reenables a user's access to IMAP4.

```
set-CASMailbox -identity cat.francis@contoso.com -ImapEnabled:$true
```

You can verify that Exchange accepted your configuration change by issuing the following command:

```
get-CASMailbox -identity cat.francis@contoso.com
```

The graphic below shows you the output from this command.

In all instances, replace "*cat.francis@contoso.com*" with the name of a user in your own environment. After you make configuration changes to the IMAP4 server, restart the server or your changes may not take effect. To restart the server using the management shell, use the following command:

```
restart-service -service msExchangeImap4
```

Exchange Server 2007 provides a number of configurable parameters that relate to the IMAP4 service. Get a complete look at how your IMAP4 service is configured by issuing the `get-imapsettings` command from the Exchange Management Shell. Figure 25-2 gives you a sample of what this output looks like.

Figure 25-2 Exchange Server 2007 IMAP4 settings

The partner command to `get-imapsettings` is `set-imapsettings` and is the way you make changes to how IMAP4 works in your environment. For example, to change the way that the IMAP4 server handles calendaring, use the command `set-imapsettings -CalendarItemRetrievalOption IntranetURL`. As usual, the Exchange Management Shell will not respond indicating that your command was successful, but the shell lets you know whether you made a mistake. Table 25-4 provides you with a complete look at the configurable parameters included with the Exchange Server 2007 IMAP4 server.

Table 25-4   Set-ImapSettings Parameters List

Parameter	Default	Possible values	Description
`Authenticated-ConnectionTimeout` *value*	1,800 seconds	30 to 86,400 seconds	Specifies the time to wait before closing an idle authenticated connection.
`Banner` *string*			This parameter specifies the banner string that is displayed after a connection to a Client Access server has been established.
`CalendarItem-RetrievalOption`	iCalendar	iCalendar, intranetUrl, InternetUrl, Custom	This parameter specifies the type of calendar item that is returned when the calendar is accessed by using IMAP4.
`DomainController` *String*			To specify the fully qualified domain name (FQDN) of the domain controller that retrieves data from the Active Directory directory service, include the `DomainController` parameter in the command.
`Instance`			The `Instance` parameter enables you to pass an entire object to the command to be processed. It is mainly used in scripts where an entire object must be passed to the command.
`LoginType`	SecureLogin	PlainTextLogin, PlainTextAuthentication, SecureLogin	This parameter specifies the authentication setting that is used for the Client Access server that is running the IMAP4 service.

Table 25-4   Set-ImapSettings Parameters List (Continued)

Parameter	Default	Possible values	Description
MaxCommandSize *value*	40 bytes	40 to 1,024 bytes	This parameter specifies the maximum size of a single command.
MaxConnection-FromSingleIP *Value*	20 connections	1 to 1,000 connections	This parameter specifies the number of connections that the specified server will accept from a single IP address.
MaxConnections *value*	2000 connections	1 to 25,000 connections	Top of Form Specifies the total number of connections the specified server will accept. This includes authenticated and unauthenticated connections.
MaxConnections-PerUser *value*	10 connections	1 to 1,000 connections	Bottom of Form This parameter specifies the maximum number of connections that the Client Access server will accept from a particular user.
MessageRetrieval-MimeFormat	BestBody-Format	TextOnly, HtmlOnly, HtmlAndTextAlternative, TextEnrichedOnly, TextEnrichedAnd-TextAlternative, BestBodyFormat>	This parameter specifies the format of the messages that are retrieved from the server.
MessageRetrieval-SortOrder	Descending	Ascending, Descending	This parameter specifies the order in which the retrieved messages are sorted.
OwaServerUrl *string*			This parameter specifies the Client Access server from which to retrieve calendar information for instances of custom Outlook Web Access calendar items.
preAuthenticated-ConnectionTimeout *value*	60 seconds	10 to 3,600 seconds	This parameter specifies the period of time to wait before closing an idle connection that is not authenticated.

Table 25-4   Set-ImapSettings Parameters List (Continued)

Parameter	Default	Possible values	Description
ProxyTargetPort *value*	43		This parameter specifies the port on the Exchange Server 2003 back-end server to which the IMAP4 service on a Client Access server will relay commands.
Server <ServerId- Parameter>			This parameter specifies an individual Client Access server in your organization for which you are specifying IMAP4 settings.
SSLBindings *MultipleValues*	993		If this parameter is specified, the cmdlet returns the IP port to use f or a Secure Sockets Layer (SSL) session.
UnencryptedOr- TLSBindings *MultipleValues*	143		This parameter specifies the IP port for communication over the Transport Layer Security (TLS)-encrypted connection or the connection that is not encrypted.
X509Certificate- Name <String>	Server name		This parameter specifies the host name in the SSL certificate from the Associated Subject field.

POP3/IMAP4 Considerations

There are a few things you should keep in mind when it comes to administering POP3 and IMAP4 on your Exchange Server 2007 server. First, if you test connections from a client to your server, bear in mind that you can't log in to an Exchange Server 2007 POP3/IMAP server using the built-in administrator account. For security reasons, Microsoft disabled this ability. Second, the biggest frustration that most people are having with POP3 and IMAP4 under Exchange Server 2007 lies with the default login security. By default, both services are locked down, meaning that you need to either loosen the server-side security restrictions or require users to use clients that support higher levels of security. Third, make absolutely sure that you restart the POP3 or IMAP4 service after you make configuration changes! Failure to do this in an initial run-through can lead to many problems. Embarrassingly, even authors of computer books can forget this crucial step. One author failed to restart services during the initial run-through of this chapter and caused himself a few hours of heartache.

Finally, if you have users connecting to your Exchange server using POP3 or IMAP4, make sure that you have the right firewall ports opened up for them. If you require secure clients, POP3 uses TCP port 995 while IMAP4 uses port 993. For unsecured, or plaintext, clients, POP3 uses port 110, and IMAP4 uses port 143.

Summary

In this chapter, you learned some of the basics of SMTP, POP3, and IMAP4. You learned how to read the more common commands of these protocols and how to log the interaction between the server and client for troubleshooting purposes.

Part VIII
Appendices

Appendix A
Default Directory Structure for Exchange Server 2007

Table A-1 lists the names of the major Microsoft Exchange directories and subdirectories created during installation, along with their contents. The path for each directory is shown relative to the default root Exchange folder, \Program Files\Microsoft\Exchange Server.

Table A-1   Default Directory Structure for Exchange Server 2007

Directory	Contents
\bin	Exchange executables and core services.
\bin\Res	DLLs for Event Viewer and System Monitor.
\clientaccess\autodiscover	Components that allow Outlook 2007 clients to perform automatic discovery of available Exchange servers and mailboxes with minimal user input.
\clientaccess\exchweb	Components for Microsoft Outlook Web Access.
\clientaccess\OAB	Components for synchronization of Offline Address Books.
\clientaccess\OWA	Components for Microsoft Outlook Web Access.
\clientaccess\PopImap	Components for POP3 and IMAP4 access.
\clientaccess\sync	Components for synchronization of offline folders.
\logging	Storage of various Exchange Server 2007 log files. See Appendix C, "Default Log File Locations," for more information.
\mailbox	Information store database files (Priv.edb, Priv.stm, Pub.edb, Pub.stm).
\Mailbox\Schema	XML files supporting the Exchange extension of the Active Directory Schema.
\scripts	Scripts for Exchange Management Shell cmdlets.
\Transport Roles	Logs for message tracking and Exchange message queues.
\Unified Messaging	Components for Unified Messaging role
\working	Working directories for message transfer.

Appendix B
Delivery Status Notification Codes

Even in the best-conceived and best-managed Microsoft Exchange environments, you are bound to have messages that just can't make it through the system. When a message experiences a fatal error and cannot be delivered, Microsoft Exchange Server 2007 (and other mail servers) returns a nondelivery report (NDR) to the sender and optionally to an administrator. Although it's rare to see NDRs generated by internal transmissions (messages sent between recipients in the same organization), it is possible. It is much more likely to see NDRs generated by non-Exchange mail servers outside the Exchange organization. Understanding the structure and coding of an NDR can help you determine where a mail flow problem is occurring.

As you recall, NDRs are system messages that report the delivery status of a message to the sender. (The structure of NDRs is defined in Request for Comments [RFC] 1893.) They are a subclass of a general message information structure referred to as *delivery status notifications* (DSNs). An NDR provides a three-digit delivery status notification code, such as 4.4.1, that identifies the failure more precisely. Each digit of the code provides information about the failure. The first digit indicates one of three different situations:

- **2.x.x** Successful transfer
- **4.x.x** Persistent transient failure
- **5.x.x** Permanent failure

Table B-1 lists the second- and third-digit codes and their meanings. For example, the code 4.4.1 indicates a persistent transient failure because the host being sent the message did not answer.

Table B-1 Standard Delivery Status Notification Codes

Code	Description
x.1.0	Other address status
x.1.1	Bad destination mailbox address
x.1.2	Bad destination system address
x.1.3	Bad destination mailbox address syntax
x.1.4	Destination mailbox address ambiguous

Table B-1   Standard Delivery Status Notification Codes (Continued)

Code	Description
x.1.5	Destination mailbox address valid
x.1.6	Mailbox has moved
x.1.7	Bad sender's mailbox address syntax
x.1.8	Bad sender's system address
x.2.0	Other or undefined mailbox status
x.2.1	Mailbox disabled, not accepting messages
x.2.2	Mailbox full
x.2.3	Message length exceeds administrative limit
x.2.4	Mailing list expansion problem
x.3.0	Other or undefined mail system status
x.3.1	Mail system full
x.3.2	System not accepting network messages
x.3.3	System not capable of selected features
x.3.4	Message too big for system
x.4.0	Other or undefined network or routing status
x.4.1	No answer from host
x.4.2	Bad connection
x.4.3	Routing server failure
x.4.4	Unable to route
x.4.5	Network congestion
x.4.6	Routing loop detected
x.4.7	Delivery time expired
x.5.0	Other or undefined protocol status
x.5.1	Invalid command
x.5.2	Syntax error
x.5.3	Too many recipients
x.5.4	Invalid command arguments
x.5.5	Wrong protocol version
x.6.0	Other or undefined media error
x.6.1	Media not supported
x.6.2	Conversion required and prohibited
x.6.3	Conversion required but not supported

Table B-1   Standard Delivery Status Notification Codes (Continued)

Code	Description
x.6.4	Conversion with loss performed
x.6.5	Conversion failed
x.7.0	Other or undefined security status
x.7.1	Delivery not authorized, message refused
x.7.2	Mailing list expansion prohibited
x.7.3	Security conversion required but not possible
x.7.4	Security features not supported
x.7.5	Cryptographic failure
x.7.6	Cryptographic algorithm not supported
x.7.7	Message integrity failure

Appendix C
Default Log File Locations

Table C-1 lists the default storage locations of the major log files in Microsoft Exchange Server 2007.

Table C-1   Exchange Server 2007 Log File Locations

Log	Default location
Agent Logs	C:\Program Files\Microsoft\Exchange Server\TransportRoles\Logs\AgentLog
Connectivity Logs	C:\Program Files\Microsoft\Exchange Server\TransportRoles\Logs\Connectivity
Diagnostic Logging	Windows Event Viewer Application Log
HTTP Virtual Server	C:\WINDOWS\System32\LogFiles\HttpSvc#*inyymmdd*.log
Message Tracking	C:\Program Files\Microsoft\Exchange Server\TransportRoles\Logs\Message Tracking
Protocol Logs	C:\Program Files\Microsoft\Exchange Server\TransportRoles\Logs\ProtocolLog
Routing Table Logs	C:\Program Files\Microsoft\Exchange Server\TransportRoles\Logs\Routing
Setup Logs	C:\ \Exchange Setup Logs\
Trace Logs	C:\Program Files\Microsoft\Exchange Serv-er\Logging\TraceLogs
Transaction Logs	C:\Program Files\Microsoft\Exchange Server\mailbox*storagegroup*

Appendix D

Default Diagnostic Logging Levels for Exchange Processes

Table D-1 shows the Exchange processes for which you can modify the diagnostic logging levels and the default logging level for each process.

Table D-1   Event Types Displayed in Event Viewer

Exchange process	Default logging level
MSExchange ActiveSync\Requests	Lowest
MSExchange ActiveSync\Configuration	Lowest
MSExchange ADAccess\Topology	Low
MSExchange ADAccess\Validation	Low
MSExchange Antispam\General	Lowest
MSExchange Assistants\Assistants	Lowest
MSExchange Autodiscover\Core	Lowest
MSExchange Autodiscover\Web	Lowest
MSExchange Autodiscover\Provider	Lowest
MSExchange Availability\Availability Service	Lowest
MSExchange Availability\Availability Service General	Lowest
MSExchange Availability\Availability Service Authentication	Lowest
MSExchange Availability\Availability Service Authorization	Lowest
MSExchange Cluster\Move	Lowest
MSExchange Cluster\Upgrade	Lowest
MSExchange Cluster\Action	Lowest
MSExchange Common\General	Lowest
MSExchange Common\Configuration	Lowest
MSExchange Common\Logging	Lowest
MSExchange Extensibility\Transport Address Book	Lowest
MSExchange Extensibility\MExRuntime	Lowest
MSExchange EdgeSync\Synchronization	Lowest
MSExchange EdgeSync\Topology	Lowest

Table D-1   Event Types Displayed in Event Viewer (Continued)

Exchange process	Default logging level
MSExchange EdgeSync\SyncNow	Lowest
MSExchange TransportService\TransportService	Lowest
MSExchange Web Services\Core	Lowest
MSExchange IMAP4\General	Lowest
MSExchange Messaging Policies\Journaling	Lowest
MSExchange Messaging Policies\AttachFilter	Lowest
MSExchange Messaging Policies\AddressRewrite	Lowest
MSExchange Messaging Policies\Rules	Lowest
MSExchange Messaging Policies\Prelicensing	Lowest
MSExchange Antispam Update\HygieneUpdate	Lowest
MSExchange Management Application\Shell	Lowest
MSExchange Management Application\Console	Lowest
MSExchange OWA\FormsRegistry	Lowest
MSExchange OWA\Core	Lowest
MSExchange OWA\Configuration	Lowest
MSExchange OWA\Themes	Lowest
MSExchange OWA\SmallIcons	Lowest
MSExchange OWA\Proxy	Lowest
MSExchange OWA\Transcoding	Lowest
MSExchange OWA\ADNotifications	Lowest
MSExchange POP3\General	Lowest
MSExchange Process Manager\ProcessManager	Lowest
MSExchange Repl\Service	Lowest
MSExchange Repl\Exchange VSS Writer	Lowest
MSExchange Search Indexer\General	Lowest
MSExchange Search Indexer\Configuration	Lowest
MSExchange Store Driver\General	Lowest
MSExchange System Attendant Mailbox\General	Lowest
MSExchange Topology\Topology Discovery	Lowest
MSExchange Unified Messaging\UMWorkerProcess	Lowest
MSExchange Unified Messaging\UMCore	Lowest
MSExchange Unified Messaging\UMManagement	Lowest

Table D-1   Event Types Displayed in Event Viewer (Continued)

Exchange process	Default logging level
MSExchange Unified Messaging\UMService	Lowest
MSExchange Unified Messaging\UMClientAccess	Lowest
MSExchange Unified Messaging\UMCallData	Lowest
MSExchange ADAccess\General	Lowest
MSExchange ADAccess\Cache	Lowest
MSExchange ADAccess\Topology	Lowest
MSExchange ADAccess\Configuration	Lowest
MSExchange ADAccess\LDAP	Lowest
MSExchange ADAccess\Validation	Lowest
MSExchange ADAccess\Recipient Update Service	Lowest
MSExchange ADAccess\Site Update	Lowest
MSExchangeAL\Ldap Operations	Lowest
MSExchangeAL\Service Control	Lowest
MSExchangeAL\Attribute Mapping	Lowest
MSExchangeAL\Account Management	Lowest
MSExchangeAL\Address List Synchronization	Lowest
MSExchangeIS\9000 Private\Transport General	Lowest
MSExchangeIS\9000 Private\General	Lowest
MSExchangeIS\9000 Private\Transport Sending	Lowest
MSExchangeIS\9000 Private\Transport Delivering	Lowest
MSExchangeIS\9000 Private\Transfer Into Gateway	Lowest
MSExchangeIS\9000 Private\Transfer Out Of Gateway	Lowest
MSExchangeIS\9000 Private\MTA Connections	Lowest
MSExchangeIS\9000 Private\Logons	Lowest
MSExchangeIS\9000 Private\Access Control	Lowest
MSExchangeIS\9000 Private\Send On Behalf Of	Lowest
MSExchangeIS\9000 Private\Send As	Lowest
MSExchangeIS\9000 Private\Rules	Lowest
MSExchangeIS\9000 Private\Storage Limits	Lowest
MSExchangeIS\9000 Private\Background Cleanup	Lowest
MSExchangeIS\9000 Private\DS Synchronization	Lowest
MSExchangeIS\9000 Private\Views	Lowest

Table D-1   Event Types Displayed in Event Viewer (Continued)

Exchange process	Default logging level
MSExchangeIS\9000 Private\Download	Lowest
MSExchangeIS\9000 Private\Local Replication	Lowest
MSExchangeIS\9001 Public\Transport General	Lowest
MSExchangeIS\9001 Public\General	Lowest
MSExchangeIS\9001 Public\Replication DS Updates	Lowest
MSExchangeIS\9001 Public\Replication Incoming Messages	Lowest
MSExchangeIS\9001 Public\Replication Outgoing Messages	Lowest
MSExchangeIS\9001 Public\Replication NDRs	Lowest
MSExchangeIS\9001 Public\Transport Sending	Lowest
MSExchangeIS\9001 Public\Transport Delivering	Lowest
MSExchangeIS\9001 Public\MTA Connections	Lowest
MSExchangeIS\9001 Public\Logons	Lowest
MSExchangeIS\9001 Public\Access Control	Lowest
MSExchangeIS\9001 Public\Send On Behalf Of	Lowest
MSExchangeIS\9001 Public\Send As	Lowest
MSExchangeIS\9001 Public\Rules	Lowest
MSExchangeIS\9001 Public\Storage Limits	Lowest
MSExchangeIS\9001 Public\Replication Site Folders	Lowest
MSExchangeIS\9001 Public\Replication Expiry	Lowest
MSExchangeIS\9001 Public\Replication Conflicts	Lowest
MSExchangeIS\9001 Public\Replication Backfill	Lowest
MSExchangeIS\9001 Public\Background Cleanup	Lowest
MSExchangeIS\9001 Public\Replication Errors	Lowest
MSExchangeIS\9001 Public\DS Synchronization	Lowest
MSExchangeIS\9001 Public\Views	Lowest
MSExchangeIS\9001 Public\Replication General	Lowest
MSExchangeIS\9001 Public\Download	Lowest
MSExchangeIS\9001 Public\Local Replication	Lowest
MSExchangeIS\9002 System\Recovery	Lowest
MSExchangeIS\9002 System\General	Lowest
MSExchangeIS\9002 System\Connections	Lowest
MSExchangeIS\9002 System\Table Cache	Lowest

Table D-1   Event Types Displayed in Event Viewer (Continued)

Exchange process	Default logging level
MSExchangeIS\9002 System\Content Engine	Lowest
MSExchangeIS\9002 System\Performance Monitor	Lowest
MSExchangeIS\9002 System\Move Mailbox	Lowest
MSExchangeIS\9002 System\Download	Lowest
MSExchangeIS\9002 System\Virus Scanning	Lowest
MSExchangeIS\9002 System\Exchange Writer	Lowest
MSExchangeIS\9002 System\Backup Restore	Lowest
MSExchangeIS\9002 System\Client Monitoring	Lowest
MSExchangeIS\9002 System\Event History	Lowest
MSExchangeIS\9002 System\Database Storage Engine	Lowest
MSExchangeMailboxAssistants\Service	Lowest
MSExchangeMailboxAssistants\OOF Assistant	Lowest
MSExchangeMailboxAssistants\OOF Library	Lowest
MSExchangeMailboxAssistants\Resource Booking Attendant	Lowest
MSExchangeMailboxAssistants\Email_Lifecycle_Assistant	Lowest
MSExchangeMailSubmission\General	Lowest
MSExchangeMU\General	Lowest
MSExchangeSA\Clean Mailbox	Lowest
MSExchangeSA\NSPI Proxy	Lowest
MSExchangeSA\RFR Interface	Lowest
MSExchangeSA\OAL Generator	Lowest
MSExchangeSA\Proxy Generation	Lowest
MSExchangeSA\RPC Calls	Lowest
MSExchangeSA\RPC-HTTP Management	Lowest
MSExchangeTransport\SmtpReceive	Lowest
MSExchangeTransport\SmtpSend	Lowest
MSExchangeTransport\DSN	Lowest
MSExchangeTransport\Routing	Lowest
MSExchangeTransport\Logging	Lowest
MSExchangeTransport\Components	Lowest
MSExchangeTransport\RemoteDelivery	Lowest
MSExchangeTransport\Pickup	Lowest

Table D-1   Event Types Displayed in Event Viewer (Continued)

Exchange process	Default logging level
MSExchangeTransport\Categorizer	Lowest
MSExchangeTransport\PoisonMessage	Lowest
MSExchangeTransport\MessageSecurity	Lowest
MSExchangeTransport\TransportService	Lowest
MSExchangeTransport\Exch50	Lowest
MSExchangeTransport\Process	Lowest
MSExchangeTransport\ResourceManager	Lowest
MSExchangeTransport\Configuration	Lowest
MSExchangeTransport\Storage	Lowest
MSExchangeTransport\Agents	Lowest
MSExchangeFDS\General	Lowest
MSExchangeFDS\FileReplication	Lowest

Glossary

Actions pane   The area of the Exchange Management Console that displays actions you can perform based on the object selected in the Console Tree, Results pane, or Work pane.

Active Clustered Mailbox role   A highly available mailbox providing a hot standby of your mailbox database.

Active Directory   The Microsoft Windows directory service, which consists of a forest, one or more domains, organizational units, containers, and objects. Various classes of objects can be represented within Active Directory, including users, groups, computers, printers, and applications.

active/passive clusters   Usually works with a two-node arrangement, in which one node is active and maintains control over the quorum, while the other node waits in the wings. In Exchange Server 2007, log shipping and log replay keep the passive node current.

administrative group   In Exchange 2000 Server and Exchange Server 2003, a collection of Exchange servers that can be administered as a single unit. An administrative group can include policies, routing groups, public folder trees, monitors, servers, conferencing services, and chat networks. When security settings (permissions) are applied to an administrative group, all child objects in the tree inherit the same permissions as the administration group node. Exchange Server 2007 no longer supports administrative groups.

alias   An alternate e-mail name for a user that can be used when sending a message to the recipient (especially from an outside system like the Internet).

anonymous authentication   Used with OWA forms-based authentication and is the least secure authentication scheme, providing limited access for specific public folders and directory information. Supported by all clients and is the preferred method of allowing general public access to specific public folders.

Application Log   A record of events generated by applications. All Exchange Server 2007 services write their status information to this log.

asymmetric keys   A system in which the sender and recipient use different keys to encrypt and decrypt data. A public key is used to encrypt the data, and a private key is used to decrypt it.

attachment filtering   Provides a way to block potentially dangerous messages and attachments from entering the Exchange organization.

AutoDiscover Service   Obtains the details necessary to complete the configuration of an Outlook 2007 client.

Availability Service   Running on the Client Access Server, this service retrieves calendar information from individual mailboxes in real time in order to provide the best user experience possible.

basic authentication   Used with OWA forms-based authentication and uses clear text to authenticate the client with a domain controller. Because the user name and password are sent in clear text between the server and the client, using SSL is recommended to ensure safer communication.

baseline   A measurement of a system over time that can later be compared to subsequent measurements to determine whether there is any variation.

Best Practices Analyzer   A tool that automatically examines an Exchange Server deployment and determines whether the configuration is set according to Microsoft best practices.

bottleneck   An overconsumption of a resource. You will experience this as a slow response time, but you should think of it as overconsumption. Finding bottlenecks is a key goal in performance tuning.

buffer overflow   Sends a larger quantity of data to the server than is anticipated. Depending on how the overflow is executed, it could cause the server to stop working, or it might run malicious code from the attacker.

Cached Exchange Mode   Stores a copy of your Exchange mailbox on the local computer in an offline storage (OST) file. When a client computer is offline, Outlook 2007 automatically switches over to a disconnected mode, during which it periodically attempts to restore the connection. While the connection is unavailable, all the data inside the OST file is available to the user.

certificate authority (CA)   Issues certificates and enables parties to trust each other. The CA's private key is used to sign a certificate, and the certificate is needed to verify the signatures. Active Directory can maintain information that a CA needs, such as user account names, group memberships, and certificate templates, as well as information about each CA installed in the domain.

certificate templates   Define the attributes for different certificate types.

checkpoint file   Records which entries in the log files have already been written to disk. The checkpoint file can speed up recovery time by telling ESE which log file entries need to be replayed and which do not.

cipher   Plain text that has been encrypted.

circular logging   Exchange Server's dual-phase commit logging includes writing all of the transactions to log files. Circular logging is the term that refers to Exchange reusing the log files after the transactions in them have been committed to the database.

Client Access server role   Provides accessibility to the Exchange environment for clients using Outlook Anywhere, POP3, and IMAP4.

cluster continuous replication (CCR)   A multinode cluster that provides redundancy of both the data and the system resources for your Exchange mailbox servers. Two servers are configured in an active/passive arrangement with a replica of the data from the active node being shipped and replayed into the passive node.

cmdlets   A verb-noun pair that acts as a command in the Exchange Management Shell.

coexistence   Describes a configuration in which different versions of Exchange Server are installed in the same Exchange organization at the same time.

communities   See newsgroups.

Console Tree   Located on the left side of the Exchange Management Console, this area is organized by containers that represent the hierarchy of the Exchange organization. The specific containers that are displayed are based on the server roles that are installed.

content filtering   The service that evaluates inbound messages and determines the likelihood of whether a message is spam or is legitimate. Content filtering uses a statistically significant sample of messages to make its determination, thus decreasing the chance for mistakes.

connection filtering: IP Allow List   An IP Allow List specifies IP addresses that are always allowed to send mail to the organization.

connection filtering: IP Allow List Providers   A list of providers that should be considered a safe sender. In this case, the safe list includes the names of domains you trust to send only legitimate mail to your organization.

connection filtering: IP Block List   Specifies IP addresses that are never allowed to send mail to the organization.

connection filtering: IP Block List Providers   Provide a way to build on the work of others in determining whether or not mail coming from a particular sender should be regarded as spam.

containers   An object that can contain both other containers and noncontainer objects.

continuous cluster replication (CCR)   Similar to LCR, except that the database copy is housed on a separate server either in the same data center or in a remote data center.

counters   In the Performance snap-in, a measurement of a specific aspect of an object.

cross-site scripting   A vulnerability whereby an attacker places malicious code into a link that appears to be from a trusted source.

decommission   Taking a server out of service and removing it from the Exchange organization.

Denial of Service attack   An attack on a network that is undertaken in an effort to disrupt the services provided by a network or server.

diagnostics logging   Indicates the level of logging to event logs that Exchange processes perform. You can change the level of diagnostic logging for most Exchange processes when you need to troubleshoot those processes.

Dial Plan   An Active Directory container object that represents sets or groupings of PBXs that share common user extension numbers.

digital certificates   Authentication method used with a PKI deployment; especially useful for authenticating parties outside your organization.

digital signatures   Provide origin authentication because only the sender holds the private key used to generate the signature. The signature also provides data integrity because the signature is a protected hash of the message, meaning that the document is hashed and then encrypted with the signer's private encryption key and, after verification, it is decrypted with the signer's public key.

Direct file access   A feature of Outlook Web Access 2007 includes Direct file access, which provides access to documents housed in Windows file shares or in SharePoint repositories.

distinguished name   A name assigned to every object in Active Directory that identifies where the object resides in the overall object hierarchy. Distinguished names are guaranteed to be unique in the forest.

distribution group A mail-enabled group object in Active Directory. Messages sent to a group are redirected and distributed to each member of that group. Groups can contain any combination of the other types of recipients, including other groups. Distribution groups are meant to perform distribution functions. You cannot use them to assign permissions to network resources.

Dnsdiag.exe A tool that verifies DNS connectivity for a computer.

domain The core unit in Active Directory. A domain is made up of a collection of computers that share a common directory database.

Domain Name System (DNS) A widely used standards-based protocol that allows clients and servers to resolve names into IP addresses and vice versa. Windows Server 2003 extends this concept even further by supplying a dynamic DNS (DDNS) service that enables clients and servers to automatically register themselves in the database without needing administrators to manually define records.

Domain Naming Master A server that controls the addition and removal of domains in the forest. This is the only domain controller from which you can create or delete a domain.

EdgeSync The service that handles synchronization between a Hub Transport server and an Edge Transport server. EdgeSync copies the information that is required for the Edge Transport server to perform anti-spam and message security tasks and information about the connector configuration that is required to enable end-to-end mail flow.

Edge Transport server role Deployed into your company's perimeter network and handles all mail from the outside world. This server role handles message security, including attachment filtering, connection filtering, content filtering, sender and recipient filtering, spam and virus protection, and more.

encryption The process of scrambling data before sending it over a medium.

Eseutil.exe A tool used to perform database defragmentation on an Exchange database while the Information Store service is stopped.

Event Viewer A graphical interface for viewing event logs generated by Windows and other applications. Event logs include normal informational events as well as any errors or warnings generated, making Event Viewer a particularly useful troubleshooting tool.

Exchange Load Generator Simulates the delivery of messaging requests to measure the impact of MAPI clients on Exchange servers.

Exchange Management Console The graphical management interface for Exchange Server 2007.

Exchange Management Shell Provides a powerful command-line interface for executing and automating administrative tasks.

Exchange Server 2007 IP Reputation Filter An IP Block list that is offered exclusively to Exchange Server 2007 customers. Premium anti-spam services include automatic updates for this filter.

Extensible Storage Engine A transaction logging system that ensures data integrity and consistency in the event of a system crash or media failure. ESE forms the basis for the Exchange Server architecture.

failover Accidental, unforeseen occurrence in which your active node/storage fails for whatever reason. When this occurs using a high-availability solution, the process should failover to the passive node/storage either automatically or manually. A failover situation usually is not lossless, in that some data may be lost during the failure/recovery process.

Filever.exe   A tool that displays versions of .exe and .dll files.

folder contact   A user that receives copies of any status messages regarding a public folder, including nondelivery reports.

folder owner   A user that is granted all permissions in a public folder, including the ability to assign permissions.

forest   A collection of domains and domain trees. The implicit name of the forest is the name of the first domain installed. All domain controllers within a forest share the same configuration and schema naming partitions.

forms-based authentication   OWA's forms-based authentication method stores the user's user name and password in a cookie instead of in the browser. Forms-based authentication is not enabled by default.

front end/back end   In Exchange Server 2003, an Exchange configuration in which clients access a bank of protocol servers (the front end) for collaboration information, and these in turn communicate with the data stores on separate servers (the back end) to retrieve the physical data.

gateway   A connection between two different types of systems.

Global Address List   The list of all Exchange Server recipients in the entire Exchange organization. Exchange uses address lists to hold and organize the names of the recipients associated with the system.

Global Catalog server   A server that holds a complete replica of the configuration and schema naming contexts for an Active Directory forest, a complete replica of the domain naming context in which the server is installed, and a partial replica of all other domains in the forest. The Global Catalog knows about every object in the forest and has representations for them in its directory; however, it might not know about all attributes (such as job title and physical address) for objects in other domains.

Globally Unique Identifier (GUID)   An attribute consisting of a 128-bit number that is guaranteed to be unique, used by applications that need to refer to an object by an identifier that remains constant. A GUID is assigned to an object when it is created, and it will never change, even if the object is moved between containers in the same domain.

group   An object defined in Active Directory that contains other objects such as users, contacts, and possibly other groups. A group can be either a distribution group or a security group, and its scope can be local, domain, or universal.

handoff   When you purposely plan to take your active node offline, for maintenance and so forth, and hand off the responsibility of the quorum to the passive node. This type of situation is lossless, in that data should not be lost during the transition of responsibility.

heartbeats   Private communication between the active and passive members of a cluster to ensure that each is still available and/or functional.

high availability   The concept of providing redundancy of your resources. In the case of Exchange Server 2007, high availability comes in several forms, each of which offers a different methodology and varying levels of success in the event of a failover.

Hub Transport server role   The Hub Transport server role's responsibilities include message delivery to a local recipient's mailbox, to recipients in remote Active Directory sites, and, through the use of a special connector, to mailboxes residing on servers running an earlier version of Exchange.

hunt group A group of PBX resources or extension numbers that are shared by users. Hunt groups are used to efficiently distribute calls into or out of a given business unit.

Inbox Repair Tool A tool that examines personal folder files (.pst files) for possible corruption and repairs those files if possible.

Infrastructure Master A domain controller that is responsible for tracking group-to-user references whenever the user and the group are not members of the same domain.

input/output per second (IOPS) The measurement of information being read into and out of a system, such as a disk.

instance In the Performance snap-in, a particular variation of a counter. For example, if you have two disk drives on a computer, a counter for a disk-based object may have two instances—one for each physical disk.

Integrated Windows Authentication Used with OWA forms-based authentication and is meant for clients running Internet Explorer 5 or later. IWA uses Kerberos to perform authentication and offers the highest level of security. In IWA, the user's password is not sent on the line in clear text. Instead, it is encrypted so that even when the password's packets are sniffed, the attacker cannot read the password.

Internet Information Services (IIS) A Web server that provides highly reliable, manageable Web services to Windows and other server services, including Exchange. In Exchange Server 2007, IIS is required only for the Mailbox Server role and the Client Access Server role. Outlook Web Access relies heavily on IIS.

Internet Message Access Protocol version 4 (IMAP4) Developed to allow users to leave their e-mail on the server and to allow remote access to messages. Thus, IMAP4 extends the functionality of POP3 to allow both offline and online storage of messages.

IP gateway In Unified Messaging, an object that establishes a logical link between an IP/VoIP gateway, a dial plan, and single or multiple hunt groups.

Isinteg.exe A tool that checks the integrity of information stores.

Kerberos version 5 The default protocol for authentication and logon in Windows.

key An algorithm applied to encrypt data, changing it into an unreadable form

key pair A pair of public and private asymmetric keys.

leaf object An object that cannot contain other objects.

local continuous replication (LCR) A single-server solution that uses built-in asynchronous log shipping and log replay technology to create and maintain a copy of a storage group on a second set of disks that are connected to the same server as the production storage group.

logical unit number (LUN) LUNs are used to identify virtual hard drive partitions, which are used in RAID configurations.

log shipping/replay Transaction logs are used to maintain an up-to-date Exchange database. These 1-MB logs grow with the addition of mail to your server. Those logs are shipped from the active node to the passive node (or from the active storage set to the passive) and then replayed into preseeded databases.

mail contact A pointer to a mailbox in an external messaging system and most likely used by a person outside the organization

mail-enabled user   A user that has an e mail address and can receive, but not send, messages.

Mail Flow Troubleshooter   A tool that helps you diagnose common mail flow problems, such as when users' messages are not being delivered or received, or when there are long delays in message delivery.

Mailbox server role   Provides the foundation of your Exchange environment and hosts the mailbox and public folder databases.

mailbox user   A user that has an associated mailbox on an Exchange server. Each user mailbox is a private storage area that allows an individual user to send, receive, and store messages.

Malicious Software Removal Tool   Checks computers running Windows XP, Windows 2000, and Windows Server 2003 for infections by specific, prevalent malicious software—including Blaster, Sasser, and Mydoom—and helps remove any infection found.

Messaging Application Programming Interface (MAPI)   An Application Programming Interface (API) used in Windows to enable shared messaging. MAPI is both an API and a transmission protocol used by Outlook to communicate with Exchange servers.

Microsoft Baseline Security Analyzer   A tool that analyzes your existing environment and, in particular, analyzes how you have configured a number of Microsoft products.

Microsoft Entourage   An e-mail client for Apple Mac OS X that provides functionality very similar to that of Microsoft Outlook, including the ability to connect to an Exchange server.

Microsoft Exchange Server Jetstress Tool   Verifies the performance and stability of a disk subsystem prior to putting an Exchange server into production.

Microsoft Management Console   A common environment for the management of various system and network resources. MMC is actually a framework that hosts modules called snap-ins, which provide the actual tools for managing a resource.

Microsoft Outlook   The latest version of Microsoft's premier messaging client. Outlook 2007 is a component of some versions of Microsoft Office 2007 and will become widely used as organizations upgrade to this newest version of the popular Office suite.

Microsoft TechNet   An online resource from Microsoft that provides a wealth of technical resources for IT professionals, including articles, white papers, webcasts, newsletters, and access to the Microsoft Knowledge Base.

moderated folder   A public folder in which a moderator must approve all newly posted items before they are made available to the public.

naming convention   A systematic approach for creating names for the various objects in an organization.

naming partition   A self-contained section of a directory hierarchy that has its own properties, such as replication configuration and permissions structure. Active Directory includes the domain, configuration, and schema naming partitions.

Native Mode (Exchange)   A mode that provides additional functionality in Exchange Server 2007 at the expense of disallowing previous versions of Exchange Server to connect to the organization.

Native Mode (Windows)   Provides the ability to create universal security groups, group conversion, and also eliminates the possibility for adding NT-based domain controllers to the domain.

NetBIOS An application programming interface that allows applications on different computers to communicate over a local area network. Typically, NetBIOS is implemented over the TCP/IP networking protocol suite.

network attached storage (NAS) Dedicated data storage technology that can be connected to a computer over an Ethernet network to provide centralized data access and storage to heterogeneous network clients.

Network Load Balancing (NLB) Included with Windows Server 2003, a service that uses clustering in order to balance network traffic across multiple servers.

Network News Transfer Protocol (NNTP) A standards-based protocol that includes simple command verbs to transfer Usenet messages between clients and servers as well as between servers. NNTP uses TCP/IP port 119. Exchange Server 2007 no longer supports NNTP for public folder access.

newsgroups Public forums, also called communities, that allow you to interact with other users and administrators and to get opinions and ideas about specific problems.

NTLM (Windows Challenge/Response) An authentication method provided for backward compatibility with Microsoft Windows NT 4.

object In the Performance snap-in, any resource, application, or service that can be monitored and measured.

Office Customization Tool Lets you create a Setup customization file that includes custom settings and Outlook profile configuration. The Setup customization file is then applied when you install Outlook 2007 from a network installation point.

organizational units A container object that is used to organize other objects within a domain. An OU can contain user accounts, printers, groups, computers, and other OUs.

OST Integrity Check Tool A tool that examines offline folder files (.ost files) for possible corruption and repairs those files if possible.

Outlook Express The messaging client included in versions of Windows prior to Windows Vista. Windows Vista replaces Outlook Express with Windows Mail.

Outlook add-ins Program modules that can be seamlessly added to the Outlook environment to extend the functionality of the product.

Outlook Anywhere Formerly called RPC-over-HTTP, allows users to connect Outlook clients from anywhere, including outside your organization's firewall.

Outlook profile A set of information services configured for a particular user or purpose. The Exchange Server information service in a profile includes a reference to an associated Exchange server and mailbox. When a user starts Outlook, he or she uses the information in an Outlook profile to establish a connection with a particular Exchange server.

Outlook Web Access (OWA) The Web browser interface to an Exchange Server mailbox.

parameter Additional information or instructions supplied with a cmdlet in the Exchange Management Shell.

Passive Clustered Mailbox role Provides a standby backup of your cluster's active node, which can be activated in the event of a failure.

PDC emulator A server responsible for synchronizing password changes and security account updates between the Windows NT 4 servers and the Windows Server 2003 servers.

Performance snap-in   A tool that graphically charts the performance of hundreds of individual system parameters on a computer running the Windows operating system.

Performance Troubleshooter   A tool that helps diagnose performance problems related to RPC connectivity. The Performance Troubleshooter collects data from different sources, analyzes the data, and then offers advice for fixing any problems it finds.

Play on Phone   A feature of Unified Messaging that allows you to request that Exchange call you at your phone number to play messages to you over the phone.

POP3   Developed in response to Simple Mail Transfer Protocol (SMTP) and designed for workstations that don't have the resources to maintain both SMTP services and a message transfer system. POP3 clients download mail from a server for perusal on the local client.

Private Branch Exchange (PBX)   A private telephone exchange often used within a company that allows the routing of telephone calls throughout an organization.

public folder   A special form of mailbox that allows public access to users of an organization, providing centralized storage of virtually any type of document or message and allowing controlled access by any user in the organization.

public folder database   The database on a Mailbox server in which public folders are stored.

public folder referrals   Provide clients with a way to access public folders in remote routing groups.

public folder tree   A hierarchy of public folders under a single top-level public folder.

queue   A place where a request for a service sits until it can be processed. For example, when a file needs to be written to a disk, the request to write that file is first placed in the queue for the disk. The driver for the disk then reads the information out of the queue and writes that information to the disk.

quorum   The clusters configuration database. It performs two very important functions: it informs the cluster which node is active, and it intervenes in the event of a failure to communicate between nodes.

RAID-5   A striped set of hard disks with distributed parity. All but one drive in a RAID-5 set must be present, meaning that if a single disk fails, data on that disk can be reconstructed from the parity information.

RAID-6   A striped set of hard disks with dual distributed parity, which works much like RAID-5 but uses two disks of the set for parity instead of just one disk.

RAID-10   A combination of two RAID types: RAID 1 (which is a striped set) and RAID 0 (which is a mirrored set). A striped set offers no fault tolerance, but does offer increased read and write times from disk. A mirrored set offers fault tolerance by creating full mirror copies of the primary disk. RAID-10 (which is essentially RAID 1+0) is a striped set of mirrored sets., which offers both increased speed and fault tolerance.

receive connector   An inbound connection point for SMTP traffic into a particular Hub Transport server or Edge Transport server. A receive connector is valid only on the server on which the connector is created.

recipient   An object in the Active Directory directory service. These objects in turn reference resources that can receive messages through interaction with Exchange Server 2007. Such a resource might be a mailbox in the mailbox store in which one of your users gets e-mail or a public folder in which information is shared among many users.

Recipient Filtering Lets you block incoming mail from the Internet for up to 800 specified users in your organization.

Recovery Point Objective (RPO) Describes the point in time to which data must be restored in order to successfully resume processing. This is often thought of as time between the last backup and when an outage occurs and indicates the amount of data lost.

Recovery Time Objective (RTO) Determined based on the acceptable downtime in case of a disruption of operations. It indicates the latest point in time at which the business operations must resume after disaster.

Recipient Update Service Originally introduced in Exchange 2000 Server, an asynchronous service that completes the provisioning process each time you create a new Exchange user.

redundant array of independent disks (RAID) A method for combining multiple disks to work as a single volume of information. Some levels of RAID also offer fault tolerance.

Relative Distinguished Name The part of the distinguished name that is an attribute of the object. Active Directory will not allow two objects with the same relative distinguished name under the same parent container.

Relative Identifier master A domain controller that allocates sequences of RIDs to each of the domain controllers in its domain. Whereas the schema master and domain naming master perform forest-wide functions, one RID master is assigned per domain.

resource mailbox A mailbox that represents a conference room or a piece of shared equipment. Users can include resource mailboxes as resources in meeting requests, providing a simple way to schedule resource availability for an organization.

response time The amount of time required to perform a unit of work from start to finish.

Results pane The area of the Exchange Management Console that displays objects that reflect the container you have selected in the console tree.

roaming user A user who does not have a fixed physical location and might consequently log on to many different machines. To accommodate such a user, you can create a roaming user profile.

routing group In Exchange 2000 Server and Exchange Server 2003, a collection of Exchange servers that can transfer messaging data to one another in a single hop without going through a bridgehead server. In general, Exchange servers within a single routing group are connected by high-bandwidth links. Connectivity among servers in a routing group is based entirely on SMTP. Exchange Server 2007 relies on Active Directory site topology and no longer uses routing groups.

RPing A utility that comes with the Windows Server 2003 Resource Kit that allows you to test the RPC connectivity between two computers. The utility consists of two parts: a server component (rpings.exe) and a client component (rpingc.exe).

schema The set of object classes (such as users and groups) and their attributes (such as full name and phone number) that form Active Directory.

Security Configuration Wizard A tool designed to reduce the attack surface of your Windows servers by helping administrators create security policies based on running the fewest possible services on a server.

security groups   Used to group users or computers for the purpose of reducing the points of administration and providing permissions to network resources.

Security Log   A record of events based on the auditing settings specified in the local policy of a machine or by group policy that applies to the machine. This record concerns components of the system itself, including such events as device driver and network failures.

seeding   The process of copying your Exchange database from the active node/storage to the passive node/storage.

segmentation   Provides an administrator with the ability to selectively enable and disable specific Outlook Web Access features on either a per-server or per-user basis.

send connector   Represents a logical gateway through which outbound messages are sent from an Exchange Server 2007 Hub Transport server or Edge Transport server to other Exchange servers or to other mail systems. Send connectors are available organization-wide.

sender filtering   The Sender Filter services take action on messages from specific addresses outside your organization.

Sender ID   Performs checks to make sure that mail coming into your organization is actually being sent by the organization claimed in the SMTP headers.

Setup customization file   A file with an .msp extension that is created by the Office Customization Tool, which allows you to customize and automate installations of Office or Outlook.

Simple Mail Transfer Protocol (SMTP)   The standard mail transmission protocol used on the Internet and within organizations. SMTP uses the TCP/IP protocol suite to achieve its goals.

single copy cluster (SCC)   A clustered mailbox server that uses shared storage in a failover cluster configuration to allow multiple servers to manage a single copy of the storage groups. This feature is similar to the cluster features in previous versions of Exchange Server.

site   In Active Directory, a collection of IP subnets. All computers in the same site have high-speed connectivity—LAN speeds—with one another.

S/MIME   Allows recipients using non-Microsoft software to see and understand encrypted, secure messages sent from Outlook 2007 users.

snap-in   Modules that are added to MMC to provide management functionality.

spam and phishing expeditions   Spam, or junk mail, is a well-known e-mail malady and affects just about everyone that uses the communication medium. A particular type of spam, called a phishing e-mail, attempts to lure unsuspecting users into clicking on unsafe web links. These links point to web forms that ask the user to provide sensitive personal information.

SSL/TLS (Secure Sockets Layer/Transport Layer Security)   An authentication method appropriate for connection-oriented security, such as access to Web-based resources on the Internet.

storage area network (SAN)   A network that is used for the purpose of accessing storage-related technologies. Typically storage area networks are fiber channel or Ethernet networks in which SCSI is the primary encapsulated protocol. SANs generally contain storage arrays, tape libraries, and hosts.

storage group   A collection of Exchange databases on an Exchange server that share the same ESE instance and transaction log. Individual databases within a storage group can be mounted and dismounted.

storage quotas A limit on the disk space that a mailbox can consume.

symmetric keys A system in which both the sender and the recipient use the same key to encrypt and decrypt the data (also known as shared keys).

throughput A measurement of the amount of work done in a given unit of time. Most often, we think of throughput as the amount of data that can be transmitted from one point to another in a given time period. However, the concept of throughput is also applied to data movement within a computer.

transition The process of upgrading from an earlier version of Exchange to Exchange Server 2007.

transport dumpster Located on the Hub Transport server in your Exchange organization, the transport dumpster maintains a queue of recently delivered mail to a CCR mailbox cluster. This mail is retained for a specified period of time and replayed into your mailbox server in the event of a failover.

Trojans A malicious program embedded inside a normal, safe-looking program. The difference between a virus and a Trojan is that the Trojan is embedded and the virus is attached to the file or executable.

Unified Messaging A server role that allows Exchange Server 2007 to connect to telephony and fax features of a voice communications system.

Unified Messaging server role Introduced in Exchange Server 2007, enables the storage of voice and fax messages in a user's Exchange mailbox, the contents of which then become accessible either via telephone or computer.

user In Active Directory, a security principal (a user who can log on to the domain). A user might have an e-mail address and/or an Exchange mailbox, making the object mail-enabled and/or mailbox-enabled, respectively.

user principal name A name that is generated for each object is in the form username@DNSdomainname. Users can log on with their user principal name, and an administrator can define suffixes for user principal names if desired.

Volume Shadow Copy Service (VSS) Provides a backup infrastructure for the Microsoft Windows Server 2003 operating system. It enables applications (such as Microsoft Exchange Server), backup applications, and hardware providers to take point-in-time snapshots of data in a supported way.

WebReady Document Viewing A new feature in Exchange Server 2007 providing users with the ability to view file attachments from within Outlook Web Access.Clients do not need to have the native application installed in order to view attachments using WebReady Document Viewing.

Windows Mail The messaging client included with Windows Vista. Windows Mail is a replacement for Outlook Express, which was included in previous versions of Windows. Windows Mail is the default e-mail reader for Windows Vista unless Outlook or another e-mail client is installed. Windows Mail supports POP3, IMAP4, and SMTP.

Work pane The area of the Exchange Management Console that displays objects based on the server role that is selected in the Server Configuration container.

worms Programs that run by themselves. They do not embed or attach themselves to other programs nor do they need to do this to replicate. They can travel from computer to computer across network connections and are self-replicating. Worms might have portions of themselves running on many different computers, or the entire program might run on a single computer.

X.509 A standard for digital certificates.

Index

About the Authors

Walter Glenn has been working in the computer industry for 20 years and has been writing for about 10 years. Walter works in Huntsville, Alabama, as a consultant, trainer, and award-winning writer. He is a Microsoft Certified Systems Engineer (MCSE), Microsoft Certified Desktop Support Technician (MCDST), and Microsoft Certified Trainer (MCT). Walter's work with Exchange Server began with Exchange Server 5.5. He has managed Exchange organizations for small- and medium-sized businesses, including designing and building Exchange infrastructures, as well as transitioning to new versions of Exchange Server.

Walter is also the author of numerous computer-related books, articles, white papers, presentations, and courseware. Walter's recent books include *MCSA/MCSE Self-Paced Training Kit (Exam 70-270): Installing, Configuring, and Administering Microsoft Windows XP Professional*, Second Edition, (Microsoft Press, 2005), and *Linksys Networks: The Official Guide*, 3rd Edition, (McGraw-Hill Osborne Media, 2005). Walter maintains a Web site at *http://www.walterglenn.com*.

Scott Lowe, MSCE, CNA, resides in Fulton, Missouri, with his wife, Amy (who is also his chief proofreader and supporter), and two children, Ryan and Isabella. By day, Scott is the Chief Information Officer at Westminster College, where he puts his 14 years of information technology experience to work serving the needs of the campus community. By night (and sometimes weekends, lunch, and everything in between!), Scott writes technical articles for CNet's TechRepublic and Microsoft. For TechRepublic—for which he has written more than 500 articles—Scott writes the weekly Exchange newsletter tip as well as the biweekly storage newsletter. He is also the author of *Home Networking: The Missing Manual,* (O'Reilly Media, Inc., 2005).

When not working, writing, or pulling the kids off each other, Scott spends time with his wife, reading and working in the yard. Scott keeps an irregularly updated blog at *www.slowe.com*.

Joshua Maher has been focused on messaging, mobility, identity management, and business continuity throughout his career. Most recently, he has been working for EMC Corporation at their Development Center in Redmond, Washington. His primary responsibility is leading EMC's storage product integration with Microsoft's Exchange Server product line. His other roles with EMC include consulting to internal and external product, marketing, and management teams on direction and integration. Josh is a regular speaker at events and conferences and the author of various white papers on messaging and business continuity integration.

In addition to his work with EMC, Josh works with messaging and technology user groups and communities. He works with Microsoft to improve the quality of their messaging education and certification programs. He has helped to develop the technical roadmap across different delivery mechanisms, including instructor-led training, e-learning, and Microsoft Press books. Josh maintains a blog at *http://joshmaher.wordpress.com*.

2007 Microsoft® Office System Resources for Developers and Administrators

Microsoft Office SharePoint® Server 2007 Administrator's Companion

Bill English with the Microsoft SharePoint Community Experts
ISBN 9780735622821

Get your mission-critical collaboration and information management systems up and running. This comprehensive, single-volume reference details features and capabilities of SharePoint Server 2007. It delivers easy-to-follow procedures, practical workarounds, and key troubleshooting tactics—for on-the-job results.

Microsoft Windows SharePoint Services Version 3.0 Inside Out

Jim Buyens
ISBN 9780735623231

Conquer Microsoft Windows SharePoint Services— from the inside out! This ultimate, in-depth reference packs hundreds of time-saving solutions, troubleshooting tips, and workarounds. You're beyond the basics, so now learn how the experts tackle information sharing and team collaboration— and challenge yourself to new levels of mastery!

Microsoft SharePoint Products and Technologies Administrator's Pocket Consultant

Ben Curry
ISBN 9780735623828

Portable and precise, this pocket-sized guide delivers immediate answers for the day-to-day administration of Sharepoint Products and Technologies. Featuring easy-to-scan tables, step-by-step instructions, and handy lists, this book offers the straightforward information you need to get the job done—whether you're at your desk or in the field!

Inside Microsoft Windows® SharePoint Services Version 3

Ted Pattison and Daniel Larson
ISBN 9780735623200

Get in-depth insights on Microsoft Windows SharePoint Services with this hands-on guide. You get a bottom-up view of the platform architecture, code samples, and task-oriented guidance for developing custom applications with Microsoft Visual Studio® 2005 and Collaborative Application Markup Language (CAML).

Inside Microsoft Office SharePoint Server 2007

Patrick Tisseghem
ISBN 9780735623682

Dig deep—and master the intricacies of Office SharePoint Server 2007. A bottom-up view of the platform architecture shows you how to manage and customize key components and how to integrate with Office programs—helping you create custom enterprise content management solutions.

Microsoft Office Communications Server 2007 Resource Kit

Microsoft Office Communications Server Team
ISBN 9780735624061

Your definitive reference to Office Communications Server 2007—direct from the experts who know the technology best. This comprehensive guide offers in-depth technical information and best practices for planning, designing, deploying, managing, and optimizing your systems. Includes a toolkit of valuable resources on CD.

Programming Applications for Microsoft Office Outlook® 2007

Randy Byrne and Ryan Gregg
ISBN 9780735622494

Microsoft Office Visio® 2007 Programming Step by Step

David A. Edson
ISBN 9780735623798

Windows Vista™ Resources for Administrators

Windows Vista Administrator's Pocket Consultant
William Stanek
ISBN 9780735622968

Portable and precise, this pocket-sized guide delivers immediate answers for the day-to-day administration of Windows Vista. Featuring easy-to-scan tables, step-by-step instructions, and handy lists, this book offers the straightforward information you need to solve problems and get the job done—whether you're at your desk or in the field!

Windows Vista Resource Kit
Mitch Tulloch, Tony Northrup, Jerry Honeycutt, Ed Wilson, Ralph Ramos, and the Windows Vista Team
ISBN 9780735622838

Get the definitive reference for deploying, configuring, and supporting Windows Vista—from the experts who know the technology best. This guide offers in-depth, comprehensive technical guidance on automating deployment; implementing security enhancements; administering group policy, files folders, and programs; and troubleshooting. Includes an essential toolkit of resources on DVD.

MCTS Self-Paced Training Kit (Exam 70-620): Configuring Windows Vista Client
Ian McLean and Orin Thomas
ISBN 9780735623903

Get in-depth preparation plus practice for Exam 70-620, the required exam for the new Microsoft Certified Technology Specialist (MCTS): Windows Vista Client certification. This 2-in-1 kit focuses on installing client software and configuring system settings, security features, network connectivity, media applications, and mobile devices. Ace your exam prep—and build real-world job skills—with lessons, practice tests, evaluation software, and more.

MCITP Self-Paced Training Kit (Exam 70-622): Installing, Maintaining, Supporting, and Troubleshooting Applications on the Windows Vista Client – Enterprise
Tony Northrup and J.C. Mackin
ISBN 9780735624085

Maximize your performance on Exam 70-622, the required exam for the new Microsoft® Certified IT Professional (MCITP): Enterprise Support Technician certification. Comprehensive and in-depth, this 2-in-1 kit covers managing security, configuring networking, and optimizing performance for Windows Vista clients in an enterprise environment. Ace your exam prep—and build real-world job skills—with lessons, practice tests, evaluation software, and more.

MCITP Self-Paced Training Kit (Exam 70-623): Installing, Maintaining, Supporting, and Troubleshooting Applications on the Windows Vista Client – Consumer
Anil Desai with Chris McCain of GrandMasters
ISBN 9780735624238

Get the 2-in-1 training kit for Exam 70-623, the required exam for the new Microsoft Certified IT Professional (MCITP): Consumer Support Technician certification. This comprehensive kit focuses on supporting Windows Vista clients for consumer PCs and devices, including configuring security settings, networking, troubleshooting, and removing malware. Ace your exam prep—and build real-world job skills—with lessons, practice tests, evaluation software, and more.

See more resources at **microsoft.com/mspress**
and **microsoft.com/learning**

Microsoft Press® products are available worldwide wherever quality computer books are sold. For more information, contact your bookseller, computer retailer, software reseller, or local Microsoft Sales Office, or visit our Web site at **microsoft.com/mspress**. To locate a source near you, or to order directly, call 1-800-MSPRESS in the United States. (In Canada, call **1-800-268-2222**.)

What do you think of this book?

We want to hear from you!

Do you have a few minutes to participate in a brief online survey?

Microsoft is interested in hearing your feedback so we can continually improve our books and learning resources for you.

To participate in our survey, please visit:

www.microsoft.com/learning/booksurvey/

...and enter this book's ISBN-10 number (appears above barcode on back cover*).
As a thank-you to survey participants in the United States and Canada, each month we'll randomly select five respondents to win one of five $100 gift certificates from a leading online merchant. At the conclusion of the survey, you can enter the drawing by providing your e-mail address, which will be used for prize notification only.

Thanks in advance for your input. Your opinion counts!

* Where to find the ISBN-10 on back cover

ISBN-13: 000-0-0000-0000-0
ISBN-10: 0-0000-0000-0

0 0 0 0 0

0 000000 000000

Example only. Each book has unique ISBN.

Microsoft®
Press

No purchase necessary. Void where prohibited. Open only to residents of the 50 United States (includes District of Columbia) and Canada (void in Quebec). For official rules and entry dates see:

www.microsoft.com/learning/booksurvey/